Publications on Ocean Development

A SERIES OF STUDIES ON THE INTERNATIONAL, LEGAL, INSTITUTIONAL AND POLICY ASPECTS OF OCEAN DEVELOPMENT

General Editors

Alex Oude Elferink
Joanna Mossop

VOLUME 103

The titles published in this series are listed at *brill.com/pood*

Regulating Autonomous Vessels

Regulating Autonomous Vessels

International, Regional, and European Regulation of Maritime Autonomous Surface Ships

By

Eva Ricarda Lange

BRILL | NIJHOFF

LEIDEN | BOSTON

Library of Congress Cataloging-in-Publication Data

Names: Lange, Eva Ricarda, author.
Title: Regulating autonomous vessels : international, regional, and European regulation of maritime autonomous surface ships / by Eva Ricarda Lange.
Description: Leiden ; Boston : Brill/Nijhoff, 2025. | Series: Publications on ocean development, 0924-1922 ; volume 103 | Includes bibliographical references and index.
Identifiers: LCCN 2025002724 (print) | LCCN 2025002725 (ebook) | ISBN 9789004729476 (hardback) | ISBN 9789004729483 (ebook)
Subjects: LCSH: Automatic pilot (Ships) | Automatic pilot (Ships)–Safety regulations. | Ships–European Union countries–Automation. | Maritime law–European Union countries.
Classification: LCC K4176.A98 L36 2025 (print) | LCC K4176.A98 (ebook) | DDC 343.09/65–dc23/eng/20250121
LC record available at https://lccn.loc.gov/2025002724
LC ebook record available at https://lccn.loc.gov/2025002725

Typeface for the Latin, Greek, and Cyrillic scripts: "Brill". See and download: brill.com/brill-typeface.

ISSN 0924-1922
ISBN 978-90-04-72947-6 (hardback)
ISBN 978-90-04-72948-3 (e-book)
DOI 10.1163/9789004729483

This book is printed on acid-free paper and produced in a sustainable manner.

Contents

Preface

This book is based on a PhD thesis defended on September 4, 2024 at the University of Bremen, Faculty of Law. I would like to express my profound gratitude to my supervisor, Professor Gralf-Peter Calliess, for his invaluable support and revealing discussions throughout this project. His guidance and trust in my work have been instrumental in enabling me to conclude the thesis and publish this work. I would also like to thank Professor Katharina Reiling for her insights in public law of the sea and for her constructive comments and recommendations on literature.

I was privileged to have the opportunity to conduct research at the Scandinavian Institute for Maritime Law at the University of Oslo for a period of six months as part of my doctoral project. I am obliged to Professor Trond Solvang, Professor Erik Røsæg, and the entire NIFS team for their generous support, which allowed me to conduct research in Norwegian Maritime Law and to gain firsthand experience of the distinctive features of Nordic legal cooperation. The stimulating environment at the Institute facilitated an enjoyable research experience. Interviews and discussions with maritime law experts, representatives of the Norwegian Ministry for Foreign Affairs, and the Transport Department of the European Commission significantly advanced my research. Finally, cross-country skiing and hiking in the Oslo Marka and the Norwegian Fjords prompted the formulation of new ideas regarding the research questions.

Furthermore, I would like to express my gratitude to my colleagues in Bremen for numerous lively legal discussions, words of encouragement, and enjoyable lunch breaks. Having a welcoming and supportive work environment makes researching much more pleasant. Moreover, I would like to extend my sincere thanks to Heike, Konstantin, Lukas, Paul, Sebastian, and Vanessa for their assistance in the final copyediting and proofreading of the book.

The opportunity to pursue my professional career is contingent upon the constant support and encouragement of my friends and family, who have consistently provided me with the motivation to persevere in my research endeavors and interrupted me when I have become mired in legal considerations. In particular, musical activities, including singing in the Cathedral Choir of Bremen and playing the organ, have provided a source of resilience during the research project.

Bremen, October 2024

Abbreviations

1994 Implementation Agreement	Agreement relating to the implementation of Part XI of the United Nations Convention on the Law of the Sea of 10 December 1982
AFS-Convention	International Convention on the Control of Harmful Anti-fouling Systems on Ships
AI	Artificial Intelligence
Brussels Convention	Convention for the Unification of Certain Rules of Law with respect to Collisions between Vessels, 1910
CMI	Comité Maritime International
COLREG	Convention on the International Regulations for Preventing Collisions at Sea, 1972
EEA	European Economic Area
EEZ	Exclusive Economic Zone
EC	European Commission
EFTA	European Free Trade Association
EMSA	European Maritime Safety Agency
EU	European Union
FAL	Facilitation Committee of the IMO
FCN-treaties	Friendship, Commerce, and Navigation Treaties
Fish Stocks Agreement	1995 UN Fish Stocks Agreement
GAIRAS	Generally accepted international rules and standards
GATT	General Agreement on Tariffs and Trade
GNSS	Global Navigation Satellite System
GT	Gross tonnage (calculated based on the ship's total volume)
GPS	Global Positioning System
ICJ	International Court of Justice
IFSMA	International Federation of Shipmaster's Association
ILC	International Law Commission
IMO	International Maritime Organization
IMO Convention	Convention on the International Maritime Organization
IMCO	Inter-Governmental Maritime Consultative Organization
ISM Code	International Safety Management Code
ISPS Code	International Ship and Port Facility Security Code
ITLOS	International Tribunal for the Law of the Sea
KW	Kilowatt
LEG	Legal Committee of the IMO
LIDAR	Light detecting and ranging systems

MARPOL	International Convention for the Prevention of Pollution from Ships 1973
MASS	Maritime Autonomous Surface Ships
MEPC	Marine Einvironmental Protection Committee of the IMO
MCA	Maritime and Coastguard Agency, UK
MSC	Maritime Safety Committee of the IMO
MoU	Memorandum of Understanding
NGO	Non-governmental organization
nm	Nautical Mile
OSPAR Convention	Convention for the protection of the marine environment of the North-East Atlantic
RADAR	Radio detection and ranging
RCC	Remote control center
RSE	Regulatory Scoping Exercise
SOLAS	International Convention for the Safety of Life at Sea, 1974
STCW	International Convention on Standards of Training, Certification and Watchkeeping for Seafarers, 1978
TEU	Treaty on European Union
TFEU	Treaty on the Functioning of the European Union
UN	United Nations
UNCLOS	United Nations Convention on the Law of the Sea
VCLT	1969 Vienna Convention on the Law of the Treaties
VTS	Vessel Traffic System

CHAPTER 1

Introduction

A short-sea fishing support vessel undocks from the Norwegian mainland, transits to a fish farm located off the coast, holds its position during the unloading process, and returns to its point of departure. A 13 hour, 160 nautical miles trip completed autonomously and remotely-controlled. The master was located 160 km away in a remote control center and monitored the autonomous vessel operation. This success was completed in May 2023 and it demonstrates the potential of autonomous maritime navigation and its technological readiness.

Shipping, akin to other industry sectors, is undergoing significant changes due to the trend towards autonomization. The impact of the digital revolution varies across different industries. While ethical considerations might be less prominent in merchant shipping than in other sectors such as health care, the sector is marked by substantial investment costs, longstanding traditions dating back centuries, global standardization, and reliance on the formidable forces of nature embodied by the ocean. This makes implementing autonomy in the shipping industry particularly challenging. Nevertheless, several projects have proven the feasibility of autonomous maritime navigation. In addition, several studies have analyzed the economic, safety, environmental and security benefits of autonomous navigation.

Autonomy in shipping acts as a versatile tool, utilized to enhance efficiency, promote environmental sustainability, facilitate smarter operations, and ultimately advance the maritime industry. However, myriad challenges arise in constructing autonomous vessels capable of remote control, spanning engineering, cybersecurity, human-machine interactions, data management, cargo handling, requisite port infrastructure, and legal considerations. This study is devoted to the legal implications of maritime autonomy.

Maritime autonomy can take on various forms. On a small scale, single tasks such as monitoring cooling containers or communicating with vessel traffic managers could be operated autonomously. On a larger scale, maritime autonomy could encompass the entire ship operation process, including navigation, propulsion, cargo handling, and system integration. This book is devoted to maritime autonomy at a large scale, particularly autonomous maritime navigation.

Against the backdrop of economically viable autonomous maritime navigation, this book seeks to explore whether autonomous vessels can comply with the prevailing international legal framework for commercial vessel operations.

 | DOI:10.1163/9789004729483_002

In a second part, it discusses different regulatory means to prepare the legal framework for autonomous vessels. The legal challenges of both, autonomous operations and operations without a human crew on board will be discussed. The International Maritime Organization deals with autonomous vessels since 2017 and has developed the term 'Maritime Autonomous Surface Ship' (MASS) which shall be used in this study. At this point the term MASS is used to describe vessels which operate without a human crew on board and which are either remotely-controlled or operated by algorithms. The definition of MASS will explored in more detail below in chapter 2.1. Moreover, the book presents a critical analysis of the regulatory process at the International Maritime Organization, with a particular focus on the examination of regional and European approaches.

Despite the limited awareness among the public, innovation in shipping is a phenomenon that warrants serious consideration. Its potential impact and importance should not be underestimated. Since 2016, numerous projects have commenced to research autonomous shipping. The value of the autonomous shipping market is estimated at between USD 8.2 billion and USD 165 billion by 2030 with a growth rate of more than 6.5%.[1] This makes the market for autonomous ships one of the fastest growing segments in the maritime industry.

The primary economic advantage of autonomous vessels is the reduction of the operational costs. Efficiency enhancements result in less fuel consumption and optimized route planning. It will be illustrated below that reduced crew-related costs create an economic margin to invest in zero-emission fuels, further reducing greenhouse gas emissions. Ultimately, autonomy makes smaller vessels economically viable, allowing for more resilient fleet solutions. Short-sea shipping could particularly benefit from increased attractiveness, leading to a modal shift and reducing heavily congested road transportation. Eventually, autonomous vessels are expected to increase safety, as human errors due to fatigue and inattentiveness are less likely to occur. Although autonomous vessels have advantages, implementing maritime autonomy on a large scale affects the basis of the shipping industry that were unchanged since its

1 Markets and Markets, 'Autonomous Ship Market by Autonomy' (2022) <https://www.marketsandmarkets.com/Market-Reports/autonomous-ships-market-267183224.html> accessed 16 February 2024; Allied Market Research, 'Autonomous Ships Market Statistics' (2020) <https://www.alliedmarketresearch.com/autonomous-ships-market> accessed 16 February 2024; Fortune Business Insights, 'Autonomous Ships Market Size, Share, COVID-19 Impact & Russian–Ukraine War analysis' (2023) <https://www.fortunebusinessinsights.com/industry-reports/autonomous-ship-market-101797> accessed 16 February 2024

invention. This makes maritime autonomy a particularly challenging, though thrilling research topic.

Shipping is as old as mankind and shipping and civilization have co-evolved throughout history. The invention of the Portuguese caravel,[2] the advent of steamships,[3] and the introduction of standardized containers revolutionized freight transportation.[4] Means of digitalization such as electronic charts are now ubiquitous on all merchant vessels. With the next revolution on the horizon, the maritime industry is on the brink of transformation as autonomization prepares to reshape it once again.

Despite the fundamental changes brought to the shipping industry by the first three industrial revolutions,[5] the fourth industrial revolution[6] is distinct. While the first three revolutions replaced human labor, the fourth one questions the very foundation of every industry: human involvement and decision-making.

Conventionally, the master is on board the vessel, gives instructions to the helmsperson, and takes all necessary decisions for the safe operation of the vessel. Now, autonomous navigation revolutionizes vessel operations, allowing vessels to be controlled by sophisticated algorithms. The master and crew can be relocated ashore. The advancement of artificial intelligence and deep-learning technologies enables algorithms to make decisions akin to humans, expanding into the realm of complex decision-making that was once exclusive to human operators.[7]

The rise of autonomy is not unique to shipping, and the general legal issues are often alike across industries. However, in terms of regulation, international

2 Sofia Toffano, 'Global goods and international trade: two eras of globalization compared' (Master's Thesis, University of Venice 2021) 26

3 Ingo Heidbrink, 'The Business of Shipping: An Historical Perspective' in Wayne K Talley (ed), *The Blackwell companion to maritime economics* (Blackwell companions to contemporary economics. Wiley-Blackwell 2012) 40

4 Lance E Hoovestal, 'The Advent of the Container' in Lance E Hoovestal (ed), *Globalization Contained* (Palgrave Macmillan US 2013)

5 See for a brief summary of industrial revolutions occured so far: Hasan Tinmaz, 'History of Industrial Revolutions: From Homo Sapiens Hunters to Bitcoin Hunters' in Rodrigo Da Rosa Righi, Antonio M Alberti and Madhusudan Singh (eds), *Blockchain Technology for Industry 4. 0: Secure, Decentralized, Distributed and Trusted Industry Environment* (Blockchain Technologies. Springer Singapore 2020)

6 Schwab coined the term "fourth industrial revolution" at the World Economic Forum 2018: Klaus Schwab and Nicholas Davis, *Shaping the future of the Fourth Industrial Revolution: A guide to building a better world* (First American edition, Currency 2018)

7 LEG, IMO, 'LEG 111/10/2: Summary of the research of the Comité Maritime International International Working Group on MASS in relation to liability issues (Comité Maritime International)' (London 19 January 2024) 2

maritime shipping stands out. Initially, rules on vessel safety and navigation were established by merchants, evolving from private law to domestic law with the emergence of the nation-state as the primary regulatory authority.[8] Following the Titanic tragedy in 1912, the first international convention on the safety of life at sea was concluded, marking a shift towards public law in shipping regulation. After World War II, amidst growing international trade, the International Maritime Organization[9] was established. From the 1960s to the 1980s, public law took precedence in regulating shipping activities, resulting in the conclusion of several new international conventions. Growing environmental concerns have led to the resurgence of regional regulation. As a result, the European Union has become a significant player in shaping maritime regulations. Currently, the legal framework governing commercial shipping activities is characterized by multiple regulatory layers that overlap and interact.

The research target of this study are autonomous vessels and vessels without a human crew on board. However, its underlying issue is of general concern: how to approach autonomy from a regulatory perspective and how to incorporate autonomous solutions into an existing international regulatory framework. This makes this contribution valuable to all stakeholders entrusted with the task of regulating autonomy in an international legal environment. Moreover, the critical reflection on international regulation encourages consideration of alternative regulatory approaches.

1.1 Aim and Objectives

This study aims to answer two research questions. Firstly, it seeks to determine whether autonomous vessels can fulfill the requirements set out by the international legal framework for commercial shipping operations. Secondly, the study identifies the most appropriate way of addressing legal gaps to prepare the legal framework for the arrival of autonomous vessels.

The imminent advent of commercially viable autonomous vessels necessitates proactive preparation of the legal framework. Beyond pinpointing legal gaps, there is a pressing need to formulate effective regulatory solutions. Hence, this study endeavors to furnish policy recommendations for navigating the

8 See a brief summary of the history of lex maritima at: Andreas Maurer, 'Lex Maritima' in Jürgen Basedow and others (eds), *Encyclopedia of Private International Law* (vol 2. Edward Elgar Publishing 2017)

9 The organization was originally titled the 'Inter-Governmental Maritime Consultative Organization' but was renamed in 1982

legal landscape surrounding autonomous vessels. The study concentrates on procedural matters, i.e. the identification of appropriate regulatory bodies, and the choice of regulatory tools. The study is aware of the ongoing work at the International Maritime Organization and aims to assess the planned regulatory measures in a critical manner. Furthermore, it seeks to offer an alternative approach. According to the IMO road map,[10] the mandatory legal framework is expected to enter into force at the earliest in 2032. This makes the development of alternative approaches particularly valuable.

In order to achieve these aims, the study's objectives are to review ongoing technical research on autonomous vessels. Beyond economic advantages, safety and environmental benefits are summarized. The international legal framework is analyzed in the light of autonomous vessels to examine which legal gaps occur. In order to conduct a comparative analysis of various regulatory approaches, valuation standards are formulated. Eventually, regulatory solutions emanating from the international, the regional, and the supranational level are evaluated against the formulated criteria. The study concludes by recommending the most appropriate solution to cope with the legal challenges identified earlier.

1.2 Scope and Outline

The research questions determine both, the scope as well as the structure of the study. The scope of the study encompasses international commercial voyages of autonomous vessels. Inland waterway, military, non-commercial, and domestic applications are excluded as a different regulatory framework applies to these applications. Nonetheless, it is expected that autonomous solutions will also be applied in these maritime contexts, i.e. ocean observation for scientific research, military operations,[11] and urban passenger transportation.[12]

10 MSC, IMO, 'MSC 108/20: Report of the Maritime Safety Committee on its 108th Session' (London 28 June 2024) 44

11 Department of the Navy, United States of America, 'The Navy Unmanned Surface Vehicle (USV) Master Plan' (Washington, D.C. 23 July 2007); Royal Navy, 'NavyX' <https://www.royalnavy.mod.uk/news-and-latest-activity/operations/united-kingdom/navy-x> accessed 16 February 2024; U.S. Navy Office of Information, *Ghost Fleet Overlord Unmanned Surface Vessel Program Completes Second Autonomous Transit to the Pacific* (2021); Department of the Navy, United States of America (n 11); Department of the Navy, United States of America (n 11)

12 See the application of autonomous passenger ferries in Trondheim, Norway (*miliAmpere2*), Helsinki Finland (Callboats), and Stockholm, Sweden (Seabuz, *MS Estelle*)

Moreover, all entities not classified as vessels are excluded from the scope of this study. Additionally, the research question aims to evaluate autonomous vessel operations in general, rather than assessing distinct forms of maritime autonomy. Therefore, this analysis will not consider cargo-specific requirements or requirements specific to passenger transportation.

The study is divided into three parts. Firstly, it introduces autonomous shipping technology, its current state-of-the-art, and an interdisciplinary assessment of the expected benefits and risks associated with MASS. In addition, it provides an overview of the current international legal framework governing shipping operations (chapters 2 and 3). Secondly, chapter 4 conducts the legal analysis to identify gaps in the legal framework arising from the emergence of MASS. It assesses whether these gaps can be addressed by means of interpretation and identifies matters that require new regulations. Thirdly, chapter 5 introduces, analyzes, and compares various solution approaches, culminating in the recommendation of the most appropriate solution. Chapter 6 summarizes the foregoing work and provides an outlook on the future legal framework for MASS.

The study is based on the premise that a comprehensive legal analysis of emerging technology requires a profound understanding of the technology itself. Additionally, the study is aimed at a general audience without prior knowledge of maritime autonomy. Consequently, Chapter 2 begins by contextualizing maritime autonomy and explaining key terms such as automation, autonomy, and operations without human presence on board. It also explores the relationship between autonomous operations and human presence on board. To emphasize the urgency of preparing the international legal framework for MASS, section 2.2 introduces some ongoing research projects. Based on these projects, section 2.3 discusses economic, safety, security, and environmental aspects of MASS. Feasible and viable business cases are highlighted to develop policy recommendations that reflect the needs of the involved stakeholders.

Chapter 3 starts with introducing the United Nations Convention on the Law of the Sea as the constitution of the oceans.[13] Then, the legal status of ports is examined. Ports represent a transshipment point for cargo and play a pivotal role in the integration of MASS into commercial supply chains. Besides

---

13 CMI, 'Position Paper on Unmanned Ships and the International Regulatory Framework' (Antwerpen May 2018) 3; Alexander Proelß and Kerstin Güssow, 'Das Internationale Seerecht – ein potentes Regelwerk' [2011] World Ocean Review 199, 207; being ciritcal about the reception of UNCLOS as the constitution of the oceans and argueing for a quiet abandonment: Karen N Scott, 'The LOSC: 'A Constitution for the Oceans' in the Anthropocene?' (2023) 41(1) The Australian Year Book of International Law Online 269, 296

the United Nations Law of the Sea Convention, generally accepted international rules and standards are decisive for international shipping. Briefly, those conventions which are part of the generally accepted international rules and standards and which are of high priority for MASS are introduced. Eventually, the International Maritime Organization (IMO) as a specialized agency in the UN family is introduced. Since 2017, the IMO deals with MASS and it has contributed significantly to the legal approach towards MASS.

After these two introductory chapters, the legal analysis of MASS follows. The author is aware that interpretation entails making a normative choice between different possible interpretations.[14] Since the analysis aims to determine which gaps cannot be bridged by interpretation, the author generally opts for the most inclusive interpretation. As interpretation of international law is distinct from interpreting domestic law, the general rule of interpretation laid down in Article 31 of the Vienna Convention on the Law of the Treaties is introduced at the beginning of chapter 4.

The subsequent legal analysis starts with assessing the most general question of whether MASS are considered vessels and ships. Then, the safety at sea, and the duty to render assistance to people in distress at sea are analyzed in the light of MASS, particularly focusing on operations without humans on board and autonomous control. As an overarching function, the safety at sea is divided into sub aspects including the safety of navigation (4.2.2.1) and the safety of life at sea (4.2.2.2). The chapter concludes by summarizing the legal gaps that need to be addressed in order to prepare the international legal framework for MASS. It is indicated whether new provisions should be developed, whether existing provisions should be amended, or whether a particular interpretation should be safeguarded by regulatory means. As some European states have already begun to prepare their legal framework for MASS, these approaches are briefly introduced in part 4.5.

Chapter 5 ties on the findings of chapter 4 and explores different means to adapt the legal framework to MASS. For evaluating the proposed instruments, criteria internal and external to the legal system are developed.[15] Internal criteria emanate from the legal system itself, whereas external criteria include knowledge from other disciplines. The reference to other disciplines is seen as particularly fruitful in the field of regulation of new technologies and international relations. In section 5.2, the study zooms in from regulation to law and further to soft law. Moreover, rational choice theory is applied to reason states'

14 Lina Kestemont, *Handbook on legal methodology: From objective to method* (Intersentia 2018) 31

15 ibid 60–67

choices of regulatory instruments. It is argued that states adhere to international law if this contributes to an increase of their welfare. This approach departs from a normative-idealistic approach, but allows considering both, soft and hard law solutions and developing pragmatic policy recommendations. Subsequently, regulatory means at the international (5.3), the regional (5.4), and the European level (5.5) are considered consecutively. At all levels, binding and non-binding solutions are discussed and evaluated against the afore-developed criteria. This part is characterized by considering non-conventional law-making and departs from accustomed manners to regulate innovative technologies in an international setting.

Considering international law approaches, the examination focusses on delegated law-making and considerations of legitimacy. The proposed IMO road map for regulating MASS is critically assessed. Particular attention is given to the tacit acceptance procedure and its suitability for the necessary amendments. Based on a profound analysis of the intention of the legislator and drawing insights from rational choice theory and delegated law-making, it is scrutinized whether this procedure should be applied in the context of MASS. As alternative approaches, a new MASS Convention, a decision of the conference of state parties, as well as customary international law are discussed.

The study continues to address regional regulation from an interdisciplinary point of view. Focusing on Europe, different fora of regional regulation are examined for their potential to regulate MASS. Nordic Cooperation is expected to be most promising and thus its unique features are discussed in detail. Identified regulatory approaches are reconciled with insights from interviews with involved stakeholders such as government representatives.

Eventually, supranational regulation is explored. Here, the European Union's role as a regulator of maritime matters is introduced along with its competencies and available instruments. Special attention is given to the regulatory relationship between the European Union and the IMO, as well as the nuances of shared competencies between the European Union and its member states. Moreover, the advantages of a European approach to benefit from this highly institutionalized cooperation are accentuated. Nevertheless, the global scope of shipping industry is not left aside and multi-level regulatory approaches are discussed combining the advantages of different regulatory levels.

Chapter 6 provides a comprehensive summary of the study's findings and places the proposed solution within its wider context. The author is aware that legal reasoning is necessarily argumentative and does not result in a final closure of a scholarly dispute.[16] Rather, the arguments can be evaluated as more or less convincing. However, this evaluation exceeds intersubjectivity. The realization that no definite solution can be provided is particularly relevant for an issue involving policy considerations. Eventually, the implementation of the proposed solution depends on the political will of policymakers. The summary offers insights into potential avenues for further research and anticipates forthcoming international activities in the field. Moreover, it reflects on the interplay of law and policy as well as the role of legal insights for the regulation of emerging technologies in an international setting.

16 Sanne Taekema, 'Relative Autonomy: A Characterization of the Discipline of Law' in Sanne Taekema and Bart van Klink (eds), *Law and Method: Interdisciplinary Research into Law* (Politika vol 4. Mohr Siebeck 2011) 47

CHAPTER 2

Autonomous Shipping Technology

This first chapter provides an overview of the technical side of automation and thus attempts to lay the foundation for a legal discourse aware of the technical aspects of the regulatory target. Additionally, the technical feasibility of autonomous shipping and its economic and environmental advantages shall be introduced to underline the urgency to deal with legal matters. For illustrative purposes, some ongoing research projects are presented and the technology used for autonomous shipping operations is briefly introduced.

As technology develops further, experiences are gained, and new business cases are identified, so the conceptual framework will never reach an end-point. Over time, however, some form of consolidation occurs and an overarching understanding of the meaning of terms and concepts develops. In this section, an interim stage of consolidation can be presented considering the development of the past years.

2.1 Maritime Autonomy as a Concept

Since 2017, the International Maritime Organization (IMO) deals with vessels operated at a high level of autonomy.[17] For this purpose, Maritime Autonomous Surface Ships are defined as "a ship which, to a varying degree, can operate independent of human interaction".[18]

This definition delimits MASS in four dimensions. 'Maritime' limits the term to seagoing vessels and excludes vessels operating on inland waterways. This reflects the scope of IMO's competence. MASS are surface ships, so submarines or semi-submersibles are excluded, although there are several promising use cases for underwater applications of autonomy. Eventually, MASS are ships. This excludes some entities; however, the scope of the term 'ship' is debated and it will therefore receive more attention during the legal analysis below. For

17 MSC, IMO, 'MSC 98/20/2: Maritime Autonomous Surface Ships; Proposal for a regulatory scoping exercise (Denmark, Estonia, Finland, Japan, the Netherlands, Norway, the Republic of Korea, the United Kingdom and the United States)' (London 27 February 2017)

18 MSC, IMO, 'MSC.1/Circ.1638: Outcome of the Regulatory Scoping Exercise for the Use of Maritime Autonomous Surface Ships (MASS)' (London 3 June 2021)

 | DOI:10.1163/9789004729483_003

this study, the meaning of the term 'autonomous' is the most interesting and will be discussed now.

2.1.1 *Autonomy and Automation*

The terms 'autonomy' and 'automation' are often used interchangeably without being conscious of their differences. To ensure conceptual clarity and precision, it is important to explain and establish the relationship between these terms.

Automation describes the execution of a pre-defined program by an artificial system.[19] The program is structured as a strict if-then system and does not allow for any flexibility.[20] All actions taken by the system are predictable and human control is not required during the performance of the task. Automation is often used to shift repetitive and constant work from humans to machines.[21]

Nowadays, automation is indispensable in the maritime industry.[22] The majority of merchant ships are equipped with an autopilot, which is connected directly or indirectly to the vessel's steering mechanism and can maintain a set course without human involvement. Advanced autopilots can reduce fuel consumption, minimize rudder movement, and adapt the course and speed to the sea state, waves, and currents. However, autopilots are limited in their ability to respond to unforeseen events. Additionally, automated bilge wells start automatically when a certain amount of liquid is detected.[23] Here, too, automation supports the engineers and does not replace them.

With the availability of advanced technical tools for data handling and optimization, autonomy has become ubiquitous in daily and professional life. This trend has also impacted the shipping industry, offering numerous possibilities for autonomous applications. Autonomy can be considered a continuation of automation and will be introduced next.

---

19 Ørnulf J Rødseth and Håvard Nordahl, 'Definition of autonomy levels for merchant ships: Report from NFAS, Norwegian Forum for Autonomous Ships' (Trondheim 2017) 4; International Organization for Standardization, 'ISO/TS 23860:2022 – Ships and marine technology—Vocabulary related to autonomous ship systems' (Geneva 05/2022) 3.1.2 <https://www.iso.org/obp/ui/#iso:std:iso:ts:23860:ed-1:v1:en>

20 Gabler Wirtschaftslexikon Automatisierung https://wirtschaftslexikon.gabler.de/definition/automatisierung-27138

21 American Bureau of Shipping, 'Advisory on Autonomous Functionality' (Houston, Texas 2020) 8

22 Asbjørn L Aalberg and others, 'Does it do the same as we would? How trust in automated shipboard systems relates to seafarers' professional identity' (2024) 172 Safety Science, 2

23 See Regulation II-1/48 of SOLAS

Autonomy derives from the Greek word *autonomia*,[24] which is composed of 'autos' meaning 'self' and 'nomos' meaning 'law'. Autonomy, therefore, means that 'laws', i.e. abstract rules, are established and subsequently implemented by the executing system itself. An autonomous system is capable of analyzing a situation and determining the most appropriate course of action in a manner similar to that of a human. It does not merely execute pre-defined commands. Therefore, its actions are not necessarily predictable[25] and it has the capacity of self-governance, both for making and executing decisions.[26] The decision-making process of an autonomous system is based on data gained from the assessment of previously made decisions as well as external input provided by the programmer.[27] Artificial intelligence (AI) is used to analyze the data and take the necessary decisions.

If comparing autonomy and automation, it can be seen that autonomy is a particularly complex form of automation.[28] The rise of AI and thus the independence of human assistance is the striking feature driving the transition from automation to autonomy.[29] AI is able to determine the most appropriate solution without a strict pre-defined if-then rule. This enables AI to handle complex situations involving multiple variables. In contrast to automation, autonomy is not limited to repetitive tasks but can perform demanding operations previously exclusive to humans.

However, depending on the number of variables an AI can consider, the level of sophistication of autonomy differs. A system based on an AI that can process three variables of a situation would still be considered autonomous because the most appropriate response is chosen independently from

---

24 Charles T Onions (ed), *The Oxford dictionary of English etymology* (Repr, Oxford Univ. Press 1996) 64

25 Shiva S Tavallaey and Christopher Ganz, 'Automation to Autonomy' (2019 24th IEEE International Conference on Emerging Technologies and Factory Automation (ETFA), Zaragoza, Spain, 9/10/2019–9/13/2019) 31

26 Oxford English Dictionary, 'autonomy, n'. <https://www.oed.com/view/Entry/13500?redirectedFrom=autonomy#eid> accessed 16 February 2024; MSC, IMO, 'MSC 108/4/4: Definitions of terminology of MASS and autonomous systems (IACS)' 7.9

27 American Bureau of Shipping (n 21) 8

28 International Organization for Standardization (n 19); Ørnulf J Rødseth and Lars A L Wennersberg, 'A Criticism of Proposed Levels of Autonomy for MASS' (2023). Proceedings of the 3rd European Conference on Safety and Reliability 2855 <https://www.esrel2023.com>

29 K. C Morris, Craig Schlenoff and Vijay Srinivasan, 'A Remarkable Resurgence of Artificial Intelligence and its Impact on Automation and Autonomy' (2017) 14(2) IEEE transactions on automation science and engineering 407, 408

external influence or pre-defined options.[30] It should be noted that such an autonomous system is not necessarily more independent from humans than an automated system pre-programmed with all possible combinations of the three variables concerned. Therefore, the main difference between autonomy and automation is the capability of self-governance, taking decisions without previously defined paths. The decision-making process of AI is not completely transparent and replicable. This is the critical point from a legal perspective, as it allows machines to make decisions previously reserved for humans in a way that cannot be predicted or replicated.[31]

The International Organization for Standardization expresses this difference between automation and autonomy by defining autonomy as "implemented by automation, but designed and verified to operate without human assistance".[32]

When adding the aspect of machine learning or deep learning, the most successful machine learning approach,[33] a clearer differentiation between automation and autonomy becomes possible. Arthur Samuel coined the term 'machine learning' in 1959 and described it as programming computers in a way to learn from previous experience without human involvement.[34] Autonomous systems equipped with machine learning algorithms are capable not only of selecting the most appropriate solution from a predefined set, but also of improving and learning from previous decisions. To do this, the system needs to be 'trained' with a large dataset of sample situations. The learning algorithm then deduces an appropriate solution to a specific task from the samples and previous experience. This is particularly useful for situations with a large number of variables, such as recognizing and identifying an object and determining whether an evasive maneuver is necessary.[35]

To summarize, autonomy is a highly sophisticated form of automation. Adding the technology of machine learning, an autonomous system is able to determine the most appropriate solution based on external training data and experience gained from former decisions.

---

30 Henrik Ringbom and Felix Collin, 'Terminology and concepts' in Henrik Ringbom, Erik Røsæg and Trond Solvang (eds), *Autonomous ships and the law* (IMLI studies in international maritime law. Routledge 2021) 12

31 ibid 13

32 International Organization for Standardization (n 19) 3.1.3

33 Christopher Manning, 'Artificial Intelligence Definitions' (Stanford September 2020)

34 Arthur L Samuel, 'Some Studies in Machine Learning; Using the Game of Checkers' (2000) 44(1.2) IBM Journal of Research and Development 206

35 Ringbom and Collin (n 30) 10

Turning now toward the practical application of autonomy, the level of autonomy and the scope of autonomy can be distinguished. The level of autonomy can be illustrated by a gradual scale from full human control to full autonomy.[36] This scale allows for intermediate levels, such as supervised and limited autonomy, where human supervision is either constant or at the system's request in exceptional circumstances.[37] The level of human involvement decreases the further the level of autonomy increases. The scope of autonomy, in contrast, describes the range of tasks that can be conducted autonomously. Considering the operation of a ship, either single tasks, such as cargo monitoring, or the entire vessel operation process can be performed autonomously.[38]

The scope of autonomy reflects the fact that a ship is a system of systems. The question of at what point such a vessel would be deemed an autonomous vessel, i.e. how much system autonomy is required to make the whole ship autonomous[39] is beyond the scope of this thesis and potentially a more philosophical question.

In the maritime industry, autonomy is not a stand-alone concept but rather part of a transition process. Together with increased digitalization and the resulting possibility to relocate humans to the shore, autonomy opens up the possibility of thoroughly rethinking shipping. Autonomous operations and the necessity of a human presence on board are closely intertwined and mutually dependent. However, relocating the crew to another place gives rise to different legal questions than replacing crew functions on board with autonomy. The latter touches upon the issue of responsibility, liability, and ethical considerations. The former, however, prompts questions concerning traditional concepts of navigation and on board competence as well as cybersecurity.[40] In order to be able to carry out a precise legal analysis, it may be necessary to assess both aspects separately as a first step before combining them.

2.1.2 *Vessel Operation without Human Presence on Board*

Implementing autonomous technology on board a vessel makes it possible to relocate the crew to another place, the remote control center (RCC). An RCC

36 Rejecting the perception of autonomy as a sliding scale, arguing rather that autonomy is either present or not: Rødseth and Wennersberg (n 28) 2856

37 Ringbom and Collin (n 30) 13

38 ibid 14

39 This question was raised by Eero Lehtovaara, Head of Regulatory and Public Affairs at ABB Marine & Ports at the 3rd International Ship Autonomy and Sustainability Summit in Oslo in April 2022

40 Ringbom and Collin (n 30) 8

is defined as “a location remote from the [vessel] that can operate some or all aspects of the functions of the [vessel]”.[41]

The crew located in the RCC is referred to as ‘remote crew’. The person having the main responsibility in the RCC is referred to as the ‘remote master’ of a vessel. The location of the crew has to be distinguished from the availability of a competent crew to operate the vessel from either aboard or remotely. This aspect is expressed by the manning level, which can vary during different voyages or even during a single voyage.[42] Several interim stages between fully manned and fully remote controlled are conceivable. In the case of remote operation, the crew does not need to be on board. Thus, a remotely operated vessel is deemed to have no crew on board.

To allow the remote crew to navigate the vessel safely, the RCC could be constructed similar to the navigation bridge on board a vessel.[43] Sensors are installed on the vessel and a steady line of communication between the vessel and the RCC ensures a constant flow of information and commands.[44] In the RCC, all data collected from the vessel is gathered and presented to the operator. For presentation different dashboards and monitors can be combined to offer the remote operator the most overseeable set up.[45] For visualization, insights from software and system engineering and human perception research can be applied. Particularly, the konect method can be used to develop safety-critical human-machine interfaces.[46] This method combines insights from research on human perception and the design of human-machine interfaces to facilitate the development of an adequate visualization of information for monitoring tasks in safety-critical systems. Depending on the level of autonomy, the

41 MSC, IMO, ‘MSC 107/5/1: Report of the MSC-LEG-FAL Joint Working Group on MASS on its second session’ (London 2 May 2023) 27; International Organization for Standardization (n 19) 3.1.8

42 Ringbom and Collin (n 30) 11

43 MSC, IMO, ‘MSC 107/INF.14: Study on the definition and organization of a Remote Control Centre (RCC) with a view to its certification (Belgium)’ (London 28 March 2023) 65

44 Chong-Ju Chae, Mingyu Kim and Hyung-Ju Kim, ‘A Study on Identification of Development Status of MASS Technologies and Directions of Improvement’ (2020) 10(13) Applied Sciences, 8–9

45 Yemao Man and others, ‘From Desk to Field – Human Factor Issues in Remote Monitoring and Controlling of Autonomous Unmanned Vessels’ (2015) 3 Procedia Manufacturing 2674, 2675–2676; Mikael Wahlström and others, ‘Human Factors Challenges in Unmanned Ship Operations – Insights from Other Domains’ (2015) 3 Procedia Manufacturing 1038, 1044

46 Marie-Christin Harre, ‘Supporting Supervisory Control of Safety-Critical Systems with Rationally Justified Information Visualizations’ (Dissertation, Carl von Ossietzky Universität 2019)

crew is able to monitor the vessel or remotely operate the rudder and thrusters directly potentially bypassing an autonomous system.[47] The exact structure of the RCC depends on the respective application. The design of the RCC is particularly important to ensure safe navigation of the vessel. Particular attention has to be given to a frictionless human-machine interaction. Insights from other industries have revealed that a reduced sense of the vessel, information overload, and a reduced safety margin present considerable risks in remote operation.[48] Extending the KONECT method to multimodal perception including haptic and audio as well as individual interface elements can reduce these risks.[49] As an example, involving the operator actively reduces the risk of inattentiveness.[50] Moreover, operating in pairs allows for cross-checks and working next to each other reduces the risk of inattentiveness.[51] In conclusion, the setup of the RCC is critical to the safe operation of MASS. Depending on the mode of operation (remotely or autonomously controlled), the set up could vary. The different set ups of RCC s designed during research projects illustrates the manifold variations. The IMO MASS Code does not prescribe a specific set up, rather it determines functional requirements to be fulfilled and demonstrated during the verification process.[52]

2.1.3 *Autonomy and Manning*

After having introduced autonomy and remote operation as separate topics, the two concepts will be combined, considering business application of MASS. Theoretically, all combinations of manning level, level of autonomy, and scope of autonomy are conceivable. However, the benchmark in practice is the safe and economically viable operation of a vessel.

To ensure safe remote operation, the vessel needs the technical capability to communicate with the RCC, if the vessel is remotely controlled.[53] In the case of a restricted bandwidth capacity, the amount of information that can be

47 Wahlström and others (n 45) 1039

48 ibid 1040

49 Marcel Saager, Jan Patrick Osterloh and Yvonne Brück, 'KONECT: Implementation and Extension of a Method for the Development of Safety-Critical Human-Machine Interaction Interfaces' (2022) 61 Human Factor in Software and Systems Engineering 1, 6

50 Peter Barthelsson and Jacob Sagefjord, *Autonomous ships and the operator's role in a Shore Control Centre – A comparative analysis on projects in the Scandinavian region and implementing the experience of Mariners to a new field of shipping* (2017) 38; Erik Veitch and Ole A Alsos, 'Gorillas on a boat: Inattentional blindness during supervisory control of autonomous vessels' (2023) 2618(1) Journal of Physics: Conference Series, 7

51 Barthelsson and Sagefjord (n 50) 48–49

52 See Chapter 2 "Remote Operation", section 2.2 of the IMO MASS-Code

53 Ringbom and Collin (n 30) 15

transferred to the RCC is limited. Current communication technologies used in the maritime section such as satellite communication, short wave channels, and very high frequenz radio communication do not offer sufficient bandwidth for video streaming.[54] Moreover, delay in transmitting information causes a major challenge, particularly for remote operations.[55] Although technological innovation concerning maritime communication are to be awaited,[56] measures have to be implemented to ensure safe handling of communication black outs. The vessel itself should be able to prioritize the collected information. Furthermore, in case of loss of communication, a 'fallback mechanism'[57] an ample level and scope of autonomy to either maintain the current position and avoid collisions or proceed to a predetermined safe anchor place[58] are necessary to avoid maritime casualties.[59] Irrespective of the general level of autonomy, the fallback mechanism must be fully autonomous as it operates in situations where there is no reliable communication with the RCC.[60] Thus, operations without a crew on board necessitate autonomy.

In contrast, a high level of autonomy does not necessitate remote operation.[61] However, it presupposes the technical ability of the autonomous system to solve complex tasks without human intervention. The higher the level of human involvement, the lower the level of intelligence, i.e. the system's ability

54 Cunqian Yu and others, 'Maritime Broadband Communications: Applications, Challenges and an Offshore 5G-virtual MIMO Paradigm' (2020 IEEE Intl Conf on Parallel & Distributed Processing with Applications, Big Data & Cloud Computing, Sustainable Computing & Communications, Social Computing & Networking (ISPA/BDCloud/SocialCom/SustainCom), Exeter, United Kingdom, 17.12.2020–19.12.2020) 1287; Jun-Bo Wang and others, 'Unmanned Surface Vessel Assisted Maritime Wireless Communication Toward 6G: Opportunities and Challenges' (2022) 29(6) IEEE Wireless Communications 72, 72; Fahad S Alqurashi and others, 'Maritime Communications: A Survey on Enabling Technologies, Opportunities, and Challenges' (2023) 10(4) IEEE Internet Things Journal 3525, 3525

55 Yu and others (n 54) 1286; Henrik Ringbom, 'Regulating Autonomous Ships—Concepts, Challenges and Precedents' (2019) 50(2–3) Ocean Development & International Law 141, 156

56 Yu and others (n 54) 1290; Wang and others (n 54) 78

57 MSC, IMO, 'MSC 108/4/4' (n 26) 7.19

58 Michal Chwedczuk, 'Analysis of the legal status of unmanned commercial vessels in U.S. admirality and maritime law' (2016) 47(2) Journal of Maritime Law and Commerce 123

59 Ringbom and Collin (n 30) 15

60 Johan Schelin, 'The responsibility for unmanned ships – shipmaster's position' in Institut du Droit International des Transportes (ed), *N° spécial – colloque international 50ème anniversaire de l'IDIT* (2020) 42

61 Ringbom and Collin (n 30) 15; Ørnulf J Rødseth and Håvard Nordahl, 'Definitions for Autonomous Merchant Ships' (Trondheim 2017)

to solve complex goals, may be.[62] As illustrated above, the system's intelligence can be limited in several ways: the number of tasks, the number of variables considered, and the number of available solutions.[63] Especially a limited number of available solutions can pose a significant risk to safe navigation. In areas of high traffic density or situations of restricted visibility due to fog, rain, or snow, it is impossible to foresee all eventualities and provide the system with an appropriate command for each situation. Hence, a system unable to develop new solutions using machine learning technology would frequently be prevented from reacting appropriately to external circumstances. Due to the posed risk, such systems may not operate independently from humans for safety reasons.[64] Furthermore, one has to bear in mind that the level and scope of autonomy can vary during a voyage depending on the area of sailing, weather and traffic conditions, and other parameters.[65] Accordingly, the degree of human involvement can vary during a voyage.

To conclude, remote operations require some autonomy to cope with extraordinary situations such as the loss of communication with the RCC. In contrast, autonomous operations necessitate human involvement as long as the reliable and safe control of even unpredictable situations cannot be achieved through autonomous means. Since technology is constantly developing and little experience with real-life scenarios has been gained so far, the technical possibilities have not yet been fully explored.

Since discussing MASS, the IMO was aware of the conceptual difference between autonomous operations and a human presence on board, though acknowledged their actual interplay. To operationalize this aspect, the IMO developed degrees of autonomy, which shall be introduced and discussed now.

2.1.4 *Degrees of Autonomy*

The introduction so far has demonstrated that MASS can be categorized along three axes: the availability and location of a crew, and scope and level of autonomy. Each MASS could be pointed in this three-dimensional coordinate system according to its individual composition. Such an individualistic approach, however, exacerbates a general legal analysis of MASS. For operationalization four degrees of autonomy have been adopted, based on proposals from the

62 Ringbom and Collin (n 30) 10
63 ibid
64 Rødseth and Nordahl, 'Definition of autonomy levels for merchant ships' (n 19) 14
65 Ringbom and Collin (n 30) 15

United States[66] and France.[67] Several national and private stakeholders such as the Research Council of Norway,[68] MaritimeUK,[69] and the China Classification Society[70] refer to the IMO's degrees of autonomy:

- Degree One: Ship with automated processes and decision support: Seafarers are on board to operate and control shipboard systems and functions. Some operations may be automated and at times be unsupervised but with seafarers on board ready to take control.
- Degree Two: Remotely controlled ship with seafarers on board: The ship is controlled and operated from another location. Seafarers are available on board to take control and to operate the shipboard systems and functions.
- Degree Three: Remotely controlled ship without seafarers on board: The ship is controlled and operated from another location. There are no seafarers on board.
- Degree Four: Fully autonomous ship: The operating system of the ship is able to make decisions and determine actions by itself.[71]

The operability of the four degrees of autonomy is at the expense of generalization. Only a few combinations of different manning situations and autonomy levels are shown. For example, no degree combines a high level of autonomy with a crew on board; however, this can be explained by practical considerations, since a high level of autonomy does not require a crew on board and therefore saves the cost of a crew. A high degree of autonomy combined with a conventional crew is therefore unlikely in the long term.

Another aspect to criticize is that the degrees of autonomy provide only two parameters for the level of autonomy and the manning level, respectively.[72] Yet, operations with periodically reduced or no crew, e.g. during night times or parts of the voyage without high traffic density are conceivable. As of today, machinery spaces may be periodically unattended if a proper alarm system is in place giving an audible and visual alarm to the engineers' public rooms

66 MSC, IMO, 'MSC 99/5/12: Comments on document MSC 99/5/5 (United States)' (London 27 March 2018)

67 France advocated for including a degree "0" for fully human-based operation without automated systems providing decision-support to a human crew: MSC, IMO, 'MSC 99/5/4: Considerations on and proposals for the methodology to use within the framework of the regulatory scoping exercise (France)' (London 9 March 2018)

68 Norges forskningsråd, 'Maritime21' (Lysaker, Norway January 2022)

69 Maritime UK, 'Maritime Autonomous Surface Ships UK Industry Conduct Principles and Code of Practice: A voluntary Code' (London November 2021)

70 China Classification Society, 'Guidelines for Autonomous Cargo Ships: Guidance Notes GD20-2018' (Shanghai 1 October 2018)

71 MSC, IMO, 'MSC.1/Circ.1638' (n 18)

72 Ringbom and Collin (n 30) 8

and cabins.[73] Such an arrangement could be installed for the navigation bridge as well. Such interim stages, however, could be reflected by a combination of different degrees of autonomy.

Likewise, partial autonomy could be installed and limited to certain tasks. A navigation system could operate the vessel autonomously; however, the control of the propulsion system could be conventionally performed by humans. The IMO's degrees of autonomy consider the whole ship and thus do not display varying degrees of autonomy for single systems.[74] Although the IMO intended to map semi-autonomous ships,[75] this project was not pursued further.[76]

The criticizing authors conclude that the IMO's degrees of autonomy are not able to serve as a basis to develop a broader conceptual framework.[77] However, the IMO adopted the degrees of autonomy already in 2018. At that time, research projects were not quite advanced. As the purpose of the degrees of autonomy was an initial legal gap analysis, a trade-off between operability and granularity was necessary.

As an alternative to the IMO's scale, reference could be made to other scales developed by industry or academia. Depending on the purpose, the scales vary between three and eight levels of autonomy. Rødseth and Nordahl developed eight levels of autonomy considering automation, the complexity of the environment, and operator independence.[78] Chwedczuk classifies only automated vessels into three classes, namely human-directed, human-delegated, and human-monitored control.[79] Although a more precise scale for assessing different forms of autonomy would be beneficial, the practical application of this scale is significantly limited by the absence of consideration for the level of manning.

Several classification societies have issued guidelines for the approval of advanced autonomous technologies within the current legal framework. The levels of autonomy included are more detailed than the scales developed by scholars, as the aim is to classify a specific vessel.[80] The American Bureau of

73 Regulation II-1/51 of SOLAS
74 Ringbom and Collin (n 30) 8
75 MSC, IMO, 'MSC 98/23: Report of the Maritime Safety Committee on its 98th Session' (London 28 June 2017) 20.2.7
76 MSC, IMO, 'MSC 99/22: Report of the Maritime Safety Committee on its 99th Session' (London 5 June 2018) 36 MSC, IMO, 'MSC 99/WP.9: Report of the Working Group' (London 23 May 2018) Annex 1
77 Ringbom and Collin (n 30) 8
78 Rødseth and Nordahl, 'Definition of autonomy levels for merchant ships' (n 19) 12
79 Chwedczuk (n 58) 129
80 Bureau Veritas (n 80) 10; *Lloyd's register*, LR Code for Unmanned Marine Systems

Shipping provides four Smart-to-Autonomy levels,[81] however, not including the location of the crew.[82] In contrast, DNV and ClassNK refused a one-fits-all approach[83] as it prevents from considering the particularities of different systems on board. Different scales are applied for navigation[84] and engineering[85] functions. Although this allows for verifying systems on board a vessel operating at different levels of automation, an overall classification of the vessel cannot be provided.

As this short overview has illustrated, several scales of degrees or levels of autonomy have been developed. The level of detail depends on the purpose of the respective scale. If the scale is developed to enable a general assessment of regulatory, political, economic, or societal aspects, a high degree of detail makes general statements more complicated. It is, therefore, to be welcomed that the IMO adopted only four degrees of autonomy as a basis for the legal gap analysis.

Classification societies, however, adopted levels of autonomy to approve a specific vessel, which necessitates detailed scales. Scholars focused on different dimensions of autonomy when providing scales for levels of autonomy. Such an approach is advantageous for developing a comprehensive conceptual framework. For legal analysis, though, the manning aspect should be included.

The present thesis will not address MASS from the technical side but will focus on the regulatory aspects. It is not intended to provide a comprehensive taxonomy for MASS; hence, a scale of degrees of autonomy designed in a way more straightforward is sufficient for this research. Therefore, the IMO's degrees of autonomy will be referred to in this thesis when necessary.

The uncertainties of how an autonomous navigation system will react to unknown situations makes some form of human involvement at all levels of autonomy necessary.[86] The wording adopted by the IMO is not precise about the level of human involvement at degree four. Anticipating the following presentation of research projects, degree four 'fully autonomous' is understood

---

81 American Bureau of Shipping (n 21) 9

82 ibid 6

83 ClassNK, 'Guidelines for Automated and Autonomous Operation on ships (ver. 1.0): Design development, Installation and Operation of Automated Operation System/ Remote Operation System' (Chiyoda, Tokyo January 2020)

84 DNV GL AS Maritime, 'Autonomous and remotely operated ships: Class Guideline' (Høvik, Norway September 2021) DNVGL-CG-0264 50

85 ibid 66

86 Barış Soyer, 'The Future of Autonomous Shipping – The Regulatory Challenge' in Barış Soyer and Andrew Tettenborn (eds), *Artificial Intelligence and Autonomous Shipping: Developing the International Legal Framework* (Hart Publishing 2021) 166

as including vessels performing most operational tasks without active human involvement. Humans, however, constantly monitor the vessel, can take over control whenever necessary, and be called upon by the autonomous system when facing a challenging situation.[87] Degree four, therefore, includes constant human involvement.[88] The monitoring task is performed at the RCC.

2.1.5 *Conclusions*

This section paved the conceptual ground for the subsequent legal analysis of Maritime Autonomous Surface Ship. The definition and the degrees of autonomy developed by the IMO will be used.

Autonomy is defined as an advanced form of automation that can determine the most appropriate response to specific external circumstances. The addition of machine learning technology further enhances autonomy, enabling a system to respond to unforeseeable circumstances by combining a training dataset with experiences.

Increased autonomy provides the possibility of reducing the number of crew members physically present on the vessel. Relocating the crew to an RCC or eliminating direct human involvement becomes possible.

From a practical point of view, both aspects, manning and autonomy, are closely intertwined and impact each other. Consequently, the term MASS encompasses both remote and on board operation, as well as direct human and autonomous control of the ship, though human monitoring is still necessary.

As most legal challenges arise from either the removal of the crew from the vessel or the handing over of control of the vessel to algorithms, the use of the term MASS in this study will focus on vessels without a crew on board that are either remotely or autonomously controlled, i.e. degrees three and four.

Before turning towards ongoing research projects, two remarks have to be made. First, one has to keep in mind that the manning of a vessel is a gradual scale and can vary throughout a single voyage and between different voyages of a vessel depending on the area of operation, the traffic density, or other aspects.[89] The specific legal challenges caused by a steady shift of control are not discussed here but have to be kept in mind when assessing real-life scenarios.

---

87 The AUTOSHIP project adopts the same restriction of the term: Yassen A Ahmed and Carolina Salas, 'D7.4 Proposed regulatory, legal and liabilities frameworks amendments' (November 2022) 30–31

88 MSC, IMO, 'MSC 107/5/1' (n 41) 13.3; Rana Saha, Monica Lundh and Scott MacKinnon, 'The shift toward autonomous European inland waterway shipping: Identifying the gaps in the emerging socio-technical system' (2023) 2618(1) Journal of Physics: Conference Series, 5

89 Ringbom and Collin (n 30) 11

Second, some projects do not only deal with one vessel, but several vessels forming a fleet operated jointly by one RCC. Similarly, vessel train concepts are discussed.[90] In these scenarios, the conventional assignment of one crew to one vessel is disrupted.[91] The specific legal challenges of this mode of operation will not be included in this study.

2.2 Technical Development and Research Projects

This section gives an overview of ongoing research projects on MASS. The maritime industry conducts research on autonomous vessels worldwide. Since 2015, the efforts have increased and some projects managed to start operating MASS in real-life. Due to the large number of research projects and the constant emergence of new projects, no attempt has been made to provide a comprehensive overview of the projects. In 2022, more than 340 research projects were identified.[92] Here, the focus is on European projects oriented towards the operation of MASS.

Most autonomous navigation and docking system are based on the fusion of the data received by the Automatic Information System (AIS), light detecting and ranging systems (LIDAR), and radio detection and ranging systems (RADAR) together with data gathered by camera supervision. The affiliated cyber and data infrastructure requires tremendous innovation and extensive trials. Moreover, research projects are confronted with challenges regarding propulsion, mooring, and ship design.

First projects of remote control of ships can be traced back to Nikola Tesla at the beginning of the 20th century.[93] During the First and Second World War, remotely operated vessels were used for naval purposes; most of the vessels were destroyed or sunk due to technical failure.[94]

90 Hilde Meersman and others, 'Evaluating the performance of the vessel train concept' (2020) 12(1) European Transport Research Review

91 Ørnulf J Rødseth, Lars A L Wennersberg and Håvard Nordahl, 'Levels of autonomy for ships' (2022) 2311(1) Journal of Physics: Conference Series, 3

92 Institut für Seeverkehrswirtschaft und Logistik, 'Projektkatalog' (Hamburg 2022)

93 Tesla, 'Nikola Tesla Timeline' <https://teslauniverse.com/nikola-tesla/timeline/1898-tesla-demonstrates-worlds-first-wireless-remote-controlled-boat> accessed 16 February 2024; Nikola Tesla, 'My Inventions: VI. The Art of Telautomatics' (1919) 78(6) Electrical Experimenter, 600

94 Harald Fock, *Marinekleinkampfmittel* (Wehrwissenschaftliche Berichte herausgegeben vom Arbeitskreis für Wehrforschung vol 3, J. F. Lehmanns Verlag 1968) 95–96

Today, the Nordic region,[95] and Norway in particular,[96] is one of the world's leaders in respect of autonomous ships. Interviews with Norwegian maritime experts revealed that being at the forefront of maritime autonomy is an issue of national pride for Norway as a seafaring nation.[97] The accumulation of research projects in Scandinavia can be attributed to the involvement of leading maritime industry stakeholders such as Kongsberg, ABB, and Rolls-Royce. The long coastal line provides numerous domestic use cases for autonomous vessels, and the region's openness to innovative technologies further contributes to the growth of this field.

In 2015, first projects conducted research on technological, legal, and economic aspects of autonomous shipping.[98] Although the goal of building a full-scale proof of concept demonstrator[99] could only be reached by the ReVolt project,[100] the project final reports present a way forward addressing different stakeholders[101] and considering navigation, mooring,[102] maintenance,[103] and financial performance.

In 2018, Kongsberg Maritime and Wilhelmsen, a Norwegian Shipping Company, founded the joint venture 'Massterly' providing its customers with the entire value chain for autonomous ships, from design and approval by the relevant authorities to vessel operation, remote control systems, and insurance. The focus lies on short-sea shipping to shift transport capacities from road to sea. However, in the future, deep-sea shipping will also be covered by the company's activities.[104]

Massterly operates the fully autonomous zero-emission 120 TEU container ship *Yara Birkeland* on the Oslofjord.[105] The trials are very successful and both,

95 Denmark, Finland, Iceland, Norway, and Sweden

96 See for an overview of Norwegian projects: MSC, IMO, 'MSC 108/INF.16: Ongoing MASS projects in Norway (Norway)' (London 12 March 2024)

97 Kanna Rajan, Karlyn D Stanley, 'Unmanned Cargo Vessels: A Working Paper' (Santa Monica, California 2023) 8

98 Esa Jokioinen and others, 'Remote and Autonomous Ships, AAWA: The next steps' (AAWA, London 2016); DNV GL AS Maritime, 'ReVolt Report' (Høvik, Norway 27 February 2015) 2015-0170, Rev. 01

99 Jokioinen and others (n 98) 13

100 DNV GL AS Maritime, 'ReVolt Report' (n 98) 5

101 Jouni Saarni, Sini Nordberg-Davies and Antti Saurama, 'Outlook on the transition towards autonomous shipping' (Turku 2018)

102 DNV GL AS Maritime, 'ReVolt Report' (n 98) 3

103 ibid 4

104 Massterly, 'What we do' <https://www.massterly.com/what-we-do> accessed 16 February 2024

105 Ash Jones, 'Self-Propelled Ship Yara Birkeland Completes Maiden Voyage' (22 November 2021) <https://industryeurope.com/sectors/transportation/slef-propelled-ship-yara-birkland-completes-maiden-voyage/> accessed 16 February 2024

autonomous navigation and autonomous docking operations function well as reported by Svend Ødegård, remote master of the *Yara Birkeland*. The benchmark for assessing success is the operation of conventionally manned vessels. The project was initiated by the fertilizer company Yara, which aimed at reducing its greenhouse gas emissions when transporting its products to the export terminal. Previously, trucks transported the cargo through the Oslo region, causing approximately 40.000 truck journeys per year.[106] The Yara-project is characteristic of autonomous shipping projects: it is not shipping companies but industrial companies whose core business is not maritime logistics that are using and researching autonomous solutions to optimize their own processes.

The second project operated by Massterly is rather similar. The Norwegian grocery distributor ASKO developed two autonomous and zero-emission barges to deliver groceries. Again the aim was to replace freight trailer routes by waterborne transportation to take load off heavily congested roads in the capital region.[107] In January 2024, the vessels operated with only three crew members on board.[108] Ultimately, the sea drones shall operate without crew on board and remotely controlled.

More projects are ongoing and two more vessels are expected to be delivered from the yards soon. The vessels shall be employed for subsea inspection works, surveys, and maintenance work in the North Sea off the coast of Norway.[109] In 2024, the Norwegian Public Roads Administration and the Norwegian ferry company Fjord1 agreed to operate autonomous car ferries in Norway from 2027 on.[110] However, to perform all tasks relating to passenger handling, neither concept aimed for operations without human presence on board.[111]

Passenger transport as part of urban mobility provides a wide field of application for autonomous vessels: in Helsinki the Finnish company "Callboats" commissioned autonomous and fully electric catamarans for up to 30 passengers.[112] Because of regulatory constraints, a human master has to be present on

---

106 Asle Skredderberget, 'The first ever zero emission, autonomous ship' (2018) <https://www.yara.com/knowledge-grows/game-changer-for-the-environment/> accessed 16 February 2024

107 Maritime Executive, 'An Early Look at ASKO's Autonomous Freight Ferries' (18 January 2021) <https://maritime-executive.com/article/an-early-look-at-asko-s-autonomous-freight-ferry> accessed 16 February 2024

108 MSC, IMO, 'MSC 108/INF.16' (n 96) 7

109 MSC, IMO, 'MSC 108/INF.16' (n 96) 10–12

110 Dagfinn Neteland, *Signerte kontrakt om verdas første ferjesamband med sjølvgåande ferjer* (2024)

111 MSC, IMO, 'MSC 108/INF.16' (n 96) 13

112 Callboats, 'CAT 10 L' <https://callboats.com/cat-10-l/> accessed 16 February 2024

each vessel.[113] In Stockholm, the Norwegian ferry company Torghatten operates the autonomous full-electric passenger ferry *MF Estelle*.[114] During tests, the demonstrator performed in compliance with applicable navigation rules.[115] Initially, a human operator is present on board to improve social acceptance. However, there are plans to relocate the human supervisor to shore during later stages.

The European AUTOSHIP project[116] developed and tested key enabling technologies for autonomous and remotely controlled vessels.[117] Gathering partners from 5 European states autonomous short-sea shipping was approached holistically including legal, economic, and social aspects. In 2023, the project results could prove their practicability during the successful 13-hour test journey off the coast of Kristiansund, Norway.[118] An autonomous navigation system, a situational awareness system, an intelligent machinery system, and a remote control center[119] allowed the vessel to sail approx. 160 nm and to hold the position during unloading in dynamic positioning mode.[120] Ultimately, the developed technologies ought to be installed on board the *Yara Birkeland* and ASKO barges for commercial operations without a human presence on board by 2025.[121]

Also in Japan and South Korea, research on maritime autonomy is flourishing. From 2020 to 2022, the Japanese project MEGURI2040 tested successfully fully autonomous navigation systems for coastal shipping.[122] During three coastal round-trips of approx. 864 nm each, the autonomous navigation

113 Paula Kultanen, 'World's first autonomous on-demand boat in Helsinki, could turn water transport carbon-neutral' (28 September 2023) <https://forumvirium.fi/en/release/worlds-first-autonomous-on-demand-boat-in-helsinki-could-turn-water-transport-carbon-neutral/> accessed 16 February 2024

114 Zeabuz, *Torghatten and Zeabuz Make History in Stockholm* (2023)

115 Presentation by Øvind Smogeli, adjunct professor at NTNU during the annual assembly of the Norwegian Forum for Autonomous Ships, Trondheim, 16.11.2023

116 Victor Bolbot and others, 'Paving the way toward autonomous shipping development for European Waters – The AUTOSHIP project' (June 2020) 2

117 AUTOSHIP project, 'Technologies' <https://www.autoship-project.eu/technologies/> accessed 16 February 2024

118 Marco M Colella and Carolina Salas, 'D7.3_Autonomous-ships Socio-economic impacts perspective analysis' (8 February 2023) 8

119 Ahmed and Salas (n 87) 27

120 Kongsberg Maritime, KONGSBERG *successfully completes autonomous operation of coastal cargo ship as part of* EU's AUTOSHIP *project* (2023)

121 Håvard Nordahl and others, 'D8.2 Roadmap for Autonomous ship adoption and development' (March 2023) 10

122 The Nippon Foundation, MEGURI2040 *Fully Autonomous Ship Program: Successful fully autonomous navigation of large, high-speed, coastal ferry in northern Kyushu seen leading*

system of a car carrier achieved an operation rate of 96% at sea.[123] As the Japanese population declines and recruiting seafarers becomes more difficult, autonomous ships are supposed to maintain ship routes to remote islands and help to cope the labor shortage in domestic shipping.[124]

Supported by the Government's Korea Autonomous Surface Ship Project,[125] the ultra-large LNG carrier *Prism Courage* autonomously navigated from Freeport, Golf of Mexico, to South Korea. Roughly, 5000 nm were sailed by the autonomous navigation technology performing about 100 collision avoidance maneuvers and route optimization.[126] The test revealed that the target detection function using AIS, RADAR, and camera vision worked well and could provide reliable information to the operator.[127] Additionally, the fuel efficiency increased by about 7% due to route optimization.[128]

Companies from the People's Republic of China,[129] the United Kingdom,[130] Belgium,[131] and the United States[132] likewise conduct research on autonomous vessels and trialed prototypes. It is important to note that MASS need to be

---

to improved safety (2022); The Nippon Foundation, *3rd and 4th Demonstration Tests of Fully Autonomous Ship Navigation Successfully Completed* (2022)

123 Japan Radio Co. Ltd. *The Nippon Foundation* MEGURI2040 *Fully Autonomous Ship Project Demonstration test of autonomous navigation system on large* RORO *cargo* (2023)

124 Kanna Rajan, Karlyn D Stanley (n 97) 7

125 Ministry of Oceans and Fisheries, 'The Future of Korea Autonomous Surface Ship' (30 November 2020) <https://www.mof.go.kr/doc/en/selectDoc.do?docSeq=49788&searchSelect=content&recordCountPerPage=&menuSeq=485&searchEtc1=&searchEtc2=&searchEtc3=&searchEtc4=&searchEtc5=&bbsSeq=90&searchValue=autonomous&currentPageNo=1> accessed 16 February 2024

126 Sanja Pekic, 'Hyundai Heavy conducts world's first transoceanic voyage of LNG carrier on autonomous navigation' (2 June 2022) <https://www.offshore-energy.biz/hyundai-heavy-conducts-worlds-first-transoceanic-voyage-of-lng-carrier-on-autonomous-navigation/> accessed 16 February 2024

127 MSC, IMO, 'MSC 107/INF.18: Results of a transoceanic voyage test with autonomous navigation system (Republic of Korea)' (London 28 March 2023) 5

128 MSC, IMO, 'MSC 107/INF.18' (n 127) 6

129 Seatrade Maritime News, 'China's first autonomous cargo ship makes maiden voyage' (2019) <https://www.seatrade-maritime.com/technology/chinas-first-autonomous-cargo-ship-makes-maiden-voyage> accessed 16 February 2024; Andrew Cox, *China's first autonomous boxship readies to enter service* (2021)

130 Ocean infinity, 'Marine Robotics' <https://oceaninfinity.com/marine-robotics/> accessed 16 February 2024

131 Zulu Associates, *Belgian vessel innovator Zulu Associates releases latest designs for first zero emission short sea vessel featuring wind blades* (2023)

132 Wärtsilä, *Wärtsilä successfully tests remote control ship operating capability* (2017); SpaceX-Fleet, 'Just Read the Instructions' <https://spacexfleet.com/just-read-the-instructions> accessed 16 February 2024

integrated in existing logistic chains. This includes, in particular, port operations such as tug services.

The European Union (EU) is heavily engaged in funding research projects on MASS. According to the Sustainable and Smart Mobility Strategy transport by inland waterways and short-sea shipping shall increase by 25% by 2030.[133] As autonomy is one way to increase efficiency and thus the attractiveness of waterborne transport, the research and innovation funding program Horizon 2020 included projects on autonomous vessels: AEGIS, MOSES, and Seamless.[134]

The AEGIS project developed policy measures for a new European waterborne transport system[135] integrating short-sea shipping feeder services[136] in existing supply chains. Special attention was given to ports and cargo handling infrastructure. The project proposes a mother-daughter concept. A daughter ship operates autonomously[137] within sheltered waters and connects small ports and rural factories with transshipment terminals. The mother ship operates between different transshipment terminals and larger ports in a wider geographical area.[138] The AEGIS project also collaborated with the MOSES project on the demonstration of an autonomous container crane to integration of small ports without any cargo-handling infrastructure.[139]

In this project, the integration of short-sea shipping and inland water transport was examined.[140] Additionally, an autonomous docking system was developed including a swarm of autonomous tugboats.[141] In autumn 2023, the project could demonstrate an autonomous feeder vessel performing all parts of the voyage (undocking, transit, and docking) autonomously.[142]

---

133 European Commission, 'Com(2020) 789 final – Sustainable and Smart Mobility Strategy – putting European transport on track for the future' (Brussels 9 December 2020) 45

134 Seamless, 'Seamless – Safe, Efficient and Autonomous: Multimodal Library of European Shortsea and Inland Solutions' (April 2023)

135 Nelson F Coelho, Jan van Tatenhove and Jesper Raakjær, 'D6.1 – Public policy recommendations for a new European waterborne transport system' (Trondheim 1 June 2023)

136 Ørnulf J Rødseth and others, 'AEGIS: Advanced, efficient and green intermodal systems' (2020) 929(1) IOP Conference Series: Materials Science and Engineering, 3–4

137 Odd E Mørkrid and others, 'D2.6 – Roadmap for automated waterborne transport' (2023) 18

138 ibid 14

139 ibid 19; Eleni S Krikigianni and others, 'Automating vessels berthing, docking and stevedorage operations: The MOSES project' (2023)

140 Eleni S. Krikigianni and others (n 139) 3

141 MOSES, 'MOSES Fact Sheet' (2020)

142 Bas de Kruif, 'Autonomous sailing from port to port' (Wageningen, Netherlands, 14 September 2023)

These EU-funded projects contribute greatly to the integration of MASS into existing logistic flows. The integration of MASS into existing transport systems enables the creation of a business case and is necessary for the commercial operation of MASS. Innovative technologies are not pursued without an expected business case.

Additionally, national maritime and port authorities from Finland, Norway, Denmark, China, the Netherlands, Singapore, and Korea have joined forces to launch the MASSport initiative in 2020. The aim of the network is to develop common guidelines for MASS trials in ports, forms and standards of communication in ports and data exchange systems.[143] The Port Authority of Singapore was also involved in trials for autonomous tugboats.[144]

In conclusion, the extensive range of research projects illustrates the diverse applications of MASS. The utilization of autonomous technology in diverse marine environments demonstrates the prospective influence of autonomy across the maritime industry. The projects did not concentrate on specific scenarios but rather addressed the fundamental elements of maritime operations, namely the transportation of goods. Consequently, the projects validated the potential of MASS for large-scale transportation applications. Before turning to laws and regulations, the following part gives an overview of the potential advantages of MASS. Both, the presentation of some technical research projects as well as a spotlight on an interdisciplinary assessment of MASS operations are important to understand the urgency of providing a solid legal framework.

2.3 Economic, Safety, Security, and Environmental Aspects

Technological innovation is spurred by its economic benefits. Autonomy is anticipated to increase efficiency, thereby enabling to provide equivalent or improved services to customers while utilizing fewer resources, including human capital and fossil fuels. Lowering costs may result in higher revenues, decreased prices for customers, or investing in zero-emission propulsion technologies. Specifically lower freight rates enhance the overall competitiveness

143 Maritime and Port Authority of Singapore, 'Flag, Coastal and Port Authorities from Eight Countries Come Together to Encourage Development of Maritime Autonomous Surface Ships' (4 August 2020) <https://www.mpa.gov.sg/media-centre/details/flag-coastal-and-port-authorities-from-eight-countries-come-together-to-encourage-development-of-maritime-autonomous-surface-ships> accessed 16 February 2024

144 Wärtsilä, *Initial sea trials successfully completed by Wärtsilä & PSA Marine's groundbreaking 'IntelliTug' project* (2020)

of waterborne transportation.[145] It would be prudent to exercise caution when considering predictions in this area, given the possibility that other modes of transport could also undergo adaptation and innovation. Additionally, arguments based on safety, security, societal implications, and environmental aspects are put forth in favour of MASS. This section provides an overview of the benefits of MASS considering several disciplines.

2.3.1 *Economic Aspects*

The primary motivation for researching and developing MASS, like any other innovative technology, is economic gain. The first question will always be "Can [a MASS] do the job, and if so, at lower cost?"[146] Several studies have conducted cost-benefit analyses and examined the economic effects of autonomous shipping.[147] Market analysts forecast that the market for autonomous ships is set to double by 2030 compared to 2020.[148] A detailed economic analysis is beyond the scope of this study. Nevertheless, a general overview of the economic benefits of autonomous shipping will be provided.

At first glance, a high potential for reducing costs is apparent. No crew or only a reduced crew is needed, which lowers the crew-related costs such as wages, accommodation, and board. Furthermore, the deckhouse can be removed, which reduces construction costs, increases cargo capacity, and decreases wind resistance[149] as well as ship weight. This results in a lower fuel consumption.[150] An autonomous navigation system will optimize route planning and contribute to improving fuel efficiency.[151] Reduced or no crew costs

---

145 Sauli Ahvenjärvi, 'The Human Element and Autonomous Ships' (2016) 10(3) TransNav 517, 517; Lutz Kretschmann, Hans-Christoph Burmeister and Carlos Jahn, 'Analyzing the economic benefit of unmanned autonomous ships: An exploratory cost-comparison between an autonomous and a conventional bulk carrier' (2017) 25 Research in Transportation Business & Management 76

146 Roger Stokey and Michael Purcell, 'AUV bloopers or why Murphy must have been an optimist: a practical look at achieving mission level reliability in an Autonomous Underwater Vehicle' (Durham, New Hampshire, 23–25.08.1999) 40

147 Ørnulf J Rødseth and Hans-Christoph Burmeister, 'Risk Assessment for an Unmanned Merchant Ship' (2015) 9(3) TransNav 357; T. Porathe, J. Prison and Y. Man, 'Situation Awareness in Remote Control Centres for Unmanned Ships' (Human Factors in Ship Design & Operation, 26–27.02.2014); Kretschmann, Burmeister and Jahn (n 145); Barthelsson and Sagefjord (n 50); Abeera Akbar and others, 'An economic analysis of introducing autonomous ships in a short-sea liner shipping network' [2020] International Transactions in Operational Research 1

148 Allied Market Research (n 1); Markets and Markets (n 1)

149 Nordahl and others (n 121) 39

150 Chae, Kim and Kim (n 44), 7 Kretschmann, Burmeister and Jahn (n 145) 81

151 Rødseth and Nordahl, 'Definition of autonomy levels for merchant ships' (n 19) 7

could make particularly smaller vessels economically viable,[152] as the proportion of crew-related costs in total operational costs is higher for short-sea vessels compared to deep-sea vessels.[153] Operating more, but smaller vessels increases the flexibility and resilience of the fleet.[154] Moreover, increased flexibility decreases pressure on the hinterland logistic[155] and allows the regular supply of more ports.[156] The *Ever Given* accident[157] in 2021 has evidenced the severe consequences of the unavailability of one big ship. Although intercontinental oceanic transportation of goods might be more efficient with large ships, the same does not apply to short sea shipping distributing cargo within a region.

However, high investments in research and development are necessary to bring MASS into service. The costs for the RCC as well as for maintenance services to the vessel in ports have to be considered.[158] Additionally, the construction costs are higher due to the need of redundancy systems and new design requirements. Nevertheless, a study concluded that the construction costs of a MASS would need to be more than 118% compared to the construction costs of a conventional vessel to consume the cost saving potential of MASS.[159] Both, high research costs and construction costs increase the initially required investment and, thus, capital costs.[160]

Although the International Federation of Shipmasters' Association (IFSMA) emphasized that the savings of labor costs will be marginal as crew costs are relatively low,[161] a shortage of competent seafarers is to be expected, at least in

---

152 Akbar and others (n 147) 16

153 Ørnulf J Rødseth and others, 'The Societal Impacts of Autonomous Ships: The Norwegian Perspective' in Tafsir M Johansson and others (eds), *Autonomous Vessels in Maritime Affairs* (Studies in National Governance and Emerging Technologies. Springer International Publishing 2023) 359; Kanna Rajan, Karlyn D Stanley (n 97) 7

154 Marco M Colella and others, 'The AUTOSHIP project: speeding-up the transition towards a next generation of autonomous ships in the EU' (Rijswijk, the Netherlands 6 March 2023) 5 <https://www.autoship-project.eu/news-press/take-a-look-at-the-autoship-e-book/> accessed 6 March 2023

155 Rødseth and others (n 153) 368

156 ibid 360

157 Panama Maritime Authority, 'Marine Safety Investigation Report of Grounding of MV *Ever Given* at Suez Canal Egypt on March 23, 2021: R-026-2021-DIAM' (Panama 2023)

158 Kretschmann, Burmeister and Jahn (n 145) Martijn Streng and Bart Kuipers, 'Economic, social, and environmental impacts of autonomous shipping strategies' in Thierry Vanelslander and Christa Sys (eds), *Maritime Supply Chains* (Elsevier 2020) 142

159 Akbar and others (n 147) 21

160 Streng and Kuipers (n 158)

161 MSC, IMO, 'MSC 99/INF.5: Report of a survey on what maritime professionals think about autonomous shipping (IFSMA and ITF)' (London 9 February 2018)

countries having a population decline such as Western Europe and Japan.[162] The Seafarer Workforce Report 2021 emphasizes the need to improve the recruitment strategy in maritime transport; as otherwise, a shortfall of 26.000 officers is to be expected by 2026.[163] A shortage of competent personnel could increase labor costs making modes of operation with less humans involved even more attractive.

The rise of MASS may lead to a shortage of training opportunities and hence personnel in the short term,[164] as remote masters and officers will likely require training on conventional vessels. However, MASS do not provide such training opportunities on board.[165]

Another interesting aspect is the effect on the maritime employment situation in general. Newly created jobs in RCC s and companies providing soft- and hardware for autonomous navigation and monitoring systems require highly qualified experts.[166] These positions may be more appealing as seafarers are no longer exposed to the risks of being at sea and do not need to be away from home for extended periods of time.[167] This could render shipping a more attractive proposition for individuals who require a regular presence in a fixed location or those with disabilities who have previously been unable to work on board vessels. Consequently, the advent of maritime autonomy could potentially exacerbate existing inequalities. Ultimately, landlocked regions may also become involved in the maritime industry, given that remote operation is not contingent on being situated in close proximity to the coast. A survey among 38 Vietnamese seafarers enclosed the poor working conditions on board sea-going vessels as one main reason for quitting the job early in their career.[168] On

162 Takeru Suzuki, 'Challenge of Technology Development through MEGURI 2040: For Safe Navigation and Workload Reduction' [2021] ClassNK Technical Journal 51; Kanna Rajan, Karlyn D Stanley (n 97) 7

163 International Chamber of Shipping, 'Seafarer Workforce Report: The global supply and demand for seafarers 2021' (8 April 2022) <https://publications.ics-shipping.org/single-product.php?id=56> accessed 16 February 2024

164 Thanasis Karlis, 'Maritime law issues related to the operation of unmanned autonomous cargo ships' (2018) 17(1) WMU Journal of Maritime Affairs 119, 123

165 Carey proposes simulator hours for the training but emphasises the need for further consideration about the training schemes, see: Luci Carey, 'All Hands Off Deck? The Legal Barriers to Autonomous Ships' [2017] SSRN Journal, 7

166 Directorate-General for Mobility and Transport, D2 Maritime Safety, 'Study on social aspects within the maritime transport sector: Final report' (Luxembourg 2020) 49

167 Nordahl and others (n 121) 38

168 Trong T Nguyen and others, 'Current Challenges in the Recruitment and Retention of Seafarers: An Industry Perspective from Vietnam' (2014) 30(2) The Asian Journal of Shipping and Logistics 217, 232

board the vessels, in contrast, particularly low-skilled employees will lose their jobs.[169] It is predicted that the net employment effect is negative, as fewer jobs are created ashore than jobs disappear on board the vessels.[170]

Moreover, countries will be unequally affected. Countries with high-tech companies and highly skilled experts gain benefits from new jobs, whereas other countries could suffer as many citizens might lose their jobs as ratings.[171] Given the current technological limitations of MASS operations, which are primarily restricted to short-sea shipping routes, and the extended transition period before MASS will be widely implemented on deep-sea voyages, the overall negative impact is not expected to be severe. Furthermore, countries that may face adverse effects will have the opportunity to develop and implement countermeasures over the next 15–20 years. Moreover, it remains to be seen how the expected shortage of seafarers and the reduced need for ratings due to MASS affect the overall maritime labor market.

The economic analysis conducted presumed that MASS will be able to call at numerous ports worldwide. But, as MASS require specific infrastructure in ports, port operators have to adapt to the needs of MASS, i.e. install specific navigation aids, appropriate port infrastructure and adjust formal procedures to the absence of a crew. The costs for this reconstruction work could in many cases be externalized, as ports are owned by the public sector. To manage the costs efficiently, MASS operators and owners could be involved in bearing the transition costs.

Furthermore, the low operational expenses make it feasible to offer novel services, for example, ferry services in remote locations[172] or 24/7 operations in minor ports. MASS could also be employed for offshore supply services, salvage, or oil spill response.[173] Several companies are about to provide survey and inspection services with small autonomously operated vessels,[174] others propose deploying MASS for marine litter surveying[175] or other scientific

169 Rødseth and others (n 153) 366; Streng and Kuipers (n 158) 141

170 Streng and Kuipers (n 158) 142

171 ibid 141

172 Yngve K Frøyen, 'Smartere transport Møre og Romsdal L1.4 – Transportfagleg vurdering – Ålesund: Autonome båtruter med utgangspunkt i Ålesund Vurdering av passasjergrunnlag, ruteopplegg og potensielle anløp' 5

173 Sean T Pribyl and Anal M Weigel, 'How an Emerging Disruptive Technology Is Poised to Impact the Maritime Industry Much Sooner than Anticipated' (2018) 17(1) RAIL: The Journal of Robotics, Artificial Intelligence & Law 17; Martyn Wingrove, *World's first autonomous spill-response vessel opens new era in marine applications* (2019)

174 See for example Reach Subsea, Argeo, Deep BV, and Fugro to name just a few

175 Fantina Madricardo and others, 'How to Deal With Seafloor Marine Litter: An Overview of the State-of-the-Art and Future Perspectives' (2020) 7 Frontiers in Marine Science, 6

observation missions.[176] Moreover, rescue ships without a human presence on board could significantly decrease the response time to distress situations in remote areas.[177] In addition to operating MASS, remote control, cybersecurity, and the implementation of autonomous navigation systems present new business opportunities already utilized by companies.[178]

To summarize, the operation of MASS can be economically viable, particularly in the case of short-sea shipping.[179] Reduced crew and fuel consumption, along with optimized route planning, contribute significantly to operational cost reductions. Whilst constructions costs for MASS are currently higher than those for conventional vessels, short-sea shipping services become more cost-effective. The same applies to flexible and resilient fleet solutions. Additionally, several novel services can bring benefits to all stakeholders involved. Certain economic advantages can be attributed to safety, security, and environmental considerations. The following section will provide a more detailed description of these benefits.

2.3.2 *Safety and Security Aspects*

The improvement of safety and security by MASS is relevant for the entire shipping industry. As of today, 80–85% of marine casualties can be traced back to human error.[180] Mostly, bad decision-making and ignorance of rules lead to collisions and groundings. Moreover, fatigue, insufficient communication,

176 Luciana F Coelho and Roland Rogers, 'The Use of Marine Autonomous Systems in Ocean Observation Under the LOSC: Maintaining Access to and Sharing Benefits for Coastal States' in Tafsir M Johansson and others (eds), *Smart Ports and Robotic Systems* (Studies in National Governance and Emerging Technologies. Springer International Publishing 2023)

177 Aldo Chircop, Floris Goerlandt and Jinho Yoo, 'Unmanned Remotely Operated Search and Rescue Ships in the Canadian Arctic: Exploring the Opportunities, Risk Dimensions and Governance Implications' in Aldo Chircop and others (eds), *Governance of Arctic Shipping: Rethinking Risk, Human Impacts and Regulation* (Springer Polar Sciences. Springer Nature 2020) 84

178 See for example Massterly and Remota offering remote operation of vessels or zeabuz providing autonomous navigaion solutions for vessel operators

179 Pauline Bellingmo, Odd E Mørkrid and Egil Wille, 'Feasibility Study for an Unmanned Deep Sea Bulk Ship and Short Sea Container Ship, No. OC2022 A-110' (Trondheim 7 February 2023) 64

180 K. S Fung and Stephen Li, 'Maritime autonomous surface ships (MASS): implementation and legal issues' (2019) 4(4) Maritime Business Review 330, 333; Ahvenjärvi (n 145), 518; Reza Ziarati and Martin Ziarati, 'Review of Accidents with Special References to Vessels with Automated Systems – A Way Forward' [2010], 1 <https://www.semanticscholar.org/paper/Review-of-Accidents-with-Special-References-to-with-Ziarati-Ziarati/bcb58658a7f5cd095c707a75d5c838603518b808> accessed 16 March 2022

poor lookout, and inadequate use of charts are factors in marine casualties.[181] The IFSMA, however, remarked that marine accidents that can be traced back to the poor design of automated systems or a failure of the system to include new safety risks should not be attributed as 'human error'.[182]

If personnel is located in an RCC rather than on board the vessel, fatigue and bad communication between crew members will occur less frequently.[183] However, as shown above, new challenges such as over-reliance arise and need to be taken into account. Nevertheless, the level of safety is predicted to increase overall as a result of MASS. Moreover, an autonomous navigation system is less likely to ignore rules for egoistic purposes. However, technology-specific issues such as software bugs could occur. As autonomous vessels can communicate with each other before they can identify each other on the RADAR courses and speeds can be coordinated early on.[184] This prevents close-quarter situations and economically inefficient short-term course changes. Researchers have already presented reliable automatic collision avoidance systems,[185] thus the increase in safety is foreseeable.

The use of autonomous technology and reduced human error should not overshadow the fact that achieving complete safety comes at the cost of utility. The slower the speed to a vessel, the safer its operation as every potential obstacle can be detected. However, the slower a vessel the less useful it becomes for transportation purposes. Thus, the emergence of autonomous vessels makes it necessary to balance safety and utility. Leading researchers in autonomous transportation advocate moving away from the ideal of absolute safety in autonomous operations.

Accidents lead to loss of lives, personal injury, damage and loss of equipment, cargo, and the vessel. The shipping industry suffers about 900 fatalities annually. This number is almost double the number of fatalities in land-based industries comparable to the shipping industry.[186] MASS enable various maritime operations without exposing humans to the risks at sea. Although it cannot be ruled out that humans are harmfully affected by MASS, the number of fatal injuries is likely to decrease significantly. A quantitative assessment of

181 Ziarati and Ziarati (n 180) 3

182 MSC, IMO, 'MSC 99/INF.5' (n 161) 9

183 Ahvenjärvi (n 145) 518

184 Utredningen om självkörande fordon på väg and SOU 2018:16, *Vägen till självkörande fordon: Introduktion slutbetänkande* (Statens offentliga utredningar 2018:16, Norstedts Juridik 2018) 187

185 Shinya Nakamura and Naoki Okada, 'Development of Automatic Collision Avoidance System and Quantitative Evaluation of the Manoeuvring Results' (2019) 13(1) TransNav 133

186 DNV GL AS Maritime, 'ReVolt Report' (n 98) 4

the impact of autonomous shipping on maritime safety was conducted, and the findings indicated that nearly 70% of all fatalities could be averted when operating all seagoing cargo ships constructed after 1980 without a human crew on board.[187] This corresponds to approximately 98% of the world's merchant fleet.[188] Moreover, fewer collisions and groundings reduce the incidents of marine pollution and oil spills.[189] Hence, MASS operations contribute to environmental protection.

Although MASS have several advantages, one also has to consider the threats posed by MASS. Several authors highlight the risk of cyberattacks.[190] Autonomous navigation systems rely on the Global Navigation Satellite System (GNSS) and need uninterrupted access to determine their position and course. This global system is composed of regional systems, the US' NAVSTAR Global Positioning System, Russia's Global'naya Navigatsionnaya Sputnikovaya Sistema, China's BeiDou Navigation Satellite System, and Europe's Galileo, and provides global coverage.[191] However, the number of incidents where false signals were sent intentionally to mislead the receiver increased recently.[192] Research projects aimed at developing methods to counteract the threat of GNSS disruptions and could provide ready-to-use solutions.[193] Conventionally manned vessels also rely on GNSS and can be harmed by jamming. However,

187 Jiri de Vos, Robert G Hekkenberg and Osiris A Valdez Banda, 'The Impact of Autonomous Ships on Safety at Sea – A Statistical Analysis' (2021) 210 Reliability Engineering & System Safety, 9

188 Danish Ship Finance, 'Shipping Market Review' (Kopenhagen November 2021) 29 <https://www.shipfinance.dk/media/2159/shipping-market-review-november-2021.pdf> accessed 8 April 2022

189 DNV GL AS Maritime, 'ReVolt Report' (n 98) 47

190 Streng and Kuipers (n 158) 143; Mohamed A Ben Farah and others, 'Cyber Security in the Maritime Industry: A Systematic Survey of Recent Advances and Future Trends' (2022) 13(1) Information 22; Kimberly Tam and Kevin Jones, 'Cyber-Risk Assessment for Autonomous Ships' (2018 International Conference on Cyber Security and Protection of Digital Services (Cyber Security), Glasgow, 6/11/2018–6/12/2018); Frank Akpan and others, 'Cybersecurity Challenges in the Maritime Sector' (2022) 2(1) Network 123; Georgios Kavallieratos, Sokratis Katsikas and Vasileios Gkioulos, 'Cyber-Attacks Against the Autonomous Ship' in Sokratis K Katsikas and others (eds), *Computer Security: ESORICS 2018 International Workshops, CyberICPS 2018 and SECPRE 2018, Barcelona, Spain, September 6–7, 2018, Revised Selected Papers* (Springer International Publishing 2019) 35

191 European Union Agency for the Space Programme, 'What is GNSS?' (15 December 2023) <https://www.euspa.europa.eu/european-space/eu-space-programme/what-gnss> accessed 16 February 2024

192 Andrzej Felski and Karolina Zwolak, 'The Ocean-Going Autonomous Ship—Challenges and Threats' (2020) 8(1) Journal of Marine Science and Engineering 41, 46

193 ibid

terrestrial and celestial navigation is still taught at maritime schools and serves as backup methods for navigation.[194]

Besides the navigation system, an autonomous vessel is equipped with control systems for electromechanical systems on board, radio detection and ranging (RADAR), and communication systems. All these systems can be attacked by hackers or malicious actors.[195] When a hacker gains remote control of the vessel, important and confidential information can be stolen, and the vessel can be misled or even used in other harmful ways.[196]

Another aspect to be considered is that, as of today, minor repair tasks and maintenance of cargo are performed by the crew almost daily.[197] Electric propulsion systems are less in need of regular repairs as fewer rotatable elements are used.[198] Redundancy systems need to be installed in case a system breaks down. Moreover, humans have already equipped space missions for several years of operation without the need for regular repair work. MASS, therefore, could benefit in this aspect from experience made in the space or aviation industry although the external circumstances differ.[199]

2.3.3 *Environmental Aspects*

Regularly, MASS are associated with zero-emission seaborne transportation.[200] Although most MASS projects combine maritime autonomy with innovative propulsion systems[201] and route optimization techniques resulting in lower

194 Hochschule Emden/Leer, 'Modulhandbuch Nautik und Seeverkehr' (Emden 26 January 2021) 3

195 Akpan and others (n 190) 126

196 ibid; Donald Liu, 'Autonomous Vessel Technology, Safety, and Ocean Impacts' in Dirk Werle (ed), *The future of ocean governance and capacity development: Essays in honor of Elisabeth Mann Borgese (1918–2002)* (Essays in Honor of Elisabeth Mann Borgese (1918–2002). Brill Nijhoff 2018) 493

197 MSC, IMO, 'MSC 99/INF.5' (n 161) 2

198 DNV GL AS Maritime, 'ReVolt Report' (n 98) 4

199 Felski and Zwolak (n 192) 43

200 All projects presented above use zero-emission propulsion systems. Moreover, almost all MASS projects identified in the global report operate zero-emission: PCCG Point Conception Consulting GmbH and others, 'Internationale Umfeldanalyse zu Anwendungsfällen von Autonomen Maritimen Systemen (AMS)' (Hamburg 22 June 2022). Furthermore, conventional diesel engines require frequent maintenance work which conflicts with the intention to operate without human presence on board. Although the combination of zero-emission propulsion systems and autonomous operation is not coercing, most projects combine both innovative technologies

201 DNV GL AS Maritime, 'ReVolt Report' (n 98) 4–5; Jones (n 105); Chae, Kim and Kim (n 44) 7

or even zero-emission transport, both aspects are not necessarily intertwined. However, there are several practical and economic reasons for the combination.

One reason for using non-conventional propulsion systems for MASS is maintenance. Most breakdowns of the machinery are related to defects of rotating elements.[202] As conventional diesel engines consist of several moving and rotating parts, this propulsion systems demand high-maintenance. As a South Korean contribution to the IMO points out, a transition to propulsion systems requiring less maintenance is necessary to enable vessel operations without a human presence on board.[203] Maintenance on such vessels can only be conducted during port calls and ought to be planned beforehand to ensure the availability of competent personnel. A propulsion system relying on constant maintenance is not compatible with such a mode of operation.

Electric batteries or fuel cell technologies are examples of low-maintenance propulsion solutions.[204] A side effect of these novel technologies is the reduced emission of polluting substances. However, fuel cell technology and electric batteries are not limited to MASS as several electrically powered, though conventionally manned vessels[205] as well as several research projects on the reduction of greenhouse gas emissions from ship engines[206] illustrate. In addition to autonomous technology, zero-emission propulsion represents a second significant area of research and development in the maritime industry. In light of the ambitious emission reduction targets set forth by the IMO,[207] it is reasonable to anticipate a number of innovations in the coming years. While the adoption of zero-emission propulsion is a desirable outcome, it is important to recognize the challenges associated with it, including lower energy density and limited range. These challenges must be addressed.

In respect of the environmental impact of MASS, another aspect has to be considered: comparing the carbon dioxide emissions per tonne-kilometer (tkm) caused by different modes of transport, the shipping sector emits the

---

202 DNV GL AS Maritime, 'ReVolt Report' (n 98) 4

203 MSC, IMO, 'MSC 105/7/6: Comments on documents MSC 105/7 (Republic of Korea)' (London 1 March 2022) 3

204 MSC, IMO, 'MSC 105/7/6' (n 203) 3

205 Chris Randall, 'World's largest electric ferry launches in Norway' (2 March 2021) <https://www.electrive.com/2021/03/02/worlds-largest-electric-ferry-yet-goes-into-service-in-norway/> accessed 16 February 2024

206 Just see for an overview of current research trends: Päivi T Aakko-Saksa and others, 'Reduction in greenhouse gas and other emissions from ship engines: Current trends and future options' (2023) 94 Progress in Energy and Combustion Science 101055

207 MEPC, IMO, 'Res. MEPC.377(80) – 2023 IMO Strategy on Reduction of GHG Emissions from Ships' (London 7 July 2023) 6

least despite the use of fossil fuels.[208] Additionally, maritime transport generates the lowest external costs in €-cent per tkm compared to other modes of transport.[209] External costs do not only include emissions and air pollution but all costs incurred by third parties who are not part of the transport. Even when zero-emission transport modes are compared, shipping generates the fewest external costs by far. Non-greenhouse gas emissions, such as road congestion and accidents, remain considerably high for other modes of transport, particularly truck transport.[210] Hence, making zero-emission maritime transport more competitive and attractive is not only beneficial from an economic point of view but allows for a promotion of zero-emission transport and low external costs.

Increasing the competitiveness of waterborne transport is important as truck transport is increasing although this mode of transportation causes the highest external costs.[211] Especially short-sea shipping vessels could replace truck transport and thereby reduce the external costs per tkm. A modal shift from road to water would relieve heavily congested roads and help to ease traffic congestion, especially in urban centers. This is particularly the case in regions where inland waterways have been underutilized for transportation purposes to date. The fully electric *Yara Birkeland*, for example, carried around 15,000 containers between April 2022 and November 2023, replacing around 8,000 truck journeys in the Oslo region. This example provides evidence of the positive environmental impact of MASS. However, trucks will be necessary for covering the last mile.[212]

Lower external costs and reduced emissions make zero-emission shipping preferable. However, zero-emission fuels and propulsion systems are still more expensive than conventional systems. Thus, from an economic point of view, it is not viable to invest in zero-emission transportation. At this point, autonomy provides an advantage as it creates an economic margin to finance more expensive zero-emission propulsion systems.[213] Both, reduced costs for crew and optimized routes reducing fuel consumption create the necessary

---

208 Claus Doll and others, 'Methodology for GHG Efficiency of Transport Modes Final Report' (Karlsruhe, Delft 30 November 2020) 64

209 Colella and others (n 154) 4

210 Marco M Colella and Anastasiya Azarko, 'Autonomy is not what you think: assessing the external costs of autonomous shipping through the AUTOSHIP IWW use case study' (July 2023) 2 <https://www.autoship-project.eu/wp-content/uploads/2023/07/Autonomy-is-not-what-you-think-assessing-the-external-costs-of-autonomous-shipping-through-the-AUTOSHIP-IWW-use-case-study.pdf>

211 Huib van Essen and others, 'State of play of Internalisation in the European Transport Sector' (May 2019) 43

212 Nordahl and others (n 121) 29

213 One Sea Autonomous maritime ecosystem, 'Autonomous ships and safety at sea: White Paper' (Tampere, Finland June 2021) 3

financial scope necessary for zero-emission propulsion. Autonomy thus leverages zero-emission waterborne transportation.

2.3.4 *Conclusions*

This part introduced maritime autonomy in the context of Maritime Autonomous Surface Ships, presented some ongoing research projects, and discussed the economic, safety, and environmental benefits of MASS. The advent of commercially operated autonomous vessels is imminent. The operation of MASS is economically viable, environmentally desirable, and increases safety. There is a business case for MASS in Europe.

A survey conducted between September 2020 and January 2021 among several involved stakeholder groups such as ship owners, operators, national authorities, and academia revealed that most participants agreed that there is a demand for a transition towards autonomous vessels.[214] Håvard Gåseidnes, former Head of the Department for vessels and seafarers with the Norwegian Maritime Authority, concluded the demand for common regulations correctly by saying that "it is time to act" at the 3rd International Ship Autonomy and Sustainability Summit in Oslo on April 5, 2022.

To act appropriately as a legal scholar, however, a comprehensive analysis of the legal challenges caused by the advent of MASS is necessary. If gaps arise, it is the role of legal scholarship not only to identify the challenges but also to propose appropriate solutions, including amendments to the legal framework. This task is addressed in Chapter 5.

Humans are no longer present on such vessels and the operation of the vessel is handed over to algorithms. These two aspects challenge the very foundation of shipping operations: humans control the vessel from aboard. Consequently, all shipping conventions addressing the master or crew of a vessel or stipulating tasks that have to be performed on board are affected by the advent of MASS. However, some legal requirements pose a greater challenge to MASS than others do. Before delving into a legal analysis of MASS, the current legal framework is introduced. This study does not provide a comprehensive textbook-like chapter on law of the sea. Rather, only those legal texts and institutions relevant to international commercial shipping are presented in an overview. Readers who are familiar with the law of the sea, the International Maritime Organization, and the conventions forming part of the generally accepted international rules and standards are referred to Chapter 4.

---

214 Gerasimos Theotokatos and others, 'Autonomous shipping – an analysis of the maritime stakeholder perspective' (2023) 22 WMU Journal of Maritime Affairs 5, 12

CHAPTER 3

International Regulatory Framework for Commercial Shipping

The set of rules governing international commercial shipping emanate from the international, supranational, and national level. Moreover, public and private law applies. The following section gives an overview of the public law provisions discussed in more detail below in section 4.

Under the auspices of the United Nations (UN), the Third UN Conference on the Law of the Sea adopted the United Nations Convention on the Law of the Sea (UNCLOS). Its zonal approach managing states' jurisdiction in respect of international shipping will be presented below. Special consideration will be given to the status of ports and the scope of port state jurisdiction.

With respect to vessels, UNCLOS refers to 'generally accepted international regulations, procedures, and practices' which includes conventions developed under the auspices of the IMO and supplementing codes. In this section, the IMO, as the regulator of international shipping, and those conventions discussed in section 4 are introduced briefly.

3.1 The United Nations Convention on the Law of the Sea

UNCLOS was adopted in 1982, entered into force in 1994,[215] and has been ratified by 168 states. Although leading industrial nations like the United States and Turkey have not ratified UNCLOS, all principles and provisions reflecting customary international law[216] apply to all states irrespectively of their membership to UNCLOS.

UNCLOS looks back on a long codification process. In 1930, the first codification attempt failed,[217] however, 1958, five conventions addressing on the

215 United Nations Convention on the Law of the Sea, No. 31363 10 December 1982

216 See for an overview of identified provisions that reflect customary international law: J. A Roach, 'Today's Customary International Law of the Sea' (2014) 45(3) Ocean Development & International Law 239

217 Yoshifumi Tanaka, 'Law of the Sea' in Simon Chesterman and others (eds), *The Oxford Handbook of United Nations Treaties* (Oxford University Press 2019) 521

 | DOI:10.1163/9789004729483_004

law of the sea could be adopted.[218] Given the rise of the exploitation of natural resources of the seabed in the 1960s,[219] and several new member states to the UN,[220] the Third UN Conference on the Law of the Sea was convened and adopted UNCLOS.[221]

During the negotiations, an effort was made to achieve an agreement by unanimity[222] on politically sensitive issues.[223] Moreover, a package-deal approach ensured that only the entire final treaty could be accepted.[224] This compelled opposing parties, particularly coastal and flag states, to reach a compromise between the geographical scope of a coastal state's jurisdictional and flag states' navigational rights and freedoms.[225] However, the plurality of opinions on some issues permitted only for an agreement at the lowest common denominator.[226]

Since its entry into force, UNCLOS was not formally amended. In 1994, the Agreement relating to the implementation of Part XI of UNCLOS was adopted[227] and in 1995, the Fish Stock Agreement[228] completed the provisions on the management of marine living resources. For the purposes of this

218 Convention on the Territorial Sea and the Contiguous Zone; No. 7477 29 April 1958; Convention on the Continental Shelf, No. 7302 29 April 1958; The Convention on the High Seas, No. 6465 29 April 1958; Convention on Fishing and Conservation of the Living Resources of the High Seas, No. 8164 29 April 1958; Optional Protocol of Signature concerning the Compulsory Settlement of Disputes 29 April 1958

219 Robin R Churchill, Vaughan Lowe and Amy Sander, *The law of the sea* (Melland Schill studies in international law, Manchester University Press 2022) 22

220 Thomas G Weiss and Danielle A Zach, 'Virtual issue: 70 years of the United Nations in International Affairs' (2022) 98(3) International Affairs e1–e19, e5

221 United Nations General Assembly, 'Res. A.2750(XXV) – peaceful purpose of the sea-bed and the ocean floor' (Geneva 17 December 1970)

222 Third United Nations Conference on the Law of the Sea, 'Rules of Procedure: A/CONF.62/30/Rev.3' (New York 1981)

223 Tanaka, 'Tanaka 2019' (n 217) 527–528

224 ibid 528; Alan Boyle, 'Further Development of the 1982 Convention on the Law of the Sea: Mechanisms for Change' in David Freestone, Richard Barnes and David M Ong (eds), *The law of the sea: Progress and prospects* (Oxford University Press 2006) 41

225 Thomas A Mensah, 'Foreword' in Sam Bateman and Donald R Rothwell (eds), *Navigational Rights and Freedoms and the New Law of the Sea* (Publications on ocean development vol 35. Brill|Nijhoff 2000) VII–VIII

226 Erik Franckx, 'Helsinki Conference (1996)' in Erik Franckx (ed), *Vessel-Source Pollution and Coastal State Jurisdiction: The Work of the ILA Committee on Coastal State Jurisdiction Relating to Marine Pollution (1991–2000)* (Brill 2001) 11

227 United Nations General Assembly, 'Res. A/Res/48/263 – Agreement relating to the implementation of Part XI of the United Nations Convention on the Law of the Sea of 10 December 1982' (New York 28 July 1994)

228 Agreement for the Implementation of the Provisions of the United Nations Convention on the Law of the Sea of 10 December 1982 relating to the Conservation and Management of Straddling Fish Stocks and Highly Migratory Fish Stocks; New York, 4 August 1995

legal analysis, it is of particular interest to examine the provisions of UNCLOS regarding flag state jurisdiction and the zonal approach. These will be introduced in this section.

3.1.1 *Flag State Jurisdiction*

A vessel may be subject to the jurisdiction of up to two states. First, each ship is subject to the jurisdiction of its flag state. Second, depending on the location of the ship, it may also be subject to the coastal or port state's jurisdiction. This section will delve into the flag state jurisdiction and nationality of vessels.

Per Article 91 of the UNCLOS each state may grant its nationality to ships by issuing a flag state certificate. Then, the vessel has the nationality of its flag state. For the registration there has to be a genuine link between the flag state and the ship. Although the draft of Article 91 of the UNCLOS elaborated further on the concept of genuine link, this was dropped in the final formulation.[229]

Article 94(1) of the UNCLOS obliges the flag state to exercise effective jurisdiction over the vessels flying its flag, and their crew and master in technical, social, and administrative matters. According to Article 94(5) of the UNCLOS, the flag state has to, as a minimum, conform to the generally accepted international regulations, procedures, and practices when adopting such measures at the least.

Following the oil crisis in 1973,[230] states begun to reduce the safety and security demands,[231] taxation,[232] and administrative procedures. These states issuing 'flags of convenience' became very attractive[233] and major flag states.[234]

---

229 International Law Commission (ILC), 'A/CN.4/104 – Report of the International Law Commission on the Work of its Eighth Session, Official Records of the General Assembly, Eleventh Session, Supplement No. 9 (A/3159)' [1956] Yearbook of the International Law Commission 253, 279

230 Christoph Ilg, *Die Rechtsetzungstätigkeit der International Maritime Organization: Zur Bedeutung der IMO bei der Weiterentwicklung des Meeresumweltrechts* (Campus Druck 2001) 116–117

231 Doris König and Tim R Salomon, 'Flag of Convenience' in Anne Peters (ed), *Max Planck Encyclopedia of Public International Law* (MPEPIL) (Oxford University Press) 4

232 Craig H Allen, 'Revisiting the Thames Formula: The Evolving Role of the International Maritime Organization and Its Member States in Implementing the 1982 Law of the Sea Convention' (2009) 10 San Diego International Law Journal 265, 303; König and Salomon (n 231) 5

233 Douglas Guilfoyle, 'Article 91 – Nationality of Ships' in Alexander Proelß and others (eds), *United Nations Convention on the Law of the Sea: A commentary* (1st edition. C.H. Beck; Hart; Nomos 2017) 10–11; Robin R Churchill, Vaughan Lowe and Amy Sander, *The law of the sea* (Melland Schill studies in international law, 4th edn, Manchester University Press 2022) 258–259

234 United Nations Conference on Trade and Development, 'UNCTAD Handbook of Statistics 2021: Factsheet #14 Merchant fleet' (Geneva 9 December 2021) 4 <https://unctad.org/system/files/official-document/tdstat46_FS14_en.pdf> accessed 4 May 2022

Although the rate of casualties and detentions for vessels flying a flag of convenience is still higher than the rate of vessels flying the flag of a state requiring a closer connection between the flag state and the vessel,[235] one should not assume that all vessels flying a flag of convenience are so-called 'substandard ships'.[236] Most of the vessels are fully compliant with all international regulations. Especially Liberia and Panama, the two world-leading flag states, appear receptive to environmental and maritime safety concerns.[237]

Some states attempted to oppose flags of convenience by arguing that the genuine link[238] requirement was not met. Notwithstanding the existence of certain international principles pertaining to the registration of ships,[239] no consensus was reached with regard to the inclusion of specific registration requirements in text of UNCLOS' predecessor convention[240] or UNCLOS itself.[241] In 1999 and 2014, the International Tribunal for the Law of the Sea (ITLOS) stated that the genuine link requirement does not entitle other states to challenge the validity of registration. Rather, it shall strengthen the effective implementation of the duties of the flag state.[242]

In conclusion, any state may grant its nationality to vessels. A flag state is obligated to exercise effective jurisdiction over vessels that fly its flag. The genuine link requirement is not a prerequisite for registration; rather, it is a consequence of registration. The jurisdiction of the flag state is exclusive on the high sea, in other maritime zones; however, the scope of jurisdiction of the flag state must be balanced with the interest of the adjacent coastal states. UNCLOS provides a fine-tuned regime for the jurisdiction of flag and coastal states, which will be presented below.

3.1.2 *The Zonal Approach*

UNCLOS divides the area of the sea off the coast of a state into different jurisdictional zones and lays down the scope of the coastal state's jurisdiction in

---

235 König and Salomon (n 231) 3

236 See the definition of 'substandard ship' at: IMO, 'Res. A.1155(32): Procedures for Port State Control' (London 28 January 2022) 7

237 Ilg (n 230) 120

238 Article 91 of the UNCLOS

239 International Law Commission (ILC), '121st Meeting' [1951] Yearbook of the International Law Commission 327, 56

240 ibid 127

241 Vincent P Cogliati-Bantz, 'Disentangling the "Genuine Link": Enquiries in Sea, Air and Space Law' (2010) 79(3) Nordic Journal of International Law 383, 397

242 *The M/V Saiga (No. 2) Case* (1999) 1999 ITLOS Reports 10 42 (International Tribunal for the Law of the Sea) *The M/V "Virginia G" Case, Panama v. Guinea-Bissau* [2014] [2014] ITLOS Reports 4 (International Tribunal for the Law of the Sea) 110, 113

respect of each jurisdictional zone. In general, the further a vessel moves away from the coast towards the high sea, the smaller the influence of the adjacent coastal state becomes. The gradually decreasing scope of jurisdiction of a coastal state balances the freedom of navigation and exclusive jurisdiction of the flag state over the ship with the territorial sovereignty of the coastal state.[243]

UNCLOS establishes five zones: the internal waters,[244] the territorial sea,[245] the contiguous zone,[246] the exclusive economic zone (EEZ),[247] and the high sea.[248] The baseline divides the internal waters from the territorial sea.[249] Special regimes are included for archipelagic states[250] and straits used for international navigation.[251]

Article 87(1) of the UNCLOS grants all vessels freedom of navigation on the high seas. This principle was first described by Hugo Grotius in 1608.[252] For the subsequent legal analysis, UNCLOS' regulations on the coastal states' jurisdiction in the territorial sea, straits used for international navigation, and archipelagic waters and port states' jurisdiction are most important.

3.1.3 *Coastal State Jurisdiction*

The sovereignty of the coastal state extends to the territorial sea located off the baseline and extending to a maximum of 12nm, Articles 2(1), 3 of the UNCLOS. Articles 17 of the UNCLOS, however, codifying customary international law,[253] limits the coastal state's sovereignty rights by ensuring the right of innocent passage for foreign-flagged vessels. This right includes either traversing the

243 Moira L McConnell, 'Darkening Confusion Mounted upon Darkening Confusion: The Search for the Elusive Genuine Link' (1985) 16(3) Journal of Maritime Law and Commerce 365, 379 <https://trid.trb.org/view/223978>

244 Article 8 of the UNCLOS

245 Part II, sections 1–3 of the UNCLOS

246 Part II, section 4 the UNCLOS

247 Part V of the UNCLOS

248 Part VII of the UNCLOS

249 UNCLOS provides for two methods to determine the baseline. Either, the low-water line along the coast marks the baseline, Article 5 of UNCLOS. Alternatively, for localities with indented or cut-in coastlines, or islands near the coastline, the straight baseline is employed, Article 7 of the UNCLOS

250 Part IV of the UNCLOS

251 Part III of the UNCLOS

252 Hugo Grotius, *The freedom of the seas, or, The right which belongs to the Dutch to take part in the East Indian Trade* (translated by Ralph Van Deman Magoffin, Oxford University Press 1916) 7

253 *Case Concerning Military and Paramilitary Activities in and against Nicaragua* [1986] [1986] ICJ Reports 14 (International Court of Justice) 214

territorial sea without entering internal water or proceeding to or from internal waters.[254] Article 21(2) of the UNCLOS safeguards the right of innocent passage by preventing the coastal state from adopting laws and regulations concerning

> [...] the design, construction, manning or equipment of foreign ships unless [the measures] are giving effect to generally accepted international rules and standards.

This provision balances the concurring jurisdiction of flag and coastal states over vessels sailing in foreign territorial waters[255] and ensures that national laws do not factually prevent innocent passage. Article 21(2) of the UNCLOS grants legislative jurisdiction to coastal states, but it remains silent about enforcement jurisdiction.[256] Article 24(1)(a) of the UNCLOS prevents coastal states from adopting laws that have the practical effect of denying innocent passage. Thus, expelling foreign vessels from territorial waters could be prohibited. Nevertheless, alternative enforcement mechanisms, such as the imposition of fines, may be employed. Furthermore, the majority of enforcement measures are carried out in port, where the port state may exercise its exclusive jurisdiction. Moreover, innocent passage may be suspended temporarily for the protection of national security, Article 25(3) of the UNCLOS.

The coastal state's jurisdiction is further limited in straits used for international navigation[257] because international shipping depends on the right to use the most convenient way. In such straits, Article 38(1) of the UNCLOS grants the right of transit passage to foreign vessels. Compared to innocent passage, the right of transit passage is more difficult to restrict.[258] Similar to Article 21(2)

---

254 Article 18(1) of the UNCLOS

255 Aldo Chircop, 'Testing International Legal Regimes: The Advent of Automated Commercial Vessels' (2017) 60 The German Yearbook on International Law 109, 120; Satya N Nandan, Shabtai Rosenne and Neal R Grandy, *Articles 1 to 85, Annexes I and II, Final Act, Annex II* (United Nations Convention on the Law of the Sea, 1982: a commentary/ Center for Oceans Law and Policy, University of Virginia. Myron H Nordquist [Ed.-in-Chief] vol 2, Kluwer Academic Publishers Group 1993) 21.11 (f)

256 Richard Barnes, 'Article 21 – Laws and regulations of the coastal State relating to innocent passage' in Alexander Proelß and others (eds), *United Nations Convention on the Law of the Sea: A commentary* (1st edition. C.H. Beck; Hart; Nomos 2017) 25

257 Article 37 of the UNCLOS; known examples are: the Strait of Gibraltar between Morocco and Spain, the Great Belt between the Danish islands of Funen and Zealand, and the Bab-el-Mandeb between Yemen and Djibouti

258 Karin M Burke and Deborah A DeLeo, 'Innocent Passage and Transit Passage in the United Nations Convention on the Law of the Sea' (1983) 9(2) Yale Journal of World Public Order, 389, 403

of the UNCLOS,[259] transiting vessels have to comply per Article 39(2) of the UNCLOS with generally accepted international regulations, procedures, and practices in respect of safety at sea and pollution prevention.

Eventually, Part IV includes provisions on archipelagic states, i.e. states constituted wholly or by one group of islands.[260] The archipelagic waters within the baseline around the outermost parts of the archipelago form part of the territory of the archipelagic state.[261] Article 52(1) of the UNCLOS grants foreign-flagged vessels the right of innocent passage through archipelagic waters. In respect of the duties of the archipelagic state and passing vessels, the regime for straits used for international navigation applies, Article 54 of the UNCLOS.

Towards the mainland, the territorial sea is joined by the internal waters, including ports,[262] located behind the baseline. As port calls are an inevitable part of international shipping, the jurisdictional aspects of ports will be discussed next.

3.2 Port State Jurisdiction

Ports lie within the internal waters of a state where it enjoys exclusive jurisdiction not governed by UNCLOS.[263] Consequently, there is no right of innocent passage[264] except for the situation described in Article 8(2) of the UNCLOS.[265] However, the right to enter foreign ports and, the right of port states to determine conditions upon entry to the port deserve further attention. Additionally, the port state control regime will be introduced.

259 IMO, 'Implications of the United Nations Convention on the Law of the Sea for the International Maritime Organization: Study by the Secretariat of the International Maritime Organization' (LEG/MISC.8, London 30 January 2014) LEG/MISC.8 8; Robert Beckman and Zhen Sun, 'The Relationship between UNCLOS and IMO Instruments' (2017) 2(2) Asia-Pacific Journal of Ocean Law and Policy 201, 221

260 Article 46 of the UNCLOS

261 Article 49(1) of the UNCLOS

262 Per Article 11 of the UNCLOS, ports form part of the coast, thus ports are within the internal waters of a state. See also: Vasilos Tasikas, 'The Regime of Maritime Port Access: A Relook at Contemporary International and United States Law' (2007) 5(1) Loyola Maritime Law Journal 1, 28; Clive R Symmons, 'Article 11 – Ports' in Alexander Proelß and others (eds), *United Nations Convention on the Law of the Sea: A commentary* (1st edition. C.H. Beck; Hart; Nomos 2017)

263 Article 2(1) the UNCLOS

264 Churchill, Lowe and Sander, *Churchill et al. 2022* (n 233) 60

265 Article 8(2) of the UNCLOS grants a right of innocent passage through internal waters if the straight baseline per Article 7 of the UNCLOS "has the effect of enclosing as internal waters areas which had not previously been considered as such"

3.2.1 *Access to Ports*

Since early times, the state's right to decide which of its ports shall be open for merchant vessels is generally accepted.[266] Nevertheless, states are highly incentivized to open their ports for foreign vessels due to the economic benefits.[267] However, discussions about a right to enter foreign ports based on customary international law or treaties continues.

A regulation is considered customary international law if the rule is jointly practiced by states, which act based on an 'opinio iure'. Opinio iure means that the practicing states believe that their behavior is determined by legally binding regulations.[268] Customary international law is binding for all states, not only for those participating in the common practice.

Although most commercial ports are open for almost all merchant vessels, the existence of an opinio iure is lively discussed.[269] The affirmation of the *Aramco* Tribunal[270] was criticized[271] and eventually refuted by the International Court of Justice (ICJ) in the Nicaragua Case in 1986.[272] The Legal Committee of the Inter-Governmental Maritime Consultative Organization (IMCO)[273] confirmed the ICJ's judgment and denied unanimously a customary international right to enter foreign ports.[274]

Turning to treaty-based access rights, UNCLOS dedicates port areas to the internal waters[275] and does not stipulate a right of port access. Rather, the port state's sovereignty over its ports and the right to deny the port access for a foreign-flagged vessel shall be respected.[276] Port states are therefore allowed to

---

266 Vaughan Lowe, 'The Right of Entry into Maritime Ports in International Law' (1977) 14(3) San Diego Law Review 597

267 Vladimir D Degan, 'Internal waters' (1986) 17 Netherlands Yearbook of International Law 3, 8; 18

268 Tullio Treves, 'Customary International Law' in Anne Peters (ed), *Max Planck Encyclopedia of Public International Law* (MPEPIL) (Oxford University Press) 8

269 Grotius (n 252) 7; La Fayette (n 269), 1; Tasikas (n 262) 8

270 Arbitration Tribunal, 'Saudi Arabia v. Arabian American Oil Company (Aramco)' (1963) 27 International Law Reports 117, 212

271 Churchill, Lowe and Sander, *Churchill et al. 2022* (n 233) 61; La Fayette. 'Access to Ports in International Law' (above, n. 90), p. 16.; Lowe (n 266); Tasikas. 'The Regime of Maritime Port Access: A Relook at Contemporary International and United States Law' (above, n. 85) p. 13

272 *International Court of Justice 1986* (n 253)

273 The IMCO was renamed to IMO in 1982

274 Tasikas (n 262) 23

275 ibid

276 *International Court of Justice 1986* (n 253) 213; Tasikas (n 262) 30

deny access to their ports based on a general test of reasonableness respecting non-discrimination and proportionality.[277]

Rather, other regional and bilateral treaties grant port access for foreign-flagged ships[278] such as the Convention and Statute on the International Regime of Maritime Ports adopted in Geneva on 9 December 1923[279] or Article V of the General Agreement on Tariffs and Trade (GATT). Additionally, several bilateral agreements, so-called Friendship, Commerce, and Navigation Treaties (FCN-Treaties) grant the right to port access. As hundreds of such bilateral agreements were entered into, most merchant vessels enjoy the right to enter foreign ports.[280] But, in bilateral agreements as well as in the GATT[281] the member states are not deprived of the right to deny access to the port for the purpose of maintaining or restoring international peace or protecting essential security interests.[282]

In contrast to the controversially discussed question of a right to enter a port, scholars unanimously agree that Article 25(2) of the UNCLOS confirms the right for port states to set up conditions for entry into their ports. This corresponds to the state's interest in controlling their ports as part of their internal waters.[283] The right to adopt national legislation finds its boundaries in general principles, such as Article 300 of the UNCLOS, which obliges the states not to abuse the rights granted by UNCLOS, and other international legal instruments, such as the GATT, FCN-treaties, or codes adopted by the IMO.[284] Additionally, the principle of non-discrimination is widely accepted in international law of the sea and it limits the state's right to impose conditions for entry into a port.[285] When in port, a vessel is subject to the exclusive jurisdiction of the port state. Reacting

---

277 Paul Dean and Henry Clack, 'Autonomous shipping and maritime law' in Barış Soyer and Andrew Tettenborn (eds), *New Technologies, Artificial Intelligence and Shipping Law in the 21st Century* (Maritime and transport law library. Informa Law from Routledge 2019) 73

278 Erik J Molenaar, 'Port State Jurisdiction: Toward Comprehensive, Mandatory and Global Coverage' (2007) 38(1–2) Ocean Development & International Law 225

279 Convention and Statute on the International Régime of Maritime Ports, No. 1379 9 December 1923

280 Churchill, Lowe and Sander, *Churchill et al. 2022* (n 233) 63

281 Articles XX and XXI of the GATT 1947

282 See as an example Article XXIV of the Treaty of Friendship, Commerce and Navigation, No. 3943 29 October 1954

283 Richard Barnes, 'Article 25 – Right of protection of the coastal State' in Alexander Proelß and others (eds), *United Nations Convention on the Law of the Sea: A commentary* (1st edition. C.H. Beck; Hart; Nomos 2017) 9

284 Erik J Molenaar, '13 Port and Coastal States' in Donald R Rothwell and others (eds), *The Oxford Handbook of the Law of the Sea* (Oxford University Press 2015) 285

285 ibid

upon insufficient flag state jurisdiction, port states begun to conduct port state controls. These controls and their implications for international shipping will be investigated next.

3.2.2 *Port State Control*

Besides the adoption and enforcement of specific national laws, port states commenced to use their exclusive jurisdiction in ports to enforce international shipping regulations as a reaction to insufficient flag state enforcement, particularly by flags of convenience.[286]

Vessels that are not properly manned, not equipped with the necessary navigation and radio communication equipment, or which pollute the marine environment can cause substantial damage to and in the territory of the port state. Thus, port states have an interest in ensuring compliance of foreign vessels with international rules and regulations and, if necessary, to enforce international law towards foreign-flagged vessels.

The legal basis for this enforcement activity lies in the exclusive jurisdiction of the port state over vessels calling at their ports. States in Western Europe were the first to join to form port state control cooperation to increase the effectiveness of port state controls.[287] As the inspection procedures were harmonized and repetitive inspections occurred less frequently, more vessels could be inspected.[288] In 1982, Paris Memorandum of Understanding (Paris MoU) was adopted.[289] Encouraged by the IMO,[290] maritime authorities in other world regions followed the Paris MoU example and grouped together to adopt regional MoU's.[291] The Coast Guard of the United States retains a separate port state control regime per Title 46, Chapter 33 of the U.S. Code.[292]

---

286 Guilfoyle, 'Guilfoyle 2017' (n 233) 10–11; Allen, 'Allen 2009' (n 232) 307

287 Despina Kiltidou, 'From The Flag State Duty For Inspections To The Remote Port State Control. The Necessity For Distant Controls' (2020) 14(4) TransNav 963

288 See for a detailed description of the port state control process provided by the Paris MoU: Ho-Sam Bang and Duck-Jong Jang, 'Recent Developments in Regional Memorandums of Understanding on Port State Control' (2012) 43(2) Ocean Development & International Law 170, 171; Z. O Özçayir, 'The Use of Port State Control in Maritime Industry and Application of the Paris MoU' (2008) 14(2) Ocean and Coastal Law Journal 201

289 Paris MoU on PSC, 'History' <https://www.parismou.org/about-us/history> accessed 16 February 2024

290 IMO, 'Res. A.682(19): Regional Cooperation in the Control of ships and Discharges' (London 21 November 1991); IMO, 'Res. A.1155(32)' (n 236)

291 Asia and the Pacific (Tokyo MoU); Latin America (Acuerdo de Viña del Mar); Caribbean (Caribbean MoU); West and Central Africa (Abuja MoU); the Black Sea region (Black Sea MoU); the Mediterranean (Mediterranean MoU); the Indian Ocean (Indian Ocean MoU); and the Arab States of the Gulf (Riyadh MoU)

292 United States Coast Guard, 'Marine Safety: Port State Control' (Washington, D.C. 20 September 2021)

The MoUs are not legally binding as they have been concluded between maritime authorities rather than governments.[293] The language used in the MoU indicates that the intention was not to create a legally-binding international treaty. Instead, the objective was to facilitate transnational cooperation between national public authorities.[294] Consequently, port state MoU can be categorized as international administrative agreements.[295] Although most MoU share great commonalities, differences exist in respect of implementation as some states lack the necessary technology, financial capacity, and infrastructure to effectively operated the MoU.[296]

If a foreign-flagged vessels calls at a port, the port state authority inspects the vessel for compliance with the standards laid down in 13[297] Conventions and Codes. For each ship, a risk profile is determined based on the flag of the vessel and other safety factors, such as the age and type of the vessel. The scope, frequency, and intensity of the inspection depend on the risk profile of the ship.[298] When identifying deficiencies, the port state authority endeavors to ensure the rectification of the deficiencies. In exceptional circumstances, the authority may detain the vessel until the deficiencies have been remedied to the satisfaction of the authority or until continuation to a repair yard was permitted.[299]

Besides harmonizing the inspection process, the MoU aim for the exchange of information among the participating inspection authorities and the publication of inspection data by the Secretariat. Although the port state control system can compensate for some deficiencies in the exercise of flag state jurisdiction, it is limited to vessels calling voluntarily in foreign ports.[300] It should therefore be borne in mind that port state controls cannot substitute effective flag state jurisdiction.[301]

The port state control measures set out in the Paris MoU were made legally binding for EU member states,[302] resulting in a more rigorous application of

293 Erik J Molenaar, 'The EC Directive on Port State Control in Context' (1996) 11(2) International Journal of Marine and Coastal Law 241, 246

294 Katharina Reiling, *Seeverwaltungsrecht als interantionales Verwaltungsrecht* (no date) 228

295 Özçayir (n 288) 210

296 See for an overview and comparison of all nine port state control regimes: Bang and Jang (n 288) 172–183

297 As examples: Section 2 of the Tokyo MoU: 14 instruments; Section 2 of the Caribbean MoU: 20 instruments; Section 1.1.1 of the Annex I to the Mediterranean MoU: 17 instruments

298 See for example Section 3.2 and Annexes 7 and 8 of the Paris MoU

299 Bang and Jang (n 288) 173

300 Allen, 'Allen 2009' (n 232) 311

301 Özçayir (n 288) 201

302 Directive 2009/16/EC of the European Parliament and of the Council of 23 April 2009 on port State control (2009) Official Journal of the European Union L 131, p. 57

port state controls.[303] The European Maritime Safety Agency (EMSA) shall support the European Commission (EC) in ensuring a convergent and effective implementation of the port state control system. Since 2010, the Directive applies to members of the European Free Trade Association as well.[304] Nevertheless, shortcomings in the inspection, the quality of the inspection, and the training of the port state control officers can still be identified.[305]

3.2.3 *Conclusions*

Every vessels is under the exclusive jurisdiction of its flag state. The genuine link requirement is not a prerequisite for the registration and cannot be challenged by third states. The zonal approach establishes five maritime zones off the coast of a state. In territorial waters, foreign vessels enjoy the right of innocent passage, which may not be hampered. However, the coastal state can adopt national laws and regulations giving effect to generally accepted international rules and standards.

In ports, vessels are exclusive subject to the jurisdiction of the port state. Several international treaties grant a right to access foreign ports. Limited by non-discrimination clauses, however, port states can establish requirements for entry into their ports. As a reaction to the emergence of flags of convenience, port states started to inspect vessels calling at their ports collectively for compliance with international conventions and codes. As of today, most regions of the world are covered by port state control agreements. The total number of sub-standard vessels has decreased. In the recent past, port state jurisdiction was used to prevent Russian vessels from calling at ports in the European Union.[306]

Besides UNCLOS several other conventions, codes, guidelines, and instruments affect international shipping. Most of these other instruments can be affiliated with the IMO. Therefore, the remainder of part C is dedicated to the IMO, its relation to UNCLOS, and the conventions adopted under the auspices of the IMO which are of high importance for the legal analysis in part D.

---

303 Bang and Jang (n 288) 173

304 EEA Joint Committee, 'No 134/2010 – amending Annex XIII (Transport) to the EEA Agreement' (Geneva, Brussels 10 December 2010)

305 Armando Graziano, Maximo Q Mejia and Jens-Uwe Schröder-Hinrichs, 'Achievements and challenges on the implementation of the European Directive on Port State Control' (2018) 72 Transport Policy 97, 106

306 Council Regulation (EU) 2022/576 – amending Regulation (EU) No 833/2014 concerning restrictive measures in view of Russia's actions destabilising the situation in Ukraine 8 April 2022, 11

3.3 The IMO and UNCLOS

3.3.1 *The Competent International Organization*

UNCLOS refers in several provisions to the 'competent international organization'.[307] Although the IMO is only explicitly mentioned once in Annex VIII, Article 2 of the UNCLOS, it is internationally agreed that these references point to the IMO.[308] The IMO is entrusted with facilitating maritime navigation,[309] and fostering cooperation for the development of rules, procedures, and practices for marine environmental protection,[310] the transfer of marine technology.[311]

Additionally, the IMO shall support the interaction with other international organizations such as the International Seabed Authority[312] and serves as a hub for information about routeing measures, flag state enforcement measures and pollution of the marine environment. Moreover, the Technical Cooperation Committee[313] of the IMO is engaged in providing technical and financial support to developing countries for facilitating the implementation of IMO instruments.[314]

Most important, the IMO shall further develop the framework provided by UNCLOS as an institutionalized and permanent body of support and expertise for the member states.[315] Regular meetings at the IMO facilitate following current topics and developments closely and adapting processes.[316] The link between the rule-setting of the IMO and UNCLOS is UNCLOS' reference to

307 See for example Articles 22(3)(a); 41(4),(5); 53(9); 60(3),(5) of the UNCLOS

308 IMO, 'Implications of the United Nations Convention on the Law of the Sea for the International Maritime Organization' (n 259) 7; Zhen Sun and Robert Beckman, 'The Development of the Polar Code and challenges to Its Implementation' in Keyuan Zou (ed), *Global Commons and the Law of the Sea* (Maritime cooperation in east asia volume 5. Brill 2018) 308; Beckman and Sun (n 259), 218; Aldo Chircop, 'The International Maritime Organization' in Donald R Rothwell and others (eds), *The Oxford Handbook of the Law of the Sea* (Oxford University Press 2015) 429

309 Recommendations for sea lanes and traffic separation schemes, Article 22(3)(a); 41(4); 53(9) of the UNCLOS; authorizing extended safety zones around artificial islands, structures, or installations, Article 60(5) of the UNCLOS; assigning radio frequencies, Article 39(3)(b) of the UNCLOS

310 Article 197 of the UNCLOS

311 Article 271 of the UNCLOS

312 Chircop, 'Chircop 2015' (n 308) 434

313 ibid 433

314 See Article 203 of the UNCLOS providing for preferential treatment of developing states

315 Chircop, 'Chircop 2015' (n 308) 430

316 Allen, 'Allen 2009' (n 232) 284

'generally accepted international rules and standards'. This rule of reference[317] or renvoi clause shall be discussed further now, before going into detail about the IMO's structure and work.

3.3.2 *Generally Accepted International Rules and Standards*

UNCLOS uses 'rules of reference' to include other legal instruments in its scope. Although the wording differs slightly,[318] the substantial scope is the same for all references.[319] This book will refer to them in the further course as 'generally accepted international rules and standards' (GAIRAS).

The reference to the detailed GAIRAS has considerable advantages. First, it underlines the constitutional character of UNCLOS. As an umbrella convention,[320] UNCLOS determines responsibilities, general obligations, and fundamental aspects and leaves detailed regulations to the IMO and its member states. This prevents a lock-in of any technological solutions and allows UNCLOS to keep pace with advancing technologies and increased needs for environmental protection.[321] Thus, UNCLOS can develop and be adapted to subsequent changes without changing the text of UNCLOS.[322] As the reference is only to *generally accepted* rules, UNCLOS ensures that only widely supported provisions are included. This ensures uniformity of the international legal framework and encourages states to find as many supporters as possible for new regulations in order to overcome the threshold of general acceptance.[323] Second, the reference ensured coherency with the IMO's framework already in place when UNCLOS was negotiated.

---

317 Robin R Churchill, 'The 1982 United Nations Convention on the Law of the Sea' in Donald R Rothwell and others (eds), *The Oxford Handbook of the Law of the Sea* (Oxford University Press 2015) 31; Douglas Guilfoyle, 'Article 94 – Duties of the flag State' in Alexander Proelß and others (eds), *United Nations Convention on the Law of the Sea: A commentary* (1st edition. C.H. Beck; Hart; Nomos 2017) 11

318 See for a comprehensive list of used formulations: Beckman and Sun (n 259), 245, Appendix II

319 IMO, 'Implications of the United Nations Convention on the Law of the Sea for the International Maritime Organization' (n 259) 8

320 Shabtai Rosenne, 'The International Maritime Law Organization Interface with the Law of the Sea' in Myron H Nordquist and John N Moore (eds), *Current maritime issues and the international maritime organization* (Martinus Nijhoff Publishers 1999) 252

321 Allen, 'Allen 2009' (n 232) 276

322 Beckman and Sun (n 259) 227; Irina Buga, 'Between Stability and Change in the Law of the Sea Convention: Subsequent Practice, Treaty Modification, and Regime Interaction' in Donald R Rothwell and others (eds), *The Oxford Handbook of the Law of the Sea* (Oxford University Press 2015) 66

323 CMI, 'Position Paper on Unmanned Ships and the International Regulatory Framework' (n 13) 4

The impact of GAIRAS on flag and coastal states varies.[324] Flag states have to "conform to" GAIRAS when exercising its jurisdiction over the vessels flying its flag,[325] thus GAIRAS are the minimum standard and more strict requirements may be imposed. Coastal states' laws, however, shall not exceed GAIRAS.[326] The duties correspond to each other and ensure a coherent regime of rights and duties in respect of vessels.[327] As all states are bound by GAIRAS as flag or coastal states,[328] these rules could be subject to a dispute under the UNCLOS dispute resolution scheme in Part XV of UNCLOS.[329]

Although UNCLOS often refers to GAIRAS, it does not determine the scope of it. Although the international courts could not yet consider the matter,[330] the scholarly discussion on the scope of GAIRAS is intense. For an instrument to be included in GAIRAS, two requirements have to be fulfilled: Firstly, the instruments must be within the scope of 'regulations', 'standards', 'practices' or 'rules'. Secondly, the instrument must be 'generally accepted'.

The first requirement is rather comprehensive and does not serve as a limiting factor. Binding and non-binding instruments,[331] instruments adopted by the IMO, and those adopted by diplomatic conferences are included.[332] This highlights the great influence IMO law-making has on the law of the sea and the relevance of informal law-making.[333]

Several scholars discussed the scope of 'generally accepted' and three views have emerged. The most limited interpretation requires global acceptance,

324 IMO, 'Implications of the United Nations Convention on the Law of the Sea for the International Maritime Organization' (n 259) 8

325 Article 94(5) of the UNCLOS

326 Article 21(2) of the UNCLOS

327 Rüdiger Wolfrum, 'IMO Interface with the Law of the Sea Convention' in Myron H Nordquist and John N Moore (eds), *Current maritime issues and the international maritime organization* (Martinus Nijhoff Publishers 1999) 229

328 Guilfoyle, 'Guilfoyle 2017' (n 317) 11

329 Zhen Sun, 'Unconventional Lawmaking in the Compliance Mechanism for the International Regulation of Shipping' in Natalie Klein (ed), *Unconventional Lawmaking in the Law of the Sea* (Oxford University Press 2022) 100

330 Churchill (n 317)

331 Natalie Klein, 'Meaning, Scope, and Significance of Informal Lawmaking in the Law of the Sea' in Natalie Klein (ed), *Unconventional Lawmaking in the Law of the Sea* (Oxford University Press 2022) 16; Wolfrum, 'Wolfrum 1999' (n 327) 230; Lene Korseberg, 'The Law-Making Effects of the FAO Deep-Sea Fisheries Guidelines' (2018) 67(4) International and Comparative Law Quarterly 801, 805

332 Wolfrum, 'Wolfrum 1999' (n 327) 230

333 Klein (n 331) 16

i.e. acceptance by all states, for a rule to be 'generally accepted'.[334] Thus, the reference would not add any provisions, which are not binding in any way.[335] The same[336] applies if equaling 'generally accepted' with customary international law.[337]

On the contrary, all instruments adopted by the IMO could be deemed 'generally accepted'. As the IMO adopts legally non-binding recommendations with the majority of the members present and voting, a rather small group could establish standards that are binding for all UNCLOS members.[338] This view should therefore be refused.

Moderately, most scholars require a broad support, however, not global acceptance. The determination of broad support should be based on the number and relevance of the supporting states.[339] The combination of a quantitative and qualitative requirement ensures that most of the world's leading shipping nations including ship-owning as well as flag states accept the respective instrument. The determination of whether an instrument is generally accepted must be made on a case-by-case basis for each individual instrument.

UNCLOS obliges all member states to adhere to GAIRAS in their capacity as flag, coastal, and port states irrespective of their membership to the concerned GAIRAS instrument.[340] This does not conflict with the principle of '*pacta tertiis nec nocent nec prosunt*'[341] as all UNCLOS member states where

---

334 Rüdiger Wolfrum, *Die Internationalisierung staatsfreier Räume: Die Entwicklung einer internationalen Verwaltung für Antarktis, Weltraum, Hohe See und Meeresboden* (Teilw. zugl.: Bonn, Univ. Habil.-Schr. 1980/81. Beiträge zum ausländischen öffentlichen Recht und Völkerrecht vol 85, Springer 1984) 638; Gennady M Danilenko, *Law-making in the international community* (Developments in international law vol 15, Nijhoff 1993) 74

335 Matthias Frenzel, *Sekundärrechtsetzungsakte internationaler Organisationen: Völkerrechtliche Konzeption und verfassungsrechtliche Voraussetzungen* (Jus Internationale et Europaeum vol 54, 1. Auflage, Mohr Siebeck 2011) 163

336 Bernard H Oxman, 'The Duty to Respect Generally Accepted International Standards' (1991) 24(1) New York University Journal of International Law and Politics 109, 146 <https://repository.law.miami.edu/cgi/viewcontent.cgi?article=1403&context=fac_articles> accessed 9 May 2022

337 Willem van Reenen, 'Rules of Reference in the new Convention on the Law of the Sea, in particular in connection with the pollution of the sea by oil from tankers' (1980) 12 Netherlands Yearbook of International Law 3, 11

338 Jurij D Aston, *Sekundärgesetzgebung internationaler Organisationen zwischen mitgliedstaatlicher Souveränität und Gemeinschaftsdisziplin* (Schriften zum Völkerrecht vol 158, Duncker & Humblot 2011) 165

339 Oxman (n 336), 157; Guilfoyle, 'Guilfoyle 2017' (n 317) 11; Frenzel (n 335) 165; Aston (n 338) 165

340 Wolfrum, 'Wolfrum 1999' (n 327) 231

341 See also Article 34 of the Vienna Convention on the Law of the Treaties

aware of the reference when ratifying UNCLOS. Moreover, most member states of UNCLOS are also a member to the IMO and can therefore participate in the rule-setting.[342] Diplomatic conferences convened by the IMO to adopt international conventions are not limited to IMO members, but are open to all states.

Article 311(2) of the UNCLOS addresses the relation between IMO treaties and UNCLOS and states that UNCLOS

> [...] shall not alter the rights and obligations of States Parties which arise from other agreements compatible with this Convention and which do not affect the enjoyment by other States Parties of their rights or the performance of their obligations under this Convention.

This provision departs from the general principle that the latter treaty should prevail over the earlier treaty ('*lex posterior derogat lex priori*')[343] laid down in Article 30(3) of the Vienna Convention on the Law of the Treaties (VCLT). It allows for the exercise of past and future treaties as long as these treaties are compatible with UNCLOS.[344] Here, the supremacy of UNCLOS and its framework character are highlighted.[345]

The practice has shown that a contradiction between UNCLOS and IMO instrument is highly unlikely. Firstly, most members of the IMO are also a member of UNCLOS, thus consider UNCLOS during law-making activities at the IMO. Secondly, most IMO conventions contain non-prejudice clauses[346] to

342 Only Laos, Burkina Faso, Lesotho, Mali and Niger are only members of the UNCLOS but not a member of the IMO; see: United Nations Treaty Collection, '6. United Nations Convention on the Law of the Sea' <https://treaties.un.org/Pages/ViewDetailsIII.aspx?src=TREATY&mtdsg_no=XXI-6&chapter=21&Temp=mtdsg3&clang=_en> accessed 16 February 2024; IMO, 'Member States' <https://www.imo.org/en/OurWork/ERO/Pages/MemberStates.aspx> accessed 16 February 2024; also Wolfrum, 'Wolfrum 1999' (n 327) 232

343 Nele Matz-Lück, 'Treaties, Conflicts between' in Anne Peters (ed), *Max Planck Encyclopedia of Public International Law* (MPEPIL) (Oxford University Press) 8

344 Nele Matz-Lück, 'Article 311 – Relation to other conventions and international agreements' in Alexander Proelß and others (eds), *United Nations Convention on the Law of the Sea: A commentary* (1st edition. C.H. Beck; Hart; Nomos 2017) 11

345 ibid 12

346 See e.g. Article 5 (4) of the STCW "Nothing in the Convention shall prejudice the codification and development of the law of the sea by the United Nations Conference on the Law of the Sea convened pursuant to resolution 2750 C(XXV) of the General Assembly of the United Nations, nor the present or future claims and legal views of any State concerning the law of the sea and the nature and extent of coastal and flag State jurisdiction"

prevent any conflicts with UNCLOS. Eventually, the IMO secretariat took part in the drafting process of UNCLOS to ensure no overlapping or inconsistency.[347]

3.3.3 *High-Priority Instruments for MASS*

In total, the IMO has drafted more than 40 conventions covering a much wider range of topics than just navigational safety. Conventions addressing the protection of the marine environment,[348] the safety of vessels,[349] liability issues,[350] liability for oil pollution,[351] and carriage of goods by sea[352] form part of the international framework for shipping. The only major subject not covered by IMO conventions is third party and contractual liability.[353] These topics are dealt with in other conventions not discussed here. Additionally, over a thousand non-binding IMO instruments have contributed to a globally harmonized framework for commercial shipping.[354]

In the initial section of the book, general matters are introduced to provide a solid foundation for the subsequent legal analysis in Chapter D. In accordance with the IMO's prioritization, the legal analysis will focus on three high-priority instruments. These will be briefly introduced here, although it should be noted that GAIRAS includes a multitude of conventions beyond these three, namely: the International Convention for the Safety of Life at Sea (SOLAS), the International Convention on Standards of Training, Certification and Watchkeeping

347 IMO, 'Implications of the United Nations Convention on the Law of the Sea for the International Maritime Organization' (n 259) 11

348 See as a prominent example the International Convention for the Prevention of Pollution from Ships (MARPOL), 1973

349 See the Load Lines Convention, 1966

350 See for example the Convention on Limitation of Liability for Maritime Claims, 1976; Nairobi International Convention on the Removal of Wrecks, 2007

351 See for example the International Convention on Civil Liability for Oil Pollution Damage, 1969; International Convention on the Establishment of an International Fund for Compensation for Oil Pollution Damage 1971 and the 1992 Protocol to the International Convention on the Establishment of an International Fund for Compensation for Oil Pollution Damage

352 International Convention for the Unification of Certain Rules of Law relating to Bills of Lading and Protocol of Signature (Hague Rules), 1924; Protocol of 23 February 1968 (Visby Rules); United Nations Convention on the Carriage of Goods by Sea (Hamburg rules), 1978, UN Convention on Contracts for the International Carriage of Goods Wholly or Partly by Sea (Rotterdam Rules) 2004

353 Chircop, 'Chircop 2015' (n 308) 417

354 Sun (n 329) 93; Rosalie P Balkin, 'The IMO and Global Ocean Governance: Past, Present, and Future' in David J Attard, Rosalie P Balkin and Donald W Greig (eds), *The IMLI Treatise on Global Ocean Governance: Volumen III: IMO and Global Ocean Governance* (First edition. Oxford University Press 2018) 2

for Seafarers (STCW), and the Convention on the International Regulations for Preventing Collisions at Sea (COLREG).

These three conventions are included in GAIRAS, as all are binding upon 95–99% of the world's total tonnage.[355] With regard to COLREG, Article 39(2)(a) of the UNCLOS serves as an additional argument as it states that ships in transit passage shall comply with the "generally accepted international regulations, procedures and practices for safety at sea, including the International Regulations for Preventing Collisions at Sea". It should be kept in mind, however, that not all conventions developed under the auspices of the IMO have acquired generally acceptance. The Nairobi International Convention on the Removal of Wrecks from 2007, for example, has been ratified by 65 states representing 79.6% of the world's total tonnage. It is therefore not yet regarded as belonging to GAIRAS.[356]

The first version of SOLAS was adopted in 1914[357] following the sinking of the Titanic.[358] Updated versions of SOLAS were adopted in 1948[359] and 1960.[360] The latest version was adopted in 1974.[361]

SOLAS consists of the main articles of the convention, an annex with fourteen chapters, three appendixes, and two annexes including certificates and documents required to be carried on board ships and a list of resolutions adopted by the SOLAS Conferences. In 1978, a protocol addressing the application of Articles II, III, IV, VI, VII, and VIII of SOLAS was adopted.[362] A 1988 protocol amends some of the provisions of Annex I.[363] SOLAS is ratified by 168 states, the 1978 protocol by 123 states, and the 1988 protocol by 127 states.[364]

---

355 Guilfoyle, 'Guilfoyle 2017' (n 317) 12; IMO, 'Implications of the United Nations Convention on the Law of the Sea for the International Maritime Organization' (n 259) 8; Satya N Nandan and Myron H Nordquist (eds), *United Nations Convention on the Law of the Sea, 1982: a commentary; Vol. III; Articles 86 to 132 and Documentary Annexes* (Brill|Nijhoff 1995) 147–148

356 Chircop, 'Chircop 2015' (n 308) 431; Iva Parlov, 'The 2007 Nairobi International Convention on the Removal of Wrecks: The Implications for the Law of the Sea' (2022) 36(1) Ocean Yearbook Online 659, 669

357 International Convention for the Safety of Life at Sea 20 January 1914

358 Rosenne (n 320) 261

359 International Convention for the Safety of Life at Sea 10 June 1948

360 International Convention for the Safety of Life at Sea 17 June 1960

361 International Convention for the Safety of Life at Sea, no. 18961 1974

362 Protocol Relating to the International Convention for the Safety of Lift at Sea, No. 18961 17 February 1978 (IMCO Conference on Tanker Safety and Pollution Prevention)

363 Protocol of 1988 Relating to the International Convention for the Safety of Life at Sea, 1974 11 November 1988 (Conference of Contracting Governments to SOLAS)

364 IMO, 'Status of Treaties' (London 19 April 2023) 2 accessed 20 June 2022

The articles of the convention address procedural aspects such as entry into force, amendments, and the use of equivalences. Article VII provides for the possibility to conclude inter-se agreements between some of the contracting governments. All substantive provisions are included in the annexes, sorted according to different subjects of regulation. SOLAS applies per Regulation I/1(a) to all vessels engaged in international voyages.

SOLAS is accompanied by numerous codes and recommendations providing more detailed technical regulations. Some codes were made mandatory by a reference in an annex chapter of SOLAS, e.g. the International Code for Ships Operating in Polar Waters (Polar Code) .[365] Article VIII SOLAS provides for different amendment procedures for the Articles of the convention and the annex. In part 5.3.2, these procedures will be discussed in detail.

STCW was adopted in 1978 and entered into force in 1984.[366] As of today, 167 states have ratified the convention.[367] Although seafarers are trained by national institutions, it is important to maintain a globally equal level of training. Moreover, global certification standards facilitate transnational employment processes. Besides qualification and training arrangements, STCW addresses the watchkeeping, which includes the presence of humans on the bridge to perceive the vessel's surroundings.

Like SOLAS, STCW compromises Articles, a supplementing protocol from 1988, and an Annex. In 2012, the Manila amendment entered into force and revised the STCW Convention and Code comprehensively.[368] As a complement, the STCW Code providing most of the substantive regulations was adopted in 1995.[369] Part A of the STCW Code is mandatory, Part B, however, provides non-binding guidance and recommendations.[370]

COLREG was adopted in 1972 and entered into force in 1977.[371] The convention replaced the collision avoidance regulations from 1960.[372] COLREG, again,

---

365 MSC, IMO, 'Res. MSC.385(94): Adoption of the Polar Code' (London 21 November 2014); MSC, IMO, 'Res. MSC.386 (94): Amendments to the International Convention for the Safety of Life at Sea, 1974' (London 21 November 2014)

366 The International Convention on Standards of Training, Certification and Watchkeeping for Seafarers, No. 23001 7 July 1978

367 IMO, 'Status of Treaties' (n 364) 2

368 Conference of Contracting Governments to STCW, 'STCW/CONF.2/32 – Final Act' (London 1 July 2010)

369 Conference of Contracting Governments to STCW, 'STCW.6/Circ.1 – STCW Code' (London 24 July 1995)

370 Regulation I/1.2 of the Annex to STCW

371 Convention on the International Regulations for Preventing Collisions at Sea, No. 15824 20 October 1972

372 IMO, 'Convention on the International Regulations for Preventing Collisions at Sea, 1972 (COLREG)' <https://www.imo.org/en/About/Conventions/Pages/COLREG.aspx> accessed 16 February 2024

is split into articles, the navigational rules, and an annex. The articles regulate procedural matters. The navigation rules provide the rules of the road[373] for the oceans. Eventually, the annexes set out technical details about lights, shapes, sound signal appliances, and distress signals. COLREG was amended just a few times since its entry into force. In 2023, China proposed a comprehensive review of COLREG as modern, electronic navigational devices and increased speed of vessels are not sufficiently considered.[374] However, the proposal was rejected by the MSC.[375] In contrast to SOLAS, Article VI COLREG provides for a single amendment procedure. Again, the MSC is entrusted to develop, discuss, and adopt amendment proposals. Additionally, the IMO Assembly has to adopt an amendment. The procedure will be discussed in below.

In the further course of the study, the term 'GAIRAS Conventions' refers collectively to COLREG, SOLAS, and STCW although there are more conventions adopted under the auspices of the IMO that are included in the scope of GAIRAS.[376]

3.3.4 *Conclusions*

UNCLOS is an umbrella convention, confers rule-making power to the IMO as the 'competent international organization', and by making GAIRAS mandatory for its member states. Although not explicitly stated by UNCLOS, GAIRAS include most of the instruments adopted by the IMO. The IMO serves as a permanent forum for the member states of UNCLOS to discuss technical and legal aspects of international shipping and develop rules. Beckman and Sun summarized the role of the IMO aptly by stating that the

> IMO has expanded beyond what is explicitly stipulated in UNCLOS. Nevertheless, the work of the IMO is within the legal framework of UNCLOS. The dynamic relationship between UNCLOS and IMO allows the legal framework to evolve and respond effectively and flexibly to new challenges and developments.[377]

373 Bredan Gogarty and Meredith Hagger, 'The Laws of Man over vehicles unmanned: the legal response to robotic revolution on sea, land and air' (2008) 19 Journal of Law, Information and Science 73, 114

374 MSC, IMO, 'MSC 107/17/16: Proposal for a new output to comprehensively review the International Regulations for Preventing Collisions at Sea, 1972 (China)' (London 28 February 2023)

375 MSC, IMO, 'MSC 107/20: Report of the Maritime Safety Committee on its 107th Session' (London 26 June 2023) 17.45

376 For example, MARPOL and the International Convention on Load Lines, 1966, are considered as being generally accepted

377 Beckman and Sun (n 259) 236

The next section follows the reference of UNCLOS to rules set by the IMO and introduces this special agency in the UN network in more details. Afterwards, the study returns to GAIRAS and introduces those conventions, which will be of special importance for the legal analysis in part D.

3.4 The International Maritime Organization

In 1897, the Comité Maritime International (CMI) was established as a non-governmental organization focusing on the development of maritime law conventions.[378] As the members of the CMI were and are not representatives of governments but national maritime law associations, the CMI could only draft conventions and propose them to specially convened international conferences. Following the establishment of the UN in 1945, the Geneva Conference of 1948 established a specialized body for shipping within the UN system. On March 6, 1948, the Inter-Governmental Maritime Consultative Organization (IMCO) was founded and the Convention on the IMCO[379] entered into force in 1958. One year later, in 1959, the IMCO met for the first time.[380] In 1982, the IMCO was renamed to International Maritime Organization.[381] According to Article 1 of the IMO-Convention, the IMO's purpose is

> (a) to provide machinery for cooperation among Governments in the field of governmental regulation and practices relating to technical matters of all kinds affecting shipping engaged in international trade; to encourage and facilitate the general adoption of the highest practicable standards in matters concerning maritime safety, efficiency of navigation and prevention and control of marine pollution from ships; and to deal with administrative and legal matters related to the purposes set out in this Article;
>
> (b)–(c) [...]

378 Nigel H Frawley, 'A Brief History: The CMI and its Relationship with IMO, the IOPC Funds and other UN Organizations' (Antwerpen 7 January 2011) 1

379 From 1982 on 'IMO-Convention'

380 IMO, 'Brief History of IMO' <https://www.imo.org/en/About/HistoryOfIMO/Pages/Default.aspx> accessed 16 February 2024

381 IMCO, 'Resolution A.358(IX). Amendments to the IMCO Convention' (London 22 December 1975)

> (d) to provide for the consideration by the Organization of any matters concerning shipping and the effect of shipping on the marine environment that may be referred to it by any organ or specialized agency of the United Nations.

In the beginning, the IMCO was limited to consultation. However, the IMO has become an important regulatory institution for maritime matters.[382] The change of name in 1982 reflects this process.

3.4.1 *Structure*

As of today, 175 states are a member of the IMO, additionally; the IMO has 3 associate members. Usually, employees of the national maritime authorities or ministries take part in the IMO meetings rather than the head of state or a minister of a state. The focus of IMO's work is, therefore, on the development of technical regulations by maritime experts.

66 intergovernmental organizations have observer status with the IMO, which includes the right to take part in meetings and conferences and to submit documents.[383] Additionally, 85 international non-governmental organizations (NGOs) representing maritime stakeholders[384] are in consultative status with the IMO which grants the privilege to take part in the meetings and conferences of the IMO, to submit documents, and to speak to any item on the agenda of special interest to the NGO.[385] The involvement of intergovernmental organizations and NGOs enables the IMO to obtain information and input from experts with special knowledge.[386] This enriches the law-making process, links provisions to the capabilities and facilities available for implementation[387] and increases the acceptance of IMO regulations within the maritime community which contributes to their implementation.[388] The NGOs, in turn, can contribute to international regulations and are aware of current discussions at the IMO. Besides participating as an observer NGO, non-state

382 Balkin (n 354) 2

383 IMO, 'Res. A.1168(32): Relations with Intergovernmental Organizations' (London 28 January 2022) 1, Annex

384 IMO, 'Non-Governmental international Organizations which have been granted consultative status with IMO' <https://www.imo.org/en/OurWork/ERO/Pages/NGOsInConsultativeStatus.aspx> accessed 16 February 2024

385 IMO, 'Rules and guidelines for consultative status of non-governmental international organizations with the International Maritime Organization' (London December 2019) 5

386 ibid 3

387 Chircop, 'Chircop 2015' (n 308) 425

388 Balkin (n 354) 6

actors can be part of the national delegations providing them with expertise on technical issues.[389]

The IMO's organizational structure is typical of an international organization within the UN system.[390] In the Assembly, all member states meet once every two years, decide on administrative matters, the work program, the budget and the rules of procedure, provide drafts for conventions, and recommend the members the adoption of regulations and guidelines.[391]

The Council of the IMO consists of thirty-two members[392] representing member states with the largest interest in shipping, Article 17 of the IMO-Convention. The Council shall prepare the Assembly meetings, gather documents provided by the Committees, coordinate the work of the other organs, and appoint the Secretary-General. The Secretary-General is responsible for all administrative tasks and its secretariat prepares the Council meetings.

The IMO has five permanent Committees dealing with different subject matters. The Maritime Safety Committee (MSC) is responsible for navigation, construction and equipment of vessels, manning, prevention of collisions, handling of cargo, salvage and rescue, and other matters concerning maritime safety.[393] Following an advisory opinion of the ICJ,[394] since 1974, all members of the IMO can send a representative to the MSC.[395]

The Legal Committee (LEG) considers any legal matters,[396] particularly the liability conventions. It was established against the background of the *Torrey Canyon* casualty in 1967.[397] Likewise, the Marine Environmental Protection Committee (MEPC) addressing environmental matters was established in the aftermath of this casualty.[398] The most prominent convention under the purview of the MEPC is the International Convention for the Prevention of Pollution from Ships, 1973 (MARPOL) which addresses ship-source pollution. Since the MEPC is also responsible for air pollution by greenhouse gas emissions, the MEPC has become increasingly important in recent years. The

389 Sun (n 329) 97

390 Allen, 'Allen 2009' (n 232) 273

391 Article 15 IMO-Convention

392 Article 16 IMO-Convention

393 Article 28 of the IMO-Convention

394 *Constitution of the Maritime Safety Committee of the inter-governmental Maritime Consultative Organization* [1960] [1960] ICJ Reports 150 (International Court of Justice)

395 IMCO, 'Resolution A.315 (IX) Amendments to the IMCO Convention' (London 17 October 1974) 11

396 Article 33 of the IMO-Convention

397 Beckman and Sun (n 259) 208

398 Chircop, 'Chircop 2015' (n 308) 424

IMO's initial strategy on the reduction of greenhouse gas emissions from ships includes the reduction of such emissions by at least 50% by 2050.[399] The MEPC is the lead manager for this ambition.

The Technical Cooperation Committee is responsible for the implementation of technical cooperation projects funded by the UN and for which the IMO acts as the executing or cooperating agency.[400] Eventually, the Facilitation Committee (FAL) aims at eliminating unnecessary formalities and facilitating international shipping[401] and has the 1965 Convention on Facilitation of International Maritime Traffic under its purview.

As MASS primarily deal with aspects of maritime safety, the work of the MSC will be of most interest for the remainder of this study.

3.4.2 *Law-Making and Implementation Activities*

Article 2 of the IMO-Convention specifies the tools, which are available to the IMO to pursue its objective: recommendations, draft conventions, agreements, and other suitable instruments.

Recommendations address the member states, though are not legally binding.[402] Most of the instruments adopted by the IMO are not termed 'recommendation', but 'Code', 'Guideline', or 'Standard' and are adopted by resolutions by a Committee or the Assembly.[403] Despite their different titles, all these instruments are recommendations in the meaning of Article 2(a) of the IMO-Convention. For technical aspects, the IMO often refers to standards developed by classification societies.[404] Most of the IMO's law-making activities is dedicated to recommendations.

Moreover, the IMO shall recommend draft conventions and other suitable instruments to governments and intergovernmental organizations and convene diplomatic conferences when necessary. This time-consuming process can result in legally binding international agreements. This path has been chosen by the IMO for the development of major codifications such as SOLAS, STCW, and MARPOL. The latest convention prepared by the IMO was the Wreck Removal Convention adopted in 2007.

In addition to the competencies laid down in the IMO-Convention, several international conventions entrust Committees of the IMO with the task

399 MEPC, IMO, 'Res. MEPC.304(72) – Initial IMO strategy on Reduction of GHG Emissions from Ships' (London 13 April 2018) 5, Nr. 3.1.3
400 Article 43 of the IMO-Convention
401 Chircop, 'Chircop 2015' (n 308) 425
402 Aston (n 338) 155; Frenzel (n 335) 150
403 Chircop, 'Chircop 2015' (n 308) 422
404 ibid 426

to adopt amendments. For example, SOLAS, STCW, and COLREG confer such powers to the MSC. When acting in this role, the MSC resembles all member states to the convention concerned.[405] In this capacity, the MSC has contributed significantly to the development of the international maritime legal framework.

Despite the fact that most IMO instruments are not legally binding, there is a strong interest in the global uniform implementation of IMO instruments. The benefits of a globally harmonized regulatory framework can only be realized with effective implementation.[406] To support flag states, the Sub-Committee on Implementation of IMO Instruments in the ambit of the MSC and the MEPC was established in 1992[407] and has issued guidelines[408] and unified interpretations.

Moreover, the IMO audit scheme,[409] mandatory since 2016,[410] promotes a consistent and effective implementation of IMO instruments and helps member states to improve their implementation capabilities.[411] The member states' performance is assessed regularly in reports.[412] As the audit reports are confidential and the IMO lacks coercive sanctioning mechanisms, member states do not fear naming and shaming and thus effectively improve their implementation mechanisms.[413]

To summarize, the IMO has moved from a technical consultative body to the main institution developing regulations for international shipping. The IMO is characterized by maritime experts taking part in the law-making process, almost global membership, a comprehensive field of competencies, and regulatory experience for more than 60 years.

Three sources of competence allow for holistically regulating international shipping: First, UNCLOS empowers the IMO to develop GAIRAS and thus adapt

405 See Article VI(2) of COLREG; Article VIII (b)(III) of SOLAS; Article XII (1)(a)(III) of STCW

406 Wolfrum, 'Wolfrum 1999' (n 327) 232

407 At its formation, the committee was named 'Sub-Committee on Flag State Implementation'. In 2013, it was renamed 'Sub-Committee on Implementation of IMO Instruments'

408 See as examples: MSC, IMO, 'MSC/Circ.1111: Guidance relating to the Implementation of SOLAS Chapter XI-2 and the ISPS Code' (London 7 June 2004); IMO, 'Res. A.1118(30): Revised Guidelines on the Implementation of the International Safety Management (ISM) Code by Administrations' (London 10 January 2017)

409 IMO, 'Res. A.1070(28): IMO Instruments Implementation Code' (London 10 December 2013)

410 MSC, IMO, 'Res. MSC.366(93): Amendments for the International Convention for the Safety of Life at Sea, IMO Instruments Implementation Code' (London 22 May 2014)

411 Beckman and Sun (n 259) 232

412 Churchill, Lowe and Sander, *Churchill et al. 2022* (n 233) 483

413 ibid 484

UNCLOS to changing circumstances and innovative developments. Additionally, the IMO is entrusted with administrative and coordinative tasks in the scope of UNCLOS. Second, the IMO-Convention allows the IMO to develop non-binding recommendations covering almost all aspects of international shipping. Third, international conventions such as SOLAS, COLREG, and STCW refer to the IMO for administrative tasks and the power to adopt amendments.

3.5 Conclusions

This section introduced the relevant conventions for the subsequent legal analysis and the IMO as the international regulator for shipping. Initially, each vessel is under the exclusive jurisdiction of its flag state. Depending on the position of the ship, coastal state jurisdiction applies. Although flag states are free in setting the legal requirements for registration, GAIRAS have to be complied with as a minimum. Conversely, coastal state law may not exceed GAIRAS with regard to foreign ships, Article 21(2) of the UNCLOS. However, UNCLOS remains silent on the consequences of non-compliance with the laws and regulations of the coastal state. The exercise of enforcement jurisdiction is thus left to the discretion of the coastal state within the limits of Article 24 of the UNCLOS. In all likelihood, a non-compliant foreign vessel cannot be expelled from the territorial sea. However, the imposition of sanctions, such as a fine, is conceivable. Port states are free in granting access to their ports and setting requirements for port entry without prejudice to other international legal obligations.

UNCLOS refers legislative tasks to the IMO to develop detailed regulations for shipping. Those instruments, which are accepted by a large number of leading maritime states, are binding for all UNCLOS member states based on the rule of reference to GAIRAS. Those GAIRAS instruments, which are relevant for the subsequent analysis, were introduced: SOLAS, STCW, and COLREG. Despite IMO's efforts to increase compliance with its instruments, the effectiveness of implementation and enforcement ultimately depends on the will and commitment of the individual states.

The international legal framework for vessel operations has been able to cope with advancing technologies such as the standard container, which has be introduced in the 1970s.[414] The next disruptive development imminent is

414 Marc Levinson, *The Box* (Princeton University Press 2016)

the advent of MASS. As Donald Liu put it already in 2018 "[a]utonomous shipping will happen; it is just a question of when, where, and how".[415]

Autonomous operations and such without a human presence on board are not explicitly reflected in the conventions and codes presented above. Consequently, before MASS can operate, the legal framework has to be examined to identify gaps and possible ways to address these gaps. This analysis shall follow now.

415 Liu (n 196) 494

CHAPTER 4

MASS and the International Legal Framework

Unlike conventional vessels, MASS at degree three and four operate autonomously without a human crew on board, posing unique legal challenges. While shipping has already seen many technological innovations, autonomous shipping affects the very foundations of shipping and therefore presents a particular regulatory challenge.[416] Developed during a manned, manually steered era, existing instruments may not fully apply to MASS. This chapter explores MASS compliance with the above-introduced 'high-priority' instruments.

Reflecting the function-based regulatory approach in the conventions, the analysis examines whether MASS can fulfill the required functions. All requirements stipulated by the conventions serve a certain function and are not means in and of themselves. The legal analysis reviews available literature scholarly contributions and the results of the Regulatory Scoping Exercise performed by the IMO.

In preparation of an appropriate legal analysis, it is necessary first to highlight the importance of GAIRAS and UNCLOS compliance for MASS and second to introduce the general rule of interpretation stipulated by Article 31 Vienna Convention on the Law of Treaties. International law is interpreted differently from national law to avoid national bias and varying interpretations depending on the jurist's legal domicile.

Some states have already prepared their national laws for the registration of MASS and lifted regulatory barriers. These national approaches will be illustrated after the legal analysis. In Norway[417] and France[418] MASS can be registered for voyages in territorial waters. The United Kingdom has adopted a Workboat Code applicable to vessels under 24m to enable the registration of

416 Anna Petrig, 'Unconventional Law for Unconventional Ships? The Role of Informal Law in the International Maritime Organization's Quest to Regulate Maritime Autonomous Surface Ships' in Natalie Klein (ed), *Unconventional Lawmaking in the Law of the Sea* (Oxford University Press 2022) 114

417 Sjøfartsdirektoratet, 'Føringer i forbindelse med bygging eller installering av automatisert funksjonalitet, med hensikt å kunne utføre ubemannet eller delvis ubemannet drift: RSV 12-2020' (Haugesund 27 August 2020). Rundskriv 5 accessed 21 June 2022

418 See: MSC, IMO, 'MSC 107/INF.12: Report on the Regulatory Framework for MASS implemented in France (France)' (London 28 March 2023) 2

 | DOI:10.1163/9789004729483_005

MASS.[419] Finnish regulations will also soon allow for MASS trials in Finnish territorial waters.[420]

4.1 Principle of Mutual Recognition

To balance the flag state principle expressed in Article 91(1) of the UNCLOS and port state jurisdiction, international shipping is based on the principle of mutual recognition of certificates. This principle is reflected by Regulation I/19(1) of SOLAS and Regulation I/10 of STCW. One could thus assume, that a MASS registered by a flag state could sail unimpededly in foreign territorial waters and call at foreign ports. However, UNCLOS links the enjoyment of these rights to the compliance with GAIRAS). Despite the right of innocent passage through territorial waters, coastal states may give effect to GAIRAS towards foreign vessels.

Upon registration, flag states have to exercise jurisdiction over vessels flying their flag effectively in administrative, social, and technical matters, Article 94(1) of UNCLOS. While adopting measures to ensure the seaworthiness of the vessels, Article 94(3), (4) of UNCLOS, flag states have to comply with the GAIRAS treaties including COLREG, SOLAS, and STCW[421] as the minimum requirement. Although a non-GAIRAS compliant MASS could sail in its flag state's territorial waters and on the high seas, other states might be eligible to initiate proceedings against the flag state for violating Article 94(5) of the UNCLOS. However, MASS are intended to transport cargo from one state to another and to enter foreign territorial waters and ports.

Coastal states have to ensure the right of innocent passage through their territorial sea, Article 17 of the UNCLOS. National regulations on the design, construction, manning, and equipment of foreign vessels can only be adopted if giving effect to GAIRAS, Article 21(2) of the UNCLOS. GAIRAS are here set as the maximum a coastal state may implement towards foreign-flagged vessels. The rationale behind this restriction is to avoid the practical ban of the right of innocent passage by differing technical standards.[422]

---

419 The Workboat Code Edition 3, The safety of small Workboats and Pilot Boats – a Code of Practice 27 November 2023

420 See especially § 13a of: 976/2018 – Lag om ändring av lagen om fartygspersonal och säkerhetsorganisation för fartyg 23 November 2018 (Eduskunta)

421 Guilfoyle, 'Guilfoyle 2017' (n 317) 12; Nandan and Nordquist (eds) (n 355) 147–148

422 Pierandrea Leucci, 'Innocent Passage in the Territorial Sea within the Framework of the Law of the Sea Convention' (2008) 10(1) KMI International Journal of Maritime Affairs and Fisheries 1, 7

Although prohibition of innocent passage for noncompliance with GAIRAS is precluded by Article 24(1) of the UNCLOS, other enforcement measures could be taken by a coastal state.[423] Such measures could include fines or inspections. In order to avoid the risk of enforcement measures, MASS should ensure compliance with GAIRAS, at least in respect of construction, design, equipment, and manning requirements. Otherwise, legitimate coastal state laws could have the effect of practically denying innocent passage for MASS.[424] The same applies to a passage through straits used for international navigation as Article 39(2)(a) of the UNCLOS links the right of transit passage to compliance with GAIRAS. Eventually, coastal states could bring an action against the flag state for violating Article 94(5) of the UNCLOS.[425]

Although MASS do not have a general right to enter foreign ports and must comply with local laws while in port,[426] port states are not at liberty to arbitrarily deny MASS entry to their ports, as the non-discrimination clauses in the GATT[427] as well as Treaties of Friendship, Commerce, and Navigation[428] safeguard port access. A port state could, therefore, decline all MASS despite the flag.[429] Considering that MASS require specific port infrastructure, port states could practically prevent MASS from entering their ports by not providing the necessary infrastructure.

More important during port calls, however, are port state controls which assess whether a vessel complies with the GAIRAS treaties. If, during the initial inspection of certificates on board the vessel, there are clear grounds to believe that the vessel does not comply with the relevant international instruments, a more detailed inspection can be carried out.[430] If deficiencies are detected, the vessel can be detained until all deficiencies have been rectified. Thus, if MASS do not comply with GAIRAS, they risk being detained in ports.

In addition to compliance with substantial provisions in the GAIRAS treaties, MASS could be confronted with a physical inspection of the vessel and

---

423 Kari Hakapää, 'Innocent Passage' in Anne Peters (ed), *Max Planck Encyclopedia of Public International Law* (MPEPIL) (Oxford University Press) 20

424 Henrik Ringbom, 'Legalizing autonomous ships' (2020) 34(1) Ocean Yearbook 431, 445

425 Churchill, Lowe and Sander, *Churchill et al. 2022* (n 233) 108

426 See on port entry and port state jurisdiction section 3.2 above

427 See Article 1(1) of the General Agreement on Traffis and Trade, 1986

428 Andreas Paulus, 'Treaties of Friendship, Commerce and Navigation' in Anne Peters (ed), *Max Planck Encyclopedia of Public International Law* (MPEPIL) (Oxford University Press) 14

429 Grit Tüngler and Sebastian tho Pesch, 'Seevölkerrechtliche Anforderungen an unbemannte Schiffe' [2017] Zeitschrift für das Recht der Transportwirtschaft 121

430 See section 3.2 and Annex 10 to the Paris MoU

the required certificates.[431] Although the IMO has paved the way for electronic documents and digital presentation of documents and certificates,[432] physical inspection remains important. If there were no harmonized regulations in place, MASS would need to check with each port beforehand whether the loading and unloading of cargo is possible. This would make MASS operations even more expensive and less attractive. Consequently, the above-mentioned economic, safety, and environmental benefits of MASS depend on the inclusion of MASS in the current legal framework.

To conclude, flag states need to consider the GAIRAS treaties as minimum, for coastal states GAIRAS presents the maximum enforceable against foreign vessels. Eventually, port state controls could result in detention if deficiencies in the compliance with the GAIRAS treaties are detected. Thus, MASS need to comply with GAIRAS to operate internationally.

4.2 Interpretation of International Law

"The interpretation of documents is to some extent an art, not an exact science".[433] Articles 31–33 of the Vienna Convention on the Law of the Treaties, 1969 (VCLT) lay down the interpretation rules for international law treaties. The purpose of treaty interpretation is to determine the ordinary meaning of the words used[434] referencing the context, object, and purpose. It is assumed that the intention of the parties is expressed in the words used.[435]

---

431 See for a list of required documents: FAL, IMO, 'FAL.2/Circ.131: List of Certificates and Documents Required to be Carried On Board Ships' (London 19 July 2017); LEG, IMO, 'LEG.2/Circ.3: List of Certificates and Documents Required to be Carried On Board Ships' (London 19 July 2017); MEPC, IMO, 'MEPC.1/Circ.873 – List of Certificates and Documents required to be Carried On Board Ships' (London 19 July 2017); MSC, IMO, 'MSC.1/Circ.1586: List of Certificates and Documents required to be carried On Board Ships' (London 19 July 2017)

432 Facilitation Committee of the International Maritime Organization, 'Guidelines for the Use of Electronic Certificates' (London 20 April 2016)

433 International Law Commission (ILC), 'Report of the International Law Commission on the work of the second part of its seventeenth session' [1966] Yearbook of the International Law Commission 169, 218

434 Donald H Regan, 'Sources of International Trade Law: Understanding What the Vienna Convention Says About Identifying and Using 'Sources For Treaty Interpretation'' in Samantha Besson and Jean d'Aspremont (eds), *The Oxford Handbook of the Sources of International Law* (vol 1. Oxford University Press 2018) 1052; Richard Gardiner, 'The Vienna Convention Rules on Treaty Interpretation' in Duncan B Hollis (ed), *The Oxford Guide to Treaties* (Oxford University Press 2012) 481

435 Reports of the Commission to the General Assembly, 'Section 3: Interpretation of treaties' [1966] Yearbook of the International Law Commission 217, 221

Although the VCLT applies in the first instance to legally binding international treaties that entered into force after 1980, Articles 1, 2(1)(a), 4 of the VCLT,[436] its customary international law character[437] allows for the transfer of the rule of interpretation to other agreements, including non-binding agreements and those that were already in force.[438] Article 31 of the VCLT sets out the method for treaty interpretation[439] and states:

> Article 31 – General rule of interpretation
> 1. A treaty shall be interpreted in good faith in accordance with the ordinary meaning to be given to the terms of the treaty in their context and in the light of its object and purpose.
> 2. The context for the purpose of the interpretation of a treaty shall comprise, in addition to the text, including its preamble and annexes:
> (a) any agreement to the treaty which between all the parties in connection with the conclusion of the treaty;
> (b) any instrument which was made by one or more parties in connection with the conclusion of the treaty and accepted by the other parties as an instrument related to the treaty.
> 3. There shall be taken into account, together with the context:
> (a) any subsequent agreement between the parties regarding the interpretation of the treaty or the application of its provisions;
> (b) any subsequent practice in the application of the treaty which establishes the agreement of the parties regarding its interpretation;
> (c) any relevant rules of international law applicable in the relations between the parties.

436 Kirsten Schmalenbach, 'Article 2 – Use of terms' in Oliver Dörr and Kirsten Schmalenbach (eds), *Vienna Convention on the Law of Treaties: A Commentary* (2. 2nd ed. 2018. Springer Berlin Heidelberg 2018) 8; International Law Commission (ILC), 'A/CN.4/167 – Third report on the law of treaties by Sir Humphrey Waldock, Special Rapporteur' [1964] Yearbook of the International Law Commission 5, 55

437 Gleider I Hernández, *International Law* (Oxford University Press 2019) 182; Lionel Yee, 'Law of Treaties' in Simon Chesterman and others (eds), *The Oxford Handbook of United Nations Treaties* (Oxford University Press 2019) 513; Antonio Cassese and others, *Cassese's International law* (Third edition, Oxford University Press 2020) 213; *Territorial Dispute – Libyan Arab Jamahiriya/Chad* [1994] [1994] ICJ Reports 6 (International Court of Justice) 41; criticizing the codification of customary international law: Gleider I Hernández, 'Interpretation' in Jörg Kammerhofer and Jean d'Aspremont (eds), *International Legal Positivism in a Post-Modern World* (Cambridge University Press 2014) 329

438 Article 38 (1)(b) of the Statue of the ICJ lists customary international law as a general source of international law

439 Christian Djeffal, 'An Interpreter's Guide to Static and Evolutive Interpretations: Solving Intertemporal Problems and the VCLT' in Georges Abi-Saab and others (eds), *Evolutionary Interpretation and International Law* (Hart Publishing 2019) 24

> 4. A special meaning shall be given to a term if it is established that the parties so intended.

The title emphasizes that there is no hierarchy between the listed authentic materials and one general rule of interpretation applies.[440] Starting from the text,[441] all possible meanings of the terms used can be determined[442] and balanced reflecting the context, object, and purpose of the treaty.[443] As a result, the ordinary meaning of the words as intended by the parties can be established.[444] Briefly, the available authentic materials for interpretation of the GAIRAS conventions and the evolutionary treaty interpretation shall be introduced.

The context of a treaty compromises the means listed in Article 31(2) of the VCLT and shall be considered together with the "external context"[445] listed in Article 31(3) of the VCLT. The materials enumerated in Article 31(2) of the VCLT bear no relevance to the legal analysis below; however, the materials listed in Article 31(3) of the VCLT deserve further attention. Extending the scope of authentic materials compared to section 2,[446] Article 31(3) of the VCLT ensures that the interpretation of a treaty considers the updated understanding of the treaty expressed by the parties.[447]

Per Article 31(3) (a) of the vclt, any subsequent agreement between the parties on the interpretation of the treaty has to be taken into account. Although not all parties need to participate such agreements,[448] the significance of the subsequent agreement increases the greater the participation rate.[449] As an

---

440 ILC, 'International Law Commission 1966' (n 433) 219; Hernández, *Hernández 2019* (n 437) 34

441 ILC, 'International Law Commission 1966' (n 433) 220

442 Yoa Li, *Exclusion from Protection as a Refugee: An Approach to a Harmonizing Interpretation in International Law* (International Refugee Law vol 9, Brill|Nijhoff 2017) 121

443 Djeffal (n 439) 24–25

444 Regan (n 434) 1055

445 Jean-Marc Sorel and Valérie B Eveno, 'Article 31' in Olivier Corten and Pierre Klein (eds), *The Vienna Conventions on the Law of Treaties* (Oxford commentaries on international law vol 2. Oxford University Press 2011) 8

446 ILC, 'International Law Commission 1966' (n 433) 220

447 Katharina Böth, *Evolutive Auslegung völkerrechtlicher Verträge: Eine Untersuchung zu Voraussetzungen und Grenzen in Anbetracht der Praxis internationaler Streitbeilegungsinstitutionen* (Schriften zum Völkerrecht vol 204, Duncker & Humblot 2013) 95

448 Arguing that all parties to the main treaty have to agree to the interpretation agreement: Regan (n 434) 1058; Oliver Dörr, 'Article 31, General rule of interpretation' in Oliver Dörr and Kirsten Schmalenbach (eds), *Vienna Convention on the Law of Treaties: A Commentary* (2. 2nd ed. 2018. Springer Berlin Heidelberg 2018) 65

449 Boyle, 'Boyle 2006' (n 224) 48

example, the 'Agreement relating to the implementation of Part XI of the United Nations Convention on the Law of the Sea of 10 December 1982' (1994 Implementation Agreement)[450] is recognized as a subsequent interpretation agreement,[451] despite the fact that only 79 of the 157 UNCLOS signatories have actively participated. The remaining parties are presumed to have tacitly consented.[452]

With regard to the GAIRAS conventions, non-binding instruments adopted by the IMO are highly relevant for the interpretation as any non-binding agreement is included in the scope of Article 31(3)(a) of the VCLT as long as the parties "are aware of [it] and accept [it]"[453] as an agreement on the interpretation.[454] Considering the IMO instruments, it could be problematic that not the state parties, but rather the IMO as a subject of international law adopted the subsequent agreements on interpretation.[455] Consequently, instruments adopted by the IMO do not fall within the scope of Article 31(3)(a) of the VCLT, whereas instruments prepared by the IMO, but adopted by a diplomatic conference are included.

Pursuant to Article 31(3)(b) of the VCLT, subsequent practice can establish a subsequent agreement on the interpretation of the treaty. Official statements, national legislative acts, executive decisions, as well as judicial decisions are considered as practice.[456] There is no minimum time requirement for the practice;[457] however, the practice must be performed consistently and repeatedly.[458]

---

450 United Nations General Assembly, 'Res. A/Res/48/263 – Agreement relating to the implementation of Part XI of the United Nations Convention on the Law of the Sea of 10 December 1982' (n 227)

451 Buga (n 322) 53–54

452 Boyle, 'Boyle 2006' (n 224) 49

453 United Nations General Assembly, 'A/CN.4/L.907 – Subsequent agreements and subsequent practice in relation to the interpretation of treaties: Text of the draft conclusions adopted by the Drafting Committee on second reading' (New York, Geneva 11 May 2018) Conclusion 10, para. 1

454 Richard K Gardiner, *Treaty interpretation* (The Oxford international law library, Second edition, Oxford University Press 2015) 247

455 Christian Walter, 'Subject of International Law' in Anne Peters (ed), *Max Planck Encyclopedia of Public International Law* (MPEPIL) (Oxford University Press) 5

456 Antonios Tzanakopoulos, 'Judicial Dialogue as a Means of Interpretation' in Helmut P Aust and Georg Nolte (eds), *The Interpretation of International Law by Domestic Courts: Uniformity, Diversity, Covergence* (Oxford University Press 2016) 92; Dörr (n 448) 79; Gardiner (n 454) 257

457 Buga (n 322) 49

458 Gardiner (n 454) 260

In line with the interpretation of Article 31(3)(a) of the VCLT, not all states have to participate in the subsequent practice. Rather, it suffices if some states perform the practice and other states react to this practice.[459] This wide understanding, however, should not be used to include merely regional particularities, as it is necessary to preserve the global character and integrity of treaties ratified by almost all states, such as UNCLOS and the GAIRAS conventions.[460]

The practice of international organizations can be included into the scope of Article 31(3)(b) of the VCLT,[461] if the international organization is entrusted with the performance of activities under the treaty.[462] The IMO is entrusted with tasks under the GAIRAS conventions and it shall develop standards and guidelines.[463] Therefore, the IMO's instruments and the practice of national administration fall within the scope of Article 31(3)(b) of the VCLT.

By agreeing on the interpretation by subsequent practice, the parties can express a revision of their intention in respect of a treaty.[464] Although some argue that subsequent practice can even amend a treaty,[465] the available modification and amendment procedures should not be circumvented. Thus, subsequent modifying practice should not be accepted.[466]

Eventually, Article 31(3)(c) of the VCLT ensures systematic integration[467] by including all sources listed in Article 38(1) of the Statute of the ICJ in the scope

459 ibid 266; ILC, 'International Law Commission 1966' (n 433) 222; United Nations General Assembly, 'A/71/10 – Report of the International Law Commission on the work of its sixty-eighth session (2 May–10 June and 4 July–12 August 2016)' (19 August 2016) Conclusion 10 [9]; Dörr (n 448) 84

460 Boyle, 'Boyle 2006' (n 224) 46

461 United Nations General Assembly, 'A/71/10 – Report of the International Law Commission on the work of its sixty-eighth session (2 May–10 June and 4 July–12 August 2016)' (n 459) Conclusion 12 [11], para. 32; Petrig (n 416) 129–130

462 Dörr (n 448) 85

463 See for example Regulations V/10.1; V/11.1; V/14.1 of SOLAS

464 United Nations General Assembly, 'A/71/10 – Report of the International Law Commission on the work of its sixty-eighth session (2 May–10 June and 4 July–12 August 2016)' (n 459) Conclusion 8 [3]

465 Dahm (n 465) 673–674; Georg Nolte, 'Court Generated State Practice: A Response to Karl Zemanek' (2015) 20 Austrian Review of International and European Law 17, 22–23; Sorel and Eveno. 'Article 31' (above, n. 465), marginal no. 42

466 Buga (n 322) 51; Karl Zemanek, 'Court Generated State Practice' (2015) 20 Austrian Review of International and European Law 3, 4; Santiago T Bernandez, 'Court Generated State Practice: (Karl Zemanek) – A Commentary' (2015) 20 Austrian Review of International and European Law 25, 27

467 United Nations General Assembly, 'A/CN.4/L.682 – Fragmentation of International Law: Difficulties Arising from the Diversification and Expansion of International Law; Report of the Study Group of the International Law Commission' (New York 13 April 2006) 208; Regan (n 434) 1062

of authentic materials.[468] To be included, a rule has to apply between the dispute parties at stake rather than between all parties to the treaty concerned.[469] Otherwise, Article 31(3)(c) of the VCLT could not be effectively applied to conventions ratified by many states due to the lack of complete congruence in membership.[470] Moreover, non-binding instruments are included[471] although the words 'rules' and 'applicable' could argue against their inclusion.[472]

The provisions of a treaty shall be interpreted in a manner that is the most effective in achieving the treaty's purpose and objective(s), thus effective interpretation can be considered a subcategory of teleological interpretation.[473] However, as, the ILC has expressed in 1966, "the maxim does not call for an "extensive" or "liberal" interpretation in the sense of an interpretation going beyond what is expressed or necessarily to be implied in the terms of the treaty".[474] The terms 'object' and 'purpose' are assumed to refer to the same concept of effet utile.[475] Often, the purpose of the treaty is expressed in the preamble.[476]

The ordinary meaning of a term can change over time due to political changes, new scientific findings, or innovative technology. To circumvent complex and often disadvantageous measures such as amendments, modification, or termination to adapt the treaty, means of interpretation can be applied to reflect the changes.[477] Nevertheless, the fine line between interpretation and revision has to be respected. Interpretation may not alter the treaty and extend the meaning of the words beyond the intention of the parties. However, treaties providing for built-in flexibility are susceptible to intertemporal or evolutionary interpretation.

468 Dörr (n 448) 95

469 Regan (n 434) 1060

470 United Nations General Assembly, 'A/CN.4/L.682 – Fragmentation of International Law: Difficulties Arising from the Diversification and Expansion of International Law; Report of the Study Group of the International Law Commission' (n 467) 237–238

471 Alan Boyle, 'Soft Law in International Law-Making' in Malcolm D Evans (ed), *International law* (Fifth edition. Oxford University Press 2018) 127; *Legal Consequences of the Construction of a Wall in the Occupied Palestinian Territory* [2004] [2004] ICJ Reports 136 (International Court of Justice) 86

472 Dörr (n 448) 100

473 Li (n 442) 123–124; Matthias Herdegen, 'Interpretation in International Law' in Anne Peters (ed), *Max Planck Encyclopedia of Public International Law* (MPEPIL) (Oxford University Press) 31

474 ILC, 'International Law Commission 1966' (n 433) 219

475 Dörr (n 448) 53; Li (n 442) 124

476 ILC, 'International Law Commission 1966' (n 433) 221

477 Georg Nolte, 'Introductory Note to the Special Issue of ICLR on the Outcome of the ILC Work on "Subsequent Agreements and Subsequent Practice in Relation to the Interpretation of Treaties"' (2020) 22 International Community Law Review 4, 5

When the VCLT was first negotiated, it was commonly accepted that subsequent changes should not be considered without further ado[478] to support the stability aspect of law. However, ignoring subsequent changes could render a treaty ineffective. The evolutionary interpretation is therefore located between the poles of stability and change.[479] It should be noted, however, that evolutionary interpretation may not exceed the intention of the parties expressed in the words used.[480]

In 1971, the ICJ recognized intertemporal law for the first time.[481] To reflect the intention of the parties, generic terms should be given the meaning prevailing at the time of interpretation.[482] However, the meaning of 'generic terms' remains ambiguous. In UNCLOS, the phrase 'generally accepted international rules and standards' opens up for advancing and intertemporal interpretation and can be considered a generic term.[483] The parties included this phrase to ensure that UNCLOS can be aligned with subsequent changes and novel technology.[484] Nevertheless, each interpretation has to be consistent with the intention of the parties and may not result in rewriting or revising the treaty.[485]

To conclude, the art of determining the ordinary meaning of the terms used as intended by the parties is led by Article 31 VCLT. The literal analysis, the context, and the purpose and object of the treaty have to be merged into a coherent whole. The crux ultimately lies in the determination of the parties' intention, which is, according to Sir Humphery Waldock "not always be easily discernible".[486]

The next section will turn to the legal analysis of MASS in the legal framework created by UNCLOS and the GAIRAS conventions. For this analysis,

478 ILC, 'International Law Commission 1966' (n 433) 222
479 Nolte, 'Nolte 2020' (n 477) 5
480 Eirik Bjorge, *The Evolutionary Interpretation of Treaties* (Oxford University Press 2014) 188
481 *Legal Consequences for States of the Continued Presence of South Africa in Namibia* [1971] [1971] ICJ Reports 16 (International Court of Justice) 53
482 *Aegean Sea Continental Shelf Case (Greece v. Turkey)* [1978] [1978] ICJ Reports 3 (International Court of Justice) 77; *Navigational and Related Rights (Costa Rica v. Nicaragua)* [2009] [2009] ICJ Reports 213 (International Court of Justice) 66; *Case Concerning Pulp Mills on the River Uruguay* [2010] [2010] ICJ Reports 14 (International Court of Justice) 204
483 Boyle, 'Boyle 2006' (n 224) 46
484 Buga (n 322) 66; Youri van Logchem, 'International Law of the Sea and Autonomous Cargo 'Vessels'' in Barış Soyer and Andrew Tettenborn (eds), *Artificial Intelligence and Autonomous Shipping: Developing the International Legal Framework* (Hart Publishing 2021) 59
485 Boyle, 'Boyle 2006' (n 224) 46
486 Humphrey Waldock, 'The evolution of human rights concepts and the application of the european convention on human rights' in André Gross (ed), *Mélanges Offert à Paul Reuter: Le droit international: unité et diversité* (Pedone 1981) 536

recourse will be made to academic literature and the Regulatory Scoping Exercise (RSE) conducted by the IMO between 2018 and 2021. Before diving into the legal analysis, the RSE shall briefly be contextualized within the work of the IMO on MASS.

4.3 The Regulatory Scoping Exercise of the IMO

In 2017, three subcommittees of the IMO, the MSC, the LEG, and the FAL, each discussed the need to deal with vessels operated at a high degree of autonomy. All three Committees included a new output in their biennale agenda to conduct a RSE of the conventions under their purview.[487] The objective was to assess the extent to which the conventions could be affected by MASS operations and to determine the most appropriate way to address potential legal gaps.[488] Volunteering member states meet regularly to conduct the RSE.[489] The MSC[490] and the LEG[491] approved the outcome of the analysis in 2021; the FAL agreed upon the results in 2022.[492]

All three Committees applied the same methodology and split the gap analysis into two steps.[493] All four degrees of autonomy were assessed separately.[494] The first step contained an initial review of the IMO instruments to identify provisions that:

A applied to MASS and prevented MASS operations; or
B applied to MASS and did not prevent MASS operations and required no actions; or

487 FAL, IMO, 'FAL 43/20: Report of the Facilitation Committee on its 43rd Session' (London 23 April 2019) 33; MSC, IMO, 'MSC 98/23' (n 75) 79; LEG, IMO, 'LEG 105/14: Report of the Legal Committee on the Work of its 105th Session' (London 1 May 2018) 20

488 MSC, IMO, 'MSC.1/Circ.1638' (n 18)

489 Henrik Tunfors, 'Evolution of IMO's MASS: Through the Prism of the Chair' in Tafsir M Johansson and others (eds), *Autonomous Vessels in Maritime Affairs* (Studies in National Governance and Emerging Technologies. Springer International Publishing 2023) 36

490 MSC, IMO, 'MSC.1/Circ.1638' (n 18)

491 LEG, IMO, 'LEG.1/Circ.11: Outcome of the Regulatory Scoping Exercise and Gap Analysis of Conventions emanating from the Legal Committee with respect to Maritime Autonomous Surface Ships (MASS)' (London 15 December 2021)

492 FAL, IMO, 'FAL.5/Circ.49: Outcome of the Regulatory Scoping Exercise and Gap Analysis of the FAL Convention with Respect to Maritime Autonomous Surface Ships' (London 1 June 2022)

493 MSC, IMO, 'MSC 99/22' (n 76) 30–31; LEG, IMO, 'LEG 106/16: Report of the Legal Committee on the Work of its 106th Session' (London 13 May 2019) 16; FAL, IMO, 'FAL 43/20' (n 487) 33

494 MSC, IMO, 'MSC 99/22' (n 76) 36

C applied to MASS and did not prevent MASS operations but might need to be amended or clarified, and/or might contain gaps; or
D had no application to MASS operations.[495]

In the second step, the most appropriate way of addressing the identified gaps was determined. Four options were available:

I equivalences as provided for by the instruments or developing interpretations; and/or
II amending existing instruments; and/or
III developing new instruments; or
IV none of the above as a result of the analysis.[496]

The results of the analysis will be debated during the discussion of the different problems below. The RSE was the first comprehensive legal assessment of MASS in the light of the current legal framework. The extent of the RSE and the invested resources illustrate the significance of legal challenges awaited by the advent of MASS. More than 40 states representing all regions of the world voluntarily participated in the RSE.[497] This also underlines the relevance of a regulatory approach to MASS and the desire of the member states to promote this development. In the following, it is examine whether MASS fulfill the functions required by the current legal framework.

4.4 Legal Gaps for MASS in the Current Legal Framework

International shipping is regulated by conventions mostly concluded in the 1970s and 1980s, a time when autonomous vessel operations and such without a human presence on board were not conceivable.[498] As MASS are shaking the foundations of the regulatory framework by removing humans from the vessel and conferring control to algorithms many legal challenges are expected. Although all aspects of shipping regulation are affected by MASS, the focus is

495 MSC, IMO, 'MSC.1/Circ.1638' (n 18)
496 MSC, IMO, 'MSC.1/Circ.1638' (n 18) 7; Emphasis added by the author
497 MSC, IMO, 'MSC 102/5/1: Report of the Intersessional Working Group on Maritime Autonomous Surface Ships' (London 25 September 2019)
498 Soyer (n 86) 164–165

put on SOLAS, COLREG, STCW, and UNCLOS. Consequently, several challenges such as liability and responsibility issues are excluded.[499]

As illustrated above, UNCLOS and the GAIRAS conventions are closely intertwined. Additionally, the GAIRAS conventions often refer to one another and form a coherent, but tightly interwoven regulatory framework. Some aspects such as the manning of a vessel or the lookout are governed by more than one convention. However, the rationale behind the provisions is the same in all conventions, as the maritime framework applies a functional approach. This means that most requirements are not a goal in themselves. Rather they should be understood as means to fulfill the underlying function. Furthermore, many conventions only specify the required function without indicating the necessary means to achieve it.[500]

The following legal analysis reflects this functional approach by aggregating all relevant provisions for one function and analyzing them together. Such a horizontal approach also resembles the actual application of the legal framework in a real-life scenario and allows for the eventual development of helpful and actionable policy recommendations at the end.

When screening the international legal framework for shipping, numerous functions can be identified. However, the concept of seaworthiness towers above all else. This concept is used in both private maritime law[501] and public law of the sea.[502] As this study limits itself to public law issues, the private maritime law dimension of seaworthiness is not discussed. Even within public law, seaworthiness can have a broad or narrow meaning, depending on the context.[503] In its most general manifestation, the term includes the ability of the ship to sail on the sea, or a little more specific, the sufficiency of the ship to face the perils of marine adventure.[504]

---

499 An analysis of the liability question in case of collision for unmanned and autonomous vessels can be found at: Philipp Etzkorn, *Der Schiffszusammenstoß unter Beteiligung autonom fahrender Schiffe* (Schriftenreihe des Instituts für Transport- und Verkehrsrecht vol 14, 1. Auflage, Nomos 2022); Marie-Luise Herkenhoff, *Die Haftung in der unbemannte Schifffahrt* (Münsteraner Reihe vol 140, VVW GmbH 2020); Simon Baughen, 'Civil Liability all at Sea: The Challenges of Unmanned Cargo Ships' in Phillip Morgan (ed), *Tort liability and autonomous systems accidents: Common and civil law perspectives* (Edward Elgar Publishing 2023); LEG, IMO, 'LEG 111/10/2' (n 7)

500 Ringbom, 'Ringbom 2020' (n 424) 437

501 See for example Article III(1)(a) of the Hague-Visby-Rules stating that the carrier shall exercise due diligend to make the ship seaworthy

502 See for example Article 94(3)(a) of the UNCLOS

503 Thor Falkanger, Hans J Bull and Lasse Brautaset, *Scandinavian Maritime Law: The Norwegian Perspective* (4th ed. Universitetsforlaget 2017) 357

504 Nikolaos Kampantais, 'Seaworthiness in autonomous unmanned cargo ships' (Erasmus University Rotterdam 2016) 2

Seaworthiness is split into many functions within the GAIRAS conventions. Roughly, the functions could be described as 'safety of the ship and its crew', 'safety of the cargo', and 'safety of third parties'. Starting from here, an almost endless list of functions that a ship has to fulfill depending on the type of ship, the intended voyage, and the cargo could be given. Since this is beyond the scope of this study, the subsequent legal analysis focusses on the functions, that accrue from the GAIRAS conventions and that need to be fulfilled by all commercial vessels irrespective of their concrete purpose and voyage. Consequently, neither the aspect of environmental protection nor cargo surveillance will be discussed. Instead, the study takes an in-depth look at the safety at sea and the duty to conduct search and rescue operations for people in distress at sea.

The requirement of safety at sea is still quite comprehensive, so that a division into different sub-aspects is appropriate. The safety at sea includes, on the one hand, the safety of navigation to avoid collisions with other ships or permanent installations, and, on the other hand, the safety of life at sea aiming at the safety of the persons involved in the ship's operation. The safety at sea is a ship-centric function concerned with one vessel and its crew. However, from the early times on, mutual assistance and support at sea in situations of distress were of paramount importance. Article 98 UNCLOS reflects this and imposes a duty to render assistance to people in distress at sea. This duty will be discussed in the light of MASS as the second main function.

However, before discussing whether and how MASS can fulfill these functions, the applicability of the international legal framework for shipping to MASS needs to be assessed. The substantial scope of application of the UNCLOS is central in this context. Therefore, the first section is dedicated towards the question of whether MASS are ships in the meaning of the UNCLOS. In this context, the nationality and genuine link requirement for the registration will be discussed in the light of MASS. As next, the safety at sea will be assessed; first considering the safety of navigation and, second, the manning of the vessel, and, third, the safety of life at sea. Eventually, the duty to render assistance to people in distress at sea will be discussed.

4.4.1 *Flag State Registration and Genuine Link*

The first and most important legal question to answer is whether MASS fall within the scope of the UNCLOS and the other GAIRAS conventions. As the conventions adopted under the purview of the IMO apply within the framework of the UNCLOS, the scope of the UNCLOS shall be addressed first. UNCLOS provides that each ship has the nationality of its flag state and that there is a genuine link between the ship and the flag state. These aspects also need to be discussed in the light of MASS. Eventually, the scope of application of the

GAIRAS conventions will be briefly examined to determine whether they apply to MASS in general.

Most provisions of the UNCLOS address 'ships' and 'vessels'. Both terms are used interchangeably without different meanings; however, neither term is defined.[505] The question, therefore, is whether MASS fall within the scope of 'ship' and 'vessel' as used in UNCLOS. As the main difference between MASS and conventional ships lies the autonomous mode of operation and the possibility to relocate the crew ashore, it needs to be determined, whether the immediate human control and/or the human presence of competent personnel on board the entity is included in the term 'ship' as used in UNCLOS.

Although the IMO uses the term 'ship' for MASS and some authors, therefore, conclude that MASS must be ships,[506] the term must be given its ordinary meaning based on the general rule of interpretation laid down in Article 31 of the VCLT.

The general meaning given in the Oxford English Dictionary is of little help, as ship is defined as a "large seagoing vessel".[507] Consulting the definition of 'vessel' the intended ability of the entity to float upon the water for the carriage of persons or goods stands out.[508] According to these meanings, neither human presence nor human control is inherent in the terms 'ship' and 'vessel'.

Following the interpretation rule stipulated by Article 31 of the VCLT, the context of the provisions needs to be considered. In some provisions, UNCLOS addresses vessels and ships. Other provisions, however, specify the terms by adding prefixes and/or describing adjectives: warships,[509] merchant ships,[510] government ships,[511] and scientific research and hydrographic survey ships.[512] Although the different purposes of these ships make an overall definition challenging,[513] the scope of the terms 'ship' and 'vessel' has to be broad enough to

505 CMI, 'Position Paper on Unmanned Ships and the International Regulatory Framework' (n 13); Richard Barnes, 'Article 17 – Right of innocent passage' in Alexander Proelß and others (eds), *United Nations Convention on the Law of the Sea: A commentary* (1st edition. C.H. Beck; Hart; Nomos 2017) 181

506 For the term "unbemanntes Schiff": Tüngler and tho Pesch (n 429)

507 Oxford English Dictionary, 'ship, n'. 1.a.i. <https://www.oed.com/dictionary/ship_n1?tab=meaning_and_use#22916502> accessed 16 February 2024

508 Oxford English Dictionary, 'vessel, n'. 4a <https://www.oed.com/dictionary/vessel_n1?tab=meaning_and_use#15794971> accessed 16 February 2024

509 As an example: Articles 29–32 of the UNCLOS

510 As an example: Articles 27, 28 of the UNCLOS

511 As an example: Articles 31, 32, 102 of the UNCLOS

512 As an example: Articles 40, 255 of the UNCLOS

513 George K Walker (ed), *Definitions for the law of the sea: Terms not defined by the 1982 Convention* (Martinus Nijhoff Publishers 2012) 56

encompass all specialized types of enumerated water crafts.[514] All these water crafts have in common that they are floatable and enclosed spaces capable of self-propulsion. MASS fulfill these characteristics. Nevertheless, all crafts are conventionally manned and controlled from aboard.

It could be argued that UNCLOS does provide a category for crafts without a human presence on board: the device.[515] Devices do not enjoy the navigational rights enjoyed by ships. Therefore, classifying MASS as a device would not support the intent of ship-like operations. Moreover, it can be concluded from Article 19(2)(f) of the UNCLOS that military devices are small enough to be launched and recovered by ships. This is not possible, especially with larger MASS. However, Article 209(2) of the UNCLOS concerns devices flying the flag of a flag state. As only ships can be granted a flag, the meaning of 'device' is ambiguously used in UNCLOS. MASS are therefore not limited to being a device.

Article 94(3)(b) of the UNCLOS requires measures with regard to "the manning of ships". Thus, the term 'ship' does not include the manning rather a ship needs to be manned.[516] The same applies to the equipment of the vessel necessary for navigation. From a contextual, general law of the sea perspective, neither the manning nor the mode of operation are relevant for the material scope of application.[517] Moreover, an abandoned vessel does not loses its character as 'vessel' merely because humans have left the vessel. Per Article 1(4) of the Wreck Removal Convention, a ship remains a ship as long as it is not sunken or stranded. At this point, a ship becomes a wreck. Consequently, the absence of humans does not render an entity a non-ship. The context does not clearly indicate a single direction. However, arguments can be made to support the inclusion of MASS in the term 'ship' as used in UNCLOS.

As next, the purpose shall be taken into account. The purpose of UNCLOS, as stated in the preamble, is to "settle, in a spirit of mutual understanding and cooperation, all issues relating to the law of the sea". UNCLOS is intended to be a comprehensive codification, which is also clear from the amalgamation of the five predecessor conventions. As "all issues relating to the law of the sea" shall be regulated, new and advancing types of vehicles should not be excluded from the scope of application if being a "law of the sea issue". UNCLOS has

514 Craig H Allen, 'Determining the Legal Status of Unmanned Maritime Vehicles: Formalism vs Functionalism' (2018) 49(4) Journal of Maritime Law and Commerce 477, 494

515 See Articles 19(2)(f); 145(a); 194(3)(c), (d); 209(2); 274(b) of the UNCLOS

516 Alexandros X M Ntovas and others, 'Liability for operations in Unmanned Maritime Vehicles with Differing Levels of Autonomy' (Southampton 15 January 2016) 14.CAT.OP.065 20; Nikolaos Kampantais, 'Legal and regulatory implications of the unmanned ship operation' (Athens, Greece March 2018) 2

517 Tüngler and tho Pesch (n 429)

often adapted to novel technologies or state practices developed after the entry into force of UNCLOS.[518] As an example, the ITLOS confirmed that Articles 56, 62(4) of the UNCLOS included coastal states' regulations on bunkering of foreign fishing vessels in the EEZ.[519]

MASS serve the same purpose as conventional vessels, thus the same risks and needs of regulation of passage and transit rights, environmental protection, and jurisdictional matters exist. Consequently, the same regulatory framework, especially in respect of jurisdiction, should apply to both, MASS and conventional vessels.[520] Rendering UNCLOS inapplicable to advancing types of vessels bears the risk, that UNCLOS loses its general scope and constitutional character.[521]

Parker supports this line of argumentation and states that the lack of MASS-specific provisions in UNCLOS does not mean that the contracting parties wanted to exclude MASS from the scope of UNCLOS. Rather, they could not conceive MASS at the time concluding UNCLOS.[522] Including MASS in the scope of UNCLOS will ensure that the same level of safety and environmental protection is achieved. This is particularly important for the period when MASS and manned vessels operate side by side. Consequently, the purpose of UNCLOS likewise advocates for including MASS in the scope of UNCLOS.

Next, the reached conclusion shall be reconciled with the subsequent national practice. Although there is no internationally uniform prevailing understanding of the terms 'ship' and 'vessel',[523] a questionnaire circulated by the CMI[524] revealed that all 17 responding maritime law associations considered MASS to be regarded as vessels within their national law.[525] The responding

518 Chie Kojima, 'South China Sea Arbitration and the Protection of the Marine Environment: Evolution of UNCLOS Part XII Through Interpretation and the Duty to Cooperate' in Seokwoo Lee and Hee E Lee (eds), *Asian Yearbook of International Law, Volume 21 (2015)* (Brill|Nijhoff 2018); Tullio Scovazzi, 'The Progressive Development of International Law of the Sea: Within or (in Certain Cases) without the UNCLOS' (2020) 12(3) China Oceans Law Review 12; Shunji Yanai, 'Can the UNCLOS Address Challenges of the 21st Century?' (2014) 57 German Yearbook of International Law 43

519 *International Tribunal for the Law of the Sea 2014* (n 242) 217

520 CMI, 'Position Paper on Unmanned Ships and the International Regulatory Framework' (n 13) 3

521 See for maritime drones: Matt Bartlett, 'Game of Drones: Unmanned Maritime Vehicles and the Law of the Sea' (2018) 24 Auckland University Law Review 66, 76

522 Jennifer Parker, 'The Challenges Posed by the Advent of Maritime Autonomous Surface Ships for International Maritime Law' (2021) 35(1) Australian and New Zealand Maritime Law Journal 31, 34 <https://maritime.law.uq.edu.au/index.php/anzmlj/article/view/1433>

523 Walker (ed) (n 513) 60

524 CMI, 'CMI Questionnaire on unmanned ships' (Antwerpen 24 March 2017)

525 CMI, 'Summary of Responses to the CMI Questionnaire' (Antwerpen May 2018)

associations included major maritime nations such as Brazil, China, France, Germany, Japan, and Singapore. The unanimous endorsement of the inclusion of MASS in the scope of their national maritime law strongly supports a broad understanding of the terms by national states. Furthermore, the active participation of many UNCLOS members in the MASS activities of the IMO can be seen as an indication that they consider MASS to be 'ships'.[526] In 2024, the LEG of the IMO expressed that "MASS are required to conform to the relevant rules of international law, including the United Nations Convention on the Law of the Sea".[527] This confirms the assumption that states assume MASS to be 'ships' in the meaning of UNCLOS.

Eventually, it is possible that the parties intended to use the term 'ship' as a generic term including an element of evolution. The appearance and the equipment of ships have changed considerably over time and the parties of UNCLOS were aware of this development. Nevertheless, only the general term 'ship' was used. This strongly advocates for the use of 'ship' as a generic term capable of evolving over time.[528] Since the IMO's discussion on MASS did not extensively address whether MASS qualify as ships under the meaning of UNCLOS, the term 'ship' has in any event changed its meaning, even if it may has been narrower previously, i.e. including the human presence on board.

To conclude, considering the context and purpose of UNCLOS, the ordinary meaning of the terms 'ship' and 'vessel' does not include the human presence on board nor immediate human control. Consequently, MASS fall within the scope of 'ship' and 'vessel'.[529]

For the enjoyment of the navigation and passage rights, it does not suffice to be considered a ship. Rather, the ship has to fly the flag of a flag state as

526 Allen, 'Allen 2018' (n 514) 503

527 LEG, IMO, 'LEG 111/17: Report of the Legal Committee on the Work of its 111th Session' (London 16 May 2024) 32; LEG, IMO, 'LEG 111/10/5: Proposal to ensure regulating MASS within the framework of international law (United Arab Emirates)' (London 16 February 2024) 2

528 Simon McKenzie, 'When is a Ship a Ship? Use by State Armed Forces of Uncrewed Maritime Vehicles and the United Nations Convention on the Law of the Sea' (2020) 21(2) Melbourne Journal of International Law 373, 384

529 CMI, 'Position Paper on Unmanned Ships and the International Regulatory Framework' (n 13) 3; Michael Boviatsis and George Vlachos, 'Sustainable Operation of Unmanned Ships under Current International Maritime Law' (2022) 14(12) Sustainability, 3; Oliver Daum and Axel Boesch, 'Zur Aktualität der Schiffsdefinition des BGH: Sind unbemannte Wasserfahrzeuge Schiffe?' [2018] Zeitschrift für das Recht der Transportwirtschaft 41, 44; Pol Deketelaere, 'The legal challenges of unmanned vessels' (Master Dissertation, Universiteit Gent 21 May 2017); Tüngler and tho Pesch (n 429), 122; Ringbom, 'Ringbom 2020' (n 424) 437; rather reserved however: Ntovas and others (n 516) 5

only states can rely on the granted rights.[530] Consequently, MASS need to be registered in a flag state to enjoy these navigational rights. Per Article 91(1) of the UNCLOS, each state may grant its nationality to ships by registering them.

As a starting point, the registration requirements are set out in the national laws of flag states. Prima facie, nothing prevents a flag state to register a MASS. However, some specifics of MASS deserve further attention. Unlike conventional ships, MASS have an RCC from which the ship is operated or monitored. This is a new aspect that could lead to a different assessment of the nationality of the vessel and the genuine link, as there is now an element of the ship that is permanently positioned on land. Initially, the relationship between the ship, the RCC, and the flag state will be examined. Subsequently, the limit for registration stipulated by UNCLOS, the requirement of a 'genuine link' between the flag state and its vessels shall be examined in the light of MASS.[531]

Per Article 91(1) of the UNCLOS, ships can be granted nationality. Even if not all aspects of the definition of the term 'ship' can be established beyond doubt, it is undisputed that 'ships' are movable units. As a result, the RCC cannot be registered, as it is a fixed installation. Unless special rules are adopted, the RCC is subject to the jurisdiction of the state in whose territory the RCC is located. This conclusion was also reached by a study performed on behalf of the Belgian Ministry for Transport, which examined the definition and organization of an RCC.[532] Nonetheless, the RCC should be surveyed and certified by the flag state administration or a recognized organization as it plays an integral role in the operation of the vessel.[533] The certification process will be performed solely by the flag state; the host state of the RCC is not involved.[534]

After having assessed the nationality, the 'genuine link' requirement provided by Article 91(1) of the UNCLOS shall be considered in the light of MASS. As illustrated above, the ITLOS repeatedly ruled that the 'genuine link' is not a pre-requisite for the registration, but rather a consequence of it.[535] Applying the same registration principles to MASS as to conventional vessels, the genuine link is likewise not a requirement for the registration of MASS. However, the RCC, located on the shore, adds a geographical element that did not exist

530 Article 90 of the UNCLOS

531 Article 91(1) of the UNCLOS

532 MSC, IMO, 'MSC 107/INF.14' (n 43) 93

533 ISWG/MASS, 'MSC-ISWG-MASS 2-3-2 – Comments regarding ROC oversights by the flag Administration (Russian Federation)' (London 15 September 2023) 9

534 MSC, IMO, 'MSC 107/INF.14' (n 43) 93

535 *International Tribunal for the Law of the Sea 2014* (n 242) 110, 113; *International Tribunal for the Law of the Sea 1999* (n 242) 83

before. This might justify a differentiating assessment of the genuine link with regard to MASS.

The genuine link requirement shall ensure that the flag state can effectively exercise jurisdiction in administrative, technical, and social matters over vessels flying its flag. As long as the RCC is located in the flag state, the flag state authorities could enforce their national laws against the RCC. Exercising jurisdiction could even be easier compared to conventional ships, as the master, crew, and RCC will be stationary and reachable for enforcement measures.[536] If, however, the RCC were located in another state's territory, the flag state would lack immediate enforcement jurisdiction, as the flag state does not have jurisdiction in another state's territory.[537] However, diplomatic consultations with the hosting state of the RCC could be hold to enforce flag state regulations.[538] Therefore, the flag state retains the ability to exercise jurisdiction, although less effectively than if the RCC were located within its territory.[539] This prompted some authors to argue that the RCC should be located in the territory of the flag state to ensure the effective performance flag state jurisdiction.[540] The LEG discussed this issue and, despite conflicting views from several states,[541] agreed that an RCC may be located outside the flag state.[542] However, each state can determine the requirements for the location of the RCC by its national law.

In the case of autonomous MASS, the delocalization could increase. The RCC only monitors the vessel and the operation software might be in sync with multiple servers located around the world. Hence, enforcing flag state regulations could become even more challenging.[543] However, the flag state system

536 Tüngler and tho Pesch (n 429) 123

537 Samantha Besson, 'Sovereignty' in Anne Peters (ed), *Max Planck Encyclopedia of Public International Law* (MPEPIL) (Oxford University Press) 1–2; Richard Barnes, 'Flag States' in Donald R Rothwell and others (eds), *The Oxford Handbook of the Law of the Sea* (Oxford University Press 2015) 312

538 Knut Ipsen and Hans-Joachim Heintze, *Völkerrecht: Ein Studienbuch* (Kurzlehrbücher für das juristische Studium, 7. Auflage, C.H. Beck 2019) 110

539 David M Coello, 'Is UNCLOS Ready for the Era of Seafaring Autonomous Vessels?' (2023) 10(1) Journal of Territorial and Maritime Studies 21, 30

540 Bingying Dong, Lowell Bautista and Ling Zhu, 'Navigating uncharted waters: Challenges and regulatory solutions for flag state jurisdiction of Maritime Autonomous Surface Ships under UNCLOS' (2024) 161 Marine Policy, 6

541 LEG, IMO, 'LEG 111/17/Add.1: Report of the Legal Committee on the Work of its 111th Session' (London 16 May 2024) 38–42

542 LEG, IMO, 'LEG 111/17' (n 527) 34

543 Eric van Hooydonk, 'The law of unmanned merchant shipping – an exploration' [2014] Journal of International Maritime Law 403, 410

developed by UNCLOS could still be maintained regardless of the delocalization of the operation of the ship.[544]

Discussions on the effectiveness of flag state jurisdiction are, however, not new. Even in the case of conventional ships, the effective exercise of flag state jurisdiction is not guaranteed. As ships not necessarily call at their flag states' ports, the vessel and its crew are not frequently within the territory of the flag state and are therefore not subject to immediate enforcement measures by the flag state. Even today, the effective enforcement depends on diplomatic cooperation with port and coastal states, which have more often enforcement opportunities against the vessel and its master than the flag state. Ultimately, the degree of effectiveness required by UNCLOS is illustrated by the fact that UNCLOS even permits land-locked states to issue flag certificates.

Consequently, effective jurisdiction does not depend on a territorial connection between the vessel and its flag state or a physical access of the flag state to the vessel during port calls. Thus, flag state jurisdiction can be exercised over MASS. Therefore, the genuine link does not limit the registration of MASS.

To conclude, MASS fall within the scope of UNCLOS and are considered a 'ship' or a 'vessel'. MASS can be registered as conventional vessels and have the nationality of their flag state. The genuine link does not require the RCC to be located in the flag state. Based on national law, however, flag and port states can imposed such requirements. The effectiveness of flag state jurisdiction could decrease if the RCC is located in another state than the flag state. However, this situation is no different from today, given the existence of flags of convenience and the fact that ships rarely call at ports in their flag states. The advent of MASS could simply add another scenario of ineffective flag state jurisdiction. Consequently, the flag state system developed by UNCLOS could be rethought and reformed as a whole now.[545] However, this is not necessary to accommodate MASS.

Now, the scope of application of SOLAS, COLREG, and STCW shall be briefly considered to determine whether these conventions apply to MASS.

Per Regulation I/1 of SOLAS, SOLAS applies to all "ships engaged on international voyages". Moreover, each chapter stipulates a distinct scope of application. The two chapters particularly relevant here, chapters III and V, however, apply to all ships on all voyages.[546] As in the case of UNCLOS, neither human presence nor human control are inherent to the term 'ship'. As this study is

544 Coello (n 539) 30

545 ibid 31

546 See Regulation III/1.1; V/1.1. of SOLAS

concerned with vessels, operating in international trade SOLAS applies to the MASS discussed here.

Turning to COLREG, Rule 1(a) stipulates that COLREG applies to "all vessels upon high seas and in all waters connected therewith navigable by seagoing vessels". The term vessel is defined by Rule 3(a) of COLREG as including

> [...] every description of water craft, including non-displacement craft, WIG craft and seaplanes, used or capable of being used as a means of transportation on water'.

The definition is broad and does not include any limitations regarding human presence or control on board. The ability to transport something or someone does not exclude MASS engaged in international cargo voyages from the scope of application. For MASS devoted to other activities such as surveillance, research explorations, or maintenance, however, the scope of application has to be assessed separately as the characterization as a means of transport is uncertain.[547] However, it could be argued that these types of MASS are also intended to transport equipment, as the relevant task cannot be conducted without it. This thesis focuses on commercially operated MASS navigating on the high seas and in connected waters, to which COLREG applies.

Eventually, STCW applies per Article III to all "seafarers serving on board seagoing ships entitled to fly the flag of a Party". At this point, it should suffice to state that MASS are seagoing ships that are allowed to fly a flag under UNCLOS. From this point of view, STCW applies to MASS. How to deal with the limitation to "seafarers serving on board seagoing ships" shall be considered later.

In conclusion, UNCLOS and all three GAIRAS conventions apply to MASS. Next, the seaworthiness of MASS from a public law perspective and the ability of MASS to fulfil this key function will be discussed. The concept of seaworthiness includes, in particular, the safety at sea. This function is of paramount importance for MASS and will be assessed first. The duty to render assistance is of equal importance and will be considered second from the MASS perspective.

4.4.2 *Safety at Sea*

All vessels have to ensure the safety at sea. Article 94 of the UNCLOS confers the duty to ensure the safety at sea to the flag states. It states that

547 Gogarty and Hagger (n 373) 114

> 3. [e]very state shall take such measures for ships flying its flag as are necessary to ensure safety at sea with regard, inter alia, to:
> (a) the construction, equipment and seaworthiness of ships;
> (b) the manning of ships, labour conditions and the training of crews, taking into account the applicable international instruments;
> (c) the use of signals, the maintenance of communications and the prevention of collisions.
> 4. Such measures shall include those necessary to ensure:
> (a) that each ship, before registration and thereafter at appropriate intervals, is surveyed by a qualified surveyor of ships, and has on board such charts, nautical publications and navigational equipment and instruments as are appropriate for the safe navigation of the ship;
> (b) that each ship is in the charge of a master and officers who possess appropriate qualifications, in particular in seamanship, navigation, communications and marine engineering, and that the crew is appropriate in qualification and numbers for the type, size, machinery and equipment of the ship;
> (c) that the master, officers and, to the extent appropriate, the crew are fully conversant with and required to observe the applicable international regulations concerning the safety of life at sea, the prevention of collisions, the prevention, reduction and control of marine pollution, and the maintenance of communications by radio.
> 5. In taking the measures called for in paragraphs 3 and 4 each State is required to conform to generally accepted international regulations, procedures and practices and to take any steps which may be necessary to secure their observance.

The safety at sea is a comprehensive and multifaceted function and includes inter alia the safety of navigation and the safety of life at sea. The safety of navigation includes the operation of a vessel in a manner avoiding collisions with other vessels or static installations and the avoidance of unnecessary close-quarter situations. The safety of life at sea concerns measures to be taken to ensure that persons involved in the operation of the vessel do not suffer harm. This aspects needs to be distinguished from the duty to render assistance to people in distress. This duty will be considered after the safety at sea, as it concerns persons external to the ship.

The subsequent legal analysis will first introduce the relevant provisions setting out the details about the function, before, as second, discussing key questions considering the technological innovation of, on the one hand, remotely operated, and, on the other hand, autonomously operated vessels. The leading question is whether MASS can fulfill the functions described by the international conventions. Subsequently, the manning requirement as set out in UNCLOS and SOLAS is considered and it is determined whether the same function-based interpretation can be applied. Eventually, the duty to render assistance to people in distress at sea will be discussed in the light of MASS.

4.4.2.1 Safety of Navigation

Both international and national laws regulate the safety of navigation. On the international level, which will be examined here, conventions, codes, and non-binding guidelines address the safety of navigation. First, the legal framework for the safety of navigation will be introduced. Second, it will be assessed whether MASS can fulfill the function of safe navigation. This assessment is guided by two core questions that reflect the innovative aspects of MASS: Does the safety of navigation require a human presence on board the vessel? Does the safety of navigation require human decision-making?

Article 94 of the UNCLOS is the central provision on the safety of navigation. Flag states must implement measures to ensure compliance with applicable international regulations for collision prevention, taking into account the GAIRAS conventions. COLREG is pointed out by Article 94(4)(c) of the UNCLOS as the main source for collision prevention regulations.

Rule 5 of COLREG is the central provision to start with as safe navigation requires information about the state of the vessel and its surroundings. Rule 5 stipulates that

> [e]very vessel shall at all times maintain a proper look-out by sight and hearing as well as by all available means appropriate in the prevailing circumstances and conditions so as to make a full appraisal of the situation and of the risk of collision.

Here, not only the lack of human presence on board MASS could pose a challenge. The rule may require human involvement to fully appraise the situation and assess the risk of collision. The conventional human-based decision-making becomes even clearer in Rule 2(a) COLREG. This provisions states that

> [n]othing in these Rules shall exonerate any vessel, or the owner, master or crew thereof, from the consequences of any neglect to comply with these Rules or of the neglect of any precaution which may be required by the ordinary practice of seamen, or by the special circumstances of the case.

Here the critical aspect is whether MASS can fulfill the requirement to adhere to the ordinary practice of seaman. This is especially relevant for MASS operating at degree four, as algorithms will take navigational decisions. Other navigation rules in COLREG include non-quantifiable terms such as "if the circumstances of the case admit"[548] or appropriate or adapted to "the prevailing circumstances and conditions".[549] It needs to be discussed whether algorithms are able to comply with such vague terms. On the first sight, these provisions require human presence on board and human involvement in the decision-making loop. This first impression is supported by STCW and SOLAS padding the safety of navigation with more details.

The STCW regime includes provisions addressing watchkeeping arrangements. Regulation VIII/2 of STCW obliges the national administrations to monitor the watchkeeping arrangements. It stipulates that

> [a]dministrations shall require the master of every ship to ensure that watchkeeping arrangements are adequate for maintaining a safe watch or watches, taking into account the prevailing circumstances and conditions and that, under the master's general direction:
>
> .1 officers in charge of the navigational watch are responsible for navigating the ship safely during their periods of duty, when they shall be physically present on the navigating bridge or in a directly associated location such as the chartroom or bridge control room at all times;

Chapter A-VIII of the STCW Code sets out more details for the watchkeeping arrangement. Regulation A-VIII/2.24.2 of the STCW Code stipulates that

> [t]he officer in charge of the navigational watch shall in no circumstances leave the bridge until properly relieved.

The increased use of electronic means to communicate ship-to-ship and ship-to-shore has added a significant dimension to the lookout as all available means shall be used per Rule 5 of COLREG. For instant communication, radio communication is the most important technology used on all vessels. Both STCW and SOLAS reflect the need to ensure safe radio communication and radio watches. Whereas Chapter IV of STCW provides provisions on the

548 Rules 8(a), (b); 9(g); 15; 17(c); 18(d)(1) of COLREG

549 Rules 6; 19(b) of COLREG

training and qualification of radio personnel, the functional requirements are stipulated by Regulation IV/4 of SOLAS:

> 1 Every ship, while at sea, shall be capable:
>
> .1 [...] of transmitting ship-to-shore distress alerts by at least two separate and independent means, each using a different radiocommunication service;
>
> .2 of receiving shore-to-ship distress alerts;
>
> .3 of transmitting and receiving ship-to-ship distress alerts;
>
> .4 of transmitting and receiving search and rescue coordinating communications;
>
> .5 of transmitting and receiving on-scene communications;
>
> .6 of transmitting and [...] receiving signals for locating;
>
> .7 of transmitting and receiving maritime safety information;
>
> .8 of transmitting and receiving general radiocommunications to and from shore-based radio systems or networks subject to regulation 15.8; and
>
> .9 of transmitting and receiving bridge-to-bridge communications.

SOLAS reflects the lookout by providing requirements for the navigation bridge visibility, design, and equipment of the bridge. Prominently, Regulation V/22 of SOLAS provides for several technical details on the construction of the navigation bridge such as the horizontal field of vision, the height of the navigation bridge front windows, and the main steering position. Regulation V/15 of SOLAS provides guiding principles to be observed when determining the navigation bridge design. These provisions will be considered together with the lookout enshrined in COLREG and STCW.

Although they are less frequently cited, the regulations V/24, V/10, V/11, and V/12 of SOLAS are no less significant for ensuring the safety of navigation. Regulation V/24.1 of SOLAS concerns the availability of manual steering. It stipulates that

> [i]n areas of high traffic density, in conditions of restricted visibility and in all other hazardous navigational situations where heading and/or track control systems are in use, it shall be possible to establish manual control of the ship's steering immediately.

This provision could demand a human presence on board the vessel to ensure manual steering in certain situations.

Increased ship traffic and highly frequented port approaches made traffic management measures necessary to avoid collisions, close-quarter situations, and smooth clearance of all vessels. The provisions introduced now form part of this traffic management system. Regulation V/10 of SOLAS addresses ship's routeing systems adopted by the IMO upon a proposal of a contracting government. Although UNCLOS only provides for the establishment of sea lanes and traffic separation schemes in the territorial sea,[550] ship's routeing measures include additional measures such as two-way routes, recommended tracks, and precautionary areas where ships should navigate with particular caution.[551] In 1985, the IMO adopted non-binding General Provisions on Ships' Routeing Systems that should be considered when proposing new routeing systems.[552] Pursuant to Regulation V/10.7 of SOLAS, ships are required to use mandatory ships' routeing systems to ensure the safety of navigation. Here, it needs to be examined whether MASS can fulfill this requirement.

Regulations V/11, V/12 of SOLAS can be assessed together as ship reporting is usually operated as a vessel traffic service (VTS).[553] The systems differ in that the ship reporting system requires a one-way communication from the vessel to the coastal state reporting core ship data such as the name, voyage plan, port of destination, and cargo details.[554] The VTS, in turn, includes a two- or multi-way communication between the vessel, the VTS control center, and other vessels. VTS operators ensure the safety of navigation by giving traffic or meteorological hazard warnings or managing the vessel traffic in ports

550 Article 22 of the UNCLOS

551 IMO, 'Ships' routeing' <https://www.imo.org/en/OurWork/Safety/Pages/ShipsRouteing.aspx> accessed 16 February 2024

552 IMO, 'Res. A.572(14): General Provisions on Ships' Routeing' (London 20 November 1985)

553 Iva Parlov, 'Can the International Regulatory Framework on Ships' Routing, Ship Reporting, and Vessel Traffic Service (VTS) Accommodate Marine Autonomous Surface Ships (MASS)?' (2023) 54(2) Ocean Development & International Law 163, 174

554 See Regulation 3 in the IMO, 'Res. A.851(20): General Principles for Ship Reporting Systems and Ship Reporting Requirements' (London 27 November 1997)

or waterways.[555] As flag states have to ensure that vessels flying their flag comply with the provisions of a VTS per Regulation V/12.4 of SOLAS, it needs to be discussed whether MASS can fulfill the reporting duties and be integrated into VTS.

The most important international regulations setting out the details about the safety of navigation have been introduced. As seen, the provisions often refer to one another and form a coherent whole. To summarize, to ensure the safety of navigation the ship shall navigate in compliance with COLREG. This requires the making of a full appraisal of the situation of the vessel, its surroundings, and of the risk of collisions. For this, a lookout is required at all times. Per STCW, humans shall be present on the navigation bridge as this is the place from where the lookout is perform on conventional vessels. The bridge shall be designed in a way ensuring that the crew and the master are able to perform properly the lookout. In particularly congested waters and ports, ship's routeing measures, ship reporting systems, and VTS ensure that the vessel traffic runs as smoothly as possible. This demands the active (reporting duties) and passive (compliance with measures adopted) cooperation of ships.

The following analysis will now consider whether remotely operated vessels can comply with the concept of navigational safety, as concretized by the provisions presented. Remotely operated vessels are characterized by the absence of people on board. The question, therefore, is, whether the safety of navigation requires the presence of people on board the ship. If this is the case, remotely operated vessels cannot meet the safe navigation requirement. However, if safe navigation is also possible for remotely operated vessels, it can be further investigated whether autonomous vessels can meet the safe navigation requirement.

4.4.2.1.1 *Human Presence on Board for the Safety of Navigation*

To determine if a human presence is necessary for safe navigation, the state of the art is briefly outlined to provide a rough overview of the technical possibilities. This understanding is essential for the subsequent legal analysis.

To guarantee safe navigation, it is essential to maintain situational awareness of the vessel and its surroundings. On board MASS, sensors are employed to imitate human senses and react to diverse environmental stimuli. Visual surveillance is conducted by cameras, which must be of different types to cope

---

555 See especially Regulation 3 of IMO, 'Res. A.1158(32): Guidelines for Vessel Traffic Systems' (London 15 December 2021)

with rapidly changing weather conditions, poor weather, or night-time.[556] Installing multiple cameras or stereo cameras enables bird's-eye view perspective and range estimation based on triangulation.[557] Bird's-eye view perspective is particularly useful for docking operations.[558] Object detection can be based on high-definition cameras that provide color information and technology can be used to segment objects from the background based on their colors.[559] However, such high-definition cameras cannot provide high-quality pictures in severe weather conditions or during night-times. Thus, additional cameras, like long-wave infrared cameras,[560] have to be installed.

Today's navigation already uses RADAR to detect obstacles irrespective of the weather conditions. These systems are, however, not precise enough to detect small moving objects or stationary installations in close-range situations (some hundred meters). As MASS should be able to operate safely even in congested areas or waters with limited space for maneuvering, close-range object detection is important. LIDAR systems can be used as an addition to provide accurate measurements of distances.[561] However, many fast-moving parts are installed in such a system, which increases the likelihood of malfunctions due to mechanical failures.[562] Trials in Trondheim, Norway, revealed that not only the capability of different sensors has to be considered, but that the run-time of the system gathering the camera data has to be adequate to provide a reliable, comprehensive image.[563]

Besides visual surveillance, sound signals must be received as they transmit relevant information.[564] Thus, sound-reception systems need to be installed.[565] Additionally, MASS need to be able to react upon sound signals and give

556 Jokioinen and others (n 98) 23; Wahlström and others (n 45) 1042; Sarang Thombre and others, 'Sensors and AI Techniques for Situational Awareness in Autonomous Ships: A Review' (2022) 23(1) IEEE Transactions on Intelligent Transportation Systems 64, 68

557 Thombre and others (n 556) 71

558 Mathias T Paasche, Øystein K Helgesen and Edmund F Brekke, 'Real-time 360 degrees view for the operator of *milliAmpere 2*' (2023) 2618(1) Journal of Physics: Conference Series, 7

559 Jokioinen and others (n 98) 23; Thombre and others (n 556) 71

560 Jokioinen and others (n 98) 23

561 Thombre and others (n 556) 69

562 Jokioinen and others (n 98) 27

563 Paasche, Helgesen and Brekke (n 558) 4

564 See Rule 35 of COLREG setting out sound signals to be used in restricted visibility

565 Thombre and others (n 556) 72

appropriate answer signals if necessary.[566] Moreover, sensors for smoke and gas should be used to detect fire and gas leaks.[567]

Technical means to ensure radio communication and radio watches on VHF Digital selective calling Channel 70 for distress signals[568] have received less attention so far. In addition to conventional radio antennas, system would need to be installed that can process the acoustic radio signals. Other projects did not install such specific radio communication technology on the vessel, but ensured that the signals received by the conventional installations on the vessel were relayed to the RCC.[569] The same holds true for radio communication with the VTS operator or for fulfilling the ship reporting duties.

Fusing different sources of data is important to balance the drawbacks of different types of sensors and to be able to detect individual errors by verifying the data received.[570] As numerous technologies support the perception of the ship's vicinity already, future awareness systems should benefit from the use of this known and used technology. Commonly used technologies can be fused with the data received by additional sensors. The position data from the Global Positioning System (GPS) as well as the vessel information included in the AIS such as the unique identification of a vessel, its position, course, and speed can be displayed in the electronic chart display and information system. This system provides geographic information and can be utilized for nautical navigation instead of paper nautical charts. This system is already used today.

Relocating both the master and the crew ashore not only necessitates the installation of sensors but also requires the processing and transmission of received data to the RCC to ensure situational awareness by the remote crew. For the transmission of data, the available bandwidth capacity is of major importance. Remote operations are usually based on the shore-based process of the data. The operator is likewise able to follow the processing to detect errors in the analysis done by the algorithm closely. Technical failure and poor network coverage make it necessary to consider the risk of restricted bandwidth capacity and the subsequently limited transfer of data gathered on board the

566 M.C Jo and others, 'Study on the potential gaps and themes identified by IMO Regulatory Scoping Exercise (RSE) for the use of Maritime Autonomous Surface Ships (MASS)' (2020) 929 IOP Conference Series: Materials Science and Engineering, 4

567 Børge Kjeldstad, Giorgio M Kufolar and Jon H Ulvensøen, 'Using the Watchkeeping regulation to verify safe operation of Uncrewed Surface Vessels' (2023) 5

568 Regulation IV/12.1.1 of SOLAS

569 Jokioinen and others (n 98) 43

570 ibid 27; Utredningen om självkörande fordon på väg and SOU 2018:16 (n 184) 187

vessel.[571] In case of only restricted bandwidth capacity, the processing needs to happen on the vessel and only the analyzed and fused data can be transmitted to the RCC. Alternatively, the algorithm prioritizes the data on board the vessel and transmits the data labeled as high-priority to the RCC. MASS could benefit from direct communication with nearby vessels to exchange information about their route, speed, and other relevant navigation aspects. This, however, depends on the cooperation of other vessels.

Physical perception of the vessel's movements, the machine vibrations, and the state of sea are also important sources of information for masters. A study conducted with experienced masters revealed the risk of a lack of physical perception of the vessel and its motion.[572] A static office environment lacking physical perception not only excludes a human sense but could also result in a lower safety margin.[573] Especially in heavy weather situations, the master should have a physical sense of the ship's movement in the state of the sea to alter the course and speed to ensure a safe passage of the ship.[574] Studies concluded that multisensory presentation of the information in the RCC increases the situational awareness achieved by the remote operator.[575] This includes the transmission of movements to the RCC.[576]

Moreover, the risk of overreliance on the system,[577] mishaps due to inattentiveness,[578] and information overload in the RCC[579] are to be considered. Thus, not only the design and equipment of the vessel need to be reconsidered, also the setup of the RCC and the design of the human-machine interaction require attention.[580] Porathe et al. illustrated in a fictional example the potential impact of a chain of unfortunate coincidences: the afternoon sun blinding the two cameras of the autonomous MASS, a small kayak not detected

571 Oda L Fastvold, 'Legal Challenges for Unmanned Ships in International Law of the Sea' (master thesis, The Arctic University of Norway 2018) 44; Ringbom and Collin (n 30) 15

572 Man and others (n 45), 2678; Wahlström and others (n 45) 1040

573 Man and others (n 45), 2678; ISWG/MASS, 'MSC-ISWG-MASS 2-3-6 – Role of the Master for consideration in the draft MASS Code (The Nautical Institute)' (London 15 September 2023) 6

574 Porathe, Prison and Man (n 147) 107; Liu (n 196) 491

575 Wahlström and others (n 45), 1044; Man and others (n 45) 2678

576 Kjeldstad, Kufolar and Ulvensøen (n 567) 5

577 Wahlström and others (n 45) 1041

578 Barthelsson and Sagefjord (n 50) 37–38

579 Porathe, Prison and Man (n 147) 108

580 See for a comparison with other industries and lessons learned for remote operation: Magnhild Kaarstad and Alf O Braseth, 'Operating autonomous ships remotely from land-based operation centers: The current state-of-the-art' (Halden, Norway 18 December 2020)

by the RADAR, and an operator who just had a coffee break could easily result in a severe collision.[581] The serious consequences of information overload can be impressively studied using the example of flight Air France 447.[582] Due to a storm, the sensors measuring the airspeed were obstructed by ice crystals. Consequently, the autopilot disconnected and handed over the control back to the Pilot in Flight. However, the pilot was surprised and overwhelmed of contradictory display information, blinking lights, and alarm signals. The situation resulted in a "total loss of cognitive control of the situation"[583] and 228 fatal injuries. While it is crucial to consider these incidents and implement measures to minimize any remaining risk, it is worth noting that inattention and fatigue are not unique to MASS and apply to traditional vessels as well as other means of automated processes[584] too. The transition of the human role from an active involvement in the navigation process to a passive supervision increases the risk of unintentional blindness.[585] As a mere passive supervision task does not work well with the way human visual attention works, active involvement of the human operator for reporting tasks could be considered to reduce the risk of unintentional blindness.[586]

Moreover, it is important that involved personnel appropriately trusts the system. Trust is necessary to reduce complexity and foster efficiency as control loops can be reduced if the system is trusted.[587] Both, overreliance and aloofness put safe operation at risk. Interviews with Norwegian seafarers revealed that positive practical experience contribute to developing trust. Additionally, the degree of self-efficacy affects seafarers' trust in autonomous systems.[588] As a result, to facilitate efficient cooperation between humans and autonomous navigation systems, the system should be trained as a new colleague.

---

581 Thomas Porathe and others, 'At least as safe as manned shipping? Autonomous shipping, safety and "human error"' in Stein Haugen and others (eds), *Safety and Reliability – Safe Societies in a Changing World: Proceedings of ESREL 2018, June 17–21, 2018, Trondheim, Norway* (Taylor & Francis 2018)

582 Parlov, 'Parlov 2023' (n 553) 179

583 Bureau d'Enquêtes et d'Analyses pour la sécurité de l'aviation civile, 'Final Report AF 447 Rio de Janeiro – Paris' (Le Bourget July 2012) 199

584 Consider automated road and train traffic, mining processes, chemical industry processes, as well as nuclear industry; in railroad traffic dead-man's vigilante systems are used to assure that the driver remain attentive: Diego Scaccabarozzi and others, 'Monitoring of train driver's alertness: A feasibility study' (2017 IEEE International Instrumentation and Measurement Technology Conference (I2MTC), Torino, Italy, 5/22/2017–5/25/2017)

585 Veitch and Alsos (n 50) 7

586 ibid

587 Aalberg and others (n 22) 2

588 ibid 8

This approach enables experienced seafarers to gain positive experiences and develop appropriate trust in the system.

Another aspect identified by the studies is the problem of verifying the received information in the RCC. As stereo vision is limited when conventional cameras are installed[589] and double-checking the information may be complicated,[590] the REMOTE operator could be distracted by the investigation of unclear information rather than supervising the current situation on board the vessel.[591]

In conclusion, the installation of a sensor-based lookout system on board a MASS presents a substantial technical challenge that should not be underestimated. Nonetheless, the maritime industry has already implemented various technical solutions, leading to a noteworthy enhancement in maritime safety. Furthermore, the pace of technological advancement is rapid, and the emergence of reliable solutions can be anticipate in the near future. The showcased research projects and successful trials underscore the significant progress in technical development and assure that any remaining challenges will soon be effectively addressed. Experts predict that the combination of already implemented technology such as RADAR, GPS, and LIDAR and cameras and additional sensors will provide a superior basis for situational awareness than the equipment on a manned vessel paired with direct human perception.[592]

Turning now to the legal assessment, Rule 5 of COLREG prescribes that the lookout shall be performed "by sight and hearing as well as all other available means". In the case of remotely operated vessels, humans will not be present on board the vessel. Hence, there is a need to deliberate on whether transmitting the data received from a sensor system to the RCC is adequate to fulfill the requisites outlined in Rule 5 of COLREG. The subsequent processing of the data is carried out by the human remote operator, and as such, it mirrors the procedures employed in conventional ships. Consequently, this aspect does not pose any legal concerns.

Starting with a literal analysis, 'sight and hearing' refer to human capacities.[593] However, the rule addresses directly the vessel, which seems contra-

589 Wahlström and others (n 45) 1042

590 Liu (n 196) 491

591 Man and others (n 45), 2679–2680

592 Chircop, 'Chircop 2017' (n 255) 27

593 Simon Baughen, 'Who is the master now?: Regulatory and contractual challenges of unmanned vessels' in Barış Soyer and Andrew Tettenborn (eds), *New Technologies, Artificial Intelligence and Shipping Law in the 21st Century* (Maritime and transport law library. Informa Law from Routledge 2019) 134; Fastvold (n 571) 32; Tüngler and tho Pesch (n 429)

dictory, as even a conventional vessel is unable to see and hear.[594] Rule 2(a) of COLREG clarifies the circle of obliged parties and imposes the duty to comply with COLREG upon the vessel, the owner, the master, or the crew. As the vessel in the sense of the structural construction, the crew, and the cargo are usually deemed as one entity,[595] Rule 5 of COLREG is not in itself inconsistent. The human capabilities referenced can be rationalized by examining the manner in which ships were operated when adopting COLREG. Thus, the MASS, together with its remote crew has to ensure the lookout. The MSC applies the same interpretation and assumes that Rule 5 of encompasses all forms of MASS as it directly addresses the vessel rather than humans.[596]

Considering the context, the lookout shall be 'proper' and all means 'appropriate in the prevailing circumstances and conditions' shall be used. Both terms, 'proper' and 'appropriate', provide flexibility on how to maintain the lookout. Given the superiority of sensors over humans in certain circumstances,[597] it could even be argued that it is necessary to use all available sensors and not just rely on human skills. Sensors have the advantage of not getting distracted or tired and they can ensure a 360° view of the vessel and its surroundings. Moreover, during night-times and in severe weather conditions a combination of different sensors can provide a more accurate picture of the situation than humans' eyesight could do.[598]

The context encompasses not only the remaining provision but also requires consideration of other relevant provisions. Reading Rule 5 of COLREG together with provisions addressing the visibility of the navigation bridge gives an idea of what the negotiators had in mind when adopting COLREG. Regulation V/22 of SOLAS prescribes the design and equipment of the navigation bridge to ensure a proper lookout. Regulation V/22.1.1 of SOLAS delineates the mandated parameters for the range of view from the navigation bridge, encompassing considerations for blind sectors caused by cargo, the horizontal field of vision, and the visibility of the ship's sides. This regulation is designed to maximize the field of vision from the bridge, suggesting an intention for lookouts to be

---

125; Ringbom, 'Ringbom 2019' (n 55) 152–153; CMI, 'Position Paper on Unmanned Ships and the International Regulatory Framework' (n 13) 14

594 Tüngler and tho Pesch (n 429) 125

595 *International Tribunal for the Law of the Sea 1999* (n 242)

596 MSC, IMO, 'MSC 107/20' (n 375) 5.48

597 Chircop, 'Chircop 2017' (n 255) 135; Toshiyuki Miyoshi, Shoji Fujimoto and Matthew Rooks, 'Study of Principles in COLREG s and Interpretations and Amendments COLREG s for Maritime Autonomous Surface Ships (MASS)' (2021) 6(1) Transactions of Navigation 11, 15

598 Jokioinen and others (n 98) 23; Miyoshi, Fujimoto and Rooks (n 597) 15

exclusively stationed on the bridge. The concept of integrating a sensor system across the entire vessel for enhanced situational awareness was not taken into account. Moreover, Regulation V/22.1.8 of SOLAS outlines specific dimensions for the front window of the navigation bridge, referencing the average height of a person (1800 mm). This underscores the regulator's presumption that lookout duties will primarily be carried out from the navigation bridge by individuals.[599]

Nevertheless, Regulation V/22.3 of SOLAS acknowledges the possibility of non-traditional designs and allows for special approval in situations where visibility from the navigation bridge cannot adhere to the specifications in Regulations V/22.1 and 22.2 of SOLAS. This provision may be relevant to remotely operated MASS. However, it is crucial to note that adherence to SOLAS is contingent upon the administration being satisfied that a level of visibility equivalent to the prescribed arrangements has been reached.[600] Similarly, Regulation V/3.1 of SOLAS allows exemptions to be granted from, among other provisions, Regulation V/22 of SOLAS. Although some argue that MASS could rely on such exemptions, the long-term registration of MASS cannot be based on exemptions, as it would undermine the nature of this rule as an exception. Nonetheless, these rules support the view that an immediate human perception of the ship's surroundings is not necessary for the lookout.

As stipulated by Article 31(1) of the VCLT, the purpose of a provision shall be considered to determine the ordinary meaning of the words used. The purpose of Rule 5 of COLREG is to ensure the systematic collection of data about the ship and its surroundings to form a comprehensive and solid information basis for navigational decisions.[601] To fulfill this purpose, all available means, including sight and hearing, shall be employed.[602] Thus, there is no restriction to such means based on direct human sight and hearing. Based on the presumption that technical solutions are available to provide the remote operator with sufficient information about the vessel and its vicinity, some argue that the purpose of the lookout can be fulfilled without direct human perception of the ship's environment.[603]

---

599 CMI, 'Position Paper on Unmanned Ships and the International Regulatory Framework' (n 13) 10

600 See Regulation V/22.3 of SOLAS for ships of unconventional design

601 Ringbom, 'Ringbom 2019' (n 55) 153; Boviatsis and Vlachos (n 529) 10

602 Ringbom, 'Ringbom 2019' (n 55) 13

603 Baughen, 'Baughen 2019' (n 593) 134; Robert Veal, Michael Tsimplis and Andrew Serdy, 'The Legal Status and Operation of Unmanned Maritime Vehicles' (2019) 50(1) Ocean Development & International Law 23, 39; Fastvold (n 571) 35; Carey, 'Carey 2017' (n 165) 11–12

The arguments presented thus far support the perspective that a human presence on board the vessel is not deemed necessary for maintaining the lookout. Although the preparatory works of a treaty shall only be referred to in specific cases,[604] the record of the discussion on Rule 5 of COLREG at the revising conference in 1972 provides interesting insights. Responding to a Canadian question of whether the reference to sight and hearing should be understood as precluding the "possibility of ever automating lookout"[605] the British representative stated that "as far as he was aware any device which would eliminate the need for a human being on look out belonged to the distant future. A provision allowing for the substitution of such a device could be left to the amendment procedure".[606] This statement can be understood as a manifestation of the human lookout.[607] Alternatively, it is possible to interpret the situation as postponing the decision to incorporate any automated solutions to avoid a lock-in of technology. Particularly in the case of remotely operated ships, the argument based on the travaux préparatoires becomes less convincing, as human involvement in the lookout is not to be eliminated. It is questionable whether the sensor-based lookout discussed was covered by the Canadian inquiry. Additionally, it should be noted that only the UK representative expressed this opinion and it was not put to a vote. Therefore, the opinions of the other Committee members remain unknown.

Despite the possible exclusion of alternative methods to perform the lookout, the response to the emergence of enclosed bridges[608] indicates that IMO member states did not adopt a narrowly constrained conceptual interpretation of the term 'lookout'. In contrast to conventional bridges, enclosed bridges have a continuous outer facade. Consequently, sound signals like a foghorn cannot reach the master immediately. To react upon this development, SOLAS was amended by Regulation V/19, 2.1.8 prescribing a sound reception system for vessels with totally enclosed bridges. Additionally, the MSC adopted performance standards for sound reception systems setting out the functional

604 Article 32 VCLT states that recourse to the preparatory works shall only be made either to confirm the meaning resulting from the application of Article 31 or if the meaning is ambiguous or obscure

605 Conference on Revision of the International Regulations for Preventing Collisions at Sea, 'CR/CONF/C.2/SR.2 – Provisional Summary record of the second meeting' (London 5 October 1972) 4

606 ibid 5

607 Daniele Mandrioli, 'The Rise of Autonomous Ships Towards an Evolutionary Interpretation of the IMO Treaties on Safety of Navigation' (2022) 124(1) Il Diritto Maritimo 159, 176

608 Ringbom, 'Ringbom 2019' (n 55) 153

requirements.[609] Regardless of a possible, narrow understanding of the terms 'sight and hearing' at the moment of the adoption of the convention, the member states did not apply a strict literal understanding in the further course of the contract.[610] Consequently, the reference to 'sight and hearing' does not imply that the ship's environment has to be immediately perceived by humans. Rather, the lookout can be ensured by 'sight and hearing' if information transmitted to the RCC is perceived by humans.[611]

The RCC is analogous to an enclosed bridge in the sense that signals received on the outer side of the facade need to be relayed to the human operator. Nevertheless, it must be acknowledged that remote operation necessitates the transmission of all signals, not just sound signals. However, the pivotal question arises as to whether this constitutes a significant legal distinction. The literature has partially overlooked the fact that remote operation primarily involves installing sensors that transmit information about the ship's situation to land, where it undergoes evaluation. Remotely controlled ships do not aim to relinquish human involvement in the lookout and hand it over to an algorithm. Considering the relevance of digital lookout possibilities (RADAR, AIS, LIDAR), which are already used today and can be used in the same way in the RCC, the innovation is limited to the fact that direct human visual perception is no longer possible.[612] However, this is only of limited help at night, in heavy weather conditions and over long distances at sea.

To conclude, the reference in Rule 5 of COLREG to the human senses should not be understood strictly literal.[613] Rather, the purpose of the lookout, systematically collecting information to base navigational decision on a comprehensive data basis, supports a more function-based, broader interpretation. As long as a sensor system provides a lookout equivalent to one based on immediate human perception, human presence on board the vessel is not necessary to comply with Rule 5 of COLREG.[614] Thus, human presence on board the vessel is not necessary to comply with Rule 5 of COLREG.

609 MSC, IMO, 'Res. MSC.86(70): Recommendation on Performance Standards for Sound Reception Systems (Annex 1)' (London 8 December 1998)

610 Ringbom, 'Ringbom 2019' (n 55) 153

611 Fastvold (n 571) 33

612 Callum Laffey, 'Reforming the Law of the Sea for the Future of Automated Shipping' in Kyriaki Noussia and Matthew Channon (eds), *The Regulation of Automated and Autonomous Transport* (1st ed. 2023. Springer International Publishing; Imprint Springer 2023) 275

613 Ringbom, 'Ringbom 2019' (n 55) 153

614 Tüngler and tho Pesch (n 429) 125; Carey, 'Carey 2017' (n 165) 11–12; Shanice N Trowers, 'Uncharted Legal Waters: "The Applicability of the Law on Seaworthiness & Good

As explained, the lookout shall ensure that navigational decisions are taken on a comprehensive information basis. How to deal with various encounter situations is stipulated by COLREG. It regulates in which situations vessels have to stand-on or give way. It considers numerous situations including vessels not under command or restricted in their ability to maneuver (Rule 27 of COLREG), fishing vessels (Rule 26 of COLREG) and towing and pushing operations (Rule 25 of COLREG). However, not all situations are pre-determined by COLREG. Rather, it is imaginable that compliance with COLREG could even cause a collision. As collision avoidance is the ultimate goal of COLREG, Rule 2(a) of COLREG prioritizes collision avoidance as an ordinary seaman over adherence to COLREG. The ordinary practice of seaman, also referred to as good seamanship, includes a judgement based on the knowledge of COLREG, experiences, and local navigation culture.[615] However, the concept does not affect the place where the navigational decision shall be taken. Consequently, the practice of ordinary seaman does not require a human presence on board the vessel and remotely operated vessels can therefore comply with the practice of an ordinary seaman.[616] The same line of reasoning applies to the non-quantifiable terms in COLREG. Complying with them does not require a human presence on board the vessel, but rather a proper analysis of the situation, which can be performed by humans ashore.

As next, the analysis turns to Regulation VIII/2 of the STCW Convention that addresses the watchkeeping to ensure a proper lookout in compliance with Rule 5 of COLREG.[617] Central, Regulation VIII/2.2.1 of STCW prescribes that

> [a]dministrations shall require the master of every ship to ensure that watchkeeping arrangements are adequate for maintaining a safe watch or watches, [considering that][…]

Seamanship to Autonomous Vessels'". in Kyriaki Noussia and Matthew Channon (eds), *The Regulation of Automated and Autonomous Transport* (1st ed. 2023. Springer International Publishing; Imprint Springer 2023) 232; Chircop, 'Chircop 2017' (n 255) 135; Ringbom, 'Ringbom 2019' (n 55) 153; Boviatsis and Vlachos (n 529), 10; arguing for non-compliance of MASS with COLREG: L. J Meyers, 'COLREGS and Autonomous Surface Vessels' [2022] The Coast Guard Journal of Safety and Security at Sea Proceeedings 46

615 See the different definitions listed by Frank Stevens, 'Seaworthiness and good seamanship in the age of autonomous vessels' in Henrik Ringbom, Erik Røsæg and Trond Solvang (eds), *Autonomous ships and the law* (IMLI studies in international maritime law. Routledge 2021) 251

616 Laffey (n 612) 274; Trowers (n 614) 230; Baughen, 'Baughen 2019' (n 593) 134; Dean and Clack (n 277) 76; Stevens (n 615) 251

617 See Regulation A-VIII/2.4-1.14 STCW Code

> .1 officers in charge of the navigational watch […] shall be physically present on the navigating bridge or in a directly associated location such as the chartroom or bridge control room at all times.

In the STCW Code more provisions on the watchkeeping and principles to be observed when keeping navigational watches can be found. Most challenging for MASS is Regulation A-VIII/2.4-1.18 of the STCW Code that stipulates, "the bridge shall never be left unattended". The MASS officer in charge of the navigation and lookout is, however, located in the RCC ashore and not on the vessel. This may contradict with the wording of Regulation VIII/2.2.1 of STCW, unless the RCC can be considered the vessel's bridge.

The term 'bridge' is defined neither STCW instrument. The natural meaning of the word in a maritime context refers to the physical structure located on the vessel itself and not just the command center of a vessel.[618] Although the RCC can be considered as the command center of the MASS, it is not physically located on the vessel. Two aspects suggest that this conventional understanding of the term 'bridge' including its physical connection to the ship should also be used in the context of STCW.

First, Regulation A-VIII/2.4-1.17.1 of the STCW Code stipulates that the state of weather and sea and the visibility shall be taken into account when deciding on watchkeeping arrangements. Considering such aspects is only useful if they can affect the watchkeeping. With regard to a conventional human lookout performed on board the vessel, however, the state of weather significantly affects the effectiveness of the lookout. The use of sophisticated cameras and visual sensors, however, reduces the dependence on the state of weather.

Second, Regulation A-VIII/2.4-1.17.11 of the STCW Code stipulates that the field of vision available from the conning position shall be considered when determining the composition of the watch. The conning position is the place on the vessel from where the navigation bridge visibility as stipulated by Regulation V/22 of SOLAS is measured. The criteria to be taken into account per Regulation V/22 of SOLAS refer to the physical construction on board the vessel rather than to a functional control room.

Nevertheless, a compelling argument rooted in purpose can advocate for a more expansive interpretation of the term 'bridge'. The insistence on a physical presence stems from the longstanding practice of maintaining vigilant oversight from the ship's bridge, a role that doubles as the central information

618 Deep Blue Sea Training, 'A Glossary of Nautical Terms – Bridge' <http://www.deepbluesea.training/nautical-terms.html> accessed 16 February 2024; Everything about Boats, 'Bridge' <https://everythingaboutboats.org/glossary/#b> accessed 16 February 2024

hub. In the context of a MASS, where all traditional bridge functions seamlessly transition to the RCC, one could posit that the RCC serves as the 'bridge' through a functional lens.

The term 'bridge' could be a generic term allowing for an evolutionary interpretation.[619] There are, however, no indications that the parties intended to use the term 'bridge' as a generic term including an element of evolution. Given the relatively limited design developments since the invention of the steamship, the term 'bridge' was not included to incorporate major innovative developments. As a result, an evolutionary interpretation cannot be applied as it no corresponding intention of the parties can be identified. Furthermore, designating a location far from the ship as a 'bridge' would constitute a revolution rather than a gradual and incremental evolution. Considering the technical details of the bridge design included in SOLAS, it is advocated that the intention of the parties favor a more conventional, literal interpretation of the term 'bridge'.

The remarks on Article 31 of the VCLT have shown that the context, the purpose, the natural meaning of the term, and the intention of the parties have to be brought together into a coherent whole. As only the purpose-based argument supports an extensive understanding of the term 'bridge', the ordinary meaning of the term excludes the RCC. To conclude, the RCC is not considered a 'bridge' in the meaning of STCW.[620] Hence, remote masters and officers cannot comply with the STCW watchkeeping arrangements.[621]

This conclusion does not contradict with Regulation I/13 of the STCW Code stipulating that

> these regulations [i.e. the regulations included in the STCW regime] shall not prevent an Administration from authorizing ships [...] to participate in trials.

This regulation ensures that innovative technologies, including automated and integrated systems[622] can be trial without the strict boundaries set by the STCW regime. Flag state administrations are empowered to authorize trials if the same degree of safety, security, and pollution prevention as provided by conventional vessels is ensured. However, the existence of a special provision for trials indicates that, in general, deviations should not be allowed and flag

619 *International Court of Justice 2009* (n 482) 66

620 Ringbom, 'Ringbom 2019' (n 55) 158; Schelin, 'Schelin 2020' (n 60) 41

621 Fastvold (n 571) 36

622 Regulation I/13(2) of STCW Code

state administrations should not have much flexibility to approve innovative technologies for permanent operation. Regulation I/13 of the STCW Code thus supports the view the other provisions of the STCW regime should be interpreted more conservative.

Regulation A-VIII/13 of the STCW Code states, that the navigational watch shall ensure that the vessel complies with COLREG. As illustrated, a remote lookout would fulfill the requirement of COLREG. Hence, the inquiry arises as to whether Regulation VIII/2 of STCW, acting as a supplementary regulation to Rule 5 of COLREG, should necessitate requirements beyond the fundamental provisions concerning the lookout.

Article III of STCW could also help at this point. It stipulates that the STCW Convention applies to all "seafarers serving *onboard* seagoing vessels".[623] Although MASS are 'seagoing', the personnel engaged in MASS operations is not located on board the ship. It is debated whether MASS operator should be considered seafarer in the meaning of STCW.[624] Nevertheless, remote operators do not serve *on board* seagoing MASS. Thus, despite the scope of 'seafarer', the STCW Convention does not apply to remote operators located in the RCC. This view is joined by the MSC[625] and several authors.[626] Considering the drawbacks of not applying the internationally agreed framework for training and qualification of seafarers, Ringbom advocates for applying the STCW Convention in its entirety.[627] This opinion, however, ignores the clear wording of Article III of STCW and extends the STCW Convention beyond its scope of application.

To conclude, the STCW Convention does not apply to remotely controlled MASS, as the humans responsible for the navigational watch are not located on board the vessel. Consequently, Regulation VIII/2 of STCW does not require a human presence on board the vessel since it does not apply to MASS.

As the STCW Convention does not apply to MASS, the provisions on radio watches included in this convention neither apply to MASS. However, the functional requirements for radio communication established by Regulation IV/4 of SOLAS need to be met by MASS. As the mobile network coverage on the

623 Emphasis added by the author

624 MSC, IMO, 'MSC.1/Circ.1638' (n 18) 83; Karlis (n 164), 122; MSC, IMO, 'MSC 99/INF.5' (n 161) 12

625 MSC, IMO, 'MSC 107/20' (n 375) 5.45.2

626 Kampantais, 'Legal and regulatory implications of the unmanned ship operation' (n 516) 3; Tüngler and tho Pesch. 'Seevölkerrechtliche Anforderungen an unbemannte Schiffe' (above, n 98) 126

627 Ringbom, 'Ringbom 2019' (n 55) 159

oceans is not ensured, radio communication is a reliable form of communication between ships and between ships and shore-based institutions.

From a literal understanding, Regulation IV/4 of SOLAS does not pose significant challenge for remotely operated MASS, as the regulation requires the ship to be capable of transmitting and receiving radio signals. Consequently, nothing in the provision prevents from relocating the radio communication station to the RCC. Nonetheless, relaying the signals to the RCC provides an appropriate way to ensure radio communication for remotely operated MASS. Consequently, Regulation IV/4 of SOLAS does not require human presence on board the vessel.

The first step in safe navigation is to fully assess the situation and create a comprehensive information base for navigation decisions. The second step is to execute the navigation decisions safely. As the analysis revealed, the first step can be performed safely by remote operators. Now, the second step, the mode of operation, shall be discussed. Prominently, Regulation V/24 of SOLAS requires the possibility of manual control in certain circumstances. It should be noted that the competent authority can grant an exemption from Regulation V/24 of SOLAS per Regulation V/3 of SOLAS if the full application of Chapter V of SOLAS is unreasonable or unnecessary considering all circumstances of the intended voyage. Especially the length of the voyage, the maximum distance of the ship from the coast, and the absence of general navigational hazards shall be considered. Although the provisional registration of a MASS could rely on exemptions, Regulation V/3 of SOLAS does not serve as a basis for regular registrations of MASS. Consequently, it remains to be assessed how MASS can comply with the manual steering requirement of SOLAS Regulation V/24.

In Regulation V/24 of SOLAS, manual control is delineated as the counterpart to automatic control. Consequently, it does not involve direct control of the steering gear without any technical assistance or transmission. Instead, manual control pertains to exclusive human decision-making devoid of support from autopilots or track control systems. The regulation underscores the importance of having qualified personnel ready to assume manual control of the vessel, although it does not mandate a continuous human presence on board.[628]

To ensure the safety of navigation in congested waters, ship's routeing measures, ship reporting systems, and VTS were established by coastal states. It

628 Laffey (n 612) 270; Ntovas et al. *Liability for operations in Unmanned Maritime Vehicles with Differing Levels of Autonomy* (above, n 553), p. 52; Tüngler and tho Pesch. 'Seevölkerrechtliche Anforderungen an unbemannte Schiffe' (above, n 463), p. 125

shall be assessed now whether MASS can comply with these measures stipulated by Regulations V/10, 11, 12 of SOLAS.

Per Regulation V/10 of SOLAS flag states have to ensure that their vessel comply with ship's routeing measures adopted by coastal states. As these measures do not address tasks conventionally performed by humans but rather the navigation of the vessel, they do not provide a challenge for remotely operated MASS.[629] Regulation V/10.7 of SOLAS clearly places the responsibility for compliance with mandatory ship's routeing systems on the ship. However, the IMO General Provisions on Ship's Routeing assume that 'marines' use the routeing systems rather than ships.[630] Bearing in mind that these guidelines are not legally binding and that there is no definition of the term 'mariners', there is nothing to prevent the 'mariners' from being on land.[631]

Regulations V/11 and V/12 of SOLAS addressing ship reporting systems and VTS should be considered together, as reporting is often done through a VTS.[632] Both, the IMO Guidelines for Ship Reporting Systems and the Guidelines for Vessel Traffic Services address the master, though do not determine a location for the master.[633] Depending on the specific tasks, the master could be relocated ashore. The Reporting Guidelines state that communication between the shore-based authority and the participating ship shall use radio communications or any other electronic means accepted by the IMO.[634] This again provides flexibility and facilitates relocating the personnel ashore. The VTS Guidelines do not specify the technology to be employed. Instead, coastal states are encouraged to take into account future technical advancements when implementing VTS measures.[635] From a legal point, therefore, nothing prevents the master of vessel to be located ashore and perform the reporting and communication duties from the RCC. However, operational challenges should not be underestimated, especially ensuring proper reaction in emergencies.[636] It should be noted that understanding and replying to verbal communication via radio communications poses a particular challenge for autonomous

629 Parlov, 'Parlov 2023' (n 553) 172

630 See Sections 3.2.1, 3.6, 3.13, 5.7.1 of the IMO, 'Res. A.572(14)' (n 552)

631 Parlov, 'Parlov 2023' (n 553) 172

632 ibid 174

633 See Regulations 2.2.1.2 in MSC, IMO, 'Res. MSC.433(98): Guidelines and Criteria for Ship Reporting Systems' (London 16 June 2017) and Regulations 6.3 and 7.1 in IMO, 'Res. A.1158(32)' (n 555) 7.1

634 MSC, IMO, 'Res. MSC.433(98)' (n 633) 2.3.2

635 IMO, 'Res. A.1158(32)' (n 555) 5.1.4

636 Jia Chyuan Chong, 'Impact of maritime autonomous surface ships (MASS) on VTS operations' (Dissertation, World Maritime University 11 April 2018) 50–52

systems. However, in the case of remotely operated vessels, radio watches can be performed by humans in the RCC. This requires the radio signals received by the ships to be relayed to the RCC, which is technically possible.

In summary, safety of navigation regulations do not mandate a human presence on board the vessel. There exists room for interpreting these regulations in a manner that allows MASS to legally fulfill navigation safety functions. However, incorporating provisions that explicitly support this interpretation would enhance the ease of introducing and registering MASS.

As noted earlier, validating the technology for safe navigation from an RCC poses a significant challenge. It is crucial to establish harmonized standards and risk assessment methods. Regulations are required to address the specifications for sensors, principles of data processing, transmission technologies, and procedures for handling emergencies such as communication loss or limited bandwidth capacity.[637] The latter is particularly relevant to liability issues to determine the required standard of care. As next, the necessity of human involvement in the decision-making loop for the safety of navigation shall be assessed. This is especially relevant for autonomous vessels, as these vessels are not constantly operated by humans.

4.4.2.1.2 *Human Decision-Making for the Safety of Navigation*

The focus now shifts to MASS operating at degree four. Based on the findings of the foregoing analysis, humans do not need to be on board to ensure the safety of navigation. Now, the question arises of whether humans need to be involved to ensure the safety of navigation. With a focus on the operation of the vessel, this implies the aspect of whether humans need to obtain situational awareness. This decision-making dimension of Rule 5 of COLREG is expressed by the requirement to "make a full appraisal of the situation and of the risk of collision".[638] Making a full appraisal of the situation means to assess the situation comprehensively beyond mere observation of the ship's surroundings. It entails analyzing and processing the gathered information to ensure informed navigational decisions.

In this study, autonomy degree four is understood to include navigational decision taken mainly by the navigation software, i.e. the algorithms. The human will constantly monitor the ship, intervene whenever necessary, and take control if the navigation system cannot handle the situation safely. Most often, this applies to close-quarter or other particularly challenging situations.

637 Ringbom, 'Ringbom 2019' (n 55)

638 Rambøll and Core Advokatfirma, 'Analysis of regulatory barriers to the use of autonomous ships' (Korsør, Denmark December 2017) 47

Thus, both the human supervisor as well as the navigation algorithm must have situational awareness.

The reference by Rule 5 of COLREG to the human senses of seeing and hearing argues for the necessity of human involvement in the attainment of situational awareness. If algorithms process the data and take navigational decisions, humans are no longer actively involved in the navigation process. The reference to human senses and awareness – a concept requiring consciousness – make human involvement necessary. An algorithm cannot be 'aware' in the sense a human can be. Therefore, the collection of data by sensors and their transmission to the RCC will meet the requirements of the lookout as long as the human is also aware of the situation. Several scholars, therefore, assume that fully autonomous vessels are not able to fulfill the lookout duty of Rule 5 of COLREG.[639] This is further supported by Section b(IV) of the IMCO Recommendation on Navigational Watchkeeping,[640] which explicitly names the "person on lookout". Hence, the Governments adopting the Resolution assumed that humans rather than algorithms will maintain the lookout.[641] Although there is no location requirement for the involved person, human participation is clearly required by Rule 5 of COLREG. During the IMCO Conference on revision of the COLREG in 1972, an automated lookout was considered to belong to a distant future.[642]

Despite this more historic-influenced interpretation, another conclusion can be reached if focusing more on the purpose of the lookout and situational awareness. Given the fact that sensors and algorithms can perceive, process, and integrate more data in a short time than humans, a sensor-based lookout and the interpretation of the data by software can provide a more accurate picture of the vessel's surroundings than a human lookout would be able to.[643]

A comparison with the current use of autopilots illustrates the extent to which algorithms are already making navigational decisions. The transition towards a system of closely monitored autonomy is not as significant as one

---

639 Baughen, 'Baughen 2019' (n 593) 134; Veal, Tsimplis and Serdy (n 603), 39; Fastvold (n 571) 40; American Bureau of Shipping (n 21) 19; CMI, 'Position Paper on Unmanned Ships and the International Regulatory Framework' (n 13) 14

640 IMCO, 'Resolution A.285(VIII): Recommendation on Basic Principles and Operational Guidance Relating to Navigational Watchkeeping' (London 21 December 1973) 2

641 Gogarty and Hagger (n 373) 115

642 Conference on Revision of the International Regulations for Preventing Collisions at Sea (n 605) 5

643 Ringbom, 'Ringbom 2019' (n 55) 153; Chircop, 'Chircop 2017' (n 255) 27; Boviatsis and Vlachos (n 529) 10

might assume. When using an autopilot, the master dictates the route and the arrival point. The autopilot then takes control of the rudder and propulsion system to follow the instructions. However, most autopilots are able to 'cooperate' with on board sensors to take into account external factors such as weather, currents, obstacles, and other vessels. These adaptive autopilots can alter the ship's course to avoid collisions and optimize the route. The master closely monitors the autopilot's decisions and is ready to intervene if necessary. A closely monitored autonomous navigation system should be treated no differently, if the remote operator can gain situational awareness. It could be argued that by not intervening, the master is implicitly agreeing to the navigation.

The IMO has concluded during the RSE that either interpretative measures could be applied to adapt COLREG to MASS, or that amendments are required.[644] During the discussion, it became clear that the understanding of the applicable law differs widely between the contracting states.[645] The advent of MASS is a good opportunity to consolidate the understanding and interpretation of the conventions adopted in the 70s. The need for amendments for degree four can be traced back to the definition of degree four, which initially totally excluded any human involvement.[646] Later, however, the IMO adapted its understanding and now it applies the understanding used in this study.[647] However, as argued above, such a scenario is not foreseeable in the near future and therefore is not considered here.

To conclude on the lookout, the reference to human senses makes human involvement and situational awareness necessary. However, algorithms could also process the data to take informed navigational decisions. Although the conclusion reached here does not require amendments to COLREG, measures should be adopted to safeguard the proposed interpretation of COLREG. Moreover, details about the design set up of the RCC and the human-machine interface are necessary to ensure safe remote monitoring.

Turning now to Rule 2(a) of COLREG, another aspect of the safety of navigation, it needs to be discussed whether good seamanship can be performed by algorithms. The concept of good seamanship concerns the aspect of how navigational decisions are taken. Most encounter situations are clearly predetermined by COLREG. However, some rules require an individual assessment taking into account the prevailing circumstances of the situation. All

644 MSC, IMO, 'MSC.1/Circ.1638' (n 18) 86–87

645 MSC, IMO, 'MSC 102/5/3: Summary of results of the second step and conclusion of the RSE for COLREG (Marshall Islands)' (London 6 February 2020) Annex 2, p. 1

646 MSC, IMO, 'MSC.1/Circ.1638' (n 18) 3

647 MSC, IMO, 'MSC 107/5/1' (n 41) 13.3

non-quantitative provisions are a challenge for pre-programmed navigation algorithms. Terms like "early" or "substantial" in Rule 16 of COLREG or "safe speed" in Rule 19(b) of COLREG are difficult to assess by algorithms.[648] Additionally, local navigation culture needs to be considered. As an example, the high-speed ferry between Gothenburg and Fredikshavn, Kattegat, keeps "out of the way of everything that moves" due to its high speed.[649] To avoid collisions properly, such peculiarities need to be considered by autonomous navigation systems.

All these non-quantifiable terms can be summarized in the concept of good seamanship, which includes the navigation of the vessel in compliance with COLREG, experiences made by professional mariner, and the local navigation customs.[650] As expressed by Rule 2(a) of COLREG, good seamanship also includes overriding the codified rules if this is necessary to avoid collisions. Some argued that taking due account of the prevailing circumstances of the situation to avoid collisions necessitates a human judgement, i.e. human involvement in the decision-making.[651] Consequently, navigating a vessel in accordance with good seamanship cannot be preprogrammed and is therefore impossible for autonomous navigation systems.[652]

Others, however, apply a more functional approach. Though admitting that pre-programming human-like behavior is hardly possible[653] and pointing to the risk that training data could include "wrong" decisions,[654] the focus is shifted to the purpose of Rule 2(a) of COLREG. The ultimate objective of COLREG is

648 Thomas Porathe, 'Maritime Autonomous Surface Ships (MASS) and the COLREGS: Do We Need Quantified Rules Or Is "the Ordinary Practice of Seamen" Specific Enough?' (2019) 13(3) TransNav 511, 513

649 Personal comment of a officer printed at: ibid 514

650 Stevens (n 615) 251

651 CMI, 'Position Paper on Unmanned Ships and the International Regulatory Framework' (n 13) 14

652 Miyoshi, Fujimoto and Rooks (n 597), 17; Baughen, 'Baughen 2019' (n 593) 134; Dean and Clack (n 277) 76; Veal, Tsimplis and Serdy (n 603), 38; Laffey (n 612) 274; see for dissenting opinion: Xiang-Yu Zhou and others, 'A Study of the Application Barriers to the Use of Autonomous Ships Posed by the Good Seamanship Requirement of COLREG s' (2020) 73(3) Journal of Navigation 710, 715

653 Nordahl and others (n 121) 14; Stevens. 'Seaworthiness and good seamanship in the age of autonomous vessels' (above, n. 625), p. 254

654 Krzysztof Wróbel and others, 'The Vagueness of COLREG versus Collision Avoidance Techniques—A Discussion on the Current State and Future Challenges Concerning the Operation of Autonomous Ships' (2022) 14(24) Sustainability, 5; Andreas N Madsen, Magne V Aarset and Ole A Alsos, 'Safe and efficient maneuvering of a Maritime Autonomous Surface Ship (MASS) during encounters at sea: A novel approach' (2022) 3 Maritime Transport Research, 3

to prevent collisions. As it is impossible to define in advance the appropriate response to all possible encounter situations Rule 2(a) of COLREG requires a prudent judgement, taking into account all the relevant circumstances of the prevailing situation, when compliance with the sailing and steering rules contained in COLREG could bear the risk of a collision. Adherence to good seamanship is therefore not an end in itself, but a means of avoiding collisions.[655] Collision avoidance, again, is nothing more than risk minimization through safety design and engineering. Other high-risk industries such as the chemical or nuclear industries have already shown how to create a reliable framework in which AI can perform high-risk activities. Prior risk assessment, risk mitigation measures, and limiting the consequences of residual risk all contribute to the safe performance of high-risk AI activities.[656]

MASS could be programmed to avoid close-range situations that could result in a collision.[657] The advantages of autonomous navigation can then be exploited: analyzing several parameters, determining the consequences of several alternatives, not becoming tired or guided by egoistic motives.[658] From a legal point of view, therefore, compliance with good seamanship is possible for an autonomous navigation software.[659] Nevertheless, this assumes that the concept of good seamanship is no longer based on the intuitive and experiential knowledge of seasoned mariners. Rather, good seamanship must be understood as risk avoidance and prevention. Moreover, it should be borne in mind that technology is constantly developing and that the risk of autonomous navigation is unknown before its actual operation. It should not be expected that autonomous navigation eliminates all collisions.[660]

In conclusion, the non-quantifiable aspects of COLREG pose a challenge to autonomous navigation. However, neither the lookout requirement nor the duty to adhere to good seamanship require constant human involvement. As shown above, good seamanship cannot be preprogrammed, as the future behavior of human beings is unpredictable. However, the principle of avoiding collisions in all circumstances can be implemented by the navigation algorithms. Autonomous systems could then be even more efficient than humans

---

655 Stevens (n 615) 254

656 ibid

657 Nakamura and Okada (n 185) 134

658 Stevens (n 615) 255

659 Ringbom, 'Ringbom 2019' (n 55) 155; Parlov, 'Parlov 2023' (n 553) 169; Stevens (n 615) 256

660 Stevens (n 615) 255; Rosemary Rayfuse, 'Public International Law and the Regulation of Emerging Technologies' in Roger Brownsword, Eloise Scotford and Karen Yeung (eds), *The Oxford Handbook of Law, Regulation and Technology* (Oxford handbooks, First edition. Oxford University Press 2017) 506

could, as several alternatives could be calculated. Again, there is no need to change the text of COLREG, but the interpretation proposed here needs to be safeguarded by appropriate means. In addition, standards for risk assessment need to be adopted, preferably at international or regional level. The risk of information overload and its potentially fatal consequences have been illustrated above. This risk could also arise when an autonomous navigation algorithm hands control back to the human supervisor. Standards need to be developed for this human-machine interaction, including precautions to avoid human information overload. To mitigate this risk, humans could be more in the loop than necessary to ensure constant situational awareness and reduce the information overload in the case of overtaking the situation. Additionally, it has to be ensured that the remote operator is informed in due time to take appropriate actions.

The watchkeeping provisions on navigational and radio watches included in STCW do not need to be considered here as autonomous MASS at degree four operate without a human crew on board. Consequently, STCW does not apply.

Eventually, the SOLAS provisions dealing with the safety of navigation have to be considered in the light of autonomously operated MASS. Regulation V/24 of SOLAS requires that manual control can be established in situations of high traffic density, reduced visibility and any other hazardous navigational situation. As illustrated above, the provision does not require a human presence on board the vessel, but immediate human control must be possible. Recalling the meaning of autonomy degree four in this study, humans closely monitor the vessel and are ready to take control at any time. Therefore, autonomous vessels can fulfil this requirement.

Regulation V/10 of SOLAS on ship's routeing systems imposes an obligation on the ship to comply with mandatory routeing measures. Consequently, also autonomous vessels can legally fulfil this requirement. The reference to 'mariners' in the supplementary guideline[661] can be interpreted in a functional way referring to the remote supervisors. Additionally, the objective of ship's routeing systems has to be considered. It shall be ensured that all vessels irrespective of their mode of operation use the routeing systems. Therefore, if an autonomous navigation algorithm can effectively use the routeing system, the person navigating the vessel and its location are of secondary importance.[662] In particular, the supplementary guideline should not be interpreted as being more restrictive than the SOLAS regulation itself. In the case of autonomous MASS, it has to be ensured that the latest adopted routeing measures are included in the

661 See section 3.2 of IMO, 'Res. A.572(14)' (n 552)

662 Parlov, 'Parlov 2023' (n 553) 172

electrical charts used by the navigation algorithm. Ship's routeing measures are currently published by the IMO in printed form and incorporated into digital nautical charts by national hydrographic services.

The interpretation of Regulations V/11 and V/12 of SOLAS are not quite so simple. Regulation V/11 of SOLAS refers directly to the master of the ship, but without providing a definition. Although it addresses a position normally occupied by a human being, the purpose of the reporting system could argue for a broader understanding of the term. The main objective of ship reporting systems is the exchange of information between the ship and the shore-based authority. Primarily, however, only the ship reports general information and the intended route.[663] The communication must not be verbal as section 2.2.1.2 of the IMO Reporting Guidelines[664] expresses. Moreover, the communication shall not impose undue burden on masters, officers, and pilots. Therefore, automating the reporting could even improve the current situation and release the master from this duty.[665] It is therefore argued here that autonomous vessels can comply with mandatory reporting systems. However, it must be ensured that the shore-based authority can receive electronic reports and that the systems used can interact smoothly.

The integration of autonomous vessels in VTS, however, poses a considerable challenge. Especially in large ports, the VTS takes over traffic control and management. This makes instant communication between the ship and the shore-based authority as well as other ships inevitable. Usually, this verbal communication uses radio channels. To ensure efficiency, the participants need to understand each other clearly.[666] Despite the desirability of human-machine radio communication, it is not currently a possibility due to technical limitations.[667] The risk of misunderstandings or the need to double-check information received are unacceptable in narrow waters.[668] Consequently, human involvement is necessary for the communication in VTS. As MASS at degree four are supervised by humans, these humans could perform the tasks of the VTS officer.

The same applies to radio communication under Regulation IV/4 of SOLAS. Although the ship is required to maintain uninterrupted radio communication,

663 MSC, IMO, 'Res. MSC.433(98)' (n 633) 2.2.1.3
664 MSC, IMO, 'Res. MSC.433(98)' (n 633) 2.2.1.3
665 Chircop, 'Chircop 2017' (n 255) 141, Parlov. 'Can the International Regulatory Framework on Ships' Routing, Ship Reporting, and Vessel Traffic Service (VTS) Accommodate Marine Autonomous Surface Ships (MASS)?' (above, n. 577), p. 176
666 IMO, 'Res. A.1158(32)' (n 555) 7.3
667 Chircop, 'Chircop 2017' (n 255) 123
668 Parlov, 'Parlov 2023' (n 553) 177

the reliable establishment of radio communication between humans and AI is not yet a technically feasible proposition. Poor audio signals and the need for verbal communication make it impossible for autonomous MASS to participate in this communication. Therefore, remote operators will have to provide radio communication from the RCC even for MASS at degree four.

In conclusion, it can be said that the safety of navigation, as substantiated by the provisions of COLREG and SOLAS, can be ensured by MASS at degree four. Direct human involvement is only required by SOLAS regulations V/24 and V/12. The much-discussed aspect of good seamanship is less problematic if compliance is viewed less dogmatically and more in terms of meaning and purpose. Collision avoidance, i.e. safe operation, can be achieved through autonomous navigation algorithms and experience from other high-risk industries could be drawn upon. However, this view is not uncriticized and a different interpretation of the regulations is possible. The legality of MASS operating at degree four depends on the availability and readiness of technology. Although several research projects have proven the feasibility of autonomous navigation technology, there is need for more trials. Specifically, trials should be conducted in congested waters and during severe weather conditions to ensure safety in all circumstances.

To ensure the safety of navigation, UNCLOS and SOLAS include provisions on the manning of the vessel. These provisions and their implications for MASS operations shall now be assessed despite the reached conclusions on the ability of MASS to ensure safe navigation. Additionally, Article 94(4)(b) of the UNCLOS has to be review in the light of manning. Considerations about the manning requirement are not comprehensive if not discussion the competence of the persons manning the vessel. Thus, comprehensive training and qualification scheme for seafarers included in STCW will be discussed as well.

4.4.2.1.3 *Manning*

With respect to the manning for the safety of navigation, Article 94 of the UNCLOS stipulates that

> 3. [e]very State shall take such measures for ships flying its flag as are necessary to ensure safety at sea with regard, inter alia, to:
>
> (a) [...]
>
> (b) the manning of ships, labour conditions and the training of crews, taking into account the applicable international instruments.

(c) […]

4. Such measures shall include those necessary to ensure:

(a) […]

(b) that each ship is in the charge of a master and officers who possess appropriate qualifications, in particular in seamanship, navigation, communications and marine engineering, and that the crew is appropriate in qualification and numbers for the type, size, machinery and equipment of the ship.

(c) […]

The reference in Article 94(3)(b) of the UNCLOS to the "applicable international instruments" is completed by Article 94(5) of the UNCLOS[669] and points to SOLAS, especially to Regulations V/14 and IV/16 of SOLAS. These are as follows:

Regulation 14 – Ships' manning
Contracting Governments undertake, each for its national ships, to maintain, or, if it is necessary, to adopt, measures for the purpose of ensuring that, from the point of view of safety of life at sea, all ships shall be sufficiently and efficiently manned.

Regulation 16 – Radio personnel
Every ship shall carry personnel qualified for distress and safety radiocommunication purposes to the satisfaction of the Administration.

Regulation 6.2 of the International Safety Management (ISM) Code iterates the obligation to ensure the manning of the vessel.[670] Since 1994, the ISM Code is mandatory.[671]

---

669 Nandan and Nordquist (eds) (n 355) 94.8(f)

670 IMO, 'Res. A.741(18): International Management Code for the Safe Operation of Ships and for Pollution Prevention (International Safety Management (ISM) Code)' (London 17 November 1993)

671 Council of the International Maritime Organization, 'C-72-12-Add.1 – Report on the Conference of Contracting Governments to the International Convention for the Safety of Life at Sea, 1974' (London 27 May 1994) 2

None of the provisions prescribes a certain minimum number of crew members. Rather, the flag state determines the level of manning on a case-by-case basis. The IMO's non-binding guidelines with Principles of Minimum Safe Manning[672] harmonize the domestic application of the international regulations and stipulate 12 relevant factors, which shall guide national administrations when assessing the level of minimum safe manning. The flag state authority issues a certificate of safe manning which indicates the size and composition of the crew for each ship.[673] This certificate needs to be carried on board.

In contrast to the safety of navigation, the manning requirement is set out in detail in UNCLOS. In particular, Article 94(4)(b) of the UNCLOS requires that every ship shall be in charge of a master and a competent crew. UNCLOS and SOLAS foresee the manning requirement to ensure the safety at sea, the prevention of collisions, the prevention, reduction, and control of marine pollution, and the radio communications.[674] This functional approach allows a dynamic interpretation, focusing on the objective and purpose.[675] As both codifications stipulate the same purposes, this study assumes that the manning requirement is the same in UNCLOS and SOLAS. As an addition, UNCLOS demands a master and crew.

4.4.2.1.3.1 Human Presence on Board

First, it shall be considered whether the manning requirement necessitates a human presence on board. This is particularly relevant to remotely operated MASS. Second, the implications for MASS operating at degree four are considered. Following the interpretation rule enshrined in Article 31 of the VCLT, the ordinary meaning of Regulation V/14 of SOLAS will be determined. Even if MASS were unthinkable in 1974, the duty to man the vessel is placed at the service of safe navigation. Consequently, the legal analysis will focus on the context, object, and purpose of the manning requirement. In the contextual analysis, Regulation IV/16 of SOLAS as lex specialis for personnel for radio communications will be of particular importance.

Regulation V/14 of SOLAS concerns the minimum safe manning. Starting with the literal analysis, the Oxford English Dictionary describes 'manned'

672 IMO, 'Res. A.1047(27): Principles of Minimum Safe Manning' (London 20 December 2011)

673 Regulation V/14.2.2 of SOLAS

674 See Article 94(4)(c) of the UNCLOS, Regulation V/14 of SOLAS

675 Henrik Ringbom, *The EU Maritime Safety Policy and International Law* (Publications on ocean development vol 64, Brill 2008) 20–21; Alexandros X M Ntovas, 'Functionalism and Maritime Autonomous Surface Ships' in James Kraska and Young-Kil Park (eds), *Emerging technology and the law of the sea* (Cambridge University Press 2022) 219

as meaning "supplied with or guarded by people".[676] Traditionally, 'guarded' implied a physical presence. However, modern technology allows offering remote guarding, particularly for security purposes. The natural meaning of 'manned' therefore does not exclude remote operation of the vessel.[677] Some point out that 'manned' does not necessarily mean the same as 'attended'. Consequently, a crew located ashore could nevertheless man the vessel in compliance with SOLAS.[678] Turning to the context, Regulation IV/16.1 of SOLAS stipulates that

> [e]very ship shall carry personnel qualified for distress and safety radiocommunication purposes to the satisfaction of the Administration.

Interestingly, this regulation pertains to carrying and not to manning. According to the Oxford English dictionary, 'carrying' refers to the physical aspect of "transporting people from one place to another".[679] This literal meaning could make it necessary to transport the radio personnel on board the ship. Since the radio personnel are part of the overall crew, it could be concluded that the crew must also be transported. Two aspects can be argued against this assumption: first, the flexibility included in Regulation IV/16 of SOLAS and the purpose of Regulation IV/16 of SOLAS.

Regulation IV/16 of SOLAS requires the carriage of personnel to the satisfaction of the administration. Therefore, if the flag state administration is satisfied with shore-based radio officers and no radio personnel on board the vessel, there is nothing preventing them from issuing the required radio certificate. Such discretionary clauses may be employed to promote innovative technologies, including remote operations.

Per Article 31(3)(c) of the VCLT, applicable rules between the parties shall be considered together with the context. As almost all SOLAS members are a member of the IMO, the IMO's guidelines providing principles for minimum safe manning[680] can be taken into account. The guidelines aim to align

676 Oxford English Dictionary, 'manned, adj'. <https://www.oed.com/view/Entry/236238?rskey=ZhhMIx&result=2&isAdvanced=false#eid> accessed 16 February 2024

677 Applying another understanding of the term 'manned' and advocating for the non-compliance of remotely-operated MASS with Regulation V/14 of SOLAS: Trowers (n 614) 219

678 Ringbom, 'Ringbom 2019' (n 55) 157; Bernard Eder, 'Unmanned vessels: challenge ahead' in Comité Maritime International (CMI) (ed), *Yearbook 2017–2018 Annuaire* (2019) 4

679 Oxford English Dictionary, 'carry, v'. sense I.i.1.a. <https://www.oed.com/dictionary/carry_v?tab=meaning_and_use#9991414> accessed 16 February 2024

680 IMO, 'Res. A.1047(27)' (n 672)

the SOLAS manning requirement with the provisions of STCW. Accordingly, manning shall ensure that safe navigation and radio watches can be maintained in accordance with STCW.[681] As SOLAS does not add any essential aspects to the safety of navigation beyond STCW and COLREG, manning satisfies the objective of safety of navigation once the requirements of STCW and COLREG are met.

After having considered the context, the objective and purpose of the manning requirement shall be assessed. Just like Regulation V/14 of SOLAS, the carriage requirement in Regulation IV/16 of SOLAS is not an end in itself. Instead, it aims to ensure safe radio communications and the safe handling of distress situations. By taking a functional approach and considering the flexibility granted to the administration as well as the fact that safe radio watches can be maintained by remote operators, it can be concluded that Regulation IV/16 of SOLAS does not mandate the presence of human personnel on board solely for transporting radio personnel.

The manning shall ensure the safety of navigation, which is clear from the title of Chapter V of SOLAS. Studies have proven that MASS can be navigated safely when remotely controlled from a technical point of view.[682] Additionally, the legal analysis of COLREG, SOLAS, and STCW above has revealed, that a human presence is not necessary to ensure the safety of navigation. Nevertheless, the equivalent level of safety needs to be demonstrated during the registration process.[683] When applying a function-based interpretation,[684] there is no reason left for SOLAS to demand a human presence on board the vessel, as long as the safe operation of a vessel can be ensured by remote operators.[685]

Applying a purpose-based interpretation is supported by the wording of Regulation V/14 of SOLAS, which states that the manning shall be "sufficiently and efficiently".[686] Both term allow for a flexible handling of the manning requirement. Whereas 'sufficiently' more points towards a quantitative dimension, 'efficiently' addresses the qualitative dimension. If the safety of navigation can be ensured from ashore, the requirement of Regulation V/14 of SOLAS would be fulfilled.

681 IMO, 'Res. A.1047(27)' (n 672) 3.1.1.1

682 DNV GL AS Maritime, 'ReVolt Report' (n 98) 47; Chae, Kim and Kim (n 44), 11; Vos, Hekkenberg and Valdez Banda (n 187), 9; Wärtsilä, *Wärtsilä 2017* (n 132)

683 American Bureau of Shipping (n 21) 19

684 Ringbom, 'Ringbom 2020' (n 424) 435

685 Veal, Tsimplis and Serdy (n 603) 37

686 Ringbom, 'Ringbom 2019' (n 55) 157; Aristotelis Komianos, 'The Autonomous Shipping Era. Operational, Regulatory, and Quality Challenges' (2018) 12(2) TransNav 335, 341

Consequently, from the perspective of safety of navigation, a human presence on board the vessel is not required by Regulation V/14 of SOLAS. The same applies to Regulation IV/16 of SOLAS. As the analysis revealed, radio watches can be performed by remote operators. Neither from a technical nor from a legal point of view, is human presence on board the vessel necessary for this function

In conclusion, neither Regulation V/14 nor IV/16 of SOLAS requires a human presence on board a vessel.[687] The same result was reached by the IMO during the RSE.[688] It should be noted, however, that MASS have only been trialed so far. Although no collisions or dangerous close-quarter situations were reported from the trials and projects introduced above, previously unknown and unconsidered risks may be discovered when MASS start operating.[689] In order to reduce the risk of MASS operations as far as possible, the development of risk assessment tools and verification schemes for MASS is important. To facilitate mutual recognition, the development should involve several flag, coastal, and port states.[690]

After having concluded that the manning requirement does not prevent remotely operated MASS, the quantitative dimension of the manning requirement expressed in 'minimum' and 'sufficiently' shall be discussed to determine whether there has to be a human involvement in the ship operation. This analysis is particularly relevant for MASS operating at degree four.

4.4.2.1.3.2 Human Involvement in the Operation of the Vessel

SOLAS does not set a concrete number of crew members needed for a vessel.[691] Rather, flag states determine the necessary number in their national laws. Even today, the manning requirement is understood very differently by flag states. To illustrate the current differences, the manning requirements in Panama and Liberia as the two world-leading flag states and in Germany and Singapore as two important ownership economies[692] will be compared based

687 Ringbom, 'Ringbom 2019' (n 55) 152; Komianos (n 686), 341; Laffey (n 612) 271; Veal, Tsimplis and Serdy (n 603) 37

688 MSC, IMO, 'MSC.1/Circ.1638' (n 18) 32

689 Måns Jacobsson, 'What Challenges Lie Ahead for Maritime Law?' in Proshanto K Mukherjee, Maximo Q Mejia and Jingjing Xu (eds), *Maritime Law in Motion* (WMU Studies in Maritime Affairs Ser vol 8. Springer 2020) 275; Porathe and others (n 581) 423–424

690 Rayfuse (n 660) 511

691 Li Rui, 'On the Legal Status of Unmanned Ships' (2019) 2019(4) China Ocean Law Review 165, 175

692 United Nations Conference on Trade and Development (n 234) 4

on the minimum manning for a vessel engaged in international voyages, with more than 3000 GT and a propulsion power of 750–3000 kWh.

In Liberia, a Marine Notice issued by the Deputy Commissioner of Maritime Affairs[693] stipulates in section 12.2 the minimum number of crew members for vessels classed by GT and KW. For the above-described vessel, 12 people would need to man the vessel as a minimum.[694] Panamanian Law also correlates the manning to the area of operation and the size of the vessel.[695] The example vessel would need to be manned by at least 9 persons.

For a registration in the German International Shipping Register and the Singapore Registry of Ships, the minimum safe manning certificate is issued upon a proposal by the owner or operator of the vessel.[696] According to the ordinary practice of the German administration, the vessel would need to be manned by 14 persons. In Singapore, however, 8 people would be the minimum manning.[697] Notwithstanding the disparate interpretations of the minimum safe manning, all variants are deemed to comply with the SOLAS regulations. Furthermore, the safety of the ships is not contingent on the size of the crew, as the detention ratio is comparable for all four flag states.[698] It can be concluded that a larger crew is not a necessity for safety at sea.

As presented, the minimum manning varies significantly. The example vessel would need to be manned by 8–14 persons, depending on the flag state. Each national authority interprets the international regulations provided by UNCLOS, SOLAS, and the ISM Code differently albeit the guidelines issued by the IMO[699] ought to streamline the interpretation and administrative practice.

693 The Deputy Commissioner of Maritime Affairs was granted power to determine the minimum safe manning by: The Liberain Maritime Regulations, Titel 21 23 April 2018 (The Senate and House of Representatives of the Republic of Liberia in Legislature assembled) 10.292

694 Marine Notice on Manning of Vessels and Principles of Watchkeeping 02/21, MAN-001 (Office of the Deputy Commissioner of Maritime Affairs) 12.2

695 See Annex 1 of: Resolución No. 106–176-DGMM 15 December 2021 (Dirección General de Marina Mercante)

696 Schiffsbesetzungsverordnung 18 July 2013, SchBesV (Bundesministerium für Verkehr, Bau und Stadtentwicklung) para 8; Shipping Circular No. 10 of 2022 – Minimum Safe Manning Document Requirements for Singapore Ships 28 June 2022 (Maritime and Port Authority of Singapore)

697 Shipping Circular No. 10 of 2022 – Minimum Safe Manning Document Requirements for Singapore Ships (n 696) Annex C

698 Paris MoU on PSC, 'Paris MoU White List 07-2024 – 06-2025' (2023); Paris MoU on PSC, 'ParisMoU Performance List Grey List 07-2024 – 06-2025' (2023); Tokyo MoU, 'Tokyo MoU Flag performance list 2023' (2023); United States Coast Guard, 'Port State Control in the United States' (2023)

699 IMO, 'Res. A.1047(27)' (n 672)

As great as the differences are, the states recognize each other's manning certificates per Regulation I/19 of SOLAS as amended by the 1988 Protocol to SOLAS and supplemented by IMO guidelines.[700] The guidelines list the manning certificate as one of the certificates to be checked at foreign ports.[701] Although SOLAS does not permit the rejection of acceptance based on the claim that the minimum manning specified in the certificate does not guarantee safety at sea, port states may have the authority to decline certificates that indicate zero crew members – even in the RCC.

Starting with the literal understanding of 'minimum', legal scholars argue that it means "more than nothing".[702] In contrast, 'minimum' in a mathematical sense describes the "value of a quantity at the point where the quantity stops to decrease and begins to increase".[703] As there cannot be a negative number of crew members, zero is the lowest imaginable number and thus the minimum. On the one hand, such a mathematical understanding could be legitimately applied, as the word 'minimum' is used in the context of determining the number of crew members. On the other hand, the negotiators of SOLAS were mostly jurists possibly not aware of the mathematical meaning. Hence, the literal meaning of the term 'minimum' is ambiguous. The term 'sufficiently' adds a degree of flexibility. In contrast to 'minimum', 'sufficiently' does not imply any momentum of "more than nothing". However, a clear indication cannot be made regarding the acceptance of zero crew members from a purely literal perspective. Thus, the purpose of the provision has to be considered to determine the ordinary meaning of the words used.

Again, reference can be made to Regulation IV/16 of SOLAS as part of the context. As discussed above, the necessity of continuous radio communication for distress situations and safety purposes as well as VTS makes human involvement indispensable. Consequently, Regulation IV/16 of SOLAS also requires the human in the loop. As the radio personnel is part of the manning addressed in Regulation V/14 of SOLAS, zero manning is not possible considering the context. As another element of context, the IMO guidelines on minimum safe manning list the level of ship automation as a factor to be considered when

700 IMO, 'Res. A.1156(32): Survey Guidelines under the Harmonized System of Survey and Certification (HSSC), 2021' (London 15 December 2021)

701 IMO, 'Res. A.1156(32)' (n 700) Annex, 1.2.1.17

702 CMI, 'Position Paper on Unmanned Ships and the International Regulatory Framework' (n 13) 10

703 Oxford English Dictionary, 'minimum, n. and adj'. (11 May 2022) <https://www.oed.com/view/Entry/118854?redirectedFrom=minimum#eid>

establishing the minimum safe manning of a vessel.[704] The IMO therefore acknowledged the impact of automation on the manning already in 2011. This supports the possibility of zero crew members.

The purpose of Regulation V/14 of SOLAS could be construed as advocating for the complete exclusion of the human element. Some scholars argue, that eliminating the human in the loop increases the safety at sea as fewer accidents occur[705] because most marine casualties can be traced back to human errors due to fatigue or inattentiveness. Nonetheless, most MASS projects foresee the human in the loop to cope with extraordinary unforeseeable situations. Although fatigue-related accidents could be prevented by fully autonomous operation, it is unlikely that safe navigation can be ensured at all times without human intervention. Human control is especially necessary for the handling of close-quarter and unpredictable situations.[706] In such circumstances, it is incumbent upon the human operator to react accordingly to unanticipated situations. In addition to adhering to COLREG, experience and local navigation characteristics play a significant role. While algorithms can preclude risks, they are not always dependable in conflict resolution. Eventually, as illustrated above, humans are needed to ensure radio communication. Therefore, based on the technology available today, human involvement is required to ensure safety at sea. In summary, the purpose of the manning requirement advocates for a human involvement to defuse critical situations safely and adequately.

In conclusion, the manning regulations in SOLAS require human involvement in the ship operation due to the insufficient technical solutions available today. However, the degree of involvement is not defined in absolute terms. Instead, it depends on what is necessary to maintain safety at sea at all times. If the traffic and weather situation allows, a vessel may operate at degree four[707] without violating SOLAS.[708] The level of human involvement can therefore be adapted to the traffic situation and vary during the voyage. When technological innovations enable safe and autonomous handling of unpredictable situations

704 IMO, 'Res. A.1047(27)' (n 672) 1.1.3, Annex 2

705 Karlo Bratić and others, 'Review of Autonomous and Remotely Controlled Ships in Maritime Sector' [2019] Transactions on Maritime Science 253, 253 <https://www.semanticscholar.org/paper/Review-of-Autonomous-and-Remotely-Controlled-Ships-Brati%C4%87-Pavi%C4%87/cabf91d3e429ff28b94f5094bf70e0af98d40601>

706 Ahvenjärvi (n 145) 520

707 Chircop, 'Chircop 2017' (n 255) 121–122

708 Laffey (n 612) 271; MSC, IMO, 'MSC.1/Circ.1638' (n 18) 32; Ringbom. 'Legalizing autonomous ships' (above, n. 537), p. 438; Tüngler and tho Pesch (n 429) 123; different view: Trowers (n 614) 219

and radio communications, human involvement in the decision-making loop is no longer necessary.[709]

As seen from the discussion and variety of expressed opinions, clarification of the meaning of the term 'manning' would be beneficial to ensure legal certainty for industry stakeholders and to provide guidance for flag, coastal, and port states on how to interpret SOLAS with respect to MASS. While the IMO principles on minimum safe manning have not resulted in a uniform interpretation, a legal instrument explicitly allowing zero crew would facilitate the advent of MASS.

4.4.2.1.4 *Master and Crew*

Eventually, the findings must be cross-checked against UNCLOS, particularly Article 94(4)(b) of the UNCLOS. The analysis concluded so far that no human presence on board, though human involvement is required. While UNCLOS establishes a framework to be filled by GAIRAS, it is important to ensure that the interpretation of the GAIRAS Conventions remains within UNCLOS' framework. In particular, the flag state's responsibility to ensure that every vessel is in charge of a master and a competent crew, contained in Article 94(4)(b) of the UNCLOS, needs to be considered.

The terms 'master' and 'crew' are not exclusive to UNCLOS; however, their interpretation in the context of remote and autonomous operations will be discussed based on UNCLOS. This is because the GAIRAS conventions are expected to align with the fundamental concepts of these terms as included in UNCLOS.

For centuries, the common picture of a master as the incarnation of the ship has not changed significantly. Although the design of ships has evolved, the master has continued to be the person commanding the ship from the bridge located on the ship. This concept is now challenged by MASS, intending to relocate the person responsible for the navigation of the ship ashore or even substitute decision-making powers with algorithms. This innovation makes it necessary to deal in detail with the meaning of 'master'. It will be examined whether the operational concepts of remotely operated and autonomous vessels are in line with UNCLOS' concept of master and crew. First, it needs to be assessed whether the master can be located in the RCC ashore. Second, the necessary degree of human involvement in the operation of the ship will be examined.

709 Others, however, are more cautious about expecting much support for innovative technologies in existing regulations: Jokioinen and others (n 98) 44

UNCLOS does not define the place of work of the master. Recourse can be made to the duties imposed on a master in order to draw conclusions about the workplace. Pursuant to Article 94(4)(c) of the UNCLOS the master shall

> observe the applicable international regulations concerning the safety of life at sea, the prevention of collisions, the prevention, reduction and control of marine pollution, and the maintenance of communications by radio.

These duties do not require an on board presence of the master. Rather, remote operation technology allows for observing compliance with the applicable international regulations from a distance. Another task assigned to the master is to be "in charge of the vessel". Understanding this as an assignment of responsibility, this task might pose a challenge to autonomous operations, whereas relocating the master ashore seams less problematic. Particularly, the master can continue to be responsible for the vessel. Being in charge of does not necessitate on board presence.

Furthermore, Article 94(4)(b) of the UNCLOS requires the master to have appropriate qualifications in seamanship, navigation, and communications. From these qualification requirements, it can be concluded that the master is responsible for the navigation and operation of the vessel. However, this does not require the master to be present on board, as the discussion above showed that safe navigation can be ensured remotely.

The term master has always described the central person of the ship's operation. Even though only some tasks are explicitly mentioned in UNCLOS, some argue that the entire concept of the master, as it prevailed at the time of the conclusion of the treaty, was incorporated into UNCLOS.[710] Nevertheless, the tasks of the master and its role in international shipping has developed considerably. Improved communication technologies and more complex cargo handling procedures have affected the master's role. This evolution already started in the 1960s, thus the parties were aware of the evolving meaning of the term 'master'. Notwithstanding, the term 'master' was included in UNCLOS without fixing a definition. This strongly advocates for an evolutionary interpretation of the term 'master'.[711] Due to new technological options in vessel

710 Baughen, 'Baughen 2019' (n 593); Schelin, 'Schelin 2020' (n 60)

711 Dong, Bautista and Zhu (n 540) 5; Ntovas (n 675) 218 and 222; *Sümer*, Overcoming the Legal Challenges of Maritime Autonomous Surface Ships (MASS) and Compliance with UNCLOS and SOLAS – Designation of a Remote Master to Assume the Safety Duties of a Master, 259

operations, the master's location is no longer relevant to the fulfilment of the tasks assigned to the master.

Some argue that the exercise of coastal state jurisdiction as stipulated by Article 27 and 28 of the UNCLOS towards foreign-flagged vessels requires the presence of a master on board. However, two aspects have to be considered in this respect. First, the reference to the presence of a master on board the vessel during the exercise of enforcement actions shall protect the interests of the flag state, rather than the enforcement possibilities of the coastal state. The flag state, however, may decide whether to register MASS. Second, technical means such as video surveillance or the consultation with diplomatic staff of the flag state could provide a practicable alternative.[712] Thus, the limited jurisdiction of the coastal state towards foreign-flagged vessels in the territorial sea does neither require a human presence on board.

Based on the provisions of UNCLOS and the tasks assigned to the master, the parties intended the master to ensure the safety of navigation and the safety of life at sea. Both aspects can be ensured in the case of remotely operated vessels. In this way, the purpose of the provisions on the master sought by the parties can be achieved. To summarize, UNCLOS does not determine the place of work of the master.[713] Consequently, the remote operator of a MASS at degree three can be considered the master.[714]

Turning now to the required level of involvement, Article 94(4)(b) of the UNCLOS states that each vessel shall be "in charge of a master". The level of involvement required is dependent on the meaning of 'in charge of'. According to the Oxford English Dictionary, 'in charge of' means to take care of something.[715] Based on this understanding, the master needs to be part of the

712 Vanessa Ritt, *Unbemannte Schiffe im Internationalen Seerecht* (Acta Iuridica Universitatis Potsdamiensis vol 8, Universitätsverlag Potsdam 2022) 99–100

713 Contrasting: Deutscher Verkehrsgerichtstag (ed), '55. Deutscher Verkehrsgerichtstag 2017: Veröffentlichung der auf dem 55. Deutschen Verkehrsgerichtstag vom 25. bis 27. Januar 2017 in Goslar gehaltenen Vorträge, Referate und erarbeiteten Empfehlungen' (2017) 267

714 Baughen, 'Baughen 2019' (n 593) 146; Carey, 'Carey 2017' (n 165) 3; Fastvold (n 571) 26; Fastvold (n 571) 28; Ntovas and others (n 516) 19; Tomotsugu Noma, 'Existing conventions and unmanned ships – need for changes?' (World Maritime University Dissertations, 527 2016) 66; Chircop, 'Chircop 2017' (n 255) 122; Parker (n 522) 35; LEG, IMO, 'LEG 110/11/3: Measures to Address MASS in Instruments under the Purview of the Legal Committee (United Arab Emirates), Consideration of issues under UNCLOS relevant to the role of the Organization' (London 23 December 2022) 23; MSC, IMO, 'MSC 107/20' (n 375) 5.22.2.2; Junghwan Choi, 'Legal Status of Remote Operator in Maritime Autonomous Surface Ships (MASS) Under International Law: who Can be a Ship Master?' in Eric Y J Lee (ed), *Revolutionary Approach to International Law: The Role of International Lawyer in Asia* (International Law in Asia, 1st edition. Springer Nature Singapore 2023) 16

715 Oxford English Dictionary, 'charge, n'. II.IV.13.A. <https://www.oed.com/dictionary/charge_n?tab=meaning_and_use#9597041> accessed 16 February 2024

operation system of the vessel and responsible for its operation.[716] The master needs to have an overview of the whole ship, its navigation, propulsion system, crew, and cargo. Being responsible entails the ultimate power of decision. However, 'being in charge of' does not preclude that another entity, e.g. the navigation algorithm, is also engaged in the appointed service.

This is illustrated by the prevalent use of advanced assistance systems, such as adaptive autopilots, in modern navigation. Even though adaptive autopilot systems can handle multiple waypoints, execute navigation sequentially, and incorporate collision avoidance maneuvers and speed adjustments based on weather conditions, the master retains ultimate responsibility for the vessel.

To clarify the understanding of the term 'in charge of', it may also be helpful to distinguish it from the related phrase 'in command of'. The latter undoubtedly refers to immediate involvement, decision-making power, and ultimate authority. The former, however, is not limited to active decision-making but includes responsibility in a broader sense.[717] In the case of autonomous MASS, humans would closely supervise the autonomous navigation system and could intervene if necessary. Consequently, the human supervisor remains finally responsible, although decision-making power is conferred to the system. Upon the advent of autopilots and intelligent assistance systems, the role of the master as being 'in charge of' was not discussed, despite the conferral of decision-making power on these systems. As long as all autonomous operation systems are closely monitored by the remote supervisor, the master arguably is in charge of the ship.[718]

As soon as the level of human involvement further decreases and a vessel is not constantly monitored, the supervisor will lose the position of 'being in charge of' the vessel. Consequently, fully autonomous operations without any human involvement do not comply with Article 94(4)(b) of the UNCLOS.[719] Undoubtedly, the master must be a human being, as an algorithm cannot be considered a master.[720]

To conclude on the interpretation of the term 'master' as used in Article 94 UNCLOS, the author is of the opinion that both remote operators and remote

716 Ringbom, 'Ringbom 2020' (n 424) 438

717 McKenzie (n 528) 388

718 Choi (n 714) 16

719 Ahmed and Salas (n 87) 172; Fastvold (n 571) 41; Laffey (n 612) 263; LEG, IMO, 'LEG 107/8/18: Comment on documents LEG 107/8, LEG 107/8/1, LEG 107/8/5, LEG 107/8/6 and LEG 107/8/11 regarding the role of the master (IFSMA)' (London 23 January 2020) 3; Soyer (n 86) 1756-176; arguing that MASS at degree four comply with UNCLOS, though not indicating consequences for the absence of human presence: LEG, IMO, 'LEG 110/11/3' (n 714) 22

720 LEG, IMO, 'LEG 107/8/18' (n 719) 3

supervisors can fulfil the functions assigned to the master by UNCLOS. Since both are ultimately responsible for the ship and have decision-making powers, both are recognized as masters.

Now, the discussion turns to the term 'crew', which is even vaguer than the term 'master' is. The term is not defined in UNCLOS. The Oxford English Dictionary defines the term 'crew' in a nautical sense as

> [t]he whole of the men belonging to and manning a ship, boat, or other vessels afloat.[721]

Hence, the term 'crew' encompasses all persons involved in the operation of the vessel except for the master. This includes deckhands, engineers, officers, the ship's cook, and other persons. As this definition only addresses functions to be fulfilled, the personnel working ashore could be regarded as 'crew'. In particular, the manning aspect supports the possibility of a relocation as the discussion above revealed.

Several scholars have discussed this question and concluded, applying a function-based approach, that the personnel working in the RCC could man the vessel as 'crew'.[722] As MASS technology enables all necessary tasks to be performed from ashore or during port calls on the vessel, it is convincing to consider the personnel carrying out those tasks as the crew of the vessel.

In the case of autonomous MASS, it seems probable that the number of crew members will be further reduced, although it is unlikely that it will reach zero. As Article 94 (4)(b) of the UNCLOS makes the number of crew members dependent on the type, size, machinery, and equipment of the vessel, a reduced crew does not conflict with UNCLOS.

Both the terms 'master' and 'crew' can be interpreted to include remote operators and supervisors, as well as any other individuals who are immediately involved in the ship operation process. This extensive opinion can be based on an evolutionary interpretation of the term 'master'. Unlike the term 'bridge', the master's concept is multifaceted and evolved over time. A master has always existed, but its concrete tasks have changed considerably over the past centuries.

The terms are used in almost all international shipping conventions, thus, a horizontal harmonization of the meaning and scope of the terms is

721 Oxford English Dictionary, 'crew, n.'. II.6.b. <https://www.oed.com/view/Entry/44347?rskey=kZkDaG&result=1&isAdvanced=false#eid> accessed 16 February 2024

722 Chircop, 'Chircop 2017' (n 255) 21; Fastvold (n 571) 29; Komianos (n 686) 341; Noma (n 714) 66

preferred.[723] A revised definition of the term 'master' could be adopted, which takes into account the relocation of the commanding officer.[724] The MSC identified the ascertainment of the definition of the terms 'master' and 'crew' as one of the high-priority tasks in relation to MASS.[725]

When revising the terms, it can also be considered, whether all tasks performed by the master are necessarily conducted by one person or whether single tasks could be performed by another person. Carey argues in favor of a holistic approach and claims that all tasks currently performed by the master must be taken over by one other person.[726] The IMO seems to consider a similar approach as a holistic revision of the term 'master' is planned.[727] However, from a practical point of view, spreading the master's tasks on several people could be necessary; in particular, cargo related tasks could be handed over to local representatives of the ship operator.[728] Moreover, it needs to be determined whether one person can only supervise one vessel at a time or whether fleet-master are imaginable.

To conclude, UNCLOS does not prevent MASS operations as long as human involvement is ensured. In respect of the master and the crew, the expressed view is extensive and encompasses remote operators, supervisors, and all individuals directly involved in the ship operation within the category of 'master' and 'crew'. Such a comprehensive approach is supported by the constitutional character of UNCLOS.

This section was concerned with the human presence on board the vessel and the necessary human involvement to ensure the safety of navigation and the safety of life at sea. Article 94 (4)(b) of the UNCLOS, however, does not only require that each vessel is "in the charge of a master and officers". Rather, these persons need to be appropriately qualified in seamanship, navigation, communication, and marine engineering. This reference points to the STCW regime providing a globally uniform training and qualification scheme for seafarers.[729]

723 Megumi Shiokari and Susumu Ota, 'Considerations on the regulatory issues for realization of Maritime Autonomous Surface Ships' (2019) 1357 Journal of Physics: Conference Series 1, 3

724 Carey, 'Carey 2017' (n 165) 22; Noma (n 714) 67; MSC, IMO, 'MSC.1/Circ.1638' (n 18) Annex, p. 8

725 MSC, IMO, 'MSC.1/Circ.1638' (n 18) 10

726 Carey, 'Carey 2017' (n 165) 22

727 MSC, IMO, 'MSC.1/Circ.1638' (n 18) Annex, p. 8

728 Schelin, 'Schelin 2020' (n 60) 42; Steven Mallam and John Cross, 'Towards the Seafarer of Tomorrow – Maritime Worker Competencies in the Autonomous Age' (2023) 18(4) The Journal of Ocean Technology 53, 55

729 Guilfoyle, 'Guilfoyle 2017' (n 317) 10

As the competence of the personnel involved in the ship operation is linked to the manning, this aspect will be discussed now.

4.4.2.1.5 *Competencies*

The manning requirement is only meaningful if the personnel is adequately qualified. The reference in Article 94 (4)(b) of the UNCLOS to "appropriate" qualifications points to the STCW regime.[730] Besides the above-introduced regulations on watchkeeping, the main part of STCW provides a comprehensive training and qualification scheme for seafarers. Furthermore, the STCW Code provides a comprehensive list of competencies for seafarers. The author is conversant about Article III of STCW and the fact that the STCW regimes does not apply to people not located on board the vessel. However, the STCW provision on qualification are referenced here to reflect the academic discussion.

The comprehensive scheme for qualification and training of seafarers provided by STCW shall ensure the safety of navigation and the safety of life at sea, Article I(2) of STCW. Moreover, STCW ensures the mutual recognition of certificates by all 167 member states unless clear grounds for fraudulent obtainment are obvious.[731] SOLAS does not stipulate particular training demands; nevertheless, it obliges sufficient training for relevant individuals in specific circumstances.[732] The main challenge with the STCW convention is that it does not apply to remote operators and supervisors as these persons are not "working *on board* seagoing vessels".[733] Even if the non-applicability of the STCW regime makes the physical presence on the bridge superfluous, it also means that the regulations on competences are not applicable.

As a response, national regulators will then enter the face and promote domestic regulations on remote operator competencies.[734] Fragmentation does not only hamper international voyages, moreover, national legislators could cope in a race to the bottom. Moreover, an internationally agreed framework for the qualification and training of MASS operators facilitates the integration of MASS in the conventional shipping business. Conventional masters and MASS-masters can take each other's positions increasing the social acceptance of MASS and the availability of qualified MASS operators. Moreover, employing MASS in international voyages is facilitated. Therefore, Ringbom suggests applying the STCW to MASS, based on the benefits of a har-

730 ibid

731 See Article X/1 of STCW

732 See for example Regulation III/10, IV/16, V/24 of SOLAS

733 Article III of STCW Convention; emphasis added by the author

734 Ringbom, 'Ringbom 2019' (n 55) 159

monized framework for the education and training of personnel involved in the operation of ships.[735] Yet the precise wording of Article III of the STCW Convention clearly speaks against this opinion.

In order to respect the wording of Article III of the STCW Convention and still apply the training and qualification scheme to MASS, the training and qualification scheme could be applied analogously. Applying a provision by analogy requires the lack of an explicit rule for the case concerned, the presence of a rule for a similar case, and the justification that both cases should be treated in the same way.[736] As a result, the explicit provision is also applied to a case outside its actual scope.

Transferred to the present case, there is no explicit training framework for remote operators and supervisors. However, there is a scheme for the qualification and the training of seafarers serving on board seagoing vessels. The next step is to examine the comparability of the qualification requirements for remote and conventional masters.

Several researchers have analyzed the relevance of competencies listed in the STCW Code for MASS masters.[737] Although the set of training and certification requirements for MASS operators is not determined finally, the necessity of conventional maritime competencies meets with broad approval.[738] Marine professionals who were interviewed on the skills needed for the remote operation of a vessel expressed that it is important to be familiar with conventional vessel operations to be able to safely navigate or monitor a vessel from ashore.[739] As most competencies listed in STCW are required by both, conventional masters and MASS masters, a distinction based on the place of work cannot be justified. Additionally, the mutual recognition of certificates is equally beneficial for MASS and conventional vessels, as MASS will also be subject to port state controls and qualification certificates are included in the scope of inspection.[740] Consequently, the equal treatment of both is indicated.

---

735 ibid

736 Fernando L Bordin, *The Analogy between States and International Organizations* (Cambridge studies in international and comparative law vol 138, Cambridge University Press 2019) 19–20

737 Rana Saha, 'Mapping competence requirements for future shore control center operators' [2021] Maritime Policy & Management 1; Amit Sharma and others, 'Catching up with time? Examining the STCW competence framework for autonomous shipping' (Haugesund 2019)

738 Directorate-General for Mobility and Transport, D2 Maritime Safety (n 166) 53; Saha (n 737), 8; Sharma and others (n 737) 6; Boviatsis and Vlachos (n 529) 6

739 MSC, IMO, 'MSC 99/INF.5' (n 161) 12

740 See Annex 10.67 of the Paris MoU

Based on a legal study conducted by Rambøll and Core,[741] Denmark proposed an analogous application at the IMO.[742] Others, advocate for the application of the STCW training scheme to remote operators, though without referring to a dogmatic legal basis.[743] As an alternative to the analogous application, the STCW convention and code could be amended to include MASS-specific regulations.[744]

It needs to be admitted though that an analogous application does not resolve all competence issues because additional competencies, especially in respect of software handling, cybersecurity, and data fluency need to be developed for MASS operators.[745] Initiatives like 'Skillful',[746] 'SkillSea',[747] and 'MASSPeople'[748] investigate which competencies are necessary for remote masters and how to develop a training and qualification scheme. MASSPeople, for example, submitted a competence table for people involved in the operation of MASS to the MSC.[749] During the RSE, the IMO identified the training scheme for remote operators as one of the most complex issues to be addressed.[750] Despite the far advanced research projects, the MSC did not instruct the Sub-Committee on Human element, Training and Watchkeeping to develop competencies necessary for MASS operators yet.[751]

4.4.2.1.6 *Conclusions*

This section discussed the safety of navigation. Every vessel must navigate without posing a risk of collisions or close-quarter situations and must comply

741 Rambøll and Core Advokatfirma (n 638) 25

742 MSC, IMO, 'MSC 99/INF.3: Final Report: Analysis of Regulatory Barriers to the use of Autonomous Ships (Denmark)' (London 18 January 2018)

743 Choi (n 714) 10

744 Karlis (n 164), 124; Jo and others (n 566), 3; CMI, 'Position Paper on Unmanned Ships and the International Regulatory Framework' (n 13) 16; Ringbom, 'Ringbom 2019' (n 55) 159; Lei Shi, 'Successful Use of the Tacit Acceptance Procedure to Effectuate Progress in International Maritime Law' (1999) 11(2) University of San Francisco Maritime Law Journal 299, 328–329

745 CMI, 'Position Paper on Unmanned Ships and the International Regulatory Framework' (n 13) 16; Karlis (n 164) 123–124; Directorate-General for Mobility and Transport, D2 Maritime Safety (n 166) 50; World Maritime University, 'Transport 2040: Automation, Technology, Employment – The Future of Work' (Malmö 2019) 112; Mallam and Cross (n 728) 56

746 Skillful, 'The need for Skillful' <https://skillfulproject.eu/> accessed 16 February 2024

747 SkillSea, 'What is SkillSea?' (2022) <https://www.skillsea.eu/index.php/about/what-is-skillsea> accessed 16 February 2024

748 MASSPeople, 'About us' <https://www.masspeople.org/about-us> accessed 16 February 2024

749 MSC, IMO, 'MSC/ISWG/MASS 2/3/1: Bridging Competency Gaps for MASS Operators in Alignmentwith the STCW Framework (IMarEST)' (London 15 September 2023)

750 MSC, IMO, 'MSC.1/Circ.1638' (n 18) 10

751 MSC, IMO, 'MSC 107/20' (n 375) 5.19

with the accepted international standards. Primary reference for these standards is Article 94(4)(b) of the UNCLOS, which points to COLREG. Further provisions on the safety of navigation are included in SOLAS and STCW.

The initial discussion pertained to the requirement of human presence on board. Given the existence of technical solutions that enable a remote operator to navigate the ship safely though located ashore, having a person on board appears unnecessary. The STCW Convention, which mandates physical presence on the navigation bridge, only applies to seafarers serving on board seagoing ships. Therefore, it does not apply to MASS personnel.

The second part concerned the question of whether the safety of navigation could be met by MASS at degree four. While most functions can be automated, radio communications within VTS and ship-to-ship communications require human involvement. As of today, technology cannot ensure that autonomous radio communication is as effective as human-to-human communication. The standard of good seamanship does not necessitate human involvement for risk minimization as algorithms can execute the task and humans constantly monitor the vessel.

Therefore, MASS can ensure safe navigation. The existing regulations do not need to be changed. However, measures should be adopted to ensure an interpretation including MASS. Moreover, additional regulations on the equipment and design of RCC and the communication line between the RCC and the MASS are necessary. With respect to the design of the RCC, the provisions included in SOLAS on the equipment and design of the bridge could be applied by analogy to the RCC.[752]

These findings where reconsidered in the light of provisions on the manning of a vessel set out in Article 94(3)(b), (4)(b) of the UNCLOS and Regulations IV/16, V/14 of SOLAS. The manning is not a goal in itself, but rather a means to ensure safe navigation. As long as safe navigation can be ensured remotely, the manning requirement does not requires a human presence on board. Having MASS operating at degree four in mind, the qualitative dimension of the manning requirement was assessed. It has been concluded that a human involvement is necessary from a technical and legal perspective to ensure the safety of navigation. The required human involvement can be ensured by a continuous human supervision from the RCC.

Subsequently, the results were checked against Article 94(4)(b) of the UNCLOS requiring that each vessel is in the charge of a master. As the place of work is not inherent to the term 'master', the remote operator can be recognized as the master of a remotely operated MASS. With respect to MASS operating at

752 Ville Jokiranta, 'The Shipmaster in Remote & Autonomous Operations' (University of Turku 6 May 2019) 18

degree four, 'being in charge of' was distinguished from 'being in command of'. Whereas the latter refers to active and immediate human involvement, the former addresses responsibility in a broader sense. As the human supervisor remains ultimately responsible for a MASS at degree four, it is argued that the human supervisor is equal to the master.

Eventually, the requirement of appropriate qualification of the persons involved in the operation process per Article 94(4)(b) of the UNCLOS was addressed. To make advantage of the comprehensive and globally accepted training scheme set up by STCW, this study advocates for an analogous application of this framework to MASS operators. However, additional competencies reflecting the technical aspects of remote operation such as cybersecurity, data fluency, and handling of loss of communication situations need to be developed.

As next, the other main sub-aspect of seaworthiness, the safety of life at sea shall be discussed. Again, a functional approach is applied. First, it will be shown how SOLAS concretizes this concept. Second, the capability of MASS to ensure the safety of life at sea will be assessed.

4.4.2.2 Safety of Life at Sea

Eventually, the safety of life at sea shall be discussed focusing on the safety of people involved in the vessel's operation. Thus, an internal perspective is applied. In contrast, the duty to render assistance protects people that are not affiliated to the vessel before they came in distress. This external dimension will be discussed in the next section.

The safety of navigation and the manning contribute to the safety of life at sea. The risk of loss of life is reduced when collisions are avoided. In addition, as shown above, moving the crew ashore contributes to safety at sea by removing the crew and the master from the dangers of the sea.[753] Therefore, several provisions that have already been assessed also concern the safety of life at sea and it was concluded that a human presence on board is not necessary. Now, additional provisions, particularly in those to be found in SOLAS are examined.

Primarily, Chapters II-2 and III of SOLAS address design and equipment requirements contributing to the safety of life at sea. Chapter II-2 of SOLAS addresses fire protection, fire detection, fire extinction, and means required on board. Although MASS will need fire safety installations, some of the requirements set out in Chapter II-2 of SOLAS seem unnecessary for MASS.

753 Vos, Hekkenberg and Valdez Banda (n 187) 13

For example, Regulation II-2/10.3 of SOLAS stipulates the availability of portable fire extinguishers. In addition, Regulations II-2/12, 13 SOLAS require crew and passenger notification systems for fire alarms and means of escape. Neither of these are – from an operational point of view – necessary on board MASS as these vessels operate without human presence on board. Although these regulatory requirements do not prevent MASS operations, they impose an unnecessary burden on MASS.[754] Fire safety installations are expensive and add unnecessary weight to the MASS. Therefore, it is preferable to not apply these provisions to MASS.

Regulation II-2/17 of SOLAS provides an outlet as it provides the methodology for the approval of alternative design and arrangements for fire safety. As soon as the functional requirements included in Regulation II-2/2 of SOLAS and the fire safety performance criteria[755] are met, deviation from the prescriptive requirements in the previous parts of Chapter II-2 of SOLAS can be approved. Most of the functional requirements set out in Regulation II-2/2.2.1 of SOLAS can be easily met by MASS.[756] This especially holds true for

> .1 division of the ship into main vertical and horizontal zones by thermal and structural boundaries;
>
> .3 restricted use of combustible materials;
>
> .4 detection of any fire in the zone of origin;
>
> .5 containment and extinction of any fire in the space of origin;
>
> .7 ready availability of fire-extinguishing appliances; and
>
> .8 minimization of possibility of ignition of flammable cargo vapour.

However, requirements .2 and .6, the necessity to ensure the separation of accommodation spaces from the remainder of the ship and the protection of means of escape[757] could create a challenge for MASS. In this case, it could be argued that the functional requirements cannot be met as neither crew

754 CMI, 'Position Paper on Unmanned Ships and the International Regulatory Framework' (n 13) 9

755 Regulation II-2/17.7.6 of SOLAS

756 Shiokari and Ota (n 723) 9

757 Regulations II-2/2.2.2, 2.2.6 of SOLAS

accommodations nor means of escape are installed on board MASS. Thus, these parts can neither be separated nor protected. Applying a functional interpretation would therefore resolve this problem. Others, however, are of the opinion, that the fire safety regulations need to be amended to encompass MASS.[758] This view, however, ignores the availability of alternative design approval procedures.

Another aspect of safety of life at sea are life-saving appliances governed by Chapter III of SOLAS. Pursuant to Regulation III/7 of SOLAS lifebuoys, lifejackets, immersion suits, and anti-exposure suits need to be on board, additionally Regulation III/11 of SOLAS prescribes the presence of lifeboats and liferafts. These are, however, only meaningful when persons are present on board. Some of the provisions stipulate that the corresponding life-saving equipment must be available for each individual on the vessel. Thus, without humans on board, no lifejackets or immersion suits[759] would be required. It could even be argued that Regulation III/31.1.1.1 of SOLAS stipulating "one or more totally enclosed lifeboats [...] of such aggregate capacity on each side of the ship as will accommodate the total number of persons on board" does not require lifeboats on vessels without a human presence on board. In contrast, Regulation III/31.2 of SOLAS prescribes the presence of a rescue boat regardless the presence of human on board the vessel. Therefore, there are still some requirements that are not appropriate for MASS without on board crew.

To cope with these requirements, Regulation III/38 of SOLAS could be invoked. It provides the methodology to be followed for alternative design and arrangements for life-saving appliances. The alternative design has to provide a level of safety equivalent to the one stipulated by Chapter III of SOLAS. With MASS, however, it is a question of no longer having any life-saving equipment on board, because there are no longer people present who need to be saved. Pritchett has correctly pointed out that the logic behind Chapter III breaks down and becomes circular in the case of MASS.[760] Alternatively, Regulation I/4(b) of SOLAS could be relied on allowing the administration to grant exemptions for vessels which "embodies features of a novel kind" from the provisions included in Chapters II-1, II-2, III, and IV of SOLAS. However, the same applies here as for the other exemptions: exemptions apply to special situations and may allow for trial arrangements. Relying on exemptions for the permanent

758 Shiokari and Ota (n 723) 5

759 See Regulation II-2/2.2.1; 3 of SOLAS

760 Paul W Pritchett, 'Ghost Ships Why the law should embrace unmanned vessel technology' (2015) 40(1) Tulane Maritime Law Journal 197, 203

operation of MASS is not legally certain and would exceed the scope of an exemption.

Applying a functional and purpose-based interpretation of Regulation III/38 of SOLAS could allow the flag state administration to accept a MASS without life-saving appliances on board. However, such an interpretation should be safeguarded by international legal instruments to ensure that other coastal and port states apply the same functional interpretation. This point is crucial as Regulation I/19 of SOLAS includes the Cargo Ship Safety Construction Certificate, which confirms compliance with Chapter III of SOLAS, within the scope of port state control.

This section focused on design and equipment provisions concerning the safety of life at sea. In conclusion, these provisions do not hinder the operation of MASS; however, applying them incautiously could impose unnecessary requirements on MASS. However, in both cases, regulations allowing alternative design and arrangements provide flexibility.

4.4.2.3 Conclusions

This section discussed whether MASS can ensure the safety at sea as set out by UNCLOS, COLREG, STCW, and SOLAS. The two core elements, the safety of navigation and the safety of life at sea, were assessed. The legal analysis concluded that MASS operating at degree three and four are able to ensure the safety at sea as stipulated by the GAIRAS conventions. MASS operating at degree three can easily fit in the existing legal framework as only the STCW convention explicitly requires the human presence on board. According to the opinion presented here, however, this convention is not applicable to MASS.

For including MASS operating at degree four into the legal framework, more argumentative effort is needed. However, the functional approach applied in several provisions provides flexibility as to the means used to perform the function concerned. Consequently, navigation algorithms can ensure the safety of navigation from a legal point of view. Nonetheless, the manning requirement and the necessity to maintain radio watches make the involvement of humans necessary because the technology available today is not able to ensure proper AI-human radio communication and the safe handling of unanticipated close-quarter situations. Recalling the definition of degree four 'fully autonomous', a human supervisor monitors the vessel constantly and can take over control whenever necessary. Moreover, s/he can perform the radio communication. Thus, MASS operating at degree four can also ensure the safety at sea in the way it is formulated in UNCLOS and the GAIRAS conventions.

From a legal point of view, there are no provisions that apply to MASS, but prevent MASS operations. Nonetheless, legal instruments should be adopted to safeguard the interpretation proposed here. Moreover, regulations addressing the design and equipment of the RCC, cybersecurity,[761] the necessary equipment for MASS, the line of communication between the RCC and the MASS, and the training and qualification scheme for persons engaged in the remote operation need to be adopted internationally. Eventually, a risk assessment tool for the verification of MASS should be developed and harmonized among flag, coastal, and port states.

The MSC concluded in the RSE that amendments to existing provisions could fill the legal gaps and provide clarification with respect to the interpretation of certain core concepts. It is preferred to adopt a separate instrument instead of amending each affected instrument individually to avoid ambiguity surrounding the application of existing laws to conventional manned vessels.[762] However, as Henrik Tunfors points out, a stand-alone instrument entails a tremendous amount of work and the development of a new goal-based instrument would take decades if ever concluded.[763]

The safety at sea concerned primarily the safety of the vessel itself. However, mutual support in emergencies has always been of utmost importance. The duty to render assistance to people in distress at sea is included in UNCLOS and SOLAS and forms a part of seaworthiness. Additionally, the International Convention on Maritime Search and Rescue, 1979, obliges the member states to ensure the coordinated rescue of people in distress and Article 10 of the International Convention on Salvage iterates the wording of Article 98(1) of the UNCLOS. However, as neither convention is generally accepted,[764] they will not be discussed here. The ability of MASS to render assistance to people in distress at sea will be examined in the following section.

4.4.3 *Search and Rescue*

The legal basis for the duty to render assistance to people in distress at sea lies within customary international law,[765] Article 98(1) of the UNCLOS and Regulation V/33 of SOLAS, supplemented by IMO guidelines for the treatment

761 MSC, IMO, 'MSC 108/INF.2: White paper on cybersecurity aboard maritime autonomous ships (France)' (London 12 February 2024)

762 MSC, IMO, 'MSC 102/5/9: Summary of results of the second step of the RSE for SOLAS chapter V (China)' (London 11 February 2020); Jacobsson (n 689) 282

763 Tunfors (n 489) 55; Eder (n 678) 380

764 The Salvage Convention is ratified by merely 77 states. The SAR Convention is ratified by 114 states representing 80.44% of the world's total tonnage. Compared to the ratification rate of SOLAS and COLREG, neither convention achieves the benchmark of general acceptance

765 ILC, 'International Law Commission 1956' (n 229) 281

of persons rescued at sea[766] and circulars.[767] Article 98 of the UNCLOS obliges every state to

> 1. [...] require the master of a ship flying its flag, in so far as he can do so without serious danger to the ship, the crew or the passengers:
>
> (a) to render assistance to any person found at sea in danger of being lost;
>
> (b) to proceed with all possible speed to the rescue of persons in distress, if informed of their need of assistance, in so far as such action may reasonably be expected of him;
>
> (c) after a collision, to render assistance to the other ship, its crew and its passengers and, where possible, to inform the other ship of the name of his own ship, its port of registry and the nearest port at which it will call.
>
> 2. [...]

Regulation V/33.1 of SOLAS adds that

> [t]he master of a ship at sea which is in a position to be able to provide assistance, on receiving information from any source that persons are in distress at sea, is bound to proceed with all speed to their assistance, if possible informing them or the search and rescue service that the ship is doing so. [...] If the ship receiving the distress alert is unable or, in the special circumstances of the case, considers it unreasonable or unnecessary to proceed to their assistance, the master must enter in the log-book the reason for failing to proceed to the assistance of the persons in distress[...].

When assessing whether MASS are able to fulfill the requirement to render assistance to people in distress at sea two questions need to be answered: first, it must be clarified whether MASS are obliged to provide assistance at all. Second, the precise scope of the duty owed must be determined.

---

766 MSC, IMO, 'Res. MSC.167(78): Guidelines on the Treatment of Persons rescued at Sea' (London 20 May 2004)

767 MSC, IMO, 'MSC.1/Circ. 1447: Guidelines for the Development of Plans for Recovery of Persons from the Water' (London 14 December 2014); MSC, IMO, 'MSC.1/Circ. 1182: Guide to Recovery Techniques' (London 31 May 2006)

Starting with the first question, both provisions need to be implemented by flag states to apply to individuals.[768] Then, both provisions address the master rather than the vessel. As concluded above, the remote operator or supervisor of a MASS is equal to the master of a MASS. Consequently, MASS masters are the addressees of the duty to render assistance[769] and MASS, remotely operated or autonomous,[770] are not released from this duty.[771]

Any other conclusion, which would have the effect of excluding mass from the duty to render assistance to people in distress at sea, would be, as Tsimplis states, "absurd"[772] and "morally and legally unacceptable".[773] Schelin also supports the conclusion that MASS need to render assistance to people in distress at sea, as otherwise the fundamental obligation to save lives at sea could be watered down.[774]

MASS are required to provide assistance, so the specific actions owed by MASS are now discussed. The scope of these actions can be defined in two ways. Firstly, the obligation could be defined in absolute terms, meaning that the ship's design and equipment must be adapted to meet the scope of the obligation. Alternatively, the obligation could be determined on a case-by-case basis, taking into account the existing equipment and design of the ship. To integrate these two approaches into a wider ethical framework, the former approach reflects deontology, whereas the latter is associated with utilitarism. The duty to render effective assistance to people in distress could be deemed

768 Daniele Mandrioli, 'The International Duty to Assist People in Distress at Sea in the Era of Unmanned Navigation: No Place for People on Board' (2020) 26(1) Humanidades & Tecnologia (FINOM) 77, 85

769 Ntovas and others (n 516) 20; CMI, 'Position Paper on Unmanned Ships and the International Regulatory Framework' (n 13) 6; Pritchett (n 760), 208–209; Roman Dremliuga and Mohd H b M Rusli, 'The Development of the Legal Framework for Autonomous Shipping: Lessons Learned from a Regulation for a Driverless Car' (2020) 13(3) Journal of Politics and Law 295, 297; Mandrioli, 'Mandrioli 2020' (n 768) 88

770 Dissenting opinion with respect to autonomous vessels: Carey, 'Carey 2017' (n 165) 18; Jo and others (n 566) 4

771 CMI, 'Summary of Responses to the CMI Questionnaire' (n 525) 7; arguing that the duty to render assistance will lose its relevance: Juan P Rodriguez Delgado, 'The Legal Challenges of Unmanned Ships in the Private Maritime Law: What Laws Would You Change?' [2018] Port, Maritime and Transport Law between Legacies of the past and modernization 493–523, 516; van Hooydonk (n 543) 421

772 Michael Tsimplis, 'Designing Norms for Autonomous Ships: The Obligation to Call for Help and the Duty to Save Life in Danger at Sea' in Tafsir M Johansson and others (eds), *Autonomous Vessels in Maritime Affairs* (Studies in National Governance and Emerging Technologies. Springer International Publishing 2023) 112

773 ibid 114

774 Schelin, 'Schelin 2020' (n 60) 42

necessary based on the sake of the duty to protect human lives. In contrast, from a utilitarian perspective, the duty could be performed in a way maximizing the well-being of all affected individuals. This implies balancing economic interests and rescue interests. In the context of MASS, the choice of method is a significant consideration. This is because MASS do not possess the necessary facilities or equipment, such as food, water and medicines, to accommodate people in a suitable manner anyway.[775]

Up to now, innovative vessel designs had no impact on the duty to render assistance. New ship types had to have the same rescue capabilities as existing ship types. Therefore, it could be argued that MASS must also provide "the full program". However, Regulation V/33.1 of SOLAS accepts the situation that the vessel is "unable, or in the special circumstances of the case, considers it unreasonable or unnecessary to provide assistance". Likewise, Article 98(1) of the UNCLOS limits the duty to situations not causing serious danger to the ship, its crew, and passengers. Therefore, the duty to render assistance is not absolute, but has to be determined considering the prevailing circumstances and the vessel concerned.[776]

Article 98 of the UNCLOS fails to determine which acts constitute assistance.[777] Rather, the decision, which acts to perform, is fully with the master's discretion.[778] Often, however, the duty to render assistance included forwarding distress signals, the proceeding to the scene of the accident, recovering people in distress, and providing them with a sheltered accommodation.[779] Unproblematically, MASS could forward distress signals to other vessels and shore-based rescue centers and proceed to the people in distress.[780]

Although MASS would not expose humans to risk when assisting at sea,[781] providing additional assistance could be challenging for MASS. Needless to say, MASS could be equipped with life-saving appliances such as life rafts, which could be released to people in distress at sea.[782] Nutrition and water could be stored on board MASS in a sheltered space to allow for the accommodation

775 Mandrioli, 'Mandrioli 2020' (n 768) 89; Volker Bertram, 'Autonomous Ship Technology – smart for Sure, Unmanned maybe' (London January 2016) 6

776 This principle is included in the Maritime UK (n 69) 132

777 Felicity G Attard, *The Duty of the Shipmaster to Render Assistance at Sea under International Law* (Queen Mary Studies in International Law vol 41, Brill|Nijhoff 2020) 44

778 ibid

779 See sections 6.12, 6.13 of MSC, IMO, 'Res. MSC.167(78)' (n 766)

780 CMI, 'Position Paper on Unmanned Ships and the International Regulatory Framework' (n 13) 11; Bertram (n 775) 6; Baughen, 'Baughen 2019' (n 593) 136

781 Ritt (n 712) 159

782 Züngler and tho Pesch (n 429), 123; Mandrioli, 'Mandrioli 2020' (n 768) 93

of rescued people. Considering different sea states, rescuing people from the water without human presence on board the rescue ship could be impractical.[783] People in distress could potentially rescue themselves in a life raft, however, embarking the MASS is rather challenging without further assistance,[784] especially in stormy weather conditions.[785] This is proven by the fact that rescue operations using conventionally manned vessels are still challenging today.

As it is questionable what the actual benefit of such life-saving equipment on board MASS would be, MASS could be released from such advanced assistance duties. However, it should be borne in mind that it is for economic reasons that people are relocated ashore and accommodation spaces are no longer installed on board MASS. This perspective is utilitarian in nature, as the necessity to perform a specific task is determined by the consequences of the act in question.[786] Given the uncertainty surrounding the ability to maximize the happiness of those in distress, coupled with the fact that the happiness of those operating MASS is not maximized due to the necessity for considerable investments, it is utilitarian to refrain from equipping MASS with rescue installations.

It is broadly supported that economic losses due to a delay in schedule or the need to call another port than planned for the disembarkation of rescued persons do not release the master of the duty to render assistance.[787] This is supported by Regulation V/34-1 of SOLAS preventing the ship owner or the operator to limit the master's decision-making discretion. Economic interest must take a back seat to the duty to assist people in distress at sea. It could be argued, therefore, that MASS cannot rely on a limited duty to render assistance. Considering the high importance of the duty to render assistance to people in distress at sea and its foundation in international law of the sea and humanitarian law,[788] a substantial participation of MASS in search and rescue operations is important for the social acceptance of MASS.[789] Social acceptance, in turn, is necessary for economically viable business cases. As Mandrioli puts it

783 Ritt (n 712) 159; Bertram (n 775) 6

784 Ritt (n 712) 159

785 Schelin, 'Schelin 2020' (n 60) 42

786 Jeremy Bentham, *Principles of Morals and Legislation, Fragment on Government, Civil Code, Penal Law* (John Bowring ed 1 1838–1843) 121

787 Mandrioli, 'Mandrioli 2020' (n 768) 93; Irini Papanicolopulu, 'The duty to rescue at sea, in peacetime and in war: A general overview' (2016) 98(902) International Review of the Red Cross 491, 497; Attard (n 777) 14

788 Papanicolopulu (n 787) 492

789 Carey, 'Carey 2017' (n 165) 20; Tsimplis. 'Designing Norms for Autonomous Ships: The Obligation to Call for Help and the Duty to Save Life in Danger at Sea' (above, n. 770), p. 114

> it would be hard to accept this technological development [MASS] both from an ethical and juridical point of view, because it maximizes profits minimizing human lives' protection.

Whilst the extent of the obligation to render assistance to persons in distress at sea is determined on the basis of the capabilities of the ship in question, fundamental humanitarian and societal considerations require that MASS cannot retreat to the position of merely forwarding distress signals. Despite the practical and technical challenges, MASS will need to be equipped with life-saving appliances and installations to recover people in distress from the sea. An internationally agreed standard can ensure equal requirements in flag states and make sure that all stakeholders, states, ship operators, and other vessels know which rescue operations to expect from MASS.

At the IMO, the same conclusion was reached. Consequently, Section 10 of the proposed MASS Code lists functional requirements that MASS need to meet. With respect to search and rescue, each MASS shall be fitted with at least one remote rescue boat, be able to launch and recover rescue boats, and provide a sheltered space on board for accommodating people in distress.[790]

In the context of MASS and distress situations at sea, it was not only discussed whether MASS would be obliged to render assistance. Rather, the improvement of rescue operations due to the employment of MASS is discussed. As MASS do not exhibit humans to the perils at sea MASS could proceed to scenes of accidents too dangerous for manned vessels.[791] Moreover, small MASS rescue units could be located in remote areas to increase the response rate to marine casualties.[792]

4.4.4 *Conclusions*

This section discussed the seaworthiness as a core function each vessel has to fulfill. Focusing on the fundamental functions safety at sea and search and rescue, the analysis revealed that MASS at degree three and four are able to perform these functions as set out in UNCLOS and the GAIRAS conventions. Additionally, the basic concepts of nationality and genuine link can be applied to MASS.

In conclusion, MASS fall within the scope of the terms 'vessel' and 'ship' and are, hence, within the scope of international shipping legislation. MASS

790 MSC, IMO, 'MSC 107/5: Report of the MASS Correspondence Group' (London 27 February 2023) 30–31, Annex 1

791 Ritt (n 712) 159

792 Chircop, Goerlandt and Yoo (n 177)

acquire the nationality of their flag states and there must be a genuine link between the MASS and the flag state. Despite the relocation of the crew and the master, the genuine link is not assessed differently from conventional ships.

MASS can ensure the safety at sea. For clarity, the discussion was split into two parts: the safety of navigation and the safety of life at sea. The safety of navigation is set out in UNCLOS, COLREG, SOLAS, and STCW. Central, Rule 5 of COLREG stipulates the duty to maintain a proper lookout by sight, hearing, and all other available at all times. As a sensor system on board is able to provide the RCC with an accurate picture of the surroundings of the vessel, human presence on board is not required. The necessary human involvement in gaining situational awareness and maintaining radio communications can be ensured by the remote supervisor of MASS. The other elements of the safety of navigation do not pose significant legal challenges to the operation of MASS. From a technical perspective, it is feasible to program navigation algorithms to prioritize collision prevention. Although algorithms cannot adhere to the practices of ordinary seaman in the same way that humans can, the purpose – collision avoidance – is equally assured. It is proposed here to not apply the STCW convention to MASS masters and crew.

The manning requirement and the obligation that each vessel is in the charge of a master shall contribute to the safety of navigation and that humans remain ultimately responsible and can take over the operation of the vessel at any time. Safe navigation can be ensured without having humans on board. Thus, remote operators properly man the vessel. The required competencies for individuals involved in vessel operations can be inferred by analogy from STCW. However, it is necessary to identify additional skills.

The safety of life at sea is not an issue in terms of MASS, as humans are no longer exposed to the perils of sea. The implementation of regulations related to design and equipment seem to be losing their relevance when it comes to MASS. Workarounds in the form of alternative designs and arrangements can be applied. Moreover, several provisions make the availability of equipment dependent on the human presence on board.

The duty to render assistance to people in distress at sea is owed by the person equivalent to the master of the MASS, either the remote operator or supervisor. Life-saving equipment such as life rafts should be present on board the MASS and it should be feasible to recover people in distress at sea. Additionally, MASS should be equipped with a sheltered and supplied accommodation space.

In summary, MASS can be seaworthy. Means of interpretation are available to include MASS into the current legal framework. However, legal instruments should be adopted to safeguard this interpretation[793] and to ensure a common understanding of the core terms and concepts with regard to MASS. Since legal issues related to MASS are not confined in one convention, a unified horizontal strategy is required.

The analysis also revealed that several new aspects need to be regulated. When replacing the human lookout with a system of sophisticated sensors, the technical requirements for such an electronic lookout as well as the communication with the RCC must be regulated. Likewise, the setup of the RCC as the operational headquarter of the vessel requires regulations. The International Federation of Shipmasters' Associations has highlighted the importance of dealing with the training and qualification schemes for remote operators.[794] Although the traditional knowledge of seaman is important in an RCC as well,[795] competencies beyond the current training scheme are necessary for remote operators.[796] Since MASS are intended to carry valuable cargo by sea without having personnel on board, the aspect of piracy must be addressed.[797] Ensuring software security is not only important to prevent cyber piracy, but also to take precautionary steps against other forms of cyber-attacks.[798] Additionally, there is a need for synchronized standards for the risk assessment of MASS. The IMO included these novel aspects in its RSE. Therefore, the IMO concluded that either amendments to SOLAS, COLREG, and STCW must be made or new instruments need to be developed.[799]

However, before MASS can start operating, several other aspects, not discussed here, need to be resolved: Coastal states face the question of how to take enforcement measures against MASS. An extended interpretation of Articles 27(3), 28 of the UNCLOS could provide a solution.[800] Similar jurisdictional challenges arise in the continuous zone (Article 33 of the UNCLOS) and the exclusive economic zone (Article 73 of the UNCLOS). All private maritime law contracts need to be adapted to MASS. The private law dimension of the

---

793 Oluwatosin S Osaloni and Victor O Ayeni, 'The Development of Maritime Autonomous Surface Ships: Regulatory Challenges and the Way Forward' (2022) 13(3) Beijing Law Review 544, 551; Jakob Bang, Mogens Blanke and Michael Henriques, 'A pre-analysis on autonomous ships' (Lyngby, Denmark 2019) 11

794 MSC, IMO, 'MSC 99/INF.5' (n 161) 12

795 Jokioinen and others (n 98) 47; MSC, IMO, 'MSC 99/INF.5' (n 161) 12; Directorate-General for Mobility and Transport, D2 Maritime Safety (n 166) 53

796 MSC, IMO, 'MSC 99/INF.5' (n 161) 12; Jokioinen and others (n 98) 47

797 Pritchett (n 760); Ritt (n 712); Liu (n 196)

798 Baughen, 'Baughen 2019' (n 593) 146

799 MSC, IMO, 'MSC.1/Circ.1638' (n 18) 11

800 Ritt (n 712) 99

concept of seaworthiness has to be reconsidered as it traditionally includes the vessel's manning.[801] In addition, the liability for collisions laid down in the Convention for the Unification of Certain Rules of Law with respect to Collisions between Vessels (Brussels Convention) has to be reassessed[802] as the convention stipulates fault-based liability.

To summarize, relocating the crew and master away from the vessel and handing over the control to an algorithm does not only affect the safety of navigation but also almost all areas of shipping. It is now up to the legislators to prepare the legal framework for MASS. As demonstrated, there is no demand to recreate existing practices; instead, minor adaptations are necessary. Certain countries have already begun modifying their national regulations. Efforts have also been undertaken by the European Union to enable trials. The presented national initiatives will act as a contemporary foundation for the forthcoming discussion on possible legal solutions.

4.5 National Regulatory Activities on MASS

This section provides a concise overview of regulatory strategies concerning MASS adopted domestically by European states. It is essential to acknowledge that all states recognize the authority of the IMO as the primary international regulatory body for maritime affairs. However, in pursuit of fostering innovation and ensuring appropriate legal frameworks for trials, national governments have developed complementary regulatory frameworks. These frameworks enable trials while maintaining alignment with the overarching regulations set forth by the IMO.

In Europe, only Finland, Norway, the United Kingdom, and France have developed comprehensive national MASS regulations as flag states. However, all four jurisdictions limit their MASS regulations to their territorial waters. In 2023, however, Belgium, Denmark, the Netherlands, and UK signed a memorandum of understanding on cooperative MASS trails in the North Sea. The states agreed to share information and recognize each other's certificates and MASS prototypes for trials.[803] In 2024, Norway joined the memorandum.[804]

801 Kampantais, 'Kampantais 2016' (n 504) 4

802 Boviatsis and Vlachos (n 529), 12–13; CMI, 'Position Paper on Unmanned Ships and the International Regulatory Framework' (n 13) 17; PCCG Point Conception Consulting GmbH and others (n 200) 80; Etzkorn (n 499); Herkenhoff (n 499)

803 Memorandum of Understanding on Cooperation Regarding the International Operation of Maritime Autonomous Surface Ships MASS 27 November 2023

804 Nærings- og fiskeridepartementet, *Ny avtale sikrer internasjonalt samarbeid om drift av autonome skip* (2024)

Outside Europe, MASS regulations can be found in South Korea, Japan, and Australia.[805] Moreover, the Netherlands[806] and Belgium[807] have developed a regulatory framework for autonomous and remote navigation on inland waterways. As it is beyond the scope of this study to present all regulatory activities on MASS worldwide, the focus will be on European countries.

4.5.1 *Finland*

In Finland, new technical solutions in respect of manning and watchkeeping can be trialed with a special permission by the competent national maritime authority for up to two years. To enable such trials, the Act on Ships' Crews and the Safety Management of Ships[808] was amended in 2018.[809] According to section 13 of this Act, the Finnish Transport and Communications Agency can release ship owners from the manning and watchkeeping requirements and permit a trial within Finnish territorial waters. The precondition for the permission is that neither the vessel nor the environment is put at risk.

Likewise, the pilotage regime was amended to enable remote pilotage with special permission.[810] Remote pilotage is not limited to MASS but can be utilized for any vessel. Per section 16b of the Pilotage Act, the application for a special permission shall include the chosen technical solutions, the intended method, and the risk handling. Additionally, it has to be illustrated how the safety of navigation and the environment is secured. The regulation is open to different technical solutions.

4.5.2 *Norway*

Norway is one of the world's leading maritime autonomy nations and has prepared its national legal framework for the operation of MASS already in 2018. Later, the maritime strategy 2021, developed by the Ministry of Trade, Industry, and Fisheries, outlines the objective of advancing digital technologies and supporting research projects to enable the deployment of digital solutions

---

805 Australian Maritime Safety Authority, 'AMSA Policy on Regulatory Treatment of Unmanned and/or Autonomous Vessels' (20 February 2020)

806 'Beleidsregel experimenten vergaand geautomatiseerd varen rijksvaarwegen', *Staatscourant van het Koninkrijk der Nederlanden* (2018)

807 Decreet houdende diverse bepalingen over het mobiliteitsbeleid, de openbare werken en het vervoer, het verkeersveiligheidsbeleid en VVM – De Lijn (1) 26 April 2019 (Vlaamse Overheid) Art. 51, § 1

808 1687/2009 – Act on Ships' Crews and the Safety Management of Ships

809 976/2018 – Lag om ändring av lagen om fartygspersonal och säkerhetsorganisation för fartyg (n 420)

810 51/2019 – Lag om ändring av lotsningslagen 18 January 2019 (Eduskunta)

through commercialization and scaling.[811] As Norwegian shipping companies operate the fifth most valuable vessel fleet in the world, the well-being of the maritime industry is crucial to Norwegian society.[812] The regulation of new technology shall ensure that the overall policy goals are promoted; however, the innovation force shall not be negatively impacted.[813]

The Norwegian Maritime Authority ('*Sjøfartsdirektoratet*') is responsible for ship registrations. It has issued a circular describing the procedure of validation for MASS.[814] Starting from the current legal framework, autonomous systems enabling a relocation of the crew ashore are certified based on the principle of functional equivalences. The Norwegian Maritime Authority refers to the IMO Guidelines for the approval of alternatives and equivalents as provided for in various IMO instruments.[815] Independent third parties have to verify that the installed technology ensures a level of safety at least equivalent to the one maintained by conventionally manned vessels.[816] Additionally, tests in an official test area have to be performed to ensure the functionality of the used technology.[817]

Additionally, the Norwegian pilotage regulation posed an obstacle to MASS operations. The Pilotage Act ('*Losloven*') required the pilot to be on board the vessel. Remote pilotage was only possible when harsh weather conditions made it impossible for the pilot to board the vessel. To remove this obstacle for MASS operations in Norwegian territorial waters, the Pilotage Act was amended.[818] Now, the ship owner can apply for an exemption from the pilotage duty when operating a vessel either autonomously or remotely controlled. The exemption may include requirements for the navigation and maneuvering system of the vessel as well as limits to the area of operation. In 2019, the Pilotage Act was included in the harbor and fairway law ('*havne- og farvannsloven*').[819] The exemption of the pilotage duty is now included in Regulation 25 ('*autonom kystseilas*') of this Act.

811 Norges forskningsråd (n 68)
812 ibid
813 Det kongelige Samferdselsdepartement, 'Nasjonal transportplan 2022–2033: Meld. St. 20 (2020–2021)' (Oslo 19 March 2021) 58
814 Sjøfartsdirektoratet (n 417)
815 MSC, IMO, 'MSC.1/Circ.1455: Guidelines for the Approval of Alternatives and Equivalents as Provided for in Various IMO Instruments' (London 24 June 2013)
816 Sjøfartsdirektoratet (n 417) 3
817 ibid para 9
818 Det kongelige Samferdselsdepartement, 'Høring om endringer i lov om losordningen for å legge til rette for autonom kystseilas' (Oslo 30 April 2018)
819 Stortinget, 'Lovvedtak 65 om havne- og farvannsloven' (Oslo 4 June 2019)

4.5.3 *United Kingdom*

The UK government intends to implement an innovative national legal framework for MASS and, at the same time, support the IMO in developing an international regulatory framework.[820] The responsible Maritime and Coastguard Agency (MCA) is aware of the need for technology-open and prompt regulations to meet the needs of the industry. Especially the advanced Norwegian regulation for the use of maritime autonomy encourages UK regulations.[821]

Back in 2018, the MCA driven MARLab project aimed at bringing together the government, academia, and the industry[822] to examine new ways to regulate MASS.[823] The project concluded that a regulation on remotely operated vessels under 24m in length was considered most urgent from an industry perspective.[824] In 2023, the third edition of the Workboat Code was published[825] providing a legal framework for remotely operated vessels under 24m in length in Annex 2. It is unclear whether autonomous modes of operation are included as section 7.2.2.2 of Annex 2 includes the navigation of the vessel in the minimum tasks of the remote operator. Moreover, section 1.1.2 provides for certification based on a case-by-case assessment for modes of operation other than those provided for in the Code. To evade any conflicts with international regulations, the Code is limited to voyages in territorial waters.[826]

Concerning vessels longer than 24m, the Merchant Shipping Act, 1995,[827] applies. To allow MASS operations, the MCA has prepared a proposal to update the relevant provisions and provide for clarifying definitions of key terms such as 'master' and 'crew'.[828] Although the proposal has not been submitted to Parliament yet, a final impact assessment concluded that regulating ahead of

820 Department for Transport, 'Maritime 2050' (London January 2019) 106

821 Adam J Fenton and Ioannis Chapsos, 'Ships without crews: IMO and UK responses to cybersecurity, technology, law and regulation of maritime autonomous surface ships (MASS)' (2023) 5 Frontiers in Computer Science, 7

822 Maritime and Coastguard Agency, 'Maritime Autonomy Regulation Lab (MARLab) Report' (Southampton 11 November 2020) 5 <https://www.gov.uk/government/publications/maritime-autonomy-regulation-lab-marlab-report/maritime-autonomy-regulation-lab-marlab-report> accessed 9 March 2022

823 ibid 2

824 ibid 8

825 The Workboat Code Edition 3, The safety of small Workboats and Pilot Boats – a Code of Practice (n 419)

826 See section 1.1.1 of the Workboat Code, edition 3

827 Merchant Shipping Act 1995

828 Maritime and Coastguard Agency, 'Maritime Autonomy Regulation Lab (MARLab) Report' (n 822) 6.2

the IMO is the preferred policy option.[829] While there is a risk of regulatory divergence, the UK anticipates that IMO will establish binding international rules in 2030 at the earliest. As this is too late to keep pace with other leading states, waiting for IMO regulations is not an option for the UK.[830]

As an interim solution, the MCA published a Marine Guidance Notice on the Certification Process for Vessels using Innovative Technology in 2022.[831] The instrument includes more than just autonomous technology.[832] As the Norwegian Circular, the Marine Guidance Notice is based on the IMO guidelines for approval of alternatives and equivalents.[833] The verification process is based on a close cooperation between the MCA and the applicant.[834]

Maritime UK is an umbrella body for various stakeholders of the maritime sector engaged in MASS. As several research projects MASS are conducted in the UK, Maritime UK developed a Code of Practice and a set of Industry Conduct Principles. These principles shall serve as guidelines for complying with IMO instruments such as COLREG, SOLAS, and STCW.[835] Although the Code is voluntary, it serves as a basis for the certification under the Marine Guidance Notice.

To summarize, MASS are addressed in the UK at various levels. The MCA engages in developing regulatory approaches, meanwhile, Maritime UK, as a private cooperative, provides guidelines for the industry to facilitate MASS trials and operations. Eventually, the national legal framework shall be updated to address the needs and specialties of the modern and digitalized maritime sector.

4.5.4 *France*

France has prepared its national legal framework for MASS already in 2016. The Blue-Economy Act introduced Article 5511-1-1 to the Transport Code defining MASS as a vessel that is operated remotely or autonomously without the need for a human presence on board.[836] However, first in 2019, the government was

829 Department for Transport, 'Future of transport regulatory review: Maritime Autonomy and Remote Operations; Final Impact Assessment' (London 14 September 2023) 1

830 ibid 14

831 MGN 664 (M + F) Amendment 1: Certification process for vessels using innovative technology September 2023 (Maritime and Coastguard Agency)

832 Fenton and Chapsos (n 821) 8

833 MSC, IMO, 'MSC.1/Circ.1455' (n 815)

834 Fenton and Chapsos (n 821) 8–9

835 Maritime UK (n 69)

836 Direction de l'information légale et administrative, 'Loi no 2016-816 du 20 juin 2016 pour l'économie bleue (1)', *Journal officiel de la République française* (2016) Article 87

authorized to adopt more detailed regulations on the operation of autonomous vessels.[837] Eventually, the Minister for Maritime Affairs adopted a regulation concerning MASS trials in 2021.[838]

In general, autonomous vessels have to fulfill the same requirements as conventional vessels. If, however, certain provisions cannot be fulfilled due to the autonomous mode of operation, the competent authority can grant exemptions if the owner of the autonomous vessel can prove that the safety of navigation as well as a high level of environmental protection is ensured. Thus, autonomous vessels can be registered and operate in French territorial waters. The certificate is valid for two years but it can be extended on request.[839]

In addition to the regulations concerning autonomous vessels, a new vessel category was introduced. 'Maritime drones' are floatable vehicles operated without a human presence on board, either autonomously or remotely controlled, and either on the surface or as submersibles. These vehicles have to fulfill certain technical standards in respect of size, power, and speed, which are determined in secondary legislation. In particular, the size of the vessel shall not exceed 100 gt.[840]

Maritime drones are not subject to the same regulatory framework as autonomous vessels. Rather, a reduced set of rules apply. The French Government aimed at reflecting the lower operational risk of maritime drones with a less complex legal framework.[841] However, the drones need to be registered and have to display their registration information.[842] Interestingly, the international regulations on the limitation of liability for maritime claims apply to maritime drones as well.[843]

Despite the comprehensive set of rules for MASS, no major research project on MASS could be found in France. Additionally, several aspects are still unsolved, most demanding regulations on liability for MASS.[844]

---

837 Direction de l'information légale et administrative, 'LOI no 2019-1428 du 24 décembre 2019 d'orientation des mobilités (1)', *Journal officiel de la République française* (2019) Article 135 III-1

838 'Ordonnance n° 2021-1330 relative aux conditions de navigation des navires autonomes et des drones maritimes', *Journal officiel de la République française* (2021)

839 See Article L5241-3-1 of the Code du Transport

840 See Article L 5000-2-2 of the Code du Transport

841 Secrétariat d'État chargé de la Mer, *La France pionnière dans l'exploitation des drones maritimes* (2021)

842 See Article L 5111-1-2 of the Code du Transport

843 See Article L 5121-5-1 of the Code du Transport

844 Morgane Roussel, 'French Regulations on MASS: Solved and Unsolved Issues' (Comité Maritime International, Montreal, 14 June 2023)

4.6 Conclusions

This section analyzed the current legal framework in the light of MASS. Despite the fact that most conventions were adopted in the 1970s and 1980s, none of the discussed provisions prevents MASS operations. Rather, applying a functional interpretation, MASS can be seaworthy and ensure the safety of navigation and the safety of life at sea. Moreover, MASS are obliged to render assistance to people in distress at sea.

To prepare the international legal framework for MASS, three steps are necessary: First, legal challenges arising in the context of international statutory instruments can be resolved by means of interpretation. Here, the necessity of developing instruments to ensure a common understanding and harmonized interpretation arises. Second, new rules need to be developed addressing all new technical features introduced by MASS, e.g. the RCC, the ship-shore-communication, cybersecurity, and training of RCC operators. Third, technical standards need to be adapted or newly developed. The following chapter explores means to adapt the legal framework and focusses thereby on the international conventions addressed above. The development of technical standards is not discussed in detail.

Some states have already prepared their national legal framework for MASS. However, the issuance of MASS certificates is based on exemption clauses and case-by-case evaluations. In the long term, it is crucial to consider MASS as a standard vessel and not an exception.[845] As the process of approving alternatives and equivalents is cumbersome, the results are unpredictable,[846] and not all IMO conventions provide for provisions allowing alternatives and equivalents.[847] Looking into the future, the registration process should be based on clear rules and standardized procedures. The IMO has started to develop a MASS Code, but the proposed roadmap is rather optimistic and has already been extended. Moreover, national approval of MASS does not ensure that other coastal and port states accept the MASS certificates. As illustrated above, compliance with the GAIRAS conventions is of paramount importance for MASS. Thus, an internationally coordinated approach is necessary.

As stated in Article 31 of the VCLT, the interpretation of legal provisions may be influenced by various materials. Multiple solutions are conceivable,

---

845 MSC, IMO, 'MSC 106/INF.6: United Kingdom developments on Maritime Autonomous Surface Shipsresearch, legislation and industry projects (United Kingdom)' (London 1 August 2022) 3

846 Tunfors (n 489) 56

847 Soyer (n 86) 172

including international, regional, and supranational approaches as well as binding and non-binding instruments. Given the successful trials and promising business models for international MASS operations, it is now time to decide on the most appropriate way to deal with MASS through legal channels. Unlike the IMO or national jurisdictions, this study does not restrict itself to a particular legal tool. Instead, it first scrutinizes and identifies the prerequisites that the new legal framework must satisfy. Second, various international, regional, and supranational regulatory instruments are evaluated to determine the optimal method of addressing MASS.

CHAPTER 5

Means to Adapt the Legal Framework to MASS

This third chapter discusses different approaches of adapting the legal framework to MASS. To be able to determine the most appropriate approach, first, some recommendations and requirements for the regulatory framework for MASS will be discussed. Second, legal regulation is situated in the wider context of regulation in general and soft law, as a distinct form of legal regulation, will be introduced. Subsequently, international, regional, and supranational solutions will be discussed and tested against the previously established requirements. Eventually, the most appropriate way of adapting the legal framework to MASS will be determined.

5.1 Requirements and Recommendations for MASS Regulation

This part is concerned with the requirements for a legal framework for MASS. In contrast to numerous academic contributions that have discussed the regulation of technology in general, this part focuses on the particular demands MASS puts on the legal framework. Given the undesirability of the law of the horse,[848] the raison d'être of technology regulation may well be questioned.[849] However, it must be acknowledged that technology imposes specific requirements on the regulatory framework, just like any other regulatory target. To provide effective regulations, it is important to determine the parameters and requirements beforehand, considering the peculiarities of the regulatory target in question.

The regulator of emerging technologies faces the challenge that the regulatory target is unknown and rapidly evolving.[850] To mitigate ineffective regulation, rule-setting could await the finalization of technological development. Despite the fact that technological development never reaches a final stage,

848 Frank H Easterbrook, 'Cyberspace and the Law of the Horse' [1996] University of Chicago Legal Forum 207–216

849 Lyria B Moses, 'How to Think about Law, Regulation and Technology: Problems with 'Technology' as a Regulatory Target' (2013) 5(1) Law, Innovation and Technology 1, 19; Ronald Leenes, 'Regulating New Technologies in Times of Change' in Leonie Reins (ed), *Regulating new technologies in uncertain times* (ProQuest Ebook Central vol 32. Asser Press; Springer 2019) 7

850 Leenes (n 849) 13; Roger Brownsword and Morag Goodwin, *Law and the technologies of the twenty-first century: Text and materials* (Law in Context, Cambridge University Press 2012) 63

 | DOI:10.1163/9789004729483_006

waiting for mature technology does not serve the interests of neither the industry nor society. Regulation shall, on the one side, combat risks and protect third parties from negative impacts,[851] and, on the other side, facilitate beneficial technological development.[852] To serve both functions, a balanced approach is necessary. Moreover, regulation has to start with uncertainty, as complete knowledge is never available.[853] Ideally, law and technology co-evolve. To recall, MASS shall be as safe as conventionally manned vessels. Although trials have demonstrated the safe operation of MASS, it is not possible to generalize these results to all MASS. Imposing onerous safety requirements could impede innovation and development. Conversely, failing to impose any safety requirements could result in casualties and have a detrimental impact on third parties. Therefore, the requirements and standards must be as rigorous as necessary, while also being adjustable and low-burden.

The dilemma faced by the regulator when regulating emerging technologies was described by Collingridge: The more mature and widespread the technology, the more difficult it is to implement restrictive regulations. However, the more mature and widespread the technology, the easier to determine and regulate risks.[854]

One solution to this dilemma is the precautionary principle especially used in environmental protection law.[855] Article 15 of the Rio Declaration from 1992[856] reproduces the principle by stating that

851 David Roth-Isigkeit and Ronny Thomale, 'Technische Rahmenbedingungen und Rechtliche Regulierung der Digitalen Transformation' in Susanne Beck, Carsten Kusche and Brian Valerius (eds), *Digitalisierung, Automatisierung, KI und Recht: Festgabe zum 10-jährigen Bestehen der Forschungsstelle RobotRecht* (Robotik und Recht vol 20. Nomos Verlagsgesellschaft mbH & Co. KG 2020) 143; Marjolein van Asselt, Ellen Vos and Tessa Fox, 'Regulating Technologies and the Uncertainty Paradox' in M. Goodwin, Bert-Jaap Koops and Ronald Leenes (eds), *Dimensions of technology regulation* (Wolf Legal Publishers 2010) 262

852 Carolyn Abbott, 'Bridging the Gap – Non-state Actors and the Challenges of Regulating New Technology' (2012) 39(3) Journal of Law and Society 329, 330; Maria Weimer and Luisa Marin, 'The Role of Law in Managing the Tension between Risk and Innovation: Introduction to the Special Issue on Regulating New and Emerging Technologies' (2016) 7(3) European Journal of Risk Regulation 469, 469; Mark Fenwick, Wulf A Kaal and Erik P M Vermeulen, 'Regulation Tomorrow: What Happens When Technology Is Faster Than the Law?' (2016) 6(3) American University Business Law Review 561, 567

853 van Asselt, Vos and Fox (n 851) 262; *L. B. Moses*, Law, Innovation and Technology, 5(1), 2013, 1–20, 8; *Fenwick/Kaal/Vermeulen*, American University Business Law Review, 6(3), 2016, 561–594, 574

854 David Collingridge, *The Social Control of Technology* (Frances Pinter (Publishers) Ltd; St. Martin's Press 1980) 19

855 Moses (n 849), 8; Elena Pariotti, 'Law, Uncertainty and Emerging Technologies' (2010) 62 Persona & Derecho 15, 18–19

856 United Nations General Assembly, 'A/CONF.151/26/Vol. I: Rio Declaration on Environment and Development' (New York 14 June 1992)

> [i]n order to protect the environment, the precautionary approach shall be widely applied by States according to their capabilities. Where there are threats of serious or irreversible damage, lack of full scientific certainty shall not be used as a reason for postponing cost-effective measures to prevent environmental degradation.

Some criticize the precautionary principle for being "innovation-deterring" and incoherent, as it does not provide a clear principle on how to make decisions in uncertainty.[857] Nevertheless, innovations that have the potential to cause irreversible damage are, in the majority of cases, not wholly beneficial. Thus, the implementation of precautionary measures to avert irreversible damage does not impede the advancement of beneficial technological development. The precautionary principle is particularly useful in situations where fundamental aspects such as environmental protection or human rights are at stake. In consideration of the MASS aspects, however, none of these factors is of critical importance. Furthermore, MASS are already subject to regulation, as ships are generally governed by the applicable legal framework. It thus follows that MASS will not commence large-scale operations until a suitable legal framework is established. It can therefore be concluded that the risks associated with unregulated MASS are not a significant concern, and that the precautionary principle is not a relevant approach in this context.

As an alternative, flexible regulations can be adopted.[858] Such regulations can prevent a lock-in of premature state of the art and mirror technological advances by allowing for flexible changes.[859] A co-evolution of law and technology is promoted by dynamic and responsive regulation. Ever since, the

857 Ryan Hagemann, Jennifer Huddelston Skees and Adam Thierer, 'Soft Law for Hard Law Problems: The Governance of Emerging Technologies in an Uncertain Future' (2018) 17(1) Colorado Technical Law Journal 37, 56; Adam Thierer, 'How Attitudes about Risk & Failure Affect Innovation on Either Side of the Atlantic' (19 June 2015) <https://readplaintext.com/how-attitudes-about-risk-failure-affect-innovation-on-either-side-of-the-atlantic-b5f0f41c3466> accessed 16 February 2024

858 Moses (n 849), 8; Hein Kötz, 'Rechtsvereinheitlichung – Nutzen, Kosten, Methoden, Ziele' (1986) 50(1–2) The Rabel Journal of Comparative and International Private Law 1, 12

859 Bartlett (n 521), 89; Gregory N Mandel, 'Legal Evolution in Response to Technological Change' in Roger Brownsword, Eloise Scotford and Karen Yeung (eds), *The Oxford Handbook of Law, Regulation and Technology* (Oxford handbooks, First edition. Oxford University Press 2017) 243; Abbott (n 852), 330; Roger Brownsword, 'So What Does the World Need Now? Reflections on Regulating Technologies' in Roger Brownsword and Karen Yeung (eds), *Regulating Technologies: Legal Futures, Regulatory Frames and Technological Fixes* (Hart 2008) 27; Petrig (n 416) 133; Leenes (n 849) 13; Hagemann, Huddelston Skees and Thierer (n 857) 60

regulator reacted upon technological innovation and had to ensure regulatory connection.[860] The new challenge, however, lies in ever faster moving innovation cycles making it more difficult for the regulator to keep pace with the technological development.[861] The rapidness of innovation cycles is illustrated by the research projects presented above going back to 2013.[862] Within 10–11 years, the projects developed full-scale demonstrators and promising business models. Thus, a new level of flexibility is needed for emerging technologies. To summarize, the regulation for MASS should be flexible and easily amendable to reflect subsequent technological developments.

However, a regulatory framework that is excessively flexible may create uncertainty about the legal regime, which could discourage investment.[863] Therefore, legal certainty and predictability are as important as flexibility.[864] This holds especially true for MASS as its development necessitates significant financial investments.[865] As ships have long life-cycles, adapting vessels to new regulations is particularly demanding. The regulatory framework must therefore strike a balance between certainty and flexibility. Regulators are thus faced with the challenge of not being too early to regulate, so as not to stifle innovation, but not too late, so that problems arise from the lack of regulation.[866] However, an early and predictable regulatory framework facilitates development because development goals can be set.[867]

Goal-based regulations offer a balance between flexibility and predictability.[868] Unlike prescriptive rules, they focus on outlining principles or

---

860 Brownsword (n 859) 26

861 Nitin Agarwala, 'Role of policy framework for disruptive technologies in the maritime domain' (2022) 14(1) Australian Journal of Maritime & Ocean Affairs 1, 7; Fenwick, Kaal and Vermeulen (n 852), 576–577; Hagemann, Huddelston Skees and Thierer (n 857), 69

862 Ørnulf J Rødseth, 'Autonomous Ship in Activities Norway' (2023) 18(4) The Journal of Ocean Technology 45, 51

863 Department for Transport, 'Future of transport regulatory review: Maritime Autonomy and Remote Operations; Final Impact Assessment' (n 829) 13; Karlis (n 164) 126

864 Tunfors (n 489) 57; Abbott (n 852), 338; Rodriguez Delgado (n 771), 505; Petrig (n 416) 132

865 Andrew Tettenborn, 'Codification – best left to states or to someone else?' in Justyna Nawrot and Zuzanna Pepłowska-Dąbrowska (eds), *Codification of maritime law: Challenges, possibilities and experience* (Maritime and transport law library. Informa Law from Routledge 2020) 51

866 Fenwick, Kaal and Vermeulen (n 852) 571–572

867 Knut Blind, Sören S Petersen and Cesare A Riillo, 'The impact of standards and regulation on innovation in uncertain markets' (2017) 46(1) Research Policy 249, 258

868 Espen Engtrø, 'The implementation and application of the International Code for Ships Operating in Polar Waters (Polar Code): Evaluations and considerations addressing this function-based regulation's effect on safety and emergency preparedness concerning Arctic shipping' (PhD thesis, University of Stavanger 2021) 75; Karisma Karisma, 'A Pragmatic

goals without specifying implementation means.[869] This allows innovative approaches to achieve results traditionally attained through established technology.[870] Others describes this form of regulation as technology neutral[871] or principle-based.[872] This regulatory instrument is already used and positive experiences could be made. However, there are challenges to this form of regulation. For example, it is difficult to develop concrete industry standards that lead to the achievement of the goals set. This is particularly relevant for sectors that rely on interoperability such as the shipping sector. The regulation of the bill of lading is an example of regulation that is open to technology, but has so far found little application in practice. In 2013, the German Commercial Code was amended by § 516 (2) allowing for an electronic bill of lading. Later, other regulatory regimes were prepared for the use of electronic documents.[873] However, as of today, only 5% of the stakeholders have transitioned to electronic bills of lading.[874] The low prevalence of digital certificates is due to the lack of universal interoperability among electronic file formats. No entity has sufficient market power to establish a standardized solution among ports, ship operators, cargo managers, and logistics companies. Instead, multiple parallel systems exist. If goal-based regulations are adopted without sufficiently detailed technical guidelines and measures ensuring interoperability, MASS could suffer the same fate.

As previously mentioned, a significant challenge in technology regulation stems from the absence of well-defined and clear objectives for the regulation. Engaging subject matter experts can maximize the utilization of existing knowledge to formulate regulations and ensure that regulations are based on

---

Regulatory Framework for Artificial Intelligence' in Ivan Giannoccaro and Pardis M Tehrani (eds), *Regulatory Aspects of Artificial Intelligence on Blockchain* (Advances in Computational Intelligence and Robotics. IGI Global 2022) 24

869 Ntovas (n 675) 231–232

870 MSC, IMO, 'MSC.1/Circ.1394/Rev.2: Generic Guidelines for Developing IMO Goal-based Standards' (London 8 July 2019) 5

871 Brownsword and Goodwin (n 850) 65; Iván Székely, Máté Dániel Szabó and Beatrix Vissy, 'Regulating the future? Law, ethics, and emerging technologies' (2011) 9(3) Journal of Information, Communication and Ethics in Society 180, 183

872 Gary E Marchant, 'The Growing Gap Between Emerging Technologies and the Law' in Gary E Marchant, Braden R Allenby and Joseph R Herkert (eds), *The Growing Gap Between Emerging Technologies and Legal-Ethical Oversight* (Springer Science and Business Media B.V. 2011) 30; Karisma (n 868) 24

873 David Saive, 'Die Zukunft der Beförderungsdokumente' [2023] Recht der Transportwirtschaft 132, 134

874 BIMCO, 'Electronic Bills of Lading' (17 January 2023) <https://www.bimco.org/insights-and-information/general-information/20230117-ebl> accessed 16 February 2024

the most comprehensive knowledge possible. The more knowledge the regulator has, the more effective regulation will be.[875] Involving experts offers several benefits: they can analyze potential threats posed by new technologies, prevent excessive restrictions on technological advancement through regulation, and ultimately contribute to the acceptance of regulations by stakeholders. Additionally, the engagement of technical experts strengthens the connection between regulation and technology.

As of today, there is no specific international regulation addressing MASS. However, the development of MASS would be significantly facilitated if there were a regulatory framework in place. Several projects are well advanced, and ships could be in service within the next 5 years.[876] Therefore, it is crucial to establish the regulatory framework as soon as possible, at the latest within the next 5 years.

The preceding legal analysis has revealed a noteworthy correlation between the GAIRAS conventions and UNCLOS. Although each instrument has its own specific scope of application, particular terms such as 'master' and 'crew' are shared among several conventions. Furthermore, the conventions refer to each other and collectively govern the shipping industry. The present framework is highly interconnected. When revising the international framework to allow for MASS operations, the horizontal coherence of terms and concepts in the GARIAS conventions and UNCLOS should be maintained. Ensuring that one convention is interpreted in a way including MASS operations is not sufficient.

After having considered the 'when' and the 'how' of regulation, the 'where' needs to be addressed. The present regulatory framework for shipping is almost globally applicable. This reflects the need of the shipping sector, as a global industry, of globally harmonized regulations.[877]

Cross-border coherency is necessary for MASS to enable international operations and to ensure that investments can be recuperated. Ship certificates

875 Abbott (n 852) 336

876 Ziaul H Munim and others, 'Autonomous ships for container shipping in the Arctic routes' (2022) 27(1) Journal of Marine Science and Technology 320, 331

877 United Law Commission on International Trade Law, 'A/CN.9/407 – Report of the Workin Group on Electronic Data Interchange (EDI) on the Work of its 29th Session' (Vienna 16.03.01995) 30; Shi (n 744) 305; Wolfrum, 'Wolfrum 1999' (n 327) 232; Aldo Chircop, 'The quest for universality and uniformity: theory and practice of international maritime regulation' in Jason Chuah (ed), *Research handbook on maritime law and regulation* (Research Handbooks in Private and Commercial Law series. Edward Elgar Publishing 2019) 121; Proshanto K Mukherjee, *Maritime Legislation* (WMU Publications 2002) 113; A. N Yiannopoulos, 'The Unification of Private Maritime Law by International Conventions' (1965) 30(2) Law and Contemporary Problems 370, 371–372

issued by flag states should be accepted by port and coastal states and coastal states should be prevented from adopting more stringent regulations than what is agreed upon internationally. Port states, however, maintain their exclusive jurisdiction over all vessels calling their ports. It is therefore frequently called for a global and uniform legal framework for MASS.[878]

Global uniform rules are not only demanded by the shipping industry, but also states pursue international coordinated approaches towards MASS. International approaches are particularly prone to matters where national responses have a global impact,[879] e.g. registration of MASS that do not ensure a high level of safety. Such MASS could endanger the safety at sea of all states. Thus, agreeing internationally on regulations that are more stringent is preferable. Moreover, international harmonized regulations facilitate international trade. Especially states with an important import and export industry advocate for a harmonized international approach.[880] This also applies to the shipping sector. Both, the ship building and ship supply industry are truly international and would benefit from harmonized standards for MASS. However, concerning both 'global' and 'uniform' there are counterarguments in the field of MASS regulation.

First, the international framework for MASS is not and does not need to be uniform. Uniformity in its strict sense means that two items have the same character or form.[881] Conveyed to the law, uniformity requires the adoption of exactly the same rules.[882] Although almost all states have ratified UNCLOS and the GAIRAS conventions, their national application varies, as shown by the example of the required minimum safe manning. Even if UNCLOS and the GAIRAS treaties may be considered uniform upon adoption, they have

878 Chris Horrocks, 'Thoughts on the Respective Role of Flag States and Port States' in Myron H Nordquist and John N Moore (eds), *Current maritime issues and the international maritime organization* (Martinus Nijhoff Publishers 1999) 191–192; Michael Kirby, 'The Fundamental Problem of Regulating Technology' (2009) 5(1) Indian Journal of Law and Technology 1, 18; Ringbom, *Ringbom 2008* (n 675) 10; Arthur Rosett, 'Unification, Harmonization, Restatement, Codification, and Reform in International Commercial Law' (1992) 40(3) The American Journal of Comparative Law 683, 688; Mukherjee (n 877) 113

879 Gary E Marchant and Brad Allenby, 'Soft law: New tools for governing emerging technologies' (2017) 73(2) Bulletin of the Atomic Scientists 108, 109

880 ibid

881 Oxford English Dictionary, 'uniformity, n'. 1.a. <https://www.oed.com/dictionary/uniformity_n?tab=meaning_and_use#16648235> accessed 16 February 2024

882 Martin Gebauer and Felix Berner, 'Unification and Harmonization of Laws' in Anne Peters (ed), *Max Planck Encyclopedia of Public International Law* (MPEPIL) (Oxford University Press) 4

lost their uniform character due to diverting national implementations and interpretations.[883] Therefore, the existing legal regime lacks uniformity. Rather than uniform, the legal framework is harmonized.

According to the Oxford English Dictionary, 'harmony' means the combination of different parts so that they form a consistent whole.[884] A consistent whole does not necessarily require that the individual parts interact with each other in a way that is perceived as pleasing. Rather, it is sufficient if the individual elements are combined constructively. This differentiation of the term harmony is also reflected in the music-theoretical understanding of the term. The theory of harmony does not only deal with discord and concord, but with the structure of the relationship between cords.[885]

This approach to 'harmony' can be transferred to the realm of law[886] and is prevalent in international law of the sea. Different national regulations are brought into a coherent whole, allowing ships to sail freely around the world. Neither UNCLOS, STCW nor SOLAS provide concrete rules, which are directly applicable. Instead, national implementation is required and varies. The principle of mutual recognition and the possibility of legal proceedings to clarify ambiguities ensure that the different national rules are compatible, i.e. that they harmonize with each other. Extending the current legal framework to MASS will result in a harmonized legal framework for MASS. These mechanisms ensure that the different national legal requirements are coordinated and do not hamper international shipping. To summarize, MASS require a harmonized legal framework.

Second, the legal framework for MASS does not need to be global. The call for a global legal framework stems from the fact that the current legal framework is applied globally. However, MASS projects are concentrated in Northern and Western Europe and East Asia. In other parts of the world, commercial MASS projects are less advanced. Autonomous deep sea voyages are not conceivable within a midterm perspective although the safety of transoceanic voyages was proven by the trials performed in the context of the MEGURI 2040 project in Japan and in South Korea.[887] Instead, MASS will be employed on

883 ibid 25

884 Oxford English Dictionary, 'harmony, n'. 1.a. <https://www.oed.com/dictionary/harmony_n?tab=meaning_and_use#2081960> accessed 16 February 2024

885 Peter Rummenhöller, 'Harmonielehre' in Laurenz Lütteken (ed), *Musik in Geschichte und Gegenwart* (RILM, Bärenreiter, Metzler 2016)

886 Martin Boodman, 'The Myth of Harmonization of Laws' (1991) 39(4) The American Journal of Comparative Law 699, 701

887 Pekic (n 126)

short-sea shipping routes.[888] The advantages of short-sea shipping compared to deep-sea voyages for MASS have been demonstrated above. Compelling factors are regular maintenance possibilities during port calls, limited range of propulsion systems which are not maintenance intense, and particularly economic impacts of 24/7 operations, economically beneficial smaller vessels and fleet solutions, as well as a higher degree of flexibility.[889] Eventually, MASS shall contribute to a modal shift from road to water transport.[890] This shift is particularly beneficial for shorter distances within a specific region, making the deployment of MASS on short-sea shipping routes particularly viable. Although the regulatory framework for conventional shipping is global, the regulatory framework for MASS could initially be limited to certain regions. However, it should be possible to extend the scope of the MASS framework to ensure flexibility in terms of geographical coverage.

In summary, the regulatory framework should be formed upon comprehensive knowledge about MASS while refraining from impeding technical innovation, while also ensuring legal certainty and predictability. The regulations could be formulated in a goal-based manner to balance flexibility and certainty. The framework should be established promptly and guarantee the integration of MASS within the current shipping framework. For this reason, a horizontal and coherent approach is crucial. The regulation does not need to be global; rather harmonization at regional level would be sufficient to meet the needs of MASS in the medium term.

So far, the requirements for 'regulation' were discussed. Regulation, however, does not necessarily mean legal regulation. Unlike other innovative technologies like nano technologies or generative artificial intelligence, which cannot be based on an existing legal framework, MASS will be integrated into the existing legal framework for international shipping. For the integration of MASS in this framework, legal regulation is necessary. The following section situates legal regulation within the wider framework of regulation in general and subsequently concentrates soft law as a form of legal regulation explored more comprehensively in the subsequent sections.

888 Nordahl and others (n 121) 19; Colella and others (n 154) 5

889 Rødseth and others (n 153) 359

890 COM(2021) 812 final – Proposal for a Regulation of the European Parliament and of the Council on Union guidelines for the development of the trans-European transport network, amending Regulation (EU) 2021/1153 and Regulation (EU) No 913/2010 and repealing Regulation (EU) 1315/2013 14 December 2021 (European Commission) 1

5.2 Law and Regulation

The meaning of "regulation" is ambiguous and scholars provide differing definitions.[891] However, scholars agree that regulation is more than law. In its broadest meaning, regulation encompasses all modes of behavioral control. Black defines regulation as

> the sustained and focused attempt to alter the behaviour of others according to defined standards or purposes with the intention of producing a broadly identified outcome or outcomes, which may involve mechanisms of standard-setting, information-gathering and behaviour-modification.[892]

This wide range of instruments available to change the behavior of others can be classified according to the four modalities of regulation developed by Lessing. Besides law, i.e. legal regulation, other forms of regulation such as social regulation, market regulation, and regulation by architecture or, for information systems, by code, can be used to affect people's behavior.[893] Social regulation includes all norms and social conventions we feel bound by. Market regulation addresses the economic force of pricing to alter other's behavior. Regulation by architecture or code refers to the external physical and technical constraints that apply to a given situation.[894] Legal regulation encompasses all obligations that may result in sanctions by the legal system if breached.[895]

As argued above, this study is concerned with legal regulation as MASS shall be integrated in the existing legal framework for international shipping. Law is the tool of the legal system to impose obligations, ensure their enforcement, and impose sanctions in case of breach.

However, as with regulation, the concrete scope of law is discussed by scholars. Already Plato posed the question of "What is law?" in his Minos.[896] One rather broad definition of law is the one presented by Hermann Kantorowicz.

---

891 Brownsword and Goodwin (n 850) 25; Blind, Petersen and Riillo (n 867) 250; Moses (n 849) 4

892 Julia Black, 'Critial Reflections on Regulation' (2002) 27 Australian Journal of Legal Philosophy 1, 26

893 Lawrence Lessing, *Code and other laws of cyberspace* (Basic Books 1999) 88

894 ibid 87

895 ibid 89

896 Joachim Dalfen, *Platon Minos; Übersetzung und Kommentar* (Vandenhoeck & Ruprecht 2009) 13

According to him, law is "a body of social rules prescribing external conduct and considered justiciable".[897]

'Justiciable' means in this context that the rule can be applied by a judicial organ, an authority recognized by the group to which the rule applies.[898] For international shipping, the relevant body of rules lies within international law. Although there is no 'world court' or other institution recognized by all states, some rules acquire legal significance and are relevant to the relation between states and other subjects of international law. Such rules are encompassed by international law.[899] Moreover, law can originate from regional or supranational sources. Although this definition of law may narrow its scope, the ultimate boundaries of law remain vague.

Despite their justifiability, legal rules can be characterized as soft or hard, formal or informal, being binding or non-binding, enforceable or non-enforceable, effective or ineffective. This study is not limited to a specific type of law. Instead, it takes a functional approach and identifies the most appropriate solution based on the criteria outlined below. This approach is transferred from transnational law,[900] a term coined by Philip C. Jessup in 1956 as including all laws regulating a transborder situation irrespective of their origin and legal character.[901]

Identifying the origin of a legal regulation presents little challenge. However, categorizing it as 'soft', 'informal', or 'non-binding' proves more difficult due to the vagueness of these terms. As soft law is especially relevant for international relations, the following section aims to shed light on the concept of soft law and its understanding as applied in this study. The reasons why states choose soft law solutions instead of hard law solutions will be examined.

The concept of soft law appears contradictory as the term 'soft' implies informality and non-bindingness, whereas 'law', according to Lessing and Kantorowicz, denotes enforceability by the legal system. This viewpoint is prevalent among legal positivists. From a positivist perspective, soft law cannot amount to 'law'. A norm is either 'law' or not law at all. There are no nuances in the characterization as law.[902] For state conduct to be deemed a legal act, i.e. falling

---

897 Hermann Kantorowicz and A. H Campbell (eds), *The definition of Law* (Octagon Books 1980) 79

898 ibid

899 Rüdiger Wolfrum, 'International Law' in Anne Peters (ed), *Max Planck Encyclopedia of Public International Law* (MPEPIL) (Oxford University Press) 1

900 Gralf-Peter Calliess, 'Law, Transnational' (2010) 06(8) CLPE Research Paper Series 2, 3

901 Philip C Jessup, *Transnational law* (Storrs lectures on jurisprudence [1956], Yale University Press 1956) 2

902 Dinah Shelton, 'Soft Law' in David Armstrong and others (eds), *Routledge Handbook of International Law* (Routledge international handbooks. Routledge 2009) 78; Jaye Ellis,

under the scope of law, its legal consequences must stem directly from the will of the subject who adopted the act.[903] All conduct whose legal effect cannot be traced back to its originator's will is considered a legal fact rather than law. As will be shown below, the creator of soft law, however, had the converse will: direct legal effect should be prevented. From a positivist perspective, therefore, soft law cannot be considered as law. Nonetheless, it is a legal fact that can be significant for the application of another legal act.[904]

The positivist perspective upholds a highly formal comprehension of the concept of law. Especially in international law, a rigidly formal separation of hard legal provisions and soft non-legal provisions does not seem to be appropriate, as the discussion below will illustrate. The practical significance of legally non-binding instruments in international relations increased latest since 2001.[905] As Boyle puts it "If the real-world phenomenon of non-binding soft law does not fit the 'theory of the legal act' it is probably time to change the theory".[906]

This work adopts a pragmatic approach as reflected in the presented definition of 'law'. The qualification of a certain conduct as law should not only be determined by its legal binding effect, but also by its functional capacity to influence behavior and to be applied in judicial bodies. Now that the general possibility of soft law has been established, this concept will be explored more thoroughly. The first step is to clarify the terms of soft law, informal law, and non-binding law. Secondly, the understanding of soft law used in this study will be defined, followed by an assessment of why states opt for soft law solutions.

5.2.1 *Soft Law*

Soft law includes all norms not formally legally binding, though having some form of normative impact.[907] However, the scope is limited here to acts

'Shades of Grey: Soft Law and the Validity of Public International Law' (2012) 25(2) Leiden Journal of International Law 313, 333; Jan Klabbers, 'The Redundancy of Soft Law' (1996) 65 Nordic Journal of International Law 167, 168

903 Jean d'Aspermont, 'Softness in International Law: A Self-Serving Quest for New Legal Materials' (2008) 19(5) European Journal of International Law 1075, 1079

904 Prosper Weil, 'Towards Relative Normativity in International Law?' (1983) 77(3) The American Journal of International Law 413, 415

905 Boyle, 'Boyle 2018' (n 471) 123–124

906 ibid 120

907 Emily Crawford, *Non-binding Norms in International Humanitarian Law: Efficacy, legitimacy, and legality* (Oxford monographs in international humanitarian and criminal law, First edition, Oxford University Press 2021) 11; Shelton, 'Shelton 2009' (n 902) 69; Daniel Thürer, 'Soft Law' in Anne Peters (ed), *Max Planck Encyclopedia of Public International Law* (MPEPIL) (Oxford University Press) 8; Andrew T Guzmán and Timothy Meyer, 'International Soft

promulgated by states or other subjects of international law. Thus, provisions developed by private stakeholders are excluded.[908] Some scholars present the legal binding effect on a spectrum, ranging from complete legal obligation to mere political declaration.[909] Since international law falls short of national law in terms of enforceability, even when all available enforcement mechanisms have been considered,[910] the legal weight of a norm depends on several factors. A continuum approach is suitable for considering these variations.

However, other definitions of soft law are found in literature,[911] which results in an amorphous and confusing situation about the scope of soft law.[912] Although a comprehensive analysis of available definitions is beyond the scope of this study, a second, often applied understanding shall be introduced briefly. Some scholars consider vaguely worded norms as 'soft law'.[913] This understanding results in labelling formally binding provisions such as Article 2(1) of the International Covenant on Civil and Political Rights[914] as soft law due to their vague wording.[915]

Law' (2011) 2(1) The Journal of Legal Analysis 171, 173; Charlotte Ku, *International Law, International Relations, and Global Governance* (Routledge 2012) 156; Klabbers, 'Klabbers 1996' (n 902) 168; Matthias Knauff, *Der Regelungsverbund: Recht und Soft Law im Mehrebenensystem* (Zugl.: Würzburg, Univ. Habil.-Schr. 2009–2010. Ius Publicum vol 193, Mohr Siebeck 2010) 228; Boyle, 'Boyle 2018' (n 471) 121 arguing that soft law has some binding force, though not the same as hard law: Hagemann, Huddelston Skees and Thierer (n 857) 45

908 Richard R Baxter, 'International Law in "Her Infinite Variety"' (1980) 29(4) The International and Comparative Law Quarterly 549, 551; Christine Chinkin, 'The Challenge of Soft Law: Development and Change in International Law' (1989) 38(4) International and Comparative Law Quarterly 850, 852

909 Guzmán and Meyer (n 907) 173; Gregory C Shaffer and Mark A Pollack, 'Hard vs. Soft Law: Alternatives, Complements and Antagonists in International Governance' (2010) 94 Minnesota Law Review 706, 716; Gunther F Handl and others, 'A Hard Look at Soft Law' [1988] Proceedings of the Annual Meeting (American Society of International Law) 371, 376; Kenneth W Abbott and Duncan Snidal, 'Hard and Soft Law in International Governance' (2000) 54(3) International Organization 421, 422; Fabien Terpan, 'Soft Law in the European Union-The Changing Nature of EU Law' (2015) 21(1) European Law Journal 68, 73

910 Guzmán and Meyer (n 907) 182

911 Oana A Stefan and others, 'EU Soft Law in the EU Legal Order: A Literature Review' [2019] SSRN Journal, 5–8; Shaffer and Pollack (n 909) 712–715

912 Hagemann, Huddelston Skees and Thierer (n 857) 44; Nigel D White, 'Lawmaking' in Jacob K Cogan, Ian Hurd and Ian Johnstone (eds), *The Oxford handbook of international organizations* (Oxford University Press 2017) 576; Handl and others (n 909) 372; Anthony Aust, 'Alternatives to Treaty-Making: MoUs as Political Commitments' in Duncan B Hollis (ed), *The Oxford Guide to Treaties* (Oxford University Press 2012) 67

913 Weil (n 904) 414; Abbott and Snidal (n 909) 422

914 Article 2(1): "Each State Party to the present Covenant undertakes to respect and to ensure to all individuals within its territory and subject to its jurisdiction the rights recognized in the present Covenant […]" International Covenant on Civil and Political Rights, No. 14668 19 December 1966

915 Shelton, 'Shelton 2009' (n 902) 69

Eventually, the term informal law appears in the context of soft law. Petring defines informal law as instruments that regulate a situation in a general-abstract manner and have normative value. They are adopted by states or international organizations, but do not belong to the recognized sources of international law laid down in Article 38(1) of the Statute of the ICJ.[916] Aust offers a concise definition of informal law and includes all instruments adopted between state parties that are not considered a treaty since they are not intended to be legally binding.[917] Considering the understanding of soft law applied here, it encompasses those rules labeled as 'informal law' by Petring and Aust.

Now, the issue of why states opt for soft law solutions as opposed to hard law in order to structure their international relations will be examined. One contributing factor is the substantial normative value of soft law.

Several examples from international law serve as proof of the legal significance of soft law.[918] Soft law can be used to guide the interpretation of hard law as stipulated by Article 31(3)(a) of the VCLT.[919] In this role, soft law guiding the interpretation of international hard law is binding upon national courts.[920] The same holds true for Article 31(3)(c) of the VCLT, including any rule of international law applicable in the relations between the parties to the scope of authentic materials for interpretation. Here likewise, soft law is included.[921]

UNCLOS even goes a step further. As illustrated above, the reference to GAIRAS includes soft law instruments, at least if unanimously adopted by the IMO.[922] GAIRAS are not only used to support the obligations outlined in the UNCLOS. Compliance with the obligations set out in the GAIRAS conventions is mandatory for all UNCLOS member states. From a doctrinal perspective, it is significant to acknowledge that UNCLOS does not elevate the non-binding GAIRAS rules to binding obligations. Instead, UNCLOS mandates

916 Petrig (n 416) 118

917 Anthony Aust, 'The Theory and Practice of Informal International Instruments' (1986) 35(4) The International and Comparative Law Quarterly 787, 788

918 Crawford (n 907) 181–217; Knauff (n 907) 259

919 Alan Boyle, 'The Choice of a Treaty' in Simon Chesterman and others (eds), *The Oxford Handbook of United Nations Treaties* (Oxford University Press 2019) 113; Handl and others (n 909) 381; Shelton, 'Shelton 2009' (n 902) 73; United Nations General Assembly, 'A/CN.4/L.907 – Subsequent agreements and subsequent practice in relation to the interpretation of treaties' (n 453) Conclusion 10, para. 1

920 Dieter Schwampe, 'Rechtsetzung durch die International Maritime Organisation unter der Lupe – Die Unified Interpretations zur unbeschränkten Haftung nach IMO Übereinkommen' [2022] Recht der Transportwirtschaft 26, 28

921 Dörr (n 448) 100; Boyle, 'Boyle 2018' (n 471) 127

922 Frenzel (n 335) 162; Wolfrum, 'Wolfrum 1999' (n 327) 230

that non-binding obligations must be considered while fulfilling the duties UNCLOS imposes.[923]

Even without being 'generally accepted', IMO instruments effectively govern international shipping. Especially interpretation guidelines and codes are considered by national administrations when performing flag and port state jurisdiction.[924] This can be reasoned by the high level of details the IMO instruments provide and the fact that states have sufficient opportunities to take part in the development process. Thus, the IMO acts reflect the state's interests.

Soft law is also important on the enforcement level as both, international courts[925] and national courts,[926] refer to soft law as an interpretative guidance to international obligations. Two examples shall be illustrated here.

In its Advisory Opinion on Legal Consequences of the Construction of a Wall in the Occupied Palestinian Territory, the ICJ had to identify the relevant rules and principles of international law to assess the legality of the measures in question. For this purpose, the ICJ considered the Charter of the United Nations, customary international law and the resolutions adopted by the UN General Assembly.[927] This is significant, as resolutions adopted by the UN General Assembly are not legally binding.[928] Nevertheless, the court mentioned them in the same breath as customary international law and the Charter of the United Nations as recognized sources of international law. Similarly, the ICJ's Whaling judgment refers to resolutions adopted by the International Whaling Commission as relevant material for the interpretation of the convention in question, although these resolutions are likewise not legally binding.[929]

In addition, national courts refer to international soft law to ascertain the interpretation of binding international treaties. The German Federal Constitutional Court has considered the significance of international soft law in interpreting national law on several occasions. It has determined that soft law must be taken into account and that a violation of soft law indicates a violation of

923 Korseberg (n 331) 805

924 Cleopatra E Henry, *The carriage of dangerous goods by sea: The role of the International Maritime Organization in international legislation* (St. Martin's Press 1985) 82; Ilg (n 230) 60; Petrig (n 416) 120

925 Boyle, 'Boyle 2019' (n 919) 105; Klabbers, 'Klabbers 1996' (n 902) 174; Chinkin (n 908) 865

926 Handl and others (n 909) 389–390

927 *International Court of Justice 2004* (n 471) 86

928 Christian Tomuschat, 'United Nations, General Assembly' in Anne Peters (ed), *Max Planck Encyclopedia of Public International Law* (MPEPIL) (Oxford University Press) 22

929 *Whaling in the Antarctic* [2014] [2014] ICJ Reports 226 (International Court of Justice) 46

national law.[930] However, there is no obligation to comply.[931] Impetus for the decision were human right matters. Later, however, the question became virulent with respect to the Convention on the Rights of Persons with Disabilities. As of today, international environmental soft law is also relevant to the interpretation of implementing national law.[932]

The normative weight of soft law is increased by the fact that soft law obligations can be enforced in court. Consent to soft law creates a legitimate expectation that the state will comply with those soft law obligations. If, contrary to expectations, the state fails to do so, other states can invoke the principles of estoppel and good faith to challenge the violation in court.[933] Soft law, thus, contributes to shaping expectations about future state conduct.[934] In the Nuclear Tests Cases, the ICJ confirmed that unilateral non-binding declarations might give rise to a legitimate expectation of compliance.[935] Australia's request to ban France from performing future nuclear tests in the South Pacific has been met, as France has declared that it will cease to conduct such tests. Although the declarations were not legally binding and France could not prove its intention to cease nuclear testing, the ICJ considered it certain that there would be no further tests and, therefore, the justification for Australia's action had ceased to exist.

In brief, soft law encompasses all provisions that are not formally legally binding, but still hold normative value. This value is derived from Article 31(3)(a), (c) of the VCLT, the reference to GAIRAS in UNCLOS, their meticulous details, reflection of the parties' interests, and the consideration they receive in court. The impact of soft law's normative value is reflected in the fact that states declare reservations to soft law instruments.[936]

The normative value of soft law is just one aspect of the reasoning behind states' preference for using soft law instead of hard law instruments. While

930 *Beschluss der 2. Kammer des Zweiten Senats* (2007) 2 BvR 939/07 15 (The Federal Constitutional Court); *Jugendstrafvollzug* (2006) 2 BvR 1673/04; 2 BvR 2404/04 63 (The Federal Constitutional Court)

931 *UN-Behindertenrechtskonvention* (2016) 1 BvL 8/15 90 (The Federal Constitutional Court)

932 Wolfgang Durner, 'Umweltvölkerrecht' in Martin Beckmann and others (eds), *Umweltrecht: Kommentar* (September 2023, 102. supplement. C.H. Beck 2023) 37

933 Anthony Aust, *Modern treaty law and practice* (3. ed. Cambridge University Press 2013) 51; Thürer (n 907) 27

934 Guzmán and Meyer (n 907) 175

935 *Nuclear Tests Case New Zealand v. France* (1974) 1974 ICJ Reports 457 46 (International Court of Justice); *Nuclear Tests Case Australia v. France* (1974) 1974 ICJ Reports 253 43 (International Court of Justice)

936 Handl and others (n 909), 387; United Nations General Assembly, 'Official Record 29th Session, Agenda Item 51' (New York 12 December 1974) 51; Chinkin (n 908) 860

there are ranges of factors that can enhance the legal force of soft law, it will never have the legal force of a formally binding hard law instrument. Additional reasons for favoring soft law will be explored below.

The main advantage of soft law is that it is not legally binding. Even though this may seem contradictory at first glance, the specific characteristics of international law may clarify why the absence of formal legal binding force is the fundamental strength of soft law.

As private law contracts, international agreements are based on consensus. During negotiations at the international level, the prospect of a non-binding agreement makes it easier to reach a consensus. Challenges can be addressed collectively without renouncing the state's freedom to act,[937] thus states are more likely to agree if they maintain flexibility.[938] Moreover, states can participate internationally without the need to defend internationally binding legal obligations domestically.[939] This approach allows states to address new fields with international regulation and to test international cooperation on a certain issue.

As soft law is not formally binding, states can "withdraw" from the agreement whenever considered beneficial. This advantage of soft law holds particularly true for soft law implementing regulations that are more demanding. Nevertheless, it is important to acknowledge that multilateral negotiations always involve the challenge of reaching a consensus, as several different economic and legal situations need to be consolidated.[940] Negotiating a bilateral hard law agreement may prove less arduous than a multilateral soft law agreement.

A differing readiness for legalization of a certain matter among states presents another challenge to negotiations.[941] Consequently, the choice is between a soft law agreement and no agreement at all.[942] In such circumstances, soft law agreements can assist in overcoming seemingly insurmountable economic and political disparities.[943] For the purpose of harmonization and global applicability, it is preferable to have a soft law agreement that is adopted by a larger number of states, rather than a hard law agreement that is only agreed upon

---

937 Boyle, 'Boyle 2018' (n 471) 122

938 Shaffer and Pollack (n 909) 736; Dinah Shelton, 'Commitment and Compliance: The Role of Non-Binding Norms in the International Legal System' in Dinah Shelton (ed), *Commitment and Compliance: The Role of Non-binding Norms in the International Legal System* (Oxford University Press 2003) 13

939 Boyle, 'Boyle 2019' (n 919) 102

940 Cassese and others (n 437) 202

941 Abbott and Snidal (n 909) 445

942 Handl and others (n 909) 391; Shelton, 'Shelton 2009' (n 902) 78; Knauff (n 907) 261

943 Handl and others (n 909) 376

by a small group of states. For international shipping law the IMO provides an established forum for discussion and the development of consensual agreements. The negotiation process at the IMO demonstrates that the development of soft law takes considerably less time than the negotiation of an instrument that may become hard law.

For soft law negotiations, there is no mandatory procedure to follow.[944] This approach offers the opportunity to involve non-state participants,[945] including industry stakeholders, which increases connection between law and technology as well as subsequent compliance.[946]

However, flexibility could also be considered as a disadvantage as the lack of formalism risks arbitrariness for soft law.[947] Particular attention should be drawn to the choice of non-state parties involved in the negotiation process. The IMO already involves non-governmental organizations in the law-making process. While there is a potential lack of transparency in the selection of participating stakeholders,[948] the open application process for consultative status with the IMO effectively addresses this risk.

In contrast, hard law instruments are subject to a more formal negotiation process, including the convening of diplomatic conferences. However, as soft law instruments are increasingly used as governance instruments, the negotiation process has become more complex and bears resemblance to that of hard law.[949] Particularly, the pre-law function of soft law leads to complex and lengthy negotiations, including detailed discussions on the wording. As states consider soft law to be increasingly binding and courts refer to soft law agreements more frequently, negotiations become more complex and detailed in proportion to the normative weight of such agreements. Negotiating the Global Compact for Migration under the auspices of the UN, a soft law agreement, took more than two years.[950] Nevertheless, the soft law negotiation process remains more flexible and expedient than the hard law negotiation process.

944 Knauff (n 907) 251

945 Gary E Marchant, 'Addressing the Pacing Problem' in Gary E Marchant, Braden R Allenby and Joseph R Herkert (eds), *The Growing Gap Between Emerging Technologies and Legal-Ethical Oversight* (Springer Science and Business Media B.V. 2011) 203

946 Guzmán and Meyer (n 907), 191; Hagemann, Huddelston Skees and Thierer (n 857) 84; Pariotti (n 855) 25

947 Jan Klabbers, 'The Undesirability of Soft Law' (1998) 67 Nordic Journal of International Law 381, 391

948 Hagemann, Huddelston Skees and Thierer (n 857) 107

949 Knauff (n 907) 251–252

950 Maria Prietz, *Weiches Recht und normative Härtung: Eine Konzeptualisierung am Beispiel des UN-Migrationspaktes* (Jus Internationale et Europaeum vol 200, 1st edn, Mohr Siebeck 2023) 49

For soft law, the negotiation process is also simplified at the national level. Public officials can negotiate on behalf of the states[951] and government involvement is not necessarily required.[952] Additionally, states may be more willing to agree to an instrument for which they cannot be held accountable domestically.[953] Soft law is thus a preferred instrument to address politically sensitive issues, as there is less national, parliamentary discourse.[954] Both reduces the bureaucratic costs and accelerates the negotiation process.[955] However, excluding national parliaments comes at the cost of legitimacy[956] and bears the risk of shifting lengthy discussions to the implementation phase.[957] Involving the legislature early can be advantageous in increasing public support for, and therefore compliance with, the international treaty in question. Finally, depending on the national reception of soft law, constitutional problems could arise if essential aspects are regulated in a way that bypasses the national legislator.[958]

After an agreement has been reached, ratification is not necessary for soft law.[959] Unlike hard law, a high threshold for entry into force does not hinder the commencement of legal value of soft law. Therefore, soft law can be applied directly after its adoption. However, soft law also needs to be implemented nationally, which can take as much time as the implementation of a hard law obligation.[960] Since national implementation is also necessary for hard law, the entire process from conclusion to legal effect is still lengthier for hard law compared to soft law.[961]

In brief, the process for soft law to come into force is accelerated compared to hard law due to smoother negotiations, no requirement for ratification and entry into force, and the absence of a registration obligation at the UN.

951 Guzmán and Meyer (n 907) 191
952 Knauff (n 907) 249
953 Boyle, 'Boyle 2018' (n 471) 123
954 Prietz (n 950) 52
955 Guzmán and Meyer (n 907) 191; Crawford (n 907) 25; Jack L Goldsmith and Eric A Posner, *The limits of international law* (1.th edn, Oxford University Press 2005) 94
956 Prietz (n 950) 55; Knauff (n 907) 254; Baxter (n 908) 554–555
957 Goldsmith and Posner (n 955) 92–94
958 Katharina Reiling, 'Die Anwendung des Grundsatzes der Völkerrechtsfreundlichkeit auf rechtsunverbindliche internationale Standards' [2018] Zeitschrift für ausländisches öffentliches Recht und Völkerrecht 311, 333
959 Alan Boyle, 'Some Reflections on the Relationship of Treaties and Soft Law' (1999) 48(4) The International and Comparative Law Quarterly 901, 904; Shelton, 'Shelton 2003' (n 938) 13
960 Henry (n 924) 82
961 Aust, 'Aust 1986' (n 917) 790; Knauff (n 907) 255

Moreover, soft law allows innovative and agile regulatory approaches, particularly suitable for innovative technologies as a regulatory target. In essence, soft law facilitates international cooperation among states without the necessity of justifying such actions at the national level. This is particularly pertinent in the context of politically sensitive issues and emerging topics. Soft law, therefore, provides a means of regulating matters that would otherwise remain unregulated at the international level.

Like the adoption process, amending soft law is less complex than amending hard law.[962] Although formal amendment procedures can be included in soft law, states are free to choose another procedure. Usually, amendments to soft law do not require a certain minimum number of participating states, which simplifies amendments to soft law.[963] Flexibility with the amendment procedure is not just beneficial for states, but also necessary for an effective regulation of emerging technologies.[964] Flexible amendments reduce the potential for prematurely fixed regulations and the lock-in of a particular technological solution.[965] Therefore, soft law instruments are the preferred tool to react upon the Collingridges dilemma.[966] The IMO Committees meet regularly which ensures constant discussion on urgent matters. Thus, the IMO is able to react spontaneously to developments and can adopt soft law instruments at short notice.

Additionally, flexibility in amending soft law enables to test different regulatory approaches.[967] As in a regulatory sandbox, different approaches can be tested and evaluated together with private stakeholders.[968] A co-evolution of technology and regulation is possible. This is particularly useful for the regulation of emerging technologies entailing unknown risks and consequences. As an example, sunset clauses allow to test a regulatory approach to innovative technology. Such clauses are easier to implement as soft law than with a hard law instrument. In the UK, for example, a regulatory sandbox was used

962 Aust, 'Aust 1986' (n 917) 792; Knauff (n 907) 253

963 Hagemann, Huddelston Skees and Thierer (n 857) 70; Boyle, 'Boyle 2019' (n 919) 102

964 Marchant, 'Marchant 2011' (n 945) 203

965 Hagemann, Huddelston Skees and Thierer (n 857) 97; Shelton, 'Shelton 2009' (n 902) 76; Shelton, 'Shelton 2003' (n 938) 13; Patricia Birnie, 'The Status of Environmental 'Soft Law': Trends and Examples with Special Focus on IMO Norms' in Henrik Ringbom (ed), *Competing norms in the law of marine environmental protection: Focus on ship safety and pollution prevention* (International environmental law and policy series vol 46, 1. publ. Kluwer Law International 1997) 39

966 Hagemann, Huddelston Skees and Thierer (n 857) 57

967 Prietz (n 950) 50

968 Fenwick, Kaal and Vermeulen (n 852) 591

to test different regulatory approaches to MASS.[969] Moreover, fintech industry and insurance services benefitted from regulatory sandboxes to test regulatory approaches.[970] Thus, states prefer soft law if a dynamic and agile regulation is required.

However, the flexibility of soft law does not come at zero costs. Goldsmith and Posner assert that hard law benefits significantly from the existence of standard rules in the VCLT. The regulation of various aspects of general interest, including the conclusion, interpretation, modification, and termination of a binding international treaty, effectively reduces transaction costs.[971] This argument is certainly valid. However, it should be noted that most of the provisions of the VCLT codify customary international law, so that these rules are also applicable to non-binding law. The benefits of default rules are thus not exclusive to hard law.

Ultimately, the absence of legal bindingness does not impair the enforcement phase. Since international law lacks coercive enforcement measures, the enforcement of international law cannot be as effective as that of national law anyway.[972] This implies that states are never truly locked-in to an agreement, not even into a formally binding hard law treaty.[973]

International law has developed several enforcement measures such as monitoring, surveillance, dispute settlement, and sanctions.[974] Additionally, the three R's, reciprocity, reputation, and retaliation, contribute to the enforcement of international law.[975] These enforcement mechanisms can be combined and included into agreements despite their characterization as binding or non-binding. In multilateral agreements, reciprocity is only relevant if the obligations included represent an assimilation of bilateral reciprocal obligations. Otherwise, it is highly improbable for a state to terminate its cooperative behavior in response to a treaty violation by another state.[976] Due to the unsuitability of conventional dispute settlement measures for multilateral treaty obligations regarding matters of global concern, and the

969 Maritime and Coastguard Agency, 'Maritime Autonomy Regulation Lab (MARLab) Report' (n 822) 6.1

970 Thomas A Hemphill, 'Technology entrepreneurship and innovation hubs: Perspectives on the universal regulatory sandbox' (2023) 50(2) Science and Public Policy 350, 351

971 Goldsmith and Posner (n 955) 95

972 Wolfrum, 'Wolfrum' (n 899) 20; Guzmán and Meyer (n 907) 182

973 Andrew T Guzmán, *How International Law Works: A Rational Choice Theory* (Oxford University Press 2008) 149

974 Terpan (n 909) 73

975 Guzmán and Meyer (n 907) 193; Guzmán (n 973) 133

976 Guzmán and Meyer (n 907) 194

fact that non-compliance often results from a lack of capacity, knowledge, or prohibitive high implementation costs, a new generation of non-compliance mechanisms has been developed.[977] These measures depart from the conventional use of sanctions and harsh penalties and instead focus on a facilitative approach. The conference of the state parties is often responsible for administering non-compliance procedures, with an expert committee additionally set up. An example of this new generation of non-compliance mechanism can be found in Article 15 of the Paris Agreement.[978]

Reputational losses can greatly diminish the credibility of future promises, making them a costly consequence for states that rely on international law's collaborative nature. However, compared to violating hard law, violating soft law generally involves lower reputational losses.[979] However, it is argued that breaching politically binding declarations may have more serious implications than breaching a binding treaty. Therefore, the significance of the reputational damage resulting from a breach of soft law should not be underestimated.[980]

The reasons for breaching an obligation are varied. In addition to inability and arbitrary unwillingness, states may choose to breach if alternative actions offer greater benefits or lower costs.[981] Such unilateral breaches could also be considered as an implementation of unilateral amendments to a soft law instrument.[982] Soft law instruments do not have a predefined amendment procedure, which could result in unilateral departures leading to a tacitly agreed amendment of the soft law agreement, especially if other states simultaneously endorse the unilaterally proposed alternative.

Given the enforcement measures available for international shipping regulations, reciprocity can be a reliable tool, although all GAIRAS conventions are multilateral agreements. This is because most obligations are owed directly to another contracting government rather than the participating governments as a whole. However, the principle of non-discrimination[983] makes it difficult to deprive only one state of the right to enter into ports. Inevitably, the higher a state's appreciation of the existence and effectiveness of an international

977 Malgosia Fitzmaurice, 'The New Generation of Environmental Non-Compliance Procedures and the Question of Legitimacy' in Christina Voigt and Caroline Foster (eds), *International Courts versus Non-Compliance Mechanisms Comparative Advantages in Strengthening Treaty Implementation* (1st ed. Cambridge University Press 2024) 56–57

978 Paris Agreement, No. 54113 12 December 2015

979 Guzmán and Meyer (n 907) 196

980 Knauff (n 907) 256; Weil (n 904) 415

981 States as rational actors will be discussed more in section 5.2.2 below

982 Guzmán and Meyer (n 907) 198

983 Molenaar, 'Molenaar 2007' (n 278) 228

regime on a particular issue, the higher its level of compliance. Despite the reciprocity of obligations and the threat of loss of reputation, compliance ultimately depends on the will of the state.[984] Although the negotiation costs of soft law agreements are lower compared to hard law treaties, increased post-negotiation costs are expected. Since soft law lacks coercive enforcement mechanisms, enforcing and managing commitments is more expensive.[985]

For MASS, states are dependent on an internationally agreed framework to allow international operations of MASS. The need for reciprocal recognition of certificates makes unilateral deviations from the agreed framework less interesting. Therefore, there is little need for hard enforcement mechanisms, and reciprocity and reputational loss in the event of a breach may be sufficient to ensure compliance.

Another way of explaining why states obey international law is that legitimacy creates a strong compliance pull, especially in a rule-based system. A state perceives a norm as legitimate if it perceives that the norm came into force following the correct procedure.[986] This kind of legitimacy is also referred to as process[987] or through-put legitimacy.[988] The higher a state evaluates the legitimacy of a norm, the higher the compliance-pull exerted by the norm.[989] In assessing the legitimacy of IMO soft law instruments, it must first be acknowledged that the compliance pull of soft law is generally lower than that of hard law.[990] However, it can be concluded that the well-established IMO process enhances the legitimacy and thus the compliance pull of IMO soft law instruments.

So far, the positive aspects of the lack of legal bindingness have been illustrated. Opting for soft law agreements holds some disadvantages, notably the reduced commitment shown by states.[991] Nevertheless, the legal bindingness, which represents the most solemn promise a state can make,[992] ultimately

984 Thomas M Franck, 'Legitimacy in the International System' (1988) 82 American Journal of International Law 705, 705
985 Abbott and Snidal (n 909) 434
986 Franck (n 984) 706
987 Alan Boyle and Christine Chinkin, *The Making of International Law* (Foundations of public international law, 1 publ, Oxford Univ. Press 2007) 24
988 Sebastian Bautzem, 'Transnational standard setting in accounting: Organizing expertise-based self-regulation in times of crises' (2014) 27(6) Accounting, Auditing & Accountability Journal 933, 939
989 Abbott and Snidal (n 909) 429
990 Hagemann, Huddelston Skees and Thierer (n 857), 98; Handl and others (n 909) 394
991 Guzmán (n 973) 136
992 Guzmán and Meyer (n 907) 196; Boyle, 'Boyle 1999' (n 959) 905

does not add significant legal force.[993] As states are never truly locked into an agreement, implementation and compliance with hard and soft law depends on the will of the state.[994]

In summary, soft law offers various advantages, particularly significant for the regulation of emerging technologies. The absence of legal bindingness permits flexibility in procedure, participation, amendment, and modification. Whilst soft law requires domestic implementation in parallel with hard law, the highly detailed IMO instruments accelerate national implementation in the context of shipping legislation. Although soft law exerts slightly lower compliance pull, this is outweighed by the numerous advantages of soft law solutions. In conclusion, soft can be an equally effective regulatory tool compared to hard law agreements. Furthermore, soft law represents the sole viable regulatory approach in the event that a hard law agreement cannot be reached due to political, economic, or pragmatic considerations. However, soft law alone cannot solve all the legal challenges associated with the regulation of new technologies. In particular, the lack of legal binding force and thus of certainty could lead to a disincentive to invest in the development of new technologies. Soft law should therefore be seen as complementary to hard law. Both, in a symbiotic relationship, are able to regulate emerging technologies appropriately.[995]

It is important to recall that the legal significance of soft law may be determined by the contracting parties based on the design of the agreement.[996] On the one hand, the incorporation of formal amendment procedures, dispute resolution schemes, or the imposition of a self-obligation to comply increases the legal weight of a soft law provision. On the other hand, the vagueness of provisions and the emphasis on their non-binding nature reduce the legal significance of soft law. In the context of multilateral agreements, the design decision can also be understood as an approach to the problem of multilateral utility maximization.[997]

993 Frederic L Kirgis, 'Specialized Law-Making Processes' in Christopher C Joyner (ed), *The United Nations and International Law* (Cambridge Univ. Press 1997) 91

994 Franck (n 984) 705; Henry (n 924) 82; Ku (n 907) 143

995 Gary Marchant, Carlos I Gutierrez and Lucille Tournas, 'Lessons for Artificial Intelligence from Historical Uses of Soft Law Governance' (2020) 61(1) Jurimetrics 1, 13; Pariotti (n 855) 24

996 Baxter (n 908) 566

997 Andrew T Guzmán and Alan O Sykes, 'Economics of International Law' in Francesco Parisi (ed), *The Oxford handbook of law and economics: Volume 3: Public Law and Legal Institutions* (Oxford University Press 2017) 446

This section has explored various arguments in favor of and against soft law. It also illustrated why states could prefer soft law and the mechanism of action of soft law. The following section shall investigate further on state preferences and choices in international law. Various theoretical approaches have been developed to explain international relations. Considering all is beyond this study, thus, rational choice theory as a particularly convincing and inclusive approach is discussed here. In the further course of argumentation, reference is made to rational choice theory, especially when determining the appropriateness of different tools to address regulatory gaps in the context of MASS.

5.2.2 *Rational Choice Theory*

Economic analysis of law saw its boost in the 1960s starting with Coase's contribution on Social Costs.[998] First in the end of the 20th century, international relations and international law was identified as a fruitful object of investigation for economic analysis.[999] In general, the approaches developed for the economic analysis of private (national) law were transferred to the international realm and adapted where necessary.[1000] Just as national private law is intended to govern the relation between equal private parties, the aim of international law is to regulate relations between states and other subjects of international law such as international organizations.[1001] Like private law subjects at the national level, states are considered to be of equal standing at the international level. Consequently, international law treaties are perceived as the analogy to private law contracts.[1002] The main difference with private contracts is that there is no overarching enforcement body at the international level to provide coercive enforcement mechanisms.[1003] This has already been discussed above. Besides economic analysis of law, particularly international law and international relations between states and institutions are analyzed based on various different theories and approaches such as constructivist,

998 Ronald H Coase, 'The Problem of Social Cost' [1960] The Journal of Law and Economics 1

999 Armin Steinbach and Anne von Aaken, Ökonomische Analyse des Völker- und Europarechts (Anne van Aaken tr. Mohr Siebeck Lehrbuch, 1st edn, Mohr Siebeck 2019) 4

1000 Pointing towards the challenges when transferring an approach to another regime: Alexander Thompson, 'Applying Rational Choice Theory to International Law: The Promise and Pitfalls' (2002) 31(1) The Journal of Legal Studies 285–306

1001 Wolfrum, 'Wolfrum' (n 899) 1

1002 Joel Trachtman, *The Economic Structure of International Law* (Harvard University Press 2008) 120

1003 Guzmán and Meyer (n 907) 182; Guzmán and Sykes (n 997) 441

constitutional, realism, and liberalism approaches as well as regime theory.[1004] Some aspects of other theories can be included in economic analysis of law.

Different approaches can be applied within economic analysis of law, including game theory, behavioral economics, and rational choice theory. These approaches partly overlap with each other. Rational choice theory assumes that individuals aim to maximize their own utility and perform a cost-benefit analysis before making decisions. As rational choice theory deals with individuals taking decisions and international law deals with states, i.e. artificial constructions lead by governments, public choice theory transfers the premise of rational choice theory to the realm of public and international law.[1005] Thus, for economic analysis of international law the same basic assumptions apply as for economic analysis of private law: it is assumed that states act according to their preferences and seek to maximize their utility.[1006] Preferences are assumed consistent, complete, and transitive.[1007]

Preferences usually refer to the desires of individuals.[1008] However, in contrast to private law, the relevant actors in international law are states and organizations, not private individuals. International relations theory treats states as billiard balls. Collisions are to be avoided, but their innards are ignored,[1009] without neglecting the relevance of domestic legal procedures for the development of preferences.[1010] In the economic analysis of international law, individuals involved in the governance of a state are not considered relevant actors. Instead, the actions and decisions of these individuals are attributed to the state.

The preferences of states include monetizable aspects such as economic wealth, quantifiable aspects such as military power, and non-commensurable public goods such as peace, public welfare, emotions, reputation, and moral

---

1004 Georg Sørensen, Jørgen Møller and Robert H Jackson, *Introduction to international relations: Theories and approaches* (Eighth edition, Oxford University Press 2022); Richard Devetak and Jacqui True, *Theories of International Relations* (6th ed. Bloomsbury Publishing Plc 2022)

1005 Eyal Zamir and Doron Teichman, 'Administrative, Constitutional, and International Law' in Eyal Zamir and Doron Teichman (eds), *Behavioral law and economics* (Oxford University Press 2018) 395; Roger D Congleton, 'Rational Choice and Politics' in Roger D Congleton, Bernard Grofman and Stefan Voigt (eds), *The Oxford handbook of public choice* (Oxford University Press 2019) 3

1006 Steinbach and Aaken (n 999) 140; Trachtman (n 1002) 15; Guzmán and Meyer (n 907) 181; Guzmán (n 973) 160

1007 Goldsmith and Posner (n 955) 7

1008 Steinbach and Aaken (n 999) 15

1009 Trachtman (n 1002) 19

1010 ibid; Goldsmith and Posner (n 955) 5

obligations.[1011] As already indicated, public (rational) choice theory is receptive to including insights from other theoretical approaches. The identification of preferences in particular provides a gateway for the inclusion of alternative approaches.[1012] A constructivist approach to state's preference includes moral obligations and the validity of arguments in the scope of states' preferences.[1013] Moreover, it considers state's preferences to be unstable and to change according to the context and legal arrangements[1014] though without explaining the impetus for a change of preferences.[1015] However, assuming non-fixed preferences is incompatible with an economic approach because the states' preferences form the basis for explaining legal rules.[1016]

Turning now to international treaties, the economic analysis of treaties adopts 'price theory' as a sub-approach of rational choice theory to compare the costs and benefits of an agreement.[1017] As soon as the expected benefits exceed the combined costs of negotiation, implementation, and compliance, a state enters into the agreement.[1018] The same cost-benefit analysis can then be made with regard to compliance with a treaty. An international agreement is only concluded and complied with by a state, if a pareto-improvement can be achieved.[1019] Consequently, depending on the circumstances, refusing to comply with a treaty may be the more efficient option for a particular state.[1020]

The costs of a treaty include transaction costs and the costs of performance.[1021] Whereas performance costs are inherent in the nature of a treaty, transaction costs depend on the concrete circumstances of the transaction. Transaction costs include information, bargaining, decision, and enforcement costs. Prohibitively high transaction costs can prevent parties from entering into efficient agreements. Thus, reducing transaction costs is beneficial

1011 Steinbach and Aaken (n 999) 148; Steinbach and Aaken (n 999) 135; Trachtman (n 1002) 17

1012 Duncan Snidal, 'Rational Choice and International Relations' in Walter Carlsnaes, Thomas Risse and Beth A Simmons (eds), *Handbook of international relations* (SAGE Publications 2013) 87

1013 Emanuel Adler, 'Constructivism in International Relations: Sources, Contributions, and Debates' in Walter Carlsnaes, Thomas Risse and Beth A Simmons (eds), *Handbook of international relations* (SAGE Publications 2013) 124

1014 Trachtman (n 1002) 18; Adler (n 1013) 114

1015 Guzmán and Sykes (n 997) 440

1016 Arguing that rational choice theory is able to include changes in actors' preferences and international political settings: Snidal (n 1012) 101

1017 Trachtman (n 1002) 142

1018 Guzmán (n 973) 121; Goldsmith and Posner (n 955) 89

1019 Trachtman (n 1002) 129; Guzmán and Sykes (n 997) 440–441

1020 Trachtman (n 1002) 142

1021 Guzmán and Sykes (n 997) 441

and promotes efficient treaties. This relation between transaction costs and efficiency is illustrated by the Coase-Theorem.[1022] It expresses that goods are allocated among participants in a way that is efficient in the absence of transaction costs. In the case of international law, the goods allocated among states are sovereignty and jurisdictional rights. As states are aware of the potentially negative impact of high transaction costs, international agreements and international organizations are used as tools to reduce transaction costs of later transactions.[1023] Reducing transaction costs by delegated law-making will be considered in more detail below.

Another challenge for an international law cost-benefit analysis are free riders and public goods. The challenging aspect are positive externalities, thus a state investing in the production of a public good, but not capturing all the benefits.[1024] As an example, if a state invests in more safe vessels, the benefits are not entirely internalized as other states also benefit from encountering safe vessels at sea. Moreover, other states could reduce their investments in ship safety as other, safe vessels ensure collision avoidance. This example illustrates the problem of free riders and public goods. The safety of vessels as a public good cannot be achieved by one state investing in safe ships. Rather, all flag states have to ensure that their vessels are safe. As the benefits of investing in safe vessels are not fully internalized, the dominant strategy for each state would be to refuse and benefit from other state's investments. Then, however, safety at sea would not be achieved. If states enter into an enforceable agreement, the situation changes. Other states are now expected to comply due to enforcement mechanisms. Then, compliance results in a higher payoff, resulting in all states benefitting if they comply.

Trachtman illustrates this link between enforceable agreements and compliance in the context of positive externalities by referring to a Rousseauvian fable of cooperation among hunters.[1025] All hunters were more interested in a share of the stag than in a rabbit. However, all hunters needed to cooperate to catch the stag, whereas each hunter could shoot a rabbit individually. Thus, each hunter depended on the others' cooperation to achieve a higher payoff. If a hunter could be assured of the others' compliance, the hunter would ignore the rabbit and contribute to the catch of the stag. Hence, in the case of public

1022 Coase (n 998) 8
1023 Guzmán and Sykes (n 997) 449
1024 Trachtman (n 1002) 13
1025 ibid 135–137

goods that depend on the committed behavior of all parties, enforcement mechanisms, even modest ones, can be of great importance.[1026]

This supports rational choice theory adopted by states calculating costs and benefits despite the legal character of an obligation. As soft law obligations can also be supplemented by enforcement mechanisms based on reputation, retaliation, and monitoring, soft law and hard law solutions can equally incentivize compliance and are treated equally from an economic point of view.[1027] However, from a rational choice theory perspective, the weight of reputational losses to ensure compliance should not be overestimated.[1028]

To conclude, rational choice theory is one approach to analyze international relations and international treaties. States are the relevant actors and assumed to be rationalists maximizing their utility according to their preferences. Thus, states enter into agreements if the expected utility exceeds the costs. However, transaction costs occur and incomplete information can prevent pareto-efficient solutions. To reduce transaction costs and thus to allocate sovereignty as efficient as possible, states enter into agreement or establish international organizations. When dealing with public goods, cooperative behavior from all involved states is often necessary to achieve a joint surplus. Enforcement mechanisms can ensure that each state opts for complying rather than refusing. Because soft law instruments can also be enforced by means of monitoring, reputational losses, and the threat of retaliation, soft and hard law instruments can be equally effective from this point of view. Given the large number of soft law agreements, it seems that states often concluded that a soft law agreement makes them better off than a hard law instrument.

5.2.3 *Conclusions*

This section considered three general issues. Firstly, recommendations and requirements surrounding the regulation of emerging technology were discussed. Central is the need to strike a balance between flexibility and predictability. Particularly regarding MASS, it is crucial to establish the legal framework promptly and to ensure a coherent and horizontally sound integration of MASS in all GAIRAS conventions and in UNCLOS. As the current legal framework for shipping is not uniform, there is no need for uniformity, although there is a need to ensure harmonization in order to allow for transborder voyages.

1026 ibid 137

1027 Goldsmith and Posner (n 955) 90; Guzmán and Sykes (n 997) 444, they consider hard and soft law different in degree, but not in kind

1028 Goldsmith and Posner (n 955) 102–103

Concerning geographical application, the legal framework for MASS need not be global at first, as regional harmonization would satisfy the requirements. Nevertheless, later expansion should be possible.

Secondly, legal regulation was situated within the broader context of regulation and soft law was examined in detail as a distinct form of legal regulation. In this study, soft law is considered to include all norms developed by subjects of international law that are not legally binding but have some form of legal significance. The main benefit of soft law is its flexibility with regard to negotiations, the adoption procedure, amendments, and participants. Therefore, soft law instruments, particularly those adopted by the IMO, could prove to be a valuable tool in regulating MASS. Boyle summarized the relevance of soft law for international treaties by stating that

> [i]t is inconceivable that modern treaty regimes or international organizations could function successfully without resort to soft law.[1029]

Thirdly, rational choice theory as an approach within the economic analysis of law was introduced to explain state's behavior. Transferring the premise of private law analysis, states are considered rational actors aiming at maximizing their utility. As high transaction costs can prevent efficient allocation of sovereignty resulting in unnecessary high costs for states, international organizations are established to reduce future transaction costs. The IMO is one such organization. In the context of public goods such as the safety of navigation, the relevance of enforcement mechanisms encouraging states to comply has been highlighted.

The next section will discuss different legal solutions to ensure a harmonized interpretation of UNCLOS and the GAIRAS conventions in the light of MASS and the implementation of additional MASS-specific provisions. Both soft and hard law solutions will be evaluated, as well as international and regional alternatives. As a global scope of application is not the most important feature of the future legal framework for MASS and the most foreseeable business case are short-sea shipping applications, Europe as a prominent hub for MASS research will receive particular attention.

1029 Alan Boyle, 'Reflections on the Treaty as a Law-making Instrument' in Alexander Orakhelashvili and Sarah Williams (eds), *40 years of the Vienna Convention on the Law of Treaties* (British Institute of International and Comparative Law 2010) 14

5.3 Regulation at the International Level

Shipping is a global industry demanding international regulations. As illustrated above, flag states can register MASS for voyages in their territorial waters without being limited by international law. As soon as MASS leave the territorial waters or enter into the territorial waters of another state, flag, coastal, and port states have to agree on a common regulation. As the IMO is the main international regulator for shipping, available instruments at the IMO will be discussed. As touched upon above, both hard and soft law, i.e. legally binding and non-binding regulations can contribute effectively to international regulation. Starting with legally non-binding regulations, the different instruments that could be adopted by the IMO will be discussed. Moving forward to the realm of hard law, amending existing conventions will be considered second. Third, the option of adopting a new convention or taking a decision at an international conference will be analyzed. Forth, the possibility to change UNCLOS by adopting GAIRAS will be considered before assessing the appropriateness of customary international law.

5.3.1 *Non-binding Instruments of the IMO*

The legal basis for IMO's law-making activities can be found in the IMO-Convention as well as in UNCLOS. Here, the focus will be laid on the competencies granted by the IMO-Convention. The interplay of non-binding instruments on MASS and the GAIRAS will be considered in section 5.3.5 below.

The IMO-Convention empowers the IMO to adopt regulations concerning its internal affairs, e.g. the budget and rules of procedure. More important, however, the IMO can make recommendations to the members for the adoption of regulations and guidelines concerning maritime safety (Article 2(a) of the IMO-Convention), prepare drafts for international conventions, agreements, and other instruments, and convene conferences necessary for the adoption of such instruments (Article 2(b) of the IMO-Convention). The drafting competence will be considered below when discussing a new MASS convention in section 5.3.3. For convenience, the relevant passages of Article 1 and 2 of the IMO-Convention are given here:

> Article 1
> The purposes of the Organization are:
> (a) To provide machinery for co-operation among Governments in the field of governmental regulation and practices relating to technical matters of all kinds affecting shipping engaged in international trade; to

> encourage and facilitate the general adoption of the highest practicable standards in matters concerning the maritime safety, efficiency of navigation and prevention and control of marine pollution from ships; and to deal with administrative and legal matters related to the purposes set out in this Article;
>
> (b)–(e) [...].
>
> Article 2
> In order to achieve the purposes set out in Part 4 the Organization shall:
> (a) Subject to the provisions of Article 3, consider and make recommendations upon matters arising under Article 1 (a), (b) and (c) that may be remitted to it by Members, by any organ or specialized agency of the United Nations or by any other intergovernmental organization or upon matters referred to it under Article 1 (d);
>
> (b) Provide for the drafting of conventions, agreements, or other suitable instruments, and recommend these to Governments and to intergovernmental organizations, and convene such conferences as may be necessary;
>
> (c)–(e) [...].

The process of adopting a recommendation commences with the incorporation of a novel output into the biennial agenda of the competent Committee based on a proposal made by a member government or a subsidiary body.[1030] After discussing the proposal in the Committee, the Committee reports to the Council and submits its report as well as developed drafts and proposals for regulations, recommendations, and guidelines.[1031] The Council submits the documents to the Assembly or directly to the member states, Article 21(b) of the IMO-Convention. The Assembly, eventually, adopts a resolution including the recommendation to the member states, Article 15(j) of the IMO-Convention.

1030 LEG, IMO, 'LEG.1/Circ.9: Organization and Method of Work of the Legal Committee' (London 30 June 2018) 7; MSC, IMO and MEPC, IMO, 'MSC-MEPC.1/Circ.5/Rev.1: Organization and Method of Work of the Maritime Safety Committee and The Marine Environment Protection Committee and their Subsidiary Bodies' (London 13 June 2018) 6

1031 See Article 29 IMO Convention for the MSC; Article 34 IMO Convention for the LEG; Article 39 IMO Convention for the MEPC

In some cases, the Assembly can confer the competence to adopt resolutions to the Committees.[1032]

As the IMO lacks real implementation and enforcement powers and competencies, the recommendations are not legally binding. It is up to the member states to adhere to the recommendations and to implement them domestically. However, their legal significance and effectiveness should not be underestimated. Two aspects in particular increase the normative effect of recommendations: First, recommendations have become quasi-legally binding by references in statutory instruments such as the GAIRAS or national legislation.[1033] This is especially true for IMO performance standards and technical guidance. Second, classification societies tend to require compliance with IMO resolutions for their certification.[1034]

Although the IMO-Convention only mentions recommendations, the IMO Assembly has adopted more than 1000 resolutions titled as codes, guidelines, guidance, recommendations, performance standards, unified interpretation, and procedures.[1035] Despite their different names, all these resolutions are recommendatory for the member states under Article 15(j) of the IMO-Convention. Besides recommendations adopted as resolutions, the IMO issues circulars including guidelines, guidance, or unified interpretations. The following section presents different instruments endorsed by the IMO in more detail and examines their legal significance for MASS. Starting with the least formal instrument, unified interpretations, guidelines, and codes will be discussed consecutively. Performance standards and procedures are assumed to contribute less to MASS regulations and are therefore left aside.

5.3.1.1 Unified Interpretations

In 2023, the IMO Committees approved 206 unified interpretations as circulars.[1036] Unified interpretations provide detailed guidance on how to interpret a certain treaty provision and address national maritime administrations. Often, unified interpretations undergird a certain treaty provision with concrete

1032 See for example: IMO, 'Res. A.825(19): Procedure for Adoption and Amendment of Performance Standards for Radio and Navigational Equipment' (London 23 November 1995)

1033 Dong Nam, 'Identification and Analysis of the Legal Status of International Maritime Organization Instruments' (2021) 27(3) Journal of the Korean Society of Marine Environment & Safety 421, 424

1034 ibid 426

1035 Henry (n 924) 73

1036 Number infered from the Global Integrated Shipping Information System, last checked 30/01/2024

numbers[1037] or examples[1038] guiding the national administration. Moreover, they provide guidance on how to deal with cases of doubt or unclear treaty provisions.[1039] Nevertheless, unified interpretations lack legal binding power, leaving the decision of how to apply them to the discretion of the national administrations. A number of flag state administrations refers to the unified interpretations on their respective web pages. This suggests that there is some form of significance to be derived from unified interpretations.

After approval, the unified interpretations are published online and listed as non-mandatory instruments in the General Integrated Shipping Information System operated by the IMO. Additionally, the unified interpretations are included in the official publications of the IMO's statutory instruments. This increases their practical relevance as they can be read in direct conjunction with the concerned treaty provision.

The need for unified interpretations arises due to diverting national applications of a certain provision or an unclear wording of newly adopted amendments. Often, the International Association of Classification Societies, which has consultative status at the imo, proposes the approval of unified interpretations.[1040]

Considering the above-introduced requirements for the future legal framework for MASS, unified interpretations are globally applicable, flexible, and can be adopted rather quickly. In accordance with the nature of IMO instruments, the territorial scope of unified interpretations is global. All member states of the IMO can participate in the development of the unified interpretations. As the correspondence rate of national administrations to unified

1037 MSC, IMO, 'MSC.1/Circ. 1362/Rev.1: Unified Interpretation of SOLAS Chapter II-1' (London 9 May 2022); MSC, IMO, 'MSC.1/Circ. 1375/Rev.1: Unified Interpretation of SOLAS Regulation V/23' (London 28 May 2012); MSC, IMO, 'MSC.1/Circ.1323: Unified Interpretation of IBC Code' (London 10 June 2009); MSC, IMO, 'MSC.1/Circ. 1260: Unified Interpretation of COLREG' (London 22 May 2008)

1038 FAL, IMO, 'FAL.7/Circ.1: Unified Interpretation of Annex 3 to the FAL Convention' (London 7 April 2017); MSC, IMO, 'MSC.1/Circ.1637: Unified Interpretation of SOLAS Regulation II-1/3-10 Concerning The Term "Unforeseen Delay in Delivery of Ships" During the Coronavirus (Covid-19) Pandemic' (London 10 December 2020); MSC, IMO, 'MSC.1/Circ.1655: Unified Interpretations of SOLAS Chapter II-2' (London 5 December 2022)

1039 LEG, IMO, 'LEG 107/9/2: Unified Interpretation on the Test for Breaking the Owner's Right to Limit Liability under the IMO Conventions' (London 24 January 2020) 16

1040 MSC, IMO, 'MSC 102/7/5: Unified interpretation of SOLAS regulation II-1/3-10 concerning the term "unforeseen delay in delivery of ships" (China and IACS)' (London 9 March 2020); MSC, IMO, 'MSC 90/22/1: Clarification of SOLAS regulation V/23 (IACS)' (London 21 November 2011)

interpretations is high, unified interpretations seem capable of harmonizing the interpretation and advocating for a MASS-including interpretation.

In respect of their relevance for national courts, unified interpretations must be assessed in the light of the VCLT. As illustrated above, Article 31(3)(a) of the VCLT stipulates that any subsequent agreement concluded between the state parties concerning the interpretation of the treaty should be considered together with the context of a provision. Moreover, not all parties to the treaty have to participate actively in the interpretation agreement. Unified interpretations are usually approved by consensus in the IMO Committees. It should be noted, however, that the representatives of the IMO member states attending the Committee meetings do not vote as representatives of the governments of the contracting parties to an international convention, but rather as members of the IMO.[1041] This aspect could reduce the legal weight of unified interpretations in light of the VCLT.

In respect of SOLAS, COLREG, and STCW, however, one has to consider that the MSC is authorized to adopt binding amendments to the annexes of the conventions.[1042] Consequently, the state parties have conferred law-making power to the MSC. As unified interpretations are of less legal significance than legally binding amendments, it could be argued that the MSC is a fortiori empowered to approve unified interpretations as interpretation agreements on behalf of the state parties.

Besides their legal relevance for treaty interpretations, unified interpretations provide several other advantages. As unified interpretations do not require a special implementation time, they would be available at short notice. The amendment of unified interpretations necessitates only the approval of the responsible Committee, thereby facilitating the expeditious response to new technological developments.[1043] Additionally, unified interpretations could be formulated in a goal-based manner, which provides more flexibility to national administrations and promotes innovative approaches to conventional goals.

However, unified interpretations are prima facie not legally binding and thus provide only limited legal certainty. Moreover, unified interpretations only address one certain provision in a treaty.[1044] As illustrated above, MASS require regulations that transcend single conventions. Rather, the meaning of certain terms needs to be reassessed in several conventions consistently. Although it

1041 Petrig (n 416) 129–130

1042 See section 5.3.2

1043 Ntovas (n 675) 221

1044 Petrig (n 416) 127

is conceivable to approve several unified interpretations for all conventions affected by MASS, the consistency across conventions is put at risk as a coherent interpretation is up to the national administrations.

The lack of legal binding force, however, allows national governments to choose freely whether they instruct their subordinated maritime authorities to consider the unified interpretations. Depending on the national constitution, parliaments could be involved in the fundamental policy decision of whether MASS should be registered in the state concerned. As illustrated above, parliamentary involvement can increase compliance and societal support.

To conclude, unified interpretations have the advantage of being created and approved in a smooth and quick procedure. Consequently, adapting unified interpretations to new technological developments is possible in a timely manner. However, legal certainty and coherence across the legal framework are not ensured and put at risk, as unified interpretations are not legally binding for the member states of the IMO. Moreover, unified interpretation are not intended to include fundamental policy decisions, but rather technical details. The question, however, whether humans are required on board a vessel touches upon the fundamentals of shipping and should thus not be governed solely by technical instruments. Although some authors consider unified interpretations helpful in the context of MASS, other instruments are preferred ultimately.[1045] As next, guidelines will be considered.

5.3.1.2 Guidelines

The IMO Committees as well as the Assembly often chose to adopt resolutions with guidelines. Although there is no official distinction between guidelines, unified interpretations, and codes, the characteristic of guidelines can be deduced from the ones adopted by the IMO so far.

Mostly, guidelines do not add substantive regulations but provide guidance for the implementation of existing instruments or how states should react to and deal with new aspects. In distinction to unified interpretation, guidelines have a more holistic approach and address several provisions. In the context of MASS, the IMO has already adopted guidelines to assist states when approving MASS trials.[1046] The guidelines do not prescribe substantive requirements

---

1045 Legros, 'Legros 2019' (n 1045) 20; Ntovas. 'Functionalism and Maritime Autonomous Surface Ships' (above, n. 535), p. 221; Petrig (n 416) 130; Ringbom. 'Legalizing autonomous ships' (above, n. 493), p. 459; dissenting and arguing that "unified interpretations will always result in confusion and contradictions": Barbara Stępień, 'Can a ship be its own captain? Safe manning of autonomous and uncrewed vessels' (2023) 148 Marine Policy, 6

1046 MSC, IMO, 'MSC.1/Circ.1604: Interim Guidelines for MASS Trials' (London 14 June 2019)

to be fulfilled by MASS, but rather list aspects to be considered by national administrations when deciding on MASS trials.

Another aspect differentiating guidelines from unified interpretations is that guidelines can have a horizontal effect across several IMO instruments.[1047] The guidelines on the use of electronic certificates are a suitable example of a cross-convention guideline. As paper-based certificates often caused trouble during port state controls, electronic certificates were used from the 2010s on. Although many states began to issue electronic certificates, printed copies were necessary as not all port state authorities accepted electronic certificates. Thus, the FAL approved the Interim Guidelines for the Use of Printed Versions of Electronic Certificates in 2013.[1048] As the use of electronic certificates has become more widespread, the guidelines were revised in 2016. They now include further provisions on the validity and authentication of electronic certificates.[1049] As the guidelines apply to all certificates issued under any of the IMO conventions, they provide a horizontal instrument.

This aspect makes guidelines particularly interesting for the regulation of MASS as common gaps affecting several IMO instruments could be addressed.[1050] Additionally, new verification methods for MASS need to be developed. IMO guidelines could assist in this process and ensure harmonized national approaches. This, in turn, would reduce the costs for shipbuilders and equipment producers as a similar procedure would apply in all flag states. A similar effect could be achieved for port state controls if including the IMO guidelines in the port state control agreements.

In addition, guidelines can be used to adopted novel substantive rules that go beyond the scope of the existing regulatory framework. These guidelines often serve as predecessor to codes.[1051] This pre-law function could be a valuable advantage of a MASS guideline. The legally non-binding guidelines were adopted as a first approach toward a certain policy issue.[1052] The desirability and necessity of subsequent hard legislation could be assessed and national maritime authorities, shipbuilders, ship operators, and other

1047 Petrig (n 416) 127

1048 FAL, IMO, 'FAL.5/Circ.39: Interim Guidelines for the Use of Printed Versions of Electronic Certificates' (London 18 April 2013)

1049 FAL, IMO, 'FAL.5/Circ.39/Rev.2: Guidelines for the Use of Electronic Certificates' (London 20 April 2016)

1050 Jokioinen and others (n 98) 55; LEG, IMO, 'LEG 111/10/4: Proposal to develop Guidelines on the implementation of LEG Instruments by MASS (China)' (London 16 February 2024) 6

1051 Linda Senden, *Soft law in European Community law* (Modern studies in European law vol 1, Hart 2004) 120; Petrig (n 416) 130

1052 Kirgis (n 993) 84

stakeholders could already adapt their practices. As a common ground was already prepared, subsequent negotiations were facilitated. Three examples of guidelines serving as pre-law for a subsequent code shall be illustrated.

The first example depicts the law-making history of the Code for Recognized Organizations.[1053] The flag state is under Article 94(1), (5) of the UNCLOS obliged to ensure that the vessels flying its flag comply with GAIRAS. Both SOLAS[1054] and MARPOL[1055] allow the flag state authorities to entrust the inspection and survey of vessels to private organizations. As flag states increasingly made use of this conferral of powers, the IMO developed uniform procedures for the delegation of authority. Consequently, the IMO adopted the Guidelines for the Authorization of Organizations Acting on Behalf of the Administrations in 1993.[1056] This resolution was cited by SOLAS Regulation I/6, although it was not legally binding. In 1995, additional specifications were adopted.[1057] Almost 20 years later, the MSC adopted the Code for Recognized Organizations to gather all requirements in one instrument. Moreover, the Code assisted in improving the globally harmonized implementation of IMO requirements.[1058] The Code was based on the guidelines adopted in 1995. At the same time, Chapter XI-1 of the Annex of SOLAS was amended to make the Code legally binding. The amendment was deemed to have been accepted on 1 July 2014.[1059]

The second example concerns the Polar Code. Since the 1990s, the MEPC and the MSC worked on a code for vessels operating in polar waters. Although the adoption of a Polar Code was already planned in 1999,[1060] the MEPC and the MSC jointly adopted Guidelines for Ships operating in Arctic Ice-Covered Waters in 2002 as an interim step.[1061] Neither was the aim of adopting a Code reached nor could the territorial scope of the new instrument be extended

1053 MSC, IMO, 'Res. MSC.349(92): Code for Recognized Organizations' (London 21 June 2013); MEPC, IMO, 'Res. MEPC. 237(65) – Code for Recognized Organizations' (London 17 May 2013)

1054 Chapter I/6(a) of SOLAS

1055 Annex I/6, Annex II/8, Annex IV/4, Annex VI/5 of MARPOL

1056 IMO, 'Res. A.739(18): Guidelines for the Authorization of Organizations Acting on Behalf of the Administration' (London 22 November 1993)

1057 IMO, 'Res. A.789(19): Specifications on the Survey and Certification Functions of Recognized Organizations Acting on Behalf of the Administration' (London 8 December 1995)

1058 MSC, IMO, 'Res. MSC.349(92)' (n 1053)

1059 MSC, IMO, 'Res. MSC.350(92): Amendments to the International Convention for the Safety of Life at Sea, 1974' (London 21 June 2013)

1060 MEPC, IMO, 'MEPC 43/21 – Report of the MEPC on its 43rd session' (London 6 July 1999)

1061 MSC, IMO and MEPC, IMO, 'MSC/Circ.1056; MEPC/Circ.399: Guidelines for Ships Operating in Arctic Ice-Covered Waters' (London 23 December 2002)

towards the Antarctic region. However, this was achieved in 2009 and the guidelines were revised to include the Antarctic region.[1062] The MSC continued to work on a mandatory code[1063] and adopted the Polar Code two years later than estimated.[1064] It was made mandatory by adding a new chapter to the annex of SOLAS.[1065] The amendment entered into force in 2016. A total of 17 years passed between the adoption of the first guidelines and the entry into force of the Polar Code.[1066] The legislative history of the Code of Safety for Ships Using Gases and Other Low-Flashpoint Fuels is alike and started with a Norwegian request for international rules for gas fueled vessels in 2003. The code entered into force in 2017.[1067]

The third and last example concerns the Ballast Water Management and can be distinguished from the first two by its outcome. Instead of adopting a mandatory code under SOLAS, a new convention was concluded. The increased use of ballast water for the safe and effective operation of ships has led to an unwanted migration of aquatic organisms. Following the UN Conference on Environment and Development, held in Rio de Janeiro in 1992, the IMO, therefore, adopted the Guidelines for Preventing the Introduction of Unwanted Aquatic Organisms and Pathogens from Ships' Ballast Water and Sediment Discharge.[1068] In 1997, these guidelines were supplemented by another IMO resolution.[1069] However, the efforts were not sufficient to address efficiently the harm of the transfer of harmful aquatic organisms. The World Summit

---

1062 IMO, 'Res. A.1024(26): Guidelines for Ships Operating in Polar Waters' (London 2 December 2009)

1063 MSC, IMO, 'MSC 86/26: Report of the Maritime Safety Committee on its 86th session' (London 12 June 2009) 23.32

1064 MSC, IMO, 'Res. MSC.385(94)' (n 365)

1065 MSC, IMO, 'Res. MSC.386(94)' (n 365)

1066 Sun (n 329) 110

1067 Norway made the first proposal in 2003: MSC, IMO, 'MSC 78/24/8: Sub-Committees on Ship Design and Equipment and on Bulk Liquids and Gases; Proposal for developing international regulations on gas fuelled ships (Norway)' (London 19 December 2003); MSC, IMO, 'MSC 86/26' (n 1063); the final code was adopted in 2015 and made mandatory by an SOLAS amendment: MSC, IMO, 'Res. MSC.391(95): Adoption of the International Code of Safety for Ships Using Gases and Other Low-Flashpoint Fuels (IGF Code)' (London 11 June 2015); MSC, IMO, 'Res. MSC.392(95): Amendments to the International Convention for the Safety of Life at Sea, 1974' (London 11 June 2015)

1068 IMO, 'Res. A.774(18): Guidelines for Preventing the Introduction of Unwanted Aquatic Oranisms and Pathogens from Ships' Ballast Water and Sediment Discharge' (London 4 November 1993)

1069 IMO, 'Res. A.868(20): Guidelines for the Control and Management of Ships' Ballast Water to Minimize the Transfer of Harmful Aquatic Organisms and Pathogens' (London 27 November 1997)

on Sustainable Development, held in Johannesburg in 2002, called for action at all levels to intensify the measures to address invasive aquatic species. In 2004, the IMO Council convened a diplomatic conference where the International Convention for the Control and Management of Ships' Ballast Water and Sediments was adopted. In 2017, the convention entered into force.[1070] Again, guidelines were relied on as a pre-law instrument. However, the limited normative value is illustrated by the insufficient measures adopted by flag states. It is to be awaited whether compliance increases after the entry into force of the convention.

All three examples envisage the slow law-making process at the IMO to conclude binding instruments. Nevertheless, the initial adoption of non-binding guidelines as a preliminary measure in the formulation of subsequent, binding legislation can also prove advantageous: States can already adapt their national legislation and a uniform state practice can emerge.[1071] Moreover, other involved stakeholders can prepare for the new regulations. Then, the adoption of a binding instrument does not entail any significant changes. Consequently, the entry into force can be accomplished within a more abbreviated timeframe.

To conclude, guidelines can be distinguished from unified interpretations by their overarching horizontal scope and pre-law function. Both, procedural and substantial matters can be included. Furthermore, guidelines can be employed as a preliminary means of coping with innovative technologies.

With regard to MASS, four reasons militate in favor of guidelines. First, a horizontal regulation is necessary as several IMO instruments are affected by the advent of MASS. Second, flag state administrations need to develop new verification processes where IMO guidelines could help to harmonize the procedures. Third, legally binding regulations are preferable in the long term. As guidelines have proven their function as pre-law, a MASS-guideline could facilitate the subsequent process of adopting a hard law instrument. Fourth, MASS guidelines could be adopted by majority vote at the IMO Assembly or a Committee enabling timely adoption.

However, the necessary scope of MASS regulations could go beyond the usual scope of guidelines. Therefore, a code, the most formal non-binding IMO

1070 See for the lawmaking process the homepage of the IMO: IMO, 'BWM Convention and Guidelines' <https://www.imo.org/en/OurWork/Environment/Pages/BWMConventionandGuidelines.aspx> accessed 16 February 2024

1071 Boyle, 'Boyle 2019' (n 919) 103; Boyle, 'Boyle 1999' (n 959) 904; Ilg (n 230) 76; Henry (n 924) 75

instrument could serve the purpose of MASS even better. This instrument shall be considered next.

5.3.1.3 Codes

Since its inception, the IMO has adopted more than 40 codes. These instruments resemble a complex and comprehensive compendium of detailed regulations on shipping matters. The subject matter of codes is not limited to either interpretative means or procedural aspects. Rather, codes can provide substantive regulations that can also go beyond the scope of the existing legal framework.[1072] Codes are adopted by the IMO Assembly or one or several of its Committees as resolutions. Just as unified interpretations and guidelines, codes are merely recommendatory to the member states. However, their practical and legal significance is considerable. The vast number of codes and their broad scope made codes an indispensable instrument of maritime regulation.[1073]

The practical relevance of codes results from four aspects: their clear wording, horizontal effect, their model status for subsequent binding regulations, and the references to them by classification societies. Firstly, codes are formulated precisely and clearly, which facilitates national implementation.[1074] Codes are developed by national maritime experts at the IMO who focus on the practicality of regulations. In contrast to unified interpretations, codes not just supplement existing provisions but can create a new, comprehensive set of rules. States can thus transpose the codes into their national law without alteration and can use codes as model laws.[1075]

Not only clear wording facilitates national implementation. Additionally, national implementation of IMO codes is easy because the representatives at the IMO are the ones who are nationally responsible for the implementation.[1076] This is especially true for the rules that can be implemented nationally by bylaws. Nevertheless, even if parliamentary legislation is required, the preparatory work is often done by the people who represent the states at the IMO. In addition to a genuine interest in the implementation of the rules they have drawn up themselves, the extensive expert knowledge of these individuals supports national implementation.

1072 Ilg (n 230) 54
1073 ibid 54–55
1074 ibid 60
1075 Henry (n 924) 83
1076 ibid

Secondly, codes can have a horizontal effect on several conventions. This is especially true if the code provides new regulations on a subject matter covered by multiple existing conventions. During the legislative process of such a cross-convention code, all Committees responsible for the concerned conventions cooperate. As an example, the Polar Code addresses safety and environmental issues for shipping in polar waters and thus touches upon the field of regulation of SOLAS and MARPOL. Consequently, the MSC and the MEPC cooperated and jointly adopted the Polar Code.[1077] Likewise, the Code for Recognized Organizations was adopted jointly by the MSC and MEPC as it addresses the verification process in SOLAS, MARPOL, and other conventions.[1078] Codes relating to several conventions underline the overlapping system of international shipping conventions. Consequently, codes may be regarded as a conduit between the conventions that concentrate on a specific case of application.

Thirdly, codes are non-legally binding. They often serve as pre-law to later binding instruments. This pre-law function is common to guidelines and codes. As with guidelines, the pre-law function increases the practical relevance of codes in two aspects: On the one side, codes are used as a regulatory experiment to assess the necessity of regulation and the required scope and degree of detail.[1079] As codes can be amended easily, subsequent developments, especially technological innovation, can be reflected.[1080] The risk of 'locking-in' is low.

The emergence of high-speed crafts in the 1960s made additional regulations and specific safety requirements necessary. The first non-binding code was adopted by the IMO in 1977.[1081] In 1994, the MSC recognized the need for amendments due to continuous technical development and adopted the Code of Safety for High-Speed Crafts.[1082] Later, several amendments were necessary to ensure that the regulation kept pace with technological development.[1083] In

1077 MEPC, IMO, 'Res. MEPC.264(68) – International Code for Ships Operating in Polar Waters' (London 15 May 2015); MSC, IMO, 'Res. MSC.385(94)' (n 365)

1078 MEPC, IMO, 'Res. MEPC. 237(65) – Code for Recognized Organizations' (n 1053); MSC, IMO, 'Res. MSC.349(92)' (n 1053)

1079 Henry (n 924) 74; Kirgis (n 993) 84

1080 Kirgis (n 993) 87

1081 IMCO, 'Resolution A. 373(X) – Code of Safety for Dynamically Supported Craft' (14 November 1977)

1082 MSC, IMO, 'Res. MSC. 36(63): Code of Safety for High Speed Craft' (London 20 May 1994)

1083 MSC, IMO, 'Res. MSC. 174(79): Amendments to the International Code of Safety for High-Speed Craft' (London 10 December 2004); MSC, IMO, 'Res. MSC. 439(99): Amendments for the International Code of Safety for High Speed Craft' (London 24 May 2018); MSC, IMO, 'Res. MSC.259(84): Amendments to the International Code of Safety for High-Speed Craft'

this case, the advantages of non-binding codes could be utilized to provide a reliable and suitable framework for innovative technology.

In addition, the pre-law function and the transparent negotiation process at the IMO eases national implementation. All IMO member states can participate in the negotiations, influence the law-making process, and be informed about the latest developments. This allows states to assess national processes early and to form national positions on the matters concerned.

No less important is the moral or political force to adhere to the non-binding code after it has been adopted unanimously at the IMO.[1084] As retaliation is a common way of reacting to failures to comply with international law, the consequences of breaching a moral obligation can be considerable.[1085] The reciprocal dependence of port, coastal, and flag states increases the benefits of compliance with politically binding instruments. Moreover, a technical assistance program for developing states supports implementation.[1086]

Fourthly, the role of classification societies has to be considered. Classification societies often refer to IMO codes in their guidelines and thus make compliance with the recommendatory instruments quasi-mandatory.[1087] This saves work at the classification society and ensures that the states agree to the standards applied by the classes during vessel verification processes.

The illustrated practical significance of codes is further supported by different ways to increase the legal effect of codes. All codes are adopted as resolutions and codes are not legally binding for the member states. Some codes have remained in this non-legally binding status.[1088] Others, however, have been 'upgraded' by additional measures implemented on the national, supranational, or international level.

At the national level, states can decide to make a code mandatory by national legislation. The provisions of the code can be either converted into national law. Alternatively, a dynamic reference can incorporate the entire code into national law. The International Maritime Dangerous Goods Code was made mandatory nationally by 51 states[1089] before it was made mandatory

(London 16 May 2008); MSC, IMO, 'Res. MSC. 221(82): Amendments to the International Code of Safety for High-Speed Craft' (London 8 December 2006)

1084 Ilg (n 230) 56

1085 Weil (n 904) 415

1086 Chircop, 'Chircop 2015' (n 308) 434

1087 Nam (n 1033) 426

1088 IMO, 'Res. A.714(17): Code of Safe Practice for Cargo Stowage and Securing' (London 6 November 1991); IMO, 'Res. A.1021(26): Code on Alerts and Indicators' (London 2 December 2009)

1089 IMO, 'Focus on IMO – IMO and dangerous goods at sea' (London May 1996) 31–32

at the international level.[1090] However, states are reluctant to adopt national legislation exceeding international binding regulations, as they fear competitive disadvantages for their merchant fleet.

However, states acting as port states include non-binding codes in the scope of port state control regimes to intensify international compliance.[1091] As flag states suffer significant economic disadvantages if vessels flying their flags are denied access to relevant ports, the inclusion of non-binding codes in the scope of port state control regimes contributes significantly to their global acceptance and implementation.[1092] Even in the absence of an amendment to port state control agreements, the inclusion of non-favorable treatment clauses[1093] increases international compliance. Such clauses prevent states from favoring non-parties and stipulate that all vessels despite their flag have to comply with the instrument concerned.[1094] Thus, for a global legal effect, not the absolute number of national implementations matters but rather whether leading maritime states, this includes flag, port, and coastal states, have implemented a certain code.[1095] The EU has also relied on its port state clout and made non-binding parts of codes mandatory by including them into EU legislation. This co-legislation of the IMO and the EU will be considered in more detail below in section 5.5.3.

Most often, however, codes were made mandatory at the international level by including a reference to them in an international convention. Mostly, SOLAS and MARPOL were amended to include former non-binding codes. This practice extended the scope of SOLAS and MARPOL considerably and ensured that these conventions kept up with the technological development. The amendment procedure will be illustrated in the next section. Alternatively, the reference to GAIRAS in UNCLOS can make codes legally binding for all members of UNCLOS. As illustrated above,[1096] non-binding codes can fall within the scope of GAIRAS. Based on qualitative and quantitative broad support, codes can become 'generally accepted'.[1097] However, most codes are made mandatory via references in conventions and in this way included in the scope of GAIRAS.

1090 See for more nationally implemented IMO codes: Henry (n 924) 83

1091 See as an example Annex 10, Reg. 10, 74 of the Paris MoU including the certificates issued under the Special Purpose Ship Safety Code and the Mobile Offshore Drilling Unit Code

1092 Henry (n 924) 83–84

1093 Ilg (n 230) 133; IMO, 'Implications of the United Nations Convention on the Law of the Sea for the International Maritime Organization' (n 259) 12

1094 Reiling, *Reiling no date* (n 294) 386

1095 Ilg (n 230) 60

1096 See section 3.3.2

1097 Oxman (n 336) 157; Frenzel (n 335) 165

Rarely, codes are not legally binding, even though they are supported by a sufficient number of states to be 'generally accepted'.

To conclude, codes are legally non-binding instruments adopted by the IMO. Due to their precise wording and comprehensive scope, the transparent and inclusive adoption procedure, reciprocal benefits of voluntary compliance, and reference to codes by classification societies codes are an indispensable element of maritime regulation. They can gain increased legal value by incorporation in binding national or international instruments as well as based on general acceptance. Codes are therefore accorded a prominent position. Lampe categorizes codes somewhere between recommendations and binding conventions,[1098] and Kirgis labels codes as "super-recommendation".[1099] The following section briefly introduces the planned work of the IMO, which involves developing a goal-based code for MASS. Subsequently, this text will discuss the advantages and disadvantages of adopting a MASS Code.

After finalizing the RSE, the MSC agreed to develop a non-mandatory code as a first step before continuing with the development of a binding code.[1100] An intersessional working group was established and instructed to draft the MASS Code. The draft was presented in 2023.[1101] According to the road map, the MASS Code shall be adopted as a non-binding instrument in 2025 and enter into force as a binding instrument in 2032.[1102] The development of the MASS Code shall be guided by the generic guidelines for developing IMO goal-based standards.[1103] These rules for rule-setting provide a framework for the drafting of goal-based regulations. Rather than prescribing the use of a certain technology, the regulation shall indicate the goals to be achieved, the functional requirements that need to be fulfilled, and how to prove conformity during the verification process.[1104]

Considering the functional, practical, and legal significance of codes presented above, several arguments can be made in favor of a MASS Code. However, legal constraints have been raised and will be discussed subsequently.

1098 Wilhelm H Lampe, 'The "New" International Maritime Organization And Its Place In Development Of International Maritime Law' (1983) 14(3) Journal of Maritime Law and Commerce 305, 318

1099 Kirgis (n 993) 84

1100 MSC, IMO, 'MSC 105/20: Report of the Maritime Safety Committee on its 105th Session' (London 19 May 2022) 40

1101 MSC, IMO, 'MSC 107-5 – Report of the MASS Correspondence Group' (London 27 February 2023)

1102 MSC, IMO, 'MSC 108/20' (n 10) 44

1103 MSC, IMO, 'MSC.1/Circ.1394/Rev.2' (n 870)

1104 See no. 10, 11, and 16 of these regulations: MSC, IMO, 'MSC.1/Circ.1394/Rev.2' (n 870)

MASS affect almost all IMO conventions. As a coherent integration of MASS is of high importance, a MASS regulation needs to exceed the scope of a single convention and have an overarching approach. Codes can provide such cross-convention regulation.[1105] Like the Polar Code, a MASS Code could provide MASS-specific regulations and supplement the existing legal framework.[1106] All MASS provisions would be collected in one instrument making compliance easier. Therefore, a single instrument is preferable to amending each affected convention individually.[1107]

Likewise, codes are capable of providing the comprehensive scope of regulations needed for MASS. Both, new substantial provisions as well as clarifications about the meaning of certain terms such as 'manning' or 'lookout' can be incorporated in a MASS Code. Additionally, the flexibility inherent to non-binding codes suits the request for a dynamic and evolving regulation.[1108] However, the risk of premature regulations hampering further development should be borne in mind.[1109] Therefore, the involvement of classification societies in the development process[1110] as well as the phrasing as goal-based standards is important.[1111]

As correctly pointed out by some, adopting standards for a fast-evolving technology is challenging.[1112] Additionally, the persons involved in the verification process need sufficient knowledge and experience to assess properly whether the proposed solution fulfills the functional requirements.[1113]

1105 Soyer (n 86) 174

1106 MSC, IMO, 'MSC 105/7/3: Discussion on some key issues in the development of the MASS instrument and proposal for a structure of a draft MASS Code (Norway)' (London 14 January 2022) 2; Pentti Kujala and Liangliang Lu (eds), *Marine Design XIII, Volume 2: Proceedings of the 13th International Marine Design Conference (IMDC 2018), June 10–14, 2018, Helsinki, Finland* (Chapman and Hall/CRC 2018) 883; Martin Bergström and others, 'Towards the unmanned ship code' in Pentti Kujala and Liangliang Lu (eds), *Marine Design XIII, Volume 2: Proceedings of the 13th International Marine Design Conference (IMDC 2018), June 10–14, 2018, Helsinki, Finland* (Chapman and Hall/CRC 2018) 883

1107 MSC, IMO, 'MSC.1/Circ.1638' (n 18) 9; Pritchett (n 760), 223

1108 Bartlett (n 521), 89; Petrig (n 416) 132

1109 Petrig (n 416) 132

1110 Kujala and Lu (eds) (n 1106) 883; Ntovas (n 675) 231–232; Ismael C Delgado, 'The IMO: The Role of the Classification Societies in Promoting Global Ocean Governance' in David J Attard, Rosalie P Balkin and Donald W Greig (eds), *The IMLI Treatise on Global Ocean Governance: Volumen III: IMO and Global Ocean Governance* (First edition. Oxford University Press 2018) 269; Petrig (n 416) 135; van Hooydonk (n 543), 411

1111 MSC, IMO, 'MSC 105/7/3' (n 1106) 3; Petrig (n 416) 122; Fenwick, Kaal and Vermeulen (n 852) 590

1112 Bergström and others (n 1106) 883; Ringbom, 'Ringbom 2020' (n 424) 436

1113 Engtrø (n 868) 75

However, these aspects should not lead to a decision not to regulate. Rather, careful, goal-based drafting and close cooperation of all involved stakeholders can minimize the risk of inappropriate premature regulation and lacking verification competence. Moreover, the simple amendment process for codes makes necessary updates possible in a timely manner.

To conclude, codes have proven to be highly effective in regulating the shipping industry, without being necessarily legally binding. This makes a MASS Code an appropriate regulatory instrument. Although some argue that a non-binding MASS Code would not be sufficiently effective and that a binding solution should be pursued instead,[1114] it is important to acknowledge that flag states would not be obligated to register MASS and port states could discourage MASS by not providing suitable port infrastructure. Therefore, a mandatory MASS instrument may not necessarily increase the accessible area for MASS. Ultimately, MASS operation depend on the willingness of port and coastal states to provide suitable shore-based infrastructure.

In contrast, a non-binding MASS Code offers the advantage of leaving the decision to make the code mandatory to the discretion of member states. This allows them to determine the most appropriate way of implementing MASS domestically, taking into account their national maritime law framework and constitutional constraints. By doing so, the policy decision on whether MASS are desirable would be shifted from the IMO to the member states. Achieving a consensus decision at IMO is easier when only a non-binding instrument is pursued. Therefore, adopting a non-binding MASS Code can be done rather quickly.

5.3.1.4 Conclusions

This section discussed legally non-binding instruments adopted by the IMO. Having different cases of application, unified interpretations, guidelines, and codes could all be used for MASS regulation. However, a code seems the most appropriate as a comprehensive compendium of regulations touching upon several conventions could be included. Eventually, the prominent position awarded to codes facilitates broad support among all stakeholders. Guidelines could contribute to streamlining the registration and port state control procedures by prescribing a harmonized method.

As already touched upon, codes can be made mandatory by incorporation into the annex of conventions. As an incorporation of MASS regulations into hard law provides the highest possible legal certainty, several scholars advocate

1114 Parker (n 522) 41

for the amendment of the affected international conventions. Additionally, some question the capability of non-binding instruments to alter the meaning of hard law conventions. Consequently, the next section is devoted to assessing amending the existing international legal framework to cope with the legal challenges identified above.

5.3.2 *Amendments to the International Legal Framework*

The legal framework's adaptation to MASS introduced thus far relies on legally non-binding instruments, which do not provide significant legal certainty. Although the effectiveness of non-binding instruments should not be underestimated, legally binding instruments could be preferable and will be illustrated and discussed now. First, formally amending the international legal framework will be considered before turning, as second, to other instruments and procedures to change the current legal framework.

The legal analysis above revealed that new provisions and clarifications on the interpretation are necessary in the scope of SOLAS, COLREG, and UNCLOS. Developing new provisions presents undoubtedly an amendment. However, it is not straightforward to characterize a clarifying provision as an amendment, as the difference between interpretations and amendments is not always decisive.[1115]

Whether an act of a state[1116] constitutes an amendment or an interpretation depends on whether the act is adopted solely to resolve a particular case, or if the act concerns the interpretation isolated from a specific case. If a provision is applied to a given case, its application cannot result in an amendment of the provision, even if the interpretation deviates significantly from the conventional interpretation.[1117] Without the states' consent, subsequent practice cannot amend a provision.[1118] If states agree to adopt a specific interpretation in the future, this would exclude other possible interpretations, resulting in an amendment to the provision. It is worth noting, however, that such an agreement does not need to take the form of an international treaty. Instead, any subsequent action that evidences the intention of the parties to influence the

1115 Geraldo Vidigal, 'From Bilateral to Multilateral Law-making: Legislation, Practice, Evolution and the Future of Inter Se Agreements in the WTO' (2013) 24(4) European Journal of International Law 1027, 1035

1116 Gardiner (n 454) 257

1117 Iain Cameron, 'Treaties, Declarations of Interpretation' (December 2020). Max Planck Encyclopedia of Public International Law (MPEPIL) 12; Buga (n 322) 52; Regan (n 434) 1059

1118 Nolte, 'Nolte 2015' (n 465) 19; Tzanakopoulos (n 456) 92; Zemanek (n 466) 7; Dahm (n 465) 673; Bernandez (n 466) 27

treaty's interpretation beyond the specific case could lead to an amendment by fixing the treaty's interpretation.[1119] Consequently, both changes, adopting new substantive provisions and clarifying the interpretation are to be considered as amendments to the conventions.

In general, for an amendment to an international treaty to enter into force, the same procedure as that for the initial creation of the treaty applies, i.e. adoption and consent to be bound.[1120] Usually, the adoption takes place at an international conference, mostly by consensus. For multilateral agreements such as UNCLOS and the GAIRAS treaties, this would necessitate an agreement by all of the more than 160 contracting states. For the entry into force, states need to consent to be bound by the treaty. For a treaty to come into force, a specific number of states must give their consent to be bound by it. Articles 11–15 of the VCLT provide for different methods to express the consent to be bound by a treaty. For multilateral treaties, ratification in accordance with domestic rules is the most common method. Then, the ratification serves as the legal basis for the mandatory character of the amendment concerned.[1121]

However, this procedure is as time-consuming as the initial adoption of a treaty and rather inflexible. Especially reaching a unanimous agreement among all state parties and a sufficient number of ratifications prolongs amendment processes considerably.[1122] As a response, several coping mechanisms have been developed. On the one hand, treaties have incorporated alternative amendment procedures to expedite the process. On the other hand, agreements have been made without adhering to the formal amendment procedure, resulting in a de facto amendment of the primary treaty. Both formal and de facto amendments will be examined and assessed in the light of the necessary MASS amendments.

All three conventions, SOLAS, COLREG, and UNCLOS provide for formal amendment procedures. First, procedures provided by SOLAS will be

1119 Gardiner (n 454) 251; Buga (n 322) 47

1120 Hernández, *Hernández 2019* (n 437) 171

1121 ibid 169

1122 William Tetley, 'Uniformity of International Private Maritime Law – The Pros, Cons, and Alternatives to International Conventions – How to Adopt an International Convention' (2000) 24(2) Tulane Maritime Law Journal 775–856, 817; M. Bowman, 'Towards a Unified Treaty Body for Monitoring Compliance with UN Human Rights Conventions? Legal Mechanisms for Treaty Reform' (2007) 7(1) Human Rights Law Review 225, 232; Jose A E Faria, 'Future Directions of Legal Harmonisation and Law Reform: Stormy Seas or Prosperous Voyage' (2009) 14(1/2) Uniform Law Review 5, 8

considered before, as second, an amendment to COLREG is discussed. Eventually, the procedures provided by UNCLOS are assessed. After giving an overview of the explicit amendment procedure, the procedure will be discussed in the context of the MASS.

5.3.2.1 Amendments to SOLAS

Article VIII SOLAS provides for two different amendment procedures, depending on whether an article of the Convention or Chapter I of the Annex is to be amended or whether a chapter of the Annex other than Chapter I is to be amended. Both procedures shall be considered and discussed in the light of the necessary MASS-amendments.

5.3.2.1.1 *Explicit Amendment Procedure*

This section focusses on the explicit amendment procedure which shall be applied to amendments to the Articles of the Convention and Chapter I of the Annex. Article VIII stipulates the procedure and states that

> (a) The present Convention may be amended by either of the procedures specified in the following paragraphs.
>
> (b) Amendments after consideration within the Organization:
>
> (i) Any amendment proposed by a Contracting Government shall be submitted to the Secretary-General of the Organization, who shall then circulate it to all Members of the Organization and all Contracting Governments at least six months prior to its consideration.
> (ii) Any amendment proposed and circulated as above shall be referred to the Maritime Safety Committee of the Organization for consideration.
> (iii) Contracting Governments of States, whether or not Members of the Organization, shall be entitled to participate in the proceedings of the Maritime Safety Committee for the consideration and adoption of amendments.
> (iv) Amendments shall be adopted by a two-thirds majority of the Contracting Governments present and voting in the Maritime Safety Committee expanded as provided for in subparagraph (iii) of this paragraph (hereinafter referred to as "the expanded Maritime Safety Committee") on condition that at least one third of the Contracting Governments shall be present at the time of voting.

(v) Amendments adopted in accordance with subparagraph (IV) of this paragraph shall be communicated by the Secretary-General of the Organization to all Contracting Governments for acceptance.

(vi)

(1) An amendment to an article of the Convention or to chapter I of the annex shall be deemed to have been accepted on the date on which it is accepted by two thirds of the Contracting Governments.

(2) [...]

(vii)

(1) An amendment to an article of the Convention or to chapter I of the annex shall enter into force with respect to those Contracting Governments which have accepted it, six months after the date on which it is deemed to have been accepted, and with respect to each Contracting Government which accepts it after that date, six months after the date of that Contracting Government's acceptance.

(2) [...]

(c) Amendment by a Conference:

(i) Upon the request of a Contracting Government concurred in by at least one third of the Contracting Governments, the Organization shall convene a Conference of Contracting Governments to consider amendments to the present Convention.

(ii) Every amendment adopted by such a Conference by a two-thirds majority of the Contracting Governments present and voting shall be communicated by the Secretary-General of the Organization to all Contracting Governments for acceptance.

(iii) Unless the Conference decides otherwise, the amendment shall be deemed to have been accepted and shall enter into force in accordance with the procedures specified in subparagraphs (b)(VI) and (b)(VII) respectively of this article, provided that references in these paragraphs to the expanded Maritime Safety Committee shall be taken to mean references to the Conference.

(d), (e), (f) [...]

(g) The Secretary-General of the Organization shall inform all Contracting Governments of any amendments which enter into force under this article, together with the date on which each such amendment enters into force.

Section (VII)(2) reiterates the pacta tertiis principle reflected in Article 40(5) of the VCLT that an amendment to a multilateral treaty shall only bind those states that have ratified it. With regard to states that have only ratified the main treaty, the amendment shall not be applicable.

The main part of SOLAS includes only 13 articles followed by 16 chapters in the Annex. Out of the main articles, seven articles address procedural aspects such as amendments and the entry into force. Amendments to these articles are unlikely, as they do not affect substantial matters on the safety of life at sea. However, chapter I of the Annex includes provisions on the application of SOLAS and definitions in Regulation I-2 of SOLAS. Here, a MASS-amendment could be incorporated providing for specific interpretations of terms used in SOLAS such as master, manning, and crew. Therefore, SOLAS Chapter I could be amended for the purpose of MASS. In the following, the appropriateness of this solution is to be discussed.

Although an amendment to SOLAS would lead to a legally binding and thus predictable framework for MASS on a global scale there are some considerable drawbacks. First, the explicit amendment procedure is very time-consuming as it necessitates both, negotiations in the MSC or the conference of parties and a ratification process.[1123] Additionally, the time periods prescribed between submission and discussion of the proposal and before entering into force prolong the amendment process. Most important in respect of time, however, is the necessary national implementation process including the adoption of a parliamentary bill. It is not uncommon for ratifications to hang in the mills of national parliaments for a long time.[1124] Eventually, most states restrain from being first-movers and leading maritime states wait for each other to ratify an amendment. Thus, the number of ratifications stagnates as states wait for ratifications by other states.[1125]

Several examples can be brought forward evidencing the reluctance of states to ratify amendments to international agreements. SOLAS 1960 could not be amended at all as none of the amendment proposals reached the necessary quorum for entry into force.[1126] Also in newer times, the entry into force of amendments takes considerable time. In 1997, a protocol to MARPOL was

1123 MSC, IMO, 'MSC 105/7/2: Outline of the draft guidelines for MASS operations (Japan, Russian Federation and United Arab Emirates)' (London 13 January 2022) 2

1124 Shi (n 744), 304–305

1125 Faria (n 1122) 26; Bowman (n 1122) 232; Tetley (n 1122) 817

1126 MSC, IMCO, 'MSC 25/13: Amendment Procedures in Conventions for which IMCO is Depositary, Note by the Secretariat' (London 24 January 1972) 7

adopted to include a new annex that addresses air pollution from vessels.[1127] Eight years later the entry into force requirement was fulfilled,[1128] although the topic had been discussed since the 1970s.[1129]

In some cases, the threat of not achieving the required number of ratifications within a reasonable timeframe was so great that a formal amendment was not proposed. The increased use of digital means such as email to conclude arbitration agreements made a change of Article 2(2)[1130] of the 1958 Convention on the Recognition and Enforcement of Foreign Arbitral Award necessary.[1131] The United Nations Commission On International Trade Law refrained from proposing a formal amendment[1132] and concluded a recommendation on the interpretation of this article. Article 2(2) of the 1958 Convention should be interpreted in a way that the listed circumstances of conclusions for the arbitral clause should not be interpreted as being exhaustive.[1133] In the aftermath, the judicial practice of courts adapted and made a formal amendment superfluous.[1134]

Reluctance to ratify amendments occurred mostly in situations where an amendment adds stricter provisions compared to the existing situation. States

---

1127 Conference of the Parties to MARPOL, 'MP/CONF. 3/34 – Consideration and Adoption of the Protocol of 1997 to amend MARPOL' (London 28 October 1997)

1128 Pursuant to Article 6 "[t]he […] protocol shall enter into force twelve months after the date on which not less than fifteen States, the combined merchant fleets of which constitute not less than 50 per cent of the gross tonnage of the world's merchant shipping, have become Parties to it"

1129 See for an overview of the preceding discussions: IMO, 'MARPOL Annex VI history' (8 June 2021) <https://www.imo.org/en/MediaCentre/PressBriefings/Pages/MARPOL100State.aspx> accessed 16 February 2024

1130 Article 2(2) states that "[t]he term "agreement in writing" shall include an arbitral clause […] signed by the parties or contained in an exchange of letters or telegrams"

1131 Convention on the Recognition and Enforcement of Foreign Arbitral Awards, No. 4739 10 June 1958

1132 As the 1958 Convention does not provide for an amendment procedure, all contracting governments would have had to ratify the amendment. As the convention was ratifyied by more thn 160 states, the risk of legal fragmentation was considered to high

1133 UNCITRAL, 'Recommendation regarding the Interpretation of Article II (2) and Article VII (1) of the Convention on the Recognition and Enforcement of Foreign Arbitral Awards' (Vienna 7 July 2006)

1134 UNCITRAL Secretariat, 'Guide on the Convention on the Recognition and Enforcement of Foreign Arbitral Awards: New York, 1958' in Uncitral Secretariat, Emmanuel Gaillard and George A Bermann (eds), *Guide on the Convention on the Recognition and Enforcement of Foreign Arbitral Awards: New York 1958* (Brill 2017) 50–52

suspect economic disadvantages when implementing stricter provisions than other states. This is especially relevant for flag states as ship owners can easily change the flag of their vessels. From a port state's perspective, ships might refrain from calling at ports where stricter requirements apply. The MASS amendments, however, would not impose stricter regulations but rather enlarge the possible modes of operation. MASS operations, currently uncertain from a legal perspective, would be enabled and safeguarded by legal means. States could face an economic advantage of being a first mover and providing a regulatory framework for MASS. Industry could be attracted to settle and make business in states ratifying the MASS amendments. Whether the will to present itself as an innovation-friendly shipping location outweighs the reluctance to ratify amendments as first remains to be seen. Nevertheless, two thirds of the contracting governments to SOLAS, i.e. 111 states, would need to ratify the amendment for its entry into force.

Secondly, even if 111 states would ratify the amendment, the risk of legal fragmentation occurs. As pointed out above, an amendment to chapter I of SOLAS only applies inter partes, i.e. only between states which have ratified the amendment. The consequence would be two different, parallel regimes, depending on whether the involved states have ratified the amendment or not. The example of the international rules for the international carriage of goods by sea impressively demonstrates the negative consequences of parallel regimes. The first codification was adopted in 1924 and ratified by 86 states. Following an amendment in 1968,[1135] the regime was referred to as "Hague-Visby-Rules" and ratified by only 24 states. Another amendment, the SDR protocol, was concluded in 1979[1136] and it changed the unit of account from pound sterling to special drawing rights. It was ratified by 19 states. One year earlier, the United Nations Convention on the carriage of goods by sea[1137] also referred to as the 'Hamburg Rules' was adopted to reflect multimodal transport and containerization. However, only 35 states, mostly developing states, ratified this convention. The latest attempt to consolidate the fragmented legal regime was

1135 Protocol to Amend the International Convention for the Unification of Certain Rules of Law Relating to Bills of Lading, No. 23643 23 February 1968

1136 Protocol Amending the International Convention for the Unification of Certain Rules of Law Relating to Bills of Lading, as amended by the protocol of 23.02.1968, No. 23643 21 December 1979

1137 United Nations Convention on the carriage of goods by sea, No. 29215 31 March 1978

undertaken in 2008/2009 and lead to the adoption of the Rotterdam Rules.[1138] As of 2023, only 5 states ratified these rules and they have not yet entered into force. All attempts to change the initially adopted Hague-Rules increased legal fragmentation. As there are five different regimes on the carriage of goods by sea, which partly overlap, determining the applicable law has become a true challenge. Although a provision that exempts amendments from requiring ratification by all state parties to the main treaty can expedite the process of entry into force, it has the potential to foster legal fragmentation.

With regard to MASS, the disadvantages of fragmentation are significantly lower than in comparison to other regulatory targets. As illustrated above, MASS do not necessarily require a globally harmonized legal framework. It would suffice the needs of MASS if, at first, only some states ratify the MASS amendments. Moreover, coordinate regional approaches might mitigate the risk of legal fragmentation. Such approaches are discussed in the section on regional and European regulation on MASS in more detail. Although MASS will be mainly deployed in regional feeder services, the ship building and ship supply industry are international and would benefit from internationally coherent regulations. Moreover, implementing international amendments, which rely on regional coordination for being effective, is not advisable.

Thirdly, the lack of flexibility is used as an argument against the formal amendment procedure. As a result of the time-consuming nature of this procedure and the risk of lack of universal acceptance, several successive amendments are unlikely. This leads to a lock-in situation where the law is unable to respond adequately to technological innovation. This is what occurred in the above-introduced example of the 1958 Convention on the recognition of arbitral awards. This effect of fixing a particular state-of-the-art in international conventions is also known as the 'petrification effect'.[1139] Locked-in technologies cannot be released due to the absence of flexible and practical amendment procedures. The term is based on Kronke's German term 'Versteinerung', which describes the phenomenon of regulations becoming locked-in within international treaties due to insurmountable requirements for amendments.[1140]

1138 United Nations General Assembly, 'Res. A/Res/63/122 – United Nations Convention on Contracts for the International Carriage of Goods Wholly or Partly by Sea' (New York 2 February 2009)

1139 Herbert Kronke, 'Ziele—Methoden, Kosten—Nutzen: Perspektiven der Privatrechtsharmonisierung nach 75 Jahren UNIDROIT' (2001) 56(23) JuristenZeitung 1149, 1152

1140 ibid

However, as illustrated above, flexibility of regulation is especially important for emerging technologies such as MASS. Although the IMO has adopted guidelines for the development of goal-based standards prescribing goals to be achieved and functions to be fulfilled,[1141] a lock-in effect could occur when formally amending SOLAS. The lack of flexibility has an even more serious consequence, as the IMO's consensus practice often means that only the lowest common denominator can be decided.[1142] Despite the existence of mechanisms designed to mitigate the risk of petrification, it is unclear whether these will be included in the SOLAS amendments. For instance, dynamic review mechanisms permit the regular evaluation of regulations. However, these mechanisms only address the issue of identifying outdated regulations. Consequently, the necessary amendments must be adopted using the formal and time-consuming amendment procedure.

Eventually, the effect of a SOLAS amendment on the interpretation of COLREG is rather questionable. Although a provision shall be interpreted considering the applicable law between the parties[1143] so that a SOLAS amendment can impact COLREG's interpretation, it would only be one of several authentic materials to be taken into account for interpretation. However, the importance of a horizontal coherent regulation for MASS was pointed out above.

To conclude, the explicit amendment procedure as laid down in SOLAS is very time-consuming, though it ensures legal certainty as a ratified amendment is legally binding for the contracting states. Additionally, the long time needed to acquire a sufficient number of ratifications could prevent future amendments if the technology further develops. Although states could abstain from setting a high entry into force threshold and the risk of legal fragmentation is negligible, a SOLAS amendment could not provide a coherent horizontal integration of MASS. As concluded in the legal analysis above, an amendment to SOLAS would not suffice the needs of MASS. Rather, all discussed conventions, SOLAS, COLREG, and UNCLOS would need to be addressed to ensure a coherent interpretation including MASS operations. An amendment to SOLAS is not able to fulfill this requirement. An amendment to chapter I of SOLAS applying the explicit amendment procedure is not recommended. Besides the discussed explicit amendment procedure, SOLAS provides for a simplified tacit acceptance procedure. This procedure shall be discussed in the following section.

1141 MSC, IMO, 'MSC.1/Circ.1394/Rev.2' (n 870)

1142 Ilg (n 230) 25

1143 Article 31(3)(c) VCLT

5.3.2.1.2 *Tacit Acceptance Procedure*

The current version of SOLAS is the successor of three SOLAS conventions, SOLAS 1914, SOLAS 1948, and SOLAS 1960. Its predecessor conventions provided only for an explicit amendment procedure applicable to the text and the annex of the convention.[1144] The need for a revision arose due to the failed amendment history of SOLAS 1960,[1145] in addition to the importance of reflecting technological innovations in conventions[1146] and raising awareness about safety at sea. Following a review of the problem and possible alternative amendment procedures,[1147] the MSC and the LEG prepared, upon request of the council,[1148] a draft proposal for an accelerating amendment procedure in 1973.[1149] In essence, acceleration should be achieved by transferring amendment authority to the IMO. Since the success of amending the IMO-Convention was uncertain, the IMO should be empowered to adopt amendments by each convention separately.[1150] The LEG prepared draft provisions for the tacit acceptance procedure that could be used during the negotiations of future conventions.[1151]

The first convention including the novel tacit acceptance procedure was SOLAS 1974. Subsequently, the tacit acceptance procedure was included in STCW, MARPOL, and, with minor adjustments, COLREG. The success of the tacit acceptance procedure is overwhelming and this procedure has accelerated the amendment process.[1152] All conventions were amended successfully several times.[1153] In respect of SOLAS, the success of the tacit acceptance

1144 See Article 74 of the Convention for the Safety of Life at Sea signed at London, January 20, 1914; Article IX of SOLAS 1948 and SOLAS 1960

1145 MSC, IMCO (n 1126) 7

1146 ibid 9

1147 IMCO, 'A VII/12 – Amendment Procedures in Conventions for which IMCO is Depositary' (London 2 August 1971) 1

1148 IMCO, 'Resolution A.249 (VII): Amendment Procedures in Conventions for which IMCO is Depositary' (London 3 November 1971) 1

1149 IMCO, 'Amendment Procedure for Conventions for which IMCO is the Depository' (London 20 September 1973)

1150 ibid 9

1151 ibid Annex II

1152 J. A Roach, 'A Note on Making the Polar Code Mandatory' in Suzanne Lalonde and Ted L McDorman (eds), *International law and politics of the Arctic Ocean: Essays in honor of Donat Pharand* (Koninklijke Brill 2015) 127

1153 IMO, 'List of Conventions and their Amendments' (London 15 October 2021) <https://view.officeapps.live.com/op/view.aspx?src=https%3A%2F%2Fwwwcdn.imo.org%2Flocalresources%2Fen%2FAbout%2FConventions%2FStatusOfConventions%2FList%2520of%2520the%2520Conventions%2520and%2520their%2520amendments.docx&wdOrigin=BROWSELINK>

procedure has surpassed itself. Thus, the MSC decided on a four-year cycle for the entry into force of amendments to SOLAS in 1991 and 2014.[1154] The next entry into force dates for amendments are 2028 and 2032. After illustrating the procedure, its application to make a MASS Code mandatory will be discussed.

In general, an amendment must be adopted and accepted to enter into force. The tacit acceptance procedure affects the second step, the acceptance of an amendment. States are not required to accept the amendment explicitly; rather, it is deemed to have been accepted after a certain period of time has elapsed, unless a group of states has raised an objection. The first step of the amendment procedure, the adoption, is identical to the explicit amendment procedure. The tacit acceptance procedure shall only apply to amendments to the Annex other than Chapter I. Article VIII(b)(VI)(2) of SOLAS stipulates for the acceptance of an amendment that

> [a]n amendment to the annex other than chapter I shall be deemed to have been accepted:
>
> (aa) at the end of two years from the date on which it is communicated to Contracting Governments for acceptance; or
>
> (bb) at the end of a different period, which shall not be less than one year, if so determined at the time of its adoption by a two-thirds majority of the Contracting Governments present and voting in the expanded Maritime Safety Committee.
>
> However, if within the specified period either more than one-third of Contracting Governments, or Contracting Governments the combined merchant fleets of which constitute not less than fifty per cent of the gross tonnage of the world's merchant fleet, notify the Secretary-General of the Organization that they object to the amendment, it shall be deemed not to have been accepted.

Pursuant to Article VIII(c) of SOLAS, the same procedure applies to an amendment that was adopted by a specifically convened conference of the contracting governments. The distinctive feature of the tacit acceptance procedure is that the ratification of an amendment is not necessary for the entry into force. Thus, states can remain tacit and be bound by the amendment. This procedure

1154 MSC, IMO, 'MSC.1/Circ. 1481: Guidance on Entry Into Force of Amendments to the 1974 SOLAS Convention and Related Mandatory Instruments' (London 11 June 2014)

deviates from the general rule of international law that explicit consent is required.[1155]

The tacit acceptance procedure delegates law-making power to the IMO, an international organization. Delegated law-making can also be considered in the wider context of state sovereignty and international relations. Delegating law-making power is by no means confined to the international level, rather most national administrative governance systems are built upon the delegation of law-making power.[1156] However, compared to the national level, the delegation chain is even more extended at the international level. The national representatives at the IMO are mostly lower public officials and maritime experts.[1157] Seldom, the representatives are directly accountable to national parliaments. Delegation is chosen to reduce transaction costs of decision-making, particularly in international relations.[1158]

As illustrated, SOLAS was among the first international conventions including far-reaching delegation of law-making power to an international organization. Later, other international organizations such as the World Health Organization or the World Meteorological Organization were granted delegated regulatory power[1159] and environmental treaties like the Climate Change Convention[1160] or its Kyoto Protocol[1161] delegate law-making power to international organizations. International delegations considered in its broadest meaning "as a grant of authority by two or more states to an international body to make decisions or take actions".[1162]

1155 Malgosia Fitzmaurice and Panos Merkouris, 'Uniformity versus specialization (1): The quest for a uniform law of inter-State treaties' in Christian J Tams, Antonios Tzanakopoulos and Andreas Zimmermann (eds), *Research Handbook on the Law of Treaties* (Edward Elgar Publishing 2014) 356

1156 Hermann Pünder, 'Democratic Legitimation of Delegated Legislation – a Comparative View on the American, British and German Law' (2009) 58(2) International and Comparative Law Quarterly 353

1157 MSC, IMO, 'MSC 107/INF.1: List of Participants' (London 21 June 2023)

1158 Liesbet Hooghe and Gary Marks, 'Delegation and pooling in international organizations' (2015) 10(3) The Review of International Organizations 305, 307

1159 Ian Johnstone, 'Law-Making by International Organizations: Perspectives from IL/IR Theory' in Jeffrey L Dunoff and Mark A Pollack (eds), *Interdisciplinary Perspectives on International Law and International Relations: 'The State of the Art'* (Cambridge University Press 2013) 272

1160 United Nations Framework Convention on Climate Change, 30822 9 May 1992

1161 Kyoto Protocol to the United Nations Framework Convention on Climate Change, 30822 11 December 1997

1162 Curtis A Bradley and Judith G Kelley, 'The Concept of International Delegation' (2008) 71(1) Law and Contemporary Problems 1, 3

Moreover, eight types of delegation can be distinguished.[1163] The power of the IMO to adopted amendments to the technical annex of SOLAS can be considered as regulatory power in contrast to legislative power, which would include the adoption of amendments to the main articles and basic principles of the treaty.[1164] As illustrated, states do not have to explicitly consent to an amendment to the annex of SOLAS to be bound by it. Consequently, by delegating regulatory power to the IMO, a part of the state's sovereignty was relinquished.

Now, it is imperative to address the normative questions pertaining to the legitimacy and conditions of international delegation. Considering the ever increased use of tacit acceptance procedures omitting the ratification phase, Brunée criticizes the shift of domestic authority over international commitments as a result of the tacit acceptance procedure.[1165] In general, governments conduct international negotiations, whereas the national legislator is involved during the ratification. In the case of the tacit acceptance procedure, however, the ratification phase is omitted. This development, however, cannot be resolved at the international level, as domestic law regulates the legislative involvement in foreign affairs. Nevertheless, international law should take into account the effects of an ever-decreasing involvement of the national legislature.

Based on the assumption that states act as rational actors and weigh the benefits against the costs, they choose to delegate regulatory power to an international organization when the benefits outweigh the costs.[1166] Besides financial commitments to the operation of international organizations, states cede a share of sovereignty when empowering international organizations to adopt legally binding instruments. Therefore, the costs associated with international delegation are by some authors referred to as 'sovereignty costs'.[1167] Others criticize the term as sovereignty includes the power to dispose of it.[1168]

1163 ibid 10

1164 ibid 14; considering the IMO s powers as pooling authority rather than delegated authority. However, only taking into account the competencies granted in the IMO-Convention: Hooghe and Marks (n 1158), 309

1165 Jutta Brunnée, 'COPing with Consent: Law-Making Under Multilateral Environmental Agreements' (2002) 15(1) Leiden Journal of International Law 1, 20 <https://www.cambridge.org/core/journals/leiden-journal-of-international-law/article/coping-with-consent-lawmaking-under-multilateral-environmental-agreements/433380D1A98723786EAF4A449B22F9CF>

1166 Johnstone (n 1159) 277; Barbara Koremenos, 'When, What, and Why do States Choose to Delegate?' (2008) 71(1) Law and Contemporary Problems 151, 152

1167 Abbott and Snidal (n 909) 436; Oona A Hathaway, 'International Delegation and State Sovereignty' (2008) 71(1) Law and Contemporary Problems 115, 119

1168 Bradley and Kelley (n 1162) 28

The costs cannot be determined abstractly; rather they depend on the prevailing circumstances, the type of delegation, and the preference of the state in the case of absence of delegation.[1169] Likewise, the benefits of delegation depend on the specific case. Delegation of regulatory power e.g. facilitates coordinating national approaches and the conglomeration of expertise.[1170] In particular, global problems that require a collective approach by several states can be effectively addressed through delegated regulatory powers.[1171] Empirical evidence for the positive perception of international delegation by states can be found in the fact that more than half of all international agreements provide for delegation.[1172]

In parallel with the classical principal-agent situations, the principals (states) chose to empower the agent (international organization) if the principal's goals can be best achieved this way. States typically condition the delegation of regulatory power as the costs of granting authority may eventually outweigh the benefits.[1173] The IMO, e.g., is empowered to adopt amendments to the annex of SOLAS. However, such amendments shall be related to already existing provisions.[1174] If, despite a conditional delegation, the agent exceeds the authority granted by the principal, normative questions may arise as the delegated regulatory act is deprived of its normative basis, the consent of the state. This question is particularly important for democratic states, as the actions of international organizations are not inherently democratically legitimized.[1175] Dahl derives this conclusion from the fact that the barriers to political participation in international organizations are prohibitively high for citizens of democratic states.[1176]

States' consent may cover seemingly overriding agent acts in two situations. Firstly, states may have granted authority to an agent with the foresight of future evolutions and the necessity of evolving agent acts.[1177] In this case, the states explicitly intended for the agent to engage in innovative regulation and

1169 ibid 31
1170 ibid 26; Hathaway (n 1167) 143
1171 Andrew T Guzmán and Jennifer Landsidle, 'The Myth of International Delegation' (2008) 96(6) California Law Review 1693, 1694; Koremenos (n 1166) 169
1172 Koremenos (n 1166) 159
1173 Hathaway (n 1167), 136; Guzmán and Landsidle (n 1171) 1694
1174 LEG, IMCO, 'LEG XIV/4: Report of the Legal Committee on the Work of the 14th Session' (London 27 September 1972) 15
1175 Robert A Dahl, 'Can international organizations be democratic? A skeptic's view' in Ian Shapiro and Casiano Hacker-Cordón (eds), *Democracy's edges* (Contemporary political theory, 1. publ. Cambridge University Press 1999) 23
1176 ibid 32
1177 Hathaway (n 1167) 136

a far-reaching act is not overriding the principal's delegation. Secondly, states may implicitly extend their consent by continuing to cooperate despite the overriding act.[1178] In this instance, it can be surmised that states have reassessed their cost-benefit analysis and concluded that the benefits of cooperation continue to outweigh the costs involved.

To summarize, the tacit acceptance procedure can be contextualized in the field of international relations and delegated law-making power to international organizations. Sovereignty encompasses the ability to relinquish it, and rational states will choose to delegate as long as the benefits outweigh the costs. To mitigate negative impact, states usually opt for conditional delegations. However, if the international organization as an agent of the states exceeds the granted power, delegated acts are deprived of their basis for normative force.

The tacit acceptance procedure stipulated by Article VIII SOLAS allows an amendment to enter into force without being explicitly accepted by the contracting governments. Rather, the entry into force takes place after the lapse of time. The contracting states have limited the delegation to amendments to the technical annex of SOLAS. Basic provisions of the treaty including general provisions and administrative matters should continue to be subject to the traditional, explicit amendment procedure.[1179] Moreover, new subjects unrelated to the existing technical annex should be excluded from the scope of application of the new procedure.[1180] In view of the potential complexity in differentiating between general provisions and unrelated subjects on the one hand and technical provisions on the other, a diplomatic conference shall be convened to determine the most appropriate amendment procedure, should this be necessary.[1181]

At first glance, the restriction of the tacit acceptance procedure to technical details renders it unsuitable for the MASS amendments. Although determining various technical details concerning MASS equipment is necessary, the fundamental political issues of whether humans may be moved ashore and whether algorithms may take over the navigation of a ship seem to be more fundamental and not covered by the delegated law-making authority. Despite these considerations, the IMO plans to make the MASS Code mandatory by

---

1178 ibid 137

1179 IMCO, 'Amendment Procedure for Conventions for which IMCO is the Depository' (n 1149) 14

1180 LEG, IMCO (n 1174) 15

1181 ibid

adding a chapter to SOLAS using the tacit acceptance procedure.[1182] Additionally, other scholars welcome an application of the tacit acceptance procedure for the MASS Code.[1183] Therefore, the following shall critically examine the exact scope of the IMO's delegated law-making authority and assess whether the MASS amendments would be covered.

Keeping the limited scope of application of the tacit acceptance procedure, it needs to be discussed whether the MASS Code touches upon the general provisions of SOLAS and/or whether it is unrelated to existing technical annexes. If this were the case, the IMO would exceed its mandate when making the MASS Code mandatory utilizing the tacit acceptance procedure.

First, the general principles of SOLAS shall be reflected in the light of the MASS Code. Following its adoption, relocating the crew to an RCC and handing over the control to algorithms shall be possible. As there is no comprehensive list of general principles of SOLAS, it needs to be determined whether the presence of competent humans on board as well as human control form part of the general principles of SOLAS.

Based on the assumption that the general principles of a treaty are not congruent with the aim of the treaty and that general principles are reflected by several provisions of the treaty, the human presence on board the vessel as well as the human control of the vessel can be seen as forming part of the general principles of SOLAS.[1184]

SOLAS aims to ensure the safety of life at sea. This includes both the safety of the persons on board and the safety of third parties. As argued above, SOLAS does not prescribe the manning of the vessel as a goal in itself. However, it must be admitted, that the human presence on board is presumed by numerous provisions, such as regulations concerning life-saving appliances,[1185] fire-fighting,[1186] periodically unattended machinery spaces,[1187] and bridge design related to the average body size.[1188] To be blunt, the raison d'être of SOLAS is based on the fact that there are humans on board ships. Thus, the human presence on board is a general principle within SOLAS.

1182 Laffey (n 612) 282; Tunfors (n 489) 56; reporting from an interview with a technical officer, Subdivision for Marine Technology and Cargoes, IMO: Fenton and Chapsos (n 821) 5

1183 Soyer (n 86) 183

1184 Eva R Lange, 'Applying the tacit amendment procedure to accommodate international maritime law to Maritime Autonomous Surface Ships' (2022) 28(5) Journal of International Maritime Law 304–319, 313

1185 Regulations 7 and 10 of Chapter III of SOLAS

1186 Regulation 10 of Chapter II-2 of SOLAS

1187 Part E of Chapter II-1 of SOLAS

1188 Regulations 19, 22, and 27 of Chapter V of SOLAS

Likewise, human control rather than control by algorithms is a general principle in SOLAS. Regulations V/24, V/26, and V/34-1 of SOLAS refer to humans on board directly operating the vessel and taking navigational and operational decisions. Regulation V/27 of SOLAS prescribes the presence of updated nautical publications and nautical charts on board the vessel necessary for humans to take informed navigational decisions. Additionally, human presence on board is required, as humans need to be present to operate the vessel. It follows from this argumentation that both aspects, human presence on board and human operation of the vessel, are general principles of SOLAS.

It could be objected to this argumentation that all of the cited provisions are included in the Annex of SOLAS rather than in the articles of the conventions. As stated during the negotiations on the tacit acceptance procedure, the general principles are normally included in the articles of the convention.[1189] Against the opinion that general principles may only be found in the main articles of a convention, two arguments can be put in place.

First, the LEG itself provided flexibility by stating that the basic provisions of a treaty are normally contained in the main articles of a convention.[1190] Second, the main articles of SOLAS do not contain many substantial provisions. Out of the 13 articles of SOLAS, 9 deal with administrative matters such as amendments, entry into force, and deposit and registration. SOLAS would be deprived of general principles if these must be found solely in the main articles. Eventually, the LEG was aware of the fact that all substantial provisions are included in the annex because SOLAS 1960 also did not provide for any substantive provisions in the main articles. Consequently, the general principles can also be found in the annex of SOLAS; otherwise, there would be no general principles. To conclude, the MASS amendments touch upon the general principles of human presence on board and human control of the vessel.

Second, it should be discussed whether the intended MASS amendments are new subject matters unrelated to the existing technical annexes. If so, the MASS amendments would be beyond the scope of application intended for the tacit acceptance procedure.

The existing chapters in the annex concern, on the one hand, issues relating to all types of vessels such as life-saving appliances (Chapter III), radio communications (Chapter IV), safety of navigation (Chapter V), and special measures to enhance the maritime safety and security (Chapters XI-1, XI-2). On the other hand, chapters provide for specific requirements for certain types

1189 IMCO, 'Amendment Procedure for Conventions for which IMCO is the Depository' (n 1149) 14

1190 ibid

of vessels. Bulk carriers, high-speed crafts, and nuclear ships are each treated separately in individual chapter. Autonomy is not covered by any chapter. This could point towards novelty. The components of maritime operations affected by autonomy, namely the location of the crew and the mode of operation, however, are dealt with in Chapters III–V. It can therefore not ultimately be decided whether MASS present a novelty as envisaged by the state parties.

Earlier applications of the tacit acceptance procedure could be consulted to determine the degree of evolution the parties included in their delegation. Since 1974, the tacit acceptance procedure was applied to add new chapters to the annex of SOLAS concerning indisputably technical aspects. The ISM Code, the International Code of Safety for High Speed Craft,[1191] the International Ship and Port Facility Code (ISPS Code) ,[1192] and the Polar Code[1193] were made mandatory using the tacit acceptance procedure.

The High Speed Craft Code and the Polar Code address vessels operating with special features or operating in designated areas, respectively. Before the adoption of the codes, neither high-speed vessel operations nor vessel operations in polar waters were prohibited by SOLAS. Rather, additional safety provisions were adopted to adequately ensure the safety of life at sea.

The ISPS Code aims at increasing security in shipping operations by fostering cooperation between contracting governments, local administrations, and shipping and port industries to detect potential security threats to ships and ports and by enhancing the exchange of security-related information. The ISM Code's objectives is to provide standards for the safe management and operation of ships. Both codes prescribe procedural aspects and behavioral rules. Although not directly technical, the provisions supplement the existing provisions by adding provisions that are more concrete. The reasonable expectation of the contracting governments that the tacit acceptance procedure will only be used for amendments of technical or subordinated nature was confirmed by the recent applications. Since the proposed MASS Code cannot be compared with the other codes in terms of essentiality, using the tacit acceptance procedure would exceed the degree of evolution foreseen by the contracting states.

To summarize, the MASS amendments touch upon the basic principles of SOLAS. Moreover, they most likely present a novelty unrelated to the existing provisions in the annex. Both argues for not applying the tacit acceptance procedure for making the MASS Code mandatory as such an application would

---

1191 Council of the International Maritime Organization (n 671) 2

1192 Conference of Contracting Governments to SOLAS, 'SOLAS/CONF/5/32 – Consideration and Adoption of Amendments to the International Convention for the Safety of Life at Sea, 1974' (London 12 December 2002) 2

1193 MSC, IMO, 'Res. MSC.386 (94)' (n 365)

not be covered by the states' consent as normative basis for legal force. While the practice of delegated law-making is becoming increasingly accepted in areas of specialization, and the IMO is the competent regulator for international shipping, the delegation of authority to the IMO was not granted with the intention of fundamentally changing shipping. The aforementioned fact is also illustrated by the status of UNCLOS, which remains under the auspices of the UN rather than being allocated to the scope of competence of the IMO. Consequently, the growing acceptance of delegated law-making must be evaluated in the context of recent legislative developments. Among these activities, none can be considered as fundamental as the changes for MASS.

The state parties have foreseen such uncertainties about the application of the tacit acceptance procedure and stated that a diplomatic conference should ultimately decide about the appropriate amendment procedure.[1194] Therefore, it is suggested that the tacit acceptance procedure should not be applied unless a diplomatic conference has confirmed the application for making the MASS Code mandatory. Despite these considerations on the applicability of the tacit acceptance procedure, the IMO plans to utilize this procedure to make the MASS Code mandatory. As illustrated above, states could choose to extend their given consent and legitimize an overriding act. Some possible considerations for states to take into account in the context of a renewed cost benefit calculation are discussed below.

The tacit acceptance procedure is an exception from the general principle of customary international law[1195] that international law derives its force and authority from the consent of the states to be bound by it.[1196] Self-evident, states can agree upon another amendment procedure as they have done with the tacit acceptance procedure in SOLAS. By expressly limiting the scope of the tacit acceptance procedure, the states expressed the exemption character. As an exemption, the tacit acceptance procedure should not be applied beyond its intended scope of application to prevent negative consequences.[1197]

1194 LEG, IMCO (n 1174) 15

1195 Kerstin von der Decken, 'Article 39, General rule regarding the amendment of treaties' in Oliver Dörr and Kirsten Schmalenbach (eds), *Vienna Convention on the Law of Treaties: A Commentary* (2. 2nd ed. 2018. Springer Berlin Heidelberg 2018) 760

1196 Hernández, *Hernández 2019* (n 437) 31; *The Case of the S.S. Lotus* (1927) 10 Collection of Judgments no 9 18 (Permanent Court of International Justice); Wouter G Werner, 'State consent as foundational myth' in Catherine Brölmann and Yannick Radi (eds), *Research handbook on the theory and practice of international lawmaking* (Edward Elgar Publishing 2016)

1197 Andronico O Adede, 'Amendment Procedures for Conventions with Technical Annexes: The IMCO Experience' (1977) 17(2) Virginia Journal of International Law 201, 210

Another aspect to consider is legitimacy. Legitimacy is understood as the "normative belief that a rule [...] ought to be obeyed".[1198] In respect of a certain rule, three facets of legitimacy can be distinguished: input, output,[1199] and process[1200] or throughput[1201] legitimacy. Process or throughput legitimacy means the

> quality of a rule which derives from a perception on the part of those to whom it is addressed that it has come into being in accordance with right process.[1202]

Franck argues that legitimacy is key for the compliance pull of a rule[1203] as states tend to obey rules that came into being following a prior agreed procedure. Especially the framework developed by the IMO relies upon the will of the states to uphold the established rules,[1204] although the mutual benefits of adhering to the standards constitute a significant incentive for compliance.[1205]

When applying the tacit acceptance procedure beyond its intended scope of application process legitimacy is negatively affected. Consequently, the compliance pull could decrease. As timely and coherent implementation is especially important for MASS regulations, the readiness for compliance should not be put at risk. Additionally, the future success of the tacit acceptance procedure could be affected by an extensive application. States may be hesitant to incorporate the tacit acceptance procedure into other treaties due to concerns about its excessive application.[1206] To summarize, following the correct law-making procedure increases the process legitimacy of a rule. As legitimacy is relevant for states' compliance with a rule, adherence to the correct law-making procedure results in a higher degree of compliance pull.

If applying the tacit acceptance procedure, national parliaments are usually not involved before international obligations apply,[1207] which could lead to

1198 Boyle and Chinkin (n 987) 24
1199 Bautzem (n 988) 939
1200 Boyle and Chinkin (n 987) 24; Franck (n 984) 706
1201 Bautzem (n 988) 939
1202 Franck (n 984) 706
1203 ibid 712
1204 Sun (n 329) 100
1205 Shelton, 'Shelton 2003' (n 938) 14–15
1206 Conference of Contracting Governments to SOLAS, 'SOLAS/CONF.2/20 – Consideration and Adoption of the International Convention on the Safety of Life at Sea (United States of America)' (London 8 April 1994) 2
1207 Kirgis (n 993) 93

constitutional issues as the United States pointed out.[1208] Although such issues have to be resolved domestically, they could boomerang to the international level as national implementation might be hampered. Considering the extensive discussion on autonomous vehicles for road transport, the early involvement of national parliaments could speed up the implementation process in the long run and increase societal support of MASS, which is of paramount importance for its overall success.

Reconsidering states as rational actors, decreased legitimacy and lower societal support increase the costs associated with the act. Particularly constitutional constraints concerning the national separation of powers and the scope within governments may enter into international obligations without parliamentary involvement can increase the costs of an international commitment.

As the tacit acceptance procedure can result in a situation where states are bound by international obligations without explicitly consenting to them, especially developing states, and those with a small administration can be overcharged with building an opinion on an amendment proposal and the possibilities of complying with it within a short time.[1209] Although these states would be bound internationally, they would not be able to ensure national implementation. In this situation, the accelerated procedure would have achieved nothing.

It could be posited that states may exercise their right to opt out of the legally binding MASS Code by formally expressing their objection in accordance with the stipulations set forth in Article VIII(b)(VII)(2) of SOLAS. Consequently, the amendment would not enter into force with respect to those governments. Nevertheless, the amendment would become part of SOLAS and thus part of the GAIRAS. In consideration of the coastal state's jurisdiction over foreign-flagged vessels as outlined in Article 21(2) of the UNCLOS, it can be concluded that a coastal state is not permitted to impose more rigorous requirements on vessels seeking to pass through its waters than those stipulated by GAIRAS. Consequently, a state that has expressed its objection to MASS in general and has opted out of the binding MASS Code is nevertheless still bound as a coastal state. It is therefore evident that a state may not impede the innocent passage of MASS through its territorial waters. The opt-out would only affect the state in its capacity as a flag and port state. However, a flag state cannot be obliged to register MASS anyway. Moreover, a port state can restrict

1208 Conference of Contracting Governments to SOLAS, 'SOLAS/CONF.2/20 – Consideration and Adoption of the International Convention on the Safety of Life at Sea (United States of America)' (n 1206) 2

1209 Adede (n 1197) 208

port entry for MASS based on its port state jurisdiction. Therefore, it is evident that there is no rationale for a state to proclaim an opt-out for the MASS Code.

The illustrated considerations concerned costs of applying the tacit acceptance procedure beyond its intended scope. This should not obscure the fact that the solution pursued by IMO entails several advantages. In addition to those examined above discussing non-binding IMO solutions, applying the tacit acceptance procedure would result in a legally binding MASS Code. However, it should be borne in mind that a MASS Code supplementing SOLAS cannot guide the interpretation of COLREG or include any matter not covered by SOLAS. A MASS Code annexed to SOLAS could thus only be one puzzle piece of a holistic legal response to MASS. A MASS Code binding as an Annex to SOLAS would not fulfill the above-established criteria for a future legal framework for MASS.

The tacit acceptance procedure is a suitable method for technical and subordinate regulations. However, the use of the tacit acceptance procedure is not recommended for the adoption of more fundamental changes. It is not advisable to use the tacit acceptance process beyond its intended scope and risk reduced compliance, societal support and domestic constitutional problems if the MASS Code is unable to provide a holistic regulatory response to MASS.

Besides SOLAS, COLREG and UNCLOS also provide for specific amendment procedures. Both shall be considered, though briefly as the negative aspect of amending only one instrument has already been pointed out.

5.3.2.2 Amendments to COLREG

Article VI COLREG provides for the amendment procedure. This procedure differs from the SOLAS tacit acceptance procedure in one important respect: states cannot opt-out. In order to compensate for this limitation, a proposal for amendment must have a two-thirds majority in both the MSC and the IMO Assembly. To prevent the entry into force of an amendment, one-third of the parties have to notify the IMO of their objection.

The absence of an opt-out can be explained by the nature of the COLREG rules providing the rules of the road for navigation. If states could individually decide whether to accept an amendment, different rules would apply depending on the flag or the location of a vessel. However, uniformity of the traffic rules is particularly important to ensure safe navigation. Legal fragmentation cannot be tolerated in the interests of maritime safety.

COLREG has been amended seven times since its entry into force in 1977. In 2001, the amendment included new rules relating to Wing-In-Ground crafts, an innovation that should be reflected by specific provisions in COLREG.[1210] Even if this example could be taken as a template for the necessary MASS amendments to COLREG, it should be noted that the COLREG amendments were the only binding amendments for wing-in-ground craft in the IMO conventions. Neither SOLAS nor any other treaty required amendments. Only non-binding guidelines were adopted in 2002[1211] and updated in 2005[1212] and 2018.[1213] These were considered sufficient to ensure SOLAS-compliance of wing-in-ground crafts.

However, for the case of MASS, just amending COLREG is not sufficient. As in the case of SOLAS, an amendment to COLREG would not ensure that SOLAS would be interpreted in a way that includes MASS. Therefore, the amendments to COLREG for wing-in-ground crafts can be taken as a template for the necessary MASS amendments; however, this approach alone is not sufficient. An amendment to COLREG would need to be accompanied by amendments to all other conventions affected by the advent of MASS. Nevertheless, it has been argued that the IMO legitimately prefers the adoption of a single instrument to gather all MASS-relevant provisions in one place. Consequently, a method has to be applied which ensures that the adoption of one instrument affects all concerned conventions. As all GAIRAS conventions operate under the umbrella put up by UNCLOS, it could be appropriate to amend UNCLOS. This shall be assessed now.

5.3.2.3 Amendments to UNCLOS

UNCLOS includes two amendment procedures. Article 312 of the UNCLOS prescribes the conventional, formal, amendment procedure, first available 10 years after the entry into force of UNCLOS.[1214] Upon a proposal by a contracting government, not less than one half of the state parties have to react in favor so that the Secretary-General convenes a diplomatic conference. At this conference, an amendment can be adopted using the same procedure as at the Third United Nations Conference on the Law of the Sea. This includes, in particular, the requirement of consensus.

1210 IMO, 'Res. A.910(22): Amendments to the International Regulations for Preventing Collisions at Sea' (London 29 November 2001)

1211 MSC, IMO, 'MSC.1/Circ. 1054: Interim Guidelines for Wing-in-Ground Craft' (London 16 December 2002)

1212 MSC, IMO, 'MSC.1/Circ. 1126: Amendments to the Interim Guidelines for Wing-in-Ground Craft' (London 6 January 2005)

1213 MSC, IMO, 'MSC.1/Circ. 1592: Guidelines for Wing-in-Ground Craft' (London 18 May 2018)

1214 UNCLOS entered into force in 1994, thus the procedure was available from 2004 on

Alternatively, the simplified procedure stipulated by Article 313 of the UNCLOS could be used. In lieu of convening a diplomatic conference for adoption, the amendment shall be deemed adopted if no state has raised an objection within 12 months of its circulation by the Secretary-General. After adoption through either procedure, Article 316 of the UNCLOS requires ratification by at least two-thirds of the state parties or 60 state parties, whatever is greater for an amendment to enter into force. As UNCLOS has 168 member states, two-thirds amount to 112 states that would need to ratify an amendment for its entry into force.

Although some consider that Article 313 of the UNCLOS incorporates the internationally well-known tacit acceptance procedure,[1215] it should be noted that the tacit element concerns the adoption rather than the entry into force of an amendment. Thus, states are not internationally bound without explicitly ratifying and thereby consenting to the amendment.

Until today, neither amendment procedure has been used.[1216] As UNCLOS covers a wide range of substantial aspects, states could be afraid that proposing a formal amendment would open Pandora's Box and put the consensual package deal approach at risk.[1217] Although MASS are expected to revolutionize shipping it seems unlikely that the state parties to UNCLOS will invoke one of the formal amendment procedures to include the necessary amendments. Furthermore, the time required to obtain a sufficient number of ratifications disqualifies an amendment to UNCLOS as an approach to provide a timely legal framework for MASS.[1218] Moreover, including specific provisions on MASS in UNCLOS would jeopardize its constitutional character. Therefore, amending UNCLOS is not recommended for the purposes of MASS.

1215 Myron H Nordquist, Shabtai Rosenne and Louis B Sohn, *Volume V, Articles 279–320, Annexes V, VI, VIII and IX, Final Act, Annex I, Resolutions I, III and IV* (United Nations Convention on the Law of the Sea, 1982: a commentary vol 5, Kluwer Academic Publishers 1989) 313.1

1216 David Freestone and Alex G O Elferink, 'Flexibility and Innovation in the Law of the Sea – will the LOS Convention Amendment Procedures ever be used?' in Alex G Oude Elferink (ed), *Stability and Change in the Law of the Sea* (Nova et Vetera Iuris Gentium vol 24. Brill 2005) 177; Tullio Treves, 'The Development of the Law of the Sea since the Adoption of the UN Convention on the Law of the Sea: Achievements and Challenges for the Future' in Davor Vidas (ed), *Law, technology and science for oceans in globalisation: IUU fishing, oil pollution, bioprospecting, outer continental shelf* (Nijhoff eBook titles. Martinus Nijhoff 2010) 49

1217 Freestone and Elferink (n 1216) 220; Scott (n 13) 276

1218 Dong, Bautista and Zhu (n 540) 4

5.3.2.4 Conclusions

This section investigated the formal amendment procedures included in SOLAS, COLREG, and UNCLOS. SOLAS can be amended by applying either the explicit or the tacit acceptance procedure whereas COLREG only provides for the latter. In the case of the explicit amendment procedure, an amendment must be accepted explicitly and reach a certain number of ratifications to enter into force. The tacit acceptance procedure, however, waives the explicit ratification requirement. An amendment is deemed to have been accepted unless a coalition of objectors representing one-third of the contracting governments arises prior to an agreed date. The rich amendment history of SOLAS since 1974 depicts the resounding success of the tacit acceptance procedure to adapt the legal framework to technical innovation.

It has been negated that the necessary MASS amendments fall within the scope of the tacit acceptance procedure as provided for in SOLAS. Despite this result, and in the light of the IMO's intention, it was subsequently discussed whether the tacit acceptance procedure could still be used to make the MASS Code binding. Given the potential negative impacts of extending a procedure beyond its intended scope and its effect on the legitimacy and compliance of the adopted act, along with the inadequacy of solely amending SOLAS, it is not advisable to utilize the tacit acceptance procedure to make the MASS Code mandatory.

Subsequently, the amendment procedures provided for in COLREG and UNCLOS were briefly discussed. Both are inadequate to prepare the legal framework for MASS. An amendment to COLREG would not affect other conventions preventing a horizontal coherent approach. The amendment procedure for UNCLOS is very time-consuming, as 112 states would have to ratify an amendment for its entry into force. Moreover, UNCLOS has never been formally amended. Although van Hooydonk recognizes the emergence of MASS as a "good opportunity to give the basic concept of [UNCLOS] a thorough overhaul",[1219] the intricate amendment process of UNCLOS precludes the provision of a legal framework for MASS in the near future.

Although amending one convention seems attractive, as only one procedure has to be followed, it is of particular importance to ensure horizontal coherence in the regulatory approach to MASS. Thus, all affected conventions could be amended simultaneously; however, this would require an accurately coordinated action.[1220] Such a solution would also entail the risk of legal fragmentation as it is challenging to ensure that all amendments are synchronized and

1219 van Hooydonk (n 543) 410

1220 Ntovas (n 675) 221

applied uniformly. Therefore, the IMO preferred to adopt a single instrument rather than amending each convention separately.[1221] While it is acknowledged that a single instrument is preferable, the intended process of making the MASS Code mandatory as an annex to SOLAS does not serve the desired horizontal coherence and is detrimental from a normative point of view.

Therefore, this study continues to consider other, more pragmatic ways of amending international conventions without applying the pre-determined formal amendment procedures. UNCLOS, although never formally adopted, has evolved over time and adapted to changes. However, instead of the formal amendment procedures, more pragmatic solutions such as an implementing agreement were preferred.[1222] Likewise, SOLAS was amended by a protocol to bypass a formal amendment procedure. Particularly, the appropriateness of such an approach shall be examined in the light of MASS. Moreover, the impact of a resolution taken by the conference of states is considered. With regard to UNCLOS, the reference to GAIRAS is evaluated as a port of entry for legal changes developed by the IMO.

5.3.3 *A New MASS Convention*

The discussed amendment procedures included in the treaties provide the internal mechanisms to adapt treaties (amendments '*stricto sensu*').[1223] Alternatively, external, independent instruments, being a treaty in the meaning of Article 2(1)(a) of the VCLT themselves,[1224] can amend a treaty without applying the formal amendment procedure included in the main treaty.[1225] New provisions to supplement the treaty[1226] or interpretative guidance[1227] can be added. This non-conventional amendment procedure was applied to several shipping conventions.[1228] During the adoption of these instruments, the IMO played a

1221 MSC, IMO, 'MSC.1/Circ.1638' (n 18) 9

1222 Freestone and Elferink (n 1216) 220

1223 ILC, 'International Law Commission 1966' (n 433) 233

1224 Dorota Lost-Siemińska, 'Implementation of IMO treaties into domestic legislation: Implementation and enforcement as the key to effectiveness of international treaties' in Zuzanna Pepłowska-Dąbrowska and Justyna Nawrot (eds), *Maritime Safety in Europe: A Comparative Approach* (Taylor & Francis 2020) 11; Jutta Brunnée and Christopher Campbell-Duruflé, 'International Legislation' in Anne Peters (ed), *Max Planck Encyclopedia of Public International Law* (MPEPIL) (Oxford University Press) 14

1225 Chie Kojima and Vladlen S Vereshchetin, 'Implementation Agreements' in Anne Peters (ed), *Max Planck Encyclopedia of Public International Law* (MPEPIL) (Oxford University Press) 11

1226 Brunnée and Campbell-Duruflé (n 1224) 11

1227 Boyle, 'Boyle 2006' (n 224) 42; Brunnée and Campbell-Duruflé (n 1224) 11

1228 See a list of protocols to IMO treaties at: Lost-Siemińska (n 1224) 11 less important role than during the procedure for amendments *stricto sensu*. The IMO has prepared drafts and convened diplomatic conferences; however, the conference of the state parties adopted the amendment. Three particularly prominent agreements updating UNCLOS and SOLAS shall be introduced and briefly discussed before assessing the appropriateness of a MASS Convention to regulatory response to the advent of MASS.

UNCLOS was changed twice by self-standing international conventions. First, in 1994, an agreement relating to the implementation of Part XI of UNCLOS[1229] was adopted by the UN General Assembly[1230] to promote universal application of UNCLOS. Several developed states had not ratified UNCLOS as the original provisions in Part XI UNCLOS were considered detrimental to the development of the exploitation of deep seabed mineral resources.[1231] Thus, the 1994 Implementation Agreement altered the provisions of Part XI of UNCLOS in favor of developed states[1232] by disapplying the production limitation in Article 151 of the UNCLOS and the mandatory transfer of technology in Article 5 of Annex III to UNCLOS. Likewise, the decision-making process was altered in a way ensuring every decision required the support of Russia and the United States.[1233] Following the 1994 Agreement, several developed nations ratified UNCLOS[1234] and almost universal participation could be achieved. Although the legal characterization of the 1994 Implementation Agreement varies, scholars agree that it de facto amended UNCLOS.[1235] Nonetheless, the term 'amendment' was not used for political reasons.[1236]

1229 Agreement relating to the implementation of Part XI of the United Nations Convention on the Law of the Sea of 10 December 1982, No. 31364 28 July 1994

1230 United Nations General Assembly, 'Res. A/Res/48/263 – Agreement relating to the implementation of Part XI of the United Nations Convention on the Law of the Sea of 10 December 1982' (n 227)

1231 Freestone and Elferink (n 1216) 219; James Harrison, *Making the Law of the Sea: A study in the development of international law* (Cambridge studies in international and comparative law, Cambridge University Press 2011) 85

1232 Yoshifumi Tanaka, *The international law of the sea* (1. publ, Cambridge University Press 2012) 179

1233 ibid 182

1234 ibid 34

1235 Kojima and Vereshchetin (n 1225) 1; Boyle, 'Boyle 2006' (n 224) 42; Buga (n 322) 53; Treves, 'Treves 2010' (n 1216) 50; Harrison (n 1231) 91

1236 Tullio Scovazzi, 'The Evolution of International Law of the Sea: New Issues, new Challenges' (2000) 286 Collected Courses of the Hague Academy of International Law, 125; Harrison (n 1231) 92

Second, just one year later, the 1995 UN Fish Stocks Agreement (Fish Stocks Agreement)[1237] was adopted. It recognized at a primary level the environmental significance of fishing activities.[1238] Although it could be argued that the Fish Stocks Agreement only affects the interpretation of UNCLOS,[1239] other aspects of the Agreement clearly go beyond UNCLOS.[1240] As the 1994 Implementation Agreement, the Fish Stocks Agreement de facto amended UNCLOS.[1241] Based on the principle of pacta tertiis, the new convention was initially binding only on those states that had ratified it. However, it is expected that over time its provisions will be regarded as part of UNCLOS.[1242]

In 2023, a binding instrument on the conservation and sustainable use of marine biological diversity beyond national jurisdiction was adopted under UNCLOS.[1243] The impact on UNCLOS remains to be seen, however, submissions to the Preparatory Commission expressed that the new convention was considered an implementation agreement to UNCLOS.[1244] The title also indicates this as the agreement is concluded "under" UNCLOS.

To summarize, UNCLOS has been altered significantly by implementation agreements adopted in the aftermath of UNCLOS' adoption. These agreements did not only concern the interpretation of provisions in UNCLOS but also added substantial aspects. A MASS Convention adopted under UNCLOS could have a similar impact and ensure that terms in UNCLOS are interpreted in a way including MASS operations. Moreover, the new convention being subordinated to UNCLOS could ensure horizontal coherency. Before discussing in detail whether a new MASS Convention is appropriate to address MASS, the SOLAS Protocol shall be briefly introduced.

1237 Agreement for the Implementation of the Provisions of the United Nations Convention on the Law of the Sea of 10 December 1982 relating to the Conservation and Management of Straddling Fish Stocks and Highly Migratory Fish Stocks, No. 37924 4 August 1995

1238 Freestone and Elferink (n 1216) 193

1239 Buga (n 322) 55; Freestone and Elferink (n 1216) 192

1240 Freestone and Elferink (n 1216) 193

1241 Scott (n 13), 277; Boyle, 'Boyle 2010' (n 1029) 7

1242 Freestone and Elferink (n 1216) 203

1243 A/CONF.232/2023/4 – Agreement under the United Nations Convention on the Law of the Sea on the conservation and sustainable use of marine biological diversity of areas beyond national jurisdiction 20 June 2023 (Intergovernmental conference on an international legally binding instrument under the United Nations Convention on the Law of the Sea on the conservation and sustainable use of marine biological diversity of areas beyond national jurisdiction)

1244 European Union, 'EU and its Member States Submission to the NNBJ PrepCom' (Brussels 25 July 2016) 2; Pacific Small Island Developing States, 'PSIDS Submission to the BBNJ PrepCom' (New York 29 August 2016) 2

Before the entry into force of SOLAS, the inspection and certificate provisions included in chapter I of SOLAS were amended by the 1978 Protocol.[1245] Although the formal amendment procedure was not available, as SOLAS had not yet entered into force, it is questionable whether states would have opted for the formal procedure if it had been available. The fact that the 1978 protocol entered into force after 15 ratifications and SOLAS itself required 25 ratifications indicates that the formal procedure was considered too inflexible.

Although the agreements were titled differently, all had in common to substantially alter the provisions of the main treaty between the participating states.[1246] It shall now be discussed how a MASS Convention altering the interpretation of provisions in SOLAS, COLREG, and UNCLOS and adding additional provisions could be designed. Subsequently, the appropriateness of this approach shall be examined.

The MASS Convention could include all MASS-specific regulations. Additionally, guidance to the interpretation of key terms such as 'master' and 'crew' included in all shipping conventions and UNCLOS could be included. Likewise, the interpretation of COLREG, specifically the lookout requirement, and the duty to adhere to the practice of an ordinary seaman could be addressed by the MASS Convention. As not the IMO, but a specially convened diplomatic conference would adopt the MASS Convention, even issues beyond the mandate of the IMO could be addressed. The conference would enjoy the freedom to regulate without being constrained by the existing conventions.[1247]

Importantly, liability aspects currently regulated in the Brussels Convention under the auspices of the CMI could be addressed.[1248] An international field analysis concluded by the German Maritime Center revealed that uncertainty with respect to liability issues was one of the greatest obstacles to marketability of MASS.[1249] Without going into details, the fault-based liability as stipulated by Articles 3 and 4 Brussels Convention poses major challenges with regard to MASS[1250] and requires further specification to accommodate MASS appropriately. Currently, the CMI considers different methods to revise the Brussels Convention without putting the almost global acceptance of the convention at

1245 Protocol Relating to the International Convention for the Safety of Lift at Sea, No. 18961 (n 362)

1246 Harrison (n 1231) 92

1247 MSC, IMO, 'MSC 100/5: Report of the Correspondence Group on MASS' (London 28 September 2018) 41

1248 Soyer (n 86) 173

1249 PCCG Point Conception Consulting GmbH and others (n 200) 80

1250 CMI, 'Position Paper on Unmanned Ships and the International Regulatory Framework' (n 13) 19

risk.[1251] The issue was also widely debated in academic literature, and several scholars concluded that a liability scheme based on strict liability for MASS owners should be introduced.[1252]

Whether a MASS Convention could appropriately address the regulatory needs of MASS shall be assessed now. The MASS Convention would not be limited to the substantive scope of a specific treaty, allowing for horizontal harmonization across several conventions. Additionally, the development and elaboration of a coherent legal framework for MASS would be greatly facilitated if all provisions specifically applicable to MASS were incorporated into one instrument. As the MASS Convention would apply as lex specialis, all other conventions dealing with shipping would have to be interpreted in the light of the MASS Convention and apply the understanding of key terms and concepts as contained in the MASS Convention. This ensures horizontal integration not only in the text but also during implementation.

To achieve its objective of horizontal harmonization, the MASS Convention must be considered when interpreting the existing treaties. Its impact on interpretation shall be briefly examined. Recalling the general rule of interpretation stipulated by Article 31 of the VCLT, the intention of the parties shall be determined based on the words used, the context and the object and purpose of the provision. Being part of the context, subsequent agreements relating to the interpretation of the treaty shall be considered per Article 31(3)(a) of VCLT. Both, the 1994 Implementation Agreement and the Fish Stocks Agreement were considered such subsequent agreements relating to the interpretation of UNCLOS.[1253] Although not all state parties of UNCLOS have ratified the two subsequent agreements, Boyle argues that they have tacitly consented.[1254] Consequently, even the most restrictive interpretation of Article 31(3)(a) of the VCLT requiring participation of all state parties would be fulfilled. If this threshold cannot be reached, however, an implementing agreement is still

1251 Belgian Federal Government, 'Convention Internationale pour L'unification de Certaines Regles en Matiere d'Abordage' (Brussels 1 June 2021) <https://diplomatie.belgium.be/sites/default/files/documents/CDM1.%20Convention%20internationale%20pour%20l'unification%20de%20%5B ... %5D.pdf>

1252 Baughen, 'Baughen 2023' (n 499) 232; Luci Carey, 'Contractual and Tortious Maritime Liability Regimes and the Introduction of Autonomous Vessels: NUS Law Working Paper 2023/012' (Singapore March 2023) 28; Ivana Surian, 'A Legal Analysis of the Collision and Strict Liability Framework for the Shipowner of Unmanned and Autonomous Vessels (South Africa)' in Sanja Bauk and Stojče D Ilčev (eds), *The 1st International Conference on Maritime Education and Development* (Springer International Publishing 2021) 118; LEG, IMO, 'LEG 111/10/2' (n 7) 10

1253 Boyle, 'Boyle 2006' (n 224) 49; Buga (n 322) 53

1254 Boyle, 'Boyle 2006' (n 224) 49

a persuasive indication for the state's intention. Additionally, adhering to the implementation agreement can be considered as a subsequent practice, relevant to the interpretation per Article 31(3)(b) of the VCLT. Finally, Article 31(3)(c) of the VCLT includes any instrument applicable between the parties to a dispute in the scope of authentic interpretation material. Reading Article 31(3)(c) of the VCLT together with Article 31(4) of the VCLT parties can agree on a certain, special, meaning of terms used, even inter partes. Thus, it is conceivable that the updated meaning of the term 'master' is limited to the parties that have ratified the MASS Convention.

Additionally, neither the negotiations nor the adoption of the MASS Convention would be governed by a formal amendment procedure included in either of the affected treaties. Thus, flexibility in terms of procedure and participation would be ensured. These were two strong arguments in favour of an implementation agreement over a formal amendment.[1255]

Moreover, the possibility of a wide geographical scope argues in favour of a MASS Convention. As the Convention would be open for ratification by all states, global harmonization could be achieved. However, a geographically limited scope of application in the first time would not significantly hamper MASS developments as MASS are unlikely to be used on transoceanic voyages in the near future. Therefore, a regional application would be an adequate solution for the industry in the interim period. However, the potential of a global scope is beneficial as the emergence of concurring standards is prevented.

A further advantage of a MASS Convention would be that it would be binding on those states that have ratified it, providing predictability and legal certainty. Industry stakeholders would be assured of a binding legal framework, rather than having to rely on the impact of soft law solutions. Flag states would also benefit, as it would be easy to determine which states accept MASS in their territorial waters and ports. Although the implementation would rely on national law, goal-based formulations and a mutual obligation to accept certificates can ensure a harmonized framework among all participating flag, coastal, and port states.

The ratification requirement would ensure that domestic regulations are adjusted to comply with the new instrument before entry into force. This facilitates proper implementation and enforcement of the new instrument. In addition, states could avoid being bound internationally if they lack the capacity to fulfill the international obligations in question. Democratic opinion-forming processes can take place as part of national preparations for ratification before

1255 Boyle, 'Boyle 2010' (n 1029) 7

binding commitments are made at the international level. In order to enhance the legitimacy of the instrument and increase compliance and societal support, it is recommended to involve national parliaments at an early stage.

However, the ratification requirement is likely to be the severest disadvantage of a MASS Convention.[1256] Before entering the ratification phase, however, the convention must be adopted by a conference. Despite the flexible procedure, the adoption is the first hurdle for an international treaty to overcome and it should be discussed before considering the ratification requirement.

Diplomatic conferences need to adopt new conventions by consensus unless special rules of procedure apply.[1257] Because of competing interests and different political and economic situations and goals, a compromise has to be found to agree in consensus.[1258] The necessity to reach a compromise does not only prevent the adoption of the best rules for regulating the substantive issue.[1259] It also gives great power to states applying the brakes to the negotiation process. Often, only the lowest common denominator[1260] or vague terms[1261] can be agreed upon as reaching a consensus is difficult, though necessary.

As the MASS Convention is intended to cover horizontal aspects common to several conventions, all state parties of all affected conventions would be invited to the conference. This would result in more than 160 participating states. Besides the challenge to reach a consensus among 160 governments, negotiations between more than 160 states are time-consuming and very costly in financial terms.[1262] Additionally, the preparation time for multilateral international conferences amount usually to several years, prolonging the overall process.[1263] Moreover, the greater the complexity and extent of the regulations, the longer the negotiations will take. Van Logchem questions whether states would value maritime autonomy as important enough to warrant demanding international diplomatic consultations. He is rather skeptical[1264] based on an

1256 Soyer (n 86) 173

1257 Jacobsson (n 689) 282

1258 Cassese and others (n 437) 202

1259 Ilg (n 230) 23

1260 ibid 94

1261 Steven Walt, 'Novelty and the Risks of Uniform Sales Law' (1999) 39(3) Virginia Journal of International Law 671, 684; Baxter (n 908) 566

1262 Ilg (n 230) 21

1263 Kirsten Schmalenbach, 'Lawmaking by treaty: Negotiation of agreements and adoption of treaty texts' in Catherine Brölmann and Yannick Radi (eds), *Research handbook on the theory and practice of international lawmaking* (Edward Elgar Publishing 2016) 98

1264 van Logchem (n 484) 58

Italian response to the CMI questionnaire[1265] and the uneven distribution of economic benefits among the states. The less urgent an aspect is perceived by the negotiators, the longer the negotiations take.

Negotiating a liability regime for MASS could present a particular challenge and prolong the negotiation process.[1266] The current scheme for third-party liability foresees fault-based liability, which is advantageous for ship-owners. Renegotiating this regime will likely cause lengthy discussions between vessel and cargo owning states and a compromise will be hard to find. However, a reliable liability framework for MASS should be in place before they start operating on a regular basis. Consequently, excluding the controversial liability issue from the negotiations could accelerate the process in the short-term. Nevertheless, the matter needs to be assessed by regulators before MASS start operating. Therefore, it can be discussed and regulated along with all other aspects related to MASS.

The negotiations could be accelerated as IMO member states already discuss legal aspects of MASS since 2017. Thus, a common ground is prepared. Additionally, the IMO could prepare a draft convention based on the MASS Code proposal. Moreover, states have experienced the benefits of a globally harmonized legal framework for shipping for their merchant fleet or port industry. Consequently, reaching a consensus could be facilitated by having the benefits of a global framework in mind. Eventually, 'consensus' in international negotiations means the absence of opposition and not the positive affirmation of all participating governments.[1267] This understanding of consensus is expressed in Article 161(8)(e) of the UNCLOS. Nevertheless, the MASS Convention would give rise to a number of complex regulatory issues pertaining to operational paradigms. In comparison to the most recent amendments to UNCLOS, the requisite MASS regulations appear to be more intricate and demanding, potentially rendering negotiations more arduous. However, if this first hurdle can be overcome and a MASS Convention was adopted by a diplomatic conference, the ratification presents the next difficulty to surmount.

To be bound at the international level, states need to express their consent to be bound per Article 11 of the VCLT. Most often, state express their consent by ratification.[1268] As shown above, ratifying an international treaty through a

1265 Associazione Italiana di Diritto Maritimo, 'CMI Questionnaire on unmanned ships – Italian MLA answers' (Antwerp 05/2018) 8

1266 For a illustration of the long and unsuccessfull negotiation history of a Third Party Liability Convention at the CMI: Patrick J Griggs, 'Uniformity of Maritime Law–An International Perspective' (1999) 73(5&6) Tulane Law Review 1551

1267 Lost-Siemińska (n 1224) 9

1268 Hernández, *Hernández 2019* (n 437) 169

national bill can further constrain the already tight schedules of national parliaments. Moreover, inertia prolongs the process, as states tend to wait for each other before ratifying a treaty.[1269] Usually, ratification processes take several years.[1270]

A long ratification process is problematic, as most treaties require a certain number of ratifications for entry into force.[1271] Thus, a slow national ratification process delays the entry into force for all states. On average, the entry into force of conventions developed under the auspices of the IMO took 7 years. The Nairobi International Convention on the Removal of Wrecks, for example, was adopted in 2007 and entered into force in 2015 after 65 states have ratified it.[1272] Other conventions, however, will probably never meet the entry into force criterion.[1273] Long ratification processes are particularly disadvantageous if rapid regulations are to be achieved as in the case of MASS.

However, the requirement for a certain number of ratifications before the treaty enters into force is not a legal requirement.[1274] Article 24(1) of the VCLT states that a treaty enters into force as soon as the requirement established by the negotiating parties has been met. Most often, parties decide to determine a certain threshold for the entry into force. However, supplementing protocols often foresee a lower entry into force threshold than the main treaty[1275]

1269 Faria (n 1122) 26

1270 ibid 8; Faria (n 1122), 8; Deutscher Verkehrsgerichtstag (ed) (n 713) 268

1271 Guzmán (n 973) 145–146

1272 See Article 18(1) of the Nairobi International Convention on the Removal of Wrecks

1273 See for example the Hong Kong International Convention for the Safe and Environmentally Sound Recycling of Ships adopted in 2009. As of today, 20 states representing approximately 30% of the world merchant shipping by gross tonnage have ratified the convention. It is not assumed that more states will ratify the convention within the next years. Likewise, the United Nations Convention on Conditions for Registration of Ships adopted in 1986 has never entered into force as only 29 states have ratified the convention per 26.06.2023. For entry into force, no less than 40 states have to accept the convention

1274 Aoife O'Leary and Jennifer Brown, 'The Legal Basis for IMO Climate Measures' (New York June 2018) 11

1275 See for example the Protocol of 1988 Relating to the International Convention for the Safety of Life at Sea, 1974 requires 15 ratifications for its entry into force, whereas SOLAS entered into force after 25 states ratified the convention. Likewise, the 2005 Protocol to the Convention for the Suppression of Unlawful Acts Against the Safety of Maritime Navigation requires 12 ratifications to enter into force, whereas the main convention required 15 ratifications. The 1995 Fishstock Agreement entered into force after the thirthieth ratification, Article 40(1); UNCLOS in contrast required sixty ratifications, Article 308(1) of the UNCLOS

as a significantly lower threshold for a provisional application or the entry into force is used as a tool for coping the time-consuming ratification phase.[1276]

Shipping conventions typically come into force once a specific number of states, representing a certain percentage of the world's merchant fleet, have ratified the treaty. This is done to ensure a global level playing field. Without a threshold for entry into force, flag states that ratify early and impose more stringent requirements than others would put their merchant fleets at a significant competitive disadvantage. Alternatively, states run the risk of vessels being re-registered to a state with a more lenient legal framework. Therefore, states may choose not to ratify a convention until it has achieved a high level of participation. To limit the advantages of not ratifying a convention, several conventions include no-more-favorable-treatment clauses.[1277] These clauses stipulate that contracting parties shall apply the rules of a treaty also to vessels flying the flag of a non-state party.[1278] However, inertia continues to be the main reason for lengthy ratification processes.[1279] The MASS Convention cannot tolerate such a lengthy process, as there is an urgent need to regulate MASS quickly.

Regarding the MASS Convention, the enthusiastic participation of many states during the Regulatory Scoping Exercise at the IMO may indicate a high level of preparedness to ratify the MASS Convention.[1280] However, Soyer argues that it is legitimate to question whether the Philippines, as a seafaring nation, and the United States, with a low ratification score, would join the MASS Convention.[1281] If these two major maritime nations do not ratify the convention, other states may be less enthusiastic.

Alternatively, it could be considered to waive the requirement for a minimum number of ratifications for entry into force. The MASS Convention, unlike almost all other maritime conventions, would not impose additional requirements on existing ships but rather enable MASS operations. As there are no specific regulations on MASS, a level playing field is not at risk. Flag states would not benefit from not ratifying the MASS Convention, as non-compliant MASS would most likely be denied access to foreign ports.

If the MASS Convention were to bind each state directly upon ratification, the geographical scope would slowly expand. However, there are no significant

1276 Bowman (n 1122) 246

1277 For example Article I of SOLAS, Article 5(4) of MARPOL, Article X of STCW

1278 Reiling, *Reiling no date* (n 294) 386

1279 Bowman (n 1122) 232

1280 Laffey (n 612) 280

1281 Soyer (n 86) 173

disadvantages associated with a slow expansion of the geographical scope. On the contrary, a gradual expansion of the scope of the MASS Convention could allow states to accede to the Convention according to the needs and readiness of their industry. Some states that are more advanced in MASS technology may choose to ratify the Convention early, while others, that are less interested, may decide to wait. This does not affect the more advanced states. Reluctant states would not be pressured by more advanced states to ratify the Convention, as no minimum number of ratifications would be required for entry into force. This solution would combine a timely regulation of MASS and a high degree of legitimacy.

However, it is not enough to think about the initial entry into force of the convention, but also subsequent changes. The ratification requirement affects not only the entry into force phase, but also amendments to conventions as illustrated above. This limits flexibility and can easily lead to a lock-in of premature regulation that does not reflect the regulatory needs of the technology in question.[1282] The above-mentioned example of the 1958 New York Convention illustrates the consequences of technological lock-in impressively. The fear of an insufficient number of ratifications and corresponding fragmentation led to the decision to resort to a soft law solution to cope with the interpretation problem.[1283] Similarly, the failed amendment history of SOLAS 1960 serves to illustrate the practical impossibility of amending international treaties with a high threshold for the entry into force of amendments.

Petrification is especially detrimental to quickly evolving technologies, as illustrated above. As emerging technologies and regulations should co-evolve,[1284] adopting premature non-flexible regulations can hamper further innovation,[1285] even if formulated in a goal-based manner. As future development is unpredictable, the MASS Convention should not lock-in any regulations and provide for a flexible amendment regime.

The above-proposed waiver of the threshold for entry into force should not apply to the entry into force of amendments to the MASS Convention. As explained above, states would not be disadvantaged by an early ratification of the MASS Convention. On the contrary, these countries can present themselves as particularly open to technology and thus offer the MASS industry an attractive legal framework. With regard to amendments, however, fragmentation should be avoided. Amendments to the MASS Convention are likely to add

1282 Kronke (n 1139) 1152
1283 UNCITRAL (n 1133)
1284 Brownsword (n 859) 27
1285 Petrig (n 416) 132

stricter regulations or new legal requirements. To ensure a level playing field, amendments should not enter into force immediately upon ratification, but only after a significant number of states representing a certain percentage of the world's MASS fleet have ratified the amendment.

Similar to other conventions adopted under the auspices of the IMO, the MASS Convention can be supplemented with an annex containing technical regulations. The tacit acceptance procedure could be added to expedite changes to the technical annex. Such an arrangement can provide the requisite flexibility. As in the case of the other conventions, the IMO could be commissioned, to administer the convention, and discuss and adopt amendments.

In summary, a MASS Convention would have the advantage of a potentially broad substantive and geographical scope. It could include interpretative guidance, in particular on horizontal terms and concepts, as well as additional provisions on MASS-specific aspects even on issues beyond the mandate of the IMO. Ongoing discussions at the IMO could accelerate the negotiation process. However, negotiations on liability issues may require additional time, but they must be resolved.

Ratification would be open to all states, and could lead to a globally harmonized legal framework. Since the required number of ratifications for entry into force is high and can delay this process, it would be advisable to waive this threshold. The MASS Convention would apply directly to all states that have ratified it. Regarding potential revisions, however, it is essential to ensure broad support and continue with the conventional requirement threshold for the entry into force of amendments.

Before ultimately determining the appropriateness of a MASS Convention, one final aspect deserves consideration. Unlike the implementing agreements mentioned earlier, the MASS Convention would supplement not only one main treaty, but several. The interpretation of all conventions including the terms master, manning, and crew would be affected. It is necessary to assess whether one treaty that is adopted subsequently can affect several other treaties simultaneously.[1286]

Although most supplementing instruments were linked to one main treaty, there are examples of horizontal cross-conventional protocols. The 1988 Joint Protocol[1287] provides for conflict-of-law rules to prevent the simultaneous application of the 1963 Vienna Convention on Civil Liability for Nuclear

1286 Laffey (n 612) 281

1287 Joint Protocol Relating to the Application of the Vienna Convention and the Paris Convention 21 September 1988

Damage and the 1960 Paris Convention on Third Party Liability in the Field of Nuclear Energy. Despite the fact that there are no examples from maritime law for a cross-cutting protocol, the state parties are free to develop such an instrument. Reconsidering the discussion of Article 31(3)(c) of the VCLT, the MASS Convention applicable between the parties would be considered in the interpretation process of any other convention applicable between the parties in question.

Although the horizontal approach and potential for worldwide implementation are noteworthy benefits, the risk of outdated regulations becoming fixed and a protracted and intricate negotiation process are of greater significance. Although petrification may be addressed procedurally, the negotiation process is lengthy and the outcome is uncertain. It is imperative that a reliable international legal framework is in place as soon as possible. A solution that is global and predictable, but inflexible and time-consuming to negotiate does not seem desirable for the regulation of MASS. Given the significant practical impacts of non-binding instruments, the advantages of a MASS Convention may not surpass the limitations. Soyer and Laffey conclude similarly that the ideal academic proposal of an all-inclusive MASS Convention cannot overcome practical obstacles.[1288]

5.3.4 *Decision of a Conference of the State Parties*

Another way to change treaties is a decision by the conference of the state parties. Being an association of the state parties to a multilateral treaty, this body is concerned with continuous governance of the subject matter of the treaty.[1289] With respect to its law-making function, explicit and implicit powers must be distinguished. A treaty may explicitly transfer law-making authority to the conference of state parties. Article 312 of the UNCLOS serves as an example as it empowers the conference of state parties to adopt amendments. This function of the conference of states has be discussed above. Any secondary law-making can be based on implicit powers.

Such decisions are not necessarily legally binding, but their legal significance can be considerable and has to be assessed on a case-by-case basis.[1290] Depending on the rules of procedure governing the conference of the state

1288 Soyer (n 86) 173; Laffey (n 612) 281

1289 Volker Röben, 'Conference (Meeting) of States Parties' in Anne Peters (ed), *Max Planck Encyclopedia of Public International Law* (MPEPIL) (Oxford University Press) 1

1290 ibid 17

parties, decisions can have varying legal effects.[1291] They can have the effect of a subsequent interpretation agreement in the meaning of Article 31(3)(a) of the VCLT or give rise to subsequent practice resulting in an agreement on the interpretation of the treaty in the meaning of Article 31(3)(b) of the VCLT.[1292] In the context of UNCLOS, it is worth noting that a formal amendment, as stipulated in Articles 312 and 313 of the UNCLOS, was considered to have the same effect as a decision by the Meeting of the States Parties.[1293]

With respect to MASS, decisions of a conference of state parties could guide the interpretation of key terms. However, substantial provisions need to be added as well. It is questionable whether a conference of states would have the authority to add new substantial provisions to a treaty.

In maritime law, the conference of state parties were actively engaged in the development of the treaties. The Meeting of States Parties to UNCLOS holds annual sessions.[1294] It has substantially affected the interpretation and application of the provisions in the Annex of UNCLOS concerning the allocation of seats on the Commission on the Limits of the Continental Shelf and the International Tribunal for the Law of the Sea.[1295] Moreover, the 10-year time period for submitting particulars on the outer limits of the continental shelf, if established beyond 200 nm, as stated in Article 4, Annex II of UNCLOS, was determined to have commenced on 13 May 1999 by a decision of the Meeting of the States Parties in 2001.[1296]

Although these decisions can be interpreted as altering the provisions of UNCLOS,[1297] all decisions concerned administrative aspects.[1298] In the case of MASS, however, substantial provisions would be affected. In 1998, the Meeting

1291 Malgosia Fitzmaurice and Daniel Costelloe, 'Lawmaking by treaty: Conclusion of treaties and evolution of treaty regimes in practice' in Catherine Brölmann and Yannick Radi (eds), *Research handbook on the theory and practice of international lawmaking* (Edward Elgar Publishing 2016) 120

1292 International Law Commission (ILC), 'A/73/10 – Report of the International Law Commission on the work of its seventieth session (30 April–1 June and 2 July–10 August 2018)' (2018) 2(2) Yearbook of the International Law Commission, 71

1293 Meeting of the States Parties, 'SPLOS/73 – Report of the eleventh Meeting of States Parties' (New York 14 June 2001) 78

1294 Harrison (n 1231) 71

1295 Meeting of the States Parties, 'SPLOS/203 – Report of the nineteenth Meeting of States Parties' (New York 24 July 2009) 102; Meeting of the States Parties, 'SPLOS/14 – Report of the fifth Meeting of States Parties' (New York 20 September 1996) 15

1296 Meeting of the States Parties, 'SPLOS/73 – Report of the eleventh Meeting of States Parties' (n 1293) 81

1297 Tanaka, *Tanaka 2012* (n 1232) 35

1298 Harrison (n 1231) 80

refused to provide interpretive guidance on the term 'coastal state' for the purpose of implementing Annexes I and II of UNCLOS. It was argued that the Meeting "did not have the competence to give a legal opinion".[1299] Thus, it is unlikely that the Meeting would take a decision on the interpretation of the terms 'master' and 'crew' in the light of MASS.

The state parties to the GAIRAS conventions do not regularly hold conferences. The last meeting of the member states of SOLAS was in 2002, the COLREG member states never met. Therefore, it is unlikely that any of these conferences will be a suitable forum for the amendments related to MASS.

Moreover, the conference of state parties only resembles the member states to one treaty. States not being a member to the treaty can join the meeting as an observer.[1300] As not all important maritime nations are a member to UNCLOS, it is not advisable to adopt decisions of global concern in this forum.[1301]

Eventually, a conference of the state parties is concerned with only one multilateral treaty. However, the MASS-amendments make horizontal integration and cross-conventional approach necessary. Considering the limited scope of competence of a conference of state parties, it is not recommended to adopt a decision on MASS as a means to combat the regulatory challenges posed by the advent of MASS.

However, it is important not to underestimate the practical significance of a decision made by the conference of state parties. Therefore, a decision to complement another – soft law – instrument on MASS could be a promising solution. Nevertheless, the decision would only affect one convention. Before turning to solutions emanating from the regional and supranational level, consideration should be given to amending UNCLOS through the development of GAIRAS and customary international law.

5.3.5 *Generally Accepted International Rules and Standards*

UNCLOS is a framework convention intended to settle all issues related to the law of the sea.[1302] Thus, for most aspects UNCLOS refers to generally accepted international rules and standards providing more detailed regulations on specific matters. Moreover, the reference to GAIRAS allows reflecting subsequent changes and developments without a need to alter the text of UNCLOS.[1303]

1299 Meeting of the States Parties, 'SPLOS/31 – Report of the Eighth Meeting of States Parties' (New York 4 June 1998) 52

1300 Röben (n 1289) 5

1301 Harrison (n 1231) 73

1302 See first section of the preamble to the UNCLOS

1303 Buga (n 322) 66; van Logchem (n 484) 59

Thus, the text of UNCLOS does not need to be changed to guide the interpretation of terms included in UNCLOS.[1304] However, the development of GAIRAS may not exceed the scope of UNCLOS. The IMO is the competent organization entrusted with the development of GAIRAS.[1305] Article 94(5) of the UNCLOS obliges flag states to conform to GAIRAS when exercising their flag state duties. Complementary, coastal states have the right to impose regulations on the construction, design, equipment and manning of foreign vessels in innocent passage giving effect to GAIRAS, Article 21(2) of the UNCLOS.

The legal analysis in chapter D. revealed that UNCLOS can be interpreted in a way including MASS. Consequently, the IMO could adopt generally accepted regulations on MASS, which would be incorporated in UNCLOS based on the rule of reference. As SOLAS and COLREG are considered part of GAIRAS,[1306] amending these conventions would be sufficient to prepare UNCLOS for the advent of MASS. Moreover, soft law instruments adopted by the IMO could also be included in the scope of GAIRAS.[1307] However, not all instruments adopted by the IMO automatically are part of GAIRAS. Rather, broad support at the IMO is necessary.[1308]

Reflecting on the above-discussed approaches to response to the legal challenges created by the advent of MASS, a legally non-binding MASS Code adopted by the IMO was considered beneficial. It has to be determined whether such a non-binding code not being part of SOLAS would fall within the scope of GAIRAS.

The LEG published a list of non-binding IMO resolutions which fall within the scope of GAIRAS.[1309] However, none of these instruments includes substantially new provisions. Rather these resolutions provide for minor amendments to existing instruments[1310] or principles that should be considered when developing regulations.[1311]

1304 Jokioinen and others (n 98) 38; Beckman and Sun (n 259) 227

1305 Freestone and Elferink (n 1216) 214; Tanaka, *Tanaka 2012* (n 1232) 36

1306 Beckman and Sun (n 259) 221; Allen, 'Allen 2018' (n 514) 500

1307 Korseberg (n 331) 805; Klein (n 331) 16; Wolfrum, 'Wolfrum 1999' (n 327) 230

1308 Aston (n 338) 165; Frenzel (n 335) 162; Ringbom, 'Ringbom 2020' (n 424) 443

1309 IMO, 'Implications of the United Nations Convention on the Law of the Sea for the International Maritime Organization' (n 259) 105–139

1310 MSC, IMO, 'Res. MSC.209(81): Adoption of amendments to the Seafarers' Training, Certification and Watchkeeping Code (STCW Code)' (London 18 May 2006); IMO, 'Res. A.955(23): Amendments to the Principles of Safe Manning' (London 26 February 2004)

1311 IMO, 'Res. A.947(23): Human Element Vision, Principles and Goals for the Organization' (London 26 February 2004)

It is therefore questionable whether the MASS Code as providing for substantially new modes of operation would be part of GAIRAS and thus incorporated in UNCLOS. As the IMO does not have the competence to decide on the qualification as 'generally accepted' it would be left to judicial review and academic scholarship to discuss whether the non-binding MASS Code would be part of GAIRAS. Given the importance of a reliable regulatory framework for MASS, uncertainty is unacceptable for both governments and industry stakeholders. Flag states need to be assured that registering MASS does not conflict with their obligation to conform to GAIRAS as stipulated in Article 94(5) of the UNCLOS. Industry stakeholders, in turn, need to know how coastal states react upon MASS during innocent passage. In summary, relying on the qualification of a non-binding MASS Code as being 'generally accepted' does not serve the need for a reliable legal framework.

Alternatively, amendments to SOLAS and COLREG were discussed. Applying the tacit acceptance procedure was dismissed for normative constraints. However, using the formal amendment procedure was likewise dismissed, as the development of a horizontally coherent framework for MASS cannot be achieved by amending several conventions independently. Moreover, the long ratification phase delays the readiness of the new legal framework. However, such amendments to the GAIRAS treaties would undoubtedly affect UNCLOS.

Eventually, developing a MASS Convention was considered a promising approach, despite the risk of locking-in premature technologies. If not being adopted as a supplementary instrument to UNCLOS, the MASS Convention could still impact UNCLOS if being 'generally accepted'. To be considered such the MASS Convention would need to be ratified by a great number of states representing a significant share of the world's merchant fleet. Although the requirements cannot be given in concrete numbers, it serves as an indication that the Wreck Removal Convention was not considered 'generally accepted' although ratified by 55 states.[1312] It would take the MASS Convention several years to achieve a sufficient high number of ratifications. Thus, it is not recommended to rely on the rule of reference in UNCLOS to incorporate the MASS Convention. Rather, this instrument should be designed in a way directly affecting UNCLOS such as the 1994 Implementation Agreement and the Fish Stocks Agreement.

In conclusion, the rule of reference in UNCLOS is designed to ensure the evolution of UNCLOS without formally amending the text itself. The IMO is the competent organization for the development of generally accepted

1312 Parlov, 'Parlov 2022' (n 356) 669

international rules and standards. However, in the context of MASS, the available procedures at the IMO are not satisfactory. MASS touches upon the fundamental presumptions of shipping: human control on board the vessel. Regulations contrasting with this presumption ought not to be adopted using the same procedure as for technical details. Therefore, alternative arrangements should be endeavored to provide a reliable legal framework. All the approaches discussed hitherto have involved the development of written amendments or instruments. However, non-written approaches are also conceivable and will be briefly discussed below.

5.3.6 *Customary International Law and Subsequent State Practice*

Eventually, there are two other sources of international law discussed in academic literature as possible solutions in the field of autonomous vessels. First, a solution based on customary international law is proposed. Second, subsequent state practice establishing an agreement of the state parties regarding the interpretation of a treaty in the meaning of Article 31(3)(b) of the VCLT is discussed.

For customary international law to develop a common state practice based on an opinio iuris is necessary.[1313] Some authors argue that uniform state practice could emerge from complying with non-binding instruments.[1314] In fact, soft law is often promoted as an antecedent to customary international law.[1315] And, in fact, customary international law can alter written treaty clauses.[1316] However, with respect to MASS three aspects deserve attention: first, customary international law develops slowly. Although the ICJ stated that the time for the emergence of customary international law could be short,[1317] a certain time is necessary, on the one side, for states to develop a uniform practice, and, on the other side, for other states to consider the other states' behavior and react to it in some way.[1318] This temporal limitation reduces the feasibility of relying on customary international law to address the challenges of MASS.

1313 Treves, 'Treves' (n 268) 8

1314 White (n 912) 572; Ilg (n 230) 19; Boyle, 'Boyle 2019' (n 919) 103

1315 Boyle, 'Boyle 1999' (n 959) 904; Jon B Skærseth, 'Managing North Sea Pollution Effectively: Linking International and Domestic Institutions' [2003] International Environmental Agreements: Politics, Law and Economics 167, 179; Shelton, 'Shelton 2009' (n 902) 68

1316 Treves, 'Treves' (n 268) 88; Dahm (n 465) 679

1317 *North Sea Continental Shelf Cases* [1969] [1969] ICJ Reports 3 (International Court of Justice) 74

1318 Gennady M Danilenko, 'The Theory of International Customary Law' (1988) 31 German Yearbook of International Law 9, 30

Second, detailed regulations are required for MASS. Since customary international law is usually unwritten, it is not suitable for creating a fine tuned regulatory framework. Likewise, the need for flexible adjustments of the new legal framework has to be considered. Taking into account the slow and unpredictable evolution of customary international law, it does not provide the necessary maneuverability.

Third, uniform state practice can only emerge if states act by registering MASS. As long as the legal framework is not prepared for dealing with MASS, most states are reluctant to allow international autonomous vessel operations. Thus, the necessary state practice is unlikely to happen.[1319] In conclusion, customary international is not able to provide a solid legal basis for MASS in the near future,[1320] though, at a later point, customary international law could be invoked.[1321]

The disadvantages of subsequent state practice are very similar to those of customary international law. It is highly unlikely that a sufficient number of states will interpret the GAIRAS conventions and UNCLOS in a uniform manner amounting to an agreement on the interpretation per Article 31(3)(b) of the VCLT without any written basis. Additionally, the very possibility of altering a treaty by subsequent practice is debated.[1322] Consequently, this approach is linked to significant legal uncertainty and therefore not recommended.

5.3.7 *Conclusions*

This section discussed approaches at the international level to meet the regulatory needs of MASS. Starting with instruments available at the IMO, binding and non-binding solutions, amending the current legal framework, developing a self-standing international MASS Convention, taking a decision at the conference of state parties, and customary international law as well as subsequent state practice were discussed and compared. With regard to UNCLOS, special attention was drawn to the mechanism of the renvio clause incorporating GAIRAS developed by the IMO.

1319 Michael F Sturley, 'Can commercial law accommodate new technologies in international shipping?' in Barış Soyer and Andrew Tettenborn (eds), *New Technologies, Artificial Intelligence and Shipping Law in the 21st Century* (Maritime and transport law library. Informa Law from Routledge 2019) 26; van Logchem (n 484) 27

1320 Ilg (n 230) 58; Sturley (n 1319) 26

1321 van Logchem (n 484) 55

1322 Nolte, 'Nolte 2015' (n 465) 19; Zemanek (n 466) 4; Bernandez (n 466) 27; Buga (n 322) 47; Dahm (n 465) 673–674

Many credit the IMO for the regulatory handling of MASS.[1323] As the 'competent international organization' under UNCLOS, the IMO possesses the necessary competence, established procedures, and appropriate instruments to address international shipping. Among all available instruments, a code was considered the most suitable IMO instrument for addressing MASS. A code is not legally binding yet it can offer an all-encompassing set of regulations. Additionally, it can address numerous conventions, thus ensuring horizontal integration and coherency. Furthermore, the IMO could adopt non-binding guidelines to streamline the registration process and port state controls. In particular, risk assessment methodologies and verification processes could be harmonized through guidelines. As of today, the IMO develops a MASS Code.

To make a code legally binding, the IMO often uses the tacit acceptance procedure to add a chapter to an international convention referring to the code. The tacit acceptance procedure allows an amendment to come into force without the express consent of a specific number of states. This procedure enables the international legal framework for shipping to be quickly adapted to innovations and urgent matters. Most of the amendments to SOLAS were adopted using the tacit acceptance procedure. Therefore, the IMO plans to make the MASS Code legally binding by adding a chapter to SOLAS invoking the tacit acceptance procedure. Despite the benefits, it must be considered that MASS require a horizontal approach. Although a code can supplement several conventions, it is not preferable to make that code binding by amending one convention. Simultaneously amending multiple conventions can be a complex task and has not often been done.

In addition, the tacit acceptance procedure was developed to facilitate amendments to technical details. General principles should not be subject to the tacit acceptance procedure. MASS, as illustrated, affect the fundamentals of shipping by moving the crew and the master ashore and by handing over control of the ship to algorithms. It is not recommended to authorize such a fundamental change through a simplified procedure. Therefore, adding a chapter to SOLAS to make the MASS Code mandatory should be avoided.

As an alternative, the explicit amendment procedure could be used. However, this approach has the disadvantage of requiring time-consuming diplomatic negotiations and the potential for settling on a suboptimal solution simply to gain consensus. Additionally, horizontal integration across all involved conventions cannot be achieved.

1323 Laffey (n 612) 282; Soyer (n 86) 183; Bergström and others (n 1106) 881; CMI, 'Summary of Responses to the CMI Questionnaire' (n 525) 5

Although similar negotiations would be necessary for a new MASS Convention, this approach can ensure seamless horizontal integration of MASS into the present legal framework. Moreover, issues beyond the mandate of the IMO, in particular the implementation of UNCLOS and liability issues, could be addressed. Eventually, the usually required high number of ratifications for entry into force could be abolished. However, implementing a binding international treaty may lead to the entrenchment of premature technologies. Given the importance of a flexible and adaptable legal framework, this section concludes that a MASS Convention is not the most appropriate way to address MASS.

In conclusion, it is not possible to find a single solution at the international level that meets all the mentioned criteria simultaneously. The following section examines regional regulations, as the geographical scope of application is the least important criterion for the future legal framework for MASS.

5.4 Regulation at the Regional Level

The culmination of research projects on maritime autonomy and MASS in Northern and Western Europe renders regional solutions for the regulatory response to MASS appealing. Due to technical and economic constraints, regional MASS applications like short-sea shipping, offshore supply, maintenance, surveillance, and local or regional mobility concepts are the most promising. In addition, the states of Northern and Western Europe are jointly affected by an ageing population, resulting in a shortage of labor, which makes autonomous solutions that allow crew reductions even more attractive. Notwithstanding the existence of significant common interests among Northern and Western European states, it would be remiss not to acknowledge the existence of notable differences, particularly in the areas of maritime transportation and technological capabilities. Aiming for the co-evolution of law and MASS technology, a global framework is not necessary for the initial regional application of MASS. Consultations with industry stakeholders have identified an urgent need for an interim regulatory framework to be put in place as soon as possible, rather than an immediate global solution. Nevertheless, a regional approach may prove detrimental to the interoperability of MASS on a global scale. While MASS are initially expected to operate on a regional level, the shipbuilding industry is global in scope and dependent on worldwide interoperability. Consequently, regional approaches may potentially compromise global standards. However, regional approaches will be discussed in the following section, with these risks in mind.

Now, regional solutions to the regulatory challenges posed by the advent of MASS shall be considered. Firstly, regional cooperation will be explored from a general perspective, reflecting on terminological issues and the reasons why states opt for regional cooperation. Then, the potential of regional solutions for the above-mentioned regulatory needs related to MASS will be discussed, focusing on Northern and Western Europe and on already existing cooperation fora.

5.4.1 *Regional Cooperation*

As a starting point, the meaning of the term 'region' needs to be ascertained. Starting with a geographical point of view, a region is a part of the earth surface characterized by geographical proximity and a common feature making this region distinct from others.[1324] On the one side, regions could be delimited by natural characteristics such as climate, topographic elements, location on the globe, flora, or fauna. On the other side, regions could be determined based on human-made constructs such as nation states, culture, language, or religion. This type of identification of regions is predominant in social science and shall thus be applied here.

For a legal conception of the term 'region', the geographical scope of jurisdiction of existing regulatory entities is decisive. Depending on the subject matter or the intended regulatory success, a region can be determined along the borders of cities, municipalities, districts, provinces, and/or nation states. As the registration of MASS is governed ultimately by national law, nation states are the relevant dimension to consider here. Thus, for the purpose of this study, a region is defined as a group of states that are geographically close and share additional common characteristics.

Such common features could be a similar economic situation and shared historical and political experiences that result in common perspectives.[1325] As the regions considered here are man-made constructions, there must be a political will to belong to a particular region.[1326] For example, Liechtenstein

1324 Derek Gregory and others (eds), *The dictionary of human geography* (5th ed. Blackwell 2009) 630–631

1325 Louise Fawcett, 'Regionalism and global governance: An appraisal' in Pierre de Senarclens and Ali Kazancigil (eds), *Regulating Globalization: Critical Approaches to Global Governance* (United Nations University Press 2007) 154; Mathias Forteau, 'Regional Cooperation' in Anne Peters (ed), *Max Planck Encyclopedia of Public International Law* (MPEPIL) (Oxford University Press) 16

1326 Monica Herz, 'Regional governance and regional organizations' in Thomas G Weiss and Rorden Wilkinson (eds), *International organization and global governance* (Second edition. Routledge Taylor & Francis Group 2018) 251; Yves Berthelot, 'Regionalization and

and Norway share historical and political experiences with other European states and have comparable economic interests, but both states have deliberately chosen not to be part of the EU, a regional grouping.[1327] Nevertheless, they both decided to become a member of the European Free Trade Association.

To conclude, the regions that are significant for MASS regulation are groups of geographically close states that share common interests in economic development and environmental protection and have the political will to cooperate at the regional level. As next, the factors that prompt states to opt for regional solutions shall be illuminated.

Based on the assumption that states act rationally and enter into agreements maximizing their surplus, states engage in regional cooperation if this results in a pareto-efficient situation. In other words, states choose regional cooperation only if it provides greater benefits than other options and if the advantages outweigh the drawbacks of such cooperation.[1328] The premise of adopting a rational and efficient choice also means that regional cooperation is not an end in itself, but is chosen when it is the best option. Given the great number of regional collaborations that exist worldwide,[1329] especially among states in Northern and Western Europe, it is evident that there must be significant benefits, which will be explored now.

Every region has unique geographical, economic, socio-economic, or environmental characteristics that differentiate it from other regions. These distinctions can be more thoroughly reflected in regional cooperation than in a global forum. Additionally, more emphasis can be placed on shared interests such as safety and environmental conservation. At a global level, only a one-size-fits-all approach can be pursued. However, such an approach is not able to reflect regional needs sufficiently.[1330] This is acknowledged also by UNCLOS, promoting regional agreements of fisheries or the marine environmental protection of enclosed and semi-enclosed seas.[1331]

The ability to create tailor-made solutions for a particular region increases the social acceptability of such solutions by reflecting regional specificities.[1332] This is because most people identify with either their local region or their

globalization: Two concomitant dynamics in need of coherent institutions' in Pierre de Senarclens and Ali Kazancigil (eds), *Regulating Globalization: Critical Approaches to Global Governance* (United Nations University Press 2007) 178

1327 Berthelot (n 1326) 178

1328 ibid 187

1329 Forteau (n 1325) 8; Fawcett (n 1325) 153

1330 Berthelot (n 1326) 194; Ringbom, *Ringbom 2008* (n 675) 12

1331 See Articles 118, 123 of the UNCLOS

1332 Fawcett (n 1325) 169; Berthelot (n 1326) 195

nation-state. Identification with a larger group of nations is still considerable, but few people see themselves as citizens of the world. Thus, a legal instrument that precisely meets regional needs is generally more accepted than one that reflects a global consensus.

The like-mindedness and homogeneity of the countries in a region makes it easier to reach consensus.[1333] Furthermore, negotiations are facilitated due to the reduced number of participating states compared to the global level. This simplifies both logistical arrangements and substantial discussions.

Regional cooperation is especially advantageous for small states that make up only a fraction of the world's population.[1334] Despite every state having one vote at the international level, regardless of its size, population or economic performance, the real negotiating weight of small states is often less. In such cases, smaller states may withdraw from the global forum and focus on regional cooperation. However, the vast majority of modern society's needs require an international approach.[1335] Therefore, small states can join together in a regional grouping and communicate their interests collectively at the international level. This enhances their combined influence and allows especially small nations to advance their interests more efficiently.[1336] For example, 39 states gathered in the 'Small Island Developing States' UN regional commission to jointly advocate for their interests. Although these states only represent 65 million people and cover 0.5% of the world's surface area, they control 16.1% of the world's total EEZ.[1337] Jointly, these states have a considerable clout to promote their interests internationally. In addition, the Nordic Cooperation, discussed in more detail below, increases the strike capability of each of its member states.

Regional cooperation is not limited to small states. Likeminded states can join forces to ensure implementation of international regulations[1338] and be forerunners for the international level.[1339] The Oslo[1340] and

1333 Hagemann, Huddelston Skees and Thierer (n 857) 79; Herz (n 1326) 254
1334 Fawcett (n 1325) 151–152
1335 Berthelot (n 1326) 187
1336 ibid 202; Johan Strang, 'Nordic Political and Economic Cooperation:' (Singapore February 2016) 6
1337 United Nations, 'About Small Island Developing States (SIDS)' <https://sdgs.un.org/smallislands/about-small-island-developing-states> accessed 16 February 2024
1338 Veronica Frank, 'Consequences of the *Prestige* Sinking for European and International Law' (2005) 20(1) The International Journal of Marine and Coastal Law 1, 10
1339 Ringbom, *Ringbom 2008* (n 675) 13; Forteau (n 1325) 17
1340 Convention for the prevention of marine pollution by dumping from ships and aircrafts, No. 13269 15 February 1972

Paris[1341] Conventions, concluded in 1972 and 1974, respectively, by states bordering the North Sea and the North-East Atlantic, are examples of such regional initiatives to address challenges that have not been effectively addressed at the international level. Although negotiations on the prevention of marine pollution and the development of oil pollution prevention conventions have been underway since 1954,[1342] the concluded convention, MARPOL, was not intended to cover land-based pollution and it was not until 1999 that the North Sea was declared a special area for mandatory pollution prevention regulations.[1343] Given the increasing pollution of the North Sea and the North-East Atlantic and the *Torrey Canyon* disaster in 1967, the bordering states engaged in regional cooperation to combat marine pollution and adopted the Oslo and Paris Convention to combat ship- and land-source pollution.[1344]

Both conventions were merged into the Convention for the protection of the marine environment of the North-East Atlantic (OSPAR Convention) in 1992.[1345] Although the scope of the OSPAR Convention does not cover the promotion of MASS, the determined cooperation reflected by the prompt development[1346] and entry into force of the Oslo, the Paris, and the OSPAR Conventions underline the potential of regional cooperation. The regional law-making activities could not be hindered by a parallel development at the international level resulting in the Convention on the prevention of marine pollution by dumping of wastes and other matter, the London Convention,[1347] adopted in late 1972. While the London and the Oslo Conventions shared similarities, they were not identical, particularly with regard to the list of prohibited substances for dumping.[1348]

1341 Convention for the prevention of marine pollution from land-based sources, No. 26842 4 June 1974

1342 Jeff B Curtis, 'Vessel-Source Oil Pollution and Marpol 73/78: An International Success Story' (1985) 15(4) Environmental Law 679, 684

1343 MEPC, IMO, 'Res. MEPC.75(40) – Amendments to the Annex of the Protocol of 1978 relating to MARPOL' (London 25 September 1997)

1344 Peter Ehlers, 'The History of the International North Sea Conferences' (1990) 5(1) International Journal of Estuarine and Coastal Law 3, 4

1345 Convention for the protection of the marine environment of the North-East Atlantic, No. 42279 22 September 1992

1346 Cees van der Burgt, 'Extract from "The Oslo and Paris Commission: The First Decade"' (1984) 4 <https://www.ospar.org/site/assets/files/1201/extract_from_the_first_decade_oslo_paris_conventions.pdf>

1347 Convention on the prevention of marine pollution by dumping of wastes and other matter, No. 15749 29 December 1972

1348 Tullio Treves, 'Regional Approaches to the Protection of the Marine Environment' in Myron H Nordquist, John N Moore and Said Mahmoudi (eds), *The Stockholm declaration and law of the marine environment* (Martinus Nijhoff Publishers 2003) 141

The OSPAR Commission continued actively to shape the international level by declaring the Ballast Water Management Convention[1349] to be preliminarily applicable in 2012,[1350] following its adoption in 2004. The Convention did not enter into force until 2017. Finally, the regulatory interrelationship between the EU and the IMO must be seen as a way of shaping the international level by regional cooperation. However, this will be considered in the section on European legislation below.[1351]

Not only unilateral regional initiatives can impact the international level, also joint international proposals are conceivable. The Nordic states, for example, promoted zero-emission fuels for shipping and submitted a joint proposal to the IMO to adopt guidelines for the safety of ships using ammonia as fuel.[1352] The background for this proposal will be illustrated below when discussing the potential of Nordic cooperation for MASS. At this stage, it shall suffice to depict the joint Nordic submission to the IMO as an example of how the regional level can actively involve at the international level.

Thus, regional and international cooperation do not necessarily contradict each other, but can lead to mutual strengthening and joint promotion of initiatives.[1353] However, regional cooperation can sometimes lead to regional selfishness, exclusion of others, and an uncompromising pursuit of one's own goals. The success of regional cooperation depends on whether states perceive that cooperation with the international level will maximize their surplus. In the realm of international shipping, states are likely to favor a regional approach that considers global perspectives and cooperates internationally, rather than adopting regional instruments in a haphazard manner. This is evidenced by several regional intergovernmental maritime organizations and the IMO granting each other observer status.

Recognizing that regional cooperation may not be solely advantageous, examining any potential drawbacks is important. As a region is defined as a

1349 International Convention for the control and management of ship's ballast water and sediments, No. 55544 13 February 2004

1350 OSPAR Commission, 'OSPAR 12/22/1-E, Annex 17: Joint Notice to Shipping from the Contracting Parties of the Barcelona Convention, OSPAR and HELCOM on: – General Guidance on the Voluntary Interim Application of the D1 Ballast Water Exchange Standard by Vessels Operating between the Mediterranean Sea and the North-East Atlantic and/or the Baltic Sea' (Bonn 29 June 2012) 2.3

1351 Section 5.5.3

1352 Sub-Committee on Carriage of Cargoes and Containers, 'CCC 9-INF.7 – Supporting information to the draft interim guidelines for the safety of ships using ammonia as fuel (Denmark, Finland, Norway, and Sweden)' (London 20 June 2023)

1353 Forteau (n 1325) 25; Fawcett (n 1325) 153

group of states distinct from other states, regionalism inevitably involves an element of exclusion. States not belonging to the region cannot directly influence or benefit from the cooperative surplus. However, most regional groups are receptive to new members as long as they meet the criteria for inclusion.

Another frequently raised concern regarding regionalism is the potential for legal fragmentation.[1354] Since the establishment of the UN in 1947, the unification of international law has been a common goal. However, regional initiatives and regulatory measures may undermine this goal and lead to legal fragmentation. Nevertheless, fragmentation is not inherently problematic.[1355] Issues may arise if there is a lack of linkages between different systems and mutual recognition clauses. Put another way, fragmented law becomes an obstacle if it is not harmonized.

The above-alleged advantage of regional forerunners could also be seen as a negative aspect of regional cooperation. An agreed compromise at the international level could be counteracted by more stringent regional measures, potentially reducing the motivation for implementation by other states and putting the level playing field at risk.[1356]

In summary, regional cooperation offers significant advantages for the participating states. It facilitates consensus-building, takes into account regional specificities, and increases the acceptance of such agreements. Regional cooperation fora can be used to jointly act at the international level, consolidate efforts to implement international regulations, and promote new or updated regulations. Moreover, regional forerunner projects can serve as experiments for the global level, benefiting third parties. However, it is important to consider the risk of fragmenting international law and undermining internationally achieved agreements.

After having considered the meaning of the term 'region' and discussed the advantages and disadvantages of regional regulation in the abstract, the focus now shifts to concrete solutions for MASS. Similar to cooperation at the international level, regional cooperation requires institutionalization in some form. As it is unlikely that a new institution will emerge specifically for MASS, existing institutions for cooperation in maritime issues in Northern and Western Europe will be presented and assessed in the light of MASS.

1354 Forteau (n 1325) 8

1355 United Nations General Assembly, 'A/CN.4/577/Add. 1 – Report of the International Law Commission on the work of its fifty-eighth session (2006)' (Geneva 23 January 2007) 5

1356 Frank (n 1338), 10 Ringbom, 'Ringbom 2020' (n 424) 459

5.4.2 *Maritime Cooperation in Northern and Western Europe*

The Baltic Sea and the North Sea are covered by several regional fora for cooperation on maritime issues.[1357] In addition to non-state initiatives such as the Baltic and International Maritime Council or the CMI, intergovernmental organizations were founded to address marine challenges at this regional level. Often, marine environmental protection was the focal point of regional institutions. It is beyond the scope of this study to provide a thorough analysis of all regional cooperation fora in the Baltic and North Sea region. Therefore, the analysis will focus on those institutions that do not consider maritime aspects as a side issue, but as a main focus.

The Helsinki Commission was established by the Convention on the Protection of the Marine Environment of the Baltic Sea Area[1358] in 1974 and focuses on preventing any form of pollution in the Baltic Sea. Although there is a Working Group considering shipping aspects, promotion of technological innovations in the field of maritime navigation are not covered by the mandate of the Commission. Thus, it is not deemed an appropriate forum to develop regional regulations on MASS.

The Arctic Council, established by the Ottawa Declaration in 1996, focuses on marine environmental protection and the active involvement of Indigenous people in Arctic matters. It gathers all states bordering the Arctic waters north of the 60th degree of latitude, i.e. in addition to Northern European states, the Russian Federation, Canada, and the United States. Due to its focus on environmental protection in the Arctic region, the Arctic Council does not provide a promising forum for MASS regulations. MASS are not intended to operate primarily in the Arctic region. Moreover, environmental protection does not pose the greatest challenge to MASS, as MASS operate most likely at zero-emission.

The Council of the Baltic Sea States was established in 1992 with the aim of promoting peace, stability, and prosperity among the bordering states. It does not exclusively deal with maritime issues. Although there is an Expert Group on Sustainable Maritime Economy, no initiative on maritime autonomy was taken so far. Thus, the Council of the Baltic Sea States does not offer a viable platform for the regulation of MASS. However, there are two regional

1357 To name just a few: The Council of the Baltic Sea States, Baltic Sea Parliamentary Conference, Baltic Council of Ministers, Baltic Assembly, Barents Euro-Arctic Council, Arctic Council, Nordic Council of Ministers, Nordic Council, Baltic Marine Environment Protection Commission, Vision and Stragety aournd the Baltic Sea, Northern Dimension, EU Strategy for the Baltic Sea Region, Interreg Baltic Sea Region, Nordic-Baltic Eight cooperation format, Paris MoU

1358 Convention on the Protection of the Marine Environment of the Baltic Sea Area, No. 25986 22 March 1974

cooperation fora, which are more promising for MASS regulation. These shall thus be considered in more detail now. First, the Paris MoU on Port State Control and, second, the Nordic cooperation are discussed.

5.4.2.1 Paris Memorandum of Understanding

The Paris MoU on Port State Control was concluded in 1982 and aims to eliminate substandard ships through harmonized port state controls. Notably, the MoU is a legally non-binding agreement among national maritime authorities and does not amount to an international treaty.[1359] Rather, these agreements can be classified as international administrative agreements[1360] forming part of global administrative law.[1361] However, as discussed earlier, soft law instruments can be just as effective as hard law instruments.[1362] Therefore, the soft nature of the Paris MoU does not make it unsuitable for MASS regulation.

The Paris MoU has 28 participating maritime authorities, mostly located in Europe. Additionally, Canada participates. Considering the desired geographical scope, the Paris MoU could provide a suitable forum for MASS regulation. However, a port state control MoU does not usually contain substantive provisions but is limited to procedural aspects.[1363] It does not set the standards to be complied with, rather it provides for a procedure to check whether vessels comply with standards adopted by the IMO. It is therefore not conceivable to include interpretation guidance in the Paris MoU on how to interpret the GAIRAS treaties in respect of MASS.

However, a MoU may include the verification of certificates issued based on non-binding codes adopted by the IMO. As an example, compliance with the non-binding Code of Safety for Special Purpose Ships[1364] is required by Annex 10.10 of the Paris MoU. Similarly, examination of a MASS-Certificate[1365] issued based on the non-binding MASS Code of the IMO could be included in the scope of the Paris MoU. MASS entering a foreign port would not face difficulties during port state controls.

1359 Reiling, *Reiling no date* (n 294) 228; Graziano, Mejia and Schröder-Hinrichs (n 305), 98; Doris König, 'The Enforcement of the International Law of the Sea by Coastal and Port States' (2002) 62(1) Zeitschrift für ausländisches öffentliches Recht und Völkerrecht 1, 8

1360 Molenaar, 'Molenaar 2007' (n 278) 227; Özçayir (n 288) 210

1361 Benedict Kingsbury, 'The Concept of Law in Global Administrative Law Changing Paradigms in International Law: A Symposium' (2009) 20 European Journal of International Law 23, 25

1362 See on the advantages of MoU: Aust, 'Aust 2012' (n 912) 59–62

1363 Ilg (n 230) 139

1364 MSC, IMO, 'Res. MSC.266(84): Code of Safety for Special Purpose Ships' (London 13 May 2008)

1365 MSC, IMO, 'MSC 108/4/1: Report of the Intersessional MASS Working Group (Secretariat)' (London 8 November 2023) Annex, p. 15

However, it is important to note that a port state control MoU only addresses port states. In order to have a comprehensive regulatory solution, flag and coastal states must also be considered and addressed. One possible solution is to include the IMO MASS Code in the Paris MoU, which could create a basis of trust that member states will apply the same MASS-including interpretation as port, flag, and coastal state. This would prevent accusations of inconsistent behavior. However, this route does not allow for the inclusion of any substantive legal provisions for MASS. It would only ensure that coastal states allow innocent passage through their territorial waters by MASS. Therefore, an amendment to the MoU should be pursued to accompany an IMO MASS Code.

Pursuant to Section 8 of the Paris MoU, the MoU can be amended based on a proposal submitted by a participating authority. Depending on whether the Articles of the MoU or the Annex shall be amended, a two-thirds majority in the Committee is required. An amendment is deemed to have been accepted after a certain time period unless an objection is declared with that time period. Without going into detail about the amendment procedure, the similarities to the tacit acceptance procedure included in SOLAS are apparent. Consequently, the same concerns about the suitability of this procedure apply. In addition, the legitimacy gap is exacerbated in the case of the Paris MoU, as only the maritime authorities, rather than the states themselves, are members of the MoU.

Apart from these democratic arguments, the concept of the Paris MoU is not suitable for making a non-binding IMO Code legally binding. The aim of the Paris MoU is to harmonize port state controls, thus harmonize the enforcement and implementation of international regulations as a reaction upon substandard ships. The Paris MoU is not located on the law-making and adoption side, but rather concerned with enforcement.

This becomes apparent in Section 2 of the MoU, which outlines the relevant instruments. Section 2.2 mandates that each party shall apply those relevant instruments to which it is a party. Therefore, the application of the Paris MoU depends on joining a corresponding instrument. An instrument cannot be made mandatory by including it in the Paris MoU. This would turn the system on its head. Once the IMO MASS Code is made mandatory by another procedure, it is recommended that it is included in the Paris MoU to ensure trouble-free port state controls.

Eventually, the Paris MoU is accompanied by the EU Directive on Port State Control[1366] making compliance with the Paris MoU an EU law obligation.

1366 Directive 2009/16/EC of the European Parliament and of the Council on port State control [2009] Official Journal of the European Union 52 L 131/57

Consequently, before amending the Paris MoU, an agreement on EU level has to be achieved.[1367] EU law to regulate MASS will be considered below.

To conclude on the Paris MoU as a forum of regional cooperation, it is not a suitable forum for adopting regulations on MASS. As the Paris MoU is concerned with the enforcement of prior adopted regulations, MASS regulations would need to be adopted in another way. Subsequently, including a MASS Code in the scope of the port state control examination is advisable to ensure smooth controls and ensure legal certainty for MASS operators.

As next, the Nordic Cooperation among Denmark, Finland, Iceland, Norway, Sweden, the Faroe Islands, Greenland, and Åland shall be considered as it could provide valuable prospects for MASS regulation.

5.4.2.2 Nordic Cooperation

The Nordic Cooperation is founded on a long lasting, common history of the Nordic states.[1368] Already in 1397, the Kalmar Union joined the three kingdoms Denmark, Sweden, and Norway and provided the region with a state constitution.[1369] Over the centuries, the borders between the Nordic kingdoms shifted, and Finland even belonged to the Russian Empire for a time. It was not until the beginning of the 20th century that the current borders were consolidated[1370] and all five Nordic states became independent.[1371] The Faroe Islands, Greenland, and Åland are not independent, but are autonomous regions within the Kingdom of Denmark and Finland respectively. Although Denmark and Sweden held dominion over Norway, Finland, and the other regions for much of history, both kingdoms were aware of each other's military power and refrained from making a bid for power over the entire region.[1372] Norway, Finland, and Iceland achieved their independence without resorting to war or armed conflict, but rather through peaceful negotiations.[1373] Thus,

1367 Erik J Molenaar, 'Options for Regional Regulation of Merchant Shipping Outside IMO, with Particular Reference to the Arctic Region' (2014) 45(3) Ocean Development & International Law 272, 285

1368 See for a summary of Nordic history: Ryszard M Czarny, 'The Shaping of Norden' (2014) 4(2(8)) Journal of Geography, Politics and Society 74

1369 Øyvind Østerud, 'Det nordiske paradokset – en ambivalent region i Europa' in Johan P Olsen and Bjørn O Sverdrup (eds), *Europa i Norden: Europeisering av sordisk samarbeid* (Tano Aschehoug 1998) 124

1370 ibid 125

1371 Norway separated form Sweden in 1905, Finland declared its independence in 1917, and Iceland has been independent from Denmark since 1944

1372 Østerud (n 1369) 127

1373 ibid

the last armed conflict between Nordic states occurred in the 18th century.[1374] Today, the Nordic states have roughly the same size of population and gross domestic product.[1375]

Nordic Cooperation is not limited to a single institution. The Nordic Council and the Nordic Council of Ministers are one pillar of Nordic Cooperation. In addition, there are regular Nordic exchanges in almost every industry and profession. For legal cooperation, the Nordic Meeting of Lawyers plays a significant role for harmonization approaches. Most importantly, however, is day-to-day cooperation across all hierarchical levels of the public sector.[1376] Interviews with Nordic public officials suggest cooperation on regular administrative tasks is rooted in pragmatism, personal connections, and mutual trust. Therefore, it is common for Swedish officials to contact their Norwegian, Finnish, or Danish counterparts frequently regarding the interpretation of a specific legal term. Due to the small size of Nordic administrations, there is often a scarcity of experts on certain subjects within each individual state. This enhances cross-border cooperation, making it even more effective. Furthermore, regular meetings between Nordic civil servants working in the same domain foster personal contacts and the development of mutual trust.[1377] As all states benefit from Nordic Cooperation and the cooperation is based on mutual trust, most rules are not legally binding.

Nordic Cooperation is not limited to a certain policy field. After World War II, several areas were conquered by Nordic Cooperation. The Scandinavian Airline System was founded in 1946 by merging the Danish, Norwegian, and Swedish Airline Companies.[1378] In 1954, the states concluded an agreement on free labor mobility and, shortly after, the Nordic Passport Union was established to ensure free movement of people within the Nordic states.[1379] Several policy areas followed, such as defense sector in the 1960s resulting in the foundation of the Nordic Defense Cooperation. Recently, the project 'Future Fuels Nordic'

1374 Hans E Andersson, 'What Activates an Identity? The Case of Norden' (2010) 24(1) International Relations 46, 51

1375 Czarny (n 1368) 92

1376 Inge L Backer, 'Styrket nordisk lovsamarbeid, Muligheter og utfordringer' (Oslo 2018) 8; Iain Cameron, 'Nordic Cooperation' in Anne Peters (ed), *Max Planck Encyclopedia of Public International Law* (MPEPIL) (Oxford University Press) 24

1377 Backer (n 1376) 19

1378 Scandinavian Airline System, 'History Milestones' <https://www.sasgroup.net/about-sas/sas-history/history-milestones/> accessed 16 February 2024

1379 Bengt Sundelius and Claes Wiklund, *Femtio år av nordiskt samarbete* (Världspolitikens dagsfrågor 2002, 4, Utrikespolitiska Inst 2002) 4; Strang, 'Nordic Political and Economic Cooperation:' (n 1336) 6

was started to enhance cooperation in the establishment of green shipping corridors. This project and its impacts will be illustrated in more detail below.

To come back to the presumption that states act as rational actors, Nordic states enter into Nordic Cooperation if this results in an increased surplus. Some of the advantages shall be introduced as basis for the latter assessment of whether Nordic Cooperation could be an appropriate forum for regulating MASS.

Nordic Cooperation is about pooling of resources. The need for Nordic administrations to cooperate across borders due to their relatively small size has already been mentioned. Ever-increasing complexity and internationalization necessitate pooling resources not only for public administration purposes, but also for other specialized areas[1380] such as research on green transition in transport. As an illustration, the establishment of the Scandinavian Institute for Maritime Law at the University of Oslo dates back to 1963, subsequent to a corresponding decision by the Nordic Council of Ministers. Moreover, almost all stakeholder organizations amalgamated into Nordic umbrella associations.[1381]

The common history, similar languages, and the same religion and climate contributed to the emergence of a common Nordic mindset.[1382] Norwegian, Swedish, and Danish are North Germanic languages,[1383] which enables mutual reading and listening comprehension.[1384] About half of the Finns understand Swedish, and Danish is a mandatory school subject in Iceland. However, the competence to understand each other mutually decreases.[1385] Lutheran faith is predominant in all Nordic states[1386] and has contributed to a common cultural identity. Furthermore, the enduring proximity between the state and the church has led to a convergence of civil-legal and moral-religious norms. Although all Nordic countries have abolished their state churches, the close connection between Lutheran faith and the state has led to a high degree of law-abiding behavior and trust in the state.[1387]

1380 Backer (n 1376) 13; Pia Letto-Vanamo and Ditlev Tamm, 'Cooperation in the field of Law' in Johan Strang (ed), *Nordic cooperation, A European region in transition* (Routledge series on global order studies vol 8. Routledge 2016) 93

1381 Strang, 'Nordic Political and Economic Cooperation:' (n 1336) 11

1382 Ingvard Havnen, 'Norden – nye muligheter: Forslag til økt mobilitet og integrasjon mellom de nordiske landene' (København 2018) 9

1383 Pål K Eriksen and Camilla Wide, 'Introduction: The Nordic languages and typology' (2011) 34(2) Nordic Journal of Linguistics 75, 75

1384 Østerud (n 1369) 124

1385 Havnen (n 1382) 9; Backer (n 1376) 25

1386 Ole Lando, 'Nordic Countries, a Legal Family? A Diagnosis and a Prognosis' (2001) 1(2) Global Jurist Advances 1, 6

1387 Strang, 'Nordic Political and Economic Cooperation:' (n 1336) 3; Østerud (n 1369) 129

Especially the aspect that Nordic people identify with their region is important in the Nordic context.[1388] The other Nordic states are often referred to as "homezone"[1389] The Nordic mindset is sometimes associated with the image of a veranda around a house. The other Nordic countries are not the house itself, but neither are they the garden. Many families have Nordic rather than national biographies.[1390] The fact that a Nordic perspective is firmly rooted in the minds of the population has also meant that Nordic Cooperation has been a constant since the 1950s, despite changing governments and political orientations.[1391]

The common mindset and shared fundamental political attitudes including the relevance of human rights,[1392] international diplomatic cooperation, and a high level of social security contributed to a similar economic and social situation in all Nordic states.[1393] This again brings about that national opinions on a political issue rarely differ significantly from a common Nordic view.[1394]

As most inter-state cooperation fora, the Nordic Cooperation is based on the consensus principle respecting the national sovereignty.[1395] Nevertheless, the Nordic Cooperation does not face significant hindrances posed by the consensus requirement due to few substantial differences in national perspectives, a common mindset, and shared political values. In addition, the participation of all five countries is not a prerequisite for the Nordic Cooperation. This ensures that solitary members do not hinder joint progress.[1396] Furthermore, the consensus principle is also common practice in many Nordic political systems and is therefore well known by politicians, public officials, and the society.[1397]

Nordic Cooperation is considered here as forum for regulating MASS. As legal norms are necessary, Nordic legal cooperation is of special interest for this study and shall be now introduced.

1388 Havnen (n 1382) 9

1389 Sundelius and Wiklund (n 1379) 14; Lando (n 1386), 6

1390 Nordisk ministerråd, 'Nordisk pendlingskarta-Huvudrapport' (København 2005) 15; Ulf Andreasson and Truls Stende, 'Status för mobiliteten i Norden' (København 2018) 15

1391 Sundelius and Wiklund (n 1379) 11–12

1392 Czarny (n 1368) 92

1393 Sundelius and Wiklund (n 1379) 23

1394 ibid 22

1395 Strang, 'Nordic Political and Economic Cooperation:' (n 1336) 7; Sundelius and Wiklund (n 1379) 14

1396 Backer (n 1376) 23

1397 Sundelius and Wiklund (n 1379) 13–14; Arend Lijphart, *Patterns of Democracy* (2nd edn, Yale University Press 2012) 244

Due to the long-lasting and intertwined history between the Nordic countries, the legal history is shared among them.[1398] Nordic Law is distinct from other law families and traditions and could be considered as a concept.[1399] Nordic Law is characterized by a departure from the codification idea prevalent in central Europe in the 19th century[1400] and pragmatism.[1401] Intense legal cooperation has further diminished differences between the Nordic legal systems,[1402] promoting unity. In modern times, legal cooperation leads back until 1872 when the first Nordic lawyers meeting (*'nordiske juristmøter'*) was held.[1403] This informal and voluntary cooperation[1404] was the starting point for a profound and ongoing legal cooperation among the Nordics. Besides common law-making, preparation of legislative activities,[1405] implementation of international regulations,[1406] and legal research are conducted jointly. As a result, several Nordic journals for legal research were established.[1407] Frequently, Nordic courts refer to other Nordic states' judgments and preparatory materials for their legal reasoning.[1408] To enhance Nordic legal thinking, a collection of judgments of the Nordic supreme courts (*'Nordisk Domssamling'*) is published since 1958. Nordic legal cooperation has been particularly fruitful for the maritime sector.

1398 Letto-Vanamo and Tamm (n 1380) 95; Lando (n 1386) 6

1399 Jaakko Husa, Kimmo Nuotio and Heikki Pihlajamäki, 'Nordic Law – Between Tradition and Dynamism' in Jaakko Husa, Kimmo Nuotio and Heikki Pihlajamäki (eds), *Nordic Law – Between Tradition and Dynamism* (Ius commune europaeum vol 66. Intersentia 2007) 3

1400 Johan Schelin, 'Sjölagen: En åldrande nordisk dinosaurie?' [2007] Jurdisk Tidskrift 140, 142; Letto-Vanamo and Tamm (n 1380) 98

1401 Letto-Vanamo and Tamm (n 1380) 98

1402 Husa, Nuotio and Pihlajamäki (n 1399) 10

1403 Stanley V Anderson, *The Nordic Council: A Study of Scandinavian Regionalism* (Svenska Bokförlaget/Norstedts 1967) 23; Pauli Kettunen and others, 'The nordic model and the rise and fall of Nordic Cooperation' in Johan Strang (ed), *Nordic cooperation, A European region in transition* (Routledge series on global order studies vol 8. Routledge 2016) 71; Sjur Brækhus, 'De Norske Sjølover: Et tilbakeblikk ved 100 års jubiléet' (1993) 200 MarIus 1, 1

1404 Letto-Vanamo and Tamm (n 1380) 93

1405 Backer (n 1376) 44

1406 ibid 39; Schelin, 'Schelin 2007' (n 1400) 146

1407 See for example: Nordisk Miljörättslig Tidskrift, Retfærd. Nordisk juridisk tidsskrift, Nordic Journal of Innovation in the Public Sector, Nordic Journal of Human Rights, Nordisk administrativt tidsskrift

1408 Pia Letto-Vanamo, 'Courts and Proceedings: Some Nordic Characteristic' in Laura Ervo, Pia Letto-Vanamo and Anna Nylund (eds), *Rethinking Nordic Courts* (Ius Gentium: Comparative Perspectives on Law and Justice vol 90. Springer 2021) 26

One of the first joint projects was the development of a maritime code (*'Sjøloven'*) in the 1880s.[1409] Developed by national commissions of lawyers, judges and civil servants,[1410] the Nordic Maritime Code was not adopted as an international treaty but as national legislation in each state.[1411] Although the code was amended several times[1412] and thoroughly updated in 1994,[1413] the core parts never lost their Nordic character as amendments were developed jointly.[1414] Even if the maritime code was a Nordic success,[1415] cooperative law-making on maritime issues has declined significantly in recent years due to diverging interests.[1416]

It is not only in the area of shipping that legal cooperation has declined. Denmark's, accession to the European Community in 1973 resulted in the growing significance of EU law and European policy initiatives in the Nordic Cooperation agenda.[1417] Since both Sweden and Finland joined the EU in 1995 and 2004, respectively, Nordic Cooperation is ultimately permeated by EU law.[1418] As the EU member states have to respect EU competencies, the scope for Nordic legal cooperation shrunk.[1419] However, Nordic Cooperation provides a forum situated between national shortsightedness and European languor.[1420]

As the European and international policy considerations increasingly dominate the legislative agenda, the Nordic Cooperation has shifted its focus more towards implementation. The Nordics now cooperate for the implementation of EU legal instruments, particularly EU directives.[1421] Furthermore, the implementation of international regulations is coordinated between the Nordic states.[1422] This form of cooperation could be particularly interesting for MASS.

One forum for Nordic legal cooperation is the Nordic Council and the Nordic Council of Ministers. Both institutions will be briefly introduced before their potential for MASS regulation is assessed.

1409 Brækhus (n 1403) 2
1410 ibid 3
1411 ibid 2; Thor Falkanger and Hans J Bull, *Sjørett* (Sjørettsfondet Akademisk 2016) 4
1412 Brækhus (n 1403), 7
1413 Falkanger and Bull (n 1411) 4
1414 Brækhus (n 1403), 3; Schelin, 'Schelin 2007' (n 1400) 140
1415 Schelin, 'Schelin 2007' (n 1400) 145
1416 ibid 146
1417 Backer (n 1376) 18
1418 ibid; Strang, 'Nordic Political and Economic Cooperation:' (n 1336) 13; Schelin, 'Schelin 2007' (n 1400) 145
1419 Backer (n 1376) 37; Strang, 'Nordic Political and Economic Cooperation:' (n 1336) 13
1420 Sundelius and Wiklund (n 1379) 23
1421 Backer (n 1376) 39
1422 ibid 11; Schelin, 'Schelin 2007' (n 1400) 146

5.4.2.2.1 *The Nordic Council and the Nordic Council of Ministers*

The Nordic Council is the official body for inter-parliamentary cooperation among the Nordic states. It has 87 representatives and meets twice a year. Government representatives are invited to the sessions and can submit proposals, but have no right to vote. Additionally, parliamentary representatives can pose questions to governmental representatives, also from other states. Before the foundation of the Nordic Council of Ministers in 1971, the participation of governmental representatives ensured the adoption of the most feasible recommendations and allowed parliament members from different states to pose queries to a minister from another state.[1423] The Nordic Council is empowered to adopt non-binding recommendations directed towards national governments and to issue statements. While it has an advisory role,[1424] its significance in legal collaboration should not be underestimated.[1425]

The origins of Nordic parliamentary cooperation can be traced back until 1889, when the Nordic Inter-Parliamentarian Union was founded.[1426] In 1951, the Dane Hans Hedtoft proposed the creation of a Nordic Council.[1427] The first meeting of the Nordic Council was held in 1953; Finland became a member in 1955.[1428] Even the foundation of the Nordic Council was typically Nordic pragmatic. The Nordic Council statute was nationally adopted, rather than concluded as an international treaty.[1429] Therefore, the statute of the Nordic Council is not internationally binding[1430] and does not create a supranational institution.[1431] This makes it difficult to grasp the Nordic Council with conventional international law categories.[1432]

In the early decades, domestic party speakers and leaders often attended the meetings, leading to dramatic political controversies.[1433] In the first 10 years, more than 90% of the proposals were submitted by parliament

1423 Strang, 'Nordic Political and Economic Cooperation:' (n 1336) 9
1424 Anderson (n 1403) 26/28
1425 Backer (n 1376) 10
1426 Anderson (n 1403) 16
1427 ibid 23
1428 ibid 24
1429 Strang, 'Nordic Political and Economic Cooperation:' (n 1336) 12
1430 Gustaf Petren, 'The Nordic Council A Unique Factor in International Law' (1959) 29 Nordisk Tidskrift for International Ret 346, 347
1431 Backer (n 1376) 10
1432 Petren (n 1430), 352; Johan Strang, 'Introduction: The Nordic model as transnational cooperation?' in Johan Strang (ed), *Nordic cooperation, A European region in transition* (Routledge series on global order studies vol 8. Routledge 2016) 6
1433 Anderson (n 1403) 30–31

representatives resulting in true Nordic parliamentarian work.[1434] In 1962, the Helsinki Treaty[1435] was adopted to consolidate Nordic Cooperation. Together with the establishment of the Nordic Council of Ministers in 1971, these two events marked a turning point in Nordic parliamentary cooperation.[1436]

Similar to the Council of the European Union, the Nordic Council of Ministers meets in different configurations, depending on the subject matter. Currently, there are eleven standing configurations.[1437] In contrast to the recommendations adopted by the Nordic Council, decisions made by the Nordic Council of Ministers are binding.[1438] Per Article 64 of the Helsinki Treaty, the Nordic Council of Ministers shall report annually to the Nordic Council on the subject of Nordic cooperation and plans for future cooperation. The rise in direct governmental cooperation has resulted in decreased significance of the Nordic Council.[1439] Moreover, national administrations are confronted with an increased workload due to European and international initiatives. This necessitates prioritization, in which the Nordic Cooperation sometimes comes out on the short end.[1440]

To conclude, the Nordic Council and the later established Nordic Council of Ministers provide one official forum for Nordic legal cooperation. Although the influence of EU law has grown and international inter-governmental cooperation has become more significant, the Nordic Council persists in its activities. Extensive international and European cooperation present capacity challenges for the small administrations of Nordic countries and necessitates prioritization. Recently, however, Nordic maritime cooperation has taken off, with the joint promotion of zero-emission shipping corridors[1441] and the

---

1434 ibid 61

1435 The Helsinki Treaty; Treaty of Co-operation between Denmark, Finland, Iceland, Norway and Sweden 23 March 1962

1436 Backer (n 1376) 18

1437 Strang, 'Nordic Political and Economic Cooperation:' (n 1336) 8

1438 Article 63 Helsinki treaty

1439 Strang, 'Nordic Political and Economic Cooperation:' (n 1336) 9; Cameron, 'Cameron' (n 1376) 24

1440 Backer (n 1376) 8

1441 Nordic transport ministers from Finland, Iceland, Sweden and Norway, 'Fredrikstad Declaration' (Fredrikstad 8 November 2022); Nordic Ministers for the Environment and Climate, 'Ministerial Declaration on zero emission shipping routes between the Nordic countries' (3 May 2022) <https://www.norden.org/en/declaration/ministerial-declaration-zero-emission-shipping-routes-between-nordic-countries> accessed 16 February 2024

digitalization of the transport sector.[1442] As MASS are located at the linkage between zero-emission shipping, increased digitalization, and autonomy, it is worth considering the potential of Nordic Cooperation for the purposes of MASS regulation.

5.4.2.2.2 *Nordic Cooperation on Green Shipping*

At the outset of Nordic legal cooperation, shipping could once again serve as the unifying element. In 2022, the project 'Future Fuels Nordic' was initiated as a four-year Nordic collaboration inspired by the Norwegian Green Shipping Program.[1443] The aim of this project is to promote the implementation of zero-emission shipping in the Nordic region.[1444] Although the project is not directly oriented towards autonomous shipping, close links are apparent and the project could function as a foundation for cooperation in the field of MASS.

The Norwegian Green Shipping Program has already established the link between zero-emission shipping and autonomous vessels:[1445] one way to reduce or eliminate emissions is to increase the efficiency of fuel consumption. Autonomy can be used for this purpose and ensure operations that are as efficient as possible. Another way to encourage the use of zero-emission fuels is to reduce operating costs to compensate for the still higher prices of future fuels. As illustrated above, MASS reduce the operational costs for a conventional cargo vessel and provide a financial margin for investments in future fuel technology.

Nordic Cooperation in the field of MASS and zero-emission shipping has already started. In June 2023, the world's first autonomous passenger ferry was baptized in Stockholm, Sweden. Operated by the Norwegian ferry company Torghatten and equipped by the Norwegian technology provider Zeabuz, the *MF Estelle* navigates collision-free and autonomously in the city center of the Swedish capital. Given that there are already Nordic projects on MASS focusing on technical challenges and business case development, the Nordic enthusiasm for green shipping provides fertile ground for regulatory cooperation on MASS. Legal cooperation on MASS would integrate seamlessly into the

1442 Nordiska ministerrådet, 'Ett säkrare, grönare, friare Norden: Program för Sveriges ordförandeskap i Nordiska ministerrådet 2024' (Kopenhagen 31.13.2023) 9

1443 Eirill Bachmann Mehammer, 'Nordic roadmap for introduction of sustainable zero-carbon fuels in shipping' (Nordic Roadmap – Helsinki Conference, Helsinki, Finland, 3 May 2023)

1444 ibid

1445 Grønt Skipfartsprogram, 'Smarte fjordkrysninger' (05/2022) <https://grontskipsfartsprogram.no/wp-content/uploads/2022/05/Smarte-fjordkrysninger.pdf> accessed 17 November 2023

long-lasting cooperation on maritime issues. It would also reflect the current joint ambition to promote zero-emission shipping in the Nordic region.

Before assessing the appropriateness of Nordic cooperation for MASS, potential legal instruments for Nordic MASS cooperation are presented and placed in the context of international law. First, non-binding solutions are considered. Second, a binding intergovernmental agreement will be discussed.

5.4.2.2.3 *Nordic Cooperation on MASS*

Nordic legal cooperation is based on several pillars, as illustrated. In addition to cooperation within the Nordic Council and the Nordic Council of Ministers, non-institutionalized meetings of ministers and members of parliament, as well as administrative cooperation, are relevant for Nordic legal cooperation. All fora and available instruments shall be examined in the light of MASS now.

When considering non-binding solutions within the Nordic Cooperation for MASS, a recommendation adopted by the Nordic Council comes to mind first. Per Article 45 of the Helsinki Treaty, the Nordic Council can adopt recommendations directed towards one or more governments of the Nordic states. Two approaches to designing a recommendation are conceivable. On the one hand, a comprehensive regulatory framework for MASS, including interpretative guidance and new substantial provisions, could be developed. On the other hand, the recommendation could reference the IMO MASS Code and recommend national governments to make it mandatory at the national level. Furthermore, the inclusion of clauses regarding mutual recognition and provisions that are more detailed on central issues such as certification and risk assessment may be considered in the recommendation. Given the limited personal and timely resources of the Nordic Council, developing a self-standing framework for MASS seems an illusionary option. However, the second option may be more promising.

Following a recommendation by the Nordic Council, the governments shall report about the measures taken in respect of the recommendation to the next Nordic Council meeting.[1446] The Nordic Council shall thus be enabled to overlook the national implementation of recommendations. Added political and moral obligation could encourage governments to make the MASS Code nationally binding.

Advantageous about this solution would be that a prompt regulation could be ensured as the Nordic Council holds annual sessions. Additionally, finding

1446 See Article 65 of the Helsinki Treaty

a consensus on critical issues such as cybersecurity and risk assessment methodologies is facilitated due to alike values and expectations. Nordic Cooperation is based on usefulness (*'nordisk nytta'*).[1447] Given the high agglomeration of research projects on MASS in the Nordic region, and thus the increased need for a regulatory framework allowing interregional operations, the usefulness of a harmonized framework for MASS is self-evident. Recommendations adopted by the Nordic Council are not binding upon national governments; however, the actual impact of these instruments and the role the Nordic Council takes in coordinated law-making should not be underestimated.[1448]

Alternatively, legal cooperation could take place outside of the Nordic Council. On an administrative level, maritime authorities could meet and agree on a certain, MASS-including interpretation of international treaties. This could result in a harmonized administrative practice in respect of the registration of MASS and mutual recognition of foreign MASS. Although national authorities usually consult each other if uncertainties about the implementation of international treaties arise, it is questionable whether national authorities would formalize this form of cooperation. Discussions with representatives of the maritime authorities revealed a reluctance to formalize cooperation for MASS. Nevertheless, it turned out that informal cooperation on a case-by-case basis does take place. In addition, national constitutional considerations may restrict the authority of administrations to determine whether the current legal framework can be interpreted to cover MASS or whether a textual change is required.

In conclusion, administrative cooperation is beneficial for applying the international framework to individual cases. However, issues of general concern should be evaluated at a different level.

Non-institutionalized parliamentary cooperation was already undertaken for the development of the Maritime Code in the 1870s. Similarly, a working group could be established among national parliaments to discuss a joint MASS Act. The act could then be adopted according to each national legislative procedure and joint development and consultation before amendments would ensure uniformity. Clauses ensuring mutual acceptance of certificates issued in one state should be included to ensure smooth interregional operation. As with a recommendation adopted by the Nordic Council, developing a self-standing legal framework for MASS is unrealistic due to time and resource limitation. However, jointly implementing a non-binding MASS Code adopted by the IMO could be beneficial. In contrast to a recommendation adopted by

1447 Letto-Vanamo and Tamm (n 1380) 103

1448 Backer (n 1376) 10

the Nordic Council, an inter-parliamentary working group would not direct its results to the national governments but rather directly to the national parliaments. Governmental involvement could still be ensured at the national level. However, developing a MASS Act without deriving benefits from the expertise located at the specialized ministries could be particularly demanding.

Considering binding solutions, the Nordic Council of Ministers could adopt a decision which is binding on the member states per Article 63 of the Helsinki treaty. Again, a decision aiming at the national implementation of an IMO MASS Code is more promising than developing a self-standing regulatory framework. Although there are regular meetings of the Nordic transport ministers, Sweden opposed the establishment of a Council of Transport Ministers in November 2023.[1449] Nevertheless, the Nordic Council of Ministers could link to the Nordic Cooperation on zero-emission shipping within the Nordic region and adopt a resolution making the non-binding IMO MASS Code binding for the Nordics.

Alternatively, the Nordic states could decide to enter into a formally binding international treaty on MASS. A regional MASS Convention could include the same provisions as the above-discussed international MASS Convention adding new substantial provisions to SOLAS and interpretative guidance to SOLAS, COLREG, and UNCLOS. Considering the time and resource constraints of the Nordic states, the MASS Convention could be based on the IMO MASS Code. It could add more detailed provisions and legal value to the IMO MASS Code. From an international law standpoint, such an agreement would constitute a treaty, necessitating the formal procedure of adoption by a diplomatic conference, ratification, and entry into force.

As all Nordic states are state parties to SOLAS, COLREG, and UNCLOS,[1450] a modification agreement could be adopted among them. If a group of state parties to the main treaty decides to alter the treaty exclusively amongst themselves, these parties modify the main treaty. Like an amendment, a modification changes the main treaty, but is restricted to some of the parties to the main treaty ab initio.[1451] Although a formal amendment does not necessarily require

1449 Claes Håkansson and André H Jamholt, 'Kun Sverige er imod et nyt ministerråd for transport' (2 November 2023) <https://www.norden.org/no/node/83860> accessed 16 February 2024

1450 IMO, 'Ratification by State' (London 22 April 2022) <https://view.officeapps.live.com/op/view.aspx?src=https%3A%2F%2Fwwwcdn.imo.org%2Flocalresources%2Fen%2FAbout%2FConventions%2FStatusOfConventions%2Fx-Status.xlsx&wdOrigin=BROWSELINK> accessed 21 June 2022

1451 Kerstin von der Decken, 'Article 41, Agreements to modify multilateral treaties between certain of the parties only' in Oliver Dörr and Kirsten Schmalenbach (eds), *Vienna*

the acceptance of all state parties to the main treaty in order to enter into force,[1452] a modification differs in the fact that it is limited to a certain group of states. Therefore, modifications are also referred to as inter-se agreements.

As stated above, an agreement determining one specific interpretation is to be considered an amendment to the main treaty. Thus, a MASS Convention concluded as an inter-se agreement would constitute a modification and thus has to be challenged against the requirements for a modification provided for by international law. Before ultimately assessing the most appropriate regional approach to MASS, the admissibility of an inter-se agreement on MASS has to be determined.

5.4.3 *Admissibility of an Inter-se Agreement*

Article 41 of the VCLT sets out the requirements for modifications, unless the main treaty provides for specific provisions. It stipulates that

> 1. Two or more of the parties to a multilateral treaty may conclude an agreement to modify the treaty as between themselves alone if:
>
> (a) the possibility of such a modification is provided for by the treaty; or
>
> (b) the modification in question is not prohibited by the treaty and:
>
> (i) does not affect the enjoyment by the other parties of their rights under the treaty or the performance of their obligations;
>
> (ii) does not relate to a provision, derogation from which is incompatible with the effective execution of the object and purpose of the treaty as a whole.

Convention on the Law of Treaties: A Commentary (2. 2nd ed. 2018. Springer Berlin Heidelberg 2018) 778; International Law Commission (ILC), 'A/CN.4/191 – Report of the of the International Law Commission on the work of its Eighteenth Session, 4 May–19 July 1966' [1966] Yearbook of the International Law Commission 169, 233; ILC, 'International Law Commission 1966' (n 433) 233; Mark E Villiger, *Commentary on the 1969 Vienna Convention on the Law of Treaties* (Martinus Nijhoff Publishers 2009) Art. 41, 5

1452 Article VII (b)(VI)(2) of SOLAS requires acceptance by two thirds of the contracting governments for an amendment to enter into force; per Article 316 (1) of the UNCLOS an amendment enters into force upon ratification by either two thirds of the state parties or 60 state parties, whichever is greater

> 2. Unless in a case falling under paragraph 1 (a) the treaty otherwise provides, the parties in question shall notify the other parties of their intention to conclude the agreement and of the modification to the treaty for which it provides.

However, it must be noted that the VCLT entered into force after SOLAS, COLREG and UNCLOS have been adopted. As a result, Article 41 of the VCLT only applies to modifications of these conventions to the extent that Article 41 of the VCLT reflects customary international law.[1453] Although the detailed requirements stipulated by Article 41(1)(b) of the VCLT were novel when adopted, they were not questioned since then. Some conclude that this has led to the emergence of corresponding customary international law.[1454] Others, however, consider that Article 41 of the VCLT does not (yet) reflect customary international law.[1455]

Anyhow, it is considered customary international law that state parties can alter a multilateral treaty between themselves exclusively, unless the treaty provides otherwise.[1456] If the modification is incompatible with the object and purpose of the main treaty, it can be considered that the main treaty implicitly prohibits such modification.[1457] In addition, based on the customary international law principle of 'pacta tertiis nec nocent nec prosunt',[1458] which is reflected in Article 34 of the VCLT,[1459] and the general principle of international law 'pacta sunt servanda',[1460] a modification may not limit the rights of third parties granted by the main treaty.

Comparing the Article 41 of the VCLT requirements with those stipulated by customary international law, there is no significant difference. Only the

1453 See Article 4 of VCTL stipulating that "[…] the Convention applies only to treaties which are concluded by States after the entry into force of the present Convention with regard to such States".

1454 Villiger (n 1451) Art. 41, 18; Anne Rigaux and Denys Simon, 'Article 41 – Agreements to modify multilateral treaties between certain of the parties only' in Olivier Corten and Pierre Klein (eds), *The Vienna Conventions on the Law of Treaties* (Oxford commentaries on international law vol 2. Oxford University Press 2011) 994

1455 Decken, 'Decken 2018' (n 1451) 780

1456 ibid 781

1457 ILC, 'International Law Commission 1966' (n 433) 235

1458 Budislav Vukas, 'Treaties, Third-Party Effect' in Anne Peters (ed), *Max Planck Encyclopedia of Public International Law* (MPEPIL) (Oxford University Press) 22

1459 Villiger (n 1451) Art. 34, 1

1460 Anthony Aust, 'Pacta sunt servanda' in Anne Peters (ed), *Max Planck Encyclopedia of Public International Law* (MPEPIL) (Oxford University Press) 1

notification requirement included in Article 41(2) of the VCLT can be seen as a conventional addition. Thus, modifications to SOLAS, COLREG, and UNCLOS will be judged by the customary international law requirements for modifications and referring to the literature on Article 41 of the VCLT.

Turning now to a MASS Convention, it is appropriate to begin with Article 311(3) of the UNCLOS, which sets out specific requirements for inter-se agreements in the scope of UNCLOS. Secondly, Article VII of SOLAS, which provides for the general admissibility of inter-se agreements in the scope of SOLAS, will be examined. Remarkably, Article VII of SOLAS does not lay down detailed substantive requirements for inter-se agreements. As it can be assumed that not all inter-se agreements are permissible, customary legal requirements must be applied in addition. In the absence of particular requirements in COLREG, modifications to COLREG are to be measured directly against customary international law. This shall be considered as third. Article 311(3) of the UNCLOS stipulates that

> [t]wo or more States Parties may conclude agreements modifying or suspending the operation of provisions of this Convention, applicable solely to the relations between them, provided that such agreements do not relate to a provision derogation from which is incompatible with the effective execution of the object and purpose of this Convention, and provided further that such agreements shall not affect the application of the basic principles embodied herein, and that the provisions of such agreements do not affect the enjoyment by other States Parties of their rights or the performance of their obligations under this Convention.

Article 311(3) of the UNCLOS was brought close to Article 41 of the VCLT during the negotiations. Thus, reference can be made to the comments on Article 41 of the VCLT.[1461] Solely the requirement, that an inter-se agreement may not affect the application of the basic principles of UNCLOS was added.[1462] As a first point, the MASS Convention must not impede the achievement of the object and purpose of UNCLOS. To illustrate the purpose of this requirement, the ILC argued that a modification of a substantive provision of a disarmament treaty would torpedo the achievement of the purpose of the main treaty[1463] and thus be not permissible. According to the preamble of UNCLOS, the object and purpose of UNCLOS is to settle all questions relating to the law of the sea

1461 Nordquist, Rosenne and Sohn (n 1215) 311.7
1462 Freestone and Elferink (n 1216) 181
1463 ILC, 'International Law Commission 1966' (n 433) 235

and to establish a legal order for the seas and oceans. In respect of shipping, the peaceful use of the seas and oceans shall be ensured. Neither the presence of humans on board nor the purely human operation of vessels are within the scope of UNCLOS' objective and purpose. The MASS Convention would rather enable the seamless integration of MASS, an innovative shipping form, into UNCLOS, thereby endorsing UNCLOS' all-inclusive approach. Hence, the execution of UNCLOS' objective and purpose will not be hindered by the MASS Convention.

Secondly, it must be established whether the MASS Convention contravenes UNCLOS' basic principles. Unfortunately, there is no enumerative list of basic principles. Article 311(6) of the UNCLOS provides a hint as it prevents inter-se agreements derogating from the common principle relating to the common heritage of mankind.[1464] The prevention of pollution and the preservation of the marine environment are deemed equally important considering the comprehensive regulatory regime provided by UNCLOS on these matters.[1465] In relation to shipping, the freedom of navigation on the high seas or the right of innocent passage could potentially be considered as basic principles of UNCLOS.[1466] However, as stipulated above, the MASS Convention would only include an interpretative clarification of terms like 'master', 'crew', or 'in charge of'. Such provisions would not touch upon the freedom of navigation on the high seas and the right of innocent passage. The MASS Convention would enable the operation of MASS and conventional shipping would still be possible. Thus, regardless of whether these institutions are indeed basic principles of UNCLOS, they are not affected by the MASS Convention.

Thirdly, the MASS Convention may not hinder the enjoyment of rights or the fulfilment of obligations under UNCLOS by other contracting states. For reasons of clarity, first, the perspective of the flag state will be considered. Second, the perspective of coastal and port states, respectively, is assessed.

Per Article 91(1) of the UNCLOS, a flag state may determine the conditions for grating its nationality to ships and has to exercise its jurisdiction over the ships flying its flag effectively. As no state would be obligated to ratify the MASS Convention, flag states would maintain their rights without hindrance. The same is true for the flag states' entitlement to innocent passage and transit through international navigation straits. Despite the operation of MASS, flag states could continue to rely on the freedom of navigation and passage rights. It is worth noting that these rights do not provide protection against encounters

1464 See Article 136 of the UNCLOS

1465 Matz-Lück, 'Matz-Lück 2017' (n 344) 14

1466 ibid

with MASS. Nevertheless, Article 24(2) of the UNCLOS may require a coastal state to give due publicity to MASS operating in its territorial sea. To summarize, flag states would not be limited in the exercise of the rights and duties.

Next, the coastal state's perspective shall be considered. Central to international shipping, the coastal state shall refrain from applying national laws, which have the practical effect of denying the right of innocent passage and shall not discriminate against foreign ships based on their nationality or their port of destination or departure.[1467] Nevertheless, coastal states can adopt national laws relating to innocent passage, Article 21(1) of the UNCLOS. With respect to the construction, design, equipment, and manning, however, such laws shall not exceed the requirements set out in the GAIRAS treaties, Article 21(2) of the UNCLOS. As the interpretation set forth by the MASS Convention is applicable solely among the ratifying parties and may differ from a conventional interpretation of the GAIRAS treaties, a coastal state's law giving effect to the GAIRAS treaties could result in the practical denial of the right of innocent passage for MASS. This would conflict with Article 24(1)(a) of the UNCLOS preventing prohibitive national laws. An example shall illustrate this infliction.

A coastal state interpreted Regulation V/14 of SOLAS as requiring the presence of a master on board and has enacted a corresponding national law. Such a requirement would make innocent passage for MASS practically impossible. Although the breach of national law does not render the passage un-innocent, the coastal state could impose other enforcement measures than expelling the MASS. By adopting a national law giving effect to GAIRAS, the coastal state would have breached its obligation under Article 24(1)(a) of the UNCLOS. An archipelagic state would face the same dilemma.[1468] To avoid this dilemma, the MASS Convention could limit MASS operations to maritime zones under the jurisdiction of states that have ratified the MASS Convention. This would prevent coastal states from being caught between the right granted by Article 21(2) of the UNCLOS and the obligation imposed by Article 24(1)(a) of the UNCLOS. Section 1.2.3 of the IMO guidelines for MASS trials[1469] supports this view: it states that flag states shall obtain authorization by the coastal states where the trial shall be performed. Thus, MASS are considered exceptional in the sense that coastal states do not have to expect MASS to operate in their territorial waters. Although the IMO Guidelines do not serve as a legal basis to

1467 See Article 24(1) of UNCLOS

1468 Article 52(1) of UNCLOS renders Articles 21(2), 24(1) of UNCLOS applicable to innocent passage through archipelagic waters

1469 MSC, IMO, 'MSC.1/Circ.1604' (n 1046) 1

prevent innocent passage for MASS, they serve as an argument supporting the presented opinion.

The dynamics would shift once the MASS Convention attains the status of being 'generally accepted'. At that point, any coastal state would be limited to give effect to the MASS Convention. To become 'generally accepted', however, a large number of states representing a significant percentage of the world's merchant fleet would need to ratify the MASS Convention.[1470] While it is not possible to establish the exact number of required ratifications, the 2007 Nairobi International Convention on the Removal of Wrecks was not considered 'generally accepted' when it was ratified by 55 states representing 78.04% of the world's gross tonnage.[1471] It will be probably many years before the MASS Convention finds such broad support, particularly when adopted as a regional solution.

Another right granted to the coastal state by UNCLOS is the right to inspect foreign vessels and initiate proceedings against foreign vessels being suspected of having violated national laws on environmental protection adopted in accordance with UNCLOS, Articles 220(1), and 226 of the UNCLOS. This right could also be affected by the MASS Convention.

Depending on the place of violation, the current location of the vessel, and the severity of the consequences of the alleged violation the coastal state may initiate proceedings, request information about the ships' nationality and intended route, physically inspect the vessel, and examine the certificates a ships has to carry in accordance with the GAIRAS treaties.[1472] With respect to MASS, especially the physical inspection could present a challenge. Depending on the design, MASS cannot be boarded by humans in a conventional manner. Regardless of the design, no human would be on board to monitor the inspection. Furthermore, it is improbable that MASS will carry physical documents on board. Instead, these documents will be digitally available and could be examined electronically.

Although there are guidelines for the acceptance of electronic certificates,[1473] these guidelines are not legally binding and only address port state controls. It is therefore questionable whether coastal states would need to

1470 Section 3.3.2

1471 Parlov, 'Parlov 2022' (n 356) 669

1472 FAL, IMO, 'FAL.2/Circ.131' (n 431); MSC, IMO, 'MSC.1/Circ.1586' (n 431); MEPC, IMO, 'MEPC.1/Circ.873 – List of Certificates and Documents required to be Carried On Board Ships' (n 431); LEG, IMO, 'LEG.2/Circ.3' (n 431)

1473 FAL, IMO, 'FAL.5/Circ.39/Rev.2' (n 1049)

accept electronic certificates during examinations under Articles 220, 226 of the UNCLOS.

The purpose Articles 220, 226 is to balance the right of coastal states to enforce their laws and the interest of flag states to enjoy unhampered passage. Considering the pacta tertiis principle that shall prevent any negative impact of inter-se agreements on third parties and the fact that all conventional vessels can be physically inspected, the MASS Convention allowing MASS operations would negatively affect the right of coastal states to enforce their laws. Inspection of foreign vessels being suspected of having violated national laws would no longer be possible. Despite the design of MASS, physical inspection would be more complex and complicated than compared to conventional vessels. Even though it is unlikely that MASS will be suspected of marine pollution as MASS will transport neither chemicals or crude oil, nor will MASS be powered by conventional fossil fuels, it is necessary to exclude any negative third party impact of the MASS Convention. As an outlet, the MASS Convention should limit MASS operations to the high seas and the EEZ, territorial waters, and internal waters of contracting parties to the MASS Convention. To summarize the coastal state's perspective, an unlimited geographical application of the MASS Convention would adversely affect the rights of coastal states, which have not ratified the MASS Convention.

Eventually, the port state's perspective is considered. It has been highlighted that the zonal regime by UNCLOS does not include ports. Therefore, port states maintain exclusive jurisdiction over vessels that call at their ports. Consequently, port states can prevent MASS from entering their ports. They would not be adversely affected by a MASS Convention.

To conclude on Article 311(3) of the UNCLOS, the MASS Convention neither derogates from the object and purpose of the UNCLOS nor interferes with the achievement of the basic principles. Nevertheless, the MASS Convention could have a detrimental impact on the coastal state's right to give effect to the GAIRAS treaties vis-à-vis foreign vessels during innocent passage and on the coastal state's right to enforce national laws under Articles 220 and 226 of the UNCLOS. Therefore, it is recommended that the geographical scope is restricted to the high seas and other areas that are under the jurisdiction of the parties to the MASS Convention. The permissibility of the MASS Convention will now be assessed in accordance with SOLAS regulations.

Article VII of SOLAS stipulates that special rules can be drawn up by an agreement between all or some of the contracting governments. However, it does not add requirements that are more concrete. Thus, the permissibility of the MASS Convention must be examined in light of customary international law requirements for inter-se agreements.

As indicated by its title, the purpose of SOLAS is to ensure the safety of human life at sea. As illustrated, MASS can and will meet the safety requirements and is likely to increase the safety of life at sea. The MASS Convention will therefore not hamper the achievement of the purpose of SOLAS.

The object and purpose of SOLAS should not be confused with its basic principles and general provisions. As argued above, these would be affected by an amendment allowing MASS operations. Consequently, this study unsells the application of the tacit acceptance procedure for making the MASS Code binding. These amendments are too fundamental as to bind to all contracting parties without their explicit consent. However, the MASS Convention would not be binding on parties, which have not explicitly consented. Therefore, an inter-se agreement is admissible despite the fact that it affects basic principles.

Eventually, the MASS Convention should not have a negative impact on the exercise of rights and obligations under SOLAS. SOLAS only grants few specific rights as most of the provisions impose obligations on the contracting parties as flag states. However, Regulation I/17 of SOLAS grants the right that issued certificates are accepted by other contracting parties. This right is not affected by the MASS Convention, as the convention is not intended to inflict with the current process of inspections.

The question of whether the obligation to adhere SOLAS is owed erga omnes partes, that is, to all state parties collectively, is a matter of debate. Obligations owed erga omnes partes typically arise from multilateral treaties and serve to protect collective interests.[1474] In the case of SOLAS, the overarching collective interest is safety at sea. It must be acknowledged, however, that operating MASS complies with SOLAS and serves to achieve the object and purpose of SOLAS. Notwithstanding the characterization of an obligation under SOLAS as owed erga omnes partes, this qualification does not in any event imply the right of others to demand a particular manner of performance of the obligation. To conclude, the MASS Convention could legitimately modify SOLAS.

Eventually, the possibility to modify COLREG by the MASS Convention shall be considered in the light of the customary international law requirements. The purpose of COLREG stems from its title: preventing collisions at sea. The analysis above showed that navigation algorithms can be COLREG compliant from a legal point of view. Reflecting on the available technology, the risk of collision is most likely reduced by the introduction of MASS. It could even be argued that MASS reinforce the purpose of COLREG by reducing the number

1474 Erika de Wet, 'Invoking Obligations Erga Omnes in the Twenty-First Century: Progressive Developments since Barcelona Traction' (2013) 38 South African Yearbook of International Law 1, 3

of collisions. While flag states registering MASS must ensure that each MASS adheres to COLREG, the MASS Convention generally allowing the operation of MASS does not interfere with the purpose of COLREG.

Considering erga omnes partes obligations again, it could be argued that COLREG compliance is owed erga omnes partes. However, as argued similarly above, the specific form for ensuring compliance is not prescribed. Therefore, other states may not demand a traditional manner of complying with COLREG. Thus, third parties would not be negatively affected by additional provisions introduced by an inter-se agreement.

To conclude, the MASS Convention as an inter-se agreement would fulfill the requirements of Article 311(3) of the UNCLOS, Article VII SOLAS, and customary international law. Thus, the MASS Convention would be admissible. Per Articles 311(3) of the UNCLOS and VII SOLAS, the parties concerned must notify the other parties or the Secretary-General of their intention to enter into a modification agreement.

5.4.4 *A Regional MASS Convention*

Once the doctrinal admissibility of a regional inter-se agreement has been established, it will be discussed whether an inter-se agreement concluded by some states, e.g. the Nordic states, would meet the regulatory needs of MASS.

As adoption and ratification of an inter-se agreement as an international treaty take time, ensuring prompt readiness of a legal framework is questionable. While negotiating a legally binding convention may be more challenging and time-consuming than a soft law instrument, the like-mindedness of regional partners could facilitate agreeing in consensus.[1475] The enhanced regulatory measures targeting marine pollution during the late 1960s and early 1970s serve as a demonstration of effective cooperative regional law-making. Additionally, it serves as an example of combined regional and international law-making.

Stemming from the *Torrey Canyon* accident, the Agreement for Cooperation in Dealing with Pollution of the North Sea by Oil (Bonn Agreement)[1476] was concluded between eight states situated along the North Sea in 1969. Although this convention focused solely on promoting cooperation in monitoring and combatting oil spills, it marked the first regional agreement on protecting a segment of the world's oceans from environmental harm. In 1971, the Norwegian Government took the lead in discussing a region-wide ban of dumping

1475 Forteau (n 1325) 16

1476 Agreement for Cooperation in Dealing with Pollution of the North Sea by Oil, No. 10099 9 June 1969

activities from ships and aircrafts.[1477] Only eight months after its initiation, the Convention for the prevention of marine pollution by dumping from ships and aircraft[1478] was signed in Oslo and ratified by seven states within two years.[1479] The same group of states involved kept discussing, adopted the Paris Convention in 1974,[1480] and merged both agreements in 1992.[1481] The resulting OSPAR Convention included innovative approaches such as the polluter pays principle and the precautionary principle.[1482]

The general consent between the involved states and the shared interest in agreeing on a convention were the main drivers for the outstanding swift negotiation of the Oslo Convention.[1483] Moreover, shared political and economic interests facilitated negotiations and frequent exchanges. Although there was a parallel negotiation process at the international level leading to the London Dumping Convention, the states bordering the North Sea and Northeast Atlantic wanted to amplify their activities in environmental protection and the regional level was considered a valid alternative to the international level to develop prompt regulations.

Since all European states have an interest in maintaining a high level of safety, security, and environmental protection, negotiations on a regional treaty on MASS are likely to be concluded more quickly than a global treaty, which would have to integrate more opinions that are heterogeneous. Thus, the long negotiation and ratification period is not a major argument against a binding inter-se agreement for MASS. The limited geographical scope is neither a persuasive counterargument as the global scope is less important. In a first step, a regional solution would suffice the needs of the industry.

As the inter-se agreement is a binding treaty, any amendments would require the same procedure as for adoption. Simplified amendment procedures could be introduced to facilitate subsequent adjustments, but this may risk a lock-in of a specific technological state of the art. Alternatively, the provisions could be formulated in a goal-based manner to avoid excluding any

1477 van der Burgt (n 1346) 1

1478 Convention for the prevention of marine pollution by dumping from ships and aircrafts, No. 13269 (n 1340)

1479 Norway, Denmark, Sweden, Portugal, Spain, Iceland, and France ratified the convention between 1972 and 1974

1480 Convention for the prevention of marine pollution from land-based sources, No. 26842 (n 1341)

1481 Convention for the protection of the marine environment of the North-East Atlantic, No. 42279 (n 1345)

1482 Treves, 'Treves 2003' (n 1348) 145

1483 van der Burgt (n 1346) 4

technological solutions. Industry stakeholders, such as classification societies and ship insurers, could develop specific technical guidelines to meet the goal-based regulatory requirements. Despite the flexibility that can be achieved by goal-based standards, it is important to note that soft law solutions add a significant degree of flexibility, particularly due to the fact that industry stakeholders could be directly involved in the law-making process.

As the inter-se agreement would be concluded by states that are all parties to the GAIRAS conventions and UNCLOS, a horizontal and coherent framework could be ensured. Unlike the IMO, states could also include interpretative guidance on UNCLOS. In addition, as with non-binding regional solutions, regional specificities could be taken into account and reflected in the inter-se agreement. This is especially relevant for short-sea shipping applications, which may be subject to specific requirements. On the one side, such requirements could take into account the fact that ships operating on short-sea shipping routes regularly call at ports where maintenance work could be carried out. Furthermore, design and equipment requirements and the need for redundant systems could take account of the fact that, in the North Sea and Baltic Sea, other ships could be on the spot within a few hours to provide technical assistance to MASS. On the other side, cybersecurity requirements could reflect the increased risk of GPS jamming in the North and Baltic Sea region and an increased risk of cyber attacks.[1484]

In conclusion, a regional MASS Convention could be a suitable tool to provide a predictable legal framework for MASS. Coherency and horizontal integration into the existing framework can be ensured. As the agreement would be binding, compliance is enhanced and states can demonstrate a greater level of commitment to their contracting partners. This fosters trust that the provisions of the agreement will be respected even in the absence of specific enforcement options. In situations where cooperation occurs with regional partners at various (administrative) levels, however, violations of any agreement, regardless of their binding status, can easily result in direct retaliation via reciprocal measures or harm to one's reputation. Thus, the level of legal commitment is of lesser importance than the actual implementation and compliance with the agreed terms.[1485] In regional settings, the specific benefits of binding treaties are less relevant, and the disadvantages, including the still lengthy negotiation process and potential cumbersome amendment process, outweigh the advantages.

1484 Jacek Lamparski, 'Safety of Navigation Satellites' [2022] Annual of Navigation 29, 31; Felski and Zwolak (n 192) 46

1485 Observing a decrease in regional codification: Forteau (n 1325) 21

During interviews, representatives from ministries and administrations of the Nordic states expressed their view that a legally binding treaty on MASS at a regional level, bypassing the IMO, is not feasible. The Nordic states aim to avoid conflicting regulations at the international and regional level, as the IMO will continue its regulatory work. Therefore, no binding regulatory action will be taken at the regional level.

5.4.5 *Conclusions*

This section considered regional regulation for MASS. Based on the understanding of a region as a group of geographically proximate states sharing certain features and having a will of belonging to a region, regional groupings dealing with maritime matters in Northern and Western Europe were introduced. The Paris Memorandum of Understanding on port state controls and the Nordic Cooperation were considered the most promising for regulating MASS.

The Paris MoU is an administrative cooperation based on a legally non-binding agreement. Its purpose is to ensure the proper implementation of international shipping conventions. Therefore, it was not deemed suitable to develop substantial provisions for MASS. However, it is important to note that including a new MASS instrument within the scope of the Paris MoU is necessary to ensure frictionless port state controls.

Next, the Nordic Cooperation was examined. The Nordic states cooperate on several matters at all levels, from prime ministers to lower public servants, based on a long-standing shared history, language similarities, parallel economic and social developments, and similar political systems. The Nordic Council and the Nordic Council of Ministers have simply added an institutional framework. Particularly, legal cooperation often happens outside the Nordic Council directly between parliaments.

Since the Nordic states have agreed to work closely together to establish green shipping corridors and promote zero-emission and smart shipping, a regulation on MASS would fit in perfectly. Thus, available instruments and their admissibility from a public international law perspective were considered in more detail. Due to time and resource constraints, developing a holistic framework for MASS was considered too arduous and thus rejected.

Adopting a recommendation at the Nordic Council or taking a decision at the Nordic Council of Ministers could promote the implementation of an IMO MASS Code. The Nordic states could also adopt a legally binding international convention on MASS. This convention would amend the existing international treaties among some of the contracting governments. Thus, it would considered a modifying inter-se agreement. The admissibility of such an agreement was then examined against Article 311(3) of the UNCLOS, Article VII of SOLAS and Article 41 of the VCLT. It was concluded here, that a modification to allow MASS operations would be possible.

Finally, the appropriateness of a regional MASS Convention was assessed. It was noted that while the Nordic states have demonstrated the ability to enter into international binding commitments quickly, there is a risk of a lock-in of premature and inflexible rules. Furthermore, the value added by a legally binding treaty was deemed less significant in a regional setting, as any failure to fulfill commitments could be met with reciprocal measures. Although a legally binding inter-se agreement could otherwise meet the requirements of the industry and could even exude to whole UNCLOS,[1486] representatives of the Nordic states have expressed reluctance to adopt any regional solutions that could interfere with the IMO. Despite the numerous advantages of regional regulations for MASS, it is unlikely to happen. However, technical cooperation continues, and informal cooperation on the implementation of an international MASS Code is likely. As a third regulator, the supranational level shall be considered in the next chapter.

5.5 Regulation at the Supranational Level

As a third alternative to international and regional regulation, MASS could be regulated at the supranational,[1487] i.e. European level.[1488] As illustrated in section 2.2, most research projects focus on short-sea shipping operations of MASS and several projects are located in EU member states, Norway, and the United Kingdom. The regulation of MASS at the European level can therefore be a promising approach. Moreover, the EU has already started to develop regulations on MASS: In 2020, the non-mandatory EU Operational Guidelines for Safe, Secure, and Sustainable Trials of MASS were published to guide national authorities when designating test areas and authorizing MASS trials.[1489] Moreover, the European Maritime Safety Agency and the classification society DNV GL developed a Risk-Based Assessment Tool facilitating the preliminary

1486 Freestone and Elferink (n 1216) 181

1487 Franz C Mayer and Simon P Thies, 'European Union, Historical Evolution' in Anne Peters (ed), *Max Planck Encyclopedia of Public International Law* (MPEPIL) (Oxford University Press) 27

1488 See for a general discussion of MASS and European Maritime Policy: Leonidas Sotiropoulos, 'European Maritime Policies and the Dynamic of Autonomous Vessels' [2024] International Investment Law Journal 71

1489 European Commission, 'EU Operational Guidelines for Safe, Secure and Sustainable Trials of Maritime Autonomous Surface Ships (MASS)' (Brussels October 2020) 7

approval of MASS by national authorities. The tool was submitted to the IMO for incorporation in the MASS Code in 2023.[1490]

European regulation shares several advantages with regional regulation. In particular, the geographical proximity of the states and the like-mindedness make it easier to find a compromise. Additionally, the EU is more institutionalized, which could improve regulatory solutions.

Another option worth considering is the participation of the EU in legal solutions already discussed. This could be necessary if the EU enjoys exclusive external competence on MASS. Even if the competence rests with the member state or is shared among the EU and its member states, EU participation could be beneficial as negotiations and implementation could be streamlined and accelerated.

At this point, it should be noted that the EU is not a state in the meaning of Article 91(1) of the UNCLOS and thus not entitled to grant its flag to vessels. This right is reserved for EU member states as state parties to UNCLOS. Thus, European maritime acts addressing vessel safety and operation must address the EU member states in their capacity as flag, coastal, or port states.

A European legal framework for MASS has some considerable advantages over regional regulation. First, the EU encompasses 27 member states and thereby a wider region than the Nordic Cooperation. Although Norway is not a member state of the EU, the European Economic Area (EEA) allows for an expansion of the geographical scope of application of EU legal instruments.[1491] Second, the EU can make recourse to a well-established institutional system to adopt maritime regulations and ensure compliance at the implementation stage. The European Maritime Safety Agency supports by developing and implementing EU maritime instruments. The wide range of expertise is reflected by the comprehensive list of legal instruments on maritime issues administered by the EMSA.[1492]

Third, regulating MASS at the European level would mirror the geographical distribution of promising research projects. Research on MASS takes place in

1490 MSC, IMO, 'MSC 107/5/4: Risk-Based Assessment Tool for MASS (Austria, Belgium, Bulgaria, Croatia, Cyprus, Czechia, Denmark, Estonia, Finland, France, Germany, Greece, Hungary, Ireland, Italy, Latvia, Lithuania, Luxembourg, Malta, Netherlands (Kingdom of the), Poland, Portugal, Romania, Slovakia, Slovenia, Spain, Sweden and European Commission)' (London 20 March 2023)

1491 Lichtenstein is also part of the EEA, but as a landlocked state it is less relevant for autonomous shipping

1492 See the list of legislative texts at: European Maritime Safety Agency, 'Legislative Texts' <https://www.emsa.europa.eu/publications/legislative-texts.html> accessed 16 February 2024

Belgium, the Netherlands, UK, Germany, Greece, and France. Consequently, several EU member states and states closely affiliated to the EU are actively engaging in MASS research. Moreover, the EU has financed research projects on the operation of MASS in short-sea shipping services and as part of green and efficient transport systems.[1493]

Providing a legal framework for MASS can help to promote MASS operations in European waters. This contributes to the EU's aim of supporting innovative technologies and reducing its greenhouse gas emissions generated by the transport sector by 90% until 2050.[1494] The EU seeks a modal shift towards low- or zero-emission modes of transport and an increase of the share of short-sea shipping by 50% by 2050.[1495] As MASS make short-sea shipping economically viable and frequently operate with zero-emissions, this technology can play a significant part in the modal shift. Autonomous operation also increases efficiency, reducing fuel consumption and emissions. Although a modal shift is demanded, short-sea shipping already accumulates to 60.9% of the total sea transportation of goods to and from main EU ports.[1496] Additionally, approximately 30% of goods transported within the EU are done so through short-sea shipping.[1497] Thus, already today, short-sea shipping is important within the EU. Eventually, the EU is faced by an ageing population resulting in a shortage of competent personnel. Given the specific benefits of MASS operations in European waters, considerable motivation to pursue MASS legislation can be expected.

Fourth, the EU has already begun to adopt legal measures in the context of MASS. The EU Operational Guidelines on trials of Maritime Autonomous Surface Ships[1498] supplement the IMO's Interim Guidelines.[1499] In 2022, the EMSA

1493 See the projects introduced in section 2.2

1494 European Commission, 'COM(2020) 789 final – Sustainable and Smart Mobility Strategy – putting European transport on track for the future' (n 133) 45

1495 COM(2021) 812 final – Proposal for a Regulation of the European Parliament and of the Council on Union guidelines for the development of the trans-European transport network, amending Regulation (EU) 2021/1153 and Regulation (EU) No 913/2010 and repealing Regulation (EU) 1315/2013 (n 890) recital 3

1496 Eurostat, 'Maritime transport statistics – short sea shipping of goods' (2023) <https://ec.europa.eu/eurostat/statistics-explained/index.php?title=Maritime_transport_statistics_-_short_sea_shipping_of_goods#Short_sea_shipping_by_type_of_cargo> accessed 16 February 2024

1497 European Commission, 'Statistical Pocketbook 2023 EU transport in figures' (Luxembourg 2023) 38

1498 European Commission, 'EU Operational Guidelines for Safe, Secure and Sustainable Trials of Maritime Autonomous Surface Ships (MASS)' (n 1489)

1499 MSC, IMO, 'MSC.1/Circ.1604' (n 1046)

commissioned a study to develop a Risk-Based Assessment Tool, which was submitted to the IMO by the European Commission and the EU member states in 2023.[1500] This tool shall be included in the IMO MASS Code as one method to assess the risks of MASS operation.[1501]

On first sight, a European regulatory approach to MASS is promising. Thus, it is worth considering a European approach to MASS in more detail. Firstly, the EU's competence in the field of MASS and available instruments for a European regulatory response to MASS shall be considered, followed by a discussion of the potential of a European participation in international regulatory approaches to MASS. As next, the focus shifts to EU-only solutions. On the one hand, a self-standing EU act is considered. This means an instrument providing a comprehensive regulatory framework for MASS including guidance to the interpretation of existing treaties and additional, MASS-specific provisions. On the other hand, a European instrument complementing an IMO instrument will be examined. In the context of the second option, the relation between the EU and the IMO as well as the legal implications of the GAIRAS conventions for the EU will be explored. This shall enable a discussion of the regulatory interplay of these two international organizations. It is important to note that the EU member states, rather than the EU itself, are the members of the IMO and contracting parties to the GAIRAS treaties. However, the IMO's law-making activities are relevant to the EU from a practical standpoint. Hence, there are reasons to examine the relationship between the EU and the IMO in more detail. The situation is different with respect to UNCLOS. As this treaty concerns both, EU and member states' competencies,[1502] both are contracting parties of UNCLOS. Consequently, the reference to GAIRAS in UNCLOS can be directly relevant for the EU.[1503]

5.5.1 *EU Competence and Available Instruments*

According to the principle of conferral, laid down in Article 4(1) of the Treaty on European Union (TEU), any competence of the EU must have been delegated to it by the member states. With regard to shipping, three titles of competence could be relevant: Article 100(2) of the Treaty on the Functioning of

---

1500 MSC, IMO, 'MSC 107/5/4' (n 1490); MSC, IMO, 'MSC 107/INF.8: Risk-Based Assessment Tool for MASS (Austria, Belgium, Bulgaria, Croatia, Cyprus, Czechia, Denmark, Estonia, Finland, France, Germany, Greece, Hungary, Ireland, Italy, Latvia, Lithuania, Luxembourg, Malta, Netherlands (Kingdom of the), Poland, Portugal, Romania, Slovakia, Slovenia, Spain, Sweden and European Commission)' (London 20 March 2023)

1501 MSC, IMO, 'MSC 107/5/4' (n 1490) 2

1502 C-459/03 *Commission of the European Communities v. Ireland, MOX Plant* [2006] 120

1503 Ringbom, *Ringbom 2008* (n 675) 134

the European Union (TFEU) concerning regulations on shipping within the framework of the common transport policy and the realization of the internal market, Article 170(1) TFEU addressing trans-European transport networks, and Article 192(1) TFEU entitling the EU to enact environmental protection regulations.

Article 192(1) TFEU is of least relevance for MASS, as MASS do not require specific provisions on marine environmental protection.[1504] Nevertheless, MASS will have to comply with the same environmental regulations as conventional ships. Therefore, Article 192(1) TFEU will not be pursued further here.

Article 100(2) TFEU and Article 170(1) TFEU are more relevant to MASS. The CJEU differentiates between these two titles of competences according to the focus of the regulation in question.[1505] Others, however, consider Article 170 TFEU to be lex specialis for the regulation of transborder infrastructure.[1506] Before MASS can be integrated into European supply chains and transport networks, MASS must be allowed to operate. This is why primarily regulations focusing exclusively on MASS need to be put in place. Subsequently, MASS can be integrated into trans-European transport networks. This study focuses on the first step, the regulation of MASS as an independent transport mode. Thus, Article 170 TFEU is not applicable for this first set of regulations. Article 100(2) TFEU stipulates that

> [t]he European Parliament and the Council, acting in accordance with the ordinary legislative procedure, may lay down appropriate provisions for sea and air transport. They shall act after consulting the Economic and Social Committee and the Committee of the Regions.

This title of competence has to be read together with Article 91 TFEU[1507] stipulating that

1504 This is evidenced by the fact that the MEPC responsible for environmental issues and administering MARPOL has not concluded a RSE to identify gaps in the legal framework caused by the advant of MASS

1505 C-271/94 *European Parliament vs. Commission of the European Communities* [1996] 26

1506 Christian Calliess, 'Article 170 AEUV' in Christian Calliess and Matthias Ruffert (eds), EUV/AEUV*: Das Verfassungsrecht der Europäischen Union mit Europäischer Grundrechtecharta: Kommentar* (6. Auflage. C.H. Beck 2022) 4; Meinhard Schröder, 'Article 170 TFEU' in Rudolf Streinz and others (eds), EUV/AEUV*: Vertrag über die Europäische Union, Vertrag über die Arbeitsweise der Europäischen Union, Charta der Grundrechte der Europäischen Union* (Beck-Online Bücher Band 57, 3. Auflage. C.H. Beck 2018) 11

1507 Michael Fehling, 'Article 100 TFEU' in Hans von der Groeben, Jürgen Schwarze and Armin Hatje (eds), *Europäisches Unionsrecht: Vertrag über die Europäische Union; Vertrag über*

> 1. [f]or the purpose of implementing [a common transport policy], and taking into account the distinctive features of transport, the European Parliament and the Council shall, acting in accordance with the ordinary legislative procedure and after consulting the Economic and Social Committee and the Committee of the Regions, lay down:
>
> (a) common rules applicable to international transport to or from the territory of a Member State or passing across the territory of one or more Member States;
>
> (b) the conditions under which non-resident carriers may operate transport services within a Member State;
>
> (c) measures to improve transport safety;
>
> (d) any other appropriate provisions.
>
> 2. When the measures referred to in paragraph 1 are adopted, account shall be taken of cases where their application might seriously affect the standard of living and level of employment in certain regions, and the operation of transport facilities.

Thus, the EU is entitled to adopt measures on shipping to address the freedom to provide services, with the aim of completing the Internal Market and measures to improve safety at sea.[1508] The measures necessary to address the legal gaps identified above are necessary to improve the safety at sea and to complete the Internal Market: clarifications about the key terms such as 'master' and 'crew' contribute to the safety of navigation as tasks can be allocated to the responsible person. Additionally, provisions addressing MASS-specific aspects, such as the line of communication to the RCC and the design of sensor-based lookout systems, also contribute to navigation safety. To enable commercial MASS operations in European waters and ensure freedom to provide MASS transport services within the Internal Market, such measures are necessary.

The competence in Article 100(2) TFEU is shared between the member states and the EU according to Article 4(2)(g) TFEU. Consequently, as soon as the EU has used its competence in respect of a certain subject matter, the

die Arbeitsweise der Europäischen Union; Charta der Grundrechte der Europäischen Union (7th edn. Nomos 2015) 15

1508 ibid

member states can no longer regulate the same matter, see Article 2(2)(2) TFEU. The EU, in turn, is not prevented from regulating if the member states have exercised a shared competence. Thus, neither national law-making activities on MASS nor the activities of the EU member states at the IMO prevent a European approach. To conclude, the EU could base a MASS instrument on Article 100(2) TFEU.

For EU external competence Articles 3(2) and 216 TFEU are relevant. Again, it needs to be distinguished between exclusive and shared competence. Article 216(1) TFEU grants the EU external competence

> [...] where the Treaties so provide or where the conclusion of an agreement is necessary in order to achieve, within the framework of the Union's policies, one of the objectives referred to in the Treaties, or is provided for in a legally binding Union act or is likely to affect common rules or alter their scope.

As the treaties do not provide for an explicit external competence of the EU in maritime issues, recourse has to be made to the second and fourth alternative, i.e. when the conclusion of international agreements is necessary to achieve EU policy goals or when an international agreement is likely to affect EU law. Before the codification in the TFEU, the CJEU decided that the EU enjoys external competence if there is a corresponding internal competence to achieve a specific objective.[1509] External competence should complement internal competence so that internal competence can be used effectively to pursue the policy objective in question.

Considering the internal competence laid down in Article 100(2) TFEU to regulate maritime shipping, navigational safety, and free movement of persons, goods, and services it could be argued that, given the global scope of shipping, the conclusion of international agreements on the safety of MASS is necessary for the effective attainment of maritime safety and the completion of the Internal Market. This could support a rather comprehensive EU external competence on maritime safety issues.[1510]

1509 1/13 *Hague Convention* [2014] 67; 2/91 *Convention N° 170 of the International Labour Organization concerning safety in the use of chemicals at work* [1993] 7; *Opinion 1/03 – the new Lugano Convention* [2006] 114

1510 Ringbom, *Ringbom 2008* (n 675) 56

As next, the nature of this competence has to be determined. Based on Article 3(2) TFEU which codifies the CJEU's AETR judgement,[1511] the EU has exclusive external competence to conclude an international agreement if this

> is provided for in a legislative act of the Union or is necessary to enable the Union to exercise its internal competence, or in so far as its conclusion may affect common rules or alter their scope.[1512]

In respect of shipping, the first alternative does not apply, as there is no explicit provision concerning international maritime agreements. However, the second and third alternatives could be relevant to establish an exclusive competence of the EU for the conclusion of international shipping agreements. The conclusion of international agreements is necessary to exercise internal competence if the two are inextricably linked.[1513] In respect of maritime issues, the EU enjoys internal competence per Article 100(2) TFEU. Although shipping is an international business, some matters such as VTS and sea lanes can be regulated internally without being dependent on international regulations.

Regarding MASS, it could be argued that the EU cannot effectively exercise its internal competence without concluding an international agreement. This is because the integration of MASS into the current framework is of paramount importance. However, some aspects of MASS could be regulated without international cooperation, such as working conditions for MASS operators or additional registration requirements or design requirements for the RCC. Therefore, the second option, exclusive external competence if the internal competence cannot be performed otherwise, is not applicable in the case of MASS. Consequently, it is worth considering the third alternative, EU exclusive external competence if an international agreement "may affect common rules or alter their scope".[1514]

1511 C-22/70 *Commission of the European Communities v. Council of the European Communities* [1972]

1512 Article 3(2) TFEU

1513 Rudolf Mögele, 'Article 3 TFEU' in Rudolf Streinz and others (eds), EUV/AEUV*: Vertrag über die Europäische Union, Vertrag über die Arbeitsweise der Europäischen Union, Charta der Grundrechte der Europäischen Union* (Beck-Online Bücher Band 57, 3. Auflage. C.H. Beck 2018) 14; 1/94 *Competence of the Community to conclude international agreements concerning services and the protection of intellectual property – Article 228 (6) of the* EC *Treaty.* [1994] 86

1514 Article 3(2) TFEU

Affection or altering of rules has to be considered on a case-by-case basis. In the case of MARPOL, the CJEU refused an exclusive external EU competence, as the EU has not assumed powers in the field regulated by MARPOL.[1515] With respect to SOLAS, however, exclusive EU competence was assumed for Chapter XI-2 and the ISPS Code as this code was integrated into community law.[1516] The decision's impact is significant because the EU has integrated several IMO Codes and parts of SOLAS into EU law.[1517] Considering this judgment, the EU could have gained exclusive external competence on all these matters. The same applies to parts of the STCW Convention. Directive 2022/993[1518] integrates STCW qualification requirements for seafarers into EU law. Thus, with respect to qualification requirements, the EU enjoys exclusive external competence, as international rules would affect EU law.[1519]

In 2017, the CJEU ruled that the EU has exclusive competence to conclude international agreements on the question of who is authorized to provide maritime transport services within the EU and to third countries. As a European regulation[1520] did already regulate the application of the principle of freedom to provide services to maritime transport between member states and between member states and third countries, the concerned article of the Free Trade Agreement with Singapore was considered to touch upon this EU regulation. Consequently, the EU enjoyed exclusive external competence.[1521] Additionally, the CJEU decided with respect to the Lugano Convention in 2003, that not only the existing EU law had to be observed, but that also its future development has to be taken into account when determining whether an international agreement could affect EU law.[1522]

In conclusion, the EU has exclusive external competence in some matters regulated by the GAIRAS conventions. However, a detailed case-by-case analysis is necessary to determine the concrete scope of exclusive external

1515 C-379/92 *Peralta* [1994] 16

1516 C-45/07 *Commission of the European Communities v. Hellenic Republic* [2009] 28

1517 Ringbom, *Ringbom 2008* (n 675) 77; Judith van Leeuwen and Kristine Kern, 'The External Dimension of European Union Marine Governance: Institutional Interplay between the EU and the International Maritime Organization' (2013) 13(1) Global Environmental Politics 69, 82

1518 Directive (EU) 2022/993 on the minimum level of training of seafarers [2022] Official Journal of the European Union 65 L 169/45

1519 Ringbom, *Ringbom 2008* (n 675) 75

1520 Council Regulation (EEC) No 4055/ 86 on applying the principle of freedom to provide services to maritime transport between Member States and between Member States and third countries 22 December 1986 (Council of the European Union)

1521 2/15 *Free Trade Agreement with Singapore* [2017] 193

1522 *Court of Justice of the European Union 2006* (n 1509) 131

EU competence. It is noteworthy that none of the EU maritime instruments exclusively addresses the safety of navigation. This could argue for non-exclusivity of EU external competence in matters relevant to MASS, such as rules on navigation safety and ship operation. International regulations will not affect existing EU rules. However, it is challenging to determine whether the EU enjoys exclusive external competence due to the requirement to consider future development of the EU's legal framework.

Beyond the dogmatic question of what kind of competence the EU has, the practical exercise of exclusive and shared external competence poses a problem in day-to-day practice[1523] because the EU could not become a member to the GAIRAS conventions, as only states can ratify these conventions. Thus, the EU has exclusive external competence but cannot exercise it directly at the international level, particularly at the IMO.[1524] In this situation, it will therefore be necessary to deal with the competence issues pragmatically.[1525]

The EU member states can submit proposals to the IMO and vote because they are contracting parties to the GAIRAS conventions and members of the IMO. To respect the EU-internal division of competence and the duty of sincere cooperation, the EU member states have to coordinate their positions before acting at the IMO and have to act jointly in the interests of the Union if the subject matter falls within the scope of exclusive external EU competence.[1526] The CJEU has deduced from the duty of loyalty an "obligation both of result and of conduct".[1527] This means that member states do not only have to align their unilateral position with the common EU positions, but also to jointly develop an EU position before submitting a proposal to the IMO.[1528] Consequently, the EU can act at the international level through the medium of the member states[1529] forming a proactive coalition.[1530] This procedure of coordinated proposals and aligned positions is particularly useful if the exclusivity of the EU's competence cannot be determined ultimately.

1523 Ringbom, *Ringbom 2008* (n 675) 74

1524 This was the case here where the EU has exclusive competence with respect to the ISPS Code and Chapter XI-2 of SOLAS, but has to exercise its compentece through the member states: *Court of Justice of the European Union 2009* (n 1516)

1525 Ringbom, *Ringbom 2008* (n 675) 103

1526 C-161/20 *European Commission v. Council of the European Union* (*Organisation maritime internationale*) [2022] 69

1527 Liu Nengye and Maes Frank, 'The European Union and the International Maritime Organization: EU's External Influence on the Prevention of Vessel-Source Pollution' (2010) 41(4) Journal of Maritime Law and Commerce 581, 591

1528 *Court of Justice of the European Union 2009* (n 1516) 28

1529 *Court of Justice of the European Union 1993* (n 1509) 37

1530 van Leeuwen and Kern (n 1517) 80

In conclusion, the EU has shared internal competence and can therefore regulate MASS internally. External competence is not explicitly granted, but it follows from the internal competence. It is ultimately unclear whether an international MASS instrument would affect existing or future EU rules, and whether the EU has exclusive external competence. Nonetheless, the EU cannot exercise its competence in the IMO, as only its member states are voting members of the IMO. Therefore, the EU acts through its member states at the IMO level.

The EU and its member states have a long-standing tradition with the conclusion of mixed agreements. A mixed agreement is an international agreement concluded by the EU, its member states, and a third party.[1531] It could be considered to conclude the proposed MASS Convention as a mixed agreement. Although the negotiations are more complex when involving the EU and its member states, mixed agreements ensure that the member states remain visible actors at the international level. Moreover, the EU and its member states are co-debtors for the fulfillment of the agreement stipulating an advantage for the other parties to the agreement.[1532] In 2023, the Agreement on the conservation and sustainable use of marine biological diversity beyond national jurisdiction was adopted under UNCLOS and signed by the EU and its member states. As the agreement touches upon exclusive EU competence and shared competence with the member states, the agreement is a mixed one.[1533] The same could be done in the case of a MASS Convention. However, considering the disadvantages of a binding MASS Convention at the international level, this solution is not proposed here as the most appropriate to cope the identified legal gaps caused by MASS. Thus, the EU participation in such an international treaty will not be further explored.

1531 Marise Cremona, 'Making Treaties and Other International Agreements: The European Union' in Curtis A Bradley (ed), *The Oxford Handbook of Comparative Foreign Relations Law* (Oxford University Press 2019) 256

1532 Stefan Lorenzmeier, 'Exclusive and Shared External Competences After the Singapore Opinion of the European Court of Justice: 2/15 Revisited' in Stefan Lorenzmeier, Roman Petrov and Christoph Vedder (eds), EU *External Relations Law: Shared Competences and Shared Values in Agreements Between the* EU *and Its Eastern Neighbourhood* (Springer eBook Collection, 1st ed. Springer International Publishing 2021) 34

1533 Pascale Ricard, 'The European Union and the Future International Legally Binding Instrument on Marine Biodiversity Beyond National Jurisdiction' in Marta C C M Da Ribeiro, Fernando L Bastos and Tore Henriksen (eds), *Global challenges and the law of the sea* (Springer 2020) 384

Returning to the internal perspective, the EU has several legal instruments at its disposal to exercise its internal competence. Article 288(1) TFEU lists all instruments available for the EU to exercise its competencies: regulations, directives, decisions, recommendations, and opinions. Regulations, directives, and decisions are binding for the member states, recommendations and opinions, however, are not legally binding. Firstly, the non-binding instruments are introduced, and secondly, the focus shifts to the binding instruments.

Recommendations usually provide for a certain behavior,[1534] whereas opinions contain an expert statement of view.[1535] Although recommendations are not legally binding, national courts should take them into consideration when implementing EU law.[1536] Recommendations are relied upon when a binding instrument is deemed inappropriate for the purpose.[1537] In addition, recommendations are most often linked to another EU legal instrument to support national implementation. The interpretation of recommendations may be subject to preliminary proceedings at the CJEU.[1538] Considering MASS, an opinion seems inappropriate, as it would not provide substantial provisions. However, an opinion could be issued on certain technical aspects. A recommendation, in contrast, could be promising for the regulatory approach towards MASS. It could complement another act with more detailed guidance on its application in individual cases. However, it does not provide a suitable dress for a self-standing MASS Act.

Turning to binding instruments now, three instruments have to be considered: decisions, regulations, and directives. Decisions can have two appearances: on the one side, decisions can be addressed to a specific person or state having binding force.[1539] On the other side, decisions can be used for matters of general concern not addressed to any person or state though being legally binding.[1540] As an example of the latter, statements on the budget for and

1534 Matthias Ruffert, 'Article 288 TFEU' in Christian Calliess and Matthias Ruffert (eds), EUV/AEUV: *Das Verfassungsrecht der Europäischen Union mit Europäischer Grundrechtecharta: Kommentar* (6. Auflage. C.H. Beck 2022) 98

1535 ibid

1536 C-322/88 *Grimaldi v. Fonds des maladies professionnelles* [1989] 18

1537 ibid 13

1538 ibid 8

1539 Maria Geismann, 'Art. 288 AEUV' in Hans von der Groeben, Jürgen Schwarze and Armin Hatje (eds), *Europäisches Unionsrecht: Vertrag über die Europäische Union; Vertrag über die Arbeitsweise der Europäischen Union; Charta der Grundrechte der Europäischen Union* (7th edn. Nomos 2015) 57

1540 ibid 61

the financial rules applicable to European Agencies are often given as decisions.[1541] Considering that MASS require material provisions, a decision is not appropriate to address the regulatory needs of MASS.

Regulations and directives, as the two core legal instruments used by the EU, to regulate aspects of general concern in a general-abstract manner. Regulations are directly applicable in the member states and binding in their entirety. Directives, in contrast, are in general not directly applicable in the member states and bind the member states with regard to the result. During domestic implementation, national parliaments and authorities can decide on the form and methods to achieve the determined results. It is important to note that the CJEU consistently rejected the implementation of directives by means of continuous administrative practice or internal administrative acts such as circulars. Instead, binding normative acts must be adopted nationally.[1542] Directives are the preferred instrument for legal harmonization because they are less intrusive on the national legal system than regulations.[1543] Often regulations were considered as 'technical' instruments not causing political controversies. However, considering statistical data, controversial issues were regulated equally by regulations and directives.[1544]

In conclusion, either a regulation or a directive seem to be the most appropriate instrument for EU legislation on MASS. Both instruments are legally binding. These pieces of legislation are adopted with the ordinary procedure illustrated below. Additionally, the EC or a European Agency can be authorized to adopt complementing instruments guiding national implementation. Moreover, recommendations could be enacted to provide more details about national implementation.

Legally binding instruments based on Article 100(2) TFEU are adopted by the European Parliament and the Council in accordance with the ordinary legislative procedure as described in Articles 289(1), 294 TFEU.[1545] Per Article 294(2), the right of initiative rests exclusively with the EC. Per Article 296 TFEU,

1541 See as examples: Decision (EU) 2016/1353 concerning the financial rules of the European Defence Agency and repealing Decision 2007/643/CFSP 4 August 2016 (Council of the European Union); Decision (EU) 2023/1901 on discharge in respect of the implementation of the budget of the European Maritime Safety Agency (EMSA) for the financial year 2021 [2023] Official Journal of the European Union 66 L 242/351

1542 C-315/98 *Commission of the European Communities v. Italian Republic* [1999] 10; C-358/98 *Commission of the European Communities v. Italian Republic* [2000] 17

1543 Ruffert (n 1534) 24

1544 Steffen Hurka and Yves Steinebach, 'Legal Instrument Choice in the European Union' (2021) 59(2) Journal of Common Market Studies 278, 280

1545 Fehling (n 1507) 14

the selection of the type of act shall be based on the principle of proportionality and has to be reasoned. During up to three readings, the Parliament and the Council can agree on a joint text, which has to be adopted by both institutions. The European Parliament acts by a majority of the votes cast, Article 231 TFEU, the Council by a qualified majority, Article 16(4) TEU. Article 292 TFEU provides for a special procedure for the adoption of recommendations, excluding the Parliament and giving the power to the Council, unless the Treaties provide otherwise. Shortly after being published in the Official Journal of the European Union, the acts enter into force, Article 297 TFEU. Directives usually provide for a two-year implementation period for the member states.

To conclude, the EU enjoys internal and external competence in the field of MASS. With respect to the external competence, its exclusivity could not be determined ultimately. However, some matters fall in the scope of exclusive external EU competence such as qualification requirements for seafarers. Consequently, an international convention on MASS should be developed as a mixed agreement involving the EU and its member states. Considering potential EU internal approaches, the EU could adopt a recommendation, a directive, or a regulation to address MASS. As next, the potential of a self-standing EU act on MASS shall be assessed. The EU could address navigational safety for MASS, and determine registration and port state control processes. Additionally, member states could be addressed as coastal states to ensure unobstructed MASS operations in European waters. The appropriateness of a self-standing EU act on MASS shall now be considered.

5.5.2 *Self-Standing Act*

Although shipping is mainly shaped by international instruments, the EU has actively shaped maritime law-making since its inception. From 1985 on, several separate developments caused a boom in maritime transport regulation.[1546] In 1993, these developments culminated in the EC's Communication on "A Common Policy on Safe Seas",[1547] which provided the final impetus for proactive regulation of maritime transport. In 1995, one of the first legal instruments in the field of maritime safety was adopted concerning port state control.[1548] More than 70 acts have been adopted, covering a wide range of

1546 Ringbom, *Ringbom 2008* (n 675) 32

1547 European Commission, 'COM(93) 66 final – Communication from the Commisson 'A Common Policy on Safe Seas" (Brussels 24 February 1993)

1548 Council Directive 95/21/EC concerning the enforcement, in respect of shipping using Community ports and sailing in the waters under the jurisdiction of the Member States, of international standards for ship safety, pollution prevention and shipboard living and working conditions (port State control) 19 June 1995 (Council of the European Union)

maritime-related aspects such as maritime safety, environmental protection, and, more recently, maritime security.[1549] A European MASS Act would continue European maritime regulation and reflect ongoing European research. Considering the requirements outlined above, a European legal act could particularly meet the desire for prompt and flexible regulation.

An EU legal act can be enacted more rapidly, than an act at the international level. Both, the negotiation process as well as the phase between adoption and entry into force are shorter than at the international level. The Council seeks to decide unanimously, however, per Article 16(3) TEU decisions can be taken by a two-thirds majority. Additionally, reaching a consensus among fewer and more like-minded states is easier than at a global level. Consequently, agreeing on high standards for safety, environmental protection, and working conditions is more likely than at the IMO level. Once adopted, these acts do not need to be ratified. Regulations and directives normally enter into force twenty days after their publication in the Official Journal. Directives, meanwhile, have to be implemented at national level, so a vacatio legis of two years is often provided for. Although the average duration of the ordinary legislative procedure is about 40 months, the EU could adopt a legally binding act within 2–4 years.

Later, EU acts can be amended rather quickly to reflect new technological developments. Depending on the urgency of the topic in question, amendments to European legal instruments can be achieved within a couple of weeks only. In contrast, the amendment procedure at the IMO takes several years.

Despite the considerable advantages of European provisions for maritime operations, the EU and its member states have acknowledged the significance of international shipping conventions administered by the IMO. On issues regulated internationally, the EU is extremely cautious to adopt legal acts that have no links to international rules. Most EU maritime acts implement or supplement regulations adopted by the IMO. Consequently, self-standing EU maritime acts are extremely scarce.

One example of truly unlinked regulation can be found in Article 7 of Directive 2016/802.[1550] This rule prescribes the maximum Sulphur content of marine fuels used by ships at berth in EU ports. Although MARPOL provides for maximum Sulphur content of marine fuels in general, it does not include specific regulations for fuels used at berth in ports. In this aspect, the EU added a new rule to the international regime.[1551] Beyond this, however, the European

1549 Ringbom, *Ringbom 2008* (n 675) 31

1550 Directive (EU) 2016/802 – relating to a reduction in the sulphur content of certain liquid fuels [2016] Official Journal of the European Union 59 L 132/58

1551 Ringbom, *Ringbom 2008* (n 675) 265

legislator has exercised restraint in enacting European maritime acts on internationally regulated aspects.

There are several reasons for this legislative reluctance. Adding new, more stringent regulations for ports and/or ship owners could entail competitive disadvantages for the European maritime industry, as shipping is an international business. If operating costs increase due to stricter safety, environmental or security regulations, freight rates will also rise, making EU service providers less attractive in a global comparison. EU operators may experience a decrease in market share, or ship-owners may choose to re-flag their vessels outside of the EU. Especially ship owning and exporting states would oppose such new rules at the European level to not jeopardize their own maritime economy.

Additionally, the member states are cautious about European solo actions as their political standing at the IMO could be put at risk. Often, European states urge for imo rules, which are more stringent, and submit corresponding proposals. During the course of negotiations, the European proposal is often softened to achieve the necessary global consensus. However, if the EU is eager to adopt rules that are more stringent unilaterally, it may be more difficult to convince other states and reach a consensus at the IMO. Regularly adopting unilateral excessive legislation could undermine the credibility of the endeavor for international regulation.

Against this background, self-standing EU acts on MASS are hardly discussed in the academic literature. Ringbom briefly comments on an EU solution for MASS and rejects such proposal as it would foster and deepen disagreements between states and put the global consistency of shipping regulation at risk.[1552]

Although the EU has the competence to adopt a unilateral act on MASS and the geographical scope would meet the needs of the MASS industry, there are other disadvantages in the context of MASS that should be taken into account. With the IMO working intensively on a MASS Code, EU member states are currently very reluctant to introduce unilateral regulations. Another aspect to consider, particularly in the case of MASS, is that EMSA has a staff of around 280. The IMO Secretariat, on the other hand, has around 300 staff. In addition, national delegations and maritime authorities provide expertise and human resources to develop complex regulatory frameworks on maritime aspects at the IMO. The EU does not have such significant resources. Moreover, the IMO has been pursuing the regulatory approach to MASS since 2017. EMSA would have to play catch-up to develop a stand-alone EU instrument on MASS. Given the time and resource constraints, this seems rather unlikely. The author

1552 Ringbom, 'Ringbom 2020' (n 424) 449–450

confirmed the reluctance of EU member states in this case through personal discussions with national representatives at the IMO and the EU.

On the other side, the relevance of an EU act for the interpretation of international law is uncertain. This means that it is not obvious whether the targeted goal can be achieved with an independent EU act at all. An EU MASS Act would need to provide guidance on how to interpret the GAIRAS conventions in a way including MASS. Terms like 'manning', 'master', and 'lookout' would need to be re-defined in the light of MASS. The implications of such a European legal act for the interpretation of the GAIRAS conventions need to be considered from both perspectives, the European and the international one.

At the international level, Article 31 of the VCLT offers several gateways to consider subsequent practices and agreements of the states concerning the interpretation of an international treaty. Especially Article 31(3)(a) of the VCLT could provide a gateway for EU acts to become relevant for the interpretation of international law as it stipulates that subsequent agreements on the interpretation of a treaty shall be taken into account together with the context. Although the term 'agreement' is wider than the term 'treaty' as defined in Article 2(1)(a) of the VCLT,[1553] it seems problematic that the EU itself, rather than the contracting states of the concerned international treaties, would develop the interpretation agreement. To recall, the EU is not a contracting party of any of the GAIRAS conventions. All these treaties limit the right to sign to states. Ambitions to include clauses in the treaties to allow the EU to adhere to the GAIRAS conventions were not successful. Although international organizations can adopt interpretation agreements concerning treaties developed under their auspices,[1554] the EU is not the international organization administering the GAIRAS treaties.

Even if an EU legal act were considered to have been adopted by the EU member states as contracting parties to the GAIRAS treaties, the necessary broad participation for an agreement in the meaning of Article 31(3)(a) of the VCLT would still be lacking. Only 27 out of more than 160 contracting parties would have been able to participate in the negotiations of the subsequent European interpretative agreement. Although the participation of all contracting states is not required, a participation rate of 17% is not sufficient. Thus, EU legislation is excluded from the scope of Article 31(3)(a) of the VCLT. Nevertheless, EU law could be relevant in the scope of Article 31(3)(c) of the VCLT or as a supplementing means of interpretation. However, the small number of participating states will significantly reduce its persuasiveness.

1553 Dörr (n 448) 66
1554 ibid

As a European interpretation act would only affect some of the contracting states of the GAIRAS conventions, one could also think of a modification, Article 41 of the VCLT. However, according to Article 41 of the VCLT, only some of the *contracting states* can agree to modify the treaty among them. Again, it is the lack of a state party status that makes it impossible for the EU to agree upon a modification. Needless to say, the EU member states could agree on a modification as contracting states of the GAIRAS conventions. In this case, however, it would be a new treaty under international law, as discussed above in section 5.3.3.

To conclude, from an international law perspective, EU legislation is of little relevance for the interpretation of international treaties. The EU as a non-contracting party to the GAIRAS conventions is not capable of concluding interpretation or modification agreements. Thus, the need to ensure an interpretation of the GAIRAS treaties including MASS cannot be achieved with a self-standing EU act. Such an act cannot safeguard a certain interpretation of international law.

From the perspective of European law, it must be noted that EU legislation is binding upon the EU member states and prevails over national law.[1555] As most international law is ratified by a national law, EU law could also prevail over implementing national law. Thus, the situation could arise that an EU act stipulates a specific interpretation that cannot be reached applying the general rule of interpretation stipulated by Article 31 of the VCLT. In this case, national courts may find themselves in a dilemma: on the one hand, EU law is binding; on the other hand, it cannot be used to interpret the IMO treaties due to the rules of the VCLT.

The EU has a duty of sincere cooperation[1556] to prevent such situations and must take into account the legal obligations of its member states, even if the EU is not a contracting party to the relevant international treaty.[1557] In its Intertanko judgment, the CJEU interpreted an EU Directive on ship-source pollution by "taking into account" the provisions of MARPOL, although the EU is not a member state of MARPOL. The CJEU based its consideration of MARPOL on the international law principle of good faith and the principle of sincere cooperation.[1558] Likewise, in the Kadi decision, the court demanded that

1555 C-06/64 *Costa v.* ENEL [1964]

1556 Article 4(3) Treaty on European Union (TEU)

1557 C-308/06 *Intertanko, Intercargo, Greek Shipping Co-operation Committee, Lloyd's Register, International Salvage Union v. Secretary of State for Transport* [2008] 52

1558 At the time of the judgment, Article 10 of the Treaty establishing the European Community contained this principle

international obligations of the member states are "taken into due account" when implementing these obligations at a European level.[1559] Although not undisputed,[1560] these judgments can be understood as promoting the principle of consistent interpretation of European and international law.[1561]

Despite the ambiguous meaning of 'taking into account', EU law has to be interpreted in a way that is open to international law and aims for coherence. This approach is supported by the EU's commitment to international law manifested in Articles 3(5); 21(2)(b), (3)(1) TEU. Moreover, the rule of customary international law on interpretation requires that international law shall be taken into account, especially when interpreting rules of a partial legal order of international law, such as EU law.[1562] Consequently, the adoption of an EU act expressing a particular interpretation of international law that is contrary to the interpretation reached at the international level would be inconsistent with the duty of sincere cooperation and consistent interpretation.[1563]

Another, more dogmatic argument could be that the EU origin of EU legal acts prevents them from being relevant to the interpretation of non-EU law acts, such as the GAIRAS conventions.[1564] Therefore, considering the legal uncertainties about the application of an EU legal act on the interpretation of the GAIRAS treaties and the fact that the EU wants to prevent diverting EU and IMO regulations, it is not advised here that the EU adopts a legal instrument providing substantial provisions for MASS and guiding the interpretation of the GAIRAS conventions in a way including MASS.

However, this does not imply that the EU has no options to act. Implementing acts could greatly facilitate the operation of MASS in European waters. The EU could support the IMO in providing legal binding force for an IMO MASS Code and could impact international law-making. This option will be considered next.

1559 C-402/05 P and C-415/05 P *Kadi and Al Barakaat International Foundation v Council and Commission* [2008] 296

1560 Allan Rosas, 'The Status in EU Law of International Agreements Concluded by EU Member States' (2011) 34(5) Fordham International Law Journal 1304, 1341

1561 Katja S Ziegler, 'The Relationship between EU Law and International Law' in Anna Södersten and Dennis M Patterson (eds), *A companion to European Union law and international law* (Wiley Blackwell 2016) 49

1562 ibid 51

1563 Being more reluctant about the openes of EU law towards international law: Jan Klabbers, 'Straddling the Fence: The EU and International Law' in Anthony Arnull and Damian Chalmers (eds), *The Oxford handbook of European Union law* (Oxford University Press 2017) 63

1564 Cécile Legros, 'Interpreting International Shipping Law with EU Soft Law Instruments' (2015) 7(1) European Journal of Commercial Contract Law 32, 34

5.5.3 *Implementing Act*

Both, the EU and the IMO are international organizations established by an international treaty. Since 1974, the EC, not the EU as such, enjoys an observer status with the IMO.[1565] This status gives the right to take part in the meetings of the IMO Assembly and IMO Committees as well as the right to submit proposals. However, the EC has no right to vote at the IMO. Conversely, there is no right of participation for the IMO at the EU level.

Prior to the establishment of the EU, the IMO had a monopoly on maritime regulation. However, since its inception, the EU has been actively involved in maritime regulation, resulting in increased interaction with the IMO.[1566] In most co-legislative situations, EU legislation implemented, strengthened, or extended the scope of IMO instruments. In addition, non-binding IMO instruments have been made legally binding for EU member states. While this approach enhanced the effectiveness of the IMO's non-binding instruments, it was criticized by the international community for jeopardizing global consensus by going beyond IMO rules.[1567]

Despite the criticism, a European implementing act brings about several advantages in the context of MASS. Therefore, the merits of an implementing act will be examined, taking into account examples of EU maritime legislation going beyond its IMO counterparts or other international sources of maritime regulation.

One of the principal advantages of implementing non-binding international rules with binding EU legal instruments is the enhanced effectiveness that this approach offers. The port state control regime exemplifies this well. Based on the exclusive jurisdiction of port states over ships calling at their ports, port states have begun to inspect visiting ships' compliance with GAIRAS.[1568] To increase the efficiency of combatting substandard ships, regional port state control regimes were established. The first of these was the Paris MoU, signed in 1982 by all the countries that are now members of the EU.[1569] In the following years, however, the number of substandard ships in European ports

1565 IMO, 'Intergovernmental Organizations which have concluded agreements of cooperation with IMO' <https://www.imo.org/en/OurWork/ERO/Pages/IGOsWithObserverStatus.aspx> accessed 16 February 2024

1566 See chapters 4, 5, 6 on the EU acting as flag, port, and coastal state, respectively, in: Ringbom, *Ringbom 2008* (n 675) 252; *van Leeuwen/Kern*, Global Environmental Politics, 13(1), 2013, 69–87, 77

1567 van Leeuwen and Kern (n 1517) 82

1568 See the discussion on port state control in section 3.2.2

1569 Paris MoU on PSC (n 289)

did not decrease, but increased.[1570] The rate of inspections varied considerably between the Paris MoU member states,[1571] leading to distortions of competition and making it more attractive for owners of substandard ships to avoid proper inspections by calling at certain ports.[1572] As a response, the EU adopted a directive on port state control in 1995,[1573] which made the Paris MoU commitments legally binding[1574] and added substantial elements.[1575] Subsequently, the Paris MoU was amended to catch up with the Directive.[1576] The increased operational strength[1577] could be ensured by powerful enforcement measures originating from EU law.

As EU law is binding for EU member states, the compliance-pull is greater than that of non-binding instruments. Moreover, powerful enforcement mechanisms are available to ensure compliance.[1578] The EC can collect information, carry out checks,[1579] and initiate proceedings at the CJEU in the case of an infringement of EU law per Article 258 TFEU.[1580] Ultimately, sanctions under Article 260 TFEU can be imposed.[1581] Additionally, the EC has established a compliant system where everyone can submit a complaint about a violation of EU law by a national authority. The EC then decides on taking further actions.[1582] These mechanisms increase the costs of non-compliance that a

1570 Roberto Salvarani, 'EC Directive on Port State Control: A Policy Statement' (1996) 11(2) The International Journal of Marine and Coastal Law 225, 228

1571 ibid

1572 See the recitals to: Council Directive 95/21/EC – concerning the enforcement, in respect of shipping using Community ports and sailing in the waters under the jurisdiction of the Member States, of international standards for ship safety, pollution prevention and shipboard living and working conditions (port State control) 19 June 1995 (Council of the European Union)

1573 Council Directive 95/21/EC concerning the enforcement, in respect of shipping using Community ports and sailing in the waters under the jurisdiction of the Member States, of international standards for ship safety, pollution prevention and shipboard living and working conditions (port State control) (n 1548)

1574 Reiling, *Reiling no date* (n 294) 208; van Leeuwen and Kern (n 1517) 82

1575 Salvarani (n 1570) 228

1576 Özçayir (n 288) 228

1577 Bang and Jang (n 288) 173

1578 Anu Bradford, *The Brussels Effect: How the European Union Rules the World* (Oxford University Press 2020) 31

1579 See Article 337 TFEU

1580 The European Commission initiated proceedings againt Italy for not fully compyling the with Port State Control Directive: *Commission of the European Communities v. Italian Republic* (1999) C-315/98 (Court of Justice of the European Union)

1581 König (n 1359) 9

1582 European Commission, 'How to make a complaint at EU level' <https://commission.europa.eu/about-european-commission/contact/problems-and-complaints/complaints

state must take into account when deciding whether to breach an international obligation, compared to the costs of breaching non-binding IMO instruments. A breach is thus in fewer situations preferable for a state which increases compliance. Thus, supplementing EU legal instruments making non-binding IMO codes mandatory increase their effectiveness and compliance pull.

The possibility of bringing a case before the CJEU not only increases effectiveness, but also ensures a common interpretation, thereby ensuring the greatest possible uniformity.[1583] Article 267(a) TFEU requires a national court to refer a question to the CJEU for a preliminary ruling if it considers that the interpretation of a European instrument is unclear but relevant to the case. Although uniformity is not a necessary condition for the future legal framework for MASS, it supports maritime autonomy. Component suppliers, in particular, benefit from a uniform interpretation across the EU, as their products can be sold throughout the Internal Market without having to comply with divergent national requirements.

Turning back to the EU Port State Control Directive, the increased legal weight of the duty to perform port state controls had a considerable impact on the rate of inspections and performance of controls.[1584] In 2005, the EC started to develop a revised version of the Directive,[1585] which entered into force in 2009.[1586] Shortly after, the Directive was included in the EEA Agreement, extending its scope of application to the states of the European Free Trade Association.[1587] The most relevant innovation was that the EMSA, established in 2002,[1588] was given considerable control powers.[1589]

A study performed in 2018 revealed a dramatic increase in national implementation and concluded that the Port State Control Directive has been successfully implemented by 25 EU and EEA member states.[1590] The European port state control regime is considered as one of the most effective systems in

-about-breaches-eu-law-member-states/how-make-complaint-eu-level_en> accessed 16 February 2024

1583 Gebauer and Berner (n 882) 12

1584 Bang and Jang (n 288) 173

1585 European Commission, 'COM(2005) 588 final – proposal for a Directive on port State control' (Brussels 23 November 2005)

1586 Directive 2009/16/EC of the European Parliament and of the Council on port State control (n 1366)

1587 EEA Joint Committee, 'No 134/2010 – amending Annex XIII (Transport) to the EEA Agreement' (n 304) Article 1(2)

1588 Regulation (EC) No 1406/2002 establishing a European Maritime Safety Agency [2002] Official Journal of the European Communities 45 L 208/1

1589 See Recital 10 of Directive 2009/16/EC and Article 2(b)(I) of Regulation EC No 1406/2002

1590 Graziano, Mejia and Schröder-Hinrichs (n 305) 107

the world for combating substandard shipping. The added legal force to the obligations emanating from the Paris MoU have played a significant role in achieving this result. The conversion of non-binding commitments into legally binding ones through European legal instruments is particularly noteworthy.

The EU not only promoted the implementation of and compliance with non-binding instruments but also supported the implementation of internationally binding conventions. The International Convention on the Control of Harmful Anti-fouling Systems on Ships (AFS Convention) was adopted in 2001 and entered into force in 2008.[1591] However, the EU developed a Regulation on the prohibition of organotin compounds on ships, which became binding for the member states already in 2003.[1592] The Regulation ensured compliance with the deadline for using organotin compounds as biocides in anti-fouling systems, as outlined by the AFS Convention, regardless of the Convention's entry into force. Consequently, the Regulation compelled EU member states to adhere to the previously non-binding Convention when acting as flag states.

However, the EU Regulation did not address the member states as port states, thus vessels calling at EU ports flying a non-EU flag were not affected.[1593] Nevertheless, the timely implementation of the ban on organotin compounds had a significant impact on the environment, as tributyltin[1594] concentrations in European waters already dropped considerably just a few years after the adoption of the EU Regulation.[1595]

Another example from this category is the Ship Recycling Regulation adopted in 2013.[1596] The regulation became effective from 2019 on; however, the Hong Kong Convention[1597] will enter into force on 26 June 2025.[1598] Per

1591 IMO, 'International Convention on the Control of Harmful Anti-fouling Systems on Ships' <https://www.imo.org/en/About/Conventions/Pages/International-Convention-on-the-Control-of-Harmful-Anti-fouling-Systems-on-Ships-(AFS).aspx> accessed 16 February 2024

1592 Regulation (EC) No 782/2003 on the prohibition of organotin compounds on ships [2003] Official Journal of the European Union 46 L 115/1-11

1593 ibid recital 15

1594 Especially coating containing tributyltin are harmful towards the marine environment

1595 Miléne Rato and others, 'Temporal evolution of imposex in Nassarius reticulatus (L.) along the Portuguese coast: the efficacy of EC regulation 782/2003' (2009) 11(1) Journal of Environmental Monitoring 100, 106

1596 Regulation (EU) No 1257/2013 on ship recycling and amending Regulation (EC) No 1013/2006 and Directive 2009/16/EC [2013] Official Journal of the European Union 56 L 330/1

1597 The Hong Kong International Convention for the Safe and Environmentally Sound Recycling of Ships, adopted 15.05.2009 in Hong Kong

1598 IMO, *Hong Kong ship recycling Convention set to enter into force* (2023)

Article 7(2)(a) of the Ship Recycling Regulation, a ship recycling plan has to be developed according to the provisions set out in the Hong Kong Convention. Thus, recycling of EU-flagged vessel has to comply with the requirements included in the Hong Kong Convention seven years before its entry into force.

Additionally, the adoption of unilateral provisions by the EU can strongly encourage IMO law-making.[1599] The legislative process concerning double-hulls for oil tankers illustrates this effect of EU legislation at the IMO level impressively.

Although the transport of crude oil by tanker ships increased sharply in the 1970s, the safety requirements did not rise to the same extent. Consequently, most tankers continued to be designed with a single hull, increasing the risk of significant oil spills in the event of an accident. Being confronted with the unilateral regulation of the U.S.[1600] following the major oil spill caused by the *Exxon Valdez* single-hull oil tanker in 1989, the MEPC amended MARPOL in 1992.[1601] New oil tankers needed to be equipped with a double-hull now. Unlike the U.S. regulation, however, existing tankers were not given an expiration date, rather, an enhanced program of inspection was imposed.

The phasing-out of existing single-hull tankers was accelerated after the *Erika* accident in 1999 off the coast of Bretagne, France. Just 4 months later, the EC proposed a regulation on the accelerated phasing-in of double-hull or equivalent design requirements for single-hull oil tankers,[1602] which was adopted in 2002.[1603] Single-hull tankers were allowed to operate until 2007.[1604] The EU regulation founded on the member states' port state jurisdiction and imposed a ban on oil tankers that the exceed age limits or operation deadlines from entering ports. As the EU is one of the world's largest economies, unilateral legislative acts can effectively regulate global markets. This effect is called the 'Brussels effect'.[1605] Based on a proposal by European states, the

1599 van Leeuwen and Kern (n 1517) 83

1600 Oil Pollution Act, PL 101-380 18 August 1990

1601 MEPC, IMO, 'Res. MEPC.52(32) – Amendments to the Annex of the Protocol of 1978 relating to MARPOL, new regulation 13F and 13G and related amendments to Annex I of MARPOL, 73/78' (London 6 March 1992)

1602 COM(2000) 142 final – Proposal for a regulation of the European Parliament and of the Council on the accelerated phasing-in of double hull or equivalent design requirements for single hull oil tankers 22 March 2000 (European Commission)

1603 Regulation (EC) Nr 417/2002 on the accelerated phasing-in of double hull or equivalent design requirements for single hull oil tankers and repealing Council Regulation (EC) No 2978/94 [2002] Official Journal of the European Communities 45 L 64/1

1604 Article 4(a) of Regulation (EC) No 417/2002

1605 Bradford (n 1578) 13–14

MEPC amended MARPOL to include the same deadlines as the European regulation.[1606]

Shortly afterwards, the *Prestige* accident in November 2000 resulted in changes in the European regulation. The deadline for the operation of single-hull tankers was preponed to 2005.[1607] During the discussions on EU level, all member states and the EC proposed another amendment to MARPOL,[1608] which was adopted in December 2003.[1609] It followed the European regulation.[1610] Eventually, the EU adopted a recasting regulation in 2012.[1611] Scholars examining this legislative process assert that the swift agreement on MARPOL amendments owes much to the presence of unilateral EU regulations, which created a sense of urgency and compelled action.[1612] The same threatening scenario was used to encourage rules on the Sulphur content in certain liquid fuels used for seagoing ships, which are more stringent. Again, the IMO agreed to tighten the regulations to avoid unilateral European standard-setting.[1613]

Transferring this approach to MASS, the EU could adopt an instrument making a non-binding IMO MASS Code binding for the member states acting as flag, coastal, and port states. The EMSA could be involved supporting the EC to ensure compliance and provide guidance for the member states for proper implementation. As the EMSA has already developed European instruments on MASS, the agency is particularly competent to prepare an implementing EU MASS Act.

1606 MEPC, IMO, 'Res. MEPC.95(46) – Amendments to the Annex of the Protocol of 1978 relating to MARPOL, amendments to regulation 13G of Annex I to MARPOL 73/78' (London 27 April 2001)

1607 Regulation (EC) No 1726/2003 – amending Regulation (EC) No 417/2002 on the accelerated phasing-in of double-hull or equivalent design requirements for single-hull oil tankers [2003] Official Journal of the European Union 46 L 249/1

1608 MEPC, IMO, 'MEPC 49/16/1 – Proposed amendments to Annex I of MARPOL 73/78 (Austria, Belgium, Denmark, Finland, France, Germany, Greece, Ireland, Italy, Luxembourg, the Netherlands, Portugal, Spain, Sweden, the United Kingdom and the European Commission)' (London 10 April 2003)

1609 MEPC, IMO, 'Res. MEPC.111(50) – Amendments to regulation 13G, addition of new regulation 13H and consequential amendments to the Supplement to the IOPP Certificate of Annex I to MARPOL 73/78' (London 4 December 2003)

1610 van Leeuwen and Kern (n 1517) 81

1611 Regulation (EU) No 530/2012 of the European Parliament and of the Council of 13 June 2012 on the accelerated phasing-in of double-hull or equivalent design requirements for single-hull oil tankers [2012] Official Journal of the European Union 55 L 172/3

1612 Frank (n 1338), 22; van Leeuwen and Kern (n 1517), 81; Nengye and Maes Frank (n 1527) 590

1613 van Leeuwen and Kern (n 1517) 81

From a technical and economic perspective, short-sea shipping represents the most promising business case for MASS in the short and medium term. Nevertheless, global voyages are imminent, thus the establishment of a harmonized legal framework on a regional basis represents merely the initial step in meeting the needs of the MASS industry. The proposed EU MASS Act would only add binding legal force and details about the implementation. All substantial provisions would be included in the non-binding IMO MASS Code having worldwide impact.

The prospect of a binding instrument at the European level could encourage the IMO's legislative process and facilitate the adoption of stringent safety rules for MASS. To recall, the MASS Code currently under development at the IMO includes provisions on the interpretation of key terms in the GAIRAS conventions and additional, MASS-specific provisions. Additionally, each MASS would be issued a MASS-certificate after an initial or renewal survey.[1614] Despite the considerable progress already made by the IMO, further engagement is required to ensure that the deadline for the adoption of a binding code by 2026 is met. Currently, diverging preferences among IMO member states, coupled with concurrent legislative projects vying for the IMO's attention, pose a significant threat to the achievement of the ambitious goal.

In addition to the possible rapid adoption of European legislative instruments, the adoption of an implementing EU act would ensure the necessary flexibility. As the legislative history on double-hull tankers has shown, the EU is able to react quickly to new developments. Preliminary, new provisions could be adopted at the EU level, paired with a joint proposal at the IMO level to amend the MASS Code. As any amendment to the MASS Code adopted by the IMO would automatically be included in the EU MASS Act, there would be two options for updating.

Such an EU act could contribute to a harmonized level playing field within the EU greatly facilitating the operation of MASS in this region. The instrument would oblige flag states to adhere to the MASS Code if registering MASS. Port states, in turn, would need to accept the MASS-certificate issued by another member state and would be prevented from imposing additional national requirements on MASS calling at their ports.

Coastal states could also be addressed. Coastal states have to ensure the right of innocent passage; however, Article 21(2) of the UNCLOS grants coastal states the right to impose national laws giving effect to GAIRAS. The coastal state must observe EU law when exercising its rights under international law.

1614 MSC, IMO, 'MSC 107/WP.9: Report of the MASS-Working Group' (London 7 June 2023) Annex 1, p. 4

This duty arises from the duty of sincere cooperation, which includes refraining from any act that could undermine the effectiveness of EU law.[1615] Any interpretation of the GAIRAS treaties that conflicts with the adopted MASS Code would undermine the effectiveness of the EU MASS Act and would therefore be prohibited. Therefore, a binding MASS Code at EU level would prevent a coastal state from adopting prohibitive national legislation on the construction, design, equipment and manning of the ship.

As illustrated, the EC, supported by the EMSA, has a great tool-box of measures to take to ensure effective implementation of EU law. An EU legal instrument making the MASS Code binding for the member states would ensure thorough implementation and non-compliance could be penalized efficiently. Ship operators could be assured that flag, coastal, and port states apply the same MASS-including interpretation of the GAIRAS treaties. Thus, the need for legal certainty could be met with an implementing EU legal act.

Particular for Europe, a legally binding MASS Code would be beneficial. As MASS will most likely be used on short-sea rather than deep-sea shipping routes in the near future, the North Sea and the Baltic Sea are particularly interesting areas of operation. Due to its geographical situation, Europe could initially benefit more from a legally binding MASS Code than other world regions. The interests of the stakeholders involved would therefore be sufficiently taken into account if there were an internationally non-binding but regionally binding set of rules.

Additionally, an EU legal act would have a higher degree of democratic legitimacy than a binding IMO instrument. Despite the EU's complex structure and far-reaching competencies, it is built upon the principle of state sovereignty rather than the sovereignty of the people.[1616] The institutionalizing treaties were adopted by state representatives and ratified according to national procedures.[1617] In this aspect, the EU is not distinct from any other international organization, including the IMO. Although the degree of democratic legitimization has increased since its foundation in 1957, legitimacy is primarily

---

1615 Wolfgang Kahl, 'Article 4 TEU' in Christian Calliess and Matthias Ruffert (eds), EUV/AEUV: *Das Verfassungsrecht der Europäischen Union mit Europäischer Grundrechtecharta: Kommentar* (6. Auflage. C.H. Beck 2022) 168

1616 Dieter Grimm, 'Zum Stand der demokratischen Legitimation der Europäischen Union nach Lissabon' in Nabila Abbas, Annette Förster and Emanuel Richter (eds), *Supranationalität und Demokratie: Die Europäische Union in Zeiten der Krise* (Staat – Souveränität – Nation, 1. Aufl. Springer VS 2014) 19

1617 In 2007, the Treaty on European Union and the Treaty on the Functioning of the European Union were adopted. Both entered into force in 2009

conferred by national parliaments and governments and is only supplemented by the legitimacy conferred by the European Parliament.[1618]

Recalling the ordinary legislative procedure stipulated by Articles 289(1), 294 TFEU, the European Parliament and the Council cooperate and adopt a legal instrument jointly. Although the European Parliament is not able to represent the body of sovereign European people as a national parliament represents its sovereign,[1619] the involvement of the European Parliament, which is directly elected by the European people, increases the legitimacy of European legal acts. Additionally, the Council is composed of members from national governments, directly accountable to the national parliaments.[1620] In addition, several member states have introduced an obligation for governments to inform their respective national parliaments of ongoing negotiations in the council. In Germany, the Act on Cooperation between the Federal Government and the German Bundestag in Matters concerning the European Union[1621] stipulates an obligation for the government to inform the parliament about any matters concerning the EU. In urgent matters, the European Affairs Committee is entitled to exercise the parliaments' rights.[1622] In summary, Article 10 TEU establishes a dual legitimation model for European legal acts, which differs according to the legislative procedure.[1623]

At the IMO, however, only the MSC adopts the MASS Code. Therefore, decisions are not legitimized by a double track. Furthermore, technical experts or lower-level public servants represent most states at the IMO.[1624] These representatives are neither directly accountable to national parliaments nor elected by the people.

1618 *Lissabon* (2009) 2 BvE 2/08 262 (German Constitutional Court)

1619 ibid 280

1620 See Article 19(2) Treaty on European Union

1621 Gesetz über die Zusammenarbeit von Bundesregierung und Deutschem Bundestag in Angelegenheiten der Europäischen Union (EUZBBG) 4 July 2013 (Deutscher Bundestag)

1622 See on the involvement of the European Affairs Committee of the German Bundestag in EU matters: Heike Baddenhausen, 'Ausschuss für die Angelegenheiten der Europäischen Union' in Martin Morlok, Utz Schliesky and (Keine Angabe) (eds), *Parlamentsrecht: Praxishandbuch* (1. Auflage. Nomos 2016)

1623 Jelena von Achenbach, *Demokratische Gesetzgebung in der Europäischen Union: Theorie und Praxis der dualen Legitimationsstruktur europäischer Hoheitsgewalt* (Beiträge zum ausländischen öffentlichen Recht und Völkerrecht vol 248, Springer 2014) 313

1624 View the list of participants at the 2023 MSC meeting. The majority of representatives are public servants from national transport ministries or shipping agencies: MSC, IMO, 'MSC 107/INF.1' (n 1157)

Comparing these two chains of legitimation, it becomes apparent that the IMO instruments are much less legitimized than EU legal acts.[1625] In order to ensure that ethical considerations in relation to autonomous shipping are taken into due account and to achieve a high level of social acceptance, it is recommended that the legal instrument providing for the first time for the general authorization of autonomous shipping should have a high degree of legitimacy. An EU legal instrument can provide the necessary degree of legitimacy.

Moreover, public consultations and low-threshold participation opportunities such as the "Have your say" initiative of the EC[1626] enable participation of a great number of stakeholders. This can be particularly relevant in the area of MASS. The advent of autonomous shipping is a revolutionary change in the shipping sector that affects numerous stakeholders. To ensure societal acceptance and a co-evolution of law and technology, it is important to involve as many stakeholders as possible in the legislative procedure. Although the IMO includes non-state actors as advisors, the formalized participation process at the IMO does not allow for the involvement of regional organizations, which are particularly affected by MASS operating on short-sea shipping routes.

To summarize, an EU act implementing an IMO instrument and making it binding for the EU member states entails several advantages. Not only would legal certainty and predictability be increased, but it would also be possible to respond flexibly to new experiences and regional particularities. The act would ensure a level playing field within the Union and have a high degree of legitimacy.

Although the EU has often overtaken the IMO in terms of regulation, the EU has rarely made instruments binding that were intended to remain non-binding at the IMO level.[1627] Usually, the EU has acted to anticipate the entry into force of an IMO instrument or international treaty. However, Regulation 725/2004 on enhancing ship and port facility safety[1628] makes Part B of the ISPS Code mandatory by Article 3(4). Part B of the ISPS Code, however, is intended to remain non-binding as stipulated by Regulation XI-2/1.1.12 of SOLAS. Thus,

1625 See for a comparison of nine regional economic organizations in respect of democratic legitimacy: Francesco Duina and Tobias Lenz, 'Democratic legitimacy in regional economic organizations: the European Union in comparative perspective' (2017) 46(3–4) Economy and Society 398, 412

1626 European Commission, 'Welcome to Have your say' <https://ec.europa.eu/info/law/better-regulation/have-your-say_en> accessed 16 February 2024

1627 See for some rare examples: Ringbom, *Ringbom 2008* (n 675) 250–251

1628 Regulation (EC) No 725/2004 on enhancing ship and port facility security [2004] Official Journal of the European Union 47 L 129/6

the EU has already applied the proposed approach and made a non-binding part of a Code mandatory.

In addition to making the MASS Code mandatory, the EU could include more detailed provisions on the registration process and the validation of equipment and components. The EU has already applied such an approach for marine equipment[1629] to harmonize the safety requirements for marine equipment among the member states.[1630] To facilitate cross-border usage of marine equipment, Directive 2014/90 provides for harmonized safety standards for marine equipment installed on board a vessel flying the flag of an EU member state. The same could be done for safety requirements for MASS-specific equipment. It would not only facilitate that MASS could be more easily operated and registered in other member states, but would also further the market for MASS components and equipment. Article 8(2) of Directive 2014/90/EU, empowering the EC to adopt technical standards if such standards are not available at the international level, but necessary to remove a serious threat to maritime safety, could be taken as a role model for the EU MASS Act. The EC would thus adopt technical standards as delegated legal acts.

It was proposed that the EU act could address port states and ensure that port states accept MASS certificates issued by another EU member state. As the question of acceptance of certificates arises during port state controls, it will be necessary to amend the Port State Control Directive simultaneously.[1631] Within the scope of Article 2 of this Directive, the MASS Code, as a non-binding IMO Code, should be included in the scope of the list of instruments with which compliance will be assessed during port state control.

For MASS, verification of the navigation and operating systems is of particular importance. It is crucial to ensure that the navigation algorithm adheres to COLREG, even in unforeseeable situations. In addition, it must be ensured that collision avoidance is given the highest priority. In exceptional situations collisions avoidance has to take precedence over literal COLREG compliance.[1632] As there are no technical standards available for MASS currently, the verification should be based on a risk assessment to identify potential risks and mitigate them as far as possible. For this process, a risk assessment methodology

1629 Directive 2014/90/EU on marine equipment and repealing Council Directive 96/98/EG [2014] Official Journal of the European Union 57 L 257/146

1630 See recitals 1 and 2 of Directive 2014/90

1631 Directive 2009/16/EC of the European Parliament and of the Council on port State control (n 1366)

1632 This is necessary to comply with Rule 2(a) of COLREG, which requires a departure from the rules in accordance with the practice of ordinary seamen if compliance would result in a collision

was prepared by EMSA and submitted to the IMO.[1633] The IMO MASS Code stipulates that the flag state can chose among different assessment methodologies[1634] including the European and a methodology submitted by China.[1635] The EU MASS act could make the EU's methodology binding for the EU member states acting as flag states.

The EU has already opted for implementing IMO instruments on MASS and adding more detailed provisions. The EU adopted supporting implementation provisions for MASS trials[1636] referring to the IMO Interim Guidelines on MASS trials.[1637] The EU guidelines, however, provided more details and reflecting regional particularities such as the elements to be considered for identifying test areas. The same approach could be applied to the IMO MASS Code.

Given the history of legislative cooperation between the EU and the IMO, unilateral action by the EU has not always been welcomed. In particular, the IMO and international academics pointed to the risk that a global consensus reached in the IMO could be rendered obsolete if the EU adopted more stringent rules on the same subject.[1638] As the EU is one of the world's largest economies and a major import market, unilateral action can effectively regulate the global shipping industry.[1639] The regulatory process on double-hull tankers has demonstrated this effect. Despite international criticism, the EU has continued to shape international shipping unilaterally. Most recently, the inclusion of shipping in the European Emission Trading System[1640] has surpassed the efforts of the IMO.[1641]

1633 MSC, IMO, 'MSC 107/5/4' (n 1490)

1634 MSC, IMO, 'MSC 107/20' (n 375) 5.13

1635 MSC, IMO, 'MSC 106/5/3: Proposal for incorporation of risk assessment into MASS instrument (China)' (London 30 August 2022)

1636 European Commission, 'EU Operational Guidelines for Safe, Secure and Sustainable Trials of Maritime Autonomous Surface Ships (MASS)' (n 1489)

1637 MSC, IMO, 'MSC.1/Circ.1604' (n 1046)

1638 Ringbom, *Ringbom 2008* (n 675) 252

1639 Nengye and Maes Frank (n 1527) 590; Bradford (n 1578) 29

1640 See Articles 3ga et sequentes of: Directive (EU) 2023/959 amending Directive 2003/87/EC establishing a system for greenhouse gas emission allowance trading within the Union and Decision (EU) 2015/1814 concerning the establishment and operation of a market stability reserve for the Union greenhouse gas emission trading system [2023] Official Journal of the European Union 66 L 130/134

1641 Ellen J Eftestøl and Emilie Yliheljo, 'International Shipping: Who Levels the Playing Field?' in Abhinayan B Bal (ed), *Regulation of Risk: Transport, Trade and Environment in Perspective* (International Law E-Books Online, Collection 2023. Brill|Nijhoff 2022)

However, the MASS Code stands apart from prior instances in a pivotal manner: it does not impose more stringent requirements on ongoing shipping operations but instead facilitates the integration of innovative technologies. New technology would be integrated without excluding existing technology. It is about enabling more, not excluding what already exists. In contrast, the examples given on double-hull tankers and Sulphur emissions were about setting stricter standards at the EU level than at the IMO level. This would not be the case with the MASS Code. Thus, the EU MASS legislation is not expected to be subject to the same criticism as other EU legislation on IMO regulated aspects.

After discussing and affirming the appropriateness of an EU legal act making a non-binding IMO MASS Code mandatory, it will be considered whether a directive, a regulation, or a recommendation would be most appropriate.

To recall, a regulation is binding in its entirety and directly applicable in all member states. Directives, in contrast, are binding with respect to the result to be achieved. The member states can chose the form and method to achieve the set result.[1642] In accordance with the principle of proportionality, the European institutions select the type of act to be adopted on a case-by-case basis where the treaties do not provide for it.[1643] The principle of proportionality requires the institutions to "not exceed what is necessary to achieve the objectives of the Treaties".[1644] The aim is to preserve the sovereignty of the member states as far as possible. A directive is therefore generally considered less interventionist than a regulation.[1645]

Thus far, the EU has enacted 26 regulations and 36 directives pertaining to shipping matters.[1646] Given that the EU MASS Act aims to make the IMO MASS Code legally binding and to establish standards for the registration process, including the risk assessment methodology and verification details, a regulation may be preferable to ensure uniformity. Moreover, regulations are directly applicable in all member states, bypassing the phase of national implementation and achieving a uniform legal framework more quickly.

1642 See Article 288 TFEU

1643 See Article 296 TFEU

1644 See Article 5(4) TEU

1645 Martin Gellermann, 'Article 296 TFEU' in Rudolf Streinz and others (eds), EUV/AEUV: *Vertrag über die Europäische Union, Vertrag über die Arbeitsweise der Europäischen Union, Charta der Grundrechte der Europäischen Union* (Beck-Online Bücher Band 57, 3. Auflage. C.H. Beck 2018) 3

1646 European Maritime Safety Agency, 'Legislative Texts' <https://www.emsa.europa.eu/publications/legislative-texts.html>

In contrast, a directive would have to be implemented by the member states, requiring a vacatio legis of usually 2 years. Thus, the readiness of the legal framework is delay. However, national sovereignty is less affected. Although it may seem contradictory at first, the EU has often been able to achieve standardization through a directive. Articles 1 and 15(1) of the Marine Equipment Directive[1647] ensure the uniform application of relevant international instruments relating to marine equipment and that all marine equipment placed on board vessels flying the flag of an EU member state is assessed by a notified body. However, member states can designate the notifying bodies and decide which national instrument to choose for implementation. This example demonstrates that standardization through directives is possible. Likewise, port state controls could be harmonized by a directive.

For MASS, a directive could provide a reliable and timely legal framework. The IMO MASS Code would include the substantial provisions, and member states would have the freedom to choose how to make them mandatory at the national level. It is unnecessary to prescribe the procedure for registration at the European level from a harmonization perspective, as each member state already has a legal system for registering ships. Moreover, regulating the registration of MASS through a specific regulation, while excluding conventional vessels, could lead to confusion and the application of different procedures in parallel. To ensure the smoothest possible integration of MASS into conventional shipping, it is advisable to apply the same registration procedure to MASS as to conventional vessels, adapting only certain verification procedures. The standards that a MASS and its equipment must meet should be stipulated at the European level. This can be achieved through a European directive.

The EU directive would enter into force two years later than a regulation, as the member states require a period of time to implement the directive. Nevertheless, the technical challenges that must be overcome before MASS can be operated on a large scale render the delay in providing a binding legal framework less significant. Moreover, member states having a particular interest in MASS could adopt their national law earlier.

To conclude, the EU has the competence to adopt legislative acts on maritime shipping. Both, free movement of services and goods as well as maritime safety can be addressed by European acts. A self-standing EU act was rejected due to time and resource constraints and reluctance of the EU member states to adopt a parallel regime to the one developed by the IMO. However, a European instrument implementing a non-binding IMO MASS Code was deemed

1647 Directive 2014/90/EU on marine equipment and repealing Council Directive 96/98/EG (n 1629)

appropriate. This section examined past EU-IMO co-legislative acts and could determine that implementing EU acts considerably contribute to the effectiveness of non-binding or binding IMO instruments. Moreover, the appropriateness of a regional regulation for the North and Baltic Sea was highlighted.

The proposed EU Directive making the IMO MASS Code legally binding could additionally add more detailed provisions on the registration and verification process. Particular, the risk-based assessment methodology developed by the EMSA could be made mandatory. Moreover, the Port State Control Directive could be amended to include the MASS Code in the scope of port state controls and ensure the recognition of MASS-certificates.

Eventually, the implications of EU legal acts for the member states of the EEA shall be touched upon briefly. As can be seen from the presentation of national research and legislative projects, Norway plays a globally leading role in respect of MASS. As Norway is not a member state of the EU, EU acts do not apply directly to Norway. However, the effectiveness of any EU act on MASS would increase if it had a legal effect in Norway. Inversely, Norway could be interested in harmonizing its own regulations with those adopted by the EU, as the EU member states are important import and export trading partners of Norway.[1648]

Norway is part of the European Free Trade Association (EFTA). Three EFTA states form together with the EU member states the EEA.[1649] The EEA Agreement[1650] entered into force in 1994 and it extends the EU Internal Market to the EEA/EFTA states. As all EU member states are subject to EU legislation, the EEA/EFTA states need to adopt such EU legislation that is relevant to the common trade in the EEA. Based on a decision of the EEA Joint Committee, all EU acts with EEA relevance are continuously incorporated into the Annex of the EEA Agreement[1651] and they acquire binding force pursuant to Article 7 of the EEA Agreement. Acts corresponding to an EU regulation shall be directly applicable in the EEA/EFTA states, whereas acts corresponding to an EU directive shall be binding with regard to the goal, but not the form and method of implementation.

1648 Statistisk sentralbyrå, 'Utenrikshandel med varer' (15 February 2024) Tabell 4 <https://www.ssb.no/utenriksokonomi/utenrikshandel/statistikk/utenrikshandel-med-varer> accessed 16 February 2024

1649 Switzerland is a member states of the EFTA, but not of the EEA

1650 Agreement on the European Economic Area 1994

1651 See for an overview of the implementation procedure: Standing Committee of the EFTA States, 'How EU acts become EEA acts and the need for adaptations' (Geneva, Brussels 23 May 2013) Ref. 1113623

An EU legal act is EEA relevant if one of the areas covered by the EEA Agreement is affected by the act. As illustrated above, transport is included in the EEA Agreement as part of the free movement of services. Moreover, Annex XIII to the EEA Agreement makes most EU maritime acts applicable to the EEA/EFTA states and Annex II includes EU acts on technical standardization. Particularly, both referenced acts, Directive 2014/90 on standards for the verification of marine equipment[1652] and Regulation 725/2004 on ship and port facility security[1653] have been implemented in the EEA agreement. As a MASS Act will affect the free movement of goods, people, and services, a MASS Act is relevant for the Internal Market and is thus deemed to have EEA relevance. It should be noted that the EEA/EFTA states are members of the EMSA,[1654] though without a right to vote.

The UK, a leading state in promoting maritime autonomy withdrew from the EU in 2020. The withdrawal agreement[1655] does not contain any provisions on the application of post-2020 EU laws in the UK. Thus, the EU MASS Directive would not be applicable in the UK. The UK is not a member state of the EFTA or the EEA, thus the EEA Agreement does not apply to the UK. Nevertheless, the UK could pass a corresponding piece of domestic legislation.

5.5.4 *Conclusions*

This section explored the potential of European regulation of MASS. The EU has shared internal competence based on Article 100(2) TFEU to adopt instruments on MASS addressing maritime safety aspects. Corresponding external competence arises from Articles 3(2), 216(1) TFEU. However, it could not be ultimately determined whether the external competence is exclusive or shared between the EU and its member states. Some aspects of an international MASS Convention fall undoubtedly in the scope of exclusive EU competence, such as qualification requirements. Other aspects, however, such as the design of the RCC or equipment necessary on board MASS are not so easy to categorize.

1652 EEA Joint Committee, 'Decision No 163/2016 amending Annex II (Technical regulations, standards, testing and certification) to the EEA Agreement [2018/384]' (Brussels 26 August 2016)

1653 EEA Joint Committee, 'Decision No 14/2005 – amending Annex XIII (Transport) to the EEA Agreement' (Brussels 8 February 2005)

1654 EEA Joint Committee, 'No. 81/2003 – amending Annex XIII (Transport) to the EEA Agreement' (20 June 2003)

1655 Agreement on the withdrawal of the United Kingdom of Great Britain and Northern Ireland from the European Union and the European Atomic Energy Community 12 November 2019 (European Union; European Atomic Energy Community; United Kingdom)

Thus, it is proposed here that an international MASS Convention should be concluded as a mixed agreement, involving the EU and its member states.

The study went further to explore self-standing EU legal acts on MASS. The advantages, particularly the accelerated negotiation process, and the measure available to ensure compliance have been pointed out. Nevertheless, the lead of the IMO in regulating MASS and the limited personnel capacities of the EMSA make it rather unlikely that the EU will adopt a self-standing instrument on MASS. Additionally, the risk of hampering the negotiations at the IMO by developing unilateral measures was considered. Eventually, this proposal was rejected.

As an alternative, the discussion centered on the adoption of a European legal instrument implementing a non-binding IMO MASS Code. Most European maritime legal instruments refer to instruments adopted by the IMO or otherwise at the international level. Therefore, making a non-binding MASS Code binding at the European level would fit perfectly with the existing IMO EU co-legislation. The benefits of implementing such acts were highlighted, with a focus on their potential to promote legislative acts at the IMO and increase compliance by the EU member states. Examples of successful EU IMO co-legislation were cited, including the regulatory approach to double-hull oil tankers and Sulphur emissions. Unilateral European approaches have been criticized for potentially undermining the internationally agreed consensus and implementing regulations that are more stringent without an international counterpart. It is important to note that due to the economic power of the EU, unilateral acts have a significant impact on global shipping. However, regarding MASS, it is not a question of stricter regulations, but one of more generous ones. The EU will allow MASS operations in its waters, which may not be possible in other countries' territorial waters. Therefore, it is unlikely that a unilateral instrument on MASS, which would make the non-binding IMO Code binding, would receive the same level of criticism as other measures.

In terms of instruments, recommendations, directives, and regulations were compared. Given the importance of a binding solution and the principle of proportionality, a directive was considered most appropriate to make an IMO MASS Code legally binding. Although a directive needs to be implemented nationally, it is less intrusive in national legal orders. By incorporating the IMO MASS Code subsequent changes are automatically included making an amendment process superfluous. Additionally, the EC and the EMSA could be empowered to adopt delegated legal acts providing for technical details and verification methodologies.

As a final point, the impact of an EU act on the EEA/EFTA states was considered. This was necessary to ensure that Norway, as a world-leading maritime autonomy nation, would be included in the geographical scope of the proposed MASS Directive. The MASS Directive is relevant to the Internal Market and the free movement of services, goods, and people. Therefore, the act is assumed relevant to the EEA. Consequently, the MASS Directive would be included in the EEA agreement, extending its scope of application to all EEA/EFTA states, including Norway. The UK, though a leading maritime autonomy nation, cannot be included, as the Withdrawal Agreement does not provide for a clause on the application of post-Brexit EU legislation. However, the UK could align its national legislation with the act adopted by the EU.

Conclusions and Outlook

This section summarizes the foregoing parts, contextualizes the findings, and gives an outlook on the future development of regulating autonomous vessels.

The international commercial shipping sector is facing a shortage of competent personnel and increased costs due to the green transition. In this scenario, autonomy is being used as a tool to improve efficiency, to overcome the shortage of labor and to create the economic margin to invest in zero-emission propulsion systems. Thus, autonomous vessels are situated at the intersection of digitalization, autonomization, and more sustainable, environmentally friendly shipping.

Autonomy refers to the ability to react to unforeseen situations in a human-like manner, as opposed to automation. Autonomous systems do not follow strict predetermined if-then commands. Instead, they use artificial intelligence and deep learning algorithms to deduce an appropriate reaction based on previous experiences and learning data. Although means of automation are indispensable for modern shipping operations, autonomy has not yet captured the bridges of commercial vessels. Implementing autonomy in the international commercial shipping sector is challenging from a technical, engineering, management, and legal point of view.

Technical research projects have demonstrated that autonomous shipping technology is gaining ground and that, from a technical perspective, it is foreseeable that autonomous vessels will be viable for commercial use within the next 5–8 years. Most likely, the first commercial autonomous vessels will be deployed on regional shipping routes linking geographically proximate ports. Deep-sea voyages, meanwhile, are on the horizon, albeit further away. Autonomous short-sea shipping services bring about several benefits, such as more flexible and resilient fleet solutions and the possibility to relieve congested roads and support modal shift.

As the implementation of deep learning algorithms and autonomy allows for the handover of core vessel functions, such as navigation and propulsion, to autonomous systems, constant human presence on board the vessel becomes unnecessary. The master and crew can be relocated ashore to a remote control center (RCC). To guarantee safe operation, especially in cases of communication loss, vessel operations without a human presence on board require a certain degree of autonomy. Depending on the degree and scope of autonomy, a vessel can be either remotely controlled by humans or autonomously controlled and supervised by a human. This study referenced the IMO term 'Maritime Autonomous Surface Ships' (MASS) and the associated degrees of

 | DOI:10.1163/9789004729483_007

autonomy. Degree three – remote operation without crew on board – and degree four – fully autonomous operation without crew on board – were of specific interest for this legal analysis.

Although MASS are not expected to operate on a global scale in the near future, the international law of the sea applies as soon as a MASS operates in the territorial waters of more than one state. It is necessary to integrate MASS into the existing regulatory framework for international commercial vessel operations, given their purpose of transporting cargo between different ports. Although some states have already prepared their respective national regulatory frameworks for autonomous vessel trials and preliminary operations, an international solution has not yet been found.

International law of the sea has a three-tier structure. Above all, UNCLOS governs all marine shipping activities and coordinates flag, coastal, and port states' rights. A finely tuned zonal management ensures that the freedom of navigation is balanced against the territorial jurisdiction of coastal and port states. Ports are not governed by UNCLOS and port states have exclusive jurisdiction over vessels calling their ports. For detailed regulations on shipping, UNCLOS refers to generally accepted international rules and standards developed by the IMO.

Since its foundation, the IMO actively shaped international shipping law and contributed to increased law-making activities. Most of the international maritime conventions, i.e. SOLAS, COLREG, STCW, and MARPOL are administered by the IMO. In order to ensure uniform implementation, several secondary legal instruments such as codes, guidelines, recommendations, unified interpretations, and circulars were adopted by the IMO. As the IMO resembles almost universal participation, it was stage of conflicts between cargo and ship owning states, ship owning and flag states, and flag and coastal states. Ever since, the IMO aimed at finding a consensus among diverting interest for the sake of global uniformity.

Following the general rule of interpretation laid down in Article 31 of the VCLT this study concluded that MASS fit into the GAIRAS conventions[1656] and UNCLOS. First, the fundamental question of whether MASS fall within the scope of the terms 'ship' and 'vessel' was answered in the affirmative. The definition of ship and vessel does not include the presence of competent personnel on board or the exclusive control by humans. Consequently, MASS can be registered with a flag state, obtain the flag state's nationality, and enjoy the freedom of navigation as granted by UNCLOS.

1656 GAIRAS refers to 'generally accepted international rules and standards'. The term 'GAIRAS Conventions' includes SOLAS, COLREG, and STCW

Second, MASS adhere to the concept of seaworthiness in its public law dimension, which encompasses navigation safety, safety of life at sea, and the duty to render assistance to persons in distress at sea.

The safety of navigation ensures that the vessel operates without causing collisions or close-quarter situations and complies with the GAIRAS conventions. This implies that vessels have to ensure a proper lookout, compliance with the navigation rules provided for in COLREG, and the ordinary practice of seaman, radio communications, proper response to vessel traffic services and ships' routeing systems as well as the manning of the vessel. Having a purpose-based regulation in mind and reflecting on available technical solutions it is concluded that MASS can navigate safely. Human presence is not necessary, nor is autonomous control prevented. However, some human involvement is necessary, particularly for synchronous radio communications. The manning requirement does not necessitate a human presence on board. Although each vessel must be in charge of a master and competent crew, this requirement is met by assigning each vessel to a suitably qualified remote operator. The STCW Convention that requires a human presence on board the navigation bridge does not apply to remote operators.

The safety of life at sea is of less relevance for MASS operating at degree three and four as no humans on board are exposed to the perils at sea. Although SOLAS stipulates the presence of life-saving appliances on board each vessel for crew members, regulations are available that allow the acceptance of alternative designs and arrangements. Thus, MASS operating at degree three and four can ensure the safety of life at sea.

Like conventional vessels, MASS are obliged to render assistance to people in distress at sea. Unlike conventional ships, MASS are not inherently equipped to provide assistance to people in distress. Although practical and technical constraints make rescue operations for MASS particularly challenging, humanitarian and societal reasons require MASS to be equipped with lifesaving appliances for people in distress and installations to recover people from distress at sea. Consequently, MASS can fulfill the obligation to render assistance to people in distress at sea.

Thus, the international legal framework established by the GAIRAS conventions and UNCLOS can be interpreted in a way including MASS. None of the provisions needs to be changed. However, additional provisions on MASS specific aspects such as qualification requirements for remote operators, the design and equipment of RCCs, and matters related to cybersecurity need to be developed. Both, primary, abstract-general legislation as well as secondary, supplementing instruments are needed. Moreover, legal instruments need to be developed to ensure a common understanding and harmonized interpretation of the conventions discussed above. Relying on flag, coastal, and port states to interpret the international legal framework similarly and including MASS does not provide a solid legal basis for the needed investments in autonomous technology and the operation of MASS. The need for new legal instruments was addressed in the fourth part. Various regulatory instruments were analyzed to determine the most appropriate way of accommodating MASS within the current international legal framework.

The future legal framework for MASS needs to reflect the novelty of autonomous maritime technology and its ongoing development. Innovative technology often challenges long-standing traditions, which requires reflection on the meaning and importance of conventional legal concepts. Regulating innovative technology requires regulation under uncertainty. The earlier a predictable legal framework is established, the better technology can align with it. However, if the framework is developed later, it can better reflect the peculiarities of the technology concerned and does not hinder the freedom to innovate. This dilemma can be addressed by the co-evolution of law and technology.

For MASS legal certainty, predictability and flexibility need be provided without limiting innovative freedom or locking-in technical solutions. To achieve this goal, MASS regulations should be formulated in a goal-based manner. Furthermore, MASS should be integrated into the current global legal framework for shipping, despite not being expected to operate on a global scale in the near future. This requirement rules out national approaches and necessitates an international strategy. Ultimately, a new framework must be established promptly to avoid hindering innovation and impeding the desirable operation of MASS. However, when comparing regulatory approaches to MASS, it is important to balance technical enthusiasm with legal sobriety. This is due to the progress of research projects and the expected benefits of MASS.

Concerning the legal character, soft law and hard law solution complement each other. The absence of coercive enforcement mechanisms in international law implies that soft and hard law solutions are almost equally effective. Based on rational choice theory, states comply with international law if compliance results in utility maximization. Moreover, international organizations such as the IMO were established to reduce transaction costs and effectively regulate public goods such as the freedom of navigation. For this purpose, international organizations are equipped with sovereignty rights to adopt binding regulations for their member states. However, transferring sovereignty to international organizations is costly for states and must be outweighed by the benefits of delegated lawmaking.

International law offers various alternatives for adjusting legal frameworks to changes. Besides non-binding instruments adopted by the IMO, binding amendments to treaties, new binding instruments, and customary international law are available. With regard to MASS, various approaches deserve a closer look. The IMO deals with MASS since 2017 and works on a non-binding code for MASS, which shall be adopted in 2025. At the IMO level, this instrument is the most suitable as it can provide a comprehensive set of rules and address multiple conventions simultaneously. In this context, the activities of the IMO are to be welcomed.

However, in the case of a non-binding instrument, legal certainty takes a back seat. Therefore, additional means to adopt a binding set of rules for MASS were discussed. Even if it seems appropriate at first glance, an amendment to SOLAS and COLREG is rejected. Both amendment procedures, the tacit acceptance procedure as well as the formal amendment procedure, implicate considerable drawbacks. The tacit acceptance procedure was developed to adapt minor technical details in the annexes to subsequent developments. Even if technical details need to be adapted for MASS, the fundamental question of whether autonomous navigation and vessel operations without a human presence on board should be possible goes beyond the scope of technical details. This question is of a more basic nature. It is not advisable to extend the tacit acceptance procedure beyond its intended scope and to use it to make the MASS Code legally binding as an annex to SOLAS. Although the formal amendment procedure would be appropriate for the MASS amendments in terms of scope, it is rejected because of the time-consuming negotiation and ratification process.

Moreover, an amendment to SOLAS, despite the procedure used, cannot ensure the necessary horizontal integration across several conventions. The same applies to an amendment of COLREG, which is likewise rejected due to the long ratification period and the inability to ensure a horizontal, coherent regulatory approach across several conventions. In addition, an amendment to UNCLOS is not expectable and deemed inappropriate.

Neither is it appropriate to develop a MASS Convention. An intricate negotiation and ratification process outweighs the benefits of a comprehensive and global convention. Although the initial entry into force could be accelerated by waiving the requirement to achieve a certain number of ratifications, this cannot be extended to subsequent amendments in order to maintain consistency. Thus, a MASS Convention is inflexible. Other means of international law, a decision of a Conference of States Parties, customary international law, and subsequent practice are inappropriate for the purpose of MASS.

In contrast to most scholars, international regulation was not considered without any alternative. The claim "international regulation for international shipping" was not taken as given, but scrutinized against the backdrop of ongoing regional research projects. Ever increased globalization betrayed legal scholars into focusing on international law to combat global challenges. This approach shall not be criticized or trivialized. However, reflections on whether a global solution is most appropriate should not be left aside. Considering the particularities of autonomous shipping, the regional level seamed more appropriate for providing a binding legal framework than the international level. Regulatory cooperation between European states on MASS trials and extended experiments prove the feasibility of a European regulatory approach to MASS.

There are several regional fora dealing with marine matters. However, only the Nordic Cooperation and port state control cooperation are considered potentially beneficial for regulating MASS. The Paris MoU has proven its ability to increase compliance with international law substantially. Nevertheless, it is inappropriate to introduce new substantial provisions and therefore not suitable for the necessary MASS regulations. Yet, it should be amended to include any new MASS instruments in the scope of port state controls within the Paris MoU region.

Nordic Cooperation is based on a long tradition of cooperation between the five Nordic countries. Shipping in particular has been approached from a Nordic rather than a national perspective. In this sense, a common maritime code was the first prestigious project of Nordic legal cooperation at the end of the 19th century, and the code is still considered a Nordic project today. Moreover, projects on green shipping and sustainable transport by water have gained ground in the last years and most research projects on autonomous vessels are located in the Nordic states. Although this could have been a promising basis for a regulation on MASS, discussions with representatives of the relevant ministries revealed that a Nordic solo effort is not expected. Rather, international rules would have to be developed, at least at the European level. In addition, a comprehensive regulatory project poses capacity challenges for the rather small administrations of the Nordic countries. Ultimately, a regional regulation of MASS is dismissed.

Eventually, a European approach was discussed and considered most appropriate. The EU enjoys internal and external legislative competence in the field of MASS. Again, the findings of discussions with experts at the EC led to a rejection of unilateral European action on MASS. Nevertheless, the benefits of a European regulatory approach can be harnessed for MASS. A European directive implementing the non-binding IMO MASS Code best combines the global scope of shipping with the desire for a timely, predictable, flexible, and certain legal framework. The IMO-Code ensures coherency across all affected conventions, and making it mandatory by a European directive makes the legal framework certain and predictable. Moreover, it gives appropriate democratic accountability and legitimacy to the binding set of rules.

The legal framework could be in place in 2026. All European states would apply the same regulations, acting as port, flag, or coastal states creating a large level playing field for MASS operations. The MASS Code could be easily amended by the IMO if subsequent technological developments make adaptations necessary. Moreover, the EU could include more detailed rules on the implementation and risk assessment methodology. The EU directive as an instrument on transport can be included in the Annex of the EEA Agreement integrating Norway in the scope of the European directive. Perspectively, other states could make the IMO MASS Code mandatory further expanding range of MASS.

The EC and all member states are involved in the IMO's work on a MASS Code. Therefore, the implementing directive could already be prepared and discussed. It is now for the EC to draw up a proposal and submit it to the European Parliament and the Council. In addition, EMSA should start developing implementation guidelines and more specific technical standards for MASS in cooperation with relevant industry stakeholders.

Despite these advantages of a joint IMO-EU approach, it appears that most states are pursuing the mandatory adoption of the MASS Code through the addition of a chapter to the Annex of SOLAS utilizing the tacit acceptance procedure. As argued, this is detrimental from a legal, dogmatic point of view. In practice, however, dogmatic-normative considerations are unlikely to prevail over politically desirable outcomes, such as an internationally binding MASS Code. Although there is a theoretical possibility of proceedings about the legislative procedure, the likelihood converges to zero. Ultimately, political considerations, including economic, safety, security, diplomatic, and environmental arguments, are decisive for making the MASS Code binding.

Regulating autonomous vessels is about politics. Legal research proved that MASS can be included in the regulatory framework and that a non-binding code developed by the IMO and made mandatory by a European directive is the most appropriate way of addressing MASS from a legal perspective. However, the decision to initiate the necessary legislative process is a political one. It depends on whether, from a political point of view, the benefits of MASS outweigh the drawbacks and risks. This is a decision to be taken by society, elected representatives, governments, public administrations, and private stakeholders.

Even if the proposed approaches are very different, it is likely that the public law issues related to autonomous shipping will be clarified and an appropriate legal framework will be established in the coming years. It is therefore worth looking at the development of private law issues related to MASS. As with public shipping law, almost all facets of private maritime law are affected by MASS. This makes it necessary to comprehensively review contractual arrangements and adapt them to MASS where necessary. Moreover, new, MASS-specific aspects need to be reflected by private law. The ongoing research projects have shown that new players enter the maritime market. Remote operation as a service has to be couched. In addition, cargo owners took over parts of the logistics' chain themselves and entered the market as ship-owners. It remains to be seen how these developments will affect the shipping market over time. Finally, MASS require a large amount of cyber equipment, bringing new suppliers into the world of shipbuilding and ship supply.

The most prominent debate in private maritime law is that of third-party liability in the event of a collision involving MASS. Despite being extensively discussed in academic literature, a widely accepted solution has yet to be found. The venerable Brussels Convention of 1910 poses a particular challenge, as it provides for fault-based liability in the event of a ship collision. Establishing fault in the case of MASS is particularly challenging because fault requires a person to be blamed. Closely related to liability issues are insurance contracts, which also need to be revised in the light of MASS. The same applies to contracts for the carriage of goods by sea. These contracts focus on the carrier's duty to ensure the seaworthiness of the vessel, which encompasses all the characteristics of the ship. As MASS challenge the conventional set-up including a master present on board the vessel, this concept needs to be re-evaluated in the light of MASS.

Regulating MASS is a marathon. While many challenges have already been overcome, more lie ahead and more will emerge as MASS enters permanent operation. The more technology evolves, the more is known about the regulatory target, the better regulation and technology can fit together. Law can facilitate beneficial technology, promote improvements, and balance competing interests, resulting in the efficient use of resources and increased welfare. However, law can also prevent positive developments, hamper innovation, and lock in premature technology. In the case of MASS, it is hoped that the law continues on the first path.

References

Aakko-Saksa PT and others, 'Reduction in greenhouse gas and other emissions from ship engines: Current trends and future options' (2023) 94 Progress in Energy and Combustion Science 101055.

Aalberg AL and others, 'Does it do the same as we would? How trust in automated shipboard systems relates to seafarers' professional identity' (2024) 172 Safety Science.

Abbott C, 'Bridging the Gap – Non-state Actors and the Challenges of Regulating New Technology' (2012) 39(3) Journal of Law and Society 329.

Abbott KW and Snidal D, 'Hard and Soft Law in International Governance' (2000) 54(3) International Organization 421.

Achenbach J von, *Demokratische Gesetzgebung in der Europäischen Union: Theorie und Praxis der dualen Legitimationsstruktur europäischer Hoheitsgewalt* (Beiträge zum ausländischen öffentlichen Recht und Völkerrecht vol 248, Springer 2014).

Adede AO, 'Amendment Procedures for Conventions with Technical Annexes: The IMCO Experience' (1977) 17(2) Virginia Journal of International Law 201.

Adler E, 'Constructivism in International Relations: Sources, Contributions, and Debates' in Walter Carlsnaes, Thomas Risse and Beth A Simmons (eds), *Handbook of international relations* (SAGE Publications 2013).

Agarwala N, 'Role of policy framework for disruptive technologies in the maritime domain' (2022) 14(1) Australian Journal of Maritime & Ocean Affairs 1.

Agreement on the withdrawal of the United Kingdom of Great Britain and Northern Ireland from the European Union and the European Atomic Energy Community 12 November 2019 (European Union; European Atomic Energy Community; United Kingdom).

Ahmed YA and Salas C, 'D7.4 Proposed regulatory, legal and liabilities frameworks amendments' (November 2022).

Ahvenjärvi S, 'The Human Element and Autonomous Ships' (2016) 10(3) TransNav 517.

Akbar A and others, 'An economic analysis of introducing autonomous ships in a short-sea liner shipping network' [2020] International Transactions in Operational Research 1.

Akpan F and others, 'Cybersecurity Challenges in the Maritime Sector' (2022) 2(1) Network 123.

Allen CH, 'Revisiting the Thames Formula: The Evolving Role of the International Maritime Organization and Its Member States in Implementing the 1982 Law of the Sea Convention' (2009) 10 San Diego International Law Journal 265.

Allen CH, 'Determining the Legal Status of Unmanned Maritime Vehicles: Formalism vs Functionalism' (2018) 49(4) Journal of Maritime Law and Commerce 477.

Allied Market Research, 'Autonomous Ships Market Statistics' (2020) <https://www.alliedmarketresearch.com/autonomous-ships-market> accessed 16 February 2024.

Alqurashi FS and others, 'Maritime Communications: A Survey on Enabling Technologies, Opportunities, and Challenges' (2023) 10(4) IEEE Internet Things Journal 3525.

American Bureau of Shipping, 'Advisory on Autonomous Functionality' (Houston, Texas 2020).

Anderson SV, *The Nordic Council: A Study of Scandinavian Regionalism* (Svenska Bokförlaget/Norstedts 1967).

Andersson HE, 'What Activates an Identity? The Case of Norden' (2010) 24(1) International Relations 46.

Andreasson U and Stende T, 'Status för mobiliteten i Norden' (København 2018).

Associazione Italiana di Diritto Maritimo, 'CMI Questionnaire on unmanned ships – Italian MLA answers' (Antwerp 05/2018).

Aston JD, *Sekundärgesetzgebung internationaler Organisationen zwischen mitgliedstaatlicher Souveränität und Gemeinschaftsdisziplin* (Schriften zum Völkerrecht vol 158, Duncker & Humblot 2011).

Attard FG, *The Duty of the Shipmaster to Render Assistance at Sea under International Law* (Queen Mary Studies in International Law vol 41, Brill|Nijhoff 2020).

Aust A, 'Pacta sunt servanda' in Anne Peters (ed), *Max Planck Encyclopedia of Public International Law* (MPEPIL) (Oxford University Press).

Aust A, 'The Theory and Practice of Informal International Instruments' (1986) 35(4) The International and Comparative Law Quarterly 787.

Aust A, 'Alternatives to Treaty-Making: MoUs as Political Commitments' in Duncan B Hollis (ed), *The Oxford Guide to Treaties* (Oxford University Press 2012).

Aust A, *Modern treaty law and practice* (3. ed. Cambridge University Press 2013).

Australian Maritime Safety Authority, 'AMSA Policy on Regulatory Treatment of Unmanned and/or Autonomous Vessels' (20 February 2020).

AUTOSHIP project, 'Technologies' <https://www.autoship-project.eu/technologies/> accessed 16 February 2024.

Bachmann Mehammer E, 'Nordic roadmap for introduction of sustainable zero-carbon fuels in shipping' (Nordic Roadmap – Helsinki Conference, Helsinki, Finland, 3 May 2023).

Backer IL, 'Styrket nordisk lovsamarbeid, Muligheter og utfordringer' (Oslo 2018).

Baddenhausen H, 'Ausschuss für die Angelegenheiten der Europäischen Union' in Martin Morlok, Utz Schliesky and (Keine Angabe) (eds), *Parlamentsrecht: Praxishandbuch* (1. Auflage. Nomos 2016).

Balkin RP, 'The IMO and Global Ocean Governance: Past, Present, and Future' in David J Attard, Rosalie P Balkin and Donald W Greig (eds), *The IMLI Treatise on Global Ocean Governance: Volumen III: IMO and Global Ocean Governance* (First edition. Oxford University Press 2018).

Baltic and International Maritime Council (BIMCO), 'Electronic Bills of Lading' (17 January 2023) <https://www.bimco.org/insights-and-information/general-information/20230117-ebl> accessed 16 February 2024.

Bang H-S and Jang D-J, 'Recent Developments in Regional Memorandums of Understanding on Port State Control' (2012) 43(2) Ocean Development & International Law 170.

Bang J, Blanke M and Henriques M, 'A pre-analysis on autonomous ships' (Lyngby, Denmark 2019).

Barnes R, 'Flag States' in Donald R Rothwell and others (eds), *The Oxford Handbook of the Law of the Sea* (Oxford University Press 2015).

Barnes R, 'Article 17 – Right of innocent passage' in Alexander Proelß and others (eds), *United Nations Convention on the Law of the Sea: A commentary* (1st edition. C.H. Beck; Hart; Nomos 2017).

Barnes R, 'Article 21 – Laws and regulations of the coastal State relating to innocent passage' in Alexander Proelß and others (eds), *United Nations Convention on the Law of the Sea: A commentary* (1st edition. C.H. Beck; Hart; Nomos 2017).

Barnes R, 'Article 25 – Right of protection of the coastal State' in Alexander Proelß and others (eds), *United Nations Convention on the Law of the Sea: A commentary* (1st edition. C.H. Beck; Hart; Nomos 2017).

Barthelsson P and Sagefjord J, *Autonomous ships and the operator's role in a Shore Control Centre – A comparative analysis on projects in the Scandinavian region and implementing the experience of Mariners to a new field of shipping* (2017).

Bartlett M, 'Game of Drones: Unmanned Maritime Vehicles and the Law of the Sea' (2018) 24 Auckland University Law Review 66.

Baughen S, 'Who is the master now?: Regulatory and contractual challenges of unmanned vessels' in Barış Soyer and Andrew Tettenborn (eds), *New Technologies, Artificial Intelligence and Shipping Law in the 21st Century* (Maritime and transport law library. Informa Law from Routledge 2019).

Baughen S, 'Civil Liability all at Sea: The Challenges of Unmanned Cargo Ships' in Phillip Morgan (ed), *Tort liability and autonomous systems accidents: Common and civil law perspectives* (Edward Elgar Publishing 2023).

Baxter RR, 'International Law in "Her Infinite Variety"' (1980) 29(4) The International and Comparative Law Quarterly 549.

Beckman R and Sun Z, 'The Relationship between UNCLOS and IMO Instruments' (2017) 2(2) Asia-Pacific Journal of Ocean Law and Policy 201.

Belgian Federal Government, 'Convention Internationale pour L'unification de Certaines Regles en Matiere d'Abordage' (Brussels 1 June 2021) <https://diplomatie.belgium.be/sites/default/files/documents/CDM1.%20Convention%20internationale%20pour%20l'unification%20de%20%5B ... %5D.pdf>.

Bellingmo P, Mørkrid OE and Wille E, 'Feasibility Study for an Unmanned Deep Sea Bulk Ship and Short Sea Container Ship, No. OC2022 A-110' (Trondheim 7 February 2023).

Ben Farah MA and others, 'Cyber Security in the Maritime Industry: A Systematic Survey of Recent Advances and Future Trends' (2022) 13(1) Information 22.

Bentham J, *Principles of Morals and Legislation, Fragment on Government, Civil Code, Penal Law* (vol 1, 1838–1843).

Bergström M and others, 'Towards the unmanned ship code' in Pentti Kujala and Liangliang Lu (eds), *Marine Design XIII, Volume 2: Proceedings of the 13th International Marine Design Conference (IMDC 2018), June 10–14, 2018, Helsinki, Finland* (Chapman and Hall/CRC 2018).

Bernandez ST, 'Court Generated State Practice: (Karl Zemanek) – A Commentary' (2015) 20 Austrian Review of International and European Law 25.

Berthelot Y, 'Regionalization and globalization: Two concomitant dynamics in need of coherent institutions' in Pierre de Senarclens and Ali Kazancigil (eds), *Regulating Globalization: Critical Approaches to Global Governance* (United Nations University Press 2007).

Bertram V, 'Autonomous Ship Technology – smart for Sure, Unmanned maybe' (London January 2016).

Besson S, 'Sovereignty' in Anne Peters (ed), *Max Planck Encyclopedia of Public International Law* (MPEPIL) (Oxford University Press).

Birnie P, 'The Status of Environmental 'Soft Law': Trends and Examples with Special Focus on IMO Norms' in Henrik Ringbom (ed), *Competing norms in the law of marine environmental protection: Focus on ship safety and pollution prevention* (International environmental law and policy series vol 46, 1. publ. Kluwer Law International 1997).

Bjorge E, *The Evolutionary Interpretation of Treaties* (Oxford University Press 2014).

Black J, 'Critial Reflections on Regulation' (2002) 27 Australian Journal of Legal Philosophy 1.

Blind K, Petersen SS and Riillo CA, 'The impact of standards and regulation on innovation in uncertain markets' (2017) 46(1) Research Policy 249.

Bolbot V and others, 'Paving the way toward autonomous shipping development for European Waters – The AUTOSHIP project' (June 2020).

Boodman M, 'The Myth of Harmonization of Laws' (1991) 39(4) The American Journal of Comparative Law 699.

Bordin FL, *The Analogy between States and International Organizations* (Cambridge studies in international and comparative law vol 138, Cambridge University Press 2019).

Böth K, *Evolutive Auslegung völkerrechtlicher Verträge: Eine Untersuchung zu Voraussetzungen und Grenzen in Anbetracht der Praxis internationaler Streitbeilegungsinstitutionen* (Schriften zum Völkerrecht vol 204, Duncker & Humblot 2013).

Botzem S, 'Transnational standard setting in accounting: Organizing expertise-based self-regulation in times of crises' (2014) 27(6) Accounting, Auditing & Accountability Journal 933.

Boviatsis M and Vlachos G, 'Sustainable Operation of Unmanned Ships under Current International Maritime Law' (2022) 14(12) Sustainability.

Bowman M, 'Towards a Unified Treaty Body for Monitoring Compliance with UN Human Rights Conventions? Legal Mechanisms for Treaty Reform' (2007) 7(1) Human Rights Law Review 225.

Boyle A, 'Some Reflections on the Relationship of Treaties and Soft Law' (1999) 48(4) The International and Comparative Law Quarterly 901.

Boyle A, 'Further Development of the 1982 Convention on the Law of the Sea: Mechanisms for Change' in David Freestone, Richard Barnes and David M Ong (eds), *The law of the sea: Progress and prospects* (Oxford University Press 2006).

Boyle A, 'Reflections on the Treaty as a Law-making Instrument' in Alexander Orakhelashvili and Sarah Williams (eds), *40 years of the Vienna Convention on the Law of Treaties* (British Institute of International and Comparative Law 2010).

Boyle A, 'Soft Law in International Law-Making' in Malcolm D Evans (ed), *International law* (Fifth edition. Oxford University Press 2018).

Boyle A, 'The Choice of a Treaty' in Simon Chesterman and others (eds), *The Oxford Handbook of United Nations Treaties* (Oxford University Press 2019).

Boyle A and Chinkin C, *The Making of International Law* (Foundations of public international law, 1 publ, Oxford Univ. Press 2007).

Bradford A, *The Brussels Effect : How the European Union Rules the World* (Oxford University Press 2020).

Bradley CA and Kelley JG, 'The Concept of International Delegation' (2008) 71(1) Law and Contemporary Problems 1.

Brækhus S, 'De Norske Sjølover: Et tilbakeblikk ved 100 års jubiléet' (1993) 200 MarIus 1.

Bratić K and others, 'Review of Autonomous and Remotely Controlled Ships in Maritime Sector' [2019] Transactions on Maritime Science 253 <https://www.semanticscholar.org/paper/Review-of-Autonomous-and-Remotely-Controlled-Ships-Brati%C4%87-Pavi%C4%87/cabf91d3e429ff28b94f5094bf70e0af98d40601>.

Brownsword R, 'So What Does the World Need Now? Reflections on Regulating Technologies' in Roger Brownsword and Karen Yeung (eds), *Regulating Technologies: Legal Futures, Regulatory Frames and Technological Fixes* (Hart 2008).

Brownsword R and Goodwin M, *Law and the technologies of the twenty-first century: Text and materials* (Law in Context, Cambridge University Press 2012).

Brunnée J, 'COPing with Consent: Law-Making Under Multilateral Environmental Agreements' (2002) 15(1) Leiden Journal of International Law 1.

Brunnée J and Campbell-Duruflé C, 'International Legislation' in Anne Peters (ed), *Max Planck Encyclopedia of Public International Law* (MPEPIL) (Oxford University Press).

Buga I, 'Between Stability and Change in the Law of the Sea Convention: Subsequent Practice, Treaty Modification, and Regime Interaction' in Donald R Rothwell and others (eds), *The Oxford Handbook of the Law of the Sea* (Oxford University Press 2015).

Bureau d'Enquêtes et d'Analyses pour la sécurité de l'aviation civile, 'Final Report AF 447 Rio de Janeiro – Paris' (Le Bourget July 2012).

Bureau Veritas, 'Guidelines for Autonomous Shipping: Guidance Note NI 641 DT R01 E' (Paris October 2019).

Burke KM and DeLeo DA, 'Innocent Passage and Transit Passage in the United Nations Convention on the Law of the Sea' (1983) 9(2) Yale Journal of World Public Order, 389.

Callboats, 'CAT 10 L' <https://callboats.com/cat-10-l/> accessed 16 February 2024.

Calliess C, 'Article 170 AEUV' in Christian Calliess and Matthias Ruffert (eds), *EUV/AEUV: Das Verfassungsrecht der Europäischen Union mit Europäischer Grundrechtecharta: Kommentar* (6. Auflage. C.H. Beck 2022).

Calliess G-P, 'Law, Transnational' (2010) 06(8) CLPE Research Paper Series 2.

Cameron I, 'Nordic Cooperation' in Anne Peters (ed), *Max Planck Encyclopedia of Public International Law* (MPEPIL) (Oxford University Press).

Cameron I, 'Treaties, Declarations of Interpretation' (December 2020). Max Planck Encyclopedia of Public International Law (MPEPIL).

Carey L, 'All Hands Off Deck? The Legal Barriers to Autonomous Ships' [2017] SSRN Journal.

Carey L, 'Contractual and Tortious Maritime Liability Regimes and the Introduction of Autonomous Vessels: NUS Law Working Paper 2023/012' (Singapore March 2023).

Cassese A and others, *Cassese's International law* (Third edition, Oxford University Press 2020).

Chae C-J, Kim M and Kim H-J, 'A Study on Identification of Development Status of MASS Technologies and Directions of Improvement' (2020) 10(13) Applied Sciences.

China Classification Society, 'Guidelines for Autonomous Cargo Ships: Guidance Notes GD20-2018' (Shanghai 1 October 2018).

Chinkin C, 'The Challenge of Soft Law: Development and Change in International Law' (1989) 38(4) International and Comparative Law Quarterly 850.

Chircop A, 'The International Maritime Organization' in Donald R Rothwell and others (eds), *The Oxford Handbook of the Law of the Sea* (Oxford University Press 2015).

Chircop A, 'Testing International Legal Regimes: The Advent of Automated Commercial Vessels' (2017) 60 The German Yearbook on International Law 109.

Chircop A, 'The quest for universality and uniformity: theory and practice of international maritime regulation' in Jason Chuah (ed), *Research handbook on maritime law and regulation* (Research Handbooks in Private and Commercial Law series. Edward Elgar Publishing 2019).

Chircop A, Goerlandt F and Yoo J, 'Unmanned Remotely Operated Search and Rescue Ships in the Canadian Arctic: Exploring the Opportunities, Risk Dimensions and

Governance Implications' in Aldo Chircop and others (eds), *Governance of Arctic Shipping: Rethinking Risk, Human Impacts and Regulation* (Springer Polar Sciences. Springer Nature 2020).

Choi J, 'Legal Status of Remote Operator in Maritime Autonomous Surface Ships (MASS) Under International Law: who Can be a Ship Master?' in Eric Y J Lee (ed), *Revolutionary Approach to International Law: The Role of International Lawyer in Asia* (International Law in Asia, 1st edition. Springer Nature Singapore 2023).

Churchill RR, 'The 1982 United Nations Convention on the Law of the Sea' in Donald R Rothwell and others (eds), The Oxford Handbook of the Law of the Sea (Oxford University Press 2015)

Churchill RR, Lowe V and Sander A, *The law of the sea* (Melland Schill studies in international law, 4th edn, Manchester University Press 2022).

Chwedczuk M, 'Analysis of the legal status of unmanned commercial vessels in U.S. admirality and maritime law' (2016) 47(2) Journal of Maritime Law and Commerce 123.

Class NK, 'Guidelines for Automated and Autonomous Operation on ships (ver. 1.0): Design development, Installation and Operation of Automated Operation System/ Remote Operation System' (Chiyoda, Tokyo January 2020).

Coase RH, 'The Problem of Social Cost' [1960] The Journal of Law and Economics 1.

Coelho LF and Rogers R, 'The Use of Marine Autonomous Systems in Ocean Observation Under the LOSC: Maintaining Access to and Sharing Benefits for Coastal States' in Tafsir M Johansson and others (eds), *Smart Ports and Robotic Systems* (Studies in National Governance and Emerging Technologies. Springer International Publishing 2023).

Coelho NF, van Tatenhove J and Raakjær J, 'D6.1 – Public policy recommendations for a new European waterborne transport system' (Trondheim 1 June 2023).

Coello DM, 'Is UNCLOS Ready for the Era of Seafaring Autonomous Vessels?' (2023) 10(1) Journal of Territorial and Maritime Studies 21.

Cogliati-Bantz VP, 'Disentangling the "Genuine Link": Enquiries in Sea, Air and Space Law' (2010) 79(3) Nordic Journal of International Law 383.

Colella MM and others, 'The AUTOSHIP project: speeding-up the transition towards a next generation of autonomous ships in the EU' (Rijswijk, the Netherlands 6 March 2023) <https://www.autoship-project.eu/news-press/take-a-look-at-the-autoship-e-book/> accessed 6 March 2023.

Colella MM and Azarko A, 'Autonomy is not what you think: assessing the external costs of autonomous shipping through the AUTOSHIP IWW use case study' (July 2023) <https://www.autoship-project.eu/wp-content/uploads/2023/07/Autonomy-is-not-what-you-think-assessing-the-external-costs-of-autonomous-shipping-through-the-AUTOSHIP-IWW-use-case-study.pdf>.

Colella MM and Salas C, 'D7.3_Autonomous-ships Socio-economic impacts perspective analysis' (8 February 2023).

Collingridge D, *The Social Control of Technology* (Frances Pinter (Publishers) Ltd; St. Martin's Press 1980).

Collingridge D, 'Position Paper on Unmanned Ships and the International Regulatory Framework' (Antwerpen May 2018).

Collingridge D, 'Summary of Responses to the CMI Questionnaire' (Antwerpen May 2018).

Comité Maritime International (CMI), 'CMI Questionnaire on unmanned ships' (Antwerpen 24 March 2017).

Congleton RD, 'Rational Choice and Politics' in Roger D Congleton, Bernard Grofman and Stefan Voigt (eds), *The Oxford handbook of public choice* (Oxford University Press 2019).

Cox A, *China's first autonomous boxship readies to enter service* (2021).

Crawford E, *Non-binding Norms in International Humanitarian Law: Efficacy, legitimacy, and legality* (Oxford monographs in international humanitarian and criminal law, First edition, Oxford University Press 2021).

Cremona M, 'Making Treaties and Other International Agreements: The European Union' in Curtis A Bradley (ed), *The Oxford Handbook of Comparative Foreign Relations Law* (Oxford University Press 2019).

Curtis JB, 'Vessel-Source Oil Pollution and Marpol 73/78: An International Success Story' (1985) 15(4) Environmental Law 679.

Czarny RM, 'The Shaping of Norden' (2014) 4(2(8)) Journal of Geography, Politics and Society 74.

Dahl RA, 'Can international organizations be democratic? A skeptic's view' in Ian Shapiro and Casiano Hacker-Cordón (eds), *Democracy's edges* (Contemporary political theory, 1. publ. Cambridge University Press 1999).

Dahm G, *Völkerrecht* (Jost Delbrück and Rüdiger Wolfrum trs, 2nd edn, de Gruyter 2002).

Dalfen J, *Platon Minos; Übersetzung und Kommentar* (Vandenhoeck & Ruprecht 2009).

Danilenko GM, 'The Theory of International Customary Law' (1988) 31 German Yearbook of International Law 9.

Danilenko GM, *Law-making in the international community* (Developments in international law vol 15, Nijhoff 1993).

Danish Ship Finance, 'Shipping Market Review' (Kopenhagen November 2021) <https://www.shipfinance.dk/media/2159/shipping-market-review-november-2021.pdf> accessed 8 April 2022.

d'Aspermont J, 'Softness in International Law: A Self-Serving Quest for New Legal Materials' (2008) 19(5) European Journal of International Law 1075.

Daum O and Boesch A, 'Zur Aktualität der Schiffsdefinition des BGH: Sind unbemannte Wasserfahrzeuge Schiffe?' [2018] Zeitschrift für das Recht der Transportwirtschaft 41.

Dean P and Clack H, 'Autonomous shipping and maritime law' in Barış Soyer and Andrew Tettenborn (eds), *New Technologies, Artificial Intelligence and Shipping Law in the 21st Century* (Maritime and transport law library. Informa Law from Routledge 2019).

Decken K von der, 'Article 39, General rule regarding the amendment of treaties' in Oliver Dörr and Kirsten Schmalenbach (eds), *Vienna Convention on the Law of Treaties: A Commentary* (2. 2nd ed. 2018. Springer Berlin Heidelberg 2018).

Decken K von der, 'Article 41, Agreements to modify multilateral treaties between certain of the parties only' in Oliver Dörr and Kirsten Schmalenbach (eds), *Vienna Convention on the Law of Treaties: A Commentary* (2. 2nd ed. 2018. Springer Berlin Heidelberg 2018).

Deep Blue Sea Training, 'A Glossary of Nautical Terms – Bridge' <http://www.deepbluesea.training/nautical-terms.html> accessed 16 February 2024.

Degan VD, 'Internal waters' (1986) 17 Netherlands Yearbook of International Law 3.

Deketelaere P, 'The legal challenges of unmanned vessels' (Master Dissertation, Universiteit Gent 21 May 2017).

Delgado IC, 'The IMO: The Role of the Classification Societies in Promoting Global Ocean Governance' in David J Attard, Rosalie P Balkin and Donald W Greig (eds), *The IMLI Treatise on Global Ocean Governance: Volumen III: IMO and Global Ocean Governance* (First edition. Oxford University Press 2018).

Delgado IC, 'Future of transport regulatory review: Maritime Autonomy and Remote Operations; Final Impact Assessment' (London 14 September 2023).

Department for Transport, 'Maritime 2050' (London January 2019).

Delgado IC, 'Nasjonal transportplan 2022–2033: Meld. St. 20 (2020–2021)' (Oslo 19 March 2021).

Department of the Navy, United States of America, 'The Navy Unmanned Surface Vehicle (USV) Master Plan' (Washington, D.C. 23 July 2007).

Det kongelige Samferdselsdepartement, 'Høring om endringer i lov om losordningen for å legge til rette for autonom kystseilas' (Oslo 30 April 2018).

Deutscher Verkehrsgerichtstag (ed), '55. Deutscher Verkehrsgerichtstag 2017: Veröffentlichung der auf dem 55. Deutschen Verkehrsgerichtstag vom 25. bis 27. Januar 2017 in Goslar gehaltenen Vorträge, Referate und erarbeiteten Empfehlungen' (2017).

Devetak R and True J, *Theories of International Relations* (6th ed. Bloomsbury Publishing Plc 2022).

Directorate-General for Mobility and Transport, D2 Maritime Safety, 'Study on social aspects within the maritime transport sector: Final report' (Luxembourg 2020).

Djeffal C, 'An Interpreter's Guide to Static and Evolutive Interpretations: Solving Intertemporal Problems and the VCLT' in Georges Abi-Saab and others (eds), *Evolutionary Interpretation and International Law* (Hart Publishing 2019).

Djeffal C, 'Autonomous and remotely operated ships: Class Guideline' (Høvik, Norway September 2021) DNVGL-CG-0264.

DNV GL AS Maritime, 'ReVolt Report' (Høvik, Norway 27 February 2015) 2015–0170, Rev. 01.

Doll C and others, 'Methodology for GHG Efficiency of Transport Modes Final Report' (Karlsruhe, Delft 30 November 2020).

Dong B, Bautista L and Zhu L, 'Navigating uncharted waters: Challenges and regulatory solutions for flag state jurisdiction of Maritime Autonomous Surface Ships under UNCLOS' (2024) 161 Marine Policy.

Dörr O, 'Article 31, General rule of interpretation' in Oliver Dörr and Kirsten Schmalenbach (eds), *Vienna Convention on the Law of Treaties: A Commentary* (2. 2nd ed. 2018. Springer Berlin Heidelberg 2018).

Dremliuga R and Rusli MHbM, 'The Development of the Legal Framework for Autonomous Shipping: Lessons Learned from a Regulation for a Driverless Car' (2020) 13(3) Journal of Politics and Law 295.

Duina F and Lenz T, 'Democratic legitimacy in regional economic organizations: the European Union in comparative perspective' (2017) 46(3–4) Economy and Society 398.

Durner W, 'Umweltvölkerrecht' in Martin Beckmann and others (eds), *Umweltrecht: Kommentar* (September 2023, 102. supplement. C.H. Beck 2023).

Easterbrook FH, 'Cyberspace and the Law of the Horse' [1996] University of Chicago Legal Forum 207–216.

Eder B, 'Unmanned vessels: challenge ahead' in Comité Maritime International (CMI) (ed), *Yearbook 2017–2018 Annuaire* (2019).

Eftestøl EJ and Yliheljo E, 'International Shipping: Who Levels the Playing Field?' in Abhinayan B Bal (ed), *Regulation of Risk: Transport, Trade and Environment in Perspective* (International Law E-Books Online, Collection 2023. Brill|Nijhoff 2022).

Ehlers P, 'The History of the International North Sea Conferences' (1990) 5(1) International Journal of Estuarine and Coastal Law 3.

Ellis J, 'Shades of Grey: Soft Law and the Validity of Public International Law' (2012) 25(2) Leiden Journal of International Law 313.

Engtrø E, 'The implementation and application of the International Code for Ships Operating in Polar Waters (Polar Code): Evaluations and considerations addressing this function-based regulation's effect on safety and emergency preparedness concerning Arctic shipping' (PhD thesis, University of Stavanger 2021).

Eriksen PK and Wide C, 'Introduction: The Nordic languages and typology' (2011) 34(2) Nordic Journal of Linguistics 75.

Etzkorn P, *Der Schiffszusammenstoß unter Beteiligung autonom fahrender Schiffe* (Schriftenreihe des Instituts für Transport- und Verkehrsrecht vol 14, 1. Auflage, Nomos 2022).

European Commission, 'Welcome to Have your say' <https://ec.europa.eu/info/law/better-regulation/have-your-say_en> accessed 16 February 2024.

European Commission, 'COM(93) 66 final – Communication from the Commisson 'A Common Policy on Safe Seas" (Brussels 24 February 1993).

European Commission, 'EU Operational Guidelines for Safe, Secure and Sustainable Trials of Maritime Autonomous Surface Ships (MASS)' (Brussels October 2020).

European Commission, 'Com(2020) 789 final – Sustainable and Smart Mobility Strategy – putting European transport on track for the future' (Brussels 9 December 2020).

European Commission, 'Statistical Pocketbook 2023 EU transport in figures' (Luxembourg 2023).

European Commission, 'Legislative Texts' <https://www.emsa.europa.eu/publications/legislative-texts.html>.

European Commission, 'How to make a complaint at EU level' <https://commission.europa.eu/about-european-commission/contact/problems-and-complaints/complaints-about-breaches-eu-law-member-states/how-make-complaint-eu-level_en> accessed 16 February 2024.

European Maritime Safety Agency, 'Legislative Texts' <https://www.emsa.europa.eu/publications/legislative-texts.html> accessed 16 February 2024.

European Union, 'EU and its Member States Submission to the NNBJ PrepCom' (Brussels 25 July 2016).

European Union Agency for the Space Programme, 'What is GNSS?' (15 December 2023) <https://www.euspa.europa.eu/european-space/eu-space-programme/what-gnss> accessed 16 February 2024.

Eurostat, 'Maritime transport statistics – short sea shipping of goods' (2023) <https://ec.europa.eu/eurostat/statistics-explained/index.php?title=Maritime_transport_statistics_-_short_sea_shipping_of_goods#Short_sea_shipping_by_type_of_cargo> accessed 16 February 2024.

Everything about Boats, 'Bridge' <https://everythingaboutboats.org/glossary/#b> accessed 16 February 2024.

Falkanger T and Bull HJ, *Sjørett* (Sjørettsfondet Akademisk 2016).

Falkanger T, Bull HJ and Brautaset L, *Scandinavian Maritime Law: The Norwegian Perspective* (4th ed. Universitetsforlaget 2017).

Faria JAE, 'Future Directions of Legal Harmonisation and Law Reform: Stormy Seas or Prosperous Voyage' (2009) 14(1/2) Uniform Law Review 5.

Fastvold OL, 'Legal Challenges for Unmanned Ships in International Law of the Sea' (master thesis, The Arctic University of Norway 2018).

Fawcett L, 'Regionalism and global governance: An appraisal' in Pierre de Senarclens and Ali Kazancigil (eds), *Regulating Globalization: Critical Approaches to Global Governance* (United Nations University Press 2007).

Fehling M, 'Article 100 TFEU' in Hans von der Groeben, Jürgen Schwarze and Armin Hatje (eds), *Europäisches Unionsrecht: Vertrag über die Europäische Union; Vertrag über die Arbeitsweise der Europäischen Union; Charta der Grundrechte der Europäischen Union* (7th edn. Nomos 2015).

Felski A and Zwolak K, 'The Ocean-Going Autonomous Ship—Challenges and Threats' (2020) 8(1) Journal of Marine Science and Engineering 41.

Fenton AJ and Chapsos I, 'Ships without crews: IMO and UK responses to cybersecurity, technology, law and regulation of maritime autonomous surface ships (MASS)' (2023) 5 Frontiers in Computer Science.

Fenwick M, Kaal WA and Vermeulen EPM, 'Regulation Tomorrow: What Happens When Technology Is Faster Than the Law?' (2016) 6(3) American University Business Law Review 561.

Fitzmaurice M, 'The New Generation of Environmental Non-Compliance Procedures and the Question of Legitimacy' in Christina Voigt and Caroline Foster (eds), *International Courts versus Non-Compliance Mechanisms Comparative Advantages in Strengthening Treaty Implementation* (1st ed. Cambridge University Press 2024).

Fitzmaurice M and Costelloe D, 'Lawmaking by treaty: Conclusion of treaties and evolution of treaty regimes in practice' in Catherine Brölmann and Yannick Radi (eds), *Research handbook on the theory and practice of international lawmaking* (Edward Elgar Publishing 2016).

Fock H, *Marinekleinkampfmittel* (Wehrwissenschaftliche Berichte herausgegeben vom Arbeitskreis für Wehrforschung vol 3, J. F. Lehmanns Verlag 1968).

Forteau M, 'Regional Cooperation' in Anne Peters (ed), *Max Planck Encyclopedia of Public International Law* (MPEPIL) (Oxford University Press).

Fortune Business Insights, 'Autonomous Ships Market Size, Share, COVID-19 Impact & Russian-Ukraine War analysis' (2023) <https://www.fortunebusinessinsights.com/industry-reports/autonomous-ship-market-101797> accessed 16 February 2024.

Franck TM, 'Legitimacy in the International System' (1988) 82 American Journal of International Law 705.

Franckx E, 'Helsinki Conference (1996)' in Erik Franckx (ed), *Vessel-Source Pollution and Coastal State Jurisdiction: The Work of the ILA Committee on Coastal State Jurisdiction Relating to Marine Pollution (1991–2000)* (Brill 2001).

Frank V, 'Consequences of the *Prestige* Sinking for European and International Law' (2005) 20(1) The International Journal of Marine and Coastal Law 1.

Frawley NH, 'A Brief History: The CMI and its Relationship with IMO, the IOPC Funds and other UN Organizations' (Antwerpen 7 January 2011).

Freestone D and Elferink AGO, 'Flexibility and Innovation in the Law of the Sea – will the LOS Convention Amendment Procedures ever be used?' in Alex G Oude Elferink (ed), *Stability and Change in the Law of the Sea* (Nova et Vetera Iuris Gentium vol 24. Brill 2005).

Frenzel M, *Sekundärrechtsetzungsakte internationaler Organisationen: Völkerrechtliche Konzeption und verfassungsrechtliche Voraussetzungen* (Jus Internationale et Europaeum vol 54, 1. Auflage, Mohr Siebeck 2011).

Frøyen YK, 'Smartere transport Møre og Romsdal L1.4 – Transportfagleg vurdering – Ålesund: Autonome båtruter med utgangspunkt i Ålesund Vurdering av passasjergrunnlag, ruteopplegg og potensielle anløp'.

Fung KS and Li S, 'Maritime autonomous surface ships (MASS): implementation and legal issues' (2019) 4(4) Maritime Business Review 330.

Gardiner R, 'The Vienna Convention Rules on Treaty Interpretation' in Duncan B Hollis (ed), *The Oxford Guide to Treaties* (Oxford University Press 2012).

Gardiner RK, *Treaty interpretation* (The Oxford international law library, Second edition, Oxford University Press 2015).

Gebauer M and Berner F, 'Unification and Harmonization of Laws' in Anne Peters (ed), *Max Planck Encyclopedia of Public International Law* (MPEPIL) (Oxford University Press).

Geismann M, 'Art. 288 AEUV' in Hans von der Groeben, Jürgen Schwarze and Armin Hatje (eds), *Europäisches Unionsrecht: Vertrag über die Europäische Union; Vertrag über die Arbeitsweise der Europäischen Union; Charta der Grundrechte der Europäischen Union* (7th edn. Nomos 2015).

Gellermann M, 'Article 296 TFEU' in Rudolf Streinz and others (eds), EUV/AEUV*: Vertrag über die Europäische Union, Vertrag über die Arbeitsweise der Europäischen Union, Charta der Grundrechte der Europäischen Union* (Beck-Online Bücher Band 57, 3. Auflage. C.H. Beck 2018).

Gogarty B and Hagger M, 'The Laws of Man over vehicles unmanned: the legal response to robotic revolution on sea, land and air' (2008) 19 Journal of Law, Information and Science 73.

Goldsmith JL and Posner EA, *The limits of international law* (1.th edn, Oxford University Press 2005).

Graziano A, Mejia MQ and Schröder-Hinrichs J-U, 'Achievements and challenges on the implementation of the European Directive on Port State Control' (2018) 72 Transport Policy 97.

Gregory D and others (eds), *The dictionary of human geography* (5th ed. Blackwell 2009).

Griggs PJ, 'Uniformity of Maritime Law—An International Perspective' (1999) 73(5&6) Tulane Law Review 1551.

Grimm D, 'Zum Stand der demokratischen Legitimation der Europäischen Union nach Lissabon' in Nabila Abbas, Annette Förster and Emanuel Richter (eds), *Supranationalität und Demokratie: Die Europäische Union in Zeiten der Krise* (Staat – Souveränität – Nation, 1. Aufl. Springer VS 2014).

Grønt Skipfartsprogram, 'Smarte fjordkrysninger' (05/2022) <https://grontskipsfartsprogram.no/wp-content/uploads/2022/05/Smarte-fjordkrysninger.pdf> accessed 17 November 2023.

Grotius H, *The freedom of the seas, or, The right which belongs to the Dutch to take part in the East Indian Trade* (translated by Ralph Van Deman Magoffin, Oxford University Press 1916).

Guilfoyle D, 'Article 91 – Nationality of Ships' in Alexander Proelß and others (eds), *United Nations Convention on the Law of the Sea: A commentary* (1st edition. C.H. Beck; Hart; Nomos 2017).

Guilfoyle D, 'Article 94 – Duties of the flag State' in Alexander Proelß and others (eds), *United Nations Convention on the Law of the Sea: A commentary* (1st edition. C.H. Beck; Hart; Nomos 2017).

Guzmán AT, *How International Law Works: A Rational Choice Theory* (Oxford University Press 2008).

Guzmán AT and Landsidle J, 'The Myth of International Delegation' (2008) 96(6) California Law Review 1693.

Guzmán AT and Meyer T, 'International Soft Law' (2011) 2(1) The Journal of Legal Analysis 171.

Guzmán AT and Sykes AO, 'Economics of International Law' in Francesco Parisi (ed), *The Oxford handbook of law and economics: Volume 3: Public Law and Legal Institutions* (Oxford University Press 2017).

Hagemann R, Huddelston Skees J and Thierer A, 'Soft Law for Hard Law Problems: The Governance of Emerging Technologies in an Uncertain Future' (2018) 17(1) Colorado Technical Law Journal 37.

Håkansson C and Jamholt AH, 'Kun Sverige er imod et nyt ministerråd for transport' (2 November 2023) <https://www.norden.org/no/node/83860> accessed 16 February 2024.

Hakapää K, 'Innocent Passage' in Anne Peters (ed), *Max Planck Encyclopedia of Public International Law* (MPEPIL) (Oxford University Press).

Handl GF and others, 'A Hard Look at Soft Law' [1988] Proceedings of the Annual Meeting (American Society of International Law) 371.

Harre M-C, 'Supporting Supervisory Control of Safety-Critical Systems with Rationally Justified Information Visualizations' (Dissertation, Carl von Ossietzky Universität 2019).

Harrison J, *Making the Law of the Sea: A study in the development of international law* (Cambridge studies in international and comparative law, Cambridge University Press 2011).

Hathaway OA, 'International Delegation and State Sovereignty' (2008) 71(1) Law and Contemporary Problems 115.

Havnen I, 'Norden – nye muligheter: Forslag til økt mobilitet og integrasjon mellom de nordiske landene' (København 2018).

Heidbrink I, 'The Business of Shipping: An Historical Perspective' in Wayne K Talley (ed), *The Blackwell companion to maritime economics* (Blackwell companions to contemporary economics. Wiley-Blackwell 2012).

Hemphill TA, 'Technology entrepreneurship and innovation hubs: Perspectives on the universal regulatory sandbox' (2023) 50(2) Science and Public Policy 350.

Henry CE, *The carriage of dangerous goods by sea: The role of the International Maritime Organization in international legislation* (St. Martin's Press 1985).

Herdegen M, 'Interpretation in International Law' in Anne Peters (ed), *Max Planck Encyclopedia of Public International Law* (MPEPIL) (Oxford University Press).

Herkenhoff M-L, *Die Haftung in der unbemannte Schifffahrt* (Münsteraner Reihe vol 140, VVW GmbH 2020).

Hernández GI, 'Interpretation' in Jörg Kammerhofer and Jean d'Aspremont (eds), *International Legal Positivism in a Post-Modern World* (Cambridge University Press 2014).

Hernández GI, *International Law* (Oxford University Press 2019).

Herz M, 'Regional governance and regional organizations' in Thomas G Weiss and Rorden Wilkinson (eds), *International organization and global governance* (Second edition. Routledge Taylor & Francis Group 2018).

Hochschule Emden/Leer, 'Modulhandbuch Nautik und Seeverkehr' (Emden 26 January 2021).

Hooghe L and Marks G, 'Delegation and pooling in international organizations' (2015) 10(3) The Review of International Organizations 305.

Hoovestal LE, 'The Advent of the Container' in Lance E Hoovestal (ed), *Globalization Contained* (Palgrave Macmillan US 2013).

Horrocks C, 'Thoughts on the Respective Role of Flag States and Port States' in Myron H Nordquist and John N Moore (eds), *Current maritime issues and the international maritime organization* (Martinus Nijhoff Publishers 1999).

Hurka S and Steinebach Y, 'Legal Instrument Choice in the European Union' (2021) 59(2) Journal of Common Market Studies 278.

Husa J, Nuotio K and Pihlajamäki H, 'Nordic Law – Between Tradition and Dynamism' in Jaakko Husa, Kimmo Nuotio and Heikki Pihlajamäki (eds), *Nordic Law – Between Tradition and Dynamism* (Ius commune europaeum vol 66. Intersentia 2007).

Ilg C, *Die Rechtsetzungstätigkeit der International Maritime Organization: Zur Bedeutung der IMO bei der Weiterentwicklung des Meeresumweltrechts* (Campus Druck 2001).

International Law Commission (ILC), 'A/CN.4/104 – Report of the International Law Commission on the Work of its Eighth Session, Official Records of the General Assembly, Eleventh Session, Supplement No. 9 (A/3159)' [1956] Yearbook of the International Law Commission 253.

International Law Commission (ILC), 'A/CN.4/167 – Third report on the law of treaties by Sir Humphrey Waldock, Special Rapporteur' [1964] Yearbook of the International Law Commission 5.

International Law Commission (ILC), 'A/CN.4/191 – Report of the of the International Law Commission on the work of its Eighteenth Session, 4 May–19 July 1966' [1966] Yearbook of the International Law Commission 169.

International Law Commission (ILC), 'Report of the International Law Commission on the work of the second part of its seventeenth session' [1966] Yearbook of the International Law Commission 169.

International Law Commission (ILC), 'A/73/10 – Report of the International Law Commission on the work of its seventieth session (30 April–1 June and 2 July–10 August 2018)' (2018) 2(2) Yearbook of the International Law Commission.

Institut für Seeverkehrswirtschaft und Logistik, 'Projektkatalog' (Hamburg 2022).

International Chamber of Shipping, 'Seafarer Workforce Report: The global supply and demand for seafarers 2021' (8 April 2022) <https://publications.ics-shipping.org/single-product.php?id=56> accessed 16 February 2024.

International Law Commission (ILC), '121st Meeting' [1951] Yearbook of the International Law Commission 327.

International Maritime Organization (IMO), 'Brief History of IMO' <https://www.imo.org/en/About/HistoryOfIMO/Pages/Default.aspx> accessed 16 February 2024.

International Organization for Standardization, 'ISO/TS 23860:2022 – Ships and marine technology—Vocabulary related to autonomous ship systems' (Geneva 05/2022) <https://www.iso.org/obp/ui/#iso:std:iso:ts:23860:ed-1:v1:en>.

Ipsen K and Heintze H-J, *Völkerrecht: Ein Studienbuch* (Kurzlehrbücher für das juristische Studium, 7. Auflage, C.H. Beck 2019).

Krikigianni Eleni S and others, 'Automating vessels berthing, docking and stevedorage operations: The MOSES project' (2023).

Jacobsson M, 'What Challenges Lie Ahead for Maritime Law?' in Proshanto K Mukherjee, Maximo Q Mejia and Jingjing Xu (eds), *Maritime Law in Motion* (WMU Studies in Maritime Affairs Ser vol 8. Springer 2020).

Japan Radio Co. Ltd. *The Nippon Foundation MEGURI2040 Fully Autonomous Ship Project Demonstration test of autonomous navigation system on large RORO cargo* (2023).

Jessup PC, *Transnational law* (Storrs lectures on jurisprudence [1956], Yale University Press 1956).

Jia Chyuan Chong, 'Impact of maritime autonomous surface ships (MASS) on VTS operations' (Dissertation, World Maritime University 11 April 2018).

Jo M and others, 'Study on the potential gaps and themes identified by IMO Regulatory Scoping Exercise (RSE) for the use of Maritime Autonomous Surface Ships (MASS)' (2020) 929 IOP Conference Series: Materials Science and Engineering.

Johnstone I, 'Law-Making by International Organizations: Perspectives from IL/IR Theory' in Jeffrey L Dunoff and Mark A Pollack (eds), *Interdisciplinary Perspectives on International Law and International Relations: 'The State of the Art'* (Cambridge University Press 2013).

Jokioinen E and others, 'Remote and Autonomous Ships, AAWA: The next steps' (AAWA, London 2016).

Jokiranta V, 'The Shipmaster in Remote & Autonomous Operations' (University of Turku 6 May 2019).

Jones A, 'Self-Propelled Ship Yara Birkeland Completes Maiden Voyage' (22 November 2021) <https://industryeurope.com/sectors/transportation/slef-propelled-ship-yara-birkland-completes-maiden-voyage/> accessed 16 February 2024.

Kaarstad M and Braseth AO, 'Operating autonomous ships remotely from land-based operation centers: The current state-of-the-art' (Halden, Norway 18 December 2020).

Kahl W, 'Article 4 TEU' in Christian Calliess and Matthias Ruffert (eds), EUV/AEUV*: Das Verfassungsrecht der Europäischen Union mit Europäischer Grundrechtecharta: Kommentar* (6. Auflage. C.H. Beck 2022).

Kampantais N, 'Seaworthiness in autonomous unmanned cargo ships' (Erasmus University Rotterdam 2016).

Kampantais N, 'Legal and regulatory implications of the unmanned ship operation' (Athens, Greece March 2018).

Kanna Rajan, Karlyn D. Stanley, 'Unmanned Cargo Vessels: A Working Paper' (Santa Monica, California 2023).

Kantorowicz H and Campbell AH (eds), *The definition of Law* (Octagon Books 1980).

Karisma K, 'A Pragmatic Regulatory Framework for Artificial Intelligence' in Ivan Giannoccaro and Pardis M Tehrani (eds), *Regulatory Aspects of Artificial Intelligence on Blockchain* (Advances in Computational Intelligence and Robotics. IGI Global 2022).

Karlis T, 'Maritime law issues related to the operation of unmanned autonomous cargo ships' (2018) 17(1) WMU Journal of Maritime Affairs 119.

Kavallieratos G, Katsikas S and Gkioulos V, 'Cyber-Attacks Against the Autonomous Ship' in Sokratis K Katsikas and others (eds), *Computer Security:* ESORICS *2018 Inter-*

national Workshops, CyberICPS 2018 and SECPRE 2018, Barcelona, Spain, September 6–7, 2018, Revised Selected Papers (Springer International Publishing 2019).

Kestemont L, *Handbook on legal methodology: From objective to method* (Intersentia 2018).

Kettunen P and others, 'The nordic model and the rise and fall of Nordic Cooperation' in Johan Strang (ed), *Nordic cooperation, A European region in transition* (Routledge series on global order studies vol 8. Routledge 2016).

Kiltidou D, 'From The Flag State Duty For Inspections To The Remote Port State Control. The Necessity For Distant Controls' (2020) 14(4) TransNav 963.

Kingsbury B, 'The Concept of Law in Global Administrative Law Changing Paradigms in International Law: A Symposium' (2009) 20 European Journal of International Law 23.

Kirby M, 'The Fundamental Problem of Regulating Technology' (2009) 5(1) Indian Journal of Law and Technology 1.

Kirgis FL, 'Specialized Law-Making Processes' in Christopher C Joyner (ed), *The United Nations and International Law* (Cambridge Univ. Press 1997).

Kjeldstad B, Kufolar GM and Ulvensøen JH, 'Using the Watchkeeping regulation to verify safe operation of Uncrewed Surface Vessels' (2023).

Klabbers J, 'The Redundancy of Soft Law' (1996) 65 Nordic Journal of International Law 167.

Klabbers J, 'The Undesirability of Soft Law' (1998) 67 Nordic Journal of International Law 381.

Klabbers J, 'Straddling the Fence: The EU and International Law' in Anthony Arnull and Damian Chalmers (eds), *The Oxford handbook of European Union law* (Oxford University Press 2017).

Klein N, 'Meaning, Scope, and Significance of Informal Lawmaking in the Law of the Sea' in Natalie Klein (ed), *Unconventional Lawmaking in the Law of the Sea* (Oxford University Press 2022).

Knauff M, *Der Regelungsverbund: Recht und Soft Law im Mehrebenensystem* (Zugl.: Würzburg, Univ. Habil.-Schr. 2009–2010. Ius Publicum vol 193, Mohr Siebeck 2010).

Kojima C, 'South China Sea Arbitration and the Protection of the Marine Environment: Evolution of UNCLOS Part XII Through Interpretation and the Duty to Cooperate' in Seokwoo Lee and Hee E Lee (eds), *Asian Yearbook of International Law, Volume 21 (2015)* (Brill|Nijhoff 2018).

Kojima C and Vereshchetin VS, 'Implementation Agreements' in Anne Peters (ed), *Max Planck Encyclopedia of Public International Law* (MPEPIL) (Oxford University Press).

Komianos A, 'The Autonomous Shipping Era. Operational, Regulatory, and Quality Challenges' (2018) 12(2) TransNav 335.

Kongsberg Maritime, *KONGSBERG successfully completes autonomous operation of coastal cargo ship as part of EU's AUTOSHIP project* (2023).

König D, 'The Enforcement of the International Law of the Sea by Coastal and Port States' (2002) 62(1) Zeitschrift für ausländisches öffentliches Recht und Völkerrecht 1.

König D and Salomon TR, 'Flag of Convenience' in Anne Peters (ed), *Max Planck Encyclopedia of Public International Law* (MPEPIL) (Oxford University Press).

Koremenos B, 'When, What, and Why do States Choose to Delegate?' (2008) 71(1) Law and Contemporary Problems 151.

Korseberg L, 'The Law-Making Effects of the FAO Deep-Sea Fisheries Guidelines' (2018) 67(4) International and Comparative Law Quarterly 801.

Kötz H, 'Rechtsvereinheitlichung – Nutzen, Kosten, Methoden, Ziele' (1986) 50(1–2) The Rabel Journal of Comparative and International Private Law 1.

Kretschmann L, Burmeister H-C and Jahn C, 'Analyzing the economic benefit of unmanned autonomous ships: An exploratory cost-comparison between an autonomous and a conventional bulk carrier' (2017) 25 Research in Transportation Business & Management 76.

Kronke H, 'Ziele—Methoden, Kosten—Nutzen: Perspektiven der Privatrechtsharmonisierung nach 75 Jahren UNIDROIT' (2001) 56(23) JuristenZeitung 1149.

Kruif B de, 'Autonomous sailing from port to port' (Wageningen, Netherlands, 14 September 2023).

Ku C, *International Law, International Relations, and Global Governance* (Routledge 2012).

Kujala P and Lu L (eds), *Marine Design XIII, Volume 2: Proceedings of the 13th International Marine Design Conference (IMDC 2018), June 10–14, 2018, Helsinki, Finland* (Chapman and Hall/CRC 2018).

Kultanen P, 'World's first autonomous on-demand boat in Helsinki, could turn water transport carbon-neutral' (28 September 2023) <https://forumvirium.fi/en/release/worlds-first-autonomous-on-demand-boat-in-helsinki-could-turn-water-transport-carbon-neutral/> accessed 16 February 2024.

La Fayette L de, 'Access to Ports in International Law' (1996) 11(1) The International Journal of Marine and Coastal Law 1.

Laffey C, 'Reforming the Law of the Sea for the Future of Automated Shipping' in Kyriaki Noussia and Matthew Channon (eds), *The Regulation of Automated and Autonomous Transport* (1st ed. 2023. Springer International Publishing; Imprint Springer 2023).

Lamparski J, 'Safety of Navigation Satellites' [2022] Annual of Navigation 29.

Lampe WH, 'The "New" International Maritime Organization And Its Place In Development Of International Maritime Law' (1983) 14(3) Journal of Maritime Law and Commerce 305.

Lando O, 'Nordic Countries, a Legal Family? A Diagnosis and a Prognosis' (2001) 1(2) Global Jurist Advances 1.

Lange ER, 'Applying the tacit amendment procedure to accommodate international maritime law to Maritime Autonomous Surface Ships' (2022) 28(5) Journal of International Maritime Law 304–319.

Leenes R, 'Regulating New Technologies in Times of Change' in Leonie Reins (ed), *Regulating new technologies in uncertain times* (ProQuest Ebook Central vol 32. Asser Press; Springer 2019).

Legros C, 'Interpreting International Shipping Law with EU Soft Law Instruments' (2015) 7(1) European Journal of Commercial Contract Law 32.

Legros C, 'Improving international uniform transport law by creating interptative committees' in Jason Chuah (ed), *Research handbook on maritime law and regulation* (Research Handbooks in Private and Commercial Law series. Edward Elgar Publishing 2019).

Lessing L, *Code and other laws of cyberspace* (Basic Books 1999).

Letto-Vanamo P, 'Courts and Proceedings: Some Nordic Characteristic' in Laura Ervo, Pia Letto-Vanamo and Anna Nylund (eds), *Rethinking Nordic Courts* (Ius Gentium: Comparative Perspectives on Law and Justice vol 90. Springer 2021).

Letto-Vanamo P and Tamm D, 'Cooperation in the field of Law' in Johan Strang (ed), *Nordic cooperation, A European region in transition* (Routledge series on global order studies vol 8. Routledge 2016).

Leucci P, 'Innocent Passage in the Territorial Sea within the Framework of the Law of the Sea Convention' (2008) 10(1) KMI International Journal of Maritime Affairs and Fisheries 1.

Levinson M, *The Box* (Princeton University Press 2016).

Li Y, *Exclusion from Protection as a Refugee: An Approach to a Harmonizing Interpretation in International Law* (International Refugee Law vol 9, Brill|Nijhoff 2017).

Lijphart A, *Patterns of Democracy* (2nd edn, Yale University Press 2012).

Liu D, 'Autonomous Vessel Technology, Safety, and Ocean Impacts' in Dirk Werle (ed), *The future of ocean governance and capacity development: Essays in honor of Elisabeth Mann Borgese (1918–2002)* (Essays in Honor of Elisabeth Mann Borgese (1918–2002). Brill Nijhoff 2018).

Lorenzmeier S, 'Exclusive and Shared External Competences After the Singapore Opinion of the European Court of Justice: 2/15 Revisited' in Stefan Lorenzmeier, Roman Petrov and Christoph Vedder (eds), EU *External Relations Law: Shared Competences and Shared Values in Agreements Between the* EU *and Its Eastern Neighbourhood* (Springer eBook Collection, 1st ed. Springer International Publishing 2021).

Lost-Siemińska D, 'Implementation of IMO treaties into domestic legislation: Implementation and enforcement as the key to effectiveness of international treaties' in Zuzanna Pepłowska-Dąbrowska and Justyna Nawrot (eds), *Maritime Safety in Europe: A Comparative Approach* (Taylor & Francis 2020).

Lowe V, 'The Right of Entry into Maritime Ports in International Law' (1977) 14(3) San Diego Law Review 597.

Madricardo F and others, 'How to Deal With Seafloor Marine Litter: An Overview of the State-of-the-Art and Future Perspectives' (2020) 7 Frontiers in Marine Science.

Madsen AN, Aarset MV and Alsos OA, 'Safe and efficient maneuvering of a Maritime Autonomous Surface Ship (MASS) during encounters at sea: A novel approach' (2022) 3 Maritime Transport Research.

Malgosia Fitzmaurice and Panos Merkouris, 'Uniformity versus specialization (1): The quest for a uniform law of inter-State treaties' in Christian J Tams, Antonios Tzanakopoulos and Andreas Zimmermann (eds), *Research Handbook on the Law of Treaties* (Edward Elgar Publishing 2014).

Mallam S and Cross J, 'Towards the Seafarer of Tomorrow – Maritime Worker Competencies in the Autonomous Age' (2023) 18(4) The Journal of Ocean Technology 53.

Man Y and others, 'From Desk to Field – Human Factor Issues in Remote Monitoring and Controlling of Autonomous Unmanned Vessels' (2015) 3 Procedia Manufacturing 2674.

Mandel GN, 'Legal Evolution in Response to Technological Change' in Roger Brownsword, Eloise Scotford and Karen Yeung (eds), *The Oxford Handbook of Law, Regulation and Technology* (Oxford handbooks, First edition. Oxford University Press 2017).

Mandrioli D, 'The International Duty to Assist People in Distress at Sea in the Era of Unmanned Navigation: No Place for People on Board' (2020) 26(1) Humanidades & Tecnologia (FINOM) 77.

Mandrioli D, 'The Rise of Autonomous Ships Towards an Evolutionary Interpretation of the IMO Treaties on Safety of Navigation' (2022) 124(1) Il Diritto Maritimo 159.

Manning C, 'Artificial Intelligence Definitions' (Stanford September 2020).

Marchant G, Gutierrez CI and Tournas L, 'Lessons for Artificial Intelligence from Historical Uses of Soft Law Governance' (2020) 61(1) Jurimetrics 1.

Marchant GE, 'Addressing the Pacing Problem' in Gary E Marchant, Braden R Allenby and Joseph R Herkert (eds), *The Growing Gap Between Emerging Technologies and Legal-Ethical Oversight* (Springer Science and Business Media B.V. 2011).

Marchant GE, 'The Growing Gap Between Emerging Technologies and the Law' in Gary E Marchant, Braden R Allenby and Joseph R Herkert (eds), *The Growing Gap Between Emerging Technologies and Legal-Ethical Oversight* (Springer Science and Business Media B.V. 2011).

Marchant GE and Allenby B, 'Soft law: New tools for governing emerging technologies' (2017) 73(2) Bulletin of the Atomic Scientists 108.

Maritime and Coastguard Agency, 'Maritime Autonomy Regulation Lab (MARLab) Report' (Southampton 11 November 2020) <https://www.gov.uk/government/publications/maritime-autonomy-regulation-lab-marlab-report/maritime-autonomy-regulation-lab-marlab-report> accessed 9 March 2022.

Maritime and Port Authority of Singapore, 'Flag, Coastal and Port Authorities from Eight Countries Come Together to Encourage Development of Maritime Autonomous Surface Ships' (4 August 2020) <https://www.mpa.gov.sg/media-centre/details/flag-coastal-and-port-authorities-from-eight-countries-come-together-to-encourage-development-of-maritime-autonomous-surface-ships> accessed 16 February 2024.

Maritime Executive, 'An Early Look at ASKO's Autonomous Freight Ferries' (18 January 2021) <https://maritime-executive.com/article/an-early-look-at-asko-s-autonomous-freight-ferry> accessed 16 February 2024.

Maritime UK, 'Maritime Autonomous Surface Ships UK Industry Conduct Principles and Code of Practice: A voluntary Code' (London November 2021).

Markets and Markets, 'Autonomous Ship Market by Autonomy' (2022) <https://www.marketsandmarkets.com/Market-Reports/autonomous-ships-market-267183224.html> accessed 16 February 2024.

MASSPeople, 'About us' <https://www.masspeople.org/about-us> accessed 16 February 2024.

Massterly, 'What we do' <https://www.massterly.com/what-we-do> accessed 16 February 2024.

Matz-Lück N, 'Treaties, Conflicts between' in Anne Peters (ed), *Max Planck Encyclopedia of Public International Law* (MPEPIL) (Oxford University Press).

Matz-Lück N, 'Article 311 – Relation to other conventions and international agreements' in Alexander Proelß and others (eds), *United Nations Convention on the Law of the Sea: A commentary* (1st edition. C.H. Beck; Hart; Nomos 2017).

Maurer A, 'Lex Maritima' in Jürgen Basedow and others (eds), *Encyclopedia of Private International Law* (vol 2. Edward Elgar Publishing 2017).

Mayer FC and Thies SP, 'European Union, Historical Evolution' in Anne Peters (ed), *Max Planck Encyclopedia of Public International Law* (MPEPIL) (Oxford University Press).

McConnell ML, 'Darkening Confusion Mounted upon Darkening Confusion: The Search for the Elusive Genuine Link' (1985) 16(3) Journal of Maritime Law and Commerce 365.

McKenzie S, 'When is a Ship a Ship? Use by State Armed Forces of Uncrewed Maritime Vehicles and the United Nations Convention on the Law of the Sea' (2020) 21(2) Melbourne Journal of International Law 373.

Meersman H and others, 'Evaluating the performance of the vessel train concept' (2020) 12(1) European Transport Research Review.

Meeting of the States Parties, 'SPLOS/14 – Report of the fifth Meeting of States Parties' (New York 20 September 1996).

Meersman H and others, 'SPLOS/31 – Report of the Eighth Meeting of States Parties' (New York 4 June 1998).

Meersman H and others, 'SPLOS/73 – Report of the eleventh Meeting of States Parties' (New York 14 June 2001).

Meersman H and others, 'SPLOS/203 – Report of the nineteenth Meeting of States Parties' (New York 24 July 2009).

Mensah TA, 'Foreword' in Sam Bateman and Donald R Rothwell (eds), *Navigational Rights and Freedoms and the New Law of the Sea* (Publications on ocean development vol 35. Brill|Nijhoff 2000).

Meyers LJ, 'COLREGS and Autonomous Surface Vessels' [2022] The Coast Guard Journal of Safety and Security at Sea Proceeedings 46.

Ministry of Oceans and Fisheries, 'The Future of Korea Autonomous Surface Ship' (30 November 2020) <https://www.mof.go.kr/doc/en/selectDoc.do?docSeq=49788&searchSelect=content&recordCountPerPage=&menuSeq=485&searchEtc1=&searchEtc2=&searchEtc3=&searchEtc4=&searchEtc5=&bbsSeq=90&searchValue=autonomous&currentPageNo=1> accessed 16 February 2024.

Miyoshi T, Fujimoto S and Rooks M, 'Study of Principles in COLREG s and Interpretations and Amendments COLREG s for Maritime Autonomous Surface Ships (MASS)' (2021) 6(1) Transactions of Navigation 11.

Mögele R, 'Article 3 TFEU' in Rudolf Streinz and others (eds), EUV/AEUV*: Vertrag über die Europäische Union, Vertrag über die Arbeitsweise der Europäischen Union, Charta der Grundrechte der Europäischen Union* (Beck-Online Bücher Band 57, 3. Auflage. C.H. Beck 2018).

Molenaar EJ, 'The EC Directive on Port State Control in Context' (1996) 11(2) International Journal of Marine and Coastal Law 241.

Molenaar EJ, 'Port State Jurisdiction: Toward Comprehensive, Mandatory and Global Coverage' (2007) 38(1–2) Ocean Development & International Law 225.

Molenaar EJ, 'Options for Regional Regulation of Merchant Shipping Outside IMO, with Particular Reference to the Arctic Region' (2014) 45(3) Ocean Development & International Law 272.

Molenaar EJ, '13 Port and Coastal States' in Donald R Rothwell and others (eds), *The Oxford Handbook of the Law of the Sea* (Oxford University Press 2015).

Mørkrid OE and others, 'D2.6 – Roadmap for automated waterborne transport' (2023).

Morris KC, Schlenoff C and Srinivasan V, 'A Remarkable Resurgence of Artificial Intelligence and its Impact on Automation and Autonomy' (2017) 14(2) IEEE transactions on automation science and engineering 407.

Moses LB, 'How to Think about Law, Regulation and Technology: Problems with 'Technology' as a Regulatory Target' (2013) 5(1) Law, Innovation and Technology 1.

MOSES, 'MOSES Fact Sheet' (2020).

Mukherjee PK, *Maritime Legislation* (WMU Publications 2002).

Munim ZH and others, 'Autonomous ships for container shipping in the Arctic routes' (2022) 27(1) Journal of Marine Science and Technology 320.

Nærings- og fiskeridepartementet, *Ny avtale sikrer internasjonalt samarbeid om drift av autonome skip* (2024).

Nakamura S and Okada N, 'Development of Automatic Collision Avoidance System and Quantitative Evaluation of the Manoeuvring Results' (2019) 13(1) TransNav 133.

Nam D, 'Identification and Analysis of the Legal Status of International Maritime Organization Instruments' (2021) 27(3) Journal of the Korean Society of Marine Environment & Safety 421.

Nandan SN and Nordquist MH (eds), *United Nations Convention on the Law of the Sea, 1982 : a commentary; Vol. III; Articles 86 to 132 and Documentary Annexes* (Brill|Nijhoff 1995).

Nandan SN, Rosenne S and Grandy NR, *Articles 1 to 85, Annexes I and II, Final Act, Annex II* (United Nations Convention on the Law of the Sea, 1982: a commentary/ Center for Oceans Law and Policy, University of Virginia. Myron H. Nordquist [Ed.-in-Chief] vol 2, Kluwer Academic Publishers Group 1993).

Nengye L and Maes Frank, 'The European Union and the International Maritime Organization: EU's External Influence on the Prevention of Vessel-Source Pollution' (2010) 41(4) Journal of Maritime Law and Commerce 581.

Neteland D, *Signerte kontrakt om verdas første ferjesamband med sjølvgåande ferjer* (2024).

Nguyen TT and others, 'Current Challenges in the Recruitment and Retention of Seafarers: An Industry Perspective from Vietnam' (2014) 30(2) The Asian Journal of Shipping and Logistics 217.

Nolte G, 'Court Generated State Practice: A Response to Karl Zemanek' (2015) 20 Austrian Review of International and European Law 17.

Nolte G, 'Introductory Note to the Special Issue of ICLR on the Outcome of the ILC Work on "Subsequent Agreements and Subsequent Practice in Relation to the Interpretation of Treaties"' (2020) 22 International Community Law Review 4.

Noma T, 'Existing conventions and unmanned ships – need for changes?' (World Maritime University Dissertations, 527 2016).

Nordahl H and others, 'D8.2 Roadmap for Autonomous ship adoption and development' (March 2023).

Nordic Ministers for the Environment and Climate, 'Ministerial Declaration on zero emission shipping routes between the Nordic countries' (3 May 2022) <https://www.norden.org/en/declaration/ministerial-declaration-zero-emission-shipping-routes-between-nordic-countries> accessed 16 February 2024.

Nordic transport ministers from Finland, Iceland, Sweden and Norway, 'Fredrikstad Declaration' (Fredrikstad 8 November 2022).

Nordisk ministerråd, 'Nordisk pendlingskarta-Huvudrapport' (København 2005).

Nordiska ministerrådet, 'Ett säkrare, grönare, friare Norden: Program för Sveriges ordförandeskap i Nordiska ministerrådet 2024' (Kopenhagen 31.13.2023).

Nordquist MH, Rosenne S and Sohn LB, *Volume V, Articles 279–320, Annexes V, VI, VIII and IX, Final Act, Annex I, Resolutions I, III and IV* (United Nations Convention on the Law of the Sea, 1982: a commentary vol 5, Kluwer Academic Publishers 1989).

Norges forskningsråd, 'Maritime21' (Lysaker, Norway January 2022).

Ntovas AXM and others, 'Liability for operations in Unmanned Maritime Vehicles with Differing Levels of Autonomy' (Southampton 15 January 2016) 14.CAT.OP.065.

Ntovas AXM, 'Functionalism and Maritime Autonomous Surface Ships' in James Kraska and Young-Kil Park (eds), *Emerging technology and the law of the sea* (Cambridge University Press 2022).

Ocean infinity, 'Marine Robotics' <https://oceaninfinity.com/marine-robotics/> accessed 16 February 2024.

O'Leary A and Brown J, 'The Legal Basis for IMO Climate Measures' (New York June 2018).

One Sea Autonomous maritime ecosystem, 'Autonomous ships and safety at sea: White Paper' (Tampere, Finland June 2021).

Onions CT (ed), *The Oxford dictionary of English etymology* (Repr, Oxford Univ. Press 1996).

Osaloni OS and Ayeni VO, 'The Development of Maritime Autonomous Surface Ships: Regulatory Challenges and the Way Forward' (2022) 13(3) Beijing Law Review 544.

OSPAR Commission, 'OSPAR 12/22/1-E, Annex 17: Joint Notice to Shipping from the Contracting Parties of the Barcelona Convention, OSPAR and HELCOM on: – General Guidance on the Voluntary Interim Application of the D1 Ballast Water Exchange Standard by Vessels Operating between the Mediterranean Sea and the North-East Atlantic and/or the Baltic Sea' (Bonn 29 June 2012).

Østerud Ø, 'Det nordiske paradokset – en ambivalent region i Europa' in Johan P Olsen and Bjørn O Sverdrup (eds), *Europa i Norden: Europeisering av sordisk samarbeid* (Tano Aschehoug 1998).

Oxford English Dictionary, 'carry, v.' <https://www.oed.com/dictionary/carry_v?tab=meaning_and_use#9991414> accessed 16 February 2024.

Oxford English Dictionary, 'charge, n.' <https://www.oed.com/dictionary/charge_n?tab=meaning_and_use#9597041> accessed 16 February 2024.

Oxford English Dictionary, 'crew, n.' <https://www.oed.com/view/Entry/44347?rskey=kZkDaG&result=1&isAdvanced=false#eid> accessed 16 February 2024.

Oxford English Dictionary, 'harmony, n.' <https://www.oed.com/dictionary/harmony_n?tab=meaning_and_use#2081960> accessed 16 February 2024.

Oxford English Dictionary, 'manned, adj.' <https://www.oed.com/view/Entry/236238?rskey=ZhhMIx&result=2&isAdvanced=false#eid> accessed 16 February 2024.

Oxford English Dictionary, 'ship, n.' <https://www.oed.com/dictionary/ship_n1?tab=meaning_and_use#22916502> accessed 16 February 2024.

Oxford English Dictionary, 'uniformity, n.' <https://www.oed.com/dictionary/uniformity_n?tab=meaning_and_use#16648235> accessed 16 February 2024.

Oxford English Dictionary, 'vessel, n.' <https://www.oed.com/dictionary/vessel_n1?tab=meaning_and_use#15794971> accessed 16 February 2024.

Oxford English Dictionary, 'minimum, n. and adj.' (11 May 2022) <https://www.oed.com/view/Entry/118854?redirectedFrom=minimum#eid>.

Oxford English Dictionary, 'autonomy, n.' <https://www.oed.com/view/Entry/13500?redirectedFrom=autonomy#eid> accessed 16 February 2024.

Oxman BH, 'The Duty to Respect Generally Accepted International Standards' (1991) 24(1) New York University Journal of International Law and Politics 109.

Özçayir ZO, 'The Use of Port State Control in Maritime Industry and Application of the Paris MoU' (2008) 14(2) Ocean and Coastal Law Journal 201.

Paasche MT, Helgesen ØK and Brekke EF, 'Real-time 360 degrees view for the operator of *milliAmpere 2*' (2023) 2618(1) Journal of Physics: Conference Series.

Pacific Small Island Developing States, 'PSIDS Submission to the BBNJ PrepCom' (New York 29 August 2016).

Panama Maritime Authority, 'Marine Safety Investigation Report of Grounding of MV *Ever Given* at Suez Canal Egypt on March 23, 2021: R-026-2021-DIAM' (Panama 2023).

Papanicolopulu I, 'The duty to rescue at sea, in peacetime and in war: A general overview' (2016) 98(902) International Review of the Red Cross 491.

Pariotti E, 'Law, Uncertainty and Emerging Technologies' (2010) 62 Persona & Derecho 15.

Pariotti E, 'Paris MoU White List 07-2024–06-2025' (2023).

Pariotti E, 'ParisMoU Performance List Grey List 07-2024–06-2025' (2023).

Paris MoU on PSC, 'History' <https://www.parismou.org/about-us/history> accessed 16 February 2024.

Parker J, 'The Challenges Posed by the Advent of Maritime Autonomous Surface Ships for International Maritime Law' (2021) 35(1) Australian and New Zealand Maritime Law Journal 31.

Parlov I, 'The 2007 Nairobi International Convention on the Removal of Wrecks: The Implications for the Law of the Sea' (2022) 36(1) Ocean Yearbook Online 659.

Parlov I, 'Can the International Regulatory Framework on Ships' Routing, Ship Reporting, and Vessel Traffic Service (VTS) Accommodate Marine Autonomous Surface Ships (MASS)?' (2023) 54(2) Ocean Development & International Law 163.

Paulus A, 'Treaties of Friendship, Commerce and Navigation' in Anne Peters (ed), *Max Planck Encyclopedia of Public International Law* (MPEPIL) (Oxford University Press).

PCCG Point Conception Consulting GmbH and others, 'Internationale Umfeldanalyse zu Anwendungsfällen von Autonomen Maritimen Systemen (AMS)' (Hamburg 22 June 2022).

Pekic S, 'Hyundai Heavy conducts world's first transoceanic voyage of LNG carrier on autonomous navigation' (2 June 2022) <https://www.offshore-energy.biz/hyundai

-heavy-conducts-worlds-first-transoceanic-voyage-of-lng-carrier-on-autonomous-navigation/> accessed 16 February 2024.

Petren G, 'The Nordic Council A Unique Factor in International Law' (1959) 29 Nordisk Tidskrift for International Ret 346.

Petrig A, 'Unconventional Law for Unconventional Ships? The Role of Informal Law in the International Maritime Organization's Quest to Regulate Maritime Autonomous Surface Ships' in Natalie Klein (ed), *Unconventional Lawmaking in the Law of the Sea* (Oxford University Press 2022).

Porathe T and others, 'At least as safe as manned shipping? Autonomous shipping, safety and "human error"' in Stein Haugen and others (eds), *Safety and Reliability – Safe Societies in a Changing World: Proceedings of* ESREL *2018, June 17–21, 2018, Trondheim, Norway* (Taylor & Francis 2018).

Porathe T, 'Maritime Autonomous Surface Ships (MASS) and the COLREGS: Do We Need Quantified Rules Or Is "the Ordinary Practice of Seamen" Specific Enough?' (2019) 13(3) TransNav 511.

Porathe T, Prison J and Man Y, 'Situation Awareness in Remote Control Centres for Unmanned Ships' (Human Factors in Ship Design & Operation, 26–27/02/2014).

Pribyl ST and Weigel AM, 'How an Emerging Disruptive Technology Is Poised to Impact the Maritime Industry Much Sooner than Anticipated' (2018) 17(1) RAIL: The Journal of Robotics, Artificial Intelligence & Law 17.

Prietz M, *Weiches Recht und normative Härtung: Eine Konzeptualisierung am Beispiel des UN-Migrationspaktes* (Jus Internationale et Europaeum vol 200, 1st edn, Mohr Siebeck 2023).

Pritchett PW, 'Ghost Ships Why the law should embrace unmanned vessel technology' (2015) 40(1) Tulane Maritime Law Journal 197.

Proelß A and Güssow K, 'Das Internationale Seerecht – ein potentes Regelwerk' [2011] World Ocean Review 199.

Pünder H, 'Democratic Legitimation of Delegated Legislation – a Comparative View on the American, British and German Law' (2009) 58(2) International and Comparative Law Quarterly 353.

Rambøll and Core Advokatfirma, 'Analysis of regulatory barriers to the use of autonomous ships' (Korsør, Denmark December 2017).

Randall C, 'World's largest electric ferry launches in Norway' (2 March 2021) <https://www.electrive.com/2021/03/02/worlds-largest-electric-ferry-yet-goes-into-service-in-norway/> accessed 16 February 2024.

Rato M and others, 'Temporal evolution of imposex in Nassarius reticulatus (L.) along the Portuguese coast: the efficacy of EC regulation 782/2003' (2009) 11(1) Journal of Environmental Monitoring 100.

Rayfuse R, 'Public International Law and the Regulation of Emerging Technologies' in Roger Brownsword, Eloise Scotford and Karen Yeung (eds), *The Oxford Handbook of*

Law, Regulation and Technology (Oxford handbooks, First edition. Oxford University Press 2017).

Regan DH, 'Sources of International Trade Law: Understanding What the Vienna Convention Says About Identifying and Using 'Sources For Treaty Interpretation" in Samantha Besson and Jean d'Aspremont (eds), *The Oxford Handbook of the Sources of International Law* (vol 1. Oxford University Press 2018).

Regan DH, 'Die Anwendung des Grundsatzes der Völkerrechtsfreundlichkeit auf rechtsunverbindliche internationale Standards' [2018] Zeitschrift für ausländisches öffentliches Recht und Völkerrecht 311.

Reiling K, *Seeverwaltungsrecht als interantionales Verwaltungsrecht* (no date).

Reports of the Commission to the General Assembly, 'Section 3: Interpretation of treaties' [1966] Yearbook of the International Law Commission 217.

Ricard P, 'The European Union and the Future International Legally Binding Instrument on Marine Biodiversity Beyond National Jurisdiction' in Marta C C M Da Ribeiro, Fernando L Bastos and Tore Henriksen (eds), *Global challenges and the law of the sea* (Springer 2020).

Rigaux A and Simon D, 'Article 41 – Agreements to modify multilateral treaties between certain of the parties only' in Olivier Corten and Pierre Klein (eds), *The Vienna Conventions on the Law of Treaties* (Oxford commentaries on international law vol 2. Oxford University Press 2011).

Ringbom H, *The EU Maritime Safety Policy and International Law* (Publications on ocean development vol 64, Brill 2008).

Ringbom H, 'Regulating Autonomous Ships—Concepts, Challenges and Precedents' (2019) 50(2–3) Ocean Development & International Law 141.

Ringbom H, 'Legalizing autonomous ships' (2020) 34(1) Ocean Yearbook 431.

Ringbom H and Collin F, 'Terminology and concepts' in Henrik Ringbom, Erik Røsæg and Trond Solvang (eds), *Autonomous ships and the law* (IMLI studies in international maritime law. Routledge 2021).

Ritt V, *Unbemannte Schiffe im Internationalen Seerecht* (Acta Iuridica Universitatis Potsdamiensis vol 8, Universitätsverlag Potsdam 2022).

Roach JA, 'Today's Customary International Law of the Sea' (2014) 45(3) Ocean Development & International Law 239.

Roach JA, 'A Note on Making the Polar Code Mandatory' in Suzanne Lalonde and Ted L McDorman (eds), *International law and politics of the Arctic Ocean: Essays in honor of Donat Pharand* (Koninklijke Brill 2015).

Röben V, 'Conference (Meeting) of States Parties' in Anne Peters (ed), *Max Planck Encyclopedia of Public International Law* (MPEPIL) (Oxford University Press).

Rodriguez Delgado JP, 'The Legal Challenges of Unmanned Ships in the Private Maritime Law: What Laws Would You Change?' [2018] Port, Maritime and Transport Law between Legacies of the past and modernization 493–523.

Rødseth ØJ and others, 'AEGIS: Advanced, efficient and green intermodal systems' (2020) 929(1) IOP Conference Series: Materials Science and Engineering.

Rødseth ØJ, 'Autonomous Ship in Activities Norway' (2023) 18(4) The Journal of Ocean Technology 45.

Rødseth ØJ and others, 'The Societal Impacts of Autonomous Ships: The Norwegian Perspective' in Tafsir M Johansson and others (eds), *Autonomous Vessels in Maritime Affairs* (Studies in National Governance and Emerging Technologies. Springer International Publishing 2023).

Rødseth ØJ and Burmeister H-C, 'Risk Assessment for an Unmanned Merchant Ship' (2015) 9(3) TransNav 357.

Rødseth ØJ and Nordahl H, 'Definition of autonomy levels for merchant ships: Report from NFAS, Norwegian Forum for Autonomous Ships' (Trondheim 2017).

Rødseth ØJ and Nordahl H, 'Definitions for Autonomous Merchant Ships' (Trondheim 2017).

Rødseth ØJ and Wennersberg LAL, 'A Criticism of Proposed Levels of Autonomy for MASS' (2023). Proceedings of the 3rd European Conference on Safety and Reliability <https://www.esrel2023.com>.

Rødseth ØJ, Wennersberg LAL and Nordahl H, 'Levels of autonomy for ships' (2022) 2311(1) Journal of Physics: Conference Series.

Rosas A, 'The Status in EU Law of International Agreements Concluded by EU Member States' (2011) 34(5) Fordham International Law Journal 1304.

Rosenne S, 'The International Maritime Law Organization Interface with the Law of the Sea' in Myron H Nordquist and John N Moore (eds), *Current maritime issues and the international maritime organization* (Martinus Nijhoff Publishers 1999).

Rosett A, 'Unification, Harmonization, Restatement, Codification, and Reform in International Commercial Law' (1992) 40(3) The American Journal of Comparative Law 683.

Roth-Isigkeit D and Thomale R, 'Technische Rahmenbedingungen und Rechtliche Regulierung der Digitalen Transformation' in Susanne Beck, Carsten Kusche and Brian Valerius (eds), *Digitalisierung, Automatisierung, KI und Recht: Festgabe zum 10-jährigen Bestehen der Forschungsstelle RobotRecht* (Robotik und Recht vol 20. Nomos Verlagsgesellschaft mbH & Co. KG 2020).

Roussel M, 'French Regulations on MASS: Solved and Unsolved Issues' (Comité Maritime International, Montreal, 14 June 2023).

Royal Navy, 'NAVY X' <https://www.royalnavy.mod.uk/news-and-latest-activity/operations/united-kingdom/navy-x> accessed 16 February 2024.

Ruffert M, 'Article 288 TFEU' in Christian Calliess and Matthias Ruffert (eds), EUV/AEUV: *Das Verfassungsrecht der Europäischen Union mit Europäischer Grundrechtecharta: Kommentar* (6. Auflage. C.H. Beck 2022).

Rui L, 'On the Legal Status of Unmanned Ships' (2019) 2019(4) China Ocean Law Review 165.

Rummenhöller P, 'Harmonielehre' in Laurenz Lütteken (ed), *Musik in Geschichte und Gegenwart* (RILM, Bärenreiter, Metzler 2016).

Saager M, Patrick Osterloh J and Brück Y, 'KONECT: Implementation and Extension of a Method for the Development of Safety-Critical Human-Machine Interaction Interfaces' (2022) 61 Human Factor in Software and Systems Engineering 1.

Saarni J, Nordberg-Davies S and Saurama A, 'Outlook on the transition towards autonomous shipping' (Turku 2018).

Saha R, 'Mapping competence requirements for future shore control center operators' [2021] Maritime Policy & Management 1.

Saha R, Lundh M and MacKinnon S, 'The shift toward autonomous European inland waterway shipping: Identifying the gaps in the emerging socio-technical system' (2023) 2618(1) Journal of Physics: Conference Series.

Saive D, 'Die Zukunft der Beförderungsdokumente' [2023] Recht der Transportwirtschaft 132.

Salvarani R, 'EC Directive on Port State Control: A Policy Statement' (1996) 11(2) The International Journal of Marine and Coastal Law 225.

Samuel AL, 'Some Studies in Machine Learning; Using the Game of Checkers' (2000) 44(1.2) IBM Journal of Research and Development 206.

Scaccabarozzi D and others, 'Monitoring of train driver's alertness: A feasibility study' (2017 IEEE International Instrumentation and Measurement Technology Conference (I2MTC), Torino, Italy, 5/22/2017–5/25/2017).

Scandinavian Airline System, 'History Milestones' <https://www.sasgroup.net/about-sas/sas-history/history-milestones/> accessed 16 February 2024.

Schelin J, 'Sjölagen: En åldrande nordisk dinosaurie?' [2007] Jurdisk Tidskrift 140.

Schelin J, 'The responsibility for unmanned ships – shipmaster's position' in Institut du Droit International des Transportes (ed), *N° spécial – colloque international 50ème anniversaire de l'IDIT* (2020).

Schmalenbach K, 'Lawmaking by treaty: Negotiation of agreements and adoption of treaty texts' in Catherine Brölmann and Yannick Radi (eds), *Research handbook on the theory and practice of international lawmaking* (Edward Elgar Publishing 2016).

Schmalenbach K, 'Article 2 – Use of terms' in Oliver Dörr and Kirsten Schmalenbach (eds), *Vienna Convention on the Law of Treaties: A Commentary* (2. 2nd ed. 2018. Springer Berlin Heidelberg 2018).

Schröder M, 'Article 170 TFEU' in Rudolf Streinz and others (eds), EUV/AEUV*: Vertrag über die Europäische Union, Vertrag über die Arbeitsweise der Europäischen Union, Charta der Grundrechte der Europäischen Union* (Beck-Online Bücher Band 57, 3. Auflage. C.H. Beck 2018).

Schwab K and Davis N, *Shaping the future of the Fourth Industrial Revolution: A guide to building a better world* (First American edition, Currency 2018).

Schwampe D, 'Rechtsetzung durch die International Maritime Organisation unter der Lupe – Die Unified Interpretations zur unbeschränkten Haftung nach IMO Übereinkommen' [2022] Recht der Transportwirtschaft 26.

Scott KN, 'The LOSC: 'A Constitution for the Oceans' in the Anthropocene?' (2023) 41(1) The Australian Year Book of International Law Online 269.

Scovazzi T, 'The Evolution of International Law of the Sea: New Issues, new Challenges' (2000) 286 Collected Courses of the Hague Academy of International Law.

Scovazzi T, 'The Progressive Development of International Law of the Sea: Within or (in Certain Cases) without the UNCLOS' (2020) 12(3) China Oceans Law Review 12.

Seamless, 'Seamless – Safe, Efficient and Autonomous: Multimodal Library of European Shortsea and Inland Solutions' (April 2023).

Seatrade Maritime News, 'China's first autonomous cargo ship makes maiden voyage' (2019) <https://www.seatrade-maritime.com/technology/chinas-first-autonomous-cargo-ship-makes-maiden-voyage> accessed 16 February 2024.

Secrétariat d'État chargé de la Mer, *La France pionnière dans l'exploitation des drones maritimes* (2021).

Senden L, *Soft law in European Community law* (Modern studies in European law vol 1, Hart 2004).

Shaffer GC and Pollack MA, 'Hard vs. Soft Law: Alternatives, Complements and Antagonists in International Governance' (2010) 94 Minnesota Law Review 706.

Sharma A and others, 'Catching up with time? Examining the STCW competence framework for autonomous shipping' (Haugesund 2019).

Shelton D, 'Commitment and Compliance: The Role of Non-Binding Norms in the International Legal System' in Dinah Shelton (ed), *Commitment and Compliance: The Role of Non-binding Norms in the International Legal System* (Oxford University Press 2003).

Shelton D, 'Soft Law' in David Armstrong and others (eds), *Routledge Handbook of International Law* (Routledge international handbooks. Routledge 2009).

Shi L, 'Successful Use of the Tacit Acceptance Procedure to Effectuate Progress in International Maritime Law' (1999) 11(2) University of San Francisco Maritime Law Journal 299.

Shiokari M and Ota S, 'Considerations on the regulatory issues for realization of Maritime Autonomous Surface Ships' (2019) 1357 Journal of Physics: Conference Series 1.

Sjøfartsdirektoratet, 'Føringer i forbindelse med bygging eller installering av automatisert funksjonalitet, med hensikt å kunne utføre ubemannet eller delvis ubemannet drift: RSV 12-2020' (Haugesund 27 August 2020). Rundskriv 5 accessed 21 June 2022.

Skærseth JB, 'Managing North Sea Pollution Effectively: Linking International and Domestic Institutions' [2003] International Environmental Agreements: Politics, Law and Economics 167.

Skillful, 'The need for Skillful' <https://skillfulproject.eu/> accessed 16 February 2024.

SkillSea, 'What is SkillSea?' (2022) <https://www.skillsea.eu/index.php/about/what-is-skillsea> accessed 16 February 2024.

Skredderberget A, 'The first ever zero emission, autonomous ship' (2018) <https://www.yara.com/knowledge-grows/game-changer-for-the-environment/> accessed 16 February 2024.

Snidal D, 'Rational Choice and International Relations' in Walter Carlsnaes, Thomas Risse and Beth A Simmons (eds), *Handbook of international relations* (SAGE Publications 2013).

Sorel J-M and Eveno VB, 'Article 31' in Olivier Corten and Pierre Klein (eds), *The Vienna Conventions on the Law of Treaties* (Oxford commentaries on international law vol 2. Oxford University Press 2011).

Sørensen G, Møller J and Jackson RH, *Introduction to international relations: Theories and approaches* (Eighth edition, Oxford University Press 2022).

Sotiropoulos L, 'European Maritime Policies and the Dynamic of Autonomous Vessels' [2024] International Investment Law Journal 71.

Soyer B, 'The Future of Autonomous Shipping – The Regulatory Challenge' in Barış Soyer and Andrew Tettenborn (eds), *Artificial Intelligence and Autonomous Shipping: Developing the International Legal Framework* (Hart Publishing 2021).

SpaceXFleet, 'Just Read the Instructions' <https://spacexfleet.com/just-read-the-instructions> accessed 16 February 2024.

Standing Committee of the EFTA States, 'How EU acts become EEA acts and the need for adaptations' (Geneva, Brussels 23 May 2013) Ref. 1113623.

Statistisk sentralbyrå, 'Utenrikshandel med varer' (15 February 2024) <https://www.ssb.no/utenriksokonomi/utenrikshandel/statistikk/utenrikshandel-med-varer> accessed 16 February 2024.

Stefan OA and others, 'EU Soft Law in the EU Legal Order: A Literature Review' [2019] SSRN Journal.

Steinbach A and Aaken A von, Ökonomische Analyse des Völker- und Europarechts (Anne van Aaken tr. Mohr Siebeck Lehrbuch, 1st edn, Mohr Siebeck 2019).

Stępień B, 'Can a ship be its own captain? Safe manning of autonomous and uncrewed vessels' (2023) 148 Marine Policy.

Stevens F, 'Seaworthiness and good seamanship in the age of autonomous vessels' in Henrik Ringbom, Erik Røsæg and Trond Solvang (eds), *Autonomous ships and the law* (IMLI studies in international maritime law. Routledge 2021).

Stokey R and Purcell M, 'AUV bloopers or why Murphy must have been an optimist: a practical look at achieving mission level reliability in an Autonomous Underwater Vehicle' (Duham, New Hampshire, 23.-25.08.1999).

Stortinget, 'Lovvedtak 65 om havne- og farvannsloven' (Oslo 4 June 2019).

Strang J, 'Introduction: The Nordic model as transnational cooperation?' in Johan Strang (ed), *Nordic cooperation, A European region in transition* (Routledge series on global order studies vol 8. Routledge 2016).

Strang J, 'Nordic Political and Economic Cooperation:' (Singapore February 2016).

Streng M and Kuipers B, 'Economic, social, and environmental impacts of autonomous shipping strategies' in Thierry Vanelslander and Christa Sys (eds), *Maritime Supply Chains* (Elsevier 2020).

Sturley MF, 'Can commercial law accommodate new technologies in international shipping?' in Barış Soyer and Andrew Tettenborn (eds), *New Technologies, Artificial Intelligence and Shipping Law in the 21st Century* (Maritime and transport law library. Informa Law from Routledge 2019).

Sub-Committee on Carriage of Cargoes and Containers, 'CCC 9-INF.7 – Supporting information to the draft interim guidelines for the safety of ships using ammonia as fuel (Denmark, Finland, Norway, and Sweden)' (London 20 June 2023).

Sun Z, 'Unconventional Lawmaking in the Compliance Mechanism for the International Regulation of Shipping' in Natalie Klein (ed), *Unconventional Lawmaking in the Law of the Sea* (Oxford University Press 2022).

Sun Z and Beckman R, 'The Development of the Polar Code and challenges to Its Implementation' in Keyuan Zou (ed), *Global Commons and the Law of the Sea* (Maritime cooperation in east asia volume 5. Brill 2018).

Sundelius B and Wiklund C, *Femtio år av nordiskt samarbete* (Världspolitikens dagsfrågor 2002, 4, Utrikespolitiska Inst 2002).

Surian I, 'A Legal Analysis of the Collision and Strict Liability Framework for the Shipowner of Unmanned and Autonomous Vessels (South Africa)' in Sanja Bauk and Stojče D Ilčev (eds), *The 1st International Conference on Maritime Education and Development* (Springer International Publishing 2021).

Suzuki T, 'Challenge of Technology Development through MEGURI 2040: For Safe Navigation and Workload Reduction' [2021] ClassNK Technical Journal 51.

Symmons CR, 'Article 11 – Ports' in Alexander Proelß and others (eds), *United Nations Convention on the Law of the Sea: A commentary* (1st edition. C.H. Beck; Hart; Nomos 2017).

Székely I, Dániel Szabó M and Vissy B, 'Regulating the future? Law, ethics, and emerging technologies' (2011) 9(3) Journal of Information, Communication and Ethics in Society 180.

Taekema S, 'Relative Autonomy: A Characterization of the Discipline of Law' in Sanne Taekema and Bart van Klink (eds), *Law and Method: Interdisciplinary Research into Law* (Politika vol 4. Mohr Siebeck 2011).

Tam K and Jones K, 'Cyber-Risk Assessment for Autonomous Ships' (2018 International Conference on Cyber Security and Protection of Digital Services (Cyber Security), Glasgow, 6/11/2018–6/12/2018).

Tanaka Y, *The international law of the sea* (1. publ, Cambridge University Press 2012).

Tanaka Y, 'Law of the Sea' in Simon Chesterman and others (eds), *The Oxford Handbook of United Nations Treaties* (Oxford University Press 2019).

Tasikas V, 'The Regime of Maritime Port Access: A Relook at Contemporary International and United States Law' (2007) 5(1) Loyola Maritime Law Journal 1.

Tavallaey SS and Ganz C, 'Automation to Autonomy' (2019 24th IEEE International Conference on Emerging Technologies and Factory Automation (ETFA), Zaragoza, Spain, 9/10/2019–9/13/2019).

Terpan F, 'Soft Law in the European Union-The Changing Nature of EU Law' (2015) 21(1) European Law Journal 68.

Tesla, 'Nikola Tesla Timeline' <https://teslauniverse.com/nikola-tesla/timeline/1898-tesla-demonstrates-worlds-first-wireless-remote-controlled-boat> accessed 16 February 2024.

Tesla N, 'My Inventions: VI. The Art of Telautomatics' (1919) 78(6) Electrical Experimenter.

Tetley W, 'Uniformity of International Private Maritime Law – The Pros, Cons, and Alternatives to International Conventions – How to Adopt an International Convention' (2000) 24(2) Tulane Maritime Law Journal 775–856.

Tettenborn A, 'Codification – best left to states or to someone else?' in Justyna Nawrot and Zuzanna Pepłowska-Dąbrowska (eds), *Codification of maritime law: Challenges, possibilities and experience* (Maritime and transport law library. Informa Law from Routledge 2020).

Tettenborn A, *3rd and 4th Demonstration Tests of Fully Autonomous Ship Navigation Successfully Completed* (2022).

The Nippon Foundation, *MEGURI2040 Fully Autonomous Ship Program: Successful fully autonomous navigation of large, high-speed, coastal ferry in northern Kyushu seen leading to improved safety* (2022).

Theotokatos G and others, 'Autonomous shipping – an analysis of the maritime stakeholder perspective' (2023) 22 WMU Journal of Maritime Affairs 5.

Thierer A, 'How Attitudes about Risk & Failure Affect Innovation on Either Side of the Atlantic' (19 June 2015) <https://readplaintext.com/how-attitudes-about-risk-failure-affect-innovation-on-either-side-of-the-atlantic-b5f0f41c3466> accessed 16 February 2024.

Third United Nations Conference on the Law of the Sea, 'Rules of Procedure: A/CONF.62/30/Rev.3' (New York 1981).

Thombre S and others, 'Sensors and AI Techniques for Situational Awareness in Autonomous Ships: A Review' (2022) 23(1) IEEE Transactions on Intelligent Transportation Systems 64.

Thompson A, 'Applying Rational Choice Theory to International Law: The Promise and Pitfalls' (2002) 31(1) The Journal of Legal Studies 285–306.

Thürer D, 'Soft Law' in Anne Peters (ed), *Max Planck Encyclopedia of Public International Law* (MPEPIL) (Oxford University Press).

Tinmaz H, 'History of Industrial Revolutions: From Homo Sapiens Hunters to Bitcoin Hunters' in Rodrigo Da Rosa Righi, Antonio M Alberti and Madhusudan Singh (eds), *Blockchain Technology for Industry 4.0: Secure, Decentralized, Distributed and Trusted Industry Environment* (Blockchain Technologies. Springer Singapore 2020).

Toffano S, 'Global goods and international trade: two eras of globalization compared' (Master's Thesis, University of Venice 2021).

Tokyo MoU, 'Tokyo MoU Flag performance list 2023' (2023).

Tomuschat C, 'United Nations, General Assembly' in Anne Peters (ed), *Max Planck Encyclopedia of Public International Law* (MPEPIL) (Oxford University Press).

Trachtman J, *The Economic Structure of International Law* (Harvard University Press 2008).

Treves T, 'Customary International Law' in Anne Peters (ed), *Max Planck Encyclopedia of Public International Law* (MPEPIL) (Oxford University Press).

Treves T, 'Regional Approaches to the Protection of the Marine Environment' in Myron H Nordquist, John N Moore and Said Mahmoudi (eds), *The Stockholm declaration and law of the marine environment* (Martinus Nijhoff Publishers 2003).

Treves T, 'The Development of the Law of the Sea since the Adoption of the UN Convention on the Law of the Sea: Achievements and Challenges for the Future' in Davor Vidas (ed), *Law, technology and science for oceans in globalisation:* IUU *fishing, oil pollution, bioprospecting, outer continental shelf* (Nijhoff eBook titles. Martinus Nijhoff 2010).

Trowers SN, 'Uncharted Legal Waters: "The Applicability of the Law on Seaworthiness & Good Seamanship to Autonomous Vessels"'. in Kyriaki Noussia and Matthew Channon (eds), *The Regulation of Automated and Autonomous Transport* (1st ed. 2023. Springer International Publishing; Imprint Springer 2023).

Tsimplis M, 'Designing Norms for Autonomous Ships: The Obligation to Call for Help and the Duty to Save Life in Danger at Sea' in Tafsir M Johansson and others (eds), *Autonomous Vessels in Maritime Affairs* (Studies in National Governance and Emerging Technologies. Springer International Publishing 2023).

Tunfors H, 'Evolution of IMO's MASS: Through the Prism of the Chair' in Tafsir M Johansson and others (eds), *Autonomous Vessels in Maritime Affairs* (Studies in National Governance and Emerging Technologies. Springer International Publishing 2023).

Tüngler G and tho Pesch S, 'Seevölkerrechtliche Anforderungen an unbemannte Schiffe' [2017] Zeitschrift für das Recht der Transportwirtschaft 121.

Tzanakopoulos A, 'Judicial Dialogue as a Means of Interpretation' in Helmut P Aust and Georg Nolte (eds), *The Interpretation of International Law by Domestic Courts: Uniformity, Diversity, Covergence* (Oxford University Press 2016).

U.S. Navy Office of Information, *Ghost Fleet Overlord Unmanned Surface Vessel Program Completes Second Autonomous Transit to the Pacific* (2021).

UNCITRAL Secretariat, 'Guide on the Convention on the Recognition and Enforcement of Foreign Arbitral Awards: New York, 1958' in Uncitral Secretariat, Emmanuel Gaillard and George A Bermann (eds), *Guide on the Convention on the Recognition and Enforcement of Foreign Arbitral Awards: New York 1958* (Brill 2017).

United Law Commission on International Trade Law, 'A/CN.9/407 – Report of the Workin Group on Electronic Data Interchange (EDI) on the Work of its 29th Session' (Vienna 16.03.1995).

United Law Commission on International Trade Law (UNCITRAL), 'Recommendation regarding the Interpretation of Article II (2) and Article VII (1) of the Convention on the Recognition and Enforcement of Foreign Arbitral Awards' (Vienna 7 July 2006).

United Nations, 'About Small Island Developing States (SIDS)' <https://sdgs.un.org/smallislands/about-small-island-developing-states> accessed 16 February 2024.

United Nations Conference on Trade and Development, 'UNCTAD Handbook of Statistics 2021: Fact sheet #14 Merchant fleet' (Geneva 9 December 2021) <https://unctad.org/system/files/official-document/tdstat46_FS14_en.pdf> accessed 4 May 2022.

United Nations General Assembly, 'Res. A.2750(XXV) – peaceful purpose of the sea-bed and the ocean floor' (Geneva 17 December 1970).

United Nations General Assembly, 'Official Record 29th Session, Agenda Item 51' (New York 12 December 1974).

United Nations General Assembly, 'A/CONF.151/26/Vol. I: Rio Declaration on Environment and Development' (New York 14 June 1992).

United Nations General Assembly, 'Res. A/Res/48/263 – Agreement relating to the implementation of Part XI of the United Nations Convention on the Law of the Sea of 10 December 1982' (New York 28 July 1994).

United Nations General Assembly, 'A/CN.4/L.682 – Fragmentation of International Law: Difficulties Arising from the Diversification and Expansion of International Law; Report of the Study Group of the International Law Commission' (New York 13 April 2006).

United Nations General Assembly, 'A/CN.4/577/Add. 1 – Report of the International Law Commission on the work of its fifty-eighth session (2006)' (Geneva 23 January 2007).

United Nations General Assembly, 'Res. A/Res/63/122 – United Nations Convention on Contracts for the International Carriage of Goods Wholly or Partly by Sea' (New York 2 February 2009).

United Nations General Assembly, 'A/71/10 – Report of the International Law Commission on the work of its sixty-eighth session (2 May–10 June and 4 July–12 August 2016)' (19 August 2016).

United Nations General Assembly, 'A/CN.4/L.907 – Subsequent agreements and subsequent practice in relation to the interpretation of treaties: Text of the draft conclusions adopted by the Drafting Committee on second reading' (New York, Geneva 11 May 2018).

United Nations Treaty Collection, '6. United Nations Convention on the Law of the Sea' <https://treaties.un.org/Pages/ViewDetailsIII.aspx?src=TREATY&mtdsg_no=XXI-6&chapter=21&Temp=mtdsg3&clang=_en> accessed 16 February 2024.

United States Coast Guard, 'Marine Safety: Port State Control' (Washington, D.C. 20 September 2021).

United States Coast Guard, 'Port State Control in the United States' (2023).

Utredningen om självkörande fordon på väg and SOU 2018:16, *Vägen till självkörande fordon: Introduktion slutbetänkande* (Statens offentliga utredningar 2018:16, Norstedts Juridik 2018).

van Asselt M, Vos E and Fox T, 'Regulating Technologies and the Uncertainty Paradox' in M. Goodwin, Bert-Jaap Koops and Ronald Leenes (eds), *Dimensions of technology regulation* (Wolf Legal Publishers 2010).

van der Burgt C, 'Extract from "The Oslo and Paris Commission: The First Decade"' (1984) <https://www.ospar.org/site/assets/files/1201/extract_from_the_first_decade_oslo_paris_conventions.pdf>.

van Essen H and others, 'State of play of Internalisation in the European Transport Sector' (May 2019).

van Hooydonk E, 'The law of unmanned merchant shipping – an exploration' [2014] Journal of International Maritime Law 403.

van Leeuwen J and Kern K, 'The External Dimension of European Union Marine Governance: Institutional Interplay between the EU and the International Maritime Organization' (2013) 13(1) Global Environmental Politics 69.

van Logchem Y, 'International Law of the Sea and Autonomous Cargo 'Vessels" in Barış Soyer and Andrew Tettenborn (eds), *Artificial Intelligence and Autonomous Shipping: Developing the International Legal Framework* (Hart Publishing 2021).

van Reenen W, 'Rules of Reference in the new Convention on the Law of the Sea, in particular in connection with the pollution of the sea by oil from tankers' (1980) 12 Netherlands Yearbook of International Law 3.

Veal R, Tsimplis M and Serdy A, 'The Legal Status and Operation of Unmanned Maritime Vehicles' (2019) 50(1) Ocean Development & International Law 23.

Veitch E and Alsos OA, 'Gorillas on a boat: Inattentional blindness during supervisory control of autonomous vessels' (2023) 2618(1) Journal of Physics: Conference Series.

Vidigal G, 'From Bilateral to Multilateral Law-making: Legislation, Practice, Evolution and the Future of Inter Se Agreements in the WTO' (2013) 24(4) European Journal of International Law 1027.

Villiger ME, *Commentary on the 1969 Vienna Convention on the Law of Treaties* (Martinus Nijhoff Publishers 2009).

Vos J de, Hekkenberg RG and Valdez Banda OA, 'The Impact of Autonomous Ships on Safety at Sea – A Statistical Analysis' (2021) 210 Reliability Engineering & System Safety.

Vukas B, 'Treaties, Third-Party Effect' in Anne Peters (ed), *Max Planck Encyclopedia of Public International Law* (MPEPIL) (Oxford University Press).

Wahlström M and others, 'Human Factors Challenges in Unmanned Ship Operations – Insights from Other Domains' (2015) 3 Procedia Manufacturing 1038.

Waldock H, 'The evolution of human rights concepts and the application of the european convention on human rights' in André Gross (ed), *Mélanges Offert à Paul Reuter: Le droit international: unité et diversité* (Pedone 1981).

Walker GK (ed), *Definitions for the law of the sea: Terms not defined by the 1982 Convention* (Martinus Nijhoff Publishers 2012).

Walt S, 'Novelty and the Risks of Uniform Sales Law' (1999) 39(3) Virginia Journal of International Law 671.

Walter C, 'Subject of International Law' in Anne Peters (ed), *Max Planck Encyclopedia of Public International Law* (MPEPIL) (Oxford University Press).

Wang J-B and others, 'Unmanned Surface Vessel Assisted Maritime Wireless Communication Toward 6G: Opportunities and Challenges' (2022) 29(6) IEEE Wireless Communications 72.

Wärtsilä, *Wärtsilä successfully tests remote control ship operating capability* (2017).

Wärtsilä, *Initial sea trials successfully completed by Wärtsilä & PSA Marine's ground-breaking 'IntelliTug' project* (2020).

Weil P, 'Towards Relative Normativity in International Law?' (1983) 77(3) The American Journal of International Law 413.

Weimer M and Marin L, 'The Role of Law in Managing the Tension between Risk and Innovation: Introduction to the Special Issue on Regulating New and Emerging Technologies' (2016) 7(3) European Journal of Risk Regulation 469.

Weiss TG and Zach DA, 'Virtual issue: 70 years of the United Nations in International Affairs' (2022) 98(3) International Affairs e1-e19.

Werner WG, 'State consent as foundational myth' in Catherine Brölmann and Yannick Radi (eds), *Research handbook on the theory and practice of international lawmaking* (Edward Elgar Publishing 2016).

Wet E de, 'Invoking Obligations Erga Omnes in the Twenty-First Century: Progressive Developments since Barcelona Traction' (2013) 38 South African Yearbook of International Law 1.

White ND, 'Lawmaking' in Jacob K Cogan, Ian Hurd and Ian Johnstone (eds), *The Oxford handbook of international organizations* (Oxford University Press 2017).

Wingrove M, *World's first autonomous spill-response vessel opens new era in marine applications* (2019).

Wolfrum R, 'International Law' in Anne Peters (ed), *Max Planck Encyclopedia of Public International Law* (MPEPIL) (Oxford University Press).

Wolfrum R, *Die Internationalisierung staatsfreier Räume: Die Entwicklung einer internationalen Verwaltung für Antarktis, Weltraum, Hohe See und Meeresboden* (Teilw. zugl.: Bonn, Univ. Habil.-Schr. 1980/81. Beiträge zum ausländischen öffentlichen Recht und Völkerrecht vol 85, Springer 1984).

Wolfrum R, 'IMO Interface with the Law of the Sea Convention' in Myron H Nordquist and John N Moore (eds), *Current maritime issues and the international maritime organization* (Martinus Nijhoff Publishers 1999).

World Maritime University, 'Transport 2040: Automation, Technology, Employment – The Future of Work' (Malmö 2019).

Wróbel K and others, 'The Vagueness of COLREG versus Collision Avoidance Techniques—A Discussion on the Current State and Future Challenges Concerning the Operation of Autonomous Ships' (2022) 14(24) Sustainability.

Yanai S, 'Can the UNCLOS Address Challenges of the 21st Century?' (2014) 57 German Yearbook of International Law 43.

Yee L, 'Law of Treaties' in Simon Chesterman and others (eds), *The Oxford Handbook of United Nations Treaties* (Oxford University Press 2019).

Yiannopoulos AN, 'The Unification of Private Maritime Law by International Conventions' (1965) 30(2) Law and Contemporary Problems 370.

Yu C and others, 'Maritime Broadband Communications: Applications, Challenges and an Offshore 5G-virtual MIMO Paradigm' (2020 IEEE Intl Conf on Parallel & Distributed Processing with Applications, Big Data & Cloud Computing, Sustainable Computing & Communications, Social Computing & Networking (ISPA/BDCloud/SocialCom/SustainCom), Exeter, United Kingdom, 17.12.2020–19.12.2020).

Zamir E and Teichman D, 'Administrative, Constitutional, and International Law' in Eyal Zamir and Doron Teichman (eds), *Behavioral law and economics* (Oxford University Press 2018).

Zeabuz, *Torghatten and Zeabuz Make History in Stockholm* (2023).

Zemanek K, 'Court Generated State Practice' (2015) 20 Austrian Review of International and European Law 3.

Zhou X-Y and others, 'A Study of the Application Barriers to the Use of Autonomous Ships Posed by the Good Seamanship Requirement of COLREGS' (2020) 73(3) Journal of Navigation 710.

Ziarati R and Ziarati M, 'Review of Accidents with Special References to Vessels with Automated Systems – A Way Forward' [2010] <https://www.semanticscholar.org/paper/Review-of-Accidents-with-Special-References-to-with-Ziarati-Ziarati/bcb58658a7f5cd095c707a75d5c838603518b808> accessed 16 March 2022.

Ziegler KS, 'The Relationship between EU Law and International Law' in Anna Södersten and Dennis M Patterson (eds), *A companion to European Union law and international law* (Wiley Blackwell 2016).

Zulu Associates, *Belgian vessel innovator Zulu Associates releases latest designs for first zero emission short sea vessel featuring wind blades* (2023).

Table of Cases

International Court of Justice

Aegean Sea Continental Shelf Case (Greece v. Turkey) [1978] [1978] ICJ Reports 3 (International Court of Justice).

Case Concerning Military and Paramilitary Activities in and against Nicaragua [1986] [1986] ICJ Reports 14 (International Court of Justice).

Case Concerning Pulp Mills on the River Uruguay [2010] [2010] ICJ Reports 14 (International Court of Justice).

Constitution of the Maritime Safety Committee of the inter-governmental Maritime Consultative Organization [1960] [1960] ICJ Reports 150 (International Court of Justice).

Legal Consequences for States of the Continued Presence of South Africa in Namibia [1971] [1971] ICJ Reports 16 (International Court of Justice).

Legal Consequences of the Construction of a Wall in the Occupied Palestinian Territory [2004] [2004] ICJ Reports 136 (International Court of Justice).

Navigational and Related Rights (Costa Rica v. Nicaragua) [2009] [2009] ICJ Reports 213 (International Court of Justice).

North Sea Continental Shelf Cases [1969] [1969] ICJ Reports 3 (International Court of Justice).

Nuclear Tests Case Australia v. France (1974) 1974 ICJ Reports 253 (International Court of Justice).

Nuclear Tests Case New Zealand v. France (1974) 1974 ICJ Reports 457 (International Court of Justice).

Territorial Dispute – Libyan Arab Jamahiriya/Chad [1994] [1994] ICJ Reports 6 (International Court of Justice).

Whaling in the Antarctic [2014] [2014] ICJ Reports 226 (International Court of Justice).

Court of Justice of the European Union

C-22/70 *Commission of the European Communities v. Council of the European Communities* [1972].

C-45/07 *Commission of the European Communities v. Hellenic Republic* [2009].

C-459/03 *Commission of the European Communities v. Ireland, MOX Plant* [2006].

C-315/98 *Commission of the European Communities v. Italian Republic* [1999].

Commission of the European Communities v. Italian Republic (1999) C-315/98 (Court of Justice of the European Union).

C-358/98 *Commission of the European Communities v. Italian Republic* [2000].

1/94 *Competence of the Community to conclude international agreements concerning services and the protection of intellectual property – Article 228 (6) of the EC Treaty.* [1994].

2/91 *Convention N° 170 of the International Labour Organization concerning safety in the use of chemicals at work* [1993].
C-06/64 *Costa v. ENEL* [1964].
C-161/20 *European Commission v. Council of the European Union (Organisation maritime internationale)* [2022].
C-271/94 *European Parliament vs. Commission of the European Communities* [1996].
2/15 *Free Trade Agreement with Singapore* [2017].
C-322/88 *Grimaldi v. Fonds des maladies professionnelles* [1989].
1/13 *Hague Convention* [2014].
C-308/06 *Intertanko, Intercargo, Greek Shipping Co-operation Committee, Lloyd's Register, International Salvage Union v. Secretary of State for Transport* [2008].
C-402/05 P and C-415/05 P *Kadi and Al Barakaat International Foundation v Council and Commission* [2008].
Opinion 1/03 – the new Lugano Convention [2006].
C-379/92 *Peralta* [1994].

Other Court Cases

Arbitration Tribunal, 'Saudi Arabia v. Arabian American Oil Company (Aramco)' (1963) 27 International Law Reports 117.
Beschluss der 2. Kammer des Zweiten Senats (2007) 2 BvR 939/07 (The Federal Constitutional Court).
Jugendstrafvollzug (2006) 2 BvR 1673/04; 2 BvR 2404/04 (The Federal Constitutional Court).
Lissabon (2009) 2 BvE 2/08 (German Constitutional Court).
The Case of the S.S. "LOTUS" (1927) 10 Collection of Judgments no 9 (Permanent Court of International Justice).
The M/V "SAIGA" (No. 2) Case (1999) 1999 ITLOS Reports 10 (International Tribunal for the Law of the Sea).
The M/V "Virginia G" Case, Panama v. Guinea-Bissau [2014] [2014] ITLOS Reports 4 (International Tribunal for the Law of the Sea).
UN-Behindertenrechtskonvention (2016) 1 BvL 8/15 (The Federal Constitutional Court).

IMO Documents

International Maritime Organization (IMO), 'Res. A.572(14): General Provisions on Ships' Routeing' (London 20 November 1985).
International Maritime Organization (IMO), 'Res. A.714(17): Code of Safe Practice for Cargo Stowage and Securing' (London 6 November 1991).
International Maritime Organization (IMO), 'Res. A.682(19): Regional Cooperation in the Control of ships and Discharges' (London 21 November 1991).

International Maritime Organization (IMO), 'Res. A.774(18): Guidelines for Preventing the Introduction of Unwanted Aquatic Oranisms and Pathogens from Ships' Ballast Water and Sediment Discharge' (London 4 November 1993).

International Maritime Organization (IMO), 'Res. A.741(18): International Management Code for the Safe Operation of Ships and for Pollution Prevention (International Safety Management (ISM) Code)' (London 17 November 1993).

International Maritime Organization (IMO), 'Res. A.739(18): Guidelines for the Authorization of Organizations Acting on Behalf of the Administration' (London 22 November 1993).

International Maritime Organization (IMO), 'Res. A.825(19): Procedure for Adoption and Amendment of Performance Standards for Radio and Navigational Equipment' (London 23 November 1995).

International Maritime Organization (IMO), 'Res. A.789(19): Specifications on the Survey and Certification Functions of Recognized Organizations Acting on Behalf of the Administration' (London 8 December 1995).

International Maritime Organization (IMO), 'Focus on IMO – IMO and dangerous goods at sea' (London May 1996).

International Maritime Organization (IMO), 'Res. A.851(20): General Principles for Ship Reporting Systems and Ship Reporting Requirements' (London 27 November 1997).

International Maritime Organization (IMO), 'Res. A.868(20): Guidelines for the Control and Management of Ships' Ballast Water to Minimize the Transfer of Harmful Aquatic Organisms and Pathogens' (London 27 November 1997).

International Maritime Organization (IMO), 'Res. A.910(22): Amendments to the International Regulations for Preventing Collisions at Sea' (London 29 November 2001).

International Maritime Organization (IMO), 'Res. A.947(23): Human Element Vision, Principles and Goals for the Organization' (London 26 February 2004).

International Maritime Organization (IMO), 'Res. A.955(23): Amendments to the Principles of Safe Manning' (London 26 February 2004).

International Maritime Organization (IMO), 'Res. A.1021(26): Code on Alerts and Indicators' (London 2 December 2009).

International Maritime Organization (IMO), 'Res. A.1024(26): Guidelines for Ships Operating in Polar Waters' (London 2 December 2009).

International Maritime Organization (IMO), 'Res. A.1047(27): Principles of Minimum Safe Manning' (London 20 December 2011).

International Maritime Organization (IMO), 'Res. A.1070(28): IMO Instruments Implementation Code' (London 10 December 2013).

International Maritime Organization (IMO), 'Implications of the United Nations Convention on the Law of the Sea for the International Maritime Organization: Study by the Secretariat of the International Maritime Organization' (LEG/MISC.8, London 30 January 2014).

International Maritime Organization (IMO), 'Res. A.1118(30): Revised Guidelines on the Implementation of the International Safety Management (ISM) Code by Administrations' (London 10 January 2017).

International Maritime Organization (IMO), 'Rules and guidelines for consultative status of non-governmental international organizations with the International Maritime Organization' (London December 2019).

International Maritime Organization (IMO), 'List of Conventions and their Amendments' (London 15 October 2021) <https://view.officeapps.live.com/op/view.aspx?src=https%3A%2F%2Fwwwcdn.imo.org%2Flocalresources%2Fen%2FAbout%2FConventions%2FStatusOfConventions%2FList%2520of%2520the%2520Conventions%2520and%2520their%2520amendments.docx&wdOrigin=BROWSELINK>.

International Maritime Organization (IMO), 'Res. A.1156(32): Survey Guidelines under the Harmonized System of Survey and Certification (HSSC), 2021' (London 15 December 2021).

International Maritime Organization (IMO), 'Res. A.1158(32): Guidelines for Vessel Traffic Systems' (London 15 December 2021).

International Maritime Organization (IMO), 'Res. A.1155(32): Procedures for Port State Control' (London 28 January 2022).

International Maritime Organization (IMO), 'Res. A.1168(32): Relations with Intergovernmental Organizations' (London 28 January 2022).

International Maritime Organization (IMO), 'Ratification by State' (London 22 April 2022) <https://view.officeapps.live.com/op/view.aspx?src=https%3A%2F%2Fwwwcdn.imo.org%2Flocalresources%2Fen%2FAbout%2FConventions%2FStatusOfConventions%2Fx-Status.xlsx&wdOrigin=BROWSELINK> accessed 21 June 2022.

International Maritime Organization (IMO), 'Status of Treaties' (London 19 April 2023) accessed 20 June 2022.

International Maritime Organization (IMO), 'BWM Convention and Guidelines' <https://www.imo.org/en/OurWork/Environment/Pages/BWMConventionandGuidelines.aspx> accessed 16 February 2024.

International Maritime Organization (IMO), 'Convention on the International Regulations for Preventing Collisions at Sea, 1972 (COLREG)' <https://www.imo.org/en/About/Conventions/Pages/COLREG.aspx> accessed 16 February 2024.

International Maritime Organization (IMO), 'Intergovernmental Organizations which have concluded agreements of cooperation with IMO' <https://www.imo.org/en/OurWork/ERO/Pages/IGOsWithObserverStatus.aspx> accessed 16 February 2024.

International Maritime Organization (IMO), 'International Convention on the Control of Harmful Anti-fouling Systems on Ships' <https://www.imo.org/en/About/Conventions/Pages/International-Convention-on-the-Control-of-Harmful-Anti-fouling-Systems-on-Ships-(AFS).aspx> accessed 16 February 2024.

International Maritime Organization (IMO), 'Member States' <https://www.imo.org/en/OurWork/ERO/Pages/MemberStates.aspx> accessed 16 February 2024.

International Maritime Organization (IMO), 'Non-Governmental international Organizations which have been granted consultative status with IMO' <https://www.imo.org/en/OurWork/ERO/Pages/NGOsInConsultativeStatus.aspx> accessed 16 February 2024.

International Maritime Organization (IMO), 'Ships' routeing' <https://www.imo.org/en/OurWork/Safety/Pages/ShipsRouteing.aspx> accessed 16 February 2024.

International Maritime Organization (IMO), 'MARPOL Annex VI history' (8 June 2021) <https://www.imo.org/en/MediaCentre/PressBriefings/Pages/MARPOL100State.aspx> accessed 16 February 2024.

International Maritime Organization (IMO), Hong Kong ship recycling Convention set to enter into force (2023).

Council of the International Maritime Organization

Council of the International Maritime Organization, 'C-72-12-Add.1 – Report on the Conference of Contracting Governments to the International Convention for the Safety of Life at Sea, 1974' (London 27 May 1994).

Maritime Safety Committee

Maritime Safety Committee of the Inter-Governmental Maritime Consultative Organization (MSC, IMCO), 'MSC 25/13: Amendment Procedures in Conventions for which IMCO is Depositary, Note by the Secretariat' (London 24 January 1972).

Maritime Safety Committee of the International Maritime Organization (MSC, IMO), 'MSC 108/4/4: Definitions of terminology of MASS and autonomous systems (IACS)'.

Maritime Safety Committee of the International Maritime Organization (MSC, IMO), 'Res. MSC. 36(63): Code of Safety for High Speed Craft' (London 20 May 1994).

Maritime Safety Committee of the International Maritime Organization (MSC, IMO), 'Res. MSC.86(70): Recommendation on Performance Standards for Sound Reception Systems (Annex 1)' (London 8 December 1998).

Maritime Safety Committee of the International Maritime Organization (MSC, IMO), 'MSC.1/Circ. 1054: Interim Guidelines for Wing-in-Ground Craft' (London 16 December 2002).

Maritime Safety Committee of the International Maritime Organization (MSC, IMO), 'MSC 78/24/8: Sub-Committees on Ship Design and Equipment and on Bulk Liquids and Gases; Proposal for developing international regulations on gas fuelled ships (Norway)' (London 19 December 2003).

Maritime Safety Committee of the International Maritime Organization (MSC, IMO), 'Res. MSC.167(78): Guidelines on the Treatment of Persons rescued at Sea' (London 20 May 2004).

Maritime Safety Committee of the International Maritime Organization (MSC, IMO), 'MSC/Circ.1111: Guidance relating to the Implementation of SOLAS Chapter XI-2 and the ISPS Code' (London 7 June 2004).
Maritime Safety Committee of the International Maritime Organization (MSC, IMO), 'Res. MSC. 174(79): Amendments to the International Code of Safety for High-Speed Craft' (London 10 December 2004).
Maritime Safety Committee of the International Maritime Organization (MSC, IMO), 'MSC.1/Circ. 1126: Amendments to the Interim Guidelines for Wing-in-Ground Craft' (London 6 January 2005).
Maritime Safety Committee of the International Maritime Organization (MSC, IMO), 'Res. MSC.209(81): Adoption of amendments to the Seafarers' Training, Certification and Watchkeeping Code (STCW Code)' (London 18 May 2006).
Maritime Safety Committee of the International Maritime Organization (MSC, IMO), 'MSC.1/Circ. 1182: Guide to Recovery Techniques' (London 31 May 2006).
Maritime Safety Committee of the International Maritime Organization (MSC, IMO), 'Res. MSC. 221(82): Amendments to the International Code of Safety for High-Speed Craft' (London 8 December 2006).
Maritime Safety Committee of the International Maritime Organization (MSC, IMO), 'Res. MSC.266(84): Code of Safety for Special Purpose Ships' (London 13 May 2008).
Maritime Safety Committee of the International Maritime Organization (MSC, IMO), 'Res. MSC.259(84): Amendments to the International Code of Safety for High-Speed Craft' (London 16 May 2008).
Maritime Safety Committee of the International Maritime Organization (MSC, IMO), 'MSC.1/Circ. 1260: Unified Interpretation of COLREG' (London 22 May 2008).
Maritime Safety Committee of the International Maritime Organization (MSC, IMO), 'MSC.1/Circ.1323: Unified Interpretation of IBC Code' (London 10 June 2009).
Maritime Safety Committee of the International Maritime Organization (MSC, IMO), 'MSC 86/26: Report of the Maritime Safety Committee on its 86th session' (London 12 June 2009).
Maritime Safety Committee of the International Maritime Organization (MSC, IMO), 'MSC 90/22/1: Clarification of SOLAS regulation V/23 (IACS)' (London 21 November 2011).
Maritime Safety Committee of the International Maritime Organization (MSC, IMO), 'MSC.1/Circ. 1375/Rev.1: Unified Interpretation of SOLAS Regulation V/23' (London 28 May 2012).
Maritime Safety Committee of the International Maritime Organization (MSC, IMO), 'Res. MSC.349(92): Code for Recognized Organizations' (London 21 June 2013).
Maritime Safety Committee of the International Maritime Organization (MSC, IMO), 'Res. MSC.350(92): Amendments to the International Convention for the Safety of Life at Sea, 1974' (London 21 June 2013).

Maritime Safety Committee of the International Maritime Organization (MSC, IMO), 'MSC.1/Circ.1455: Guidelines for the Approval of Alternatives and Equivalents as Provided for in Various IMO Instruments' (London 24 June 2013).

Maritime Safety Committee of the International Maritime Organization (MSC, IMO), 'Res. MSC.366(93): Amendments for the International Convention for the Safety of Life at Sea, IMO Instruments Implementation Code' (London 22 May 2014).

Maritime Safety Committee of the International Maritime Organization (MSC, IMO), 'MSC.1/Circ. 1481: Guidance on Entry Into Force of Amendments to the 1974 SOLAS Convention and Related Mandatory Instruments' (London 11 June 2014).

Maritime Safety Committee of the International Maritime Organization (MSC, IMO), 'Res. MSC.385(94): Adoption of the Polar Code' (London 21 November 2014).

Maritime Safety Committee of the International Maritime Organization (MSC, IMO), 'Res. MSC.386 (94): Amendments to the International Convention for the Safety of Life at Sea, 1974' (London 21 November 2014).

Maritime Safety Committee of the International Maritime Organization (MSC, IMO), 'MSC.1/Circ. 1447: Guidelines for the Development of Plans for Recovery of Persons from the Water' (London 14 December 2014).

Maritime Safety Committee of the International Maritime Organization (MSC, IMO), 'Res. MSC.391(95): Adoption of the International Code of Safety for Ships Using Gases and Other Low-Flashpoint Fuels (IGF Code)' (London 11 June 2015).

Maritime Safety Committee of the International Maritime Organization (MSC, IMO), 'Res. MSC.392(95): Amendments to the International Convention for the Safety of Life at Sea, 1974' (London 11 June 2015).

Maritime Safety Committee of the International Maritime Organization (MSC, IMO), 'MSC 98/20/2: Maritime Autonomous Surface Ships; Proposal for a regulatory scoping exercise (Denmark, Estonia, Finland, Japan, the Netherlands, Norway, the Republic of Korea, the United Kingdom and the United States)' (London 27 February 2017).

Maritime Safety Committee of the International Maritime Organization (MSC, IMO), 'Res. MSC.433(98): Guidelines and Criteria for Ship Reporting Systems' (London 16 June 2017).

Maritime Safety Committee of the International Maritime Organization (MSC, IMO), 'MSC 98/23: Report of the Maritime Safety Committee on its 98th Session' (London 28 June 2017).

Maritime Safety Committee of the International Maritime Organization (MSC, IMO), 'MSC.1/Circ.1586: List of Certificates and Documents required to be carried On Board Ships' (London 19 July 2017).

Maritime Safety Committee of the International Maritime Organization (MSC, IMO), 'MSC 99/INF.3: Final Report: Analysis of Regulatory Barriers to the use of Autonomous Ships (Denmark)' (London 18 January 2018).

Maritime Safety Committee of the International Maritime Organization (MSC, IMO), 'MSC 99/INF.5: Report of a survey on what maritime professionals think about autonomous shipping (IFSMA and ITF)' (London 9 February 2018).

Maritime Safety Committee of the International Maritime Organization (MSC, IMO), 'MSC 99/5/4: Considerations on and proposals for the methodology to use within the framework of the regulatory scoping exercise (France)' (London 9 March 2018).

Maritime Safety Committee of the International Maritime Organization (MSC, IMO), 'MSC 99/5/12: Comments on document MSC 99/5/5 (United States)' (London 27 March 2018).

Maritime Safety Committee of the International Maritime Organization (MSC, IMO), 'MSC.1/Circ. 1592: Guidelines for Wing-in-Ground Craft' (London 18 May 2018).

Maritime Safety Committee of the International Maritime Organization (MSC, IMO), 'MSC 99/WP.9: Report of the Working Group' (London 23 May 2018).

Maritime Safety Committee of the International Maritime Organization (MSC, IMO), 'Res. MSC. 439(99): Amendments for the International Code of Safety for High Speed Craft' (London 24 May 2018).

Maritime Safety Committee of the International Maritime Organization (MSC, IMO), 'MSC 99/22: Report of the Maritime Safety Committee on its 99th Session' (London 5 June 2018).

Maritime Safety Committee of the International Maritime Organization (MSC, IMO), 'MSC 100/5: Report of the Correspondence Group on MASS' (London 28 September 2018).

Maritime Safety Committee of the International Maritime Organization (MSC, IMO), 'MSC.1/Circ.1604: Interim Guidelines for MASS Trials' (London 14 June 2019).

Maritime Safety Committee of the International Maritime Organization (MSC, IMO), 'MSC.1/Circ.1394/Rev.2: Generic Guidelines for Developing IMO Goal-based Standards' (London 8 July 2019).

Maritime Safety Committee of the International Maritime Organization (MSC, IMO), 'MSC 102/5/1: Report of the Intersessional Working Group on Maritime Autonomous Surface Ships' (London 25 September 2019).

Maritime Safety Committee of the International Maritime Organization (MSC, IMO), 'MSC 102/5/3: Summary of results of the second step and conclusion of the RSE for COLREG (Marshall Islands)' (London 6 February 2020).

Maritime Safety Committee of the International Maritime Organization (MSC, IMO), 'MSC 102/5/9: Summary of results of the second step of the RSE for SOLAS chapter V (China)' (London 11 February 2020).

Maritime Safety Committee of the International Maritime Organization (MSC, IMO), 'MSC 102/7/5: Unified interpretation of SOLAS regulation II-1/3-10 concerning the term "unforeseen delay in delivery of ships" (China and IACS)' (London 9 March 2020).

Maritime Safety Committee of the International Maritime Organization (MSC, IMO), 'MSC.1/Circ.1637: Unified Interpretation of SOLAS Regulation II-1/3-10 Concerning The Term "Unforeseen Delay in Delivery of Ships" During the Coronavirus (Covid-19) Pandemic' (London 10 December 2020).

Maritime Safety Committee of the International Maritime Organization (MSC, IMO), 'MSC.1/Circ.1638: Outcome of the Regulatory Scoping Exercise for the Use of Maritime Autonomous Surface Ships (MASS)' (London 3 June 2021).

Maritime Safety Committee of the International Maritime Organization (MSC, IMO), 'MSC 105/7/2: Outline of the draft guidelines for MASS operations (Japan, Russian Federation and United Arab Emirates)' (London 13 January 2022).

Maritime Safety Committee of the International Maritime Organization (MSC, IMO), 'MSC 105/7/3: Discussion on some key issues in the development of the MASS instrument and proposal for a structure of a draft MASS Code (Norway)' (London 14 January 2022).

Maritime Safety Committee of the International Maritime Organization (MSC, IMO), 'MSC 105/7/6: Comments on documents MSC 105/7 (Republic of Korea)' (London 1 March 2022).

Maritime Safety Committee of the International Maritime Organization (MSC, IMO), 'MSC.1/Circ. 1362/Rev.1: Unified Interpretation of SOLAS Chapter II-1' (London 9 May 2022).

Maritime Safety Committee of the International Maritime Organization (MSC, IMO), 'MSC 105/20: Report of the Maritime Safety Committee on its 105th Session' (London 19 May 2022).

Maritime Safety Committee of the International Maritime Organization (MSC, IMO), 'MSC 106/INF.6: United Kingdom developments on Maritime Autonomous Surface Shipsresearch, legislation and industry projects (United Kingdom)' (London 1 August 2022).

Maritime Safety Committee of the International Maritime Organization (MSC, IMO), 'MSC 106/5/3: Proposal for incorporation of risk assessment into MASS instrument (China)' (London 30 August 2022).

Maritime Safety Committee of the International Maritime Organization (MSC, IMO), 'MSC.1/Circ.1655: Unified Interpretations of SOLAS Chapter II-2' (London 5 December 2022).

Maritime Safety Committee of the International Maritime Organization (MSC, IMO), 'MSC 107/5: Report of the MASS Correspondence Group' (London 27 February 2023).

Maritime Safety Committee of the International Maritime Organization (MSC, IMO), 'MSC 107-5 – Report of the MASS Correspondence Group' (London 27 February 2023).

Maritime Safety Committee of the International Maritime Organization (MSC, IMO), 'MSC 107/17/16: Proposal for a new output to comprehensively review the

International Regulations for Preventing Collisions at Sea, 1972 (China)' (London 28 February 2023).

Maritime Safety Committee of the International Maritime Organization (MSC, IMO), 'MSC 107/5/4: Risk-Based Assessment Tool for MASS (Austria, Belgium, Bulgaria, Croatia, Cyprus, Czechia, Denmark, Estonia, Finland, France, Germany, Greece, Hungary, Ireland, Italy, Latvia, Lithuania, Luxembourg, Malta, Netherlands (Kingdom of the), Poland, Portugal, Romania, Slovakia, Slovenia, Spain, Sweden and European Commission)' (London 20 March 2023).

Maritime Safety Committee of the International Maritime Organization (MSC, IMO), 'MSC 107/INF.8: Risk-Based Assessment Tool for MASS (Austria, Belgium, Bulgaria, Croatia, Cyprus, Czechia, Denmark, Estonia, Finland, France, Germany, Greece, Hungary, Ireland, Italy, Latvia, Lithuania, Luxembourg, Malta, Netherlands (Kingdom of the), Poland, Portugal, Romania, Slovakia, Slovenia, Spain, Sweden and European Commission)' (London 20 March 2023).

Maritime Safety Committee of the International Maritime Organization (MSC, IMO), 'MSC 107/INF.12: Report on the Regulatory Framework for MASS implemented in France (France)' (London 28 March 2023).

Maritime Safety Committee of the International Maritime Organization (MSC, IMO), 'MSC 107/INF.14: Study on the definition and organization of a Remote Control Centre (RCC) with a view to its certification (Belgium)' (London 28 March 2023).

Maritime Safety Committee of the International Maritime Organization (MSC, IMO), 'MSC 107/INF.18: Results of a transoceanic voyage test with autonomous navigation system (Republic of Korea)' (London 28 March 2023).

Maritime Safety Committee of the International Maritime Organization (MSC, IMO), 'MSC 107/5/1: Report of the MSC-LEG-FAL Joint Working Group on MASS on its second session' (London 2 May 2023).

Maritime Safety Committee of the International Maritime Organization (MSC, IMO), 'MSC 107/WP.9: Report of the MASS-Working Group' (London 7 June 2023).

Maritime Safety Committee of the International Maritime Organization (MSC, IMO), 'MSC 107/INF.1: List of Participants' (London 21 June 2023).

Maritime Safety Committee of the International Maritime Organization (MSC, IMO), 'MSC 107/20: Report of the Maritime Safety Committee on its 107th Session' (London 26 June 2023).

Maritime Safety Committee of the International Maritime Organization (MSC, IMO), 'MSC/ISWG/MASS 2/3/1: Bridging Competency Gaps for MASS Operators in Alignmentwith the STCW Framework (IMarEST)' (London 15 September 2023).

Maritime Safety Committee of the International Maritime Organization (MSC, IMO), 'MSC 108/4/1: Report of the Intersessional MASS Working Group (Secretariat)' (London 8 November 2023).

Maritime Safety Committee of the International Maritime Organization (MSC, IMO), 'MSC 108/INF.2: White paper on cybersecurity aboard maritime autonomous ships (France)' (London 12 February 2024).

Maritime Safety Committee of the International Maritime Organization (MSC, IMO), 'MSC 108/INF.16: Ongoing MASS projects in Norway (Norway)' (London 12 March 2024).

Maritime Safety Committee of the International Maritime Organization (MSC, IMO), 'MSC 108/20: Report of the Maritime Safety Committee on its 108th Session' (London 28 June 2024).

Maritime Safety Committee of the International Maritime Organization (MSC, IMO) and Marine Environment Protection Committee of the International Maritime Organization (MEPC, IMO), 'MSC/Circ.1056; MEPC/Circ.399: Guidelines for Ships Operating in Arctic Ice-Covered Waters' (London 23 December 2002).

Maritime Safety Committee of the International Maritime Organization (MSC, IMO) and Marine Environment Protection Committee of the International Maritime Organization (MEPC, IMO), 'MSC-MEPC.1/Circ.5/Rev.1: Organization and Method of Work of the Maritime Safety Committee and The Marine Environment Protection Committee and their Subsidiary Bodies' (London 13 June 2018).

Marine Environmental Protection Committee

Marine Environment Protection Committee of the International Maritime Organization (MEPC, IMO), 'Res. MEPC.52(32) – Amendments to the Annex of the Protocol of 1978 relating to MARPOL, new regulation 13F and 13G and related amendments to Annex I of MARPOL, 73/78' (London 6 March 1992).

Marine Environment Protection Committee of the International Maritime Organization (MEPC, IMO), 'Res. MEPC.75(40) – Amendments to the Annex of the Protocol of 1978 relating to MARPOL' (London 25 September 1997).

Marine Environment Protection Committee of the International Maritime Organization (MEPC, IMO), 'MEPC 43/21 – Report of the MEPC on its 43rd session' (London 6 July 1999).

Marine Environment Protection Committee of the International Maritime Organization (MEPC, IMO), 'Res. MEPC.95(46) – Amendments to the Annex of the Protocol of 1978 relating to MARPOL, amendments to regulation 13G of Annex I to MARPOL 73/78' (London 27 April 2001).

Marine Environment Protection Committee of the International Maritime Organization (MEPC, IMO), 'MEPC 49/16/1 – Proposed amendments to Annex I of MARPOL 73/78 (Austria, Belgium, Denmark, Finland, France, Germany, Greece, Ireland, Italy, Luxembourg, the Netherlands, Portugal, Spain, Sweden, the United Kingdom and the European Commission)' (London 10 April 2003).

Marine Environment Protection Committee of the International Maritime Organization (MEPC, IMO), 'Res. MEPC.111(50) – Amendments to regulation 13G, addition of new regulation 13H and consequential amendments to the Supplement to the IOPP Certificate of Annex I to MARPOL 73/78' (London 4 December 2003).

Marine Environment Protection Committee of the International Maritime Organization (MEPC, IMO), 'Res. MEPC.237(65) – Code for Recognized Organizations' (London 17 May 2013).

Marine Environment Protection Committee of the International Maritime Organization (MEPC, IMO), 'Res. MEPC.264(68) – International Code for Ships Operating in Polar Waters' (London 15 May 2015).

Marine Environment Protection Committee of the International Maritime Organization (MEPC, IMO), 'MEPC.1/Circ.873 – List of Certificates and Documents required to be Carried On Board Ships' (London 19 July 2017).

Marine Environment Protection Committee of the International Maritime Organization (MEPC, IMO), 'Res. MEPC.304(72) – Initial IMO strategy on Reduction of GHG Emissions from Ships' (London 13 April 2018).

Marine Environment Protection Committee of the International Maritime Organization (MEPC, IMO), 'Res. MEPC.377(80) – 2023 IMO Strategy on Reduction of GHG Emissions from Ships' (London 7 July 2023).

Facilitation Committee

Facilitation Committee of the International Maritime Organization (FAL, IMO), 'FAL.5/Circ.39: Interim Guidelines for the Use of Printed Versions of Electronic Certificates' (London 18 April 2013).

Facilitation Committee of the International Maritime Organization (FAL, IMO), 'FAL.5/Circ.39/Rev.2: Guidelines for the Use of Electronic Certificates' (London 20 April 2016).

Facilitation Committee of the International Maritime Organization (FAL, IMO), 'FAL.7/Circ.1: Unified Interpretation of Annex 3 to the FAL Convention' (London 7 April 2017).

Facilitation Committee of the International Maritime Organization (FAL, IMO), 'FAL.2/Circ.131: List of Certificates and Documents Required to be Carried On Board Ships' (London 19 July 2017).

Facilitation Committee of the International Maritime Organization (FAL, IMO), 'FAL 43/20: Report of the Facilitation Committee on its 43rd Session' (London 23 April 2019).

Facilitation Committee of the International Maritime Organization (FAL, IMO), 'FAL.5/Circ.49: Outcome of the Regulatory Scoping Exercise and Gap Analysis of the FAL Convention with Respect to Maritime Autonomous Surface Ships' (London 1 June 2022).

Legal Committee

Legal Committee of the Inter-Governmental Maritime Consultative Organization (LEG, IMCO), 'LEG XIV/4: Report of the Legal Committee on the Work of the 14th Session' (London 27 September 1972).

Legal Committee of the International Maritime Organization (LEG, IMO), 'LEG.2/Circ.3: List of Certificates and Documents Required to be Carried On Board Ships' (London 19 July 2017).

Legal Committee of the International Maritime Organization (LEG, IMO), 'LEG 105/14: Report of the Legal Committee on the Work of its 105th Session' (London 1 May 2018).

Legal Committee of the International Maritime Organization (LEG, IMO), 'LEG.1/Circ.9: Organization and Method of Work of the Legal Committee' (London 30 June 2018).

Legal Committee of the International Maritime Organization (LEG, IMO), 'LEG 106/16: Report of the Legal Committee on the Work of its 106th Session' (London 13 May 2019).

Legal Committee of the International Maritime Organization (LEG, IMO), 'LEG 107/8/18: Comment on documents LEG 107/8, LEG 107/8/1, LEG 107/8/5, LEG 107/8/6 and LEG 107/8/11 regarding the role of the master (IFSMA)' (London 23 January 2020).

Legal Committee of the International Maritime Organization (LEG, IMO), 'LEG 107/9/2: Unified Interpretation on the Test for Breaking the Owner's Right to Limit Liability under the IMO Conventions' (London 24 January 2020).

Legal Committee of the International Maritime Organization (LEG, IMO), 'LEG.1/Circ.11: Outcome of the Regulatory Scoping Exercise and Gap Analysis of Conventions emanating from the Legal Committee with respect to Maritime Autonomous Surface Ships (MASS)' (London 15 December 2021).

Legal Committee of the International Maritime Organization (LEG, IMO), 'LEG 110/11/3: Measures to Address MASS in Instruments under the Purview of the Legal Committee (United Arab Emirates), Consideration of issues under UNCLOS relevant to the role of the Organization' (London 23 December 2022).

Legal Committee of the International Maritime Organization (LEG, IMO), 'LEG 111/10/2: Summary of the research of the Comité Maritime International International Working Group on MASS in relation to liability issues (Comité Maritime International)' (London 19 January 2024).

Legal Committee of the International Maritime Organization (LEG, IMO), 'LEG 111/10/4: Proposal to develop Guidelines on the implementation of LEG Instruments by MASS (China)' (London 16 February 2024).

Legal Committee of the International Maritime Organization (LEG, IMO), 'LEG 111/10/5: Proposal to ensure regulating MASS within the framework of international law (United Arab Emirates)' (London 16 February 2024).

Legal Committee of the International Maritime Organization (LEG, IMO), 'LEG 111/17: Report of the Legal Committee on the Work of its 111th Session' (London 16 May 2024).

Legal Committee of the International Maritime Organization (LEG, IMO), 'LEG 111/17/Add.1: Report of the Legal Committee on the Work of its 111th Session' (London 16 May 2024).

Intersessional Working Group on MASS

Intersessional Working Group on MASS (ISWG/MASS), 'MSC-ISWG-MASS 2-3-2 – Comments regarding ROC oversights by the flag Administration (Russian Federation)' (London 15 September 2023).

Intersessional Working Group on MASS (ISWG/MASS), 'MSC-ISWG-MASS 2-3-6 – Role of the Master for consideration in the draft MASS Code (The Nautical Institute)' (London 15 September 2023).

Inter-Governmental Maritime Consultative Organization

Inter-Governmental Maritime Consultative Organization (IMCO), 'A VII/12 – Amendment Procedures in Conventions for which IMCO is Depositary' (London 2 August 1971).

Inter-Governmental Maritime Consultative Organization (IMCO), 'Resolution A.249 (VII): Amendment Procedures in Conventions for which IMCO is Depositary' (London 3 November 1971).

Inter-Governmental Maritime Consultative Organization (IMCO), 'Amendment Procedure for Conventions for which IMCO is the Depository' (London 20 September 1973).

Inter-Governmental Maritime Consultative Organization (IMCO), 'Resolution A.285(VIII): Recommendation on Basic Principles and Operational Guidance Relating to Navigational Watchkeeping' (London 21 December 1973).

Inter-Governmental Maritime Consultative Organization (IMCO), 'Resolution A.315 (IX) Amendments to the IMCO Convention' (London 17 October 1974).

Inter-Governmental Maritime Consultative Organization (IMCO), 'Resolution A.358(IX). Amendments to the IMCO Convention' (London 22 December 1975).

Inter-Governmental Maritime Consultative Organization (IMCO), 'Resolution A. 373(X) – Code of Safety for Dynamically Supported Craft' (14 November 1977).

International Conventions and Statutory Instruments

International Conventions

A/CONF.232/2023/4 – Agreement under the United Nations Convention on the Law of the Sea on the conservation and sustainable use of marine biological diversity of areas beyond national jurisdiction 20 June 2023 (Intergovernmental conference on an international legally binding instrument under the United Nations Convention on the Law of the Sea on the conservation and sustainable use of marine biological diversity of areas beyond national jurisdiction).

Agreement for Cooperation in Dealing with Pollution of the North Sea by Oil, No. 10099 9 June 1969.

Agreement for the Implementation of the Provisions of the United Nations Convention on the Law of the Sea of 10 December 1982 relating to the Conservation and Management of Straddling Fish Stocks and Highly Migratory Fish Stocks, No. 37924 4 August 1995.

Agreement on the European Economic Area 1994.

Agreement relating to the implementation of Part XI of the United Nations Convention on the Law of the Sea of 10 December 1982, No. 31364 28 July 1994.

Conference of Contracting Governments to SOLAS, 'SOLAS/CONF.2/20 – Consideration and Adoption of the International Convention on the Safety of Life at Sea (United States of America)' (London 8 April 1994).

Conference of Contracting Governments to SOLAS, 'SOLAS/CONF/5/32 – Consideration and Adoption of Amendments to the International Convention for the Safety of Life at Sea, 1974' (London 12 December 2002).

Conference of Contracting Governments to STCW, 'STCW.6/Circ.1 – STCW Code' (London 24 July 1995).

Conference of Contracting Governments to STCW, 'STCW/CONF.2/32 – Final Act' (London 1 July 2010).

Conference of the Parties to MARPOL, 'MP/CONF. 3/34 – Consideration and Adoption of the Protocol of 1997 to amend MARPOL' (London 28 October 1997).

Conference on Revision of the International Regulations for Preventing Collisions at Sea, 'CR/CONF/C.2/SR.2 – Provisional Summary record of the second meeting' (London 5 October 1972).

Convention and Statute on the International Régime of Maritime Ports, No. 1379 9 December 1923.

Convention for the prevention of marine pollution by dumping from ships and aircrafts, No. 13269 15 February 1972.

Convention for the prevention of marine pollution from land-based sources, No. 26842 4 June 1974.

Convention for the protection of the marine environment of the North-East Atlantic, No. 42279 22 September 1992.

Convention on Fishing and Conservation of the Living Resources of the High Seas, No. 8164 29 April 1958.

Convention on the Continental Shelf, No. 7302 29 April 1958.

Convention on the International Regulations for Preventing Collisions at Sea, No. 15824 20 October 1972.
Convention on the prevention of marine pollution by dumping of wastes and other matter, No. 15749 29 December 1972.
Convention on the Protection of the Marine Environment of the Baltic Sea Area, No. 25986 22 March 1974.
Convention on the Recognition and Enforcement of Foreign Arbitral Awards, No. 4739 10 June 1958.
Convention on the Territorial Sea and the Contiguous Zone; No. 7477 29 April 1958.
International Convention for the control and management of ship's ballast water and sediments, No. 55544 13 February 2004.
International Convention for the Safety of Life at Sea 10 June 1948.
International Convention for the Safety of Life at Sea 17 June 1960.
International Convention for the Safety of Life at Sea 20 January 1914.
International Convention for the Safety of Life at Sea, no. 18961 1974.
International Covenant on Civil and Political Rights, No. 14668 19 December 1966.
Joint Protocol Relating to the Application of the Vienna Convention and the Paris Convention 21 September 1988.
Kyoto Protocol to the United Nations Framework Convention on Climate Change, 30822 11 December 1997.
Optional Protocol of Signature concerning the Compulsory Settlement of Disputes 29 April 1958.
Paris Agreement, No. 54113 12 December 2015.
Protocol Amending the International Convention for the Unification of Certain Rules of Law Relating to Bills of Lading, as amended by the protocol of 23.02.1968, No. 23643 21 December 1979.
Protocol of 1988 Relating to the International Convention for the Safety of Life at Sea, 1974 11 November 1988 (Conference of Contracting Governments to SOLAS).
Protocol Relating to the International Convention for the Safety of Lift at Sea, No. 18961 17 February 1978 (IMCO Conference on Tanker Safety and Pollution Prevention).
Protocol to Amend the International Convention for the Unification of Certain Rules of Law Relating to Bills of Lading, No. 23643 23 February 1968.
The Convention on the High Seas, No. 6465 29 April 1958.
The Helsinki Treaty; Treaty of Co-operation between Denmark, Finland, Iceland, Norway and Sweden 23 March 1962.
The International Convention on Standards of Training, Certification and Watchkeeping for Seafarers, No. 23001 7 July 1978.
Treaty of Friendship, Commerce and Navigation, No. 3943 29 October 1954.

United Nations Convention on the carriage of goods by sea, No. 29215 31 March 1978.

United Nations Convention on the Law of the Sea, No. 31363 10 December 1982.

United Nations Framework Convention on Climate Change, 30822 9 May 1992.

EU Statutory Instruments

COM(2000) 142 final – Proposal for a regulation of the European Parliament and of the Council on the accelerated phasing-in of double hull or equivalent design requirements for single hull oil tankers 22 March 2000 (European Commission).

Council Directive 95/21/EC – concerning the enforcement, in respect of shipping using Community ports and sailing in the waters under the jurisdiction of the Member States, of international standards for ship safety, pollution prevention and shipboard living and working conditions (port State control) 19 June 1995 (Council of the European Union).

Council Regulation (EEC) No 4055/ 86 on applying the principle of freedom to provide services to maritime transport between Member States and between Member States and third countries 22 December 1986 (Council of the European Union).

Council Regulation (EU) 2022/576 – amending Regulation (EU) No 833/2014 concerning restrictive measures in view of Russia's actions destabilising the situation in Ukraine 8 April 2022.

Decision (EU) 2016/1353 concerning the financial rules of the European Defence Agency and repealing Decision 2007/643/CFSP 4 August 2016 (Council of the European Union).

Decision (EU) 2023/1901 on discharge in respect of the implementation of the budget of the European Maritime Safety Agency (EMSA) for the financial year 2021 [2023] Official Journal of the European Union 66 L 242/351.

Directive (EU) 2016/802 – relating to a reduction in the sulphur content of certain liquid fuels [2016] Official Journal of the European Union 59 L 132/58.

Directive (EU) 2022/993 on the minimum level of training of seafarers [2022] Official Journal of the European Union 65 L 169/45.

Directive (EU) 2023/959 amending Directive 2003/87/EC establishing a system for greenhouse gas emission allowance trading within the Union and Decision (EU) 2015/1814 concerning the establishment and operation of a market stability reserve for the Union greenhouse gas emission trading system [2023] Official Journal of the European Union 66 L 130/134.

Directive 2009/16/EC of the European Parliament and of the Council on port State control [2009] Official Journal of the European Union 52 L 131/57.

Directive 2014/90/EU on marine equipment and repealing Council Directive 96/98/EG [2014] Official Journal of the European Union 57 L 257/146.

European Commission, 'COM(2005) 588 final – proposal for a Directive on port State control' (Brussels 23 November 2005).

Regulation (EC) No 1406/2002 establishing a European Maritime Safety Agency [2002] Official Journal of the European Communities 45 L 208/1.

Regulation (EC) No 1726/2003 – amending Regulation (EC) No 417/2002 on the accelerated phasing-in of double-hull or equivalent design requirements for single-hull oil tankers [2003] Official Journal of the European Union 46 L 249/1.

Regulation (EC) No 725/2004 on enhancing ship and port facility security [2004] Official Journal of the European Union 47 L 129/6.

Regulation (EC) No 782/2003 on the prohibition of organotin compounds on ships [2003] Official Journal of the European Union 46 L 115/1-11.

Regulation (EC) Nr 417/2002 on the accelerated phasing-in of double hull or equivalent design requirements for single hull oil tankers and repealing Council Regulation (EC) No 2978/94 [2002] Official Journal of the European Communities 45 L 64/1.

Regulation (EU) No 1257/2013 on ship recycling and amending Regulation (EC) No 1013/2006 and Directive 2009/16/EC [2013] Official Journal of the European Union 56 L 330/1.

Regulation (EU) No 530/2012 of the European Parliament and of the Council of 13 June 2012 on the accelerated phasing-in of double-hull or equivalent design requirements for single-hull oil tankers [2012] Official Journal of the European Union 55 L 172/3.

EEA Joint Committee

EEA Joint Committee, 'No 81/2003 – amending Annex XIII (Transport) to the EEA Agreement' (20 June 2003).

EEA Joint Committee, 'Decision No 14/2005 – amending Annex XIII (Transport) to the EEA Agreement' (Brussels 8 February 2005).

EEA Joint Committee, 'No 134/2010 – amending Annex XIII (Transport) to the EEA Agreement' (Geneva, Brussels 10 December 2010).

EEA Joint Committee, 'Decision No 163/2016 amending Annex II (Technical regulations, standards, testing and certification) to the EEA Agreement [2018/384]' (Brussels 26 August 2016).

Other Statutory Instruments

1687/2009 – Act on Ships' Crews and the Safety Management of Ships.

51/2019 – Lag om ändring av lotsningslagen 18 January 2019 (Eduskunta).

976/2018 – Lag om ändring av lagen om fartygspersonal och säkerhetsorganisation för fartyg 23 November 2018 (Eduskunta).

'Beleidsregel experimenten vergaand geautomatiseerd varen rijksvaarwegen', *Staatscourant van het Koninkrijk der Nederlanden* (2018).

COM(2021) 812 final – Proposal for a Regulation of the European Parliament and of the Council on Union guidelines for the development of the trans-European transport network, amending Regulation (EU) 2021/1153 and Regulation (EU) No 913/2010 and repealing Regulation (EU) 1315/2013 14 December 2021 (European Commission).

Decreet houdende diverse bepalingen over het mobiliteitsbeleid, de openbare werken en het vervoer, het verkeersveiligheidsbeleid en VVM – De Lijn (1) 26 April 2019 (Vlaamse Overheid).

Direction de l'information légale et administrative, 'Loi no 2016-816 du 20 juin 2016 pour l'économie bleue (1)', *Journal officiel de la République française* (2016).

Direction de l'information légale et administrative, 'LOI no 2019-1428 du 24 décembre 2019 d'orientation des mobilités (1)', *Journal officiel de la République française* (2019).

Gesetz über die Zusammenarbeit von Bundesregierung und Deutschem Bundestag in Angelegenheiten der Europäischen Union (EUZBBG) 4 July 2013 (Deutscher Bundestag).

Marine Notice on Manning of Vessels and Principles of Watchkeeping 02/21, MAN-001 (Office of the Deputy Commissioner of Maritime Affairs).

Memorandum of Understanding on Cooperation Regarding the International Operation of Maritime Autonomous Surface Ships MASS 27 November 2023.

MGN 664 (M + F) Amendment 1: Certification process for vessels using innovative technology September 2023 (Maritime and Coastguard Agency).

Merchant Shipping Act 1995.

Oil Pollution Act, PL 101-380 18 August 1990.

'Ordonnance n° 2021-1330 relative aux conditions de navigation des navires autonomes et des drones maritimes', *Journal officiel de la République française* (2021).

Resolución No. 106–176-DGMM 15 December 2021 (Dirección General de Marina Mercante).

Schiffsbesetzungsverordnung 18 July 2013, SchBesV (Bundesministerium für Verkehr, Bau und Stadtentwicklung).

Shipping Circular No. 10 of 2022 – Minimum Safe Manning Document Requirements for Singapore Ships 28 June 2022 (Maritime and Port Authority of Singapore).

The Liberain Maritime Regulations, Titel 21 23 April 2018 (The Senate and House of Representatives of the Republic of Liberia in Legislature assembled).

The Workboat Code Edition 3, The safety of small Workboats and Pilot Boats – a Code of Practice 27 November 2023.

Index

www.ingramcontent.com/pod-product-compliance
Lightning Source LLC
Chambersburg PA
CBHW070252260926
51849CB00001BA/275
* 9 7 8 9 0 0 4 7 2 9 4 7 6 *